UNITED STATES HISTORY

BEGINNINGS TO 1877

ISBN 978-0-544-66879-9

9 10   0868   24 23 22 21 20 19

4500786380   E F G

Educational Advisory Panel

The following educators provided ongoing review during the development of prototypes and key elements of this program.

Jose Colon

Berkeley High School
Berkeley, California

Bethany Copeland

Peach County High School
Fort Valley, Georgia

Darrel Dexter

Egyptian Community Unit School
Tamms, Illinois

Charles Dietz

Burnett Middle School
San Jose, California

John Hogan

Brevard High School
Brevard, North Carolina

Jeffrey Kaufman

Aspirations Diploma Plus High School
Brooklyn, New York

Beth E. Kuhlman

Queens Metropolitan High School
Forest Hills, New York

Beatrice Nudelman

Aptakisic Junior High School
Buffalo Grove, Illinois

Kyle Race

Greene High School
Greene, New York

Gretchen Ritter Varela

Northville High School
Northville, Michigan

Sharon Shirley

Branford High School
Branford, Connecticut

Yvette Snopkowski

Davis Junior High School
Sterling Heights, Michigan

La-Shanda West

Cutler Bay Senior High School
Cutler Bay, Florida

Contents

HISTORY Videos related to each module can be accessed through your digital Student Edition.

Module 1

Module 2

Module 3

Module 4

Module 5

***

Module 6

***

Module 7

***

Module 8

Module 9

Module 10

Module 11

Module 12

Module 13

Module 14

★

Module 15

★

Module 16

★

Module 17

★

Module 18

★

Module 19

Available Online

Reading Like a Historian

Historic Documents

Biolgraphical Dictionary

Close-Read Screencasts

Facts about the States

Presidents of the United States

Supreme Court Decisions

Economic Handbook

Geography and Map Skills Handbook

Skillbuilder Handbook

Multimedia Connections

These online lessons feature award-winning content and include short video segments, maps and visual materials, primary source documents, and more.

The Maya

Ponce de León

The American Revolution

Lewis and Clark

The Real West: Rush for Gold

Days of Darkness: The Gettysburg Civilians

HISTORY

HISTORY® is the leading destination for revealing, award-winning, original non-fiction series and event-driven specials that connect history with viewers in an informative, immersive and entertaining manner across multiple platforms. HISTORY is part of A+E Networks, a global entertainment media company that includes, among others, A&E®, HISTORY®, Lifetime®, H2®, FYI™, and LMN®.

HISTORY programming greatly appeals to educators and young people who are drawn into the visual stories our documentaries tell. Our Education Department has a long-standing record in providing teachers and students with curriculum resources that bring the past to life in the classroom. Our content covers a diverse variety of subjects, including American and world history, government, economics, the natural and applied sciences, arts, literature and the humanities, health and guidance, and even pop culture.

The HISTORY website, located at **www.history.com**, is the definitive historical online source that delivers entertaining and informative content featuring broadband video, interactive timelines, maps, games, podcasts and more.

"We strive to engage, inspire and encourage the love of learning..."

Since its founding in 1995, HISTORY has demonstrated a commitment to providing the highest quality resources for educators. We develop multimedia resources for K–12 schools, two- and four-year colleges, government agencies, and other organizations by drawing on the award-winning documentary programming of A&E Television Networks. We strive to engage, inspire and encourage the love of learning by connecting with students in an informative and compelling manner. To help achieve this goal, we have formed a partnership with Houghton Mifflin Harcourt.

The Idea Book for Educators

Classroom resources that bring the past to life

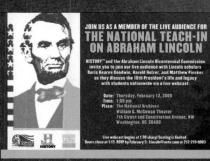
Live webcasts

HISTORY Take a Veteran to School Day

In addition to premium video-based resources, **HISTORY** has extensive offerings for teachers, parents, and students to use in the classroom and in their in-home educational activities, including:

- *The Idea Book for Educators* is a biannual teacher's magazine, featuring guides and info on the latest happenings in history education to help keep teachers on the cutting edge.

- **HISTORY Classroom (www.history.com/classroom)** is an interactive website that serves as a portal for history educators nationwide. Streaming videos on topics ranging from the Roman aqueducts to the civil rights movement connect with classroom curricula.

- **HISTORY email newsletters** feature updates and supplements to our award-winning programming relevant to the classroom with links to teaching guides and video clips on a variety of topics, special offers, and more.

- **Live webcasts** are featured each year as schools tune in via streaming video.

- **HISTORY Take a Veteran to School Day** connects veterans with young people in our schools and communities nationwide.

In addition to **Houghton Mifflin Harcourt**, our partners include the *Library of Congress,* the *Smithsonian Institution, National History Day, The Gilder Lehrman Institute of American History,* the Organization of American Historians, and many more. HISTORY video is also featured in museums throughout America and in over 70 other historic sites worldwide.

Reading Social Studies

Did you ever think you would begin reading your social studies book by reading about reading? Actually, it makes better sense than you might think. You would probably make sure you learned soccer skills and strategies before playing in a game. Similarly, you need to learn reading skills and strategies before reading your social studies book. In other words, you need to make sure you know whatever you need to know in order to read this book successfully.

Tip #1

Use the Reading Social Studies Pages

Take advantage of the two pages on reading at the beginning of every module. Those pages introduce the module themes, explain a reading skill or strategy, and identify key terms and people.

Themes

Why are themes important? They help our minds organize facts and information. For example, when we talk about baseball, we may talk about types of pitches. When we talk about movies, we may discuss animation.

Historians are no different. When they discuss history or social studies, they tend to think about some common themes: Economics, Geography, Religion, Politics, Society and Culture, and Science and Technology.

Reading Skill or Strategy

Good readers use a number of skills and strategies to make sure they understand what they are reading. These lessons will give you the tools you need to read and understand social studies.

Key Terms and People

Before you read the module, review these words and think about them. Have you heard the word before? What do you already know about the people? Then watch for these words and their meanings as you read the module.

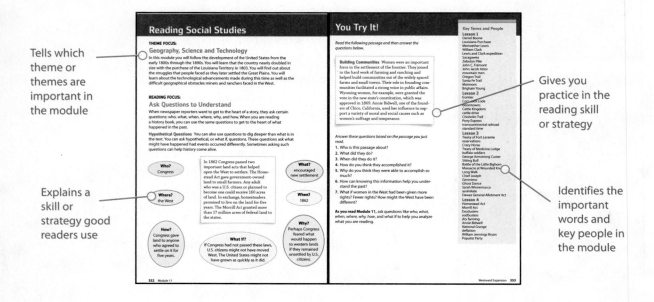

Tells which theme or themes are important in the module

Explains a skill or strategy good readers use

Gives you practice in the reading skill or strategy

Identifies the important words and key people in the module

Tip #2

Read like a Skilled Reader

You will never get better at reading your social studies book—or any book for that matter—unless you spend some time thinking about how to be a better reader.

Skilled readers do the following:

- They preview what they are supposed to read before they actually begin reading. They look for vocabulary words, titles of lessons, information in the margin, or maps or charts they should study.

- They divide their notebook paper into two columns. They title one column "Notes from the Lesson" and the other column "Questions or Comments I Have."

- They take notes in both columns as they read.

- They read like **active readers**. The Active Reading list below shows you what that means.

- They use clues in the text to help them figure out where the text is going. The best clues are called signal words.

  Chronological Order Signal Words: *first, second, third, before, after, later, next, following that, earlier, finally*

  Cause and Effect Signal Words: *because of, due to, as a result of, the reason for, therefore, consequently*

  Comparison/Contrast Signal Words: *likewise, also, as well as, similarly, on the other hand*

Active Reading

Successful readers are **active readers**. These readers know that it is up to them to figure out what the text means. Here are some steps you can take to become an active, and successful, reader.

Predict what will happen next based on what has already happened. When your predictions don't match what happens in the text, reread the confusing parts.

Question what is happening as you read. Constantly ask yourself why things have happened, what things mean, and what caused certain events.

Summarize what you are reading frequently. Do not try to summarize the entire module! Read a bit and then summarize it. Then read on.

Connect what is happening in the part you're reading to what you have already read.

Clarify your understanding. Stop occasionally to ask yourself whether you are confused by anything. You may need to reread to clarify, or you may need to read further and collect more information before you can understand.

Visualize what is happening in the text. Try to see the events or places in your mind by drawing maps, making charts, or jotting down notes about what you are reading.

Tip #3

Pay Attention to Vocabulary

It is no fun to read something when you don't know what the words mean, but you can't learn new words if you use or read only the words you already know. In this book, we know we probably have used some words you don't know. But, we have followed a pattern as we have used more difficult words.

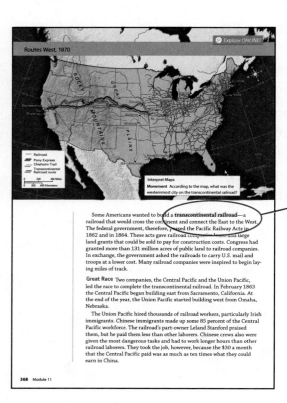

Key Terms and People

At the beginning of each lesson you will find a list of key terms and people that you will need to know. Be on the lookout for those words as you read through the lesson.

nd a **transcontinental railroad**—a ntinent and connect the East to the West e, passed the Pacific Railway Acts in

Academic
Vocabulary
facilitate to make
easier

Academic Vocabulary

When the text uses a word that is important in all classes, not just social studies, we define it in the margin under the heading Academic Vocabulary. You will run into these academic words in other textbooks, so you should learn what they mean while reading this book.

Academic and Social Studies Words

As you read this social studies textbook, you will be more successful if you know or learn the meanings of the words on this page. Academic words are important in all classes, not just social studies. Social studies words are special to the study of U.S. history and other social studies topics.

Academic Words

abstract   expressing a quality or idea without reference to an actual thing

acquire   to get

advocate   to plead in favor of

affect   to change or influence

agreement   a decision reached by two or more people or groups

aspects   parts

authority   power, right to rule

cause   the reason something happens

circumstances   surrounding situations

classical   referring to the cultures of ancient Greece or Rome

complex   difficult, not simple

concrete   specific, real

consequences   the effects of a particular event or events

contemporary   existing at the same time

contract   a binding legal agreement

criteria   rules for defining

develop/development   1. to grow or improve; 2. the process of growing or improving

distinct   separate

distribute   to divide among a group of people

effect   the result of an action or decision

efficient/efficiency   1. productive, not wasteful; 2. the quality of being efficient

element   part

execute   to perform, carry out

explicit   fully revealed without vagueness

facilitate   to bring about

factor   cause

features   characteristics

function   use or purpose

impact   effect, result

implement   to put in place

implications   effects of a decision

implicit   understood though not clearly put into words

incentive   something that leads people to follow a certain course of action

influence   change or have an effect on

innovation   a new idea or way of doing something

logic/logical   1. well-thought-out idea; 2. reasoned, well thought out

motive   a reason for doing something

neutral   unbiased, not favoring either side in a conflict

policy   rule, course of action

primary   main, most important

principle   basic belief, rule, or law

procedure   a series of steps taken to accomplish a task

process   a series of steps by which a task is accomplished

reaction   a response

role   1. a part or function; 2. assigned behavior

strategy   a plan for fighting a battle or war

structure   the way something is set up or organized

traditional   customary, time-honored

values   ideas that people hold dear and try to live by

vary/various   1. to be different; 2. of many types

Social Studies Words

AD   refers to dates after the birth of Jesus of Nazareth

BC   refers to dates before the birth of Jesus

BCE   refers to "Before Common Era," dates before the birth of Jesus

CE   refers to "Common Era," dates after the birth of Jesus

century   a period of 100 years

civilization   the culture of a particular time or place

climate   the weather conditions in a certain area over a long period of time

culture   the knowledge, beliefs, customs, and values of a group of people

custom   a repeated practice, tradition

democracy   governmental rule by the people, usually on a majority rule principle

economy   the system in which people make and exchange goods and services

geography   the study of the earth's physical and cultural features

independence   freedom from forceful rule

monarchy   governmental rule by one person, a king or queen

North   the region of the United States sometimes defined by the states that did not secede from the Union during the Civil War

rebellion   an organized resistance to the established government

society   a group of people who share common traditions

South   the region of the United States sometimes defined by the states that seceded from the Union to form the Confederate States of America

Using This Book

Studying U.S. history will be easy for you using this textbook. Take a few minutes to become familiar with the easy-to-use structure and special features of this history book. See how this U.S. history textbook will make history come alive for you!

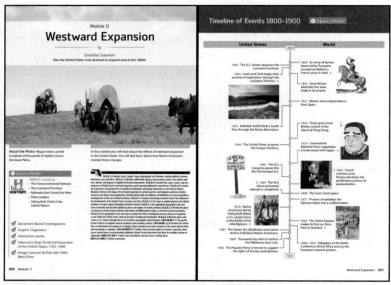

Module

Each module begins with an Essential Question and a Timeline of Events showing important dates in U.S. and world history, and ends with a Module Assessment.

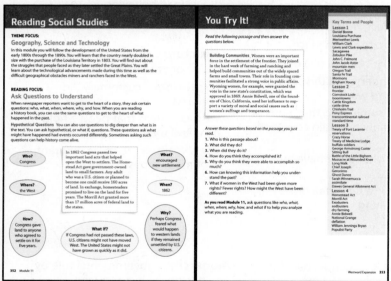

Reading Social Studies

These reading lessons teach you skills and provide opportunities for practice to help you read the textbook more successfully. There are questions in the Module Assessment to make sure you understand the reading skill.

Social Studies Skills

The Social Studies Skills lessons give you an opportunity to learn and use a skill you will most likely use again while in school. You will also be given a chance to make sure that you understand each skill by answering related questions in the Module Assessment activity.

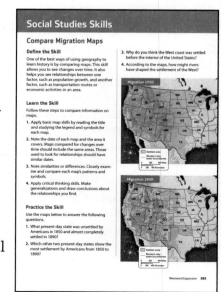

Lesson

The lesson opener includes an overarching Big Idea statement, Main Ideas, and Key Terms and People.

If YOU were there . . . introductions begin each lesson with a situation for you to respond to, placing you in the time period and in a situation related to the content you will be studying in the lesson.

Headings and subheadings organize the information into manageable chunks of text that will help you learn and understand the lesson's main ideas.

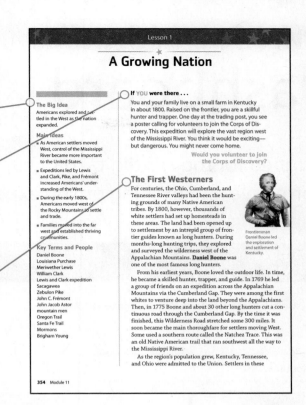

A Growing Nation

The Big Idea
Americans explored and settled in the West as the nation expanded.

Main Ideas
- As American settlers moved West, control of the Mississippi River became more important to the United States.
- Expeditions led by Lewis and Clark, Pike, and Frémont increased Americans' understanding of the West.
- During the early 1800s, Americans moved west of the Rocky Mountains to settle and trade.
- Families moved into the far west and established thriving communities.

Key Terms and People
Daniel Boone
Louisiana Purchase
Meriwether Lewis
William Clark
Lewis and Clark expedition
Sacagawea
Zebulon Pike
John C. Frémont
John Jacob Astor
mountain men
Oregon Trail
Santa Fe Trail
Mormons
Brigham Young

If YOU were there . . .
You and your family live on a small farm in Kentucky in about 1800. Raised on the frontier, you are a skillful hunter and trapper. One day at the trading post, you see a poster calling for volunteers to join the Corps of Discovery. This expedition will explore the vast region west of the Mississippi River. You think it would be exciting—but dangerous. You might never come home.

Would you volunteer to join the Corps of Discovery?

The First Westerners
For centuries, the Ohio, Cumberland, and Tennessee River valleys had been the hunting grounds of many Native American tribes. By 1800, however, thousands of white settlers had set up homesteads in these areas. The land had been opened up to settlement by an intrepid group of frontier guides known as long hunters. During months-long hunting trips, they explored and surveyed the wilderness west of the Appalachian Mountains. **Daniel Boone** was one of the most famous long hunters.

Frontiersman Daniel Boone led the exploration and settlement of Kentucky.

From his earliest years, Boone loved the outdoor life. In time, he became a skilled hunter, trapper, and guide. In 1769 he led a group of friends on an expedition across the Appalachian Mountains via the Cumberland Gap. They were among the first whites to venture deep into the land beyond the Appalachians. Then, in 1775 Boone and about 30 other long hunters cut a continuous road through the Cumberland Gap. By the time it was finished, this Wilderness Road stretched some 300 miles. It soon became the main thoroughfare for settlers moving West. Some used a southern route called the Natchez Trace. This was an old Native American trail that ran southwest all the way to the Mississippi River.

As the region's population grew, Kentucky, Tennessee, and Ohio were admitted to the Union. Settlers in these

354 Module 11

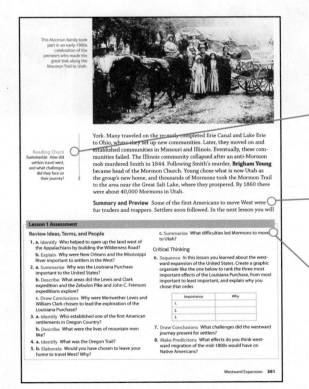

This Mormon family took part in an early-1900s celebration of the pioneers who made the great trek along the Mormon Trail to Utah.

Reading Check
Summarize How did settlers travel west, and what challenges did they face on their journey?

York. Many traveled on the recently completed Erie Canal and Lake Erie to Ohio, where they set up new communities. Later, they moved on and established communities in Missouri and Illinois. Eventually, these communities failed. The Illinois community collapsed after an anti-Mormon mob murdered Smith in 1844. Following Smith's murder, **Brigham Young** became head of the Mormon Church. Young chose what is now Utah as the group's new home, and thousands of Mormons took the Mormon Trail to the area near the Great Salt Lake, where they prospered. By 1860 there were about 40,000 Mormons in Utah.

Summary and Preview Some of the first Americans to move West were fur traders and trappers. Settlers soon followed. In the next lesson you will

Lesson 1 Assessment

Review Ideas, Terms, and People

1. **a.** Identify Who helped to open up the land west of the Appalachians by building the Wilderness Road?
   b. Explain Why were New Orleans and the Mississippi River important to settlers in the West?
2. **a.** Summarize Why was the Louisiana Purchase important to the United States?
   b. Describe What areas did the Lewis and Clark expedition and the Zebulon Pike and John C. Frémont expeditions explore?
   c. Draw Conclusions Why were Meriwether Lewis and William Clark chosen to lead the exploration of the Louisiana Purchase?
3. **a.** Identify Who established one of the first American settlements in Oregon Country?
   b. Describe What were the lives of mountain men like?
4. **a.** Identify What was the Oregon Trail?
5. **b.** Elaborate Would you have chosen to leave your home to travel West? Why?

c. Summarize What difficulties led Mormons to move to Utah?

Critical Thinking

6. **Sequence** In this lesson you learned about the westward expansion of the United States. Create a graphic organizer like the one below to rank the three most important effects of the Louisiana Purchase, from most important to least important, and explain why you chose that order.

Importance	Why
1.	
2.	
3.	

7. **Draw Conclusions** What challenges did the westward journey present for settlers?
8. **Make Predictions** What effects do you think westward migration of the mid-1800s would have on Native Americans?

Westward Expansion **361**

Reading Check questions are at the end of each main heading so you can test whether or not you understand what you have just studied.

Summary and Preview statements connect what you have just studied in the lesson to what you will study in the next lesson.

Lesson Assessment boxes provide an opportunity for you to make sure you understand the main ideas of the lesson.

HMH Social Studies
Dashboard

Designed for today's digital natives, **HMH® Social Studies** offers you an informative and exciting online experience.

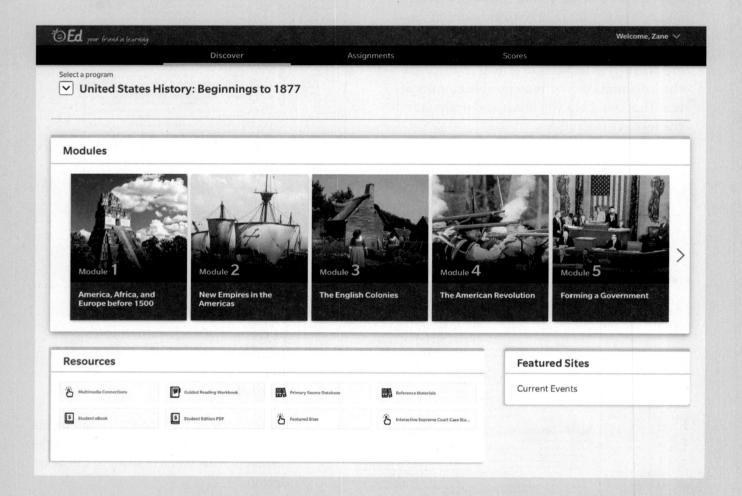

Your personalized Dashboard is organized into three main sections:

1. **Discover**—Quickly access content and search program resources

2. **Assignments**—Review your assignments and check your progress on them

3. **Scores**—Monitor your progress on the course

Explore Online ⊳
to **Experience** the **Power** of
United States History
Beginnings to 1877

Houghton Mifflin Harcourt™ is changing
the way you **experience** social studies.

By delivering an immersive experience through compelling narratives
enriched with media, we're connecting you to history through experiences that are
energizing, inspiring, and memorable. The following pages highlight
some digital tools and instructional support that will help you
approach history through active inquiry, so you can connect to the past
while becoming active and informed citizens for the future.

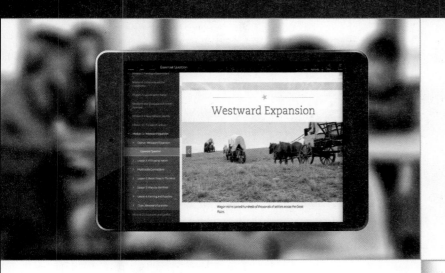

The Student eBook is the primary learning portal.

More than just the digital version of a textbook, the Student eBook serves as the primary learning portal for you. The narrative is supported by a wealth of multimedia and learning resources to bring history to life and give you the tools you need to succeed.

Bringing Content to Life

HISTORY® videos and Multimedia Connections bring content to life through primary source footage, dramatic storytelling, and expert testimonials.

In-Depth Understanding

Close Read Screencasts model an analytical conversation about primary sources.

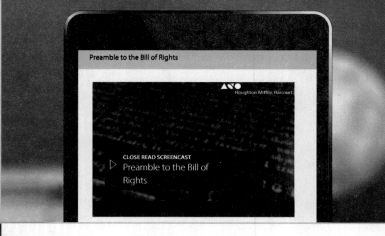

Content in a Fun Way

Interactive Features, Maps, and **Games** provide quick, entertaining activities and assessments that present important content in a fun way.

Investigate Like a Historian

Document-Based Investigations in every lesson build to end-of-module DBI performance tasks so you can examine and assess primary sources as historians do.

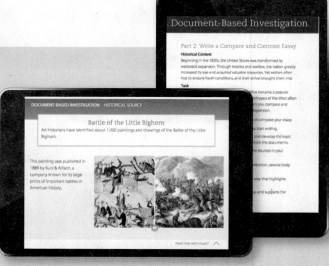

Full-Text Audio Support

You can listen while you read.

Skills Support

Point-of-use support is just a click away, providing instruction on critical reading and social studies skills.

Personalized Annotations

My Notes encourages you to take notes while you read and allows you to customize them to your study preferences. You can easily access them to review later as you prepare for exams.

Interactive Lesson Graphic Organizers

Graphic organizers help you process, summarize, and keep track of your learning for end-of-module performance tasks.

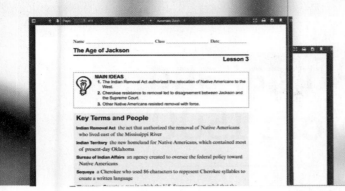

The **Guided Reading Workbook** and **Spanish/English Guided Reading Workbook** offer you lesson summaries with vocabulary, reading, and note-taking support.

Current Events features trustworthy articles on today's news that connect what you learn in class to the world around you.

No Wi-Fi®? No problem!

HMH Social Studies United States History: Beginnings to 1877 will allow you to connect to content and resources by downloading them when online and accessing them when offline.

Module 1

America, Africa, and Europe before 1500

★

Essential Question

Why might a U.S. historian study the Americas, Africa, and Europe before 1500?

About the Photo: American buffalo were a vital food source for many Native American groups.

▶ Explore ONLINE!

HISTORY.

VIDEOS, including...
- Mexico's Ancient Civilizations
- Corn
- Machu Picchu
- Salt
- Origins of Western Culture
- Rome Falls
- The First Crusade

☑ Document-Based Investigations

☑ Graphic Organizers

☑ Interactive Games

☑ Interactive Map: Migrations of Early People

☑ Image with Hotspots: The Chinook

☑ Image Carousel: Empires of Gold and Salt

In this module you will learn the histories of three regions—the Americas, West Africa, and Europe—whose people would come together and forever change North America.

What You Will Learn ...

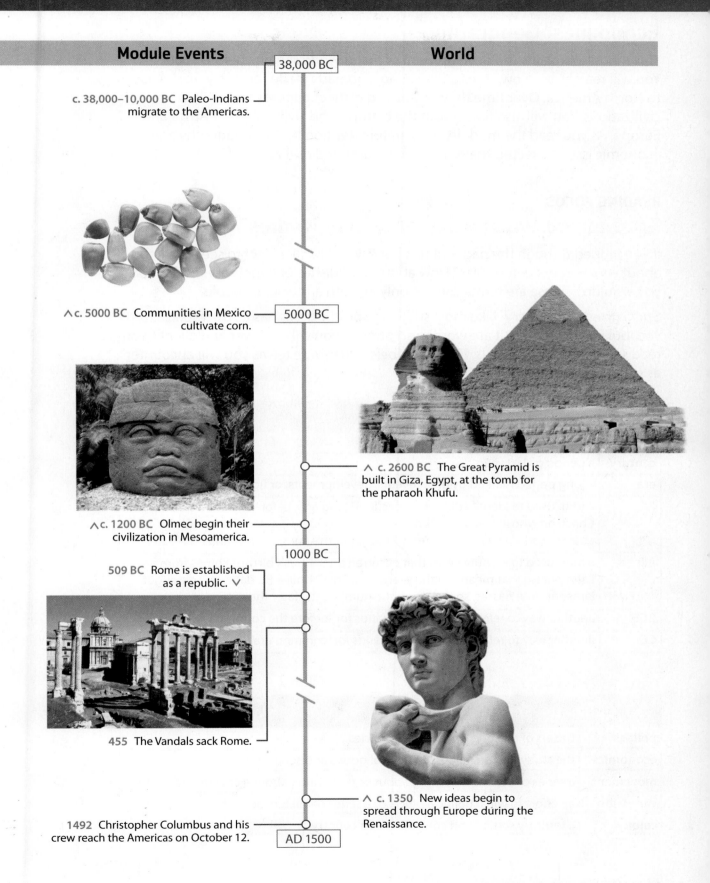

Module Events		World
	38,000 BC	

c. 38,000–10,000 BC Paleo-Indians migrate to the Americas.

∧ **c. 5000 BC** Communities in Mexico cultivate corn. — **5000 BC**

∧ **c. 2600 BC** The Great Pyramid is built in Giza, Egypt, at the tomb for the pharaoh Khufu.

∧ **c. 1200 BC** Olmec begin their civilization in Mesoamerica.

1000 BC

509 BC Rome is established as a republic. ∨

455 The Vandals sack Rome.

∧ **c. 1350** New ideas begin to spread through Europe during the Renaissance.

1492 Christopher Columbus and his crew reach the Americas on October 12.

AD 1500

Reading Social Studies

THEME FOCUS:

Economics, Geography

This module explains the development of major world regions before 1600. You will read about how, during the Ice Age, nomads made their way from Asia to North America. Over time they developed distinct cultures and built great civilizations. You will also read about the cultures and civilizations of Africa and Europe. As you read the module, pay careful attention to how geography and economic issues affected the growth of cultures and civilizations.

READING FOCUS:

Specialized Vocabulary of Social Studies

If you flipped through the pages of this book, would you expect to see anything about square roots or formulas? How about petri dishes or hypotheses? Of course you wouldn't. Those are terms you see only in math and science books.

Specialized Vocabulary Like most subjects, social studies has its own specialized vocabulary. Included in it are words and phrases you will see over and over as you read social studies materials. The charts below list some terms you will encounter as you read this book.

Terms about Time	
decade	a period of 10 years
century	a period of 100 years
era	a long period marked by great events, developments, or figures
BC	a term used to identify dates that occurred long ago, before the birth of Jesus Christ, on whose teachings Christianity was founded; it means "before Christ." BC dates get smaller as time passes, so the larger the number, the earlier the date.
AD	a term used to identify dates that occurred after Jesus's birth; it comes from a Latin phrase that means "in the year of our Lord." Unlike BC dates, AD dates get larger as time passes, so the larger the number, the later the date.
BCE	another way to refer to BC dates; it stands for "before the common era"
CE	another way to refer to AD dates; it stands for "common era"

Terms about Government and Society	
politics	the art of creating government policies
economics	the study of the creation and use of goods and services
movement	a series of actions that bring about or try to bring about a change in society
campaign	an effort to win a political office, or a series of military actions
colony	a territory settled and controlled by a country

You Try It!

The following passage shows you how some specialized vocabulary is defined in context.

> **North and Northwest** Native Americans in the Pacific Northwest carved images of **totems**—ancestor or animal spirits—on tall, wooden poles. Totem poles held great religious and historical significance for Native Americans of the Northwest. Feasts called potlatches were another unique, or unusual, aspect of these Native Americans' culture.

Use the clues to understand meaning.

1. In the first sentence, find the word *totems*. Notice that the term is **highlighted** in yellow. Highlighted terms appear in a list under Key Terms and People on the first page of each lesson. Why do you think some specialized vocabulary terms are highlighted, while others are not?

2. Again, find the word *totems*. The phrase after the **dash** is the definition. Often in this book, specialized vocabulary words are defined after a dash. So be on the lookout for dashes.

3. The word *potlatches* is defined in the third sentence. The clue to finding this definition is the word **called**. Words like **called** and **known as** can indicate that a definition is coming up. In this case, the word *feasts* is a definition of potlatches.

4. The word *unique* is defined in the final sentence. The clue to finding this definition is the **comma** followed by the word **or**. So be on the lookout for commas followed by *or*.

As you read Module 1, keep track of the specialized vocabulary terms you learn.

The Earliest Americans

The Big Idea

Native American societies developed across North and South America.

Main Ideas

- Climate changes allowed Paleo-Indians to migrate to the Americas.
- Major civilizations developed in Mesoamerica and South America.

Key Terms and People

Bering Land Bridge
Paleo-Indians
migration
hunter-gatherers
environments
culture

If YOU were there . . .

You are living in North America about 10,000 years ago, close to the end of the Ice Age. For weeks, your group has been following a herd of elk across a marshy landscape. This trip has taken you far from your usual hunting grounds. The air is warmer here. There are thick grasses and bushes full of berries. You decide to camp here for the summer and perhaps stay a while.

How would settling here change your way of life?

Early Migrations to the Americas

Many scientists believe that the first people arrived in North America during the last Ice Age. At the start of the Ice Age, Earth's climate became intensely cold. Large amounts of water froze into huge, moving sheets of ice called glaciers. As a result, ocean levels dropped more than 300 feet lower than they are today. When the sea level fell, a land bridge between northeastern Asia and present-day Alaska was exposed. Geographers call this strip of land the **Bering Land Bridge**. Although no one knows exactly when or how people crossed into North

Mammoths, such as the skeleton shown here, were present during the Ice Age and were hunted by early peoples in North America.

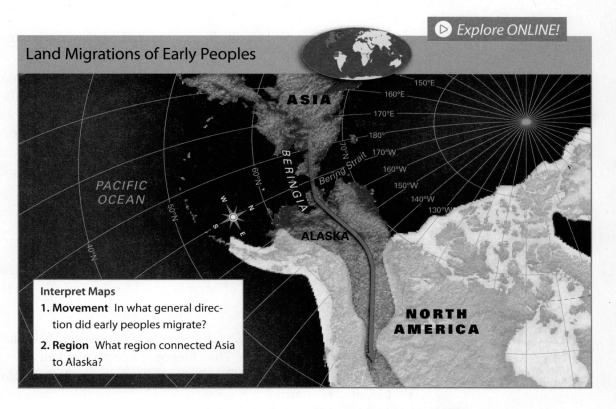

ASIA

150°E
160°E
170°E
180°
170°W
160°W
150°W
140°W
130°W

70°N
60°N
50°N
40°N

BERINGIA

Bering Strait

PACIFIC
OCEAN

ALASKA

NORTH
AMERICA

Interpret Maps
1. **Movement** In what general direction did early peoples migrate?
2. **Region** What region connected Asia to Alaska?

America, evidence suggests that people called **Paleo-Indians** crossed this bridge into Alaska between 38,000 and 10,000 BC.

This **migration**—a movement of people or animals from one region to another—took place over a long time. It is believed that Paleo-Indians traveled south into Canada, the United States, and Mexico following herds of animals. Over time, their descendants went as far as the southern tip of South America. These people were **hunter-gatherers**, people who hunted animals and gathered wild plants for food.

About 8000 BC Earth's climate grew warmer, and the Ice Age ended. Rising temperatures melted glaciers. Water levels in the oceans rose, and the Bering Land Bridge was covered with water.

Although most scholars agree that early peoples crossed the Bering Land Bridge into the Americas, some researchers have proposed other theories about the continents' settlement. Those scientists point to sites in South America that were occupied by humans long before people could have migrated to those places from Beringia, the area surrounding the Bering Land Bridge. One theory in particular provides an explanation. That theory says that people from East Asia came to the west coast of North and South America by boat. They could have stayed in sight of land as they traveled north and then south along the coast.

The warmer climate that developed at the end of the Ice Age created new **environments**—climates and landscapes that surround living things. Large herds of animals such as buffalo and deer ate new short grasses that thrived in the warm climate. As the number of these animals grew, Paleo-Indians hunted them for resources such as meat, hides, and bones.

Varied environments influenced the development of different Native American societies, or groups that share a culture. **Culture** is a group's set

Reading Check
Draw Conclusions
How did climate
change affect early
peoples' migrations?

Academic
Vocabulary
develop the process of
growing or improving

of common values and traditions, including language, government, and family relationships.

Like all societies, Native American groups changed over time. People planted seeds, and eventually they learned to breed animals, farm, and grow plants. Maize, or corn, was one of their most important early crops. Later, they learned to grow beans and squash. Farming allowed people to stop moving around looking for food and to settle in one place. With adequate food supplies, settlements could support larger populations. As populations grew, more advanced societies began to develop.

Early Mesoamerican and South American Societies

Some of the earliest American cultures arose in Mesoamerica, a region that includes the southern part of what is now Mexico and the northern parts of Central America.

Olmec and Maya Around 1200 BC the Olmec **developed** the earliest-known civilization in Mesoamerica. The Olmec are known for their use of stone in architecture and sculpture. They built the first pyramids in the Americas, and they created sculptures of huge stone heads. When their civilization ended around 400 BC, trade had spread Olmec culture throughout the region.

This pyramid is one of five that the Maya built in Tikal, Guatemala, which was an important Maya trading post.

Like the Olmec, the Maya grew maize and other crops and lived in small villages. These villages traded goods with each other, and by about AD 200, the Maya were building large cities.

Maya cities had pyramids, large stone temples, palaces, and bridges. The Maya also paved large plazas for public gatherings and built canals to control the flow of water through the cities.

In the 900s Maya civilization began to collapse. Historians are still not sure what caused this great civilization's decline. Theories include disease, soil exhaustion, and long-term drought, among others.

Aztec The Aztec were fierce warriors, and their superior military ability was key to their success. Around the mid-1100s AD, the Aztec migrated south to central Mexico. There they settled down, conquered many towns, made alliances to build their empire, and controlled a huge trade network.

In AD 1325 the Aztec founded their capital, Tenochtitlán (tay-nawch-teet-LAHN), on an island in Lake Texcoco. Raised roads called causeways connected the island to the shore, making trade and travel easier. Tenochtitlán became the greatest city in the Americas and one of the world's largest cities.

Trade and tribute paid by conquered people in the form of cotton, gold, and food made the Aztec rich. By the early 1500s, they ruled the most powerful state in Mesoamerica.

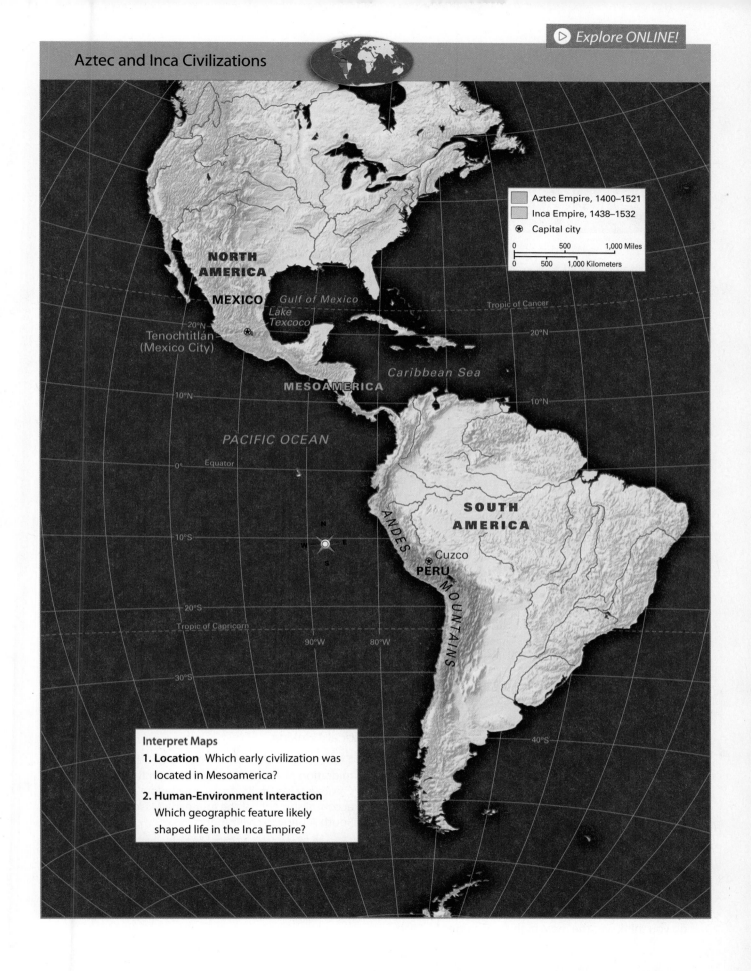

Explore ONLINE!

Aztec Empire, 1400–1521
Inca Empire, 1438–1532
⊛ Capital city

0   500   1,000 Miles
0   500   1,000 Kilometers

NORTH
AMERICA

MEXICO   Gulf of Mexico
                Lake
                Texcoco   Tropic of Cancer
20°N   20°N
Tenochtitlán
(Mexico City)

                                Caribbean Sea
10°N   10°N
        MESOAMERICA

PACIFIC OCEAN

0°   Equator

                                        SOUTH
                                        AMERICA
10°S
        N
    W   E
        S
                        Cuzco
20°S   PERU

Tropic of Capricorn
        90°W   80°W

30°S

40°S

Interpret Maps

1. **Location** Which early civilization was
   located in Mesoamerica?

2. **Human-Environment Interaction**
   Which geographic feature likely
   shaped life in the Inca Empire?

Aztec Calendar of the World

This map is from an illustrated book of the Aztec calendar dating to the 1400s. The map shows the world in the shape of a cross. Each branch is a direction—east (top), west (bottom), north (left), and south (right).

The Aztec used mathematics and their observations of the heavens to create a calendar. The calendar was made up of two cycles that together formed a 52-year period. Among other Aztec achievements were jade and stone carvings, the use of medicinal herbs, and maintenance of a road system. They also had a writing system made up of signs and symbols. The Aztec spoke Nahuatl, a language that still has some 1.5 million speakers, most of whom live in Central Mexico.

Inca The Inca began as a small tribe in the Andes Mountains of South America. They named their capital city Cuzco (KOO-skoh). In the mid-1400s, the Inca began to expand their territory. By the 1500s the empire stretched along the Pacific coast from what is now northern Ecuador to central Chile. In time, the empire was home to about 12 million people. The Inca formed a strong central government with a king as ruler. The official language of the empire was Quechua.

Because they had no written language, the Inca kept records with a system of knotted strings called *quipu*. They also used *quipu* for mathematics. The knots and their positions on the string indicated numbers, while the strings' colors represented different types of information. For example, red strings may have been used to count warriors or yellow strings to count gold. The Inca also developed a device much like a calculator, allowing them to multiply, divide, and use fractions.

The Inca are known for building and for art. Massive buildings and forts were made of huge stone blocks. An advanced system of highways ran the length of the empire. Paved roads and rope bridges connected all parts of Inca territory. This enabled the Inca to communicate with and control their large empire.

Reading Check
Summarize
What early civilizations existed in Mesoamerica and South America?

Summary and Preview Early people migrated into North and South America and developed societies. In the next lesson you will learn about Native American cultures in North America.

Lesson 1 Assessment

Review Ideas, Terms, and People

1. a. Recall What was the Ice Age?

b. Summarize Why were early peoples able to use the Bering Land Bridge?

c. Draw Conclusions Why do you think the migration early peoples in the Americas flowed north to south?

2. a. Identify What was the earliest civilization in the Americas, and where was it located?

b. Analyze How did the Aztec build such a powerful, rich state?

c. Evaluate Which of the four civilizations discussed do you think was the most highly developed? Explain.

Critical Thinking

3. Categorize In this lesson you learned about the migration of early peoples and about their societies. Create a table similar to the one below and identify accomplishments of the four early Mesoamerican and South American civilizations.

	Significant Accomplishments
Olmec	
Maya	
Aztec	
Inca	

Native American Cultures

Many diverse Native American cultures developed across the different geographic regions of North America.

Main Ideas

- Several early societies developed in North America long before Europeans explored the continent.

- Geographic areas influenced Native American cultures.

- Language united Native American groups and contributed to cultural diversity.

- Despite their differences, Native American cultures shared similar beliefs and practices.

Key Terms and People

pueblos
kivas
totems
teepees
matrilineal
Iroquois League

If YOU were there . . .

You live in the North American Southwest about 1,000 years ago. You've been working in the fields for several hours today. The maize crop looks good this summer, and you are hoping for a successful harvest. After finishing your work, you walk home. The opening to your house is in a cliff wall 30 feet above a canyon floor. You must use ladders to get to the opening.

Do you like the location of your home? Why?

Early Societies

The earliest people in North America were hunter-gatherers. After 5000 BC some of these people learned how to farm and settled in villages. In time, many diverse and complex societies developed throughout North America. Although they left no written record, historians have learned about them by studying artifacts, or the objects that they made and used.

Anasazi By 1500 BC the people who lived in the North American Southwest, like those who lived in Mesoamerica, were growing maize. One of the early farm cultures in the Southwest was the Anasazi (ah-nuh-SAH-zee). The Anasazi lived in the Four Corners region, where present-day Arizona, Colorado, New Mexico, and Utah meet. Anasazi farmers adapted to their dry environment and grew maize, beans, and squash. Over time, they began to use irrigation to increase food production. By the time the Anasazi settled in the area, they were already skilled basket makers. They wove straw, vines, and yucca to make containers for food and other items, and they eventually became skilled potters as well.

The early Anasazi lived in pit houses dug into the ground. After about AD 750 they built **pueblos**, or aboveground houses made of a heavy clay called adobe. The Anasazi built these houses on top of each other, creating large multistoried complexes. Some pueblos had several hundred rooms and

Anasazi Cliff Dwellings
Dwellings like these were built into cliffs for safety. Often, ladders were needed to reach the buildings. The ladders could be removed, keeping invaders from reaching the dwellings.

could house 1,000 people. The Anasazi often built their houses in canyon walls and had to use ladders to enter their homes. These cliff dwellings provided a strong defense against enemies. The Anasazi also built **kivas**, underground ceremonial chambers, at the center of each community. Kivas were sacred areas used for religious ceremonies. Some of these rituals focused on the life-giving forces of rain and maize.

The Anasazi thrived for hundreds of years. After AD 1300, however, they began to abandon their villages. Scholars believe that drought, disease, or raids by nomadic tribes from the north may have caused the Anasazi to move away from their pueblos.

Mound Builders Several farming societies developed in the eastern part of North America after 1000 BC. The Hopewell lived along the Mississippi, Ohio, and lower Missouri river valleys. They supported their large population with agriculture and trade. They built large burial mounds to honor their dead.

By AD 700 the Hopewell culture had declined and another culture, the Mississippian, began to thrive in the same area. Skilled farmers and traders, the Mississippian built large settlements. Their largest city, Cahokia, was located near present-day Saint Louis, Missouri. It had a population of 30,000.

The Mississippian people built hundreds of mounds for religious ceremonies. Cahokia alone had more than 100 temple and burial mounds. These mounds had flat tops, and temples were built on top of the mounds. Many of the mounds were gigantic. Monks Mound, near Collinsville, Illinois, for example, was 100 feet high and covered 16 acres.

Reading Check
Summarize
Why did some Native American groups build mounds?

Several other mound-building cultures thrived in eastern North America. More than 10,000 mounds have been found in the Ohio River valley alone. Some of these mounds are shaped like birds and snakes. The mound-building cultures had declined by the time European explorers reached the Southeast. Their societies no longer existed by the early 1700s.

Native American Culture Areas

Researchers use culture areas—the geographic locations that influenced societies—to help them describe ancient Native American peoples. North America is divided into several culture areas.

North and Northwest The far north of North America is divided into the Arctic and Subarctic culture areas. Few plants grow in the Arctic because the ground is always frozen beneath a thin top layer of soil. This harsh environment was home to two groups of people, the Inuit and the Aleut. The Inuit lived in present-day northern Alaska and Canada. Their homes were igloos, hide tents, and huts. The Aleut, whose home was in western and southern Alaska, lived in multifamily houses that were partially underground. The two groups shared many cultural features, including language. Both groups survived by fishing and hunting large mammals. The Aleut and Inuit also depended on dogs for many tasks, such as hunting and pulling sleds.

South of the Arctic lies the Subarctic, home to groups such as the Dogrib and Montagnais peoples. While they followed the seasonal migrations of deer, these peoples lived in shelters made of animal skins. At other times, they lived in villages made up of log houses. Farther south, the Kwakiutl and the Chinook thrived, thanks to the rich supply of game animals, fish, and wild plants that allowed large populations to increase without the need for farming.

Native Americans in the Pacific Northwest carved images of **totems**—ancestor or animal spirits—on tall, wooden poles. Totem poles held great religious and historical significance for Native Americans of the Northwest. Feasts called potlatches were another unique, or unusual, aspect of these Native Americans' culture. At these gatherings, hosts, usually chiefs or wealthy people, gave away most of their belongings as

People in different culture areas created unique artifacts. The bird-shaped pipe (left) is from the Northwest Coast culture area. The sewing tool (center) with a carved bone handle was used in the Great Plains. The human figure (right) was created by someone who lived in the Southwest culture area.

gifts. Those gifts would likely be distributed to friends or even neighboring tribes. By displaying their generosity, potlatch hosts increased their social status and power. Potlatches were also occasions for defining roles within the group and for granting economic privileges.

West and Southwest Farther south along the Pacific coast was the California region, which included the area between the Pacific and the Sierra Nevada mountain range. Food sources were plentiful, so farming was not necessary. One major plant food was acorns, which were ground into flour. People also fished and hunted deer and other game. Most Native Americans in the California region lived in groups of families of about 50 to 300. Among these groups, including the Hupa, Miwok, and Yokuts, more than 100 languages were spoken.

The area east of the Sierra Nevada, the Great Basin, received little rain. To survive, Native Americans adapted to the drier climate by gathering seeds, digging roots, and trapping small animals for food. Most groups in this area, including the Paiute, Shoshone, and Ute, spoke the same language.

The Southwest culture region included the present-day states of Arizona and New Mexico and parts of Colorado and Texas. Pueblo groups, such as the Hopi and Zuni, lived there. Like the Anasazi, these Native Americans also adapted to a dry climate. The Pueblo irrigated the land and grew maize, squash, and beans. These crops were vital to southwestern peoples. The Pueblo religion focused on two key areas of Pueblo life—rain and maize. The Pueblo performed religious rituals hoping to bring rain and a successful maize crop to their people.

Pueblo peoples were settled and built multistoried houses out of adobe bricks. Over time their towns grew larger, and some towns had more than 1,000 residents. Pueblo peoples made fine pottery that featured beautifully painted designs.

The Apache and Navajo also lived in the Southwest. These groups were nomadic—they moved from place to place hunting small animals and foraging for food. The Apache and Navajo also supported themselves by raiding the villages of the Pueblo and others.

Great Plains The huge Great Plains region stretches south from Canada into Texas. This culture area is bordered by the Mississippi Valley on the east and the Rocky Mountains on the west. The Plains were mainly grassland, home to millions of buffalo. Deer, elk, and other game also thrived there.

Most Great Plains peoples were nomadic hunters. Many groups hunted buffalo using bows and spears. Blackfoot and Arapaho hunters sometimes chased the animals over cliffs, drove them into corrals, or trapped them in a ring of fire. Native Americans on the Plains used buffalo skins for shields, clothing, and coverings for their **teepees**— cone-shaped shelters. Buffalo skins were also trade items.

Some Plains groups were farmers, while others depended more on gathering foods in addition to hunting. For example, some groups of Sioux

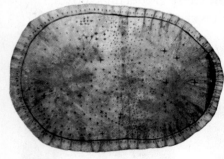

Pawnee Star Chart

The Pawnee carefully observed the night sky. This map of the night sky dates to the 1700s, but historians believe that Plains Indians used similar maps before 1500.

gathered wild rice and speared fish. The Mandan and Pawnee settled in villages and grew corn, beans, and squash. The Pawnee lived in round lodges made of dirt.

Like some other Native American groups, Pawnee society was **matrilineal**. This means that people traced their ancestry through their mothers, not their fathers. In some groups, such as the Sioux, women organized societies focused on the community's well-being. Men of the Sioux belonged to military societies that acted as a police force.

Northeast and Southeast Eastern North America was rich in sources of food and shelter. Animals, plant foods, fish, and wood for housing were plentiful in the region's woodlands and river valleys.

Most southeastern groups, including the Cherokee, Creek, and Seminole, lived in farming villages governed by village councils. In the Northeast, groups like the Algonquian survived by hunting and gathering plants. Those in the south farmed, hunted, gathered plants, and fished. Many tribes used strings of beads known as wampum for money.

To the east of the Algonquian lived the Iroquois (or Haudenosaunee). They were farmers, hunters, and traders. Among their crops were squash, corn, and beans. During the cold winters, the Iroquois cut holes in the ice over rivers and lakes to catch fish. In the spring, they tapped the region's maple trees to make syrup. The Iroquois lived in longhouses, or rectangular homes made from logs and bark, that housed eight to ten families.

Five Iroquois nations—the Cayuga, Mohawk, Oneida, Onondaga, and Seneca—formed a political alliance called the **Iroquois League**. This is also

Iroquois Longhouse

Northeastern Native Americans such as the Iroquois lived in longhouses made of tree bark. The drawing at right shows the longhouses in one Iroquois village.

Why do you think a fence was built around the longhouses?

Modus muniendi apud Mahikanenses

Maniere van Woonplaetsen ofte Dorpen der Mahicans ende andre Natien huer geburen

Native American Culture Areas

▶ Explore ONLINE!

Legend:
- Arctic
- Subarctic
- Northwest Coast
- Plateau
- Great Plains
- Northeast
- Great Basin
- California
- Southwest
- Southeast

0   250   500 Miles
0   250   500 Kilometers

Inuit
Inuit
Aleut
Ingalik
Han
Saschutkenne
Inuit
Eyak
Tagish
Dogrib
Tlingit
Slave
Beaver
Chipewyan
Inuit
Naskapi
Beothuk
Tongass
Haisla
Carrier
Swampy Cree
Montagnais
Haida
Heiltsuk
Micmac
Kwakiutl
Nootka
Shuswap
Squamish
Makah
Nooksack
Chimakum
Coast Salish
Columbia
Spokane
Blackfoot
Plains Cree
Plains Ojibway
NORTH AMERICA
Algonquian
Ottawa
Massachuset
Wampanoag
Narragansett
Chinook
Yakima
Huron
Pequot
Mohegan
Klickitat
Walla Walla
Nez Percé
Crow
Mandan
Great Lakes
Iroquois Mohawk
Oneida
Onondaga
Cayuga
Seneca
Yaquina
Molala
Umpqua
Modoc
Northern Paiute
Santee Sioux
Sauk
Fox
Potawatomi
Delaware
Susquehanna
Tolowa
Achomawi
Northern Shoshone
Teton Sioux
Cheyenne
Kickapoo
Miami
Hupa
Washo
Maidu
ROCKY MOUNTAINS
Omaha
Iowa
Illinois
Powhatan
Yuki
Wappo
Miwok
Western Shoshone
Arapaho
Pawnee
Missouri
Shawnee
ATLANTIC OCEAN
Costanoan
Esselen
Yokuts
Chumash
Mono
Kawaiisu
Ute
Kansa
Cahokia
Osage
Cherokee
Cheraw
Hopi (Pueblo)
Navajo
Zuni (Pueblo)
Apache
Kiowa
Chickasaw
Tuskegee
Cusabo
Mohave
Comanche
Creek
Alabama
Yuma
Apache
Suma
Wichita
Choctaw
Mobile
Apalachee
Nakipa
Pima
Jumano
Caddo
Tonkawa
Cochimi
Seri
Tarahumara
Karankawa
Seminole
Calusa
Ignacieno
Yaqui
Gulf of Mexico
Tropic of Cancer
Taino
Waicura
Lagunero
Guachichil
MESOAMERICA
Caribbean Sea
PACIFIC OCEAN
Hudson Bay
Arctic Circle

Interpret Maps

1. **Region** Why did some culture areas have fewer groups of people than other culture areas did?

2. **Human-Environment Interaction** What natural features served as boundaries between culture areas?

known as the Iroquois Confederation. In 1722, a sixth nation, the Tusca-rora, joined the league. The Confederation kept peace among its members and waged war to protect its territory from invasion.

Highly organized and extremely powerful, the Iroquois Confederation held strong for hundreds of years. Its government was founded in the Great Law of Peace, an oral constitution that emphasized the equality of all people. The confederation made decisions through representatives and consensus, or agreement. Some scholars propose that the constitution and structure of the Iroquois Confederation inspired the framers of the U.S. Constitution.

Reading Check
Generalize
How did environment influence Native American cultures in North America?

Native American Languages

As you can see on the "Native American Culture Areas" map, some culture areas, such as the Arctic, occupied large regions, but had few distinct groups of people. By contrast, the California and Northwest Coast areas were home to many groups. Language played an important part in the cultural diversity of these regions.

At the time of European contact, about 300 languages were spoken in North America. Most could be grouped into 29 language families, or languages that descend from a common ancestor. Present-day California was home to more than 70 languages and 20 language families, some of which covered areas no larger than a modern county. Other language families occupied broader territory. One of the largest, the Uto-Aztecan language family, covered about a fourth of what is now the continental United States. Today the Shoshone in the Great Basin and the Hopi in the Southwest continue to speak Uto-Aztecan languages.

Reading Check
Make Inferences
How were Native American culture areas and languages connected?

Similar Beliefs and Practices

Despite their differences, Native American groups of North America shared a number of similar beliefs and practices. For example, Native Americans held similar spiritual and religious ideas. One was a spiritual connection to the natural world. A chief of a Wabanaki nation in the Northeast once described this idea by saying "The Great Spirit is our father, but the Earth is our mother."

In many belief systems, a tree stood at the center of the earth. For the Iroquois it was a white pine; for the Sioux, a mighty flowering tree. Animals, too, were thought to be powerful spirits. Hunters often carried out rituals to honor the spirit of an animal they were about to kill. Many groups chose an animal as their symbol and spirit guide.

Native Americans also had similar ideas about land ownership. Generally speaking, they did not believe that land could be bought, sold, or owned by individuals. Rather, land was held for the use of everyone in a group to hunt, fish, or gather and grow food as needed. Many believed that they should preserve the land and its resources for future generations. These beliefs contrasted sharply with those of Europeans, who believed that land and everything on it could be bought and owned by individuals. This difference would cause conflict for hundreds of years.

Though Native Americans did not own land, they did have other forms of private property. For example, in the Great Plains, women owned tepees and most household goods.

Among all the peoples of North America, women played essential roles in the groups' survival. Women performed many tasks, such as making baskets and clothing, cooking, hunting, child rearing, and gathering wild foods. Among the Inuit, women had to prepare meat obtained on a hunt before the cold air froze the meat. In farming societies, women were usually responsible for growing crops. In many North American groups, women owned property in their own right and held considerable power. For example, Iroquois clanmothers—older, respected women of the community—appointed the chief. The clanmothers could also fire the chief if he proved to be a poor leader.

Though they held similar traits in common, the diverse culture groups of North America generally did not join together into large political units. For most Native American peoples, respected elders and chiefs led local groups. Native Americans were, however, connected by thousands of miles of trade networks. Along with foodstuffs, raw materials, and exotic goods, trade networks carried ideas from place to place. One of the most famous routes began in Iroquois country and ran southward through mountain valleys to present-day North Carolina. It crossed the territory of the Shawnee, Choctaw, Cherokee, and other nations.

Summary and Preview People of North America formed many complex societies. In the next lesson you will read about societies in West Africa.

Reading Check
Identify Points of View What beliefs and practices did Native American groups share?

Lesson 2 Assessment

Review Ideas, Terms, and People

1. **a. Recall** Why did the Anasazi build kivas?

   b. Summarize What different types of housing were built by the Anasazi?

   c. Draw Conclusions Why do you think that some mounds were built in the shapes of birds and snakes?

2. **a. Identify** What are culture areas?

   b. Contrast How did food sources for Native Americans of the North and Northwest differ from those living in the West and Southwest?

   c. Elaborate Why was the formation of the Iroquois League considered to be a significant political development?

3. **a. Recall** About how many languages were spoken in North America at the time of European contact?

   b. Analyze What role did language have in the various regions of North America?

   c. Make Generalizations What generalization can you make about Native American languages in what is now California?

4. **a. Recall** How did Native Americans view land ownership?

   b. Analyze What role did nature play in the religious ideas of Native Americans?

   c. Explain Why do you think women held positions of power and influence in many Native American groups?

Critical Thinking

5. **Compare and Contrast** In this lesson you learned about early societies and culture areas. Create a graphic organizer like the one below to compare and contrast early Native American culture groups.

North and Northwest	
West and Southwest	
Great Plains	
Northeast and Southeast	

★
Trading Kingdoms of West Africa

The Big Idea

Using trade to gain wealth, Ghana, Mali, and Songhai were West Africa's most powerful kingdoms.

Main Ideas

- The Empire of Ghana was the first of three great West African trading kingdoms.

- Like Ghana, the empires of Mali and Songhai grew strong by controlling trade.

Key Terms and People

Berbers
Mansa Musa
hajj
mosques
Askia the Great

If YOU were there . . .

You are a trader's assistant from the Middle East, traveling in a caravan headed for West Africa. The caravan carries many goods, but the most precious is salt. Your job is to trade the salt for gold and return the gold to your employer immediately. Your boss never meets the traders face to face.

Why is your boss so secretive?

Empire of Ghana

By 1500 West Africa was well known for its trading kingdoms. Since ancient times, despite the dangers of the Sahara, trade routes crisscrossed West Africa. For many years, **Berbers**, a group of people from northern Africa, controlled these routes. In time, however, a series of three great trading empires arose thanks to the control of the salt and gold trades. Ghana (GAH-nuh) was the first of these empires.

The Rise of Ghana Historians think the first people in Ghana were farmers along the Niger River. Sometime after AD 300 these farmers, the Soninke (soh-NING-kee), were threatened by nomadic herders. The herders wanted to take the farmers' water and pastures. For protection, groups of Soninke families began to band together. This banding together was the beginning of Ghana.

Ghana was in an ideal position to become a trading center. To the north lay the vast Sahara, the source of much of the salt. Ghana itself was rich in gold. People wanted gold for its beauty, but they needed salt in their diets to survive. Salt, which could be used to preserve food, also made bland food tasty. These qualities made salt very valuable. In fact, Africans sometimes cut up slabs of salt and used the pieces as money.

As the gold and salt trade increased, Ghana's rulers gained power. Eventually, they built up armies equipped with iron weapons that were superior to the weapons of nearby people. Over time, Ghana conquered its neighbors and took control over trade in the region.

Ghana's rulers grew wealthy by controlling trade in salt and gold. Salt came from the north in large slabs, and gold came from the south.

By 800 Ghana was firmly in control of West Africa's trade routes. Nearly all trade between northern and southern Africa passed through Ghana. With so many traders passing through their lands, Ghana's rulers looked for ways to make money from them. One way they raised money was by forcing traders to pay taxes. All traders who entered Ghana had to pay a special tax on the goods they carried. Then they had to pay another tax on any goods they took with them when they left. Ghana's rulers gained incredible wealth from trade, taxes on traders and on the people of Ghana, and their own personal stores of gold. They used their wealth to build an army and an empire.

Islam in Ghana Extensive trade routes brought the people of Ghana into contact with people of many different cultures and beliefs. As the kingdom of Ghana extended into the Sahara, increased contact with Arab traders from the east brought the religion of Islam to Ghana.

Islam was founded in the 600s by an Arab man named Muhammad. Muslims, followers of Islam, believe that God had spoken to Muhammad through an angel and had made him a prophet, someone who tells of God's messages. After Muhammad's death, his followers wrote down his teachings to form the book known as the Qur'an. Islam spread quickly through the Arabian Peninsula.

In the 1060s a Muslim group called the Almoravids (al-muh-RAH-vuhdz) attacked Ghana in an effort to force its leaders to convert to Islam. The Almoravids weakened Ghana's empire and cut off many trade routes.

Reading Check
Identify
How did Ghana become wealthy through trade?

Without its trade, Ghana could not support its empire, and the empire eventually fell. The influence of Islam, however, remained strong. By the late 1400s Islam would become the most practiced religion in the region.

The Empires of Mali and Songhai

For about 150 years after Ghana's decline, no one kingdom controlled trade across the Sahara. Then two new trading empires rose to power in the region—Mali (MAH-lee) followed by Songhai (SAWNG-hy).

Kingdom of Mali Like Ghana, Mali lay along the upper Niger River. This area's fertile soil helped Mali grow. In addition, Mali's location on the Niger allowed its people to control trade on the river. Through this control of trade, the empire grew rich and powerful. According to legend, Mali's rise to power began under a ruler named Sundiata. Sundiata

Mansa Musa was a descendant of Sundiata, the first emperor to rule a united Mali.

won back his country's independence and conquered nearby kingdoms, including Ghana.

Mali's most famous ruler, however, was a Muslim king named **Mansa Musa** (MAHN-sah moo-SAH). Under his leadership, Mali reached the height of its wealth, power, and fame.

Mansa Musa ruled Mali for about 25 years, from 1312 to 1337. During that time, Mali added many important trade cities, including Timbuktu (tim-buhk-TOO), Djenné (je-NAY), and Gao (GOW), to its empire. Traders came to Timbuktu from the north and the south to trade for salt, gold, metals, shells, and many other goods.

Religion was also very important to Mansa Musa. In 1324 he left Mali on a **hajj**, or pilgrimage to Mecca. Making this journey once in their lives is the spiritual duty of all Muslims. As he traveled to Mecca, Mansa Musa introduced his empire to the world. The stories of Mali's wealth and religion spread far and wide. Because of Mansa Musa's influence, Islam spread through a large part of West Africa.

Mansa Musa wanted all Muslims to be able to read the Qur'an. Therefore, he stressed the importance of learning to read and write the Arabic language. He sent scholars to study in Morocco. These scholars later set up schools in Mali for studying the Qur'an.

To encourage the spread of Islam in West Africa, Mansa Musa brought back artists and architects from other Muslim countries to build **mosques**, or buildings for Muslim prayer, throughout his lands.

▷ Explore ONLINE!

Empires of West Africa, 800–1500

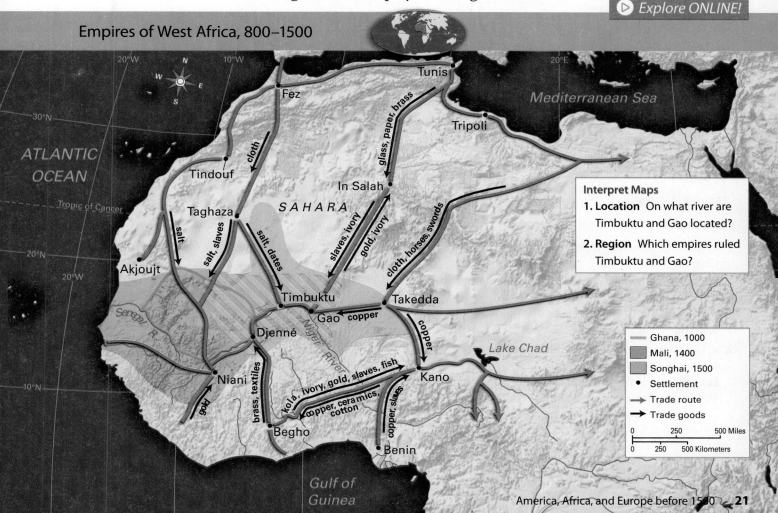

Interpret Maps

1. **Location** On what river are Timbuktu and Gao located?

2. **Region** Which empires ruled Timbuktu and Gao?

Ghana, 1000
Mali, 1400
Songhai, 1500
• Settlement
→ Trade route
→ Trade goods

0   250   500 Miles
0 250 500 Kilometers

Askia the Great became ruler of Songhai when he was nearly 50 years old. He ruled Songhai for about 35 years.

Reading Check
Compare
What did Mali and Songhai have in common?

The architectural advances in cities like Timbuktu as well as an organized government, an emphasis on education, and an expansion of trade all combined to make Mansa Musa Mali's most successful ruler. Much of Mali's success depended on strong leaders. After Mansa Musa died, poor leadership weakened the empire. By 1500 nearly all of the lands the kingdom once ruled were lost. Only a small area of Mali remained.

Songhai Empire In the 1300s Mansa Musa had conquered a rival kingdom of people called the Songhai, who also lived along the Niger River. As the Mali Empire weakened in the 1400s, the Songhai grew wealthy by trading goods along the Niger. They took advantage of Mali's decline, regained their independence, and eventually conquered most of Mali.

One of Songhai's greatest rulers was Muhammad Ture, who chose the title *askia*, a title of military rank. He became known as **Askia the Great**. Like Mansa Musa, Askia the Great was a devout Muslim who supported education and learning. Under his rule, the cities of Gao and Timbuktu flourished. They contained great mosques, universities, schools, and libraries. People came from all parts of West Africa to study mathematics, science, medicine, grammar, and law.

Askia understood that an empire needed effective government. He created a professional army, and to improve the government, he set up five provinces within Songhai. He removed local leaders and appointed new governors who were loyal to him. He also created specialized departments to oversee various tasks, much like modern-day government offices do.

Soon after Askia the Great lost power, the empire of Songhai declined. Songhai was invaded by the Moroccans, the kingdom's northern neighbors. The Moroccans wanted to control the Saharan salt mines. They had superior military power and were able to take over Timbuktu and Gao. Changes in trade patterns completed Songhai's fall.

Summary and Preview Trade was important to the kingdoms of West Africa. In the next lesson you will learn about Europe before 1500.

Lesson 3 Assessment

Review Ideas, Terms, and People

1. a. Identify How did trade contribute to the rise of Ghana?

   b. Explain Why did Ghana's rulers tax traders passing through their kingdom?

   c. Evaluate Which resource do you think was more valuable to Ghana, gold or salt? Why?

2. a. Describe How did Mansa Musa introduce his empire to the world?

   b. Compare How did Islam affect the achievements of Mali and Songhai?

   c. Evaluate What do you think was the most important achievement of Askia the Great? Explain.

Critical Thinking

3. Compare and Contrast In this lesson you learned about African kingdoms and trade. Create a chart like the one below and identify the similarities and differences that led to the fall of the kingdoms of Ghana, Mali, and Songhai.

Fall of Ghana, Mali, and Songhai	Similarities	Differences

Europe before 1500

The Big Idea
New ideas and trade changed Europeans' lives.

Main Ideas
- The Greeks and Romans established new forms of government.
- During the Middle Ages, society eventually changed from a feudal system to a system with a middle class of artisans and merchants.
- The Renaissance was a time of rebirth in the arts and in learning.

Key Terms and People
Socrates
Plato
Aristotle
reason
democracy
knights
Black Death
Michelangelo
Leonardo da Vinci
Johannes Gutenberg
joint-stock companies

Academic Vocabulary
classical referring to the cultures of ancient Greece or Rome

If YOU were there . . .
You are a peasant in the Middle Ages, living on the land of a noble. Although you and your family work very hard from sunrise to sundown, much of the food you grow goes to the noble. Your house is very small and has a dirt floor. Your parents are tired and weak, and you wish you could do something to improve their lives.

Is there any way you could change your life?

Greek and Roman Influences

By 1500 European culture had been shaped by centuries of civilization and cultural development. Among the most significant and lasting contributions were those made by the ancient Greeks and Romans.

Greek Philosophers and Government Ancient Greeks valued human reason and believed in the power of the human mind to think, explain, and understand life. Three of the greatest Greek thinkers, or philosophers, were **Socrates**, **Plato**, and **Aristotle**. Socrates, a great teacher, wanted to make people think and question their own beliefs. Plato, a philosopher and teacher, wrote a work called *The Republic*. It describes an ideal society based on justice and fairness for everyone. Aristotle taught that people should live their lives based on **reason**, or clear and ordered thinking.

Greek scientists and mathematicians also gained fame for their contributions to geometry and for accurately calculating the size of Earth. Doctors studied the human body to understand how it worked. One Greek engineering invention that is still used today is a water screw, which brings water to farm fields.

One of the Greeks' most lasting contributions, however, is their political system. During the time known as the **Classical** Period, around the fifth and fourth centuries BC, Greece was organized into several hundred independent

The Roman Senate played a principal role in the Roman government.

city-states, which became the foundation for Greek civilization. Athens was the first Greek city-state to establish **democracy**—a form of government in which people rule themselves. All male citizens in Athens had the right to participate in the assembly, a gathering of citizens, to debate and create the city's laws. Every citizen voted on every issue. Because all male citizens in Athens participated directly in government, we call the Greek form of government a direct democracy.

Roman Law and Government Later, Rome followed Greece's example by establishing a form of democratic government. The Roman Republic was created in 509 BC. Each year freeborn male citizens of Rome elected officials to rule the city. These officials acted on behalf of the citizens and debated ideas at an assembly of representatives. They had many powers, but stayed in power for only one year. Although this early republic was not a direct democracy, it did allow input from citizens. Later, the Romans changed their government into one with three parts. These three parts were made up of elected representatives who protected the city and its residents.

Roman laws were written and kept on public display so all people could know them. Roman concepts of equality before the law and innocent until proven guilty protected Roman citizens' rights.

The political ideas of Greece and Rome survived to influence governments around the world, including that of the United States. In the U.S. political system, citizens vote for representatives, making the nation a democratic republic.

Reading Check
Analyze
How did Roman and Greek governments influence the United States?

Middle Ages

As the Roman Empire fell, groups from the north and east moved into former Roman lands. By the early 500s Europe was divided into many small kingdoms. This marked the beginning of the Middle Ages, a period that lasted about a thousand years.

Feudalism In the 480s a powerful group called the Franks conquered Gaul, the region we now call France. The Franks created a huge empire in

The structure of feudal society has been likened to a pyramid, with kings sitting at the very top of society and peasants at the bottom.

Europe. When invaders began to attack European settlements in the 800s, the Frankish kings could not defend their empire. Nobles had to defend their own lands. As a result, the power of nobles grew, and kings became less powerful. Although loyal to the king, nobles ruled their lands as independent territories.

Nobles needed soldiers to defend their lands. Nobles gave **knights**, warriors who fought on horseback, land in exchange for military service. Nobles who gave land to knights so the knights would defend the land were called lords. A knight who promised to support the noble in battle was called a vassal. This system of promises between lords and vassals is known as feudalism.

Peasants owned no land, so they were not part of the feudal system. They did, however, need to grow food to live. As a result, a new economic system developed. Knights allowed peasants to farm land on their large estates, called manors. In return, the peasants had to give the knights food or other goods as payment.

Because of its structure, feudalism promoted the separation of territories and people. The Catholic Church, however, served as a strong unifying force among the states and people of Europe. During the Middle Ages, nearly everyone in Europe was Christian. Life revolved around the local church with markets, festivals, and religious ceremonies.

The Crusades In the late 1000s a long series of wars called the Crusades began between the European Christians and Muslims in Southwest Asia.

The Turks had captured Palestine, also known as the Holy Land because it was where Jesus had lived. Christians no longer felt safe to travel there on pilgrimages. Christians were called upon to go to war with the Turks to recapture Palestine.

Although the Crusades failed, they changed Europe forever. Trade between Europe and Asia began to grow, introducing Europeans to new products such as apricots, rice, and cotton cloth, as well as the ideas of Muslim thinkers.

Travel, Trade, and Towns In the Middle Ages, towns were small. After about 1000, this situation began to change. New technology meant farmers could produce larger harvests. As farmers grew more food, the population increased.

Travel became safer as increased protection from stronger rulers kept larger territories secure. Over time, kingdoms became nation-states—organized political units with central governments. This development provided even more protection to merchants.

The rulers of the Mongols made routes like the Silk Road (a caravan route that started in China and ended at the Mediterranean Sea) safe for travelers and traders. Among these traders was Marco Polo. In 1271 he journeyed from Europe to China along part of the old Silk Road. He spent 20 years living and traveling in Asia. When Marco Polo returned to Europe, he brought back stories of spices, coal, and paper money.

Timeline: Key Events in the Middle Ages

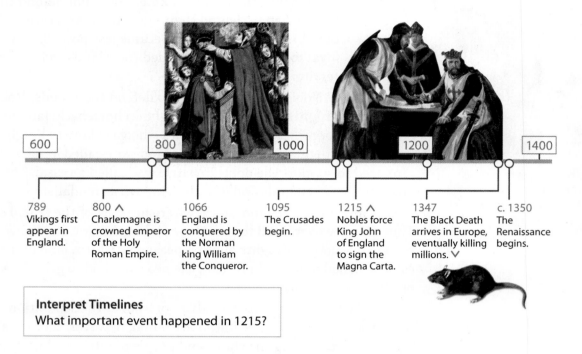

| 600 | 800 | 1000 | 1200 | 1400 |

789
Vikings first appear in England.

800 ∧
Charlemagne is crowned emperor of the Holy Roman Empire.

1066
England is conquered by the Norman king William the Conqueror.

1095
The Crusades begin.

1215 ∧
Nobles force King John of England to sign the Magna Carta.

1347
The Black Death arrives in Europe, eventually killing millions. ∨

c. 1350
The Renaissance begins.

Interpret Timelines
What important event happened in 1215?

Trade routes spread all across Europe. Merchants brought goods from Asia and Africa to sell in European markets. Their ships also brought back rats infected with the plague. The disease, known as the **Black Death**, spread across Europe, killing an estimated 25 million people. The European economy was dramatically affected by the shortage of workers. Peasants and serfs could now demand payment for their labor. They began to move to cities, which began to grow in size.

In time, the growth of trade led to the decline of feudalism and the manor system. A new middle class of artisans and merchants emerged, and trade cities became commercial centers. Trade associations called guilds became an influential part of European life.

Reading Check
Draw Conclusions
How did travel and trade affect the feudal system?

Renaissance

The Renaissance period brought new ways of thinking to Europe, weakening the old feudal system even more. The word *Renaissance* means "rebirth" and refers to the period that followed the Middle Ages in Europe. This movement began in Italy and eventually spread to other parts of Europe.

During the Renaissance, European rulers began to increase their power over the nobles in their countries. Fewer invasions from outside forces helped bring a period of order and stability to Europe.

Search for Knowledge Love of art and education was a key feature of the Renaissance. As Turks conquered much of the Byzantine Empire in the East, scholars fled to Italy. They brought ancient classical writings with them. Some of the works were by Greek thinkers like Plato.

Excited by the discoveries brought by Byzantine scholars, European scholars went looking for ancient texts in Latin. They discovered many

Latin texts in monasteries, which had preserved works by Roman writers. As Italian scholars read these ancient texts, they rediscovered the glories of Greece and Rome.

The search for knowledge and learning spread to all fields, including art, literature, science, and political thought. The Renaissance emphasized the importance of people rather than focusing on religion. This new focus on human value and the study of humanities was called humanism. People's interest in the humanities led them to respect those who could write, create, or speak well. During the Middle Ages, most people had worked only to glorify God.

Italian artists created some of the most beautiful paintings and sculptures in the world. Their art reflected the basic Renaissance idea—the value of human beings. They rejected flat, two-dimensional images used in medieval art in favor of classical forms and techniques such as perspective. **Michelangelo** and **Leonardo da Vinci** are two of the greatest Renaissance artists. They are known for their work in the fields of painting, sculpture, and architecture. Leonardo was also an inventor, engineer, and mapmaker.

Italian writers also penned great works of literature. Dante Alighieri was a politician and poet. Before Dante, most authors wrote in Latin, the language of the church. But Dante chose to write in Italian, the common language of the people. This gave ordinary people the opportunity to read Dante's work.

Many texts that Europeans rediscovered in the 1300s dealt with science. After reading these works, Renaissance scholars went on to make their own scientific advances. They also studied ancient math texts and built on the ideas they read about. For example, they created symbols for the square root and for positive and negative numbers. Astronomers discovered that Earth moves around the sun. Other scientists used measurements and made calculations to create better, more accurate maps.

By 1450 Johannes Gutenberg had refined his invention of the printing press.

The development of the printing press was a giant step forward in spreading new ideas. In the mid-1400s, a German man, **Johannes Gutenberg** (GOOT-uhn-berk), developed a printing press that used movable type. This allowed an entire page to be printed at once. For the first time in history, thousands of people could read the same books and share ideas about them.

Economic Changes Affect Trade The growth in trade and services at the beginning of the Renaissance sparked a commercial revolution. This also brought a rise in mercantilism. Mercantilism is an economic system that unifies and increases the power and wealth of a nation.

Four northern Italian cities, Florence, Genoa, Milan, and Venice, developed into important trading centers. These cities played two major roles in trade. They served as ports along the Mediterranean Sea. They also served as manufacturing centers and specialized in certain crafts. This economic activity made some families in these cities very wealthy.

As trade and commerce grew, the need for banks arose. Bankers in Florence, Italy, kept money for merchants from all over Europe. The bankers also made money by charging interest on funds they loaned to merchants. The greatest bankers in Florence were from the Medici family. Although Florence was already wealthy from trade, banking increased that wealth.

Reading Check
Draw Conclusions
How did the Renaissance lead to trade and a commercial revolution?

During this time, merchants began to create **joint-stock companies**, or businesses in which a group of people invest together. In a joint-stock company, the investors share in the company's profits and losses. Forming joint-stock companies allowed investors to take fewer risks.

Summary and Preview Greek and Roman civilizations, the Middle Ages, and the Renaissance were major forces that shaped European history. In the next module you will read about how the Renaissance paved the way for exploration of the Americas.

Lesson 4 Assessment

Review Ideas, Terms, and People

1. **a. Identify** What is the difference between a direct democracy and a republic?
   b. Elaborate What is the importance of having a written law code?
2. **a. Describe** What was the relationship between knights and nobles?
   b. Elaborate How did the Crusades affect the feudal system?
3. **a. Identify** What does the term *Renaissance* mean?
   b. Analyze What is the relationship among trade, banking, and joint-stock companies?
   c. Elaborate What do you think was the greatest accomplishment of the Renaissance?

Critical Thinking

4. **Support a Point of View** You learned about the major changes that took place in Europe during the periods discussed in this lesson. Create a chart similar to the one below and identify which period you think was the most important and explain why.

Most Important	Why

Interpret Diagrams

Understand the Skill

Diagrams are drawings that use lines and labels to explain or illustrate something. Different types of diagrams have different purposes. *Pictorial diagrams* show an object in simple form, much like it would look if you were viewing it. *Cutaway diagrams* show the "insides" of an object. *Component diagrams* show how an object is organized by separating it into parts. Such diagrams are sometimes also called *schematic drawings*. The ability to interpret diagrams will help you to better understand a historical object, its function, and how it worked.

Learn the Skill

Use these basic steps to interpret a diagram:

1. Determine what type of diagram it is.

2. Read the diagram's title or caption to find out what the diagram represents.

3. Look for any labels and read them carefully. Most diagrams include text that identifies the object's parts or explains relationships among the parts.

4. If a legend is present, study it to identify and understand any symbols and colors that are used in the diagram.

5. Look for numbers or letters that might indicate a sequence of steps. Also, look for any arrows that might show direction or movement.

An Early Castle

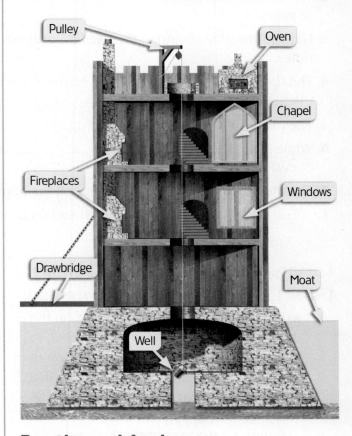

Practice and Apply

Interpret the diagram of an early castle and answer the following questions.

1. What type of diagram is this?

2. What labels in the diagram suggest how the castle was heated?

3. What was the purpose of the pulley?

4. Of what materials was the castle made?

5. What features of the castle helped make it secure against attack?

Module 1 Assessment

Review Vocabulary, Terms, and People

Complete each sentence by filling in the blank with the correct term or person.

1. During the Ice Age, a narrow strip of land called the _____ was exposed.

2. The _____ of Paleo-Indians from North to South America took thousands of years.

3. Native Americans living in the Pacific Northwest carved _____ on tall poles.

4. The first political confederation of Native Americans in North America was the _____.

5. The most famous ruler of Mali was _____.

6. While Mali's leader was on a _____, or pilgrimage to Mecca, he introduced his empire to the world.

7. The most famous ruler of Songhai took the name _____.

8. _____ describes an ideal society based on justice in *The Republic*.

Comprehension and Critical Thinking

Lesson 1

9. a. **Describe** How did early peoples in the Americas get their food?
   b. **Analyze** What led to the development of different culture groups in the Americas?
   c. **Elaborate** What features did the early civilizations of Mesoamerica and South America have in common?

Lesson 2

10. a. **Identify** Which early Native American society built cliff dwellings and which built mounds?
   b. **Analyze** How did Native Americans' religious beliefs affect their lives in North America?
   c. **Evaluate** Do you think it was easier for Native Americans to live in the dry climate of the Southwest, where rainfall was scarce, or in the North, where the cold climate presented a constant challenge?

Lesson 3

11. a. **Describe** Which two major trade goods made Ghana rich?
   b. **Compare** What characteristics did Mansa Musa and Askia the Great have in common?
   c. **Elaborate** How did geography contribute to the rise of Ghana, Mali, and Songhai?

Lesson 4

12. a. **Recall** What role did Greek and Roman traditions play in the development of the United States?
   b. **Summarize** How did the Crusades in Southwest Asia and the travels of Marco Polo in Asia contribute to the growth of trade in Europe?
   c. **Evaluate** Which do you think contributed the most to the advances in learning that occurred during the Renaissance—writing in the common language of a people or inventing the printing press?

Module 1 Assessment, continued

Review Themes

13. Geography How did changes in climate lead to migration to the Americas?

14. Economics Describe the development of the European economy during the Middle Ages.

Reading Skills

Specialized Vocabulary of Social Studies *Use the Reading Skills taught in this module to answer the question about the reading selection below.*

> To encourage the spread of Islam in West Africa, Mansa Musa brought back artists and architects from other Muslim countries to build **mosques**, or buildings for Muslim prayer, throughout his lands.

15. What is the definition of the word *mosques* in the sentence above?

Social Studies Skills

Interpret Diagrams *Use the Social Studies Skills taught in this module to answer the question below.*

16. Look back at the diagram of a castle on the Social Studies Skills page. Which of the following is the main way to enter the castle?
   a. well
   b. moat
   c. drawbridge
   d. windows

Focus on Writing

17. Write a Travelogue In a travelogue, you describe a journey you have taken to an area. Someone who is not familiar with the area can learn about it from your descriptions. You have read about many cultures across a long span of history. Pick one area that you found the most interesting in the module. Organize your thoughts about the kinds of people you would have met, the sights and sounds you would have experienced, and the kind of things you would have done if you had traveled there during the time discussed.

Try to include information about a culture's history, customs, beliefs, practices, economies, political systems, and natural environments. Write a paragraph about what you might have liked or disliked about your trip. Be sure to include a main idea sentence and several sentences that support the main idea with evidence.

THE
Maya

The Maya developed one of the most advanced civilizations in the Americas, but their story is shrouded in mystery. Around AD 250, the Maya began to build great cities in southern Mexico and Central America. They developed a writing system, practiced astronomy, and built magnificent palaces and pyramids with little more than stone tools. Around AD 900, however, the Maya abandoned their cities, leaving their monuments to be reclaimed by the jungle and, for a time, forgotten.

Explore some of the incredible monuments and cultural achievements of the ancient Maya online. You can find a wealth of information, video clips, primary sources, activities, and more through your online textbook.

Destroying the Maya's Past

Watch the video to learn how the actions of one Spanish missionary nearly destroyed the written record of the Maya world.

Finding the City of Palenque

Watch the video to learn about the great Maya city of Palenque and the European discovery of the site in the eighteenth century.

Pakal's Tomb

Watch the video to explore how the discovery of the tomb of a great king helped archaeologists piece together the Maya past.

"Thus let it be done!
Let the emptiness be filled!
Let the water recede and
make a void, let the earth
appear and become solid; let it
be done . . . "Earth!" they said,
and instantly it was made."

The Popol Vuh

Read the document to learn how the Maya believed the world was created.

Module 2

New Empires in the Americas

Essential Question
How did Europeans change life in the Americas?

About the Photo: The ships of explorer Christopher Columbus sail again in the form of these replicas.

▶ *Explore ONLINE!*

VIDEOS, including...
• Columbus Sails West

☑ Document-Based Investigations

☑ Graphic Organizers

☑ Interactive Games

☑ Interactive Map: Magellan's Voyage Around the World

☑ Image with Hotspots: Tenochtitlán

☑ Image Carousel: Key Events in Europe, 1450 – 1588

In this module you will learn about the Europeans who colonized the Americas.

What You Will Learn ...

Timeline of Events 1400–1700

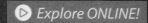
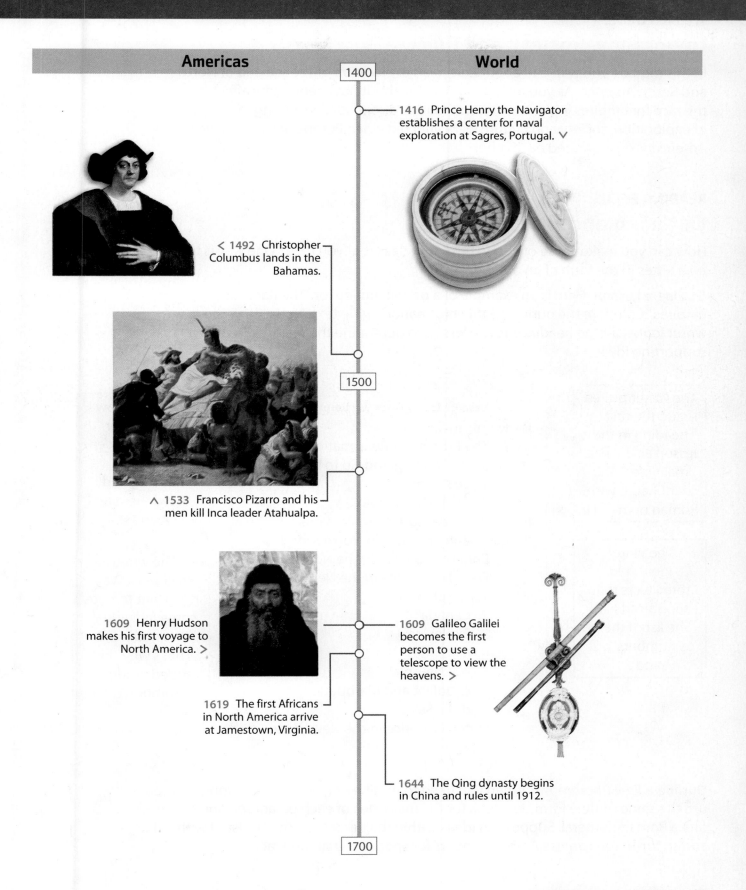

Americas		World
	1400	

1416 Prince Henry the Navigator establishes a center for naval exploration at Sagres, Portugal. ∨

< **1492** Christopher Columbus lands in the Bahamas.

1500

∧ **1533** Francisco Pizarro and his men kill Inca leader Atahualpa.

1609 Henry Hudson makes his first voyage to North America. >

1609 Galileo Galilei becomes the first person to use a telescope to view the heavens. >

1619 The first Africans in North America arrive at Jamestown, Virginia.

1644 The Qing dynasty begins in China and rules until 1912.

1700

Reading Social Studies

THEME FOCUS:

Geography, Society and Culture

In this module you will read about European exploration of the sea and of North and South America. As you read you will learn about how geography affected the race for empires in the New World. You will also read how, during journeys of exploration, society and culture were affected when Europeans and Native Americans encountered each other.

READING FOCUS:

Outlining and History

How can you make sense of all the facts and ideas that you read? One way is to take notes in the form of an outline.

Outline a Lesson Here is an example of a partial outline for "The Race for Empires." Compare the outline to the information in the text. Notice how the writer looked at the headings in the lesson to determine the main and supporting ideas.

The writer picked up the first heading in the lesson as the first main idea. She identified it with Roman numeral I.

The writer identified three facts that supported III.B. She listed them as numbers 1, 2, and 3.

The writer saw two smaller headings under the bigger heading and listed them as A and B.

The writer decided it was important to note some individual facts under B.3. That's why she added points a through d.

Lesson 4: The Race for Empires

I. Events in Europe
   A. The Protestant Reformation
   B. Spain and England Go to War
      1. Sea dogs
      2. Spanish Armada
II. Search for a Northwest Passage
III. European Presence in North America
   A. English Presence in the New World
   B. French Presence in the New World
      1. Huguenots
      2. Canada
      3. Explorers
         a. Cartier
         b. Champlain
         c. Jolliet and Marquette
         d. La Salle
   C. Dutch Presence in the New World

Outline a Few Paragraphs When you need to outline only a few paragraphs, you can use the same outline form. Just look for the main idea of each paragraph and give each one a Roman numeral. Supporting ideas within the paragraph can be listed with A, B, and so forth. You can use Arabic numbers for specific details and facts.

You Try It!

Read the following passage. Then fill in the blanks to complete the outline below.

Conquest of the Aztec Empire Moctezuma ruled the Aztec Empire, which was at the height of its power in the early 1500s. Moctezuma's capital, Tenochtitlán, was built in the middle of Lake Texcoco, near the present-day site of Mexico City. Tenochtitlán was a large city with temples, a palace, and buildings that were built on an island in the middle of the lake. The buildings and riches of the city impressed the Spaniards. They saw the Aztec Empire as a good source of gold and silver. They also wanted to convert the Aztec to Christianity.

The Aztec had thousands of warriors. In contrast, Cortés had only 508 soldiers, about 100 sailors, 16 horses, and some guns. Cortés hoped that his superior weapons would bring him victory.

Complete this outline based on the passage you just read.

I. Moctezuma and the Aztec Empire were at the height of power in the early 1500s.

   A. Tenochtitlán was the capital

     1. Built in Lake Texcoco

     2. _____

   B. The buildings and riches impressed the Spaniards

     1. _____

     2. Christianity

II. _____

   A. Cortés had fewer soldiers

   B. _____

As you read Module 2, practice outlining a few paragraphs to help you make sense of the facts and ideas you have read.

Key Terms and People

Lesson 1
Leif Eriksson
Henry the Navigator
astrolabe
caravels

Lesson 2
Christopher Columbus
Line of Demarcation
Treaty of Tordesillas
Ferdinand Magellan
circumnavigate
Columbian Exchange

Lesson 3
conquistadors
Hernán Cortés
Moctezuma II
Francisco Pizarro
encomienda system
plantations
Bartolomé de Las Casas

Lesson 4
Protestant Reformation
Protestants
Spanish Armada
Northwest Passage
Jacques Cartier
charter

Europeans Set Sail

The Big Idea

Europeans explored the world, searching for new lands and new trade routes.

Main Ideas

- Vikings were skilled sailors, and they were the first Europeans to reach North America.
- Prince Henry the Navigator established a school for sailors and provided financial support that enabled the Portuguese to start exploring the oceans.
- Portuguese sailors sailed around Africa and found a sea route to Asia.

Key Terms and People

Leif Eriksson
Henry the Navigator
astrolabe
caravels

If YOU were there . . .

You are a sailor living in Portugal in the mid-1400s. Several of your friends are excited about joining an expedition to sail to new, unexplored lands. Although Portuguese navigators have made improvements to sailing ships and advancements in ocean travel, you have heard about the dangers other sailors have faced on the open seas.

Will you join the expedition or stay behind? Why?

Viking Sailors Reach North America

The Vikings were the first Europeans to make contact with North America. They came from Scandinavia, a peninsula that includes the present-day countries of Denmark, Norway, and Sweden. The Vikings were skilled sailors who developed a new style of ship, called the longship, which curved up at both ends. Viking vessels traveled the rough North Atlantic seas better than earlier ships because their designs were more stable.

The Vikings raided countries throughout Europe, but they also developed large trading networks. Viking ships sailed to the British Isles and the Mediterranean and Black seas. Eventually, the Vikings sailed west into the North Atlantic. There they founded a settlement on the island of Iceland in about 874. More than 100 years later, Viking Erik the Red, who had been convicted of crimes in Iceland, was sent away as punishment. He went to Greenland and brought settlers there.

Leif Eriksson, the son of Erik the Red, was also an adventurer. In the year 1000, he was sailing west from Norway to Greenland when strong winds blew his ship off course and carried it all the way to the North American coast.

Eriksson and his crew landed on the Labrador Peninsula in

Norwegian explorer Leif Eriksson led a group of Vikings to North America in about 1000.

present-day Canada. The Vikings then sailed farther south to the island of Newfoundland, and perhaps to what is now

New England. According to their myths, Vikings saw forests, meadows, and rivers that held "larger salmon than they had ever seen."

Eriksson settled in a coastal area he called Vinland. The Vikings left after only a few years. Attacks by Native Americans posed a constant threat, and the area may have been too far from other Viking settlements to be supported.

After the Vikings left North America, Europeans did not return to the continent for centuries. In the 1400s, however, a growing interest in discovery and exploration spread across Europe.

Reading Check
Sequence List the stages of exploration that led to the Vikings' landing in North America.

Looking toward the Sea

Exploration was necessary for European trade. One reason was that European mines were running out of silver and gold. Merchants needed more of the precious metals to conduct business. In addition, new forms of production, such as spinning wheels and windmills, made manufacturing more efficient. As a result, workers needed more raw materials, and merchants needed new markets where they could sell the manufactured goods. Traders also sought products—from incense to silk—that could only be found in the East.

Since the 1200s Europeans had been traveling east by land. The Crusades had introduced them to knowledge, products, markets, and natural resources found across Asia. For a time, land routes to the east were relatively safe. The Mongols, who had conquered much of the continent, provided protection. When the Muslim Ottomans conquered Constantinople in 1453, however, they blocked the land trade routes to Asia. In response, the European powers began to compete in a race to find a sea route to Asia.

Riches and Religion During the 1400s Europeans had several reasons to explore the world. First, they wanted Asian spices. They hoped to bypass the merchants who had a monopoly on, or economic control of, the Asian products that reached the Mediterranean. If a sea route to Asia could be found, countries could buy spices and other items directly. Second, religion played a role in exploration. Christians in Europe wanted to convert more people to their faith. Third, many Europeans had become interested in Asian cultures. Explorer Marco Polo wrote a book about his travels throughout Asia. It remained popular in Europe long after his death in 1324. Many Europeans wanted to learn more about Asia and the money they could make by trading with Asians.

Portugal Leads the Way Portugal became a leader in world exploration. Prince **Henry the Navigator**, in particular, was responsible for advances that would make exploration more successful. Although he never set out on a voyage himself, Henry greatly advanced Portugal's exploration efforts.

In the early 1400s Prince Henry built an observatory and founded a school of navigation to teach better methods of sailing. He also financed research by mapmakers and shipbuilders. Finally, he paid for expeditions to explore the west coast of Africa.

The Caravel

A special type of ship called the caravel became the workhorse of many European explorers. Though small, caravels were sturdy. They could sail across huge oceans and up small rivers. Caravels featured important advances in sailing technology.

Triangular sails enabled the caravel to sail into the wind.

The smooth rounded hull handled high seas well.

The large center rudder made quick turns possible.

Analyze Visuals
What features made the caravel an excellent sailing ship?

Scientific and Technological Advances Scientific and geographical knowledge about the Earth had increased, thanks in part to rediscovery of Roman sources and to overland journeys by European merchants. This knowledge led to better maps. Sailors had more, although still incomplete, information about the sea and lands beyond it. New technology also played a major role in advancing world exploration. Sailors began to use tools such as the magnetic compass, which indicated all directions by always pointing north. In addition, sailors had the **astrolabe**, a device that enabled navigators to learn their ship's location by charting the position of the stars. Better instruments made it possible for sailors to travel the open seas without landmarks to guide them.

The Portuguese also made advances in shipbuilding. They began designing ships that were smaller, lighter, and easier to steer than the heavy galleons they had used before. These new ships, called **caravels** (KER-uh-velz), used triangular sails that, unlike traditional square sails, allowed ships to sail against the wind. By placing rudders at the back of the ship, the Portuguese also improved the steering of ships.

Reading Check
Summarize What factors led to increased exploration?

A Sea Route to Asia

By the 1400s Portugal had several motives, financial support, and the technology necessary for exploration. Portuguese explorers set out to find new lands.

Rounding Africa Even with new technology, travel on the open seas was dangerous and difficult. One person described the **effect** on sailors of a voyage south from Portugal.

> "Those which survived could hardly be recognized as human. They had lost flesh and hair, the nails had gone from hands and feet. . . . They spoke of heat so incredible that it was a marvel that ships and crews were not burnt."
>
> —Sailor, quoted in *World Civilizations*, edited by Edward McNall Burns, et al.

In spite of the dangers, Portuguese explorers continued sailing south, setting up trading posts along the way.

In 1488 Portuguese navigator Bartolomeu Dias led an expedition from Portugal southward along the African coast. A storm blew his ships around the southern tip of Africa. This point became known as the Cape of Good Hope. Dias wanted to continue his voyage, but his men did not. Since supplies were very low, Dias decided to call off the voyage and return to Portugal.

Later, King Manuel of Portugal sent another explorer, Vasco da Gama, on an expedition around the Cape of Good Hope. Da Gama left Lisbon, Portugal, in July 1497 and arrived in southwestern India the next year. Portugal had won the European race for a sea route to Asia.

When da Gama reached the Indian port of Calicut, Muslim traders met him and his men. The Muslims surprised the sailors by speaking to them in Portuguese. Soon, da Gama and his crew learned that the people of India had been trading with Muslim and Italian merchants who knew Portuguese. Da Gama made two more trips back to India. He even governed a small colony there.

Results of Exploration Portugal's explorations would have major results, including the start of the Atlantic slave trade. As Portuguese sailors explored the west coast of Africa, they negotiated for gold, ivory, and slaves. The slave trade devastated African communities. It led to increased warfare among kingdoms and broke up many families. The Portuguese sent

Causes and Effects of the Discovery of a Sea Route to Asia

Several factors led to the discovery of a sea route from Europe to Asia.

Causes
- Financial backing from Prince Henry the Navigator
- New technology (caravel and mariner's astrolabe)
- Seeking trade with Asia and financial gain
- Converting people to Christianity
- Curiosity

Effects
- Discovery of a sea route to Asia
- Face-to-face contact with traders in distant lands
- Awareness of different cultures and ways of life

Analyze Information
Why was trade with Asia so important to Europeans?

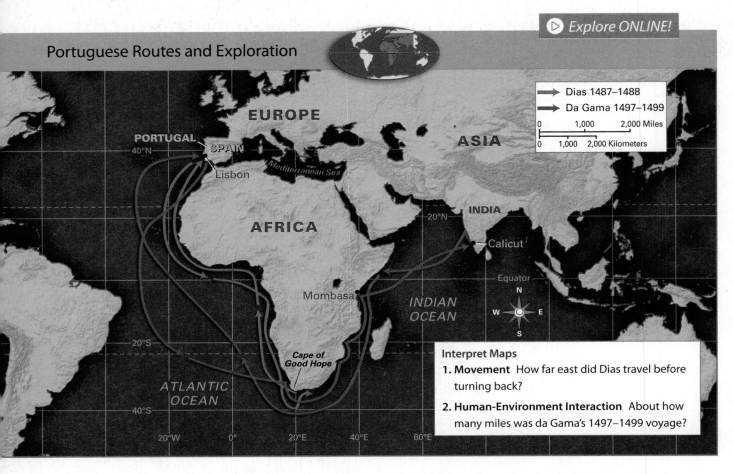

Interpret Maps

1. **Movement** How far east did Dias travel before turning back?

2. **Human-Environment Interaction** About how many miles was da Gama's 1497–1499 voyage?

many enslaved Africans to Europe and to islands in the Atlantic, where they lived and worked under brutal conditions.

The other nations of Europe watched as new trade routes brought increased wealth and power to Portugal. They soon launched voyages of exploration to find their own water routes to Asia.

Reading Check
Predict How would continued exploration affect Africans?

Summary and Preview In the 1400s the Portuguese started a new era of exploration. In the next lesson you will learn how Europeans reached the American continents.

Lesson 1 Assessment

Review Ideas, Terms, and People

1. **a. Identify** Who was Leif Eriksson?

   b. Summarize How did the Vikings eventually establish Vinland?

   c. Draw Inferences Why do you think the Vikings did not try to colonize the Americas?

2. **a. Identify** Who was Prince Henry the Navigator?

   b. Summarize Why were European merchants concerned about the supply of gold and silver?

3. **a. Recall** Who was the first explorer to find a sea route from Europe to Asia?

   b. Explain How did Muslims living in India learn Portuguese?

c. Draw Conclusions How did the slave trade affect African communities?

Critical Thinking

4. **Summarize** In this lesson you learned about European exploration. Create a chart similar to the one below and explain the reason for the explorations, the technology that made explorations possible, and the results of the explorations.

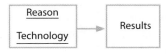

Europeans Reach the Americas

The Big Idea

Christopher Columbus's voyages led to new exchanges between Europe, Africa, and the Americas.

Main Ideas

- Christopher Columbus sailed across the Atlantic Ocean and reached a continent that was previously unknown to him.

- After Columbus's voyages, other explorers sailed to the Americas.

Key Terms and People

Christopher Columbus
Line of Demarcation
Treaty of Tordesillas
Ferdinand Magellan
circumnavigate
Columbian Exchange

If YOU were there . . .

You are a European explorer who just returned to your homeland from the Americas. While you were gone, you tried new and different foods, including corn, potatoes, and cocoa. You have brought some of these foods back with you. You want your friends and family to sample these items, but they resist.

What will you say about these new foods?

Columbus Sails across the Atlantic

Stories of fabulous kingdoms and wealth in Asia captured the imagination of **Christopher Columbus**, a sailor from Genoa, Italy. Columbus was convinced that he could reach Asia by sailing west across the Atlantic Ocean.

Columbus knew that the Earth was round. In fact, the Earth's shape was well known among educated Westerners. Columbus's plans included errors, however. He thought the Earth was much smaller than it is. He also thought that Asia extended farther east and, therefore, that the lands he sought were closer to Europe.

The Journey Begins Columbus asked King Ferdinand and Queen Isabella of Spain to pay for an expedition across the Atlantic. He promised them great riches, new territory, and Catholic converts. It took Columbus several years to convince the king and queen, but they finally agreed to help finance the journey. Ferdinand and Isabella ordered Columbus to bring back any items of value and to claim for Spain any lands he explored.

On August 3, 1492, Columbus's three ships set sail. The *Niña* and the *Pinta* were caravels. Columbus sailed in the larger *Santa María*. The ships carried about 90 sailors and a year's worth of supplies. They made a stop in the Canary Islands, and then on September 6, they resumed their journey. Soon, they passed the limits of Columbus's maps and sailed into uncharted seas. After more than a month with no sight of land, the crew grew restless.

Soon the crew saw signs of land—birds and floating tree branches. Columbus promised a reward "to him who first sang out that he saw land." On October 12, 1492, a lookout cried, "Land! Land!" ending the long journey from the Canary Islands.

The ships landed on an island in the Bahamas. Columbus thought he had found a new route to Asia. Instead, he had reached another continent that was unknown to him. Columbus called the island San Salvador, which means "Holy Savior." Columbus also visited another island he called Hispaniola. There he met a group of native people called the Taino (TY-noh). At that time Europeans called Asia the Indies, so Columbus, believing he was in Asia, called these Native Americans Indians.

The Taino lived in small farming communities. In his journal, Columbus wrote that the Taino were "so generous . . . that no one would believe it who has not seen it." However, Columbus and his crew were not interested in Taino culture, but in gold. After three months of exploring, looking for gold, and collecting exotic plants and animals, Columbus returned to Spain.

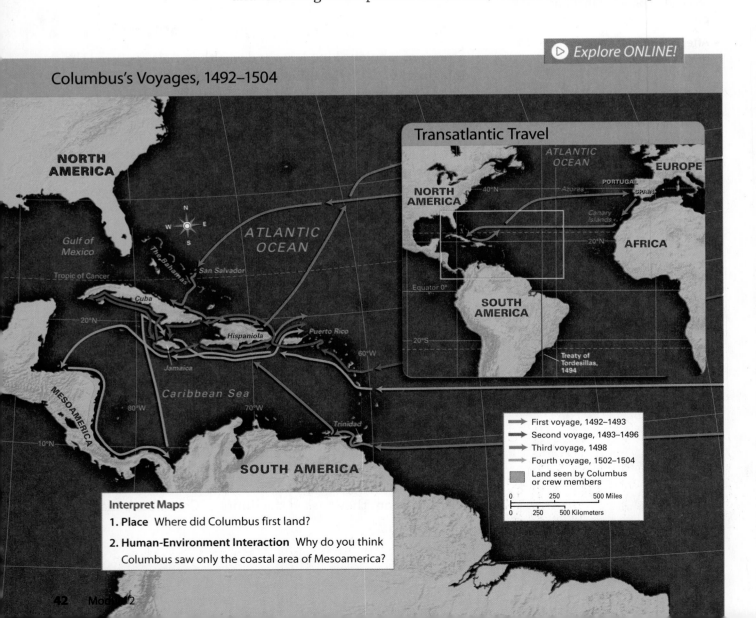

Columbus's Voyages, 1492–1504

Transatlantic Travel

First voyage, 1492–1493
Second voyage, 1493–1496
Third voyage, 1498
Fourth voyage, 1502–1504
Land seen by Columbus or crew members

Interpret Maps

1. **Place** Where did Columbus first land?

2. **Human-Environment Interaction** Why do you think Columbus saw only the coastal area of Mesoamerica?

Columbus made three more journeys to the Americas during his lifetime. In 1504 he returned to Spain in poor health. Columbus died two years later, still believing that he had reached Asia.

Impact of Columbus's Voyages The voyages of Columbus changed the way Europeans thought of the world and their place in it. A new era of interaction between Europe and the Americas had begun. Moreover, Columbus's voyages and the voyages of explorers who came after him would set in motion the development of American society.

Columbus's discovery also created conflict between European countries. Both Spain and Portugal wanted to add these lands to their growing empires. In 1493 Pope Alexander VI, originally from Spain, issued a decree that drew a new boundary for Spain and Portugal. This imaginary **Line of Demarcation** divided the Atlantic Ocean. Spain could claim all land west of the line.

The Portuguese king believed that this arrangement favored Spain. To prevent war, the two leaders signed the **Treaty of Tordesillas**, which moved the Line of Demarcation 800 miles farther west. This gave Portugal more opportunity to claim lands unexplored by other Europeans.

The pope's decree and the Treaty of Tordesillas helped establish the idea that a country that explored a newly found land was entitled to own and

DOCUMENT-BASED INVESTIGATION   Historical Source

Christopher Columbus's Letter, 1494

Two years after discovering the island of Hispaniola, Columbus wrote a letter to the Spanish king and queen outlining his ideas of its colonization.

Analyze Historical Sources
What were Columbus's main concerns in founding a colony on Hispaniola?

Most High and Mighty Sovereigns,
    In the first place, as regards the Island of Espanola: Inasmuch as the numb colonists who desire to go thither [there] amounts to two thousand, owing to the land being safer and better for farming and trading. . . .
1. That in the said island there shall be founded three or four towns. . . .
2. That for the better and more speedy colonization of the said island, no one shall have liberty to collect gold in it except those who have taken out colonists' papers. . . .
3. That each town shall have its alcalde [mayor]. . . .
4. That there shall be a church, and parish priests or friars to administer the sacraments, to perform divine worship, and for the conversion of the Indians.

—Christopher Columbus, letter to the king and queen of Spain, 1494

rule it. This idea came to be known as the "Doctrine of Discovery." By this doctrine, native peoples who had lived on the land for generations were considered occupants, not owners with property rights. The policy would have a devastating effect on Native Americans for centuries to come.

Other Explorers Sail to the Americas

Columbus's discoveries inspired others to sail across the Atlantic Ocean. In 1501 explorer Amerigo Vespucci (vuh-SPOO-chee) led a Spanish fleet to the coast of present-day South America. He was convinced the land he reached was not Asia. Instead, Vespucci believed he had found a "new world." A German mapmaker labeled the continents across the ocean *America* in honor of Vespucci. Europeans began using the names North America and South America for these lands.

In a Spanish settlement in present-day Panama, another explorer, Vasco Núñez de Balboa (NOON-yays day bahl-BOH-uh), heard stories from local Native Americans about another ocean farther west. Balboa set out to find it. For weeks he and his men struggled through thick jungle and deadly swamps. In 1513 they reached the top of a mountain. From this spot Balboa saw a great blue sea—the Pacific Ocean—stretching out before him.

In 1519 **Ferdinand Magellan** (muh-JEHL-uhn), a Portuguese navigator, set out with a Spanish fleet to sail down the east coast of South America. After sailing around the southern tip of the continent, Magellan continued into the Pacific even though his ships were dangerously low on food and fresh water.

Portuguese navigator Ferdinand Magellan's ships were the first to sail full circle around the globe.

Magellan's fleet sailed across the Pacific Ocean. In the Philippines, Magellan was killed in a battle with native peoples. Down to three ships, the expedition continued sailing west into the Indian Ocean. In 1522 the voyage's only remaining ship returned to Spain. Only 18 members of Magellan's original crew survived. These sailors were the first people to **circumnavigate**, or go all the way around, the globe. Their entire journey was some 40,000 miles long.

European explorers and settlers took plants and animals with them to the Americas. They also brought back a variety of new plants and animals to Europe, Asia, and Africa. This transfer became known as the **Columbian Exchange** because it started with Columbus's explorations.

European explorers found many plants in the Americas that were unknown to them, including corn, potatoes, squash, tobacco, and cocoa. They brought these items to Europe, where they were highly valued. Turkeys, too, made the journey from the Americas to Europe. The explorers introduced horses, cattle, and pigs to the Americas. Native Americans came to use these animals for food and transportation. They also started to farm European grains such as wheat and barley. Citrus fruits and sugarcane were other plants that came from Europe. These became important crops over time.

Without intending to do so, the explorers also introduced deadly new diseases to the Americas. Native Americans had no natural resistance to European diseases. As a result, diseases such as smallpox killed from 80 to 95 percent of the native population within 150 years of Columbus's arrival. Not only did these deaths devastate Native American communities, they also had a terrible long-term effect. Soon after they established colonies, Europeans, especially the Spanish, forced Native Americans to work as laborers, raising food and mining for gold and silver. But because so many native people died from the new diseases, a labor shortage soon developed. The Europeans began looking for a new source of workers. They turned to Africa and began importing enslaved Africans. Over many years, Europeans shipped millions of slaves to the New World colonies.

The Columbian Exchange changed the world for all time. Environments, agriculture, trade relationships, and even entire cultures were affected in Europe, Africa, and the Americas. Some changes, such as the death of Native Americans from new diseases, happened very quickly. Others happened more gradually. For example, as some mountain-dwelling Native Americans acquired horses, which had come from Europe, they moved down to the Great Plains. There these peoples adopted lifestyles that depended on the buffalo herds.

Over time, a trading pattern involving the exchange of raw materials, manufactured products, and slaves developed among Europe, Africa, and the Americas. This trading pattern would affect many aspects of history, both in the New World and the old.

Summary and Preview Columbus's voyages to America inspired other Europeans to explore the "New World." This led to new exchanges between both sides of the Atlantic. In the next lesson you will learn about Spain's empire in the Americas.

Reading Check
Evaluate What were the negative aspects of the Columbian Exchange?

Lesson 2 Assessment

Review Ideas, Terms, and People

1. a. **Recall** What agreement did Christopher Columbus make with Queen Isabella and King Ferdinand of Spain?

   b. **Explain** Where did Columbus think he had landed when he reached the Bahamas?

   c. **Evaluate** How did Columbus's voyage lead to a dispute between Spain and Portugal?

2. a. **Identify** Who was the first European explorer to see the Pacific Ocean?

   b. **Summarize** What route did Ferdinand Magellan's ships take to circumnavigate the globe?

   c. **Draw Conclusions** How did the Columbian Exchange and the slave trade affect the economies and the people of Europe, Africa, and the Americas? Why would the people involved in the Columbian Exchange have had different perspectives on the events?

Critical Thinking

3. **Support a Point of View** In this lesson you learned about European exploration. Create a graphic organizer like the one below and rank, in order, the most important results of European voyages to the Americas. Explain your choices in the "Why" column. Add more rows as necessary.

Most Important	Why

Spain Builds an Empire

The Big Idea

Spain established a large empire in the Americas.

Main Ideas

- Spanish conquistadors conquered the Aztec and Inca empires.

- Spanish explorers traveled through the borderlands of New Spain, claiming more land.

- Spanish settlers treated Native Americans harshly, forcing them to work on plantations and in mines.

Key Terms and People

conquistadors
Hernán Cortés
Moctezuma II
Francisco Pizarro
encomienda system
plantations
Bartolomé de Las Casas

If YOU were there . . .

You are an Aztec warrior living in central Mexico in the 1500s. You are proud to serve your ruler, Moctezuma II. One day several hundred foreigners arrive on your shores. They are pale, bearded men, and they have strange animals and equipment.

From where do you think these strangers have come?

Spanish Conquistadors

The Spanish sent **conquistadors** (kahn-kees-tuh-DAWS), soldiers who led military expeditions in the Americas. Conquistador **Hernán Cortés** left the island of Cuba to sail to present-day Mexico in 1519. Cortés had heard of a wealthy land to the west ruled by a king named **Moctezuma II** (mawk-tay-SOO-mah).

Conquest of the Aztec Empire Moctezuma ruled the Aztec Empire, which was at the height of its power in the early 1500s. Moctezuma's capital, Tenochtitlán, was built in the middle of Lake Texcoco, near the present-day site of Mexico City. Tenochtitlán was a large city with temples, a palace, and buildings that were built on an island in the middle of the lake. The buildings and riches of the city impressed the Spaniards. They saw the Aztec Empire as a good source of gold and silver. They also wanted to convert the Aztec to Christianity.

The Aztec had thousands of warriors. In contrast, Cortés had only 508 soldiers, about 100 sailors, 16 horses, and some guns. Cortés hoped that his superior weapons would bring him victory. Cortés also sought help from enemies of the Aztec. An Indian woman named Malintzin (mah-LINT-suhn) helped Cortés win allies.

Spanish conquistadors (left), benefited from having stronger weapons and defenses than Aztec warriors (right).

At first Moctezuma believed Cortés to be a god and welcomed him. Cortés then took Moctezuma prisoner and seized control of Tenochtitlán. Eventually, Tenochtitlán was

Reasons for Spanish Victory

Several advantages helped the Spanish defeat the Aztec and Inca.

Causes of the Aztec and Inca Defeat

- Spanish steel armor and weapons
- Spanish horses
- European diseases
- Spanish alliances with Aztec and Inca enemies

▼

Effects

- Reduced Native American population
- Spanish rule of the Americas
- Columbian Exchange

Analyze Information
Which cause do you think was most important to the Spanish victory?

destroyed and Moctezuma was killed. Smallpox and other diseases brought by the Spanish quickened the fall of the Aztec Empire.

Conquest of the Inca Empire Another Spanish conquistador, **Francisco Pizarro** (puh-ZAHR-oh), heard rumors of the Inca cities in the Andes of South America. The Inca ruled a large territory that stretched along the Pacific coast from present-day Chile to northern Ecuador.

Pizarro had fewer than 400 men in his army. But the Inca, like the Aztec, had no weapons to match the conquistadors' swords and guns. Though outnumbered, Pizarro's troops captured the great Inca capital at Cuzco in present-day Peru and killed the Inca leaders. By 1534 Pizarro and his Native American allies had conquered the entire Inca Empire.

In only a few years, the Spanish had conquered two great American empires. During the conquest, the Spanish and their allies killed thousands of Inca and Aztec and looted their settlements. Moreover, possibly more than three-quarters of the Aztec and Inca populations were killed by the diseases the Europeans brought.

Spanish Settlements The Spanish began to settle their vast empire, which they called New Spain. Spain's government wanted to control migration to the Americas. Most of the emigrants were Spanish, though a few non-Spanish subjects of the king also migrated. Jews, Muslims, and non-Christians were forbidden to settle in New Spain. At first, most emigrants were men. The government then encouraged families to migrate. Eventually, women comprised one-quarter of the total emigration from Spain.

Spain ruled its large American empire through a system of royal officials. At the top was the Council of the Indies, formed in 1524 to govern the Americas from Spain. The Council appointed two viceroys, or royal governors. The Viceroyalty of Peru governed most of South America. The Viceroyalty of New Spain governed all Spanish territories in Central America, Mexico, and the southern part of what is now the United States.

The Spanish established three kinds of settlements in New Spain. Pueblos served as trading posts and sometimes as centers of government. Priests started missions, where they converted local Native Americans to Catholicism. The Spanish also built presidios, or military bases, to protect towns and missions.

Reading Check
Analyze How did the Spanish conquer the great Aztec and Inca empires?

To connect some of the scattered communities of New Spain, Spanish settlers built *El Camino Real,* or "the Royal Road." This network of roads ran for hundreds of miles, from Mexico City to Santa Fe. The roads later stretched to settlements in California.

Exploring the Borderlands of New Spain

Spain's American empire was not limited to lands taken from the conquered Aztec and Inca empires. Many other Spanish explorers came to North America. They explored the borderlands of New Spain and claimed many new lands for the Spanish crown.

Exploring the Southeast In 1508 explorer Juan Ponce de León landed on the Caribbean island of Puerto Rico. By 1511 he had conquered the island for Spain and founded the city of San Juan. Ponce de León also discovered gold on Puerto Rico. Spanish officials appointed him governor of the colony.

In 1513 Ponce de León discovered the coast of present-day Florida. According to legend, Ponce de León heard that a Fountain of Youth, whose waters could make old people young again, could be found in Florida. However, this story did not appear until after his death. Whatever his goal might have been, Ponce de León set out to explore the area.

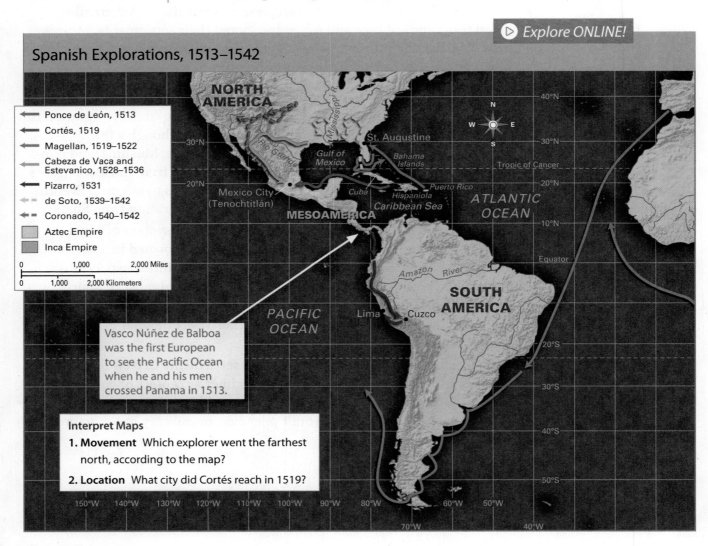

Explore ONLINE!

Spanish Explorations, 1513–1542

Key:
← Ponce de León, 1513
← Cortés, 1519
← Magellan, 1519–1522
← Cabeza de Vaca and Estevanico, 1528–1536
← Pizarro, 1531
← de Soto, 1539–1542
← Coronado, 1540–1542
▢ Aztec Empire
▢ Inca Empire

0 1,000 2,000 Miles
0 1,000 2,000 Kilometers

Vasco Núñez de Balboa was the first European to see the Pacific Ocean when he and his men crossed Panama in 1513.

Interpret Maps

1. **Movement** Which explorer went the farthest north, according to the map?

2. **Location** What city did Cortés reach in 1519?

Although he had royal permission to colonize Florida, he did not succeed in doing so.

Two decades later another explorer traveled through Florida. Royal officials gave Hernando de Soto permission to explore the coastal region of the Gulf of Mexico. In 1539 his expedition landed in an area near the present-day city of Tampa Bay, Florida. De Soto then led his men north through what is now Georgia and the Carolinas. In 1540, while in present-day Alabama, de Soto encountered the Muscogee peoples. De Soto took the Muscogee chief, Tuscaloosa, hostage as a way to gain supplies. Arguments between the Spaniards and the Muscogee led to a fierce battle. Several thousand Muscogee were killed. Although the Spaniards won the battle, they lost many men and almost all their supplies. Still, de Soto continued his journey, discovering the Mississippi River in 1541. The explorers then traveled west into present-day Oklahoma. De Soto died in 1542 on this journey.

Exploring the Southwest The Spanish also explored what is now the southwestern United States. In 1528 explorer Álvar Núñez Cabeza de Vaca joined conquistador Pánfilo de Narváez on an expedition to North America. Their group of 300 men first landed on the Florida coast. They faced many severe problems, including a shortage of food.

The group built boats, which made it possible for them to travel around the Florida panhandle. The explorers continued along the Gulf Coast and eventually reached the Mississippi River. Severe weather hit this group hard, and many members of the expedition died. Cabeza de Vaca's boat shipwrecked on what is now Galveston Island in Texas. Only Cabeza de Vaca and three other men survived. One of the survivors was a Moroccan-born slave named Estevanico. His Spanish slave-holder also survived.

Estevanico was an enslaved African who traveled with Cabeza de Vaca.

Each of the four survivors was captured and enslaved by local Native American groups. After six years of captivity, the men finally escaped. They journeyed on foot throughout the North American Southwest, receiving help from Native Americans they met along the way. In 1536, after turning south, the group reached Spanish settlements in Mexico.

Soon after their journey ended, Estevanico's slaveholder sold him to a Spanish viceroy. The viceroy assigned Estevanico to serve as a guide for a new expedition he was sending into the Southwest. Native Americans killed the enslaved African in 1539.

Cabeza de Vaca eventually returned to Spain, where he called for better treatment of Native Americans. He later wrote about his experiences in the first European book exclusively devoted to North America. Cabeza de Vaca's book increased Spanish interest in the New World. His writings fueled the rumors that riches could be found in North America.

> "For two thousand leagues did we travel, on land, and by sea in barges, besides ten months more after our rescue from captivity; untiringly did we walk across the land. . . . During all that time we crossed from one ocean to the other. . . . We heard that on the shores of the South there are pearls and great wealth, and that the richest and best is near there."
>
> —Cabeza de Vaca, *The Journey of Álvar Núñez Cabeza de Vaca*

Cabeza de Vaca's account inspired other explorers to travel to North America. In 1540 Francisco Vásquez de Coronado set out to explore the North American Southwest. He wanted to find the legendary Seven Cities of Gold that were rumored to exist there. His expedition went through present-day New Mexico and Arizona, where a group of his men discovered the Grand Canyon. Coronado trekked through Texas and Oklahoma, going as far north as Kansas before turning around. He never found the fabled cities of gold.

Reading Check
Compare How were the expeditions of Hernando de Soto and Francisco Vásquez de Coronado similar?

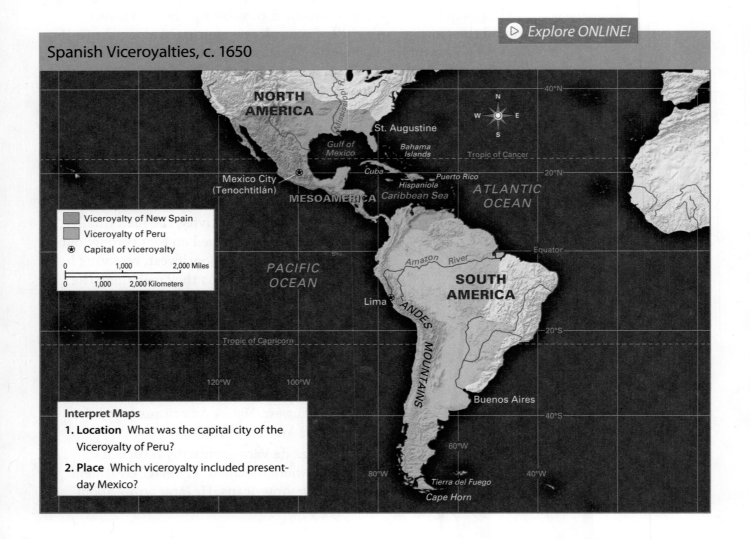

Spanish Viceroyalties, c. 1650

Explore ONLINE!

Viceroyalty of New Spain
Viceroyalty of Peru
⊛ Capital of viceroyalty

0   1,000   2,000 Miles
0   1,000   2,000 Kilometers

Interpret Maps
1. **Location** What was the capital city of the Viceroyalty of Peru?
2. **Place** Which viceroyalty included present-day Mexico?

The Devastation of the Indies: A Brief Account

Bartolomé de Las Casas, a Catholic priest in New Spain, wrote a book that encouraged better treatment of Native Americans.

"When they [Spaniards] have slain all those who fought for their lives or to escape the tortures they would have to endure, that is to say, when they have slain all the native rulers and young men (since the Spaniards usually spare only the women and children, who are subjected to the hardest and bitterest servitude [slavery] ever suffered by man or beast), they enslave any survivors. With these infernal [devilish] methods of tyranny they debase and weaken countless numbers of those pitiful Indian nations."

—Bartolomé de Las Casas, from *The Devastation of the Indies: A Brief Account*

Analyze Historical Sources
How did Las Casas's view of the treatment of Native American groups differ from the views of other Spaniards?

Spanish Treatment of Native Americans

The journeys of the Spanish explorers allowed Spain to claim a huge empire in the Americas. Spain's American colonies helped make the country very wealthy. From 1503 to 1660, Spanish fleets loaded with treasure carried 200 tons of gold and 18,600 tons of silver from the former Aztec and Inca empires to Spain. Mexico and Peru also grew food to help support Spain's growing empire. However, these gains came with a price for Native Americans. Native peoples suffered greatly at the hands of the Spanish.

Forced Labor By 1650 the Spanish Empire in the Americas had grown to some 3 to 4 million people. Native Americans made up about 80 percent of the population. The rest were whites, Africans, and people of mixed racial background. Settlers who came from Spain were called *peninsulares* (pay-neen-soo-LAHR-ays) and usually held the highest government positions. To reward settlers for their service to the Crown, Spain established the **encomienda** (ayn-koh-mee-AYN-dah) **system**. It gave settlers the right to tax local Native Americans or to make them work. In exchange, these settlers were supposed to protect the Native American people and convert them to Christianity. Instead, most Spanish treated the Native Americans as slaves. Native Americans were forced to work in terrible conditions. They faced cruelty and desperate situations on a daily basis.

The Spanish operated many **plantations**, large farms that grew just one kind of crop. Plantations throughout the Caribbean colonies made huge profits for their owners. It took many workers to run a plantation, however, so colonists forced thousands of Native Americans to work in the fields. Indians who were taken to work on haciendas, the vast Spanish estates in Central and South America, had to raise and herd livestock. Other Native Americans were forced to endure the backbreaking work of mining gold and silver. The forced labor and harsh treatment killed many native people in New Spain.

The Role of the Catholic Church The Catholic Church played a major role in the interactions of the Spanish with Native Americans. The Spanish king commanded priests to convert the local people to the Christian faith. Some Native Americans combined Spanish customs with their own. Others rejected Spanish ideas completely.

Reading Check
Find Main Ideas
How did the encomienda system strengthen Spanish rule?

Some European settlers in the Americas protested the terrible treatment of Native Americans. A priest named **Bartolomé de Las Casas** said that the Spanish should try to convert Native Americans to Christianity by showing them love, gentleness, and kindness. The Spanish monarchs agreed, but the colonists did not always follow their laws.

Summary and Preview In the 1500s Spain built a vast empire in the Americas. The Spanish treated the Native Americans harshly in their new empire. In the next lesson you will learn about other European empires in the Americas.

Lesson 3 Assessment

Review Ideas, Terms, and People

1. a. **Identify** Who was Moctezuma II?
   b. **Analyze** How was Hernán Cortés able to conquer the Aztec Empire?
   c. **Elaborate** What advantages did the Spanish have over Native Americans?
2. a. **Recall** Which Spanish explorer received permission to colonize Florida?
   b. **Analyze** Why do you think Cabeza de Vaca wrote of great riches that could be found in the Americas?
   c. **Evaluate** Why do you think Cabeza de Vaca called for better treatment of Native Americans after having been held prisoner by them?
3. a. **Identify** What was the encomienda system?
   b. **Analyze** Why do you think the king of Spain commanded Catholic priests to teach Native Americans about Christianity?

Critical Thinking

4. **Categorize** In this lesson you learned about Spanish conquest and settlement in the Americas. Copy the graphic organizer below and use it to explain the impact Spain had on the Americas.

Spanish America	
government	.
religion	
labor	

The Race for Empires

The Big Idea

Other European nations challenged Spain in the Americas.

Main Ideas

- Events in Europe affected settlement of North America.
- Several explorers searched for a Northwest Passage to the Pacific Ocean.
- European nations raced to establish empires in North America.

Key Terms and People

Protestant Reformation
Protestants
Spanish Armada
Northwest Passage
Jacques Cartier
charter

If YOU were there . . .

The people of your village in France have always belonged to the same church. Now, in the 1600s, your village is divided over religious beliefs. You have heard about the Dutch colony of New Netherland in America, where people can practice any religion freely. You would like to leave for America, but your parents are unwilling to leave their home.

How would you persuade your family to emigrate?

Events in Europe

Many significant events took place in Europe in the 1500s. Disagreements about religion threw Europe into turmoil. Some of these disagreements eventually led to wars. At the same time, several European nations began to compete for land and power overseas.

The Protestant Reformation In 1517 a German priest named Martin Luther publicly criticized the Roman Catholic Church. Luther charged that the church was too wealthy and that it abused its power. Criticisms like Luther's started the **Protestant Reformation**. This religious movement began in small German towns but quickly spread to much of Europe.

Martin Luther nailed his 95 theses to a church door in Wittenberg, Germany.

It became a part of many political disputes as well. The **Protestants** were reformers who protested some of the Catholic Church's practices. Many Protestants believed God meant for religion to be simple.

The printing press—a machine that produces printed copies using movable type—helped spread the ideas of the Reformation. Protestants printed large numbers of Bibles as well as short essays explaining their ideas. This allowed more people to read and think about the Bible on their own, rather than relying solely on the teachings of a priest.

Johannes Gutenberg developed a movable-type printing press around 1450.

Conflicts between Catholics and Protestants took place throughout Europe, often leading to civil war. In the late 1500s French Catholics fought with French Protestants, known as Huguenots (HYOO-guh-nahts). Many Huguenots eventually immigrated to the Americas in search of religious freedom.

In 1534 King Henry VIII founded the Church of England, or the Anglican Church. By making himself the head of the church, Henry challenged the authority of the pope and angered Catholics. Political issues soon became entangled with the religious struggles.

Spain and England Go to War In the late 1500s King Philip II used Spain's great wealth to lead a Catholic Reformation against the Protestant movement. He hoped to drive the Protestants out of England. Standing in his way was the Protestant English queen Elizabeth I and her sea dogs. Sea dogs was the name given to English sailors who raided Spanish treasure ships. The most successful and daring was Sir Francis Drake.

Philip was angered by English piracy. He began gathering the **Spanish Armada**, a huge fleet of warships meant to end English plans. The

In 1588 the Spanish Armada launched an attack on England.

Armada had about 130 ships and some 27,000 sailors and soldiers. This mighty fleet was launched to invade England and overthrow Queen Elizabeth and the Anglican Church. But in July 1588 the smaller, but faster, English fleet defeated the Armada in a huge battle.

The Armada's defeat shocked the Spanish. In addition to the naval defeat, Spain's economy was in trouble. The gold and silver that Spain received from the Americas caused high inflation. Inflation is a rise in the price of goods caused by an increase in the amount of money in use. Economic problems in Spain combined with the defeat of the Spanish Armada led countries such as England, France, and the Netherlands to challenge Spanish power overseas.

Reading Check
Analyze What led to the decline of the Spanish Empire?

Search for a Northwest Passage

Europeans wanted to find a **Northwest Passage**, a water route through North America that would allow ships to sail from the Atlantic to the Pacific. The English began sending explorers to find it.

Italian sailor John Cabot knew that the king of England wanted to find such a route. Cabot offered to pay for his own expedition, asking only that the king of England grant him a royal charter to any lands he found. The

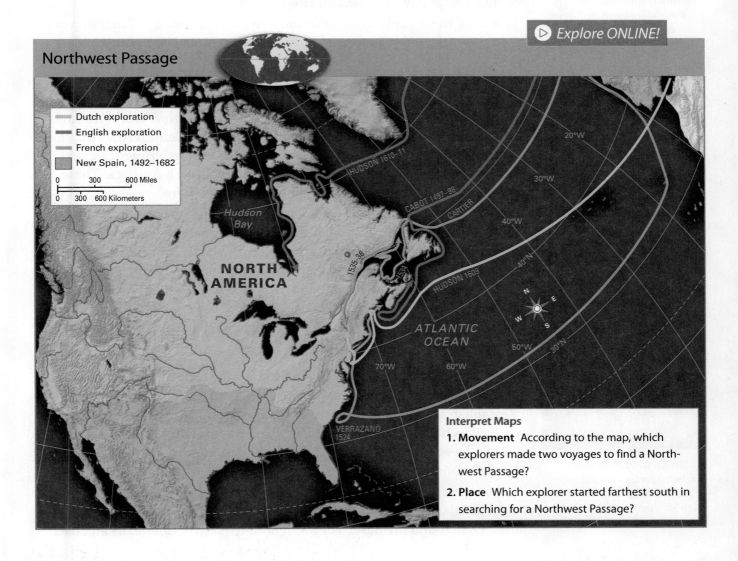

▷ *Explore ONLINE!*

Northwest Passage

Dutch exploration
English exploration
French exploration
New Spain, 1492–1682

0   300   600 Miles
0 300 600 Kilometers

Interpret Maps

1. **Movement** According to the map, which explorers made two voyages to find a Northwest Passage?

2. **Place** Which explorer started farthest south in searching for a Northwest Passage?

king agreed, and Cabot made voyages to North America for England in 1497 and 1498.

Cabot sailed to North America, but he left very few records of his journeys. It is believed that he traveled along the coast of present-day Newfoundland in Canada. Although Cabot did not find a passage to the Pacific Ocean, his voyages were successful. They became the basis of England's claim to land in North America.

In 1524 France sent an Italian captain, Giovanni da Verrazano (vayr-ah-ZAH-noh), to seek a Northwest Passage. Verrazano sailed along the coast of North America from present-day North Carolina to Maine. **Jacques Cartier** (kahr-TYAY), a French sailor, led France's next major exploration of North America. He made two trips to what is now Canada. Cartier sailed into the Saint Lawrence River and traveled all the way to present-day Montreal, claiming the areas he explored for France.

The Dutch also entered the race. They hired English captain Henry Hudson to find a Northwest Passage. Hudson first sailed to present-day New York in 1609. The following year Hudson returned to North America, sailing under the English flag. He traveled far to the north. Eventually he reached a strait that he hoped would lead to the Pacific Ocean. Instead, it led into a huge bay, later named Hudson Bay.

None of these explorers ever found a Northwest Passage. Their explorations, however, led to increased European interest in North America.

Reading Check
Find Main Ideas
Why did European explorers seek a Northwest Passage?

European Presence in North America

The Spanish and the Portuguese were the early leaders in overseas exploration. They dominated the colonization of the New World through the 1500s. However, Spain and Portugal focused on Central America, the Caribbean, and South America. They left much of North America unexplored. The English, French, and Dutch explored North America. These nations then sought to expand their own empires there.

As their empires grew throughout the 1500s and into the 1600s, Europeans acquired a new tool for understanding their world. The Mercator projection map had been created especially for sailors. Although the far northern and southern regions were distorted on the map, the regions where Europeans wanted to explore and claim land were shown fairly well. This map would have helped explorers plan their journeys. It also showed the vast areas where they might find great riches and expand their presence.

English Presence in the New World In the late 1500s England decided to set up a permanent settlement in North America. This colony was to establish an English presence in the New World. Sir Walter Raleigh received a **charter**, a document giving him permission to start a colony. In 1584 he sent an expedition that landed in present-day Virginia and North Carolina. Raleigh named the entire area Virginia.

The following year, Raleigh sent another group to found a colony on Roanoke Island, off the coast of North Carolina. The English colonists at Roanoke found life hard. They fought with Native Americans and had

In 1584, England's Queen Elizabeth granted adventurer Sir Walter Raleigh permission to establish a permanent settlement in North America.

European Exploration of the Americas, 1492–1682

Legend:
- Dutch exploration
- English exploration
- French exploration
- Spanish exploration
- New Spain, 1492–1682

0   150   300 Miles
0   150   300 Kilometers

Hudson Bay

HUDSON 1610-17

CABOT 1497-98

CARTIER 1534-35

CARTIER 1534

Newfoundland

CARTIER 1535-36

Hudson's search for a Northwest Passage led him to the bay that still bears his name.

NORTH AMERICA

Great Lakes

Quebec

Lake Champlain

HUDSON 1609

Nova Scotia

CHAMPLAIN 1609

CHAMPLAIN 1603-1615

Mississippi River

La Salle sailed down the Mississippi to its mouth and claimed for France all the land along the river and its tributaries.

LA SALLE 1679-82

New York

ATLANTIC OCEAN

Colorado River

CORONADO 1540-42

DE SOTO 1539-42

Roanoke Island

Juan Ponce de León became the first European in Florida when he arrived in 1513.

CABEZA DE VACA AND ESTEVANICO 1528-36

Rio Grande

St. Augustine

PONCE DE LEON 1513

PACIFIC OCEAN

Gulf of Mexico

Tropic of Cancer

CORTÉS 1519

Bahama Islands

Cuba

Puerto Rico

Hispaniola

Mexico City (Tenochtitlán)

The Spanish gold coin bears the images of King Ferdinand and Queen Isabella.

110°W

60°N
50°N
40°N
20°N
60°W

Interpret Maps

1. **Movement** Why do you think European explorers traveled with cannons and armaments on their vessels?

2. **Region** In what regions did Spanish explorers travel?

trouble finding and growing food. After only a year, the remaining colonists returned to England.

John White, a talented artist, and 150 colonists resettled Roanoke in the spring of 1587. White's granddaughter, Virginia Dare, was the first English colonist born in North America. After a few months, White went back to England to get more supplies. War with Spain prevented White from returning for three years. When he came back, White found the colony deserted. The only clue he found to the fate of the colonists was the word *Croatoan,* the name of a nearby island, carved into a post. Did the colonists try to escape a Native American attack by fleeing to the island? Or did they intermarry and blend with the friendly Croatan tribe? White never found out. To this day, no one is certain what happened to the "lost colony" at Roanoke.

French Presence in the New World France built its first North American settlement in Florida, when Huguenots started a few small colonies there in 1564. The Spanish soon destroyed these settlements and drove out the French. Religious wars in France slowed further French efforts to colonize North America. When the religious conflicts ended, the French renewed efforts to settle present-day eastern Canada. The explorations of Jacques Cartier and Samuel de Champlain gave France a claim to this region.

Nearly 70 years after Cartier sailed up the Saint Lawrence, French sailor Samuel de Champlain began exploring North America. He recorded his ideas about European exploration in his journal.

> "Through [exploration] we gain knowledge of different countries, regions and kingdoms; through it we attract and bring into our countries all kinds of riches; through it . . . Christianity [is spread] in all parts of the earth."
>
> –Samuel de Champlain, quoted in *Voyages of Samuel de Champlain*

Champlain followed Cartier's old paths. Over the years he made many journeys along the Saint Lawrence River. He also visited the Great Lakes, led by Native American guides. During his travels Champlain met Native Americans called the Algonquin. Some Algonquins formed alliances with the French explorer.

In 1608 Champlain founded a small colony on the Saint Lawrence River. He named the colony Quebec. This trading post opened fur-trading routes for the French throughout the region. Champlain's explorations became the basis of France's claim to much of Canada.

In the late 1600s the French began spreading out from the Saint Lawrence River. Calling their North American territory New France, French fur traders, explorers, and missionaries were all on the move.

In the 1650s French missionaries told stories about "a beautiful river, large, broad, and deep." In 1673 explorer Louis Jolliet (jahl-ee-ET) and missionary Jacques Marquette set out to find this great river, the Mississippi. (Hernando de Soto was the first European to find the Mississippi

River, in 1541.) Jolliet and Marquette reached the river and traveled down it as far as present-day Arkansas.

Nine years later René-Robert de La Salle followed the Mississippi River to the Gulf of Mexico. He claimed the Mississippi Valley for King Louis XIV of France. To honor the king, La Salle named the region Louisiana.

Starting in the 1700s, the French built new outposts. These included Detroit on the Great Lakes and Saint Louis and New Orleans along the Mississippi River. Most towns in the French territory were small. As late as 1688 there were only about 12,000 French settlers in New France. Its small population and the value of the fur trade led French settlers to ally and trade with local Native American groups.

Because of their close trading relationships, the French treated the Native Americans with more respect than some other European settlers had done. Some Algonquins allied with French settlers against English settlers and the Iroquois. In turn, many French settlers learned Native American languages and even adopted their ways of life.

Dutch Presence in the New World The English and the French were not the only European powers to seek an empire in North America. The Dutch, who had merchant fleets around the world, came in search of trade. They claimed the land between the Delaware and Hudson rivers and called it New Netherland. This area included parts of what is now New York, New Jersey, Connecticut, and Delaware.

Dutch explorers and settlers encountered the Mahican, or Mohican, peoples, farmers who lived in large settlements of longhouses. At the center of the Mahican lands was the Hudson River. Conflicts with Dutch and other settlers pushed the Mahican eastward.

In 1624 the newly formed Dutch West India Company sent about

New Amsterdam

The Dutch settlement of New Amsterdam was built next to a harbor where the Hudson River flows into the Atlantic Ocean. By 1643 more than 400 people lived there.

Inside the fort at the center of New Amsterdam was a marketplace, a church, and a windmill.

Ships arrived at the public dock on the East River.

30 families to settle in New Netherland. Two years later Peter Minuit bought Manhattan Island from local Native Americans. He paid with goods that today would be worth less than $1,100. Minuit then founded the town of New Amsterdam, today called New York City. To attract colonists, the Dutch allowed members of all religions to settle in their colony.

Minuit also helped Swedish settlers found New Sweden along the Delaware River. The first settlement, Fort Christina, was begun in 1638. The Swedish settlement was small, but the Dutch felt that it threatened Dutch lands and fur trading. The two sides fought a series of battles. Finally, the governor of New Netherland, Peter Stuyvesant (STY-vuh-suhnt), conquered New Sweden in 1655. He allowed the Swedes to continue their colony, but he called it the "Swedish Nation."

Summary and Preview The English, French, Dutch, and Swedish explored the North American continent and later established colonies there. In the next module you will learn how all of those colonies became English possessions.

Reading Check
Draw Conclusions
Were the French explorers in North America successful? Explain.

Lesson 4 Assessment

Review Ideas, Terms, and People

1. **a. Identify** What was the Protestant Reformation?
   b. Explain What role did the printing press play in the Protestant Reformation?
   c. Summarize How did events that took place in Europe affect the relationships among the British, French, Spanish, and Dutch in their quests to explore North America?

2. **a. Identify** Who was the first European to search for the Northwest Passage?
   b. Describe Which French and Dutch explorers tried to find the Northwest Passage?

3. **a. Recall** What happened to the first English settlements in North America?
   b. Evaluate Which European empire in North America do you think was most successful? Why?

Critical Thinking

4. **Sequence** In this lesson you learned about European exploration and settlement of North America. Create a timeline like the one below and place the four events you think were most important to the development of European empires in North America on the timeline. Be sure to include the date of the event, as well as a description of it and its significance.

Social Studies Skills

Frame Historical Questions

Define the Skill

One of the most valuable ways that people gain knowledge is by asking effective questions. An effective question is one that obtains the kind of information the person asking the question desires. The ability to frame, or construct, effective questions is an important life skill as well as a key to gaining a better understanding of history. Asking effective historical questions will aid you in studying history and in conducting historical research.

Learn the Skill

Effective questions are specific, straightforward, and directly related to the topic. When we do not obtain the information we want or need, often it is because we have asked the wrong questions. Asking effective questions is not as easy as it seems. It requires thought and preparation. The following guidelines will help you in framing effective questions.

1. Determine exactly what you want to know.

2. Decide what questions to ask and write them down. Having written questions is very important. They will help guide your study or research and keep you focused on your topic and goal.

3. Review each of your questions to make sure it is specific, straightforward, and directly related to your topic.

4. Rewrite any questions that are vague, too broad, or biased.

Questions that are vague or too broad are likely to produce information not directly related to what you want to know. For example, if you wanted to know more about trade and the voyages of exploration that you just read about, "What were the voyages of exploration?" may not be a good question to ask. It is too broad. Its answer would not give you the information you want.

Asking "Why was trade the most important cause of the voyages of exploration?" would not be an effective question either. This question is biased because it *assumes* trade was the main reason for the voyages, when that might not have been true. Good historical investigation assumes nothing that is not known to be fact. A more effective question, which would get the information you want, is "Were trade and the voyages of exploration connected, and, if so, in what ways?" Do you see now why wording is so important in asking effective questions and why you should write out and review your questions beforehand?

Practice the Skill

Re-read the information about Cortés and the Aztec, and then complete the activities below.

1. Suppose you wanted to learn more about Cortés's defeat of the Aztec. Decide whether each of the following would be an effective question to ask about this topic. Explain why or why not.

    a. What happened when the Aztec and the Spanish met?

    b. Why did other Indians betray the Aztec?

    c. What resources did Cortés have that helped him conquer the Aztec?

2. Frame five questions that would be effective in helping you to learn more about this topic.

Module 2 Assessment

Review Vocabulary, Terms, and People

1. The first Europeans to reach the east coast of North America were the _____.

2. _____ established a navigation school and financed expeditions to the west coast of Africa.

3. One of the most important European explorers was _____, who was the first person to claim lands in the Americas for Spain.

4. The first voyage that sailed completely around the world was headed by _____.

5. Sir Walter Raleigh founded the colony of Virginia after receiving a _____, a grant to set up a colony, from the queen of England.

6. Large farms, or _____, which specialize in growing one type of crop for profit, were common in Spanish America.

Comprehension and Critical Thinking

Lesson 1

7. **a. Recall** On which two islands did the Vikings establish settlements before coming to North America?

   b. Analyze What factors led Europeans to begin their voyages of exploration?

   c. Evaluate What do you think motivated sailors to sign on for voyages of exploration?

Lesson 2

8. **a. Recall** Why was Columbus's first voyage important?

   b. Summarize Explain the conflict that emerged between Spain and Portugal over their empires in the Americas and how it was resolved.

   c. Evaluate Do you think the Columbian Exchange improved life or made life worse in the Americas? Explain your answer.

Lesson 3

9. **a. Identify** What territories in the Americas did Spain control?

   b. Analyze What factors enabled the Spanish to defeat the Aztec and the Inca?

   c. Elaborate Why was the encomienda system important to Spanish settlers?

Lesson 4

10. **a. Describe** What were the results of the defeat of the Spanish Armada?

    b. Contrast How did French settlements and interactions with native peoples in the Americas differ from the English and Spanish settlements and interactions with native peoples?

    c. Predict What problems might arise among the different empires with settlements in North America?

Module 2 Assessment, continued

Review Themes

11. **Geography** What geographic features in North America helped and hindered the exploration and colonization of the continent?

12. **Society and Culture** How did the Spanish interactions with the Muscogee, the English interactions with the native people at Roanoke, the French interactions with the Algonquins, and the Dutch interactions with the Mahican people compare?

13. **Economics** Refer to the gold coin that bears the images of King Ferdinand and Queen Isabella on the map titled European Exploration of the Americas, 1492–1682, in Lesson 4. What does this coin indicate about the monarchs' rule?

Reading Skills

Outlining and History *Use the Reading Skills taught in this module to complete the following activity.*

14. Make a short but complete outline of the text under the heading "Spanish Treatment of Native Americans."

Social Studies Skills

Frame Historical Questions *Use the Social Studies Skills taught in this module to complete the following activity.*

15. Write a historical question for each of the four lessons of this module.

Focus on Writing

16. **Write a Letter** In this module you learned about different groups that came to the Americas. Imagine that you are a member of one of these groups and write a letter home to tell your friends and family about the people you meet and the experiences you are having in the Americas. Which details will your friends and family be most interested in? Which do you find most important?

Ponce de León

The Spanish conquistador Juan Ponce de León was the first European to set foot on land that later became part of the United States. Ponce de León first sailed to the Americas with Christopher Columbus on his second voyage in 1493. Once in the Caribbean region, he helped conquer what is now Puerto Rico and was named ruler of the island. According to legend, Ponce de León learned about a Fountain of Youth, whose waters could make old people young again. He may have been searching for this fountain when, in 1513, he made landfall on the coast of what today is the southeastern United States. He named the area Florida and claimed it for Spain.

Explore important events in the life of Ponce de León online. You can find a wealth of information, video clips, primary sources, activities, and more through your online textbook.

🎥 Caribbean Island Encounters

Watch the video to learn about the first encounters between Spanish explorers and the people of the Caribbean.

🎥 Claiming Florida for Spain

Watch the video to learn about Ponce de León's first landing on the coast of what is now Florida.

🌎 Ponce de León's 1513 Route

Study the map to learn about the region of the Americas that Ponce de León explored in 1513.

Module 3
The English Colonies

Essential Question

How did the colonial experience shape America's political and social ideals?

About the Photo: Plymouth Colony thrives again in this highly accurate re-creation.

▶ *Explore ONLINE!*

VIDEOS, including...
• Life in Jamestown

HISTORY.

☑ Document-Based Investigations

☑ Graphic Organizers

☑ Interactive Games

☑ Image with Hotspots: Jamestown Fort

☑ Image with Hotspots: New England Town

☑ Interactive Graph: America's Population, 1760

In this module you will learn about the English settlements that dotted the East Coast of North America.

What You Will Learn ...

Timeline of Events 1600–1770

▶ Explore ONLINE!

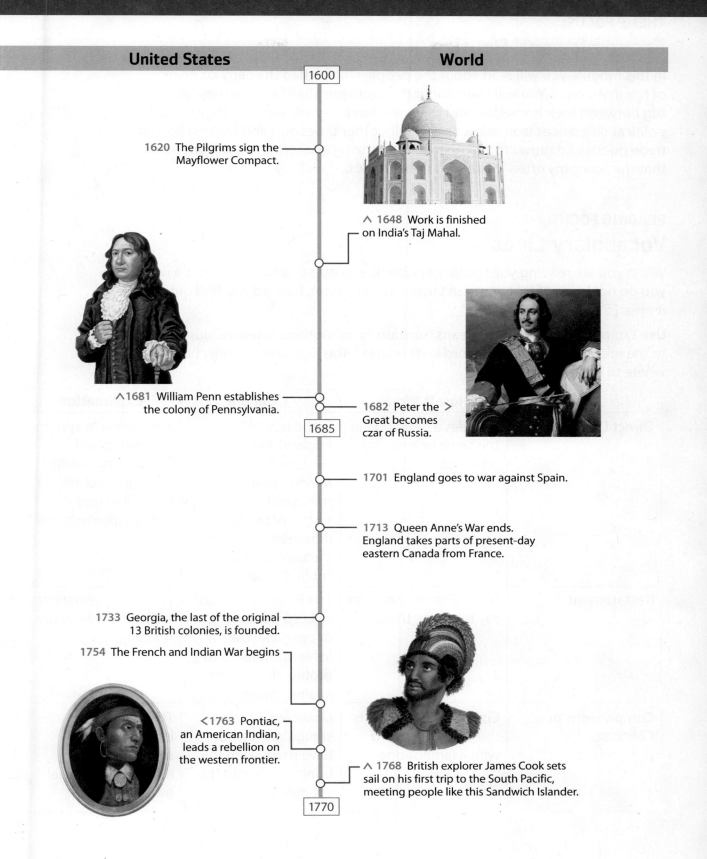

United States	World

1600

1620 The Pilgrims sign the Mayflower Compact.

∧ **1648** Work is finished on India's Taj Mahal.

∧**1681** William Penn establishes the colony of Pennsylvania.

1682 Peter the ﹀ Great becomes czar of Russia.

1685

1701 England goes to war against Spain.

1713 Queen Anne's War ends. England takes parts of present-day eastern Canada from France.

1733 Georgia, the last of the original 13 British colonies, is founded.

1754 The French and Indian War begins

﹤**1763** Pontiac, an American Indian, leads a rebellion on the western frontier.

∧ **1768** British explorer James Cook sets sail on his first trip to the South Pacific, meeting people like this Sandwich Islander.

1770

Reading Social Studies

THEME FOCUS:

Economics and Politics

In this module you will read about the people who settled the early colonies of North America. You will learn about the problems they faced as they felt the tug between their homeland and their new land. You will see how they settled political differences (sometimes peacefully, other times not) and learned how to trade goods and grow crops to establish a thriving economy. You will discover that the economy often influenced their politics.

READING FOCUS:

Vocabulary Clues

When you are reading your history textbook, you may often come across a word you do not know. If that word isn't listed as a key term, how do you find out what it means?

Use Context Clues *Context* means "surroundings." Authors often include clues to the meaning of a difficult word in its context. You just have to know how and where to look.

Clue	How It Works	Example	Explanation
Direct Definition	Includes a definition in the same or a nearby sentence	In the late 1600s England, like most western European nations, practiced mercantilism, *a system of creating and maintaining wealth through carefully controlled trade.*	The phrase "a system of creating and maintaining wealth through carefully controlled trade" defines *mercantilism*.
Restatement	Uses different words to say the same thing	The British continued to keep a standing, or *permanent*, army in North America to protect the colonists against Indian attacks.	The word *permanent* is another way to say *standing*.
Comparisons or Contrasts	Compares or contrasts the unfamiliar word with a familiar one	*Unlike legal traders*, smugglers did not have permission to bring goods into the country.	The word *unlike* indicates that smugglers are different from legal traders.

You Try It!

The following sentences are from this module. Each uses a definition or restatement clue to explain unfamiliar words. See if you can use the context to figure out the meaning of the words in italics.

> ### Context Clues Up Close
>
> 1. In 1605 a company of English merchants asked King James I for the right to *found*, or establish, a settlement.
>
> 2. The majority of workers were *indentured servants*. These servants signed a contract to work for four to seven years for those who paid for their journey to America.
>
> 3. In New England, the center of politics was the *town meeting*. In town meetings people talked about and decided on issues of local interest, such as paying for schools.

Answer the questions about the sentences you read.

1. In example 1, what does the word *found* mean? What hints did you find in the sentence to figure that out?

2. In example 2, where do you find the meaning of *indentured servants*? What does this phrase mean?

3. In example 3, you learn the definition of *town meeting* in the second sentence. Can you combine these two sentences into one sentence? Try putting a dash after the word *meeting* and using "a place where" to replace "In town meetings."

As you read Module 3, look for context clues that can help you figure out the meanings of unfamiliar words or terms.

Key Terms and People

Lesson 1
Jamestown
John Smith
Pocahontas
indentured servants
Bacon's Rebellion
Toleration Act of 1649
Olaudah Equiano
slave codes

Lesson 2
Puritans
Pilgrims
immigrants
Mayflower Compact
Tisquantum
John Winthrop
Anne Hutchinson

Lesson 3
Peter Stuyvesant
Quakers
William Penn
staple crops

Lesson 4
town meeting
English Bill of Rights
triangular trade
Great Awakening
Jonathan Edwards
Enlightenment
John Locke
Pontiac
salutary neglect

The Southern Colonies

The Big Idea
Despite a difficult beginning, the southern colonies soon flourished.

Main Ideas
- Jamestown was the first permanent English settlement in America.
- Daily life in Virginia was challenging to the colonists.
- Religious freedom and economic opportunities were motives for founding other southern colonies, including Maryland, the Carolinas, and Georgia.
- Farming and slavery were important to the economies of the southern colonies.

Key Terms and People
Jamestown
John Smith
Pocahontas
indentured servants
Bacon's Rebellion
Toleration Act of 1649
Olaudah Equiano
slave codes

If YOU were there . . .

A year ago, in 1609, you moved to the colony of Virginia. Life here has been hard. During the winter many people died of cold or sickness. Food is always scarce. Now it is spring, and a ship has come from England bringing supplies. In a week it will sail home. Some of your neighbors are giving up and returning to England. They ask you to come, too.

Would you take the ship back to England?

Settlement in Jamestown

In 1605 a company of English merchants asked King James I for the right to found, or establish, a settlement. In 1606 the king issued the First Virginia Charter that gave the company permission to settle in a region called Virginia.

Founding a New Colony The investors in the new settlement formed a joint-stock company called the Virginia Company of London. This enabled the group to share the cost and risk of establishing the colony. Members of England's growing middle class purchased stock in the company, hoping to earn money from their investment. The middle class is a social class between the upper class and working class.

On April 26, 1607, the first 105 colonists sent by the Virginia Company arrived in America. On May 14, about 40 miles up the James River in Virginia, the colonists founded **Jamestown**, the first permanent English settlement in North America. Most of the colonists hoped to find gold and get rich. Others came looking for new opportunities in North America as cities in England were crowded and jobs were hard to find.

A lack of preparation cost a lot of the colonists their lives. Most of the men who came to Jamestown were adventurers with no farming experience or useful skills

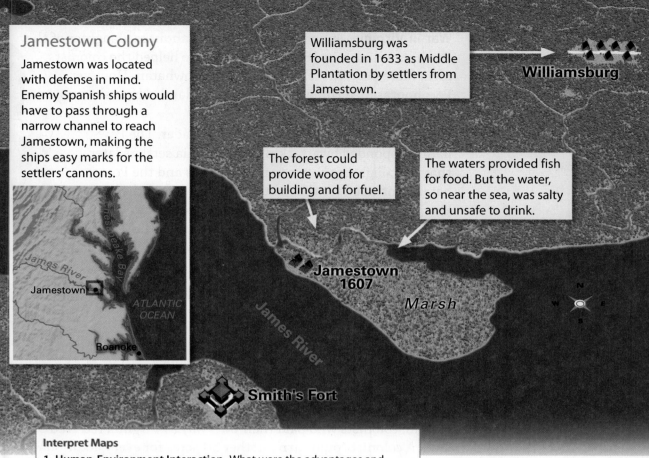

Jamestown Colony

Jamestown was located with defense in mind. Enemy Spanish ships would have to pass through a narrow channel to reach Jamestown, making the ships easy marks for the settlers' cannons.

Williamsburg was founded in 1633 as Middle Plantation by settlers from Jamestown.

Williamsburg

The forest could provide wood for building and for fuel.

The waters provided fish for food. But the water, so near the sea, was salty and unsafe to drink.

Jamestown 1607

Marsh

James River

Smith's Fort

Chesapeake Bay

James River

Jamestown

ATLANTIC OCEAN

Roanoke

Interpret Maps

1. **Human-Environment Interaction** What were the advantages and disadvantages of locating Jamestown on a river?

2. **Human-Environment Interaction** What do you think would have been a commonly used method of transportation for people in this region?

such as carpentry. Jamestown was surrounded by marshes full of disease-carrying mosquitoes. By the time winter arrived, two-thirds of the original colonists had died.

Powhatan Confederacy Jamestown fared better under **John Smith**, who took control of the colony and built a fort in 1608. He forced the settlers to work harder and to build better housing by creating rules that rewarded harder workers with food. The colonists received help from the powerful Powhatan Confederacy of Native Americans after Smith made an agreement with them. The Powhatan traded food for tools and pots to help the colonists. They also taught the colonists how to grow corn.

In 1609 some 400 more settlers arrived in Jamestown. The Powhatan realized that the colony would continue to expand. They started to view the settlers as invaders who would take over their land. In the winter of 1609–1610, the Powhatan surrounded the Jamestown fort and killed anyone who tried to reach supplies outside.

That winter, disease and famine also hit the colony. The colonists called this period the starving time. By the spring of 1610, only 60 colonists were still alive. Jamestown failed to make a profit until colonist John Rolfe introduced a new type of tobacco that sold well in England.

Academic Vocabulary
authority power, right to rule

Reading Check
Find Main Ideas
What problems did the Jamestown colonists face?

War in Virginia John Rolfe married **Pocahontas**, daughter of the Powhatan leader, in 1614. Their marriage helped the colonists form more peaceful relations with the Powhatan. However, Pocahontas died three years later in England, where she was visiting with Rolfe.

In 1622 colonists killed a Powhatan leader. The Powhatan responded by attacking the Virginia settlers later that year. Fighting between the colonists and the Powhatan continued for the next 20 years. Because the Virginia Company could not protect its colonists, the English Crown canceled the company's charter in 1624. Virginia became a royal colony and existed under the **authority** of a governor chosen by the king.

Pocahontas helped the English in Jamestown's early years.

Daily Life in Virginia

In early Virginia, people lived on scattered farms rather than in towns. Tobacco farmers established large farms called plantations. Tobacco was so valuable that it was sometimes used as money.

Headright System These plantations were made possible in part by the headright system, which was started by the Virginia Company. Under this system, colonists who paid their own way to Virginia received 50 acres of land. A colonist could earn another 50 acres for every additional person brought from England. Rich colonists who brought servants or relatives to Virginia gained large amounts of land.

Labor in Virginia Colonists in Virginia suffered very high death rates, which led to labor shortages. The majority of workers were **indentured servants**. These servants signed a contract to work for four to seven years for those who paid for their journey to America.

Expansion of Slavery Not all laborers in Virginia came from Europe. A Dutch ship brought the first Africans to Virginia in 1619. Some Africans were servants; others had been enslaved. Some African servants became successful farmers when their contracts ended.

Colonists overcame tough beginnings to create large and wealthy settlements like this one in Virginia. Churches were often the first major buildings in a growing town.

Colonial Williamsburg Foundation

Academic
Vocabulary
factors causes

The demand for workers was soon greater than the supply of people willing to work as indentured servants. Over time, the cost of slaves fell. These **factors** led some colonists to turn to slave labor. By the mid-1600s most Africans in Virginia were being kept in lifelong slavery.

Women and Children in Virginia Before 1619 most of Virginia's settlers were men. Only a few women and children lived in the colony. It was not until 1619 that the Virginia Company decided to send more women to the colony. The arrival of 90 English women in 1620 allowed more settlers to start families. As a result many settlers chose to make a permanent home in Virginia.

Women brought their skills in cooking, sewing, and making household items. Many could make and mend clothing. Others could make useful items for the home, such as soap and candles. As the Virginia colony grew, more women arrived. Many came as indentured servants.

Life was hard for children in colonial Virginia. They spent much of their time working. Boys who lived on farms helped take care of animals, plant crops, and chop firewood. Girls helped cook and clean. They also spun and wove cloth and helped make butter, soap, and candles.

Bacon's Rebellion As plantations grew, the economy of Jamestown began to expand. Soon, colonial officials began to ask for more taxes. During the mid-1600s poor colonists protested the higher taxes. They were also upset about the governor's policies toward Native Americans. They thought the colony was not well protected against attack. In 1676 a group of former indentured servants led by Nathaniel Bacon attacked some friendly American Indians. Bacon opposed the governor's policies promoting trade with American Indians. He also thought the colonists should be able to take the Indians' land. When the governor tried to stop him, Bacon and his followers attacked and burned Jamestown in an uprising known as **Bacon's Rebellion**.

At one point, Bacon controlled much of the colony. He died of fever, however, and the rebellion soon ended.

Reading Check
Analyze What factors led to the increased use of slave labor in Virginia?

Other Southern Colonies

As Jamestown was developing in Virginia, new groups of colonists began planning their move to America. Many English Catholics came to America to escape religious persecution. English Catholics had long been against England's separation from the Roman Catholic Church. For this reason they were not allowed by the Church of England to worship freely. English leaders also feared that English Catholics would ally with Catholic countries such as France and Spain in conflicts.

Maryland In the 1620s George Calvert, the first Lord Baltimore, asked King Charles I for a charter establishing a new colony in America for Catholics. In 1632 Charles issued the charter to Calvert's son, Cecilius, who took over the planning of the colony. Cecilius, known as the second Lord Baltimore, named the colony Maryland in honor of England's queen, Henrietta Maria. It was located just north of Virginia in the Chesapeake Bay area. Calvert intended for the colony to be a refuge for English

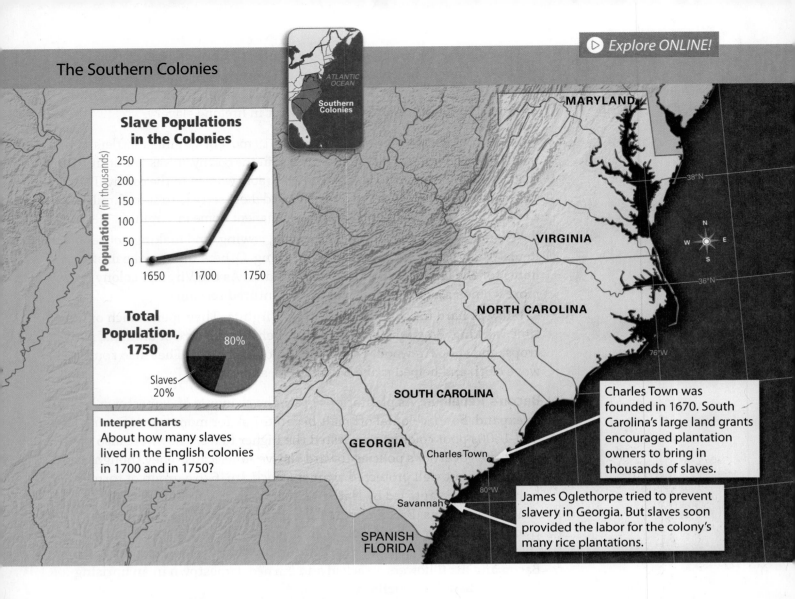

Explore ONLINE!

MARYLAND

VIRGINIA

NORTH CAROLINA

SOUTH CAROLINA

GEORGIA

Charles Town

Savannah

SPANISH FLORIDA

38°N

36°N

76°W

80°W

Slave Populations in the Colonies

Population (in thousands)

250
200
150
100
50
0

1650   1700   1750

Total Population, 1750

80%

Slaves 20%

Interpret Charts
About how many slaves lived in the English colonies in 1700 and in 1750?

Charles Town was founded in 1670. South Carolina's large land grants encouraged plantation owners to bring in thousands of slaves.

James Oglethorpe tried to prevent slavery in Georgia. But slaves soon provided the labor for the colony's many rice plantations.

Catholics. It would also be a proprietary colony. This meant that the colony's proprietors, or owners, controlled the government.

In 1634 a group of 200 English Catholics came to Maryland. Included in the group were wealthy landowners, servants, craftspeople, and farmers. Settlers in Maryland benefited from the lessons learned by the Jamestown colonists. They spent their time raising corn, cattle, and hogs so that they would have enough to eat. Before long, many colonists also began growing tobacco for profit.

Although Catholics founded Maryland, a growing number of Protestants began moving there in the 1640s. Soon, religious conflicts arose between Catholics and Protestants in the colony. To reduce tensions, Lord Baltimore presented a bill to the colonial assembly that became known as the **Toleration Act of 1649**. This bill made it a crime to restrict the religious rights of Christians. This was the first law supporting religious tolerance passed in the English colonies.

The Toleration Act did not stop all religious conflict. However, it did show that the government wanted to offer some religious freedom and protect the rights of minority groups.

The Carolinas and Georgia Colonies were also established south of Virginia. In 1663 the English king, Charles II, gave much of the land between Virginia and Spanish Florida to eight of his supporters. At first Carolina was a single colony. However, the settlements were far apart, and it was hard to govern them. In 1712 the colony separated into North and South Carolina.

Most of the colonists in North Carolina were farmers who had migrated south from Virginia. Among the earliest immigrants who settled North Carolina were the Highland Scots, a group that came from northern Scotland. Colonists primarily from Europe settled South Carolina. Those who paid their own way received large grants of land, and some brought enslaved Africans with them. By 1730 about 20,000 enslaved Africans were living in the colony, compared to some 10,000 white settlers. Both North and South Carolina had rice plantations on which enslaved Africans did much of the work.

James Oglethorpe founded the colony of Georgia in 1733.

South Carolina's proprietors managed the colony poorly, and in 1719 the proprietary government was overthrown. The Crown then purchased North and South Carolina in 1729, making them royal colonies.

In 1732 King George II granted a charter to James Oglethorpe and other trustees to found Georgia. The king hoped that Georgia would act as a shield or buffer between Britain's other colonies and Spanish Florida. In 1733 Oglethorpe and 120 colonists, mostly from England, founded the city of Savannah.

Oglethorpe wanted the Georgia colony to be a place where debtors, who had been jailed for their unpaid debts in England, could make a new start. He offered settlers a bonus of 50 acres for every debtor they brought along to help with the work on their farms. Oglethorpe hoped that the debtors would better themselves through hard work instead of spending time in prison. Only a few settlers were interested in his offer, however, and his plan failed.

Oglethorpe did not want Georgia to have large plantations owned by a few wealthy individuals. He wanted many small farmers. To reach this goal, Oglethorpe outlawed slavery and limited the size of land grants. Soon, however, the settlers grew unhappy with Oglethorpe's strict rules. In 1752 the British government made Georgia a royal colony with new laws. Coastal Georgia was soon filled with large rice plantations worked by thousands of slaves.

Reading Check
Find Main Ideas
What were some of the reasons colonists came to the southern colonies?

Economies of the Southern Colonies

The economies of the southern colonies depended on agriculture. They also exported materials for building ships, such as wood and tar. Some colonies traded with local Indians for deerskins to sell.

The colonies had many small farms and some large plantations. Farms did well because the southern colonies enjoyed a warm climate and a long growing season. Many farms grew cash crops that were sold for profit. Tobacco, rice, and indigo—a plant used to make blue dye—were the most important cash crops.

The southern colonies' cash crops required a great deal of difficult work to grow and harvest. This meant a large workforce was needed. By the 1700s enslaved Africans, rather than indentured servants, had become the main source of labor.

Slavery was a viciously brutal condition for many inhabitants of the southern colonies. One former slave named **Olaudah Equiano** recorded his experiences.

> "Tortures, murder, and every other imaginable barbarity . . . are practiced upon the poor slaves with impunity [no punishment]. I hope the slave-trade will be abolished."
>
> —Olaudah Equiano, from *The Interesting Narrative of the Life of Olaudah Equiano, or Gustavus Vassa, the African*

Reading Check
Summarize What role did slavery play in the southern plantation economy? How was it regulated?

Most of the southern colonies passed **slave codes**, or laws to control slaves. Colonies with large numbers of slaves had the strictest slave codes. For example, South Carolina's slaveholders feared that slaves would revolt. As a result, South Carolina's code said slaves could not hold meetings or own weapons. Some colonies did not allow slaveholders to free their slaves.

Summary and Preview In this lesson you read about life in the southern colonies. In the next lesson you will learn about the New England colonies.

Lesson 1 Assessment

Review Ideas, Terms, and People

1. **a. Describe** How did John Smith improve conditions in Jamestown?
   b. Explain What events led to a conflict between the Jamestown settlers and the Powhatan Confederacy?

2. **a. Recall** Why were indentured servants necessary in Virginia?
   b. Evaluate What do you think was the most serious problem faced by settlers in Virginia? Why?

3. **a. Identify** Which colony was the first to promote religious tolerance?
   b. Analyze Why did more enslaved Africans live in South Carolina than did white settlers?
   c. Predict How might the colony of Georgia have been different if Oglethorpe's plan had succeeded?

4. **a. Recall** What was the purpose of slave codes?
   b. Analyze Why were slaves in high demand in the southern colonies?

Critical Thinking

5. **Contrast** How did the want of natural resources result in cooperation between the Virginia colonists and Native Americans? How did it sometimes result in conflict?

6. **Summarize** In what ways did cultural and social influences help shape the southern colonies?

7. **Compare and Contrast** How were the experiences of indentured servants and enslaved people different from one another?

8. **Analyze** What does the idea of the Georgia colony acting as a shield from Spanish Florida tell you about England's relationship with Spain?

9. **Summarize** In this lesson you learned about the southern colonies. Create a chart similar to the one below and summarize the successes and/or failures of each colony.

Colony	Year	Why Founded	Successes/Failures

The New England Colonies

The Big Idea

English colonists traveled to New England to gain religious freedom.

Main Ideas

- The Pilgrims and Puritans came to America to avoid religious persecution.
- Religion and government were closely linked in the New England colonies.
- The New England economy was based on trade and farming.
- Education was important in the New England colonies.

Key Terms and People

Puritans
Pilgrims
immigrants
Mayflower Compact
Tisquantum
John Winthrop
Anne Hutchinson

If YOU were there . . .

You live in a town near London in the early 1700s. Some of your neighbors are starting new lives in the American colonies. You would like to go with them, but you cannot afford the cost of the trip. There is one way you can go, though. You can sign a paper promising to work as a servant for five years. After the five years, you would be free—and in a new country!

Would you sign the paper and go to America?

Pilgrims and Puritans

Religious tensions in England remained high after the Protestant Reformation. A Protestant group called the **Puritans** wanted to purify, or reform, the Anglican Church. The Puritans thought that bishops and priests had too much power over church members.

Pilgrims on the Move The most extreme English Protestants wanted to separate from the Church of England. These Separatists formed their own churches and cut all ties with the Church of England. In response, Anglican leaders began to punish Separatists.

The **Pilgrims** were one Separatist group that left England in the early 1600s to escape persecution. The Pilgrims moved to the Netherlands in 1608. The Pilgrims were **immigrants**—people who have left the country of their birth to live in another country.

The Pilgrims were glad to be able to practice their religion freely. They were not happy, however, that their children were learning the Dutch language and culture. The Pilgrims feared that their children would forget their English traditions. The Pilgrims decided to leave Europe altogether. They formed a joint-stock company with some merchants and then received permission from England to settle in the American colony of Virginia.

On September 16, 1620, a ship called the *Mayflower* left England with more than 100 men, women, and children aboard. Not all of these colonists were Pilgrims. However, Pilgrim leaders such as William Bradford sailed with the group.

The Mayflower Compact After two months of rough ocean travel, the Pilgrims sighted land far north of Virginia. The Pilgrims knew that they would thus be outside the authority of Virginia's colonial government when they landed. Their charter would not apply. So, they decided to establish their own basic laws and social rules to govern the colony they would found.

On November 21, 1620, 41 of the male passengers on the ship signed the **Mayflower Compact**, a legal contract in which they agreed to have fair laws to protect the general good. The Compact represents one of the first attempts at self-government in the English colonies.

In late 1620 the Pilgrims landed at Plymouth Rock in present-day Massachusetts. The colonists struggled through the winter to build the Plymouth settlement. Nearly half died during this first winter from sickness and the freezing weather.

DOCUMENT-BASED INVESTIGATION Historical Source

The Mayflower Compact

In November 1620 Pilgrim leaders aboard the *Mayflower* drafted the Mayflower Compact. This excerpt from the Mayflower Compact describes the principles of the Pilgrim colony's government.

> The Pilgrims describe the reasons they want to form a colony in North America.

> The Pilgrims promise to obey laws that help the whole colony.

"*We whose names are underwritten . . . having undertaken, for the glory of God, and advancement of the Christian faith, and the honour of our King and country, a voyage to plant the first colony in the northern parts of Virginia, do by these* **presents**[1] *solemnly and mutually in the presence of God, and one of another,* **covenant**[2] *and combine ourselves together into a civil body* **politic**[3] *for our better ordering and preservation and furtherance of the ends* **aforesaid**[4]*; and by* **virtue**[5] *hereof, to enact, constitute, and frame such just and equal laws,* **ordinances**[6]*, acts, constitutions, and offices . . . as shall be thought most* **meet**[7] *and convenient for the general good of the colony unto which we promise all due . . . obedience.*"

[1]*by these presents:* by this document
[2]*covenant:* promise
[3]*civil body politic:* group organized to govern
[4]*aforesaid:* mentioned above

[5]*virtue:* authority
[6]*ordinances:* regulations
[7]*meet:* fitting

Analyze Historical Sources
1. Why do you think the colonists felt the need to establish a government for themselves?
2. How do you think the Mayflower Compact influenced later governments in America?

Tisquantum served as an interpreter, adviser, and friend to the Pilgrims who settled in Plymouth Colony.

Pilgrims and Native Americans In March 1621 a Native American named Samoset walked boldly into the colonists' settlement. He spoke in broken English. Samoset had learned some English from the crews of English fishing boats. He gave the Pilgrims useful information about the peoples and places of the area. He also introduced them to a Patuxet Indian named **Tisquantum**, or Squanto. Tisquantum had at one time lived in Europe and spoke English as well.

From Tisquantum the Pilgrims learned to fertilize the soil with fish remains. He also helped the Pilgrims establish relations with the local Wampanoag Indians. Conditions in Plymouth Colony soon began to improve.

In the fall of 1621 the Pilgrims gathered their first harvest. William Bradford, governor of Plymouth Colony, decided they should have a celebration so that people could give thanks to God. He invited Wampanoag chief Massasoit and 90 other guests to celebrate their harvest. This is what many people today think of as the first Thanksgiving. However, Thanksgiving celebrations, such as the Green Corn Ceremony, have been held by Native Americans for thousands of years. The Pilgrims' Thanksgiving feast included wild turkeys, fish, and lobsters. This event marked the survival of the Pilgrims in the new colony.

Pilgrim Community Although the Pilgrims overcame many problems, their small settlement still struggled. Most Pilgrims became farmers, but the farmland around their settlement was poor. They had hoped to make money by trading furs and by fishing. Unfortunately, fishing and hunting conditions were not good in the area. Some colonists traded corn with American Indians for beaver furs. The Pilgrims made little money but were able to form a strong community. The colony began to grow stronger in the mid-1620s after new settlers arrived and, as in Jamestown, colonists began to have more rights to farm their own land.

The Pilgrims' settlement was different from Virginia's in that it had many families. The Pilgrims taught their children to read and offered some education to their indentured servants. Families served as centers of religious life, health care, and community well-being.

All family members worked together to survive during the early years of the colony. Women generally cooked, spun and wove wool, and sewed clothing. They also made soap and butter, carried water, dried fruit, and cared for livestock. Men spent most of their time repairing tools and working in the fields. They also chopped wood and built shelters.

Women in the Colony In Plymouth, women had more legal rights than they did in England. In England, women were not allowed to make contracts, to sue, or to own property. In America, Pilgrim women had the right to sign contracts and to bring some cases before local courts. Widows could also own property. From time to time, local courts recognized the ways women helped the business community. Widow Naomi Silvester received a large share of her husband's estate. The court called her "a frugal [thrifty] and laborious [hardworking] woman."

Plymouth Colony

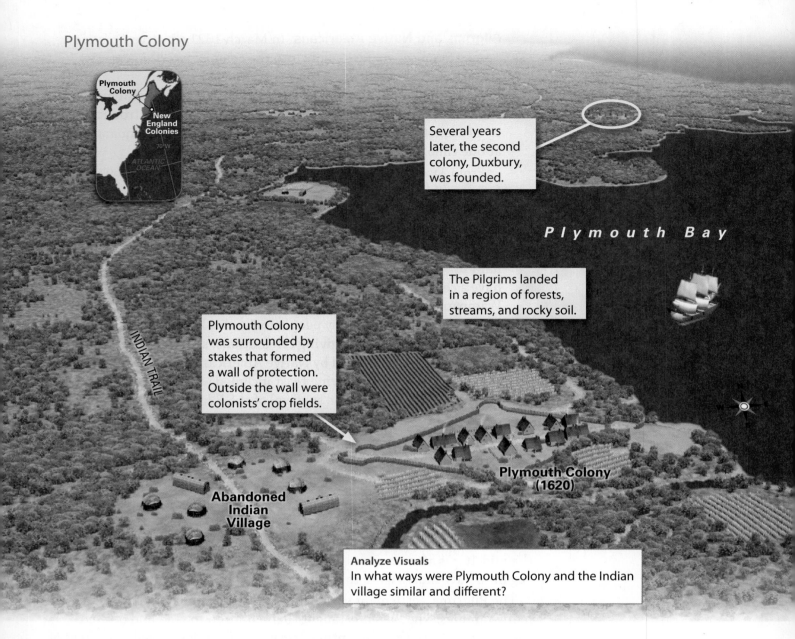

Several years later, the second colony, Duxbury, was founded.

Plymouth Bay

The Pilgrims landed in a region of forests, streams, and rocky soil.

Plymouth Colony was surrounded by stakes that formed a wall of protection. Outside the wall were colonists' crop fields.

INDIAN TRAIL

Abandoned Indian Village

Plymouth Colony (1620)

Analyze Visuals
In what ways were Plymouth Colony and the Indian village similar and different?

Puritans Leave England During the 1620s England's economy suffered. Many people lost their jobs. The English king, Charles I, made the situation worse by raising taxes. This unpopular act led to a political crisis. At the same time, the Church of England began to punish Puritans because they were dissenters, or people who disagree with official opinions. King Charles refused to allow Puritans to criticize church actions.

Great Migration These economic, political, and religious problems in England led to the Great Migration. Between 1629 and 1640 many thousands of English men, women, and children left England. More than 40,000 of these people moved to English colonies in New England and the Caribbean. In 1629 Charles granted a group of Puritans and merchants a charter to settle in New England. The group formed the Massachusetts Bay Company.

In 1630 a group of Puritan colonists seeking religious freedom sailed on a fleet of ships from England to Massachusetts. They were led by **John Winthrop**. The Puritans believed that they had made a covenant, or promise, with God to build an ideal Christian community.

Puritan leader John Winthrop was the first governor of Massachussetts Bay Colony.

A New Colony The Puritans arrived in New England well prepared to start their colony. They brought large amounts of tools and livestock with them. Like the Pilgrims, the Puritans faced little resistance from local American Indians. Trade with Plymouth Colony helped them, too. In addition, the region around Boston had a fairly healthful climate. Thus, few Puritans died from sickness. All of these things helped Massachusetts Bay Colony do well. By 1691 Massachusetts Bay Colony had expanded to include the Pilgrims' Plymouth Colony.

Reading Check
Summarize What role did religion play in the establishment of the Massachusetts Bay Colony?

Religion and Government in New England

Massachusetts Bay Colony had to obey English laws. However, the colony's charter provided more independence than did the royal charter of Virginia. For example, it created a General Court to help run the Massachusetts colony.

The Puritan colonists turned this court into a type of self-government to represent the needs of the people. Each town sent two or three delegates to the Court. After John Winthrop served as the colony's first governor, the General Court elected the governor and his assistants. In 1644 the General Court became a two-house, or bicameral, legislature.

Politics and religion were closely linked in Puritan New England. Government leaders were also church members, and ministers often had a great deal of power in Puritan communities. Male church members were the only colonists who could vote. Colonists became full members in the church by becoming what the Puritans called God's "elect," or chosen. Reaching this status was a difficult process. Individuals had to pass a public test to prove that their faith was strong.

In 1636 minister Thomas Hooker and his followers left Massachusetts to help found Connecticut, another New England colony. In 1639 Hooker wrote the Fundamental Orders of Connecticut. This set of principles made Connecticut's government more democratic. For example, the Orders allowed men who were not church members to vote. As a result, some historians call Hooker the father of American democracy. The Fundamental Orders of Connecticut also outlined the powers of the general courts.

Not all Puritans shared the same religious views. Minister Roger Williams did not agree with the leadership of Massachusetts. He called for his church to separate completely from the other New England congregations. Williams also criticized the General Court for taking land from American Indians without paying them.

Puritan leaders worried that Williams's ideas might hurt the unity of the colony. They made him leave Massachusetts. Williams took his supporters to southern New England. They formed a new settlement called Providence. This settlement later developed into the colony of Rhode

Anne Hutchinson 1591–1643

In 1634 Anne Hutchinson emigrated with her family from England to Massachusetts Bay Colony. After settling in Boston, she worked as a nurse and midwife. She also hosted a Bible-study class that met in her home. Over time, Hutchinson began to question the teachings of the local ministers. Meanwhile, her popularity grew.

After being banished from the colony, Hutchinson settled in Rhode Island and, later, Long Island. She died in an American Indian attack. Today, we remember her as a symbol of the struggle for religious freedom.

Draw Conclusions
Why do you think church leaders disliked Hutchinson's ideas?

Island. In Providence, Williams supported the separation of the church from the state. He also believed in religious tolerance for all members of the community.

In Boston an outspoken woman also angered Puritan church leaders. **Anne Hutchinson** publicly discussed religious ideas that some leaders thought were radical. For example, Hutchinson believed that people's relationship with God did not need guidance from ministers.

Hutchinson's views alarmed Puritans such as John Winthrop. Puritan leaders did not believe that women should be religious leaders. Puritan leaders put Hutchinson on trial for her ideas. The court decided to force her out of the colony. With a group of followers, Hutchinson helped found the new colony of Portsmouth, later a part of the colony of Rhode Island.

In 1643 the New England colonies made an early move toward unity. Several of the colonies formed the United Colonies of New England. This union was established by the New England Articles of Confederation. The articles were an important document in the development of self-government in the English colonies.

Perhaps the worst community conflicts in New England involved the witchcraft trials of the early 1690s. The largest number of trials were held in Salem, Massachusetts. In Salem a group of girls had accused people of casting

Church and State

QUICK FACTS

Religion Affected Government
- Government leaders were church members.
- Ministers had great authority.

Government Affected Religion
- Government leaders outlawed certain religious views.
- Government leaders punished dissenters.

spells on them. The community formed a special court to judge the witch-craft cases. The court often pressured the suspected witches to confess. Before the trials had ended, the Salem witch trials led to 19 people being put to death.

The growth of the New England colonies caused conflicts with Native Americans. As colonists spread across New England, they settled where Native Americans already lived and hunted. Each group had different ideas about land ownership. The Wampanoag and other tribes believed that no one person could own land. The English, however, believed that if they claimed an area, the land was theirs. The colonists expected the Native American tribes to leave the land. Arguments over land sometimes led to wars between the colonists and Native Americans.

New England Economy

Connecticut, Massachusetts, New Hampshire, and Rhode Island were very different from the southern colonies. The often harsh climate and rocky soil meant that few New England farms could grow cash crops. Most farming families grew crops and raised animals for their own use. There was thus little demand for farm laborers. Although some people held slaves, slavery did not become as important to this region.

Merchants Trade was vital to New England's economy. New England merchants traded goods locally, with other colonies, and overseas. Many of them traded local products such as furs, pickled beef, and pork. Many merchants grew in power and wealth, becoming leading members of the New England colonies.

Fishing Fishing became one of the region's leading industries. The rich waters off New England's coast served as home to many fish, including cod, mackerel, and halibut. Merchants exported dried fish. Colonists also began hunting for whales that swam close to shore. Whales were captured with harpoons, or spears, and dragged to shore. Whaling provided valuable oil for lighting.

Shipbuilding Shipbuilding became an important industry in New England for several reasons. The area had plenty of forests that provided materials for shipbuilding. As trade—particularly in slaves—in the New England seaports grew, more merchant ships were built. The fishing industry also needed ships. New England shipyards made high-quality, valuable vessels. Ship owners sometimes even told their captains to sell the ship along with the cargo when they reached their destination.

Skilled Craftspeople The northern economy needed skilled crafts-people. Families often sent younger sons to learn skilled trades such as blacksmithing, weaving, shipbuilding, and printing. The young boys who learned skilled trades were known as apprentices.

Apprentices lived with a master craftsman and learned from him. In exchange, the boys performed simple tasks. Apprentices promised to work for a master craftsman for a set number of years. They learned trades that

Reading Check
Identify Cause and Effect What led to religious disagreements among the Puritans, and what was the result?

were essential to the survival of the colonies. Apprentices received food and often clothing from the craftsmen. Gabriel Ginings, for example, was an apprentice in Portsmouth, Rhode Island. He received "sufficient food and raiment [clothing] suitable for such an apprentice," as his 1663 contract stated.

After a certain amount of time had passed, apprentices became journeymen. They usually traveled and learned new skills in their trade. Eventually, they would become a master of the trade themselves.

Reading Check
Categorize What types of jobs were common in the New England colonies?

Education in the Colonies

Education was important in colonial New England. Mothers and fathers wanted their children to be able to read the Bible. Massachusetts Bay Colony passed some of the first laws requiring parents to provide instruction for their children.

Public Education To be sure that future generations would have educated ministers, communities established town schools. In 1647 the General Court of Massachusetts issued an order that a school be founded in every township of 50 families.

Schoolchildren often used the *New England Primer*, which had characters and stories from the Bible. They learned to read at the same time that they learned about the community's religious values.

The availability of schooling varied in the colonies. There were more schools in New England than in the other colonies, where most children lived far from towns. These children had to be taught by their parents or by private tutors. Most colonial children stopped their education after the elementary grades. Many went to work, either on their family farm or away from home.

A meeting house and a school were located at the center of most New England towns.

Higher Education Higher education was also important to the colonists. In 1636 John Harvard and the General Court founded Harvard College. Harvard taught ministers and met the colony's need for higher education. The second college founded in the colonies, William and Mary, was established in Virginia in 1693.

By 1700 about 70 percent of men and 45 percent of women in New England could read and write. These figures were much lower in Virginia, where Jamestown was the only major settlement.

Summary and Preview In this lesson you learned about the role that religion played in the New England colonies. In the next lesson you'll learn about New York, New Jersey, and Pennsylvania.

Reading Check
Analyze Why was education important to the New England colonies?

Lesson 2 Assessment

Review Ideas, Terms, and People

1. **a. Recall** Why did the Pilgrims and Puritans leave Europe for the Americas?

   b. Elaborate Do you think the Pilgrims could have survived without the assistance of Tisquantum and Massasoit? Explain your answer.

   c. Analyze How did political problems in England encourage the Puritans to start a colony in North America?

2. **a. Describe** What role did the church play in Massachusetts?

   b. Analyze Why did some colonists disagree with the leaders of Massachusetts?

3. **a. Identify** Describe the economy in the New England colonies.

   b. Analyze Why do you think New England merchants became leading members of society?

4. **a. Describe** What are some of the steps Massachusetts Bay Colony took to promote education?

   b. Predict What are some possible benefits that New England's emphasis on education might bring?

Critical Thinking

5. **Analyze** What impact do you think the Mayflower Compact and the Fundamental Orders of Connecticut had on the creation of the United States government?

6. **Contrast** How did New England colonists and Native Americans share natural resources? How did the want of natural resources sometimes result in conflict?

7. **Identify Cause and Effect** In this lesson you learned about the reasons English colonists came to New England. Create a diagram like the one below and show how the colonists' experiences caused them to build certain types of colonies.

Causes → Effects

The Middle Colonies

The Big Idea

People from many nations settled in the middle colonies.

Main Ideas

- The English created New York and New Jersey from former Dutch territory.
- William Penn established the colony of Pennsylvania.
- The economy of the middle colonies was supported by trade and staple crops.

Key Terms and People

Peter Stuyvesant
Quakers
William Penn
staple crops

If YOU were there . . .

You are a farmer in southern Germany in 1730. Religious wars have torn your country apart for many years. Now you hear stories about a place in America where people of all religions are welcome. But the leaders of the colony—and many of its people—are English. You would not know their language or customs. Still, you would be free to live and worship as you like.

How would you feel about moving to a country full of strangers?

New York and New Jersey

The Dutch founded New Netherland in 1613 as a trading post for exchanging furs with the Iroquois and other Native American groups. The center of the fur trade in New Netherland was the town of New Amsterdam on Manhattan Island. The colonists traded Dutch goods with the Native Americans for furs and land.

Generous land grants to patroons, or lords, and religious tolerance soon brought Jews, French Huguenots, Puritans, and others to New Netherland. The patroons brought at least 50 new settlers to the colony. Following the Dutch patroon system, the settlers farmed the patroon's land and paid him rent. Director-general **Peter Stuyvesant** (STY-vuh-suhnt) led the New Netherland colony beginning in 1647.

Peter Stuyvesant was forced to surrender New Netherland to the English in 1664.

Characteristics of the Middle Colonies

Social
- New York: Dutch influence
- New Jersey: diverse population
- Pennsylvania: founded by Quakers

Economic
- successful farming of staple crops
- workforce of slaves and indentured servants
- active trade with Britain and West Indies

The first enslaved Africans were brought to New Netherland in 1626 by the Dutch West India Company. Over time, the population of enslaved Africans increased in the colony. Many were forced to work on farms, in shops, and in homes. Others had to help build ships and work on loading docks. The Dutch West India Company freed some enslaved Africans. Others were able to buy their freedom.

King Charles II of England wanted to take over the growing colony of New Netherland so England could control the entire Atlantic coast of North America. In 1664 an English fleet captured the undefended colony without firing a single shot. New Netherland was renamed New York, and New Amsterdam became New York City.

Soon after the English conquest in 1664, the Duke of York made Sir George Carteret and Lord John Berkeley proprietors of New Jersey. This colony occupied lands between the Hudson and Delaware rivers. It had a diverse population, including Dutch, Swedes, Finns, and Scots. The fur trade was important to the economies of New York and New Jersey through the end of the 1600s.

In the early 1700s New York's African population grew. By 1723 more than 6,000 Africans—both free and enslaved—lived in the colony. However, free and enslaved Africans had fewer rights under English rule than under the Dutch. It was difficult for enslaved Africans to earn their freedom under English laws. Because they were mistreated and lived under harsh conditions, some resisted slavery.

In 1712 a group of enslaved Africans led an armed revolt to escape from slavery. This uprising became known as the New York Slave Revolt of 1712. The resistors failed to gain their freedom, however. As a result, harsher laws were passed to prevent future revolts.

Reading Check
Compare How were New York and New Jersey similar?

Penn's Colony

The Society of Friends, or the **Quakers**, made up one of the largest religious groups in New Jersey. Quakers did not follow formal religious practices and dressed plainly. They believed in the equality of men and women before God. They also supported nonviolence and religious tolerance for all people. At the time, many Quaker beliefs and practices shocked most Christians. As a result, Quakers were persecuted in both England and America.

William Penn 1644–1718

William Penn was born in London as the son of a wealthy admiral. Penn joined the Quakers in 1666 and became an active preacher and writer of religious works. He supported toleration of dissenters.

In 1681 he received a charter to establish a new colony called Pennsylvania. There, Penn put his beliefs into practice. He insisted on fair dealings with local American Indians, welcomed immigrants, and promised religious toleration.

Make Generalizations
How did Penn's ideas influence the rules of the colony?

One proprietor of the New Jersey colony was a Quaker named **William Penn**. Penn wished to found a larger colony under his own control that would provide a safe home for Quakers. In 1681 King Charles II agreed to grant Penn a charter to begin a colony west of New Jersey.

Penn's colony, known as Pennsylvania, grew rapidly. Penn limited his own power and established an elected assembly. He also promised religious freedom to all Christians. His work made Pennsylvania an important example of representative self-government—a government that reflects its citizens' will—in the colonies.

Penn named the capital of his colony Philadelphia, which means "the city of brotherly love." In 1682 the Duke of York sold Penn a region to the south of Pennsylvania. This area, called Delaware, remained part of Pennsylvania until 1776.

Reading Check
Find Main Ideas
Why did William Penn establish Pennsylvania, and how did he influence its government?

Economy of the Middle Colonies

The middle colonies combined characteristics of the New England and southern colonies. With a good climate and rich land, farmers there could grow large amounts of **staple crops**—crops that are always needed. These crops included wheat, barley, and oats. Farmers also raised livestock.

Slaves were somewhat more important to the middle colonies than they were to New England. They worked in cities as skilled laborers, such as blacksmiths and carpenters. Other slaves worked on farms, onboard ships, and in the growing shipbuilding industry. However, indentured servants largely filled the middle colonies' growing labor needs. Between 1700 and 1775 about 135,000 indentured servants came to the middle colonies. About half of them moved to Pennsylvania. By 1760 Philadelphia had become the largest British colonial city. Other cities in the middle colonies, such as New York City, also grew quickly.

Trade was important to the economy of the middle colonies. Merchants in Philadelphia and New York City exported colonial goods to markets in

Britain and the West Indies. These products included wheat from New York, Pennsylvania, and New Jersey.

Throughout the colonies, women made important contributions to the economy. They ran farms and businesses such as clothing and grocery stores, bakeries, and drugstores. Some women also practiced medicine and worked as nurses and midwives. However, colonial laws and customs limited women's economic opportunities.

Most colonial women worked primarily in the home. Married women managed households and raised children. Sometimes they earned money for their families by selling products like butter. They also provided paid services such as washing clothes.

Summary and Preview In this lesson you learned about the middle colonies. In the next lesson you will read about colonial government, the slave trade, and conflicts that arose in the English colonies.

Reading Check
Find the Main Idea
On what were the economies of the middle colonies based?

Lesson 3 Assessment

Review Ideas, Terms, and People

1. **a. Describe** Name the middle colonies. Where were they located?
   b. Draw Inferences What led to the diverse populations of New York and New Jersey?
2. **a. Identify** Who are the Quakers?
   b. Analyze How did William Penn attempt to create a colonial government that would be fair to all?
3. **a. Describe** What different types of jobs did slaves in the middle colonies hold?
   b. Evaluate In what ways were women essential to the middle colonies?

Critical Thinking

4. **Analyze** What does England's capturing of the New Netherland colony tell you about its relationship with the Dutch?
5. **Compare and Contrast** In what ways was the development of the English colonies similar to the development of the Dutch colonies in North America? In what ways was it different?
6. **Analyze** What impact do you think William Penn's elected assembly had on the creation of the United States government?
7. **Sequence** In this lesson you learned about the nations that founded the middle colonies. Create a timeline like the one below and list the event that occurred on each of the dates on the timeline.

1613   1647   1664   1681

America's Growth by 1760

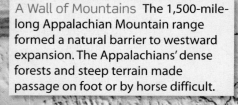

The English colonies in 1760 were located between the Atlantic Ocean and the Appalachian Mountains. The total population of the colonies was around 1.8 million. Soon, however, the colonies began to grow both in size and in population.

In 1763 Great Britain and France signed the Treaty of Paris, giving Britain control over all lands east of the Mississippi River. With the stroke of a pen, the colonies increased enormously in size. The westward expansion of the English colonies—soon to be the United States—had begun.

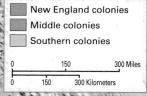

A Wall of Mountains The 1,500-mile-long Appalachian Mountain range formed a natural barrier to westward expansion. The Appalachians' dense forests and steep terrain made passage on foot or by horse difficult.

New England colonies
Middle colonies
Southern colonies

```
0        150        300 Miles
0    150    300 Kilometers
```

America's Population, 1760: 1.8 million

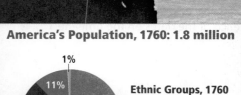

Ethnic Groups, 1760
- White/European
- African American
- Native American
- Other

1%
11%
18%
70%

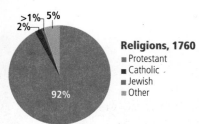

Religions, 1760
- Protestant
- Catholic
- Jewish
- Other

>1%
2%
5%
92%

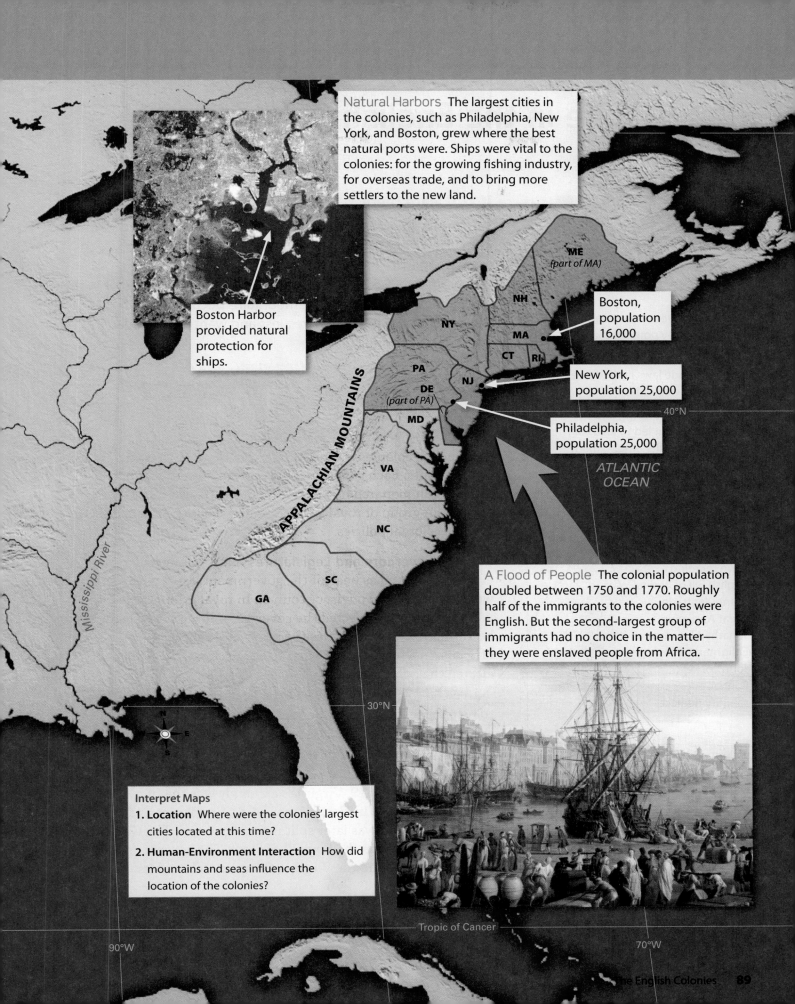

Natural Harbors The largest cities in the colonies, such as Philadelphia, New York, and Boston, grew where the best natural ports were. Ships were vital to the colonies: for the growing fishing industry, for overseas trade, and to bring more settlers to the new land.

Boston Harbor provided natural protection for ships.

ME
(part of MA)

NH

NY

MA

Boston, population 16,000

CT   RI

PA

NJ

DE
(part of PA)

MD

New York, population 25,000

40°N

Philadelphia, population 25,000

VA

ATLANTIC OCEAN

NC

A Flood of People The colonial population doubled between 1750 and 1770. Roughly half of the immigrants to the colonies were English. But the second-largest group of immigrants had no choice in the matter—they were enslaved people from Africa.

SC

GA

Mississippi River

APPALACHIAN MOUNTAINS

30°N

Interpret Maps
1. **Location** Where were the colonies' largest cities located at this time?
2. **Human-Environment Interaction** How did mountains and seas influence the location of the colonies?

Tropic of Cancer

90°W

70°W

Life in the English Colonies

The Big Idea

The English colonies continued to grow despite many challenges.

Main Ideas

- Colonial governments were influenced by political changes in England.
- English trade laws limited free trade in the colonies.
- The Great Awakening and the Enlightenment led to ideas of political equality among many colonists.
- The French and Indian War gave England control of more land in North America.

Key Terms and People

town meeting
English Bill of Rights
triangular trade
Great Awakening
Jonathan Edwards
Enlightenment
John Locke
Pontiac
salutary neglect

If YOU were there . . .

Your family migrated to America in the 1700s and started a small farm in western Pennsylvania. Now, more and more people are moving in. You would like to move farther west, into the Ohio River valley. But a new law says you cannot move west of the mountains because it is too dangerous. Still, you are restless and want more land and more freedom.

Why might you decide to break the law and move west?

Colonial Governments

The English colonies in North America all had their own governments. Each government was given power by a charter. The English monarch had ultimate authority over all of the colonies. A group of royal advisers called the Privy Council set English colonial policies.

Colonial Governors and Legislatures Each colony had a governor who served as head of the government. Most governors were assisted by an advisory council. In royal colonies the English king or queen selected the governor and the council members. In proprietary colonies the proprietors chose all of these officials. In a few colonies, such as Connecticut, the people elected the governor.

In some colonies the people also elected representatives to help make laws and set policy. These officials served on assemblies. Each colonial assembly passed laws that had to be approved first by the advisory council and then by the governor.

Established in 1619, Virginia's assembly was the first colonial legislature in North America. At first it met as a single body, but it was later split into two houses. The first house was known as the Council of State. The governor's advisory council and the Virginia Company selected its

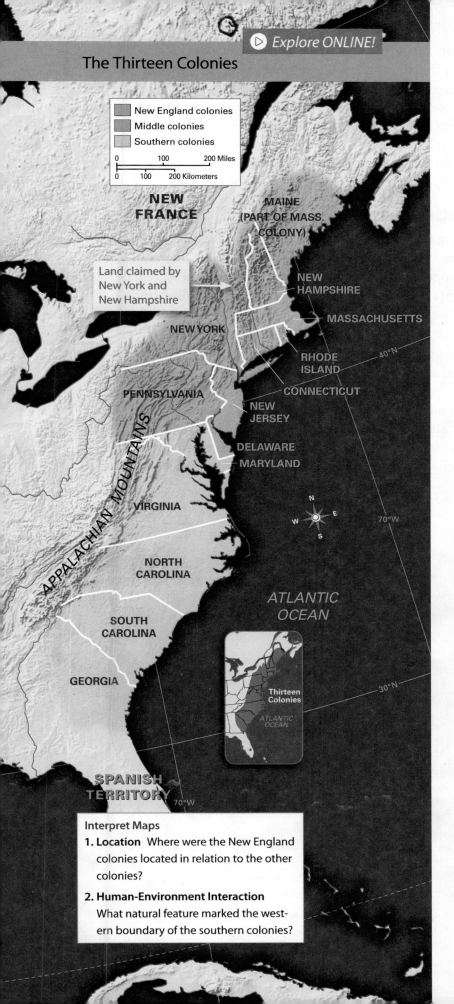

The Thirteen Colonies

▶ Explore ONLINE!

New England colonies
Middle colonies
Southern colonies

0   100   200 Miles
0   100   200 Kilometers

NEW FRANCE

MAINE (PART OF MASS. COLONY)

Land claimed by New York and New Hampshire

NEW HAMPSHIRE

MASSACHUSETTS

NEW YORK

RHODE ISLAND

40°N

CONNECTICUT

PENNSYLVANIA

NEW JERSEY

DELAWARE

MARYLAND

APPALACHIAN MOUNTAINS

VIRGINIA

70°W

NORTH CAROLINA

ATLANTIC OCEAN

SOUTH CAROLINA

Thirteen Colonies

ATLANTIC OCEAN

30°N

GEORGIA

70°W

SPANISH TERRITORY

Interpret Maps

1. **Location** Where were the New England colonies located in relation to the other colonies?

2. **Human-Environment Interaction** What natural feature marked the western boundary of the southern colonies?

members. The House of Burgesses was the assembly's second house. The members were elected by colonists.

In New England the center of politics was the **town meeting**. In town meetings people talked about and decided on issues of local interest, such as paying for schools.

In the southern colonies people typically lived farther away from one another. Therefore, many decisions were made at the county level. The middle colonies used both county meetings and town meetings to make laws.

Political Change in England In 1685 James II became king of England. He was determined to take more control over the English government, both in England and in the colonies.

James believed that the colonies were too independent. In 1686 he united the northern colonies under one government called the Dominion of New England. James named Sir Edmund Andros royal governor of the Dominion. The colonists disliked Andros because he used his authority to limit the powers of town meetings.

English Bill of Rights Parliament replaced the unpopular King James and passed the **English Bill of Rights** in 1689. This act reduced the powers of the English monarch. At the same time, Parliament gained power. As time went on, the colonists valued their own right to elect representatives to decide local issues. Following these changes, the colonies in the Dominion quickly formed new assemblies and charters.

Colonial Courts Colonial courts made up another important part of colonial governments. Whenever possible, colonists used the courts to control local affairs. In general, the courts reflected the beliefs of their local communities. For example, many laws in Massachusetts enforced the Puritans' religious beliefs. Laws based on the Bible set the standard for the community's conduct.

Reading Check
Analyze Information
Why were colonial assemblies and colonial courts created, and what did they do?

Sometimes colonial courts also protected individual freedoms. For example, in 1733 officials arrested John Peter Zenger for printing statements that criticized the governor of New York. The governor claimed that these statements were false. Andrew Hamilton, Zenger's attorney, argued that the statements were true and that he should be allowed to publish his opinions. Jury members believed that colonists had a right to voice their ideas openly and found him not guilty. The Zenger trial was important in establishing the right to freedom of the press in the colonies.

English Trade Laws

One of England's main reasons for founding and controlling its American colonies was to earn money from trade. In the late 1600s England, like most western European nations, practiced mercantilism, a system of creating and maintaining wealth through carefully controlled trade. A country gained wealth if it had fewer imports—goods bought from other countries—than exports—goods sold to other countries.

To support this system of mercantilism, between 1650 and 1696 Parliament passed a series of Navigation Acts limiting colonial trade. For example, the Navigation Act of 1660 forbade colonists from trading specific items such as sugar and cotton with any country other than England. The act also required colonists to use English ships to transport goods. Parliament later passed other acts that required all trade goods to pass through English ports, where duties, or import taxes, were added to the items.

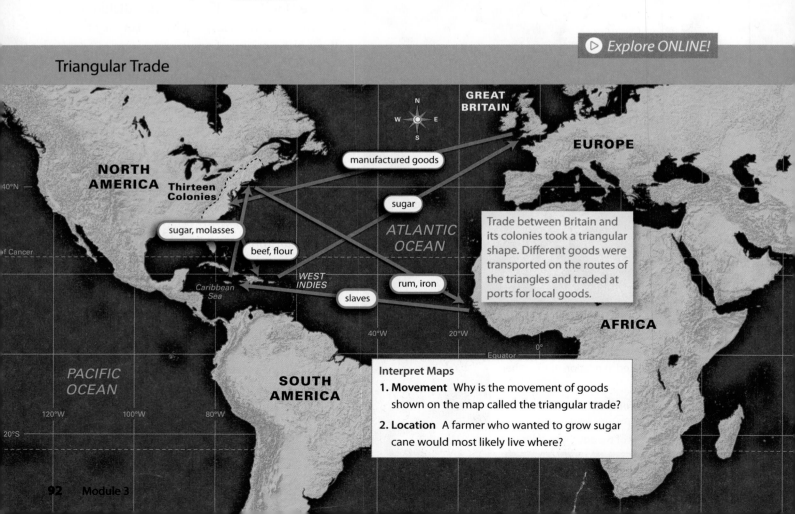

▶ *Explore ONLINE!*

Triangular Trade

manufactured goods

sugar

sugar, molasses

beef, flour

rum, iron

slaves

Trade between Britain and its colonies took a triangular shape. Different goods were transported on the routes of the triangles and traded at ports for local goods.

Interpret Maps
1. **Movement** Why is the movement of goods shown on the map called the triangular trade?
2. **Location** A farmer who wanted to grow sugar cane would most likely live where?

England claimed that the Navigation Acts were good for the colonies. After all, the colonies had a steady market in England for their goods. But not all colonists agreed. Many colonists wanted more freedom to buy or sell goods wherever they could get the best price. Local demand for colonial goods was small compared to foreign demand.

Despite colonial complaints, the trade restrictions continued into the 1700s. Some traders turned to smuggling, or illegal trading. They often smuggled sugar, molasses, and rum into the colonies from non-English islands in the Caribbean. Parliament responded with the Molasses Act of 1733, which placed duties on these items. British officials, however, rarely carried out this law.

By the early 1700s English merchants were trading around the world. Most American merchants traded directly with Great Britain or the West Indies. By importing and exporting goods such as sugar and tobacco, some American merchants became wealthy.

Triangular Trade Trade between the American colonies and Great Britain was not direct. Rather, it generally took the form of **triangular trade**—a system in which goods and slaves were traded among the Americas, Britain, and Africa. There were several routes of the triangular trade. In one route colonists exchanged goods like beef and flour with plantation owners in the West Indies for sugar, some of which they shipped to Britain. The sugar was then exchanged for manufactured products to be sold in the colonies. Colonial merchants traveled great distances to find the best markets for their goods.

Middle Passage One version of the triangular trade began with traders exchanging rum for slaves on the West African coast. The traders then sold the enslaved Africans in the West Indies for molasses or brought them to sell in the mainland American colonies.

Olaudah Equiano 1745–1797

Olaudah Equiano claimed to have been born in Africa in present-day Nigeria. His autobiography told the story of his enslavement. According to his autobiography, Equiano survived the Middle Passage, traveling in a slave ship across the Atlantic. After he arrived in the colonies, a Virginia planter purchased him and again sold him to a British naval officer. While working as a sailor, Equiano eventually earned enough money to purchase his own freedom in 1766.

Equiano later settled in England and devoted much of his life to ending slavery.

Analyze Information
How did Equiano gain his freedom?

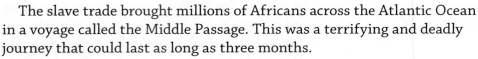

> "I received such a salutation [smell] in my nostrils, as I had never experienced in my life; . . . I became so sick and low that I was not able to eat . . .
>
> The groans of the dying, rendered [made] the whole a scene of horror almost inconceivable [unbelievable]."
>
> —Olaudah Equiano, from *The Interesting Narrative of the Life of Olaudah Equiano, or Gustavus Vassa, the African*

Enslaved Africans endured a long, terrifying trip in overcrowded ships.

The slave trade brought millions of Africans across the Atlantic Ocean in a voyage called the Middle Passage. This was a terrifying and deadly journey that could last as long as three months.

Enslaved Africans lived in a space not even three feet high. Slave traders fit as many slaves as possible on board so they could earn greater profits. Thousands of captives died on slave ships during the Middle Passage. In many cases, they died from diseases such as smallpox. As farmers began to use fewer indentured servants, slaves became even more valuable.

Enslaved Africans in the English colonies tried to deal with their hardships by keeping their culture alive. They told stories and sang songs about their African homelands. By the late 1700s the Christian religion also became a source of strength for many enslaved Africans. Some enslaved Africans resisted slavery. They rebelled by breaking tools, pretending to be sick, or working slowly.

Reading Check
Identify Cause and Effect What factors caused the slave trade to grow? How did this affect conditions on the Middle Passage?

Great Awakening and Enlightenment

In the early 1700s revolutions in both religious and nonreligious thought transformed the Western world. These movements began in Europe and affected life in the American colonies.

Great Awakening After years of population growth, religious leaders wanted to spread religious feeling throughout the colonies. In the late 1730s these ministers began holding revivals, emotional gatherings where people came together to hear sermons.

Many American colonists experienced "a great awakening" in their religious lives. This **Great Awakening**—a religious movement that swept through the colonies in the 1730s and 1740s—changed colonial religion. It also affected social and political life. **Jonathan Edwards** of Massachusetts was one of the most important leaders of the Great Awakening. His dramatic sermons told sinners to seek forgiveness for their sins or face punishment in Hell forever. British minister George Whitefield held revivals from Georgia to New England.

The Great Awakening drew people of different regions, classes, and races. Women, members of minority groups, and poor people often took part in services. Ministers from different colonies met and shared ideas with one another. This represented one of the few exchanges between people from different colonies.

The Great Awakening promoted ideas and virtues that may also have affected colonial politics. Sermons about the spiritual equality of all people led some colonists to begin demanding more political equality. Revivals became popular places to talk about political and social issues. People from those colonies with less political freedom were thus introduced to more democratic systems used in other colonies.

Enlightenment During the 1600s Europeans began to reexamine their world. Scientists began to better understand the basic laws that govern nature. Their new ideas about the universe began the Scientific Revolution. The revolution changed how people thought of the world.

Many colonists were also influenced by the **Enlightenment**. This movement, which took place during the 1700s, spread the idea that reason and logic could improve society. Enlightenment thinkers also formed ideas about how government should work.

Some Enlightenment thinkers believed that there was a social contract between government and citizens. Philosophers such as **John Locke** thought that people had natural rights such as equality and liberty. Ideas of the Scientific Revolution and the Enlightenment eventually influenced colonial leaders.

Reading Check
Summarize How did the Great Awakening and the Enlightenment influence colonial society?

In King Philip's War, Wampanoag leader Metacomet led a coalition force of Native Americans against the colonial militia.

French and Indian War

By the 1670s tensions had arisen between New England colonists and the Wampanoag. Metacomet, a Wampanoag leader also known as King Philip, opposed the colonists' efforts to take his people's lands. In 1675 these tensions finally erupted in a conflict known as King Philip's War. The colonial militia—civilians serving as soldiers—fought American Indian warriors. Both sides attacked each other's settlements, killing men, women, and children. The fighting finally ended in 1676, but only after about 600 colonists and some 3,000 Indians had been killed, including Metacomet.

Native American Allies Some Native Americans allied with the colonists to fight against Metacomet and his forces. These Indians had developed trade relations with colonists. They wanted tools, weapons, and other goods that Europeans could provide. In exchange, the colonists wanted furs, which they sold for large profits in Europe. As a result, each side came to depend upon the other.

French colonists traded and allied with the Algonquian and Huron. English colonists traded and allied with the Iroquois League, in the New York colony. This powerful group united American Indians from six different groups. Many American Indians trusted the French more than they did the English. The smaller French settlements were less threatening than the rapidly growing English colonies. No matter who their allies were,

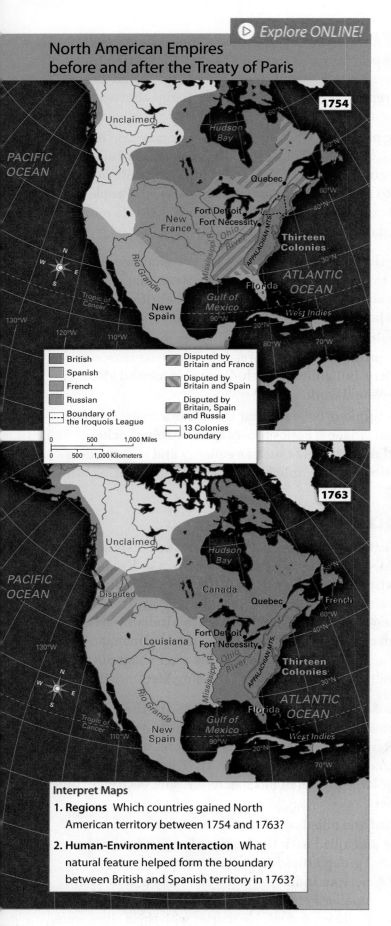

North American Empires before and after the Treaty of Paris

▶ Explore ONLINE!

1754

PACIFIC OCEAN

Unclaimed

Hudson Bay

Quebec

Fort Detroit
Fort Necessity
New France
Ohio River
Thirteen Colonies

APPALACHIAN MTS.

Florida

ATLANTIC OCEAN

New Spain

Rio Grande

Gulf of Mexico

West Indies

Mississippi R.

Tropic of Cancer

130°W 120°W 110°W 90°W 80°W 70°W 60°W 40°N 30°N 20°N

Legend:
- British
- Spanish
- French
- Russian
- Boundary of the Iroquois League
- Disputed by Britain and France
- Disputed by Britain and Spain
- Disputed by Britain, Spain and Russia
- 13 Colonies boundary

0   500   1,000 Miles
0   500   1,000 Kilometers

1763

PACIFIC OCEAN

Unclaimed

Hudson Bay

Canada

Disputed

Quebec French

Louisiana

Fort Detroit
Fort Necessity
Ohio River

APPALACHIAN MTS.

Thirteen Colonies

Florida

ATLANTIC OCEAN

New Spain

Rio Grande

Gulf of Mexico

West Indies

Mississippi R.

Tropic of Cancer

130°W 110°W 90°W 60°W 40°N 30°N 20°N 70°W

Interpret Maps

1. **Regions** Which countries gained North American territory between 1754 and 1763?

2. **Human-Environment Interaction** What natural feature helped form the boundary between British and Spanish territory in 1763?

---

many Indian leaders took care to protect their people's independence. As one leader said:

> "We are born free. We neither depend upon [the governor of New France] nor [the governor of New York]. We may go where we please . . . and buy and sell what we please."
>
> —Garangula, quoted in *A Complete History of the United States of America*, by Frederick Butler

War Erupts Until the mid-1700s France and Great Britain struggled for control of territory in North America. British colonists wanted to settle in the Ohio River valley, where they could take advantage of the valuable fur trade. The French believed this settlement would hurt their fur trade profits. A standoff developed in the Ohio River valley where the French had built three forts. Fighting erupted in 1753 as the British military moved to take over the valley.

When a young Virginian named George Washington arrived with more soldiers, he found the area under French control. Washington and his troops built a small, simple fort that he named Fort Necessity. After his troops suffered many casualties—captured, injured, or killed soldiers—Washington finally surrendered. His defeat in 1754 was the start of the French and Indian War.

Colonial leaders, such as Benjamin Franklin, met to discuss defense. The convention produced a plan called the Albany Plan of Union, based on Franklin's idea for uniting the colonies. The Iroquois tribes, or Haudenosaunee as they called themselves, took part in the convention. They may have helped shape the Albany Plan with their ideas about government. Franklin published his famous "Join, or Die" political cartoon to help convince the colonies to unite. Meanwhile, in 1756 fighting began in Europe, starting what became known as the Seven Years' War.

Treaty of Paris The turning point of the war came in 1759. That year British general James Wolfe captured Quebec, gaining the advantage in the war. However, the war dragged on for four more years. Finally, in 1763 Britain and France signed the Treaty of Paris, officially ending the war.

The terms of the treaty gave Canada to Britain. Britain also gained all French lands east of the Mississippi River except the city of New Orleans and two small islands in the Gulf of St. Lawrence. From Spain, which had allied with France in 1762, Britain received Florida. In an earlier treaty, Spain had received Louisiana, the land that France had claimed west of the Mississippi River. The Treaty of Paris changed the balance of power in North America. Soon, British settlers began moving west to settle new lands.

Western Frontier In the late 1600s and early 1700s, most colonial settlements were located along the Atlantic coast. At that time few colonists had settled the backcountry. Thick forests, steep hills, and few roads made it hard to settle. By the mid-1700s, however, many colonial settlers, or pioneers, were slowly moving into the Virginia and Carolina backcountry and the Ohio River valley. Many of these settlers were Scots-Irish immigrants. The Scots-Irish were people whose ancestors had migrated from Scotland to Ireland. A group of German immigrants called Moravians settled in the foothills of North Carolina's backcountry mountains. They were a religious group who saw themselves as a large "family."

Indian leaders like Chief **Pontiac** opposed British settlement of this new land. Pontiac's Rebellion began in May 1763, when his forces attacked British forts on the frontier. Within one month they had destroyed or captured seven forts. Pontiac then led an attack on Fort Detroit. The British held out for months.

British leaders feared that more fighting would take place on the frontier if colonists kept moving onto American Indian lands. To avoid more conflict, King George III issued the Proclamation of 1763. This law banned British settlement west of the Appalachian Mountains. The law also ordered settlers to leave the upper Ohio River valley. The right to settle and claim ownership of land was important to the colonists, so the proclamation angered them.

BIOGRAPHY

Pontiac 1720–1769

Pontiac, an Ottawa chief who had fought for France, tried to resist British settlement west of the Appalachians. Calling them "dogs dressed in red who have come to rob us," he attacked the British in the Ohio country in 1763. Pontiac's Rebellion was put down, and he surrendered in 1766.

Analyze Information
How did Pontiac try to stop the British?

Most colonists ignored the king's proclamation. They believed they had fought the war to keep the French from blocking their settlement of the western frontier. They did not like the British government telling them to stay out of those lands. As a result, fighting between the settlers and the American Indians continued.

The colonists were not used to laws being strictly enforced in the colonies. Before 1763 Britain interfered very little in colonial affairs. This hands-off policy was known as **salutary neglect**. The British Parliament passed laws to help govern the colonies, but governors rarely enforced these laws. The practice of salutary neglect encouraged individualism and self-reliance in the colonies. The colonists got accustomed to acting on their own. Soon new laws would be passed by Parliament that would further anger the colonists.

Summary and Preview In this lesson you read about colonial governments, the slave trade, and the conflicts with foreign countries and with Native Americans that the colonies faced as they grew. In the next lesson you'll learn about the increasing tension between the colonies and Great Britain that led to independence.

Reading Check
Summarize Why did George III issue the Proclamation of 1763?

Lesson 4 Assessment

Review Ideas, Terms, and People

1. a. Describe How were colonial governments organized?

   b. Analyze How did political change in England affect colonial governments?

2. a. Explain What is mercantilism?

   b. Analyze How did the Navigation Acts support the system of mercantilism?

   c. Evaluate Did the colonies benefit from mercantilism? Why or why not?

3. a. Identify What was the Great Awakening?

   b. Compare How was the Enlightenment similar to the Great Awakening?

4. a. Explain What caused the French and Indian War?

   b. Examine What were some of the outcomes of the French and Indian War?

   c. Evaluate Defend the British decision to ban colonists from settling on the western frontier.

Critical Thinking

5. Analyze What impact did colonial governments have on American politics and institutions?

6. Summarize In this lesson you learned about developments in the colonies during the late 1600s to mid-1700s. Create a chart like the one below to explain the effects of these developments. Then add a box to the bottom of your chart in which you briefly summarize how the colonies grew, changed, and faced challenges during the period.

Development	Effects
Establishment of local government	
Political change in England	
Trade laws	
Great Awakening/ Enlightenment	
French and Indian War	

How the colonies grew, changed, and faced challenges

Social Studies Skills

Interpret Timelines

Define the Skill

Knowing the sequence, or order, in which historical events took place is important to understanding these events. Timelines visually display the sequence of events during a particular period of time. They also let you easily see time spans between events, such as how long after one event a related event took place—and what events occurred in between. In addition, comparing timelines for different places makes relationships between distant events easier to identify and understand.

Learn the Skill

Follow these guidelines to read, interpret, and compare timelines.

1. Determine each timeline's framework. Note the years it covers and the periods of time into which it is divided. Be aware that a pair of timelines may not have the same framework.

2. Study the order of events on each timeline. Note the length of time between events. Compare what was taking place on different timelines around the same time period.

3. Look for relationships between events. Pay particular attention to how an event on one timeline might relate to an event on another.

Practice the Skill

Interpret the timelines below to answer the following questions.

1. What is each timeline's framework?

2. How long was England without a king?

3. What event in England allowed the colonists to get rid of the Dominion of New England in 1689?

4. Massachusetts's independence had troubled English officials for many years. What do the timelines suggest about why this colony was allowed to remain independent until 1686?

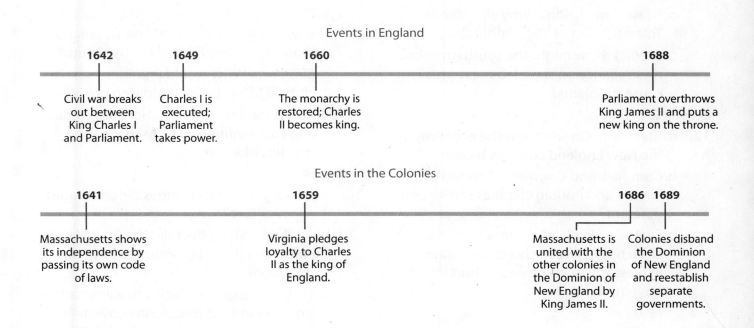

Events in England

1642	1649	1660		1688
Civil war breaks out between King Charles I and Parliament.	Charles I is executed; Parliament takes power.	The monarchy is restored; Charles II becomes king.		Parliament overthrows King James II and puts a new king on the throne.

Events in the Colonies

1641	1659	1686	1689
Massachusetts shows its independence by passing its own code of laws.	Virginia pledges loyalty to Charles II as the king of England.	Massachusetts is united with the other colonies in the Dominion of New England by King James II.	Colonies disband the Dominion of New England and reestablish separate governments.

Module 3 Assessment

Review Vocabulary, Terms, and People

Match the words in the left column with the correct definition in the right column.

1. salutary neglect
2. Jonathan Edwards
3. mercantilism
4. immigrants
5. indentured servants
6. William Penn
7. Pocahontas
8. Quakers
9. staple crops
10. town meeting

a. colonists who received free passage to North America in exchange for working without pay for a certain number of years

b. a hands-off policy under which Britain interfered very little in colonial affairs

c. crops that are continuously in demand

d. daughter of Powhatan chief whose marriage to colonist John Rolfe eased tensions between the Powhatan and the colonists

e. one of the leaders of the Great Awakening, he urged sinners to seek forgiveness

f. Protestant sect founded in England that believed salvation was available to all people

g. people who move to another country after leaving their homeland

h. political gathering at which people make decisions on local issues

i. Quaker leader who established a colony with the goal of fair government for all

j. system of creating and maintaining wealth through controlled trade

Comprehension and Critical Thinking

Lesson 1

11. a. Explain What problems did the settlers of Virginia face?

   b. Draw Conclusions Why was Maryland's Toleration Act of 1649 important?

   c. Predict How might the southern colonies' reliance on slave labor eventually cause problems?

Lesson 2

12. a. Describe On what was the economy of the New England colonies based?

   b. Compare and Contrast How were the Pilgrim and Puritan colonies similar and different?

   c. Evaluate Explain why you think the close ties between church and state in Massachusetts helped or hurt its government.

Lesson 3

13. a. Identify What types of crops were grown in the middle colonies?

   b. Draw Conclusions Why did the middle colonies have a more diverse population than either New England or the South?

   c. Elaborate Why would immigrants have chosen to live in the middle colonies?

   d. Compare and Contrast How did cultural and social influences help shape the middle colonies?

Lesson 4

14. a. Identify What challenges did the English colonies face?

   b. Analyze What effect did the Great Awakening and the Enlightenment have on the colonies?

   c. Evaluate Explain which you think had a greater impact on colonial government—the passage of the English Bill of Rights or the Great Awakening.

Module 3 Assessment, continued

Review Themes

15. Politics What political influences shaped the governments of the British colonies?

16. Economics How did mercantilism affect the economies of Great Britain and the colonies?

17. Economics In what ways were the economies of the southern, New England, and middle colonies similar to one another? In what ways were they different?

Reading Skills

Vocabulary Clues *Use the Reading Skills taught in this module to answer the question about the reading selection below.*

> King James I issued a charter, which gave the Virginia Company permission to settle Virginia.

18. According to the reading selection above, what is the best definition of *charter*?

   a. a chart that showed Virginia's location

   b. an instruction manual on how to sail a ship

   c. a contract setting a limit on the number of indentured servants

   d. a document that gives permission to start a colony

Social Studies Skills

Interpret Timelines *Use the Social Studies Skills taught in this module to answer the questions about the "Events in England" and "Events in the Colonies" timelines shown on the Social Studies Skills page.*

19. How many years after the start of the English Civil War did Parliament overthrow King James II?

20. How many years did the Dominion of New England last?

   a. 41

   b. 18

   c. 3

   d. 6

Focus on Writing

21. Write an Infomercial What if television had been invented during the time the English colonies were being founded in North America? Instead of relying on printed flyers and word of mouth to attract settlers, the founders of colonies might have made infomercials. Choose a colony and time period and make a list of reasons why English citizens might want to settle there. Then write an infomercial with at least four scenes. Each scene should have video and a voice-over telling one of the reasons for immigrating.

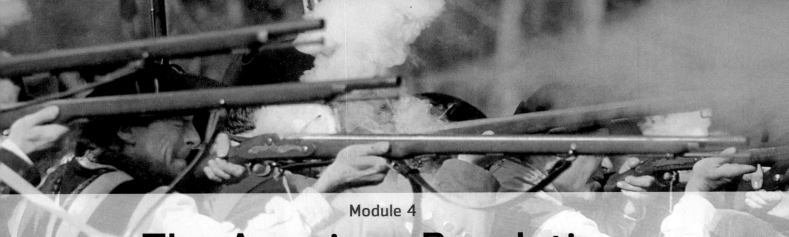

Module 4
The American Revolution

Essential Question

Why were the American Patriots willing to risk their lives for independence?

About the Photo: Soldiers fight with single-shot muskets in this reenactment of a battle during the Revolutionary War.

▷ *Explore ONLINE!*

HISTORY

VIDEOS, including...
- American Revolution: One Word
- Jefferson Writes the Declaration of Independence
- George Washington: Yorktown

✓ Document-Based Investigations

✓ Graphic Organizers

✓ Interactive Games

✓ Image with Hotspots: Battle of Bunker Hill

✓ Image with Hotspots: Winter at Valley Forge

✓ Interactive Map: Battle of Yorktown

In this module you will learn about the American War for Independence.

What You Will Learn ...

Timeline of Events 1760–1785

▶ Explore ONLINE!

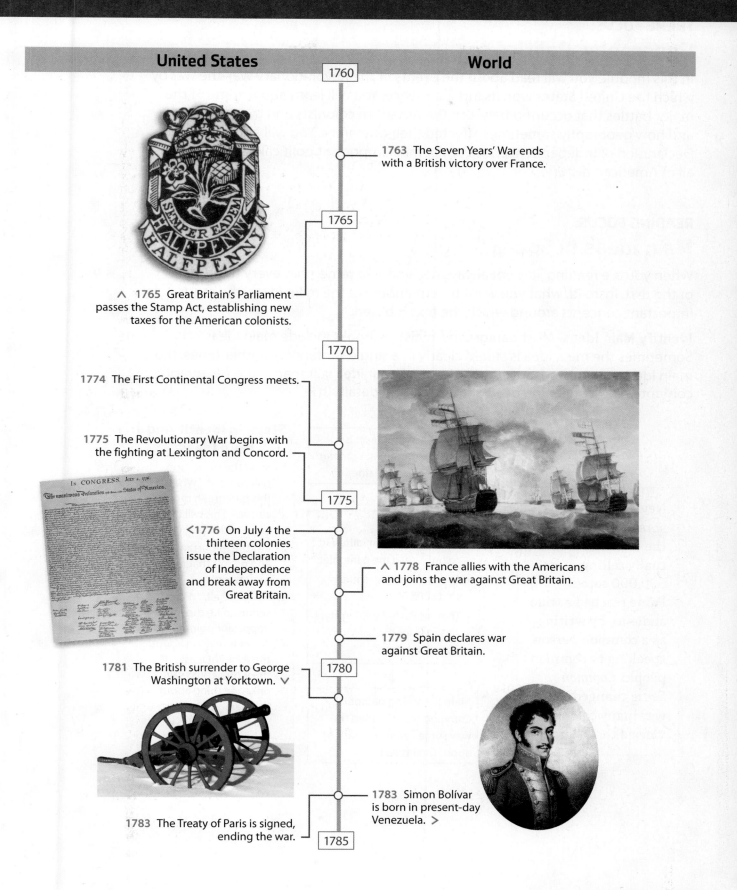

United States | **World**

1760

1763 The Seven Years' War ends with a British victory over France.

1765

∧ **1765** Great Britain's Parliament passes the Stamp Act, establishing new taxes for the American colonists.

1770

1774 The First Continental Congress meets.

1775 The Revolutionary War begins with the fighting at Lexington and Concord.

1775

<**1776** On July 4 the thirteen colonies issue the Declaration of Independence and break away from Great Britain.

∧ **1778** France allies with the Americans and joins the war against Great Britain.

1779 Spain declares war against Great Britain.

1781 The British surrender to George Washington at Yorktown. ∨

1780

1783 Simon Bolívar is born in present-day Venezuela. >

1783 The Treaty of Paris is signed, ending the war.

1785

Reading Social Studies

THEME FOCUS:

Geography, Politics

In this module you will read about the events of the Revolutionary War, the war by which the United States won its independence. You will learn about some of the major battles that occurred between the American colonists and the British army and how geography sometimes affected their outcomes. You will also read the Declaration of Independence, one of the most important political documents in all of American history.

READING FOCUS:

Main Ideas in Social Studies

When you are reading, it is not always necessary to remember every tiny detail of the text. Instead, what you want to remember are the main ideas, the most important concepts around which the text is based.

Identify Main Ideas Most paragraphs in history books include main ideas. Sometimes the main idea is stated clearly in a single sentence. At other times, the main idea is suggested, not stated. However, that idea still shapes the paragraph's content and the meaning of all of the facts and details in it.

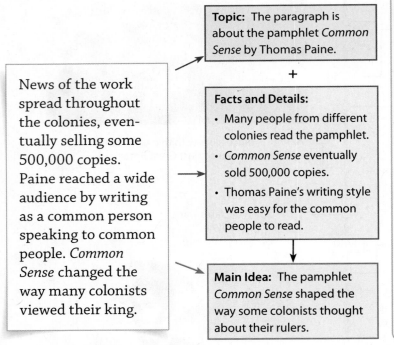

News of the work spread throughout the colonies, eventually selling some 500,000 copies. Paine reached a wide audience by writing as a common person speaking to common people. *Common Sense* changed the way many colonists viewed their king.

Topic: The paragraph is about the pamphlet *Common Sense* by Thomas Paine.

+

Facts and Details:
• Many people from different colonies read the pamphlet.
• *Common Sense* eventually sold 500,000 copies.
• Thomas Paine's writing style was easy for the common people to read.

Main Idea: The pamphlet *Common Sense* shaped the way some colonists thought about their rulers.

Steps in Identifying Main Ideas

1. Read the paragraph. Ask yourself, "What is this paragraph mostly about?" This will be the topic of this paragraph.

2. List the important facts and details that relate to that topic.

3. Ask yourself, "What seems to be the most important point the writer is making about the topic?" Or ask, "If the writer could say only one thing about this paragraph, what would it be?" This is the **main idea** of the paragraph.

You Try It!

The following passage is from the module you are about to read. Read it and then answer the questions below.

The Treaty of Paris

After Yorktown, only a few small battles took place. Lacking the money to pay for a new army, Great Britain entered into peace talks with America. Benjamin Franklin had a key role in the negotiations.

Delegates took more than two years to come to a peace agreement. In the Treaty of Paris of 1783, Great Britain recognized the independence of the United States. The treaty also set America's borders. A separate treaty between Britain and Spain returned Florida to the Spanish. British leaders also accepted American rights to settle and trade west of the original thirteen colonies.

Answer these questions based on the passage you just read.

1. The main idea of the second paragraph is stated in a sentence. Which sentence expresses the main idea?

2. What is the first paragraph about? What facts and details are included in the paragraph? Based on your answers to these questions, what is the main idea of the first paragraph?

As you read Module 4, identify the main ideas of the paragraphs you are reading.

Conflict in the Colonies

The Big Idea

Tensions developed as the British government placed tax after tax on the colonies.

Main Ideas

- British efforts to raise taxes on colonists sparked protest.
- The Boston Massacre caused colonial resentment toward Great Britain.
- Colonists protested the British tax on tea with the Boston Tea Party.
- Great Britain responded to colonial actions by passing the Intolerable Acts.

Key Terms and People

Samuel Adams
Committees of Correspondence
Stamp Act of 1765
Mercy Otis Warren
Boston Massacre
Tea Act
Boston Tea Party
Intolerable Acts
Quartering Act

If YOU were there . . .

You live in the New England colonies in the 1700s. Recently, British officials have placed new taxes on tea—your favorite beverage. You've never been very interested in politics, but you're beginning to think that people far across the ocean in Britain shouldn't be able to tell you what to do. Some of your friends have joined a group that refuses to buy British tea.

Would you give up your favorite drink to join the boycott?

Great Britain Raises Taxes

Great Britain had won the French and Indian War, but Parliament still had to pay for it. The British continued to keep a standing, or permanent, army in North America to protect the colonists against Indian attacks. To help pay for this army, Prime Minister George Grenville asked Parliament to tax the colonists. In 1764 Parliament passed the Sugar Act, which set duties on molasses and sugar imported by colonists. This was the first act passed specifically to raise money in the colonies.

British officials also tried harder to arrest smugglers. Colonial merchants were required to list all the trade goods they carried aboard their ships. These lists had to be approved before ships could leave colonial ports. This made it difficult for traders to avoid paying duties. The British navy also began to stop and search ships for smuggled goods.

Parliament also changed the colonies' legal system by giving greater powers to the vice-admiralty courts. These courts had no juries, and the judges treated suspected smugglers as guilty until proven innocent. In regular British courts, accused persons were treated as innocent until proven guilty.

Taxation without Representation Parliament's actions upset many colonists who had grown used to being independent and governing themselves. The Parliament's longtime

Voice of Protest

Leaders like Patrick Henry made speeches that encouraged colonists to protest the British government. Here, Henry is shown protesting the Crown's control of religion in front of a Virginia court.

Why were public speeches so important to protesting British rule?

practice of salutary neglect, or not enforcing most laws governing the colonies, had fostered individualism among the colonists. The government's previous hands-off approach made these actions seem even harsher to the colonists. The rising merchant class thought the taxes were unfair and hurt business. Many believed that Great Britain had no right to tax the colonies at all without popular consent.

James Otis, a colonial lawyer, argued that the power of the Crown and Parliament was limited. Otis said they could not "take from any man any part of his property, without his consent in person or by representation." Colonial assemblies had little influence on Parliament's decisions. In addition, the colonists had no direct representatives in Parliament. The colonists were subjects of the Crown instead of citizens of England.

At a Boston town meeting in May 1764, local leader **Samuel Adams** agreed with Otis. He believed that Parliament could not tax the colonists without their permission. The ideas of Otis and Adams were summed up in the slogan "No Taxation without Representation," which spread throughout the colonies.

Adams helped found the **Committees of Correspondence**. Each committee got in touch with other towns and colonies. Its members shared ideas and information about the new British laws and ways to challenge them.

A popular method of protest was the boycott, in which people refused to buy British goods. The first colonial boycott started in New York in 1765. It soon spread to other colonies. Colonists hoped that their efforts would hurt the British economy and might convince Parliament to end the new taxes.

Stamp Act The British government continued to search for new ways to tax the American colonies, further angering many colonists. For example, Prime Minister Grenville proposed the **Stamp Act of 1765**. This act required colonists to pay for an official stamp, or seal, when they bought

Colonists had to pay for a stamp, such as this halfpenny stamp, when purchasing any paper item.

paper items. The tax had to be paid on legal documents, licenses, newspapers, pamphlets, and even playing cards. Colonists who refused to buy stamps could be fined or sent to jail.

Grenville did not expect this tax to spark protest. After all, in Britain people already paid similar taxes. But colonists saw it differently. The Stamp Act was Parliament's first attempt to raise money by taxing the colonists directly, rather than by taxing imported goods. **Mercy Otis Warren**, a writer in the Massachusetts colony, disagreed with the new tax. She began writing plays that accused British leaders of being greedy.

Protests against the Stamp Act began almost immediately. Colonists formed a secret society called the Sons of Liberty. Samuel Adams helped organize the group in Boston. This group sometimes used violence to frighten tax collectors. Many colonial courts shut down because people refused to buy the stamps required for legal documents. Businesses openly ignored the law by refusing to buy stamps.

In May 1765 a Virginia lawyer named Patrick Henry presented a series of resolutions to the Virginia House of Burgesses. These resolutions stated that the Stamp Act violated colonists' rights. In addition to taxation without representation, the Stamp Act denied the accused a trial by jury. Henry's speech in support of the resolutions convinced the assembly to support some of his ideas.

Repealing the Stamp Act In Boston the members of the Massachusetts legislature called for a Stamp Act Congress. In October 1765 delegates from nine colonies met in New York. They issued a declaration that the Stamp Act was a violation of their rights and liberties.

Pressure on Parliament to repeal, or do away with, the Stamp Act grew quickly. A group of London merchants complained that their trade suffered from the colonial boycott. Parliament repealed the Stamp Act in 1766.

Members of Parliament were upset that colonists had challenged their authority. Thus, Parliament issued the Declaratory Act, which stated that Parliament had the power to make laws for the colonies "in all cases whatsoever." The Declaratory Act further worried the colonists. The act stripped away much of their independence.

Townshend Acts In June 1767 Parliament passed the Townshend Acts. These acts placed duties on glass, lead, paint, paper, and tea. To enforce the Townshend Acts, British officials used writs of assistance. These allowed tax collectors to search for smuggled goods. Colonists hated the new laws because they took power away from colonial governments.

The colonists responded to the Townshend Acts by once again boycotting many British goods. Women calling themselves the Daughters of Liberty supported the boycott. In February 1768 Samuel Adams wrote a letter arguing that the laws violated the legal rights of the colonists. The Massachusetts legislature sent the letter to other colonies' legislatures, who voted to join the protest.

Reading Check
Sequence What series of events led to the arrival of British troops in Boston in 1768?

At the same time, tax collectors in Massachusetts seized the ship *Liberty* on suspicion of smuggling. This action angered the ship's owner and the Sons of Liberty. They attacked the houses of customs officials in protest. In response, the governor broke up the Massachusetts legislature. He also asked troops to restore order. British soldiers arrived in Boston in October 1768.

Boston Massacre

Many Bostonians saw the presence of British troops as a threat by the British government against its critics in Massachusetts. Some colonists agreed with Samuel Adams, who said, "I look upon [British soldiers] as foreign enemies." The soldiers knew that they were not welcome. Both sides resented each other, and name-calling, arguments, and fights between Bostonians and the soldiers were common.

The tension exploded on March 5, 1770. A lone British soldier standing guard had an argument with a colonist and struck him. A crowd gathered around the soldier, throwing snowballs and shouting insults. Soon a small number of troops arrived. The crowd grew louder and angrier by the moment. Some yelled, "Come on you rascals . . . Fire if you dare!" Suddenly, the soldiers fired into the crowd, instantly killing three men, including African American sailor Crispus Attucks. Attucks is the best-remembered casualty of the incident. Two others died within a few days.

Samuel Adams and other protesters quickly spread the story of the shootings. They used it as propaganda—a story giving only one side in an argument—against the British. Colonists called the shootings the **Boston Massacre**. Paul Revere created an elaborate color print titled "The Bloody Massacre perpetrated in King Street."

The soldiers and their officer, Thomas Preston, were charged with murder. Two Boston lawyers, Josiah Quincy and John Adams—Samuel

Paul Revere's engraving of the Boston Massacre became an effective piece of propaganda. It stirred up anti-British feelings among the colonists.

The Boston Massacre

An account of the Boston Massacre appeared in the *Boston Gazette and Country Journal* soon after the event.

Analyze Historical Sources
Why do you think the people described were not intimidated by the soldiers?

"*The People were immediately alarmed with the Report of this horrid Massacre, the Bells were set a Ringing, and great Numbers soon assembled at the Place where this tragical Scene had been acted; their Feelings may be better conceived than expressed; and while some were taking Care of the Dead and Wounded, the Rest were in Consultation what to do in these dreadful Circumstances.*

But so little intimidated were they [Bostonians], notwithstanding their being within a few Yards of the Main Guard, and seeing the 29th Regiment under Arms, and drawn up in King street; that they kept their Station and appeared, as an Officer of Rank expressed it, ready to run upon the very Muzzles of their Muskets."

—*Boston Gazette and Country Journal,*
March 12, 1770

Reading Check
Analyze What was the significance of the Boston Massacre?

Adams's cousin—agreed to defend the soldiers. The British soldiers claimed that they acted in self-defense. Quincy and Adams argued this point in the trial. The Boston jury agreed, finding Preston and six soldiers not guilty. Two soldiers were convicted of killing people in the crowd by accident. These men were branded on the hand and released. The trial helped calm people down, but many were still angry at the British.

The Boston Tea Party

To reduce tensions in the colonies, Parliament repealed almost all of the Townshend Acts. However, it kept the tax on tea. British officials knew that the colonial demand for tea was high despite the boycott. But colonial merchants were smuggling most of this imported tea and paying no duty on it.

The British East India Company offered Parliament a solution. The company had huge amounts of tea but was not allowed to sell it directly to the colonists. If the company could sell directly to the colonists, it could charge low prices and still make money. Cheaper tea might encourage colonists to stop smuggling. Less smuggling would result in more tax money.

Parliament agreed and passed the **Tea Act** in 1773, which allowed the British East India Company to sell tea directly to the colonists. Many colonial merchants and smugglers feared that the British East India Company's cheap tea would put them out of business.

Three ships loaded with tea from the British East India Company arrived in Boston Harbor in 1773. Members of the Sons of Liberty

Angered by the passage of the Tea Act, colonists in Boston dumped chests of British tea into the harbor before it could be unloaded.

demanded that the ships leave. But the governor of Massachusetts would not let the ships leave without paying the duty. Unsure of what to do, the captains waited in the harbor.

On the night of December 16, 1773, colonists disguised as Native Americans sneaked onto the three tea-filled ships and dumped over 340 tea chests into Boston Harbor. This event became known as the **Boston Tea Party**. Soon the streets echoed with shouts of "Boston harbor is a teapot tonight!"

Reading Check
Summarize What factors led to the Boston Tea Party?

Quick Facts

The Road to Revolution

Colonists reacted to British laws with anger and violence. The British Parliament continued to pass tax after tax.

	British Actions	Colonists' Reactions
1764 The Sugar Act	The Sugar Act is passed to raise money from the colonies for Britain.	Samuel Adams founds the Committees of Correspondence to improve communication among the colonies.
1765 The Stamp Act	The Stamp Act taxes newspapers, licenses, and colonial paper products.	A series of resolutions is published, stating that the Stamp Act violates the rights of the colonists.
1770 The Boston Massacre	British soldiers fire into a crowd of colonists, killing five men.	Colonists protest and bring the soldiers to trial.
1773 The Tea Act	The Tea Act is passed, making British tea cheaper than colonial tea.	Colonists protest by dumping chests of British tea into Boston Harbor.
1774 The Intolerable Acts	Boston Harbor is closed, and British troops are quartered in colonists' homes.	Colonists' resentment toward Britain builds.

Analyze Visuals
In what year did the conflict between Britain and the colonists turn violent?

The Intolerable Acts

Lord North, the new British prime minister, was furious when he heard the news. Parliament decided to punish Boston. In the spring of 1774 it passed the Coercive Acts. Colonists called these laws the **Intolerable Acts**. The acts had several effects.

1. Boston Harbor was closed until Boston paid for the ruined tea.
2. Massachusetts's charter was canceled. The governor decided if and when the legislature could meet.
3. Royal officials accused of crimes were sent to Britain for trial. This let them face a friendlier judge and jury.
4. A new **Quartering Act** required colonists to house British soldiers.
5. The Quebec Act gave a large amount of land to the colony of Quebec.
6. General Thomas Gage became the new governor of Massachusetts.

The British hoped that these steps would bring back order in the colonies. Instead, they simply increased people's anger at Britain.

Reading Check
Analyze What was the purpose of the Intolerable Acts?

Summary and Preview In this lesson you learned about the increasing dissatisfaction between the colonists and Great Britain. In the next lesson you'll learn about the events that started the American Revolution.

Lesson 1 Assessment

Review Ideas, Terms, and People

1. **a. Explain** Why did Great Britain raise taxes in its American colonies?
   b. Evaluate Which method of protesting taxes do you think was most successful for the colonists? Why?

2. **a. Describe** What events led to the Boston Massacre?
   b. Elaborate Why do you think John Adams and Josiah Quincy agreed to defend the British soldiers who were involved in the Boston Massacre?
   c. Explain How did the colonists' and the British soldiers' viewpoints differ about the Boston Massacre?

3. **a. Recall** What was the purpose of the Tea Act?
   b. Draw Conclusions What message did the Boston Tea Party send to the British government?

4. **a. Explain** Why did Parliament pass the Intolerable Acts?
   b. Draw Conclusions Why do you think the colonists believed that these laws were "intolerable"?

Critical Thinking

5. **Identify Cause and Effect** In this lesson you learned about laws passed by the British government that impacted the American colonies. Create a chart similar to the one below to identify these laws and their results.

Law	Result
1.	
2.	
3.	
4.	
5.	

The Revolution Begins

The Big Idea

The tensions between the colonies and Great Britain led to armed conflict in 1775.

Main Ideas

- The First Continental Congress demanded certain rights from Great Britain.

- Armed conflict between British soldiers and colonists broke out with the "shot heard 'round the world."

- The Second Continental Congress created the Continental army to fight the British.

- In two early battles, the army lost control of Boston but then regained it.

Key Terms and People

First Continental Congress
Patriots
minutemen
Redcoats
Second Continental Congress
Continental army
George Washington
Battle of Bunker Hill

If YOU were there . . .

You are a member of the British Parliament in the 1770s. Some members say that the Americans are defying the king. Others point out that the colonists are British citizens who have certain rights. Now the king must decide to punish the rebellious colonists or listen to their complaints.

What advice would you give the king?

First Continental Congress

To many colonists the closing of Boston Harbor was the final insult in a long list of abuses. In response to the mounting crisis, all the colonies except Georgia sent representatives to a meeting in October 1774. This meeting, known as the **First Continental Congress**, was a gathering of colonial leaders who were deeply troubled about the relationship between Great Britain and its colonies in America. At Carpenters' Hall in Philadelphia, the leaders remained locked in weeks of intense debate. Patrick Henry and others believed that violence was unavoidable. On the other hand, delegates from Pennsylvania and New York had strict orders to seek peace.

Wisely, the delegates compromised. They encouraged colonists to continue boycotting British goods but told colonial militias to prepare for war. Meanwhile, they drafted the Declaration of Rights, a list of ten resolutions to be presented to King George III. Included was the colonists' right to "life, liberty, and property."

The First Continental Congress did not seek a separation from Britain. Its goal was to state the colonists' concerns and ask the king to correct the problems. But before they left Philadelphia, the delegates agreed to meet in 1775 if the king refused their petition.

Patrick Henry returned from the Congress and reported to his fellow Virginians. To encourage them to support the Patriot cause, Henry voiced these famous words:

Reading Check
Identify Cause and Effect Why did the delegates attend the First Continental Congress? What were the results?

"They tell us, Sir, that we are weak; unable to cope with so formidable an adversary. But when will we be stronger? Gentlemen may cry, Peace, Peace—but there is no peace. I know not what course others may take; but as for me, give me liberty or give me death."

—Patrick Henry, quoted in *Eyewitnesses and Others*

In time many colonists came to agree with Henry. They became known as **Patriots**—colonists who chose to fight for independence from Great Britain.

"Shot Heard 'round the World"

The Continental Congress planned to meet again in 1775. Before it could, the situation in the colonies had changed—for the worse.

The Ride of Paul Revere British military leaders in the colonies grew uneasy when local militias seemed to be preparing for action. The governor of Massachusetts, Thomas Gage, learned that a stockpile of weapons was stored in Concord, about 20 miles from Boston. He also heard that colonial leaders Samuel Adams and John Hancock were meeting in nearby Lexington. In April 1775 he decided to seize the supplies and arrest the two leaders.

Gage thought he had kept his plan a secret. However, Boston was full of spies for the Patriot cause. They noticed the British were preparing for action and quickly informed the Patriots. Unsure of how the British would strike, Sons of Liberty member Paul Revere enlisted the aid of Robert Newman. Newman was to climb into the steeple of the Old North Church and watch for British soldiers. If they advanced across land, Newman would display one lantern from the steeple. If they rowed across the Charles River, Newman would display two lanterns.

When Revere and fellow Patriot William Dawes saw two lights shine, they set off on horseback. Using two different routes out of Boston, they

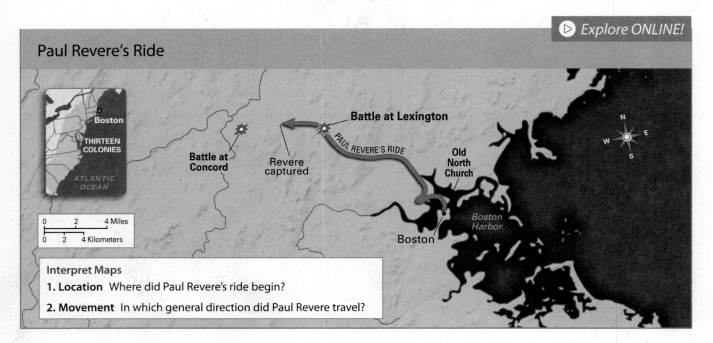

▶ Explore ONLINE!

Paul Revere's Ride

Boston
THIRTEEN COLONIES
ATLANTIC OCEAN

0   2   4 Miles
0   2   4 Kilometers

Battle at Lexington
Battle at Concord
Revere captured
PAUL REVERE'S RIDE
Old North Church
Boston
Boston Harbor

Interpret Maps

1. **Location** Where did Paul Revere's ride begin?

2. **Movement** In which general direction did Paul Revere travel?

sounded the alert. As the riders advanced, drums and church bells called out the local militia, or **minutemen**—who got their name because they were ready to fight at a minute's notice. Many minutemen were rural farmers. Others were craftsmen who lived in towns and cities.

Battles at Lexington and Concord At dawn on April 19, the British troops arrived at the town of Lexington, near Concord, where 70 armed minutemen waited. Patriot captain John Parker yelled to his troops, "Don't fire unless fired upon." Suddenly a shot rang out. To this day, no one knows who fired this "shot heard 'round the world."

The battle at Lexington ended in minutes, with only a few volleys fired. When the smoke cleared, eight of the badly outnumbered minutemen lay dead, and ten were wounded. The British, with only one soldier wounded, marched on to Concord.

Although Revere had been arrested, the citizens of Concord were warned by another rider, Samuel Prescott. Most of the weapons in Concord had already been hidden, but the few that were left were now concealed. Some of the British troops, frustrated because the stockpile had disappeared, set fire to a few buildings. In **reaction** the minutemen charged forward.

For the skilled colonial marksmen of Concord, the British soldiers made an easy target. They were wearing the British military uniform with its bright red jacket. For some time the colonists had called the British soldiers **Redcoats** because of these jackets. The British were forced to retreat to Boston, suffering many casualties along the way.

Academic Vocabulary
reaction response

Reading Check
Draw Inferences
Why did the Patriots need several riders? Why did they take different routes?

Battle of Lexington
The Battle of Lexington was the first battle of the Revolutionary War.

Second Continental Congress

King George III had refused to address the concerns listed in the Declaration of Rights. In May 1775 delegates from 12 colonies met again in Philadelphia for the **Second Continental Congress**. This second group of delegates from the colonies was still far from unified, but represented the first attempt at a Republican government in the colonies.

Some of the delegates called for a war, others for peace. Once again they compromised. Although the Congress did not openly revolt, delegates showed their growing dissatisfaction. They sent word to colonial authorities asking for new state constitutions. States set up conventions to write them. They also authorized the Massachusetts militia to become the **Continental army**. This force would soon include soldiers from all colonies and would carry out the fight against Britain. Congress named a Virginian, **George Washington**, to command the army.

As Washington prepared for war, the Congress pursued peace. On July 5 the delegates signed the Olive Branch Petition as a final attempt to restore harmony. King George refused to read it. Instead, he looked for new ways to punish the colonies.

Reading Check
Summarize
What did the Second Continental Congress accomplish?

——— BIOGRAPHY ———

George Washington
1732–1799

George Washington was a true American, born in the Virginia colony. Although he was a wealthy farmer, he spent most of his life in the military and in politics. In 1775 he served in the Second Continental Congress and was selected to be the commander of the Continental army. Leading the colonial forces to victory in the Revolutionary War, he then helped shape the new government of the United States.

On April 30, 1789, Washington was sworn in as the first president of the United States. As president, he lived in New York City and Philadelphia, the nation's first two capitals. Washington served two terms as president.

Washington inspired Americans and helped to unite them. One of his greatest accomplishments as president was to keep the peace with Britain and France. Upon leaving the presidency in 1796, he urged Americans to avoid becoming politically divided. When he retired, he returned to his plantation home at Mount Vernon, in Virginia.

Draw Conclusions
How might Washington's leadership in the Revolutionary War have prepared him for his role as president?

Early Battles

While the Congress discussed peace, the Massachusetts militia began to fight. Boston was a key city in the early days of the war. Both Patriots and the British fought to hold it.

Bunker Hill Desperate for supplies, leaders in Boston sent Benedict Arnold and a force of 400 men to New York State. Their objective was to attack the British at Fort Ticonderoga. In May 1775 Arnold captured the fort and its large supply of weapons.

Meanwhile, the poorly supplied Patriots kept the British pinned down inside Boston. Although British leaders were trying to form a battle plan, they awoke on June 17 to a stunning sight. The colonial forces had quietly dug in at Breed's Hill, a point overlooking north Boston. The Redcoats would have to cross Boston Harbor and fight their way uphill.

As the British force of 2,400 advanced, 1,600 militia members waited. Low on gunpowder, the commander ordered his troops not to fire "until you see the whites of their eyes." As they climbed the exposed hillside with their heavy packs, the British soldiers were cut down. Twice they retreated. Stepping over the dead and wounded, they returned for a third try. The colonists were now out of ammunition, and eventually they had to retreat.

This famous conflict is now known as the **Battle of Bunker Hill**, although it was actually launched from Breed's Hill. While the Patriots lost, they proved they could take on the Redcoats. For the British, the

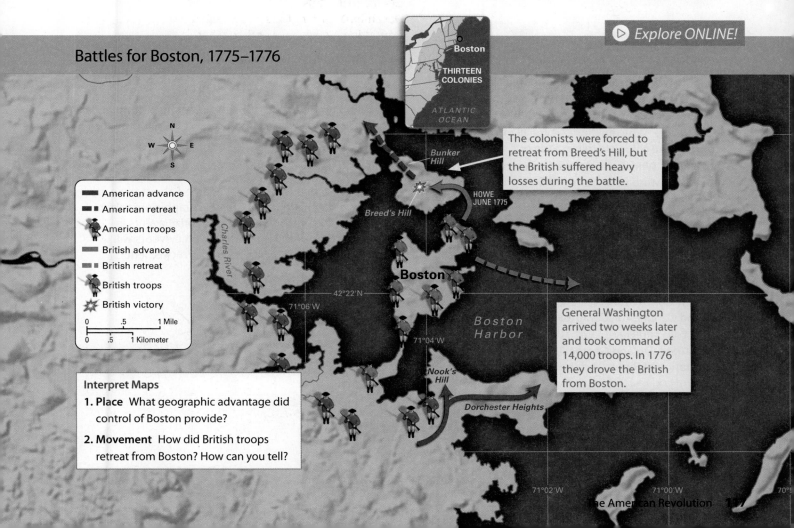

Explore ONLINE!

Battles for Boston, 1775–1776

Boston

THIRTEEN COLONIES

ATLANTIC OCEAN

Bunker Hill

The colonists were forced to retreat from Breed's Hill, but the British suffered heavy losses during the battle.

HOWE JUNE 1775

Breed's Hill

Boston

Charles River

42°22'N

71°06'W

Boston Harbor

71°04'W

Nook's Hill

Dorchester Heights

General Washington arrived two weeks later and took command of 14,000 troops. In 1776 they drove the British from Boston.

- ▬ American advance
- ▬ American retreat
- American troops
- ▬ British advance
- ▬ British retreat
- British troops
- ✸ British victory

0   .5   1 Mile
0   .5   1 Kilometer

Interpret Maps

1. Place What geographic advantage did control of Boston provide?

2. Movement How did British troops retreat from Boston? How can you tell?

71°02'W   71°00'W   70°

battle was a tragic victory. To win, they had sacrificed about double the number of Patriot soldiers.

Dorchester Heights Shortly after the Battle of Bunker Hill, General Washington arrived in Boston to command the Continental army. Washington knew that he would need heavier guns to drive the British out of Boston, and he knew where to get them—Fort Ticonderoga. Colonel Henry Knox was assigned to transport the captured cannons from Fort Ticonderoga to Boston. He successfully brought the heavy guns over 300 miles of rough terrain in the middle of winter. When Knox delivered the cannons, Washington was ready to regain control of Boston.

On March 4, 1776, Washington moved his army to Dorchester Heights, an area that overlooked Boston from the south. He stationed the cannons and his troops on Nook's Hill overlooking British general William Howe's position. When Howe awoke the next morning and saw the Patriots' well-positioned artillery, he knew he would have to retreat. "The Rebels have done more in one night than my whole army could do in months," Howe declared. On March 7 Howe retreated from Boston to Canada. The birthplace of the rebellion was now in Patriot hands.

Summary and Preview Some colonial leaders became convinced that they could not avoid war with Great Britain. In the next lesson you will read about another step toward war—the writing of the Declaration of Independence.

Reading Check
Draw Inferences
Why was the geography of the Boston area important in forming a battle plan?

Lesson 2 Assessment

Review Ideas, Terms, and People

1. a. Identify What was the First Continental Congress?

b. Make Inferences Why did the First Continental Congress send the Declaration of Rights to the king?

c. Elaborate Why did King George III refuse to consider the colonists' declaration?

2. a. Identify Who warned the colonists of the British advance toward Lexington and Concord?

b. Analyze Why did the British army march on Lexington and Concord?

c. Elaborate What is meant by the expression "shot heard 'round the world"?

3. a. Describe What was the purpose of the Second Continental Congress?

b. Draw Conclusions Were the delegates to the Second Continental Congress ready to revolt against George III? Explain.

c. Evaluate Defend George III's response to the Declaration of Rights and the Olive Branch Petition.

4. a. Identify What leader captured Fort Ticonderoga?

b. Draw Conclusions How was the Continental army able to drive British forces out of Boston?

c. Evaluate How would you evaluate the performance of the Continental army in the early battles of the war? Explain.

Critical Thinking

5. Categorize In this lesson you learned about the early battles of the Revolution. Create a graphic organizer similar to the one below and categorize events in the early days of the Revolution. Some events will be attempts at peace; others will be movement toward war.

Attempts at Peace	Movement toward War

★ Declaring Independence

The Big Idea

The colonies formally declared their independence from Great Britain.

Main Ideas

- Thomas Paine's *Common Sense* led many colonists to support independence.

- Colonists had to choose sides when independence was declared.

- The Declaration of Independence did not address the rights of all colonists.

Key Terms and People

Common Sense
Thomas Paine
Declaration of Independence
Thomas Jefferson
Loyalists

Reading Check
Support a Point of View Would you have agreed with Thomas Paine? Explain.

If YOU were there . . .

You live on a farm in New York in 1776. The conflicts with the British have torn your family apart. Your father is loyal to King George and wants to remain British. But your mother is a fierce Patriot, and your brother wants to join the Continental army. Your father and others who feel the same way are moving to British-held Canada. Now you must decide what you will do.

Would you go to Canada or support the Patriots?

Paine's *Common Sense*

"[There] is something very absurd in supporting a continent to be perpetually [forever] governed by an island." This plain-spoken argument against British rule over America appeared in **Common Sense**, a 47-page pamphlet that was distributed in Philadelphia in January 1776. *Common Sense* was published anonymously—that is, without the author's name. The author, **Thomas Paine**, had recently emigrated to the colonies from Great Britain. He argued that citizens, not kings and queens, should make laws. At a time when monarchs ruled much of the world, this was a bold idea.

News of the work spread throughout the colonies, eventually selling some 500,000 copies. Paine reached a wide audience by writing as a common person speaking to common people. He used loaded language to influence people's opinions. Loaded language is powerful words and phrases used to persuade people by appealing to their emotions. *Common Sense* changed the way many colonists viewed their king. It made a strong case for economic freedom in the colonies and for the right to military self-defense. It cried out against tyranny—that is, the abuse of government power. Thomas Paine's words rang out in his time, and they have echoed throughout American history.

In *Common Sense*, Thomas Paine argued that the colonies should claim their independence.

Independence Is Declared

Many colonists agreed with Paine. In April 1776 more than 90 percent of adult males in New Hampshire signed a document called the Association Test. Signers of this document swore to take up arms and resist British rule. Among the signers was Wentworth Cheswell, an African American teacher and government leader.

In June 1776 the Second Continental Congress formed a committee to write a document declaring the colonies' independence. A committee also created a seal for the new country with the Latin motto "*E pluribus unum*" or "out of many, one." This motto recognized the new union of states.

A New Philosophy of Government The **Declaration of Independence** formally announced the colonies' break from Great Britain. In the Preamble, **Thomas Jefferson**, the document's main author, stated why the members of the Continental Congress believed the colonies had the right to become a free nation. The Declaration of Independence expressed three main ideas. First, Jefferson argued that all people possess unalienable rights, including the rights of "life, liberty, and the pursuit of happiness." Jefferson's eloquent argument reflected the English Bill of Rights of 1689 and the ideas of philosopher John Locke and English lawyer William Blackstone about natural rights.

Next, Jefferson asserted that King George III had violated the colonists' rights by taxing them without their consent. Jefferson accused the king of passing unfair laws and interfering with colonial governments. Jefferson also believed that stationing a large British army within the colonies was a burden.

Third, Jefferson stated that the colonies had the right to break from Britain. Influenced by the Enlightenment ideal of the social contract that came from philosophers such as John Locke, Jefferson maintained that governments and rulers must protect the rights of citizens. In exchange, the people agree to be governed. Jefferson argued that King George III had broken the social contract.

On July 4, 1776, the Continental Congress approved the Declaration of Independence. This act broke all ties to the British crown. The United States of America was born. Today, the key principles of the Declaration of Independence are part of the unifying ideas of American democracy.

Choosing Sides The signing of the Declaration made the rebellion a full-scale revolt against Britain. Those who supported it would be considered traitors. Colonists who chose to side with the British were known as **Loyalists**—often called Tories. Historians estimate that 40 to 45 percent of Americans were Patriots, while 20 to 30 percent were Loyalists. The rest were neutral. In every colony there were more Patriots than Loyalists.

Because of persecution by Patriots, more than 50,000 Loyalists fled the colonies during the Revolution. Most went to Canada, where Britain allowed them more self-rule after the Revolution. In doing so, they abandoned their homes and property. Divided allegiances tore apart families and friendships—even Benjamin Franklin became separated from his

Patriot Benjamin Franklin was a printer, author, scientist, inventor, and musician. He would soon become one of America's founders.

Choosing Sides

When Ben Franklin's son William was a child, he helped his father experiment with lightning. But by the time William had grown and the Revolution started, the two men viewed the conflict differently. They exchanged letters on the subject.

In a letter to his father, William Franklin expressed his opinion that all British laws governing the American colonies should be obeyed unless legal action was taken to repeal them. He also said it was the responsibility of executive members of government to enforce these laws. Benjamin Franklin had a very different opinion about the laws that the British Parliament made for the colonies.

"I am indeed of the opinion, that the parliament has no right to make any law whatever, binding on the colonies . . . I know your sentiments differ from mine on these subjects. You are a thorough government man, which I do not wonder at, nor do I aim at converting you. I only wish you to act uprightly and steadily."

—Benjamin Franklin,
quoted in *The Private Correspondence of Benjamin Franklin*

Analyze Historical Sources
How did the two men view the British government differently?

Reading Check
Draw Conclusions
Why would Native Americans have lost out no matter who won the war?

Loyalist son William. Benjamin Franklin wrote about his political beliefs and his scientific experiments in his *Autobiography*, which was first published in 1791.

Native Americans were at first encouraged by both sides to remain neutral. By the summer of 1776, however, both Patriots and the British were aggressively recruiting Indian fighters. Many Native Americans, particularly in the South, sided with the British because the British promised to give them guns and other European goods if they agreed to help them. In northern New York, four of the six Iroquois nations fought for the British. However, the Oneida and Tuscarora helped the Patriots, even delivering food to the soldiers at Valley Forge. Other Native American groups stayed out of the fighting.

Unfinished Business

Today we recognize that the Declaration of Independence excluded many colonists. While it declared that "all men are created equal," the document failed to mention women, enslaved Africans, or Native Americans. The rights of these minorities would be subject to the rule of the majority.

Signing the Declaration of Independence
The Declaration of Independence was adopted on July 4, 1776. This painting shows 47 of the 56 signers of the document. The man sitting on the right is John Hancock, who was the president of the Second Continental Congress. He is accepting the Declaration from the committee that wrote it.

How realistic do you think this painting is?

1 John Adams
2 Roger Sherman
3 Robert Livingston
4 Thomas Jefferson
5 Benjamin Franklin
6 Charles Thomson
7 John Hancock

Women Although many colonial women were Patriots, the Declaration of Independence did not address their rights. At least one delegate's wife, Abigail Adams, tried to influence her husband, John Adams, to include women's rights in the Declaration. In a failed effort, she expressed her concerns:

"Remember the Ladies, and be more generous and favorable to them than your ancestors. Do not put such unlimited power into the hands of the Husbands . . . If particular care and attention is not paid to the Ladies we are and will not hold ourselves bound by Laws in which we have no voice, or Representation."
—Abigail Adams, from a letter from Abigail Adams to John Adams

African Americans and Native Americans The Declaration did not recognize the rights of enslaved Africans, either. The authors had compared life under British rule to living as an enslaved people. The obvious question arose: Why did any form of slavery exist in a land that valued personal freedom? Even Thomas Jefferson, the main author of the Declaration, was a slaveholder.

In July 1776 slavery was legal in all the colonies. By the 1780s the New England colonies were taking steps to end slavery. Even so, the conflict over slavery continued long after the Revolutionary War.

The Declaration of Independence also did not address the rights of Native Americans to life, liberty, or property. Despite the Proclamation of 1763, American colonists had been quietly settling on lands that belonged to Native Americans. This tendency to disregard the rights of Native Americans would develop into a pattern after the colonists won their independence from Great Britain.

Summary and Preview In 1776 the colonists declared their independence. To achieve their goal, however, they would have to win a war against the British army. In the next lesson you will learn about some of the battles of the Revolutionary War. For a time, it seemed as if the British would defeat the colonists.

Reading Check
Find Main Ideas
What groups were unrepresented in the Declaration of Independence?

Lesson 3 Assessment

Review Ideas, Terms, and People

1. **a. Identify** Who was Thomas Paine?

   b. Make Inferences Why do you think Thomas Paine originally published *Common Sense* anonymously?

   c. Elaborate Do you think that most colonists would have supported independence from Britain without Thomas Paine's publication of *Common Sense*? Explain.

2. **a. Identify** What two sides emerged in response to the Declaration of Independence? What did each side favor?

   b. Explain What arguments did the authors of the Declaration of Independence give for declaring the colonies free from British control?

   c. Predict How might some groups use the Declaration of Independence in the future to gain rights?

3. **a. Identify** Who urged her husband to "remember the ladies"?

   b. Make Inferences Why did the authors of the Declaration of Independence fail to address the rights of women, African Americans, and Native Americans in the document?

Critical Thinking

4. **Evaluate** Think about the main ideas expressed in the Declaration of Independence. In what ways are these ideas important in today's world?

5. **Compare and Contrast** Create a chart that compares the points of view of Patriots and Loyalists.

6. **Analyze** In this lesson you learned about the Declaration of Independence. Create a graphic organizer like the one below and identify three results of the Declaration of Independence.

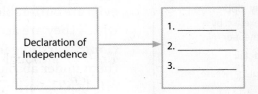

The Declaration of Independence

EXPLORE THE DOCUMENT

Thomas Jefferson wrote the first draft of the Declaration in a little more than two weeks. *How is the Declaration's idea about why governments are formed still important to our country today?*

Vocabulary

[1] **impel** force

[2] **endowed** provided

[3] **usurpations** wrongful seizures of power

[4] **evinces** clearly displays

[5] **despotism** unlimited power

[6] **tyranny** oppressive power exerted by a government or ruler

[7] **candid** fair

[8] **relinquish** release, yield

EXPLORE THE DOCUMENT

Here the Declaration lists the charges that the colonists had against King George III. *How does the language in the list appeal to people's emotions?*

In Congress, July 4, 1776
The unanimous Declaration of the thirteen united States of America,

When in the Course of human events, it becomes necessary for one people to dissolve the political bands which have connected them with another, and to assume among the Powers of the earth, the separate and equal station to which the Laws of Nature and of Nature's God entitle them, a decent respect to the opinions of mankind requires that they should declare the causes which **impel**[1] them to the separation.

We hold these truths to be self-evident, that all men are created equal, that they are **endowed**[2] by their Creator with certain unalienable Rights, that among these are Life, Liberty, and the pursuit of Happiness. That to secure these rights, Governments are instituted among Men, deriving their just powers from the consent of the governed, That whenever any Form of Government becomes destructive of these ends, it is the Right of the People to alter or to abolish it, and to institute new Government, laying its foundation on such principles and organizing its powers in such form, as to them shall seem most likely to effect their Safety and Happiness. Prudence, indeed, will dictate that Governments long established should not be changed for light and transient causes; and accordingly all experience hath shown, that mankind are more disposed to suffer, while evils are sufferable, than to right themselves by abolishing the forms to which they are accustomed. But when a long train of abuses and **usurpations**[3], pursuing invariably the same Object **evinces**[4] a design to reduce them under absolute **Despotism**[5], it is their right, it is their duty, to throw off such Government, and to provide new Guards for their future security.—Such has been the patient sufferance of these Colonies; and such is now the necessity which constrains them to alter their former Systems of Government. The history of the present King of Great Britain is a history of repeated injuries and usurpations, all having in direct object the establishment of an absolute **Tyranny**[6] over these States. To prove this, let Facts be submitted to a **candid**[7] world.

He has refused his Assent to Laws, the most wholesome and necessary for the public good.

He has forbidden his Governors to pass Laws of immediate and pressing importance, unless suspended in their operation till his Assent should be obtained; and when so suspended, he has utterly neglected to attend to them.

He has refused to pass other Laws for the accommodation of large districts of people, unless those people would **relinquish**[8] the right of

9 **inestimable**
priceless

10 **formidable**
causing dread

11 **annihilation**
destruction

12 **convulsions**
violent disturbances

13 **naturalization
of foreigners** the
process by which
foreign-born persons
become citizens

14 **appropriations of
lands** setting aside
land for settlement

15 **tenure** term

16 **a multitude of**
many

Representation in the Legislature, a right **inestimable**[9] to them and **formidable**[10] to tyrants only.

He has called together legislative bodies at places unusual, uncomfortable, and distant from the depository of their Public Records, for the sole purpose of fatiguing them into compliance with his measures.

He has dissolved Representative Houses repeatedly, for opposing with manly firmness his invasions on the rights of the people.

He has refused for a long time, after such dissolutions, to cause others to be elected; whereby the Legislative Powers, incapable of **Annihilation**[11], have returned to the People at large for their exercise; the State remaining in the mean time exposed to all the dangers of invasion from without, and **convulsions**[12] within.

He has endeavored to prevent the population of these States; for that purpose obstructing the Laws of **Naturalization of Foreigners**[13]; refusing to pass others to encourage their migration hither, and raising the conditions of new **Appropriations of Lands**[14].

He has obstructed the Administration of Justice, by refusing his Assent to Laws for establishing Judiciary Powers.

He has made Judges dependent on his Will alone, for the **tenure**[15] of their offices, and the amount and payment of their salaries.

He has erected **a multitude of**[16] New Offices, and sent hither swarms of Officers to harass our people, and eat out their substance.

He has kept among us, in times of peace, Standing Armies without the Consent of our legislature.

He has affected to render the Military independent of and superior to the Civil Power.

Mum Bett, a Massachusetts slave, believed that the words "all men are created equal" should apply to her and other enslaved Africans. She successfully sued for her freedom in 1781.

EXPLORE THE DOCUMENT
Here the Declaration calls the king a tyrant. *What do you think* tyrant *means in this passage?*

He has combined with others to subject us to a jurisdiction foreign to our constitution, and unacknowledged by our laws; giving his Assent to their Acts of pretended legislation:

For **quartering**[17] large bodies of armed troops among us:

For protecting them, by a mock Trial, from Punishment for any Murders which they should commit on the Inhabitants of these States:

For cutting off our Trade with all parts of the world:

For imposing taxes on us without our Consent:

For depriving us in many cases, of the benefits of Trial by Jury:

For transporting us beyond Seas to be tried for pretended offences:

For abolishing the free System of English Laws in a neighboring Province, establishing therein an **Arbitrary**[18] government, and enlarging its Boundaries so as to **render**[19] it at once an example and fit instrument for introducing the same absolute rule into these Colonies:

For taking away our Charters, abolishing our most valuable Laws, and altering fundamentally the Forms of our Governments:

For suspending our own Legislature, and declaring themselves invested with Power to legislate for us in all cases whatsoever.

He has **abdicated**[20] Government here, by declaring us out of his Protection and waging War against us.

He has plundered our seas, ravaged our Coasts, burnt our towns, and destroyed the lives of our people.

He is at this time transporting large armies of **foreign mercenaries**[21] to complete the works of death, desolation and tyranny, already begun with circumstances of Cruelty & **perfidy**[22] scarcely paralleled in the most barbarous ages, and totally unworthy the Head of a civilized nation.

He has constrained our fellow Citizens taken Captive on the high Seas to bear Arms against their Country, to become the executioners of their friends and Brethren, or to fall themselves by their Hands.

He has excited domestic **insurrections**[23] amongst us, and has endeavored to bring on the inhabitants of our frontiers, the merciless Indian Savages, whose known rule of warfare, is an undistinguished destruction of all ages, sexes and conditions.

In every stage of these Oppressions We have **Petitioned for Redress**[24] in the most humble terms: Our repeated Petitions have been answered only by repeated injury. A Prince, whose character is thus marked by every act which may define a Tyrant, is unfit to be the ruler of a free People.

Nor have We been wanting in attention to our British brethren. We have warned them from time to time of attempts by their legislature to extend an **unwarrantable jurisdiction**[25] over us. We have reminded them of the circumstances of our emigration and settlement here. We have appealed to their native justice and **magnanimity**[26], and we have **conjured**[27] them by the ties of our common kindred to disavow these usurpations, which, would inevitably interrupt our connections and correspondence. They too have been deaf to the voice of justice and of **consanguinity**[28]. We must, therefore, **acquiesce**[29] in the necessity, which denounces our Separation, and hold them, as we hold the rest of mankind, Enemies in War, in Peace Friends.

We, therefore, the Representatives of the united States of America, in General Congress, Assembled, appealing to the Supreme Judge of the world for the **rectitude**[30] of our intentions, do, in the Name, and by Authority of the good People of these Colonies, solemnly publish and declare, That these United Colonies are, and of Right ought to be Free and Independent States; that they are Absolved from all Allegiance to the British Crown, and that all political connection between them and the State of Great Britain, is and ought to be totally dissolved; and that as Free and Independent States, they have full Power to levy War, conclude Peace, contract Alliances, establish Commerce, and to do all other Acts and Things which Independent States may of right do. And for the support of this Declaration, with a firm reliance on the Protection of Divine Providence, we mutually pledge to each other our Lives, our Fortunes and our sacred Honor.

John Hancock	Benjamin Harrison	Lewis Morris
Button Gwinnett	Thomas Nelson, Jr.	Richard Stockton
Lyman Hall	Francis Lightfoot Lee	John Witherspoon
George Walton	Carter Braxton	Francis Hopkinson
William Hooper	Robert Morris	John Hart
Joseph Hewes	Benjamin Rush	Abraham Clark
John Penn	Benjamin Franklin	Josiah Bartlett
Edward Rutledge	John Morton	William Whipple
Thomas Heyward, Jr.	George Clymer	Samuel Adams
Thomas Lynch, Jr.	James Smith	John Adams
Arthur Middleton	George Taylor	Robert Treat Paine
Samuel Chase	James Wilson	Elbridge Gerry
William Paca	George Ross	Stephen Hopkins
Thomas Stone	Caesar Rodney	William Ellery
Charles Carroll of	George Read	Roger Sherman
Carrollton	Thomas McKean	Samuel Huntington
George Wythe	William Floyd	William Williams
Richard Henry Lee	Philip Livingston	Oliver Wolcott
Thomas Jefferson	Francis Lewis	Matthew Thornton

The Struggle for Liberty

The Big Idea
Patriot forces faced many obstacles in the war against Britain.

Main Ideas
- Many Americans supported the war effort.
- The Patriots both won and lost battles during the years 1775–1777.
- France and Spain helped the Patriots fight the British.
- The winter at Valley Forge tested the strength of Patriot troops.
- The war continued at sea and in the West.

Key Terms and People
Haym Salomon
mercenaries
Battle of Trenton
Battle of Saratoga
Marquis de Lafayette
Baron Friedrich von Steuben
Bernardo de Gálvez
John Paul Jones
George Rogers Clark

If YOU were there . . .

You are a serving maid at an inn in New York City. British soldiers often stop at the inn for a meal. You sometimes overhear their conversations, though they don't notice that you do. Now a Patriot militia officer has asked you to bring him any information that you hear. You want to help the Patriot cause. Yet, you are worried about what will happen to you if you are caught spying.

Would you agree to spy for the Patriots?

Supporting the War Effort

George Washington's chief task as the Continental army's Commander in Chief was to raise troops. During the war, more than 230,000 soldiers served in the Continental army, and another 145,000 enlisted in local militias. The typical soldier was young, often under the legal age of 16, and had little money or property. The army offered low pay, harsh conditions, and a big chance of becoming a casualty. Yet the Patriots knew they were fighting for their homes and their freedom.

Finding and keeping dedicated soldiers would be a constant challenge throughout the war. In time, the Continental Congress required states to supply soldiers. Men who could afford it often paid others, such as slaves or apprentices, to fight in their places.

One question facing General Washington was whether to recruit African Americans. Many white southerners, particularly wealthy planters, were against the idea, and at first Washington banned African Americans from serving. When the British promised freedom to any enslaved person who fought on their side, however, thousands of African Americans joined the British army. In response, the Continental army began to recruit free African Americans to fight on their side.

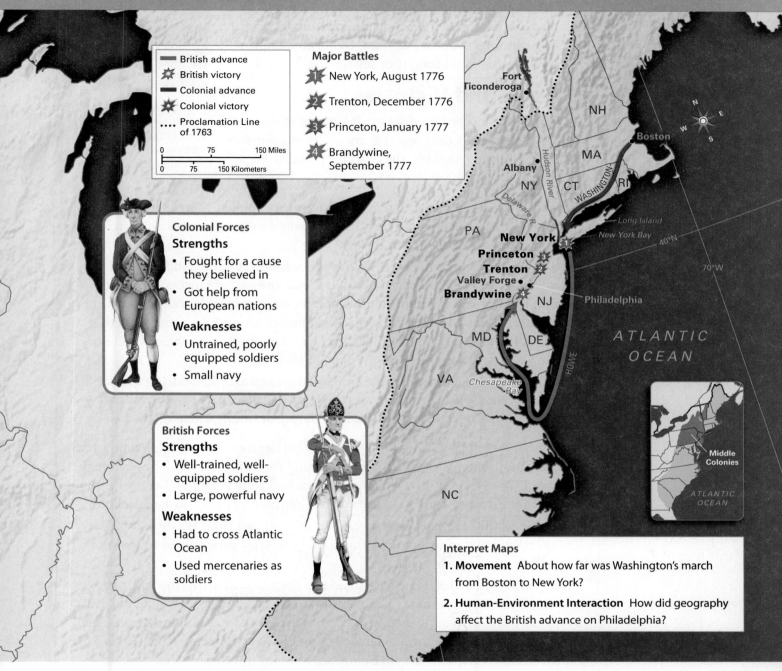

Battles in the Middle Colonies, 1776–1777

Explore ONLINE!

Legend

— British advance
✸ British victory
— Colonial advance
✸ Colonial victory
···· Proclamation Line of 1763

0   75   150 Miles
0   75   150 Kilometers

Major Battles

1. New York, August 1776
2. Trenton, December 1776
3. Princeton, January 1777
4. Brandywine, September 1777

Colonial Forces

Strengths
- Fought for a cause they believed in
- Got help from European nations

Weaknesses
- Untrained, poorly equipped soldiers
- Small navy

British Forces

Strengths
- Well-trained, well-equipped soldiers
- Large, powerful navy

Weaknesses
- Had to cross Atlantic Ocean
- Used mercenaries as soldiers

Interpret Maps

1. **Movement** About how far was Washington's march from Boston to New York?
2. **Human-Environment Interaction** How did geography affect the British advance on Philadelphia?

While men served as soldiers, many women ran farms and businesses. Others helped the Continental army by raising money for supplies or making clothing. Women served as messengers, nurses, and spies. A man from Massachusetts noted:

"At every house Women and children [are] making Cartridges, running Bullets . . . and at the same time animating [encouraging] their Husbands and Sons to fight."

—Anonymous, quoted in *The Literary Diary of Ezra Stiles*

The American Revolution **129**

Perhaps the best-known woman to fight in the war was Mary Ludwig Hays. She was called Molly Pitcher because she brought water to the troops. When her husband was wounded in a 1778 battle, she took his place loading cannons. Another woman, Deborah Sampson, dressed as a man and fought in several battles.

Mary Ludwig Hays, better known as Molly Pitcher, loaded cannons during the Battle of Monmouth after her husband fell in battle.

Defeats and Victories

As the Revolution gathered steam, it became more deadly. At first the Continental army suffered a number of defeats. In time, though, the Patriots' patience began to pay off.

Canada In part because the army was short on supplies, many Patriot leaders favored fighting a defensive war. Others wanted to invade British-controlled Canada and make it the "14th colony."

Patriot troops led by General Richard Montgomery captured Montreal in November 1775. The next major target was the city of Quebec. Benedict Arnold, now a general, led his troops north on a remarkable trek through the rough backcountry of Maine. He reached Quebec around the same time that Montreal fell to Montgomery. Since his first attempt to take the city failed, Arnold waited for Montgomery's troops to join his.

Taking an immense chance, the combined armies attacked during a fierce blizzard on New Year's Eve. They were quickly defeated. The Americans had suffered a crushing loss, and the Patriots' hopes of taking Canada faded.

New York New York City became the next battleground. General Washington had moved his troops to New York, expecting the British arrival. Sure enough, in June 1776, a fleet of British ships approached New York Bay. Led by General William Howe, the British forced the Continental army off Long Island.

Howe's 32,000 soldiers were much better equipped than Washington's 23,000 men, most of whom were militia. The Patriot general had to use all of his skills just to save his army.

In a series of battles, Howe pounded the Continental army, forcing it to retreat farther and farther. The Redcoats captured Patriots as well as supplies. Eventually, the British pushed Washington across the Hudson River into New Jersey. Howe's revenge for his defeat at Boston was complete. When Howe captured New York City, **Haym Salomon**, a recent immigrant from Poland, stayed there and spied for the Patriots. He later used his skills as a banker to help fund the American Revolution.

During the New York campaigns, a young Connecticut officer named Nathan Hale went behind British lines to get secret information. Seized by the British with documents hidden in the soles of his shoes, Hale was ordered to be hanged. Before his execution, he is said to have declared, "I regret that I have but one life to lose for my country."

After the British gained control of New York City and Long Island, some Patriots left those areas and the Loyalist population grew. Many of these Loyalists fled from other colonies. In the inland part of the New York colony, however, the Patriots still greatly outnumbered the Loyalists.

Crossing the Delaware

George Washington and his troops crossed the partially frozen Delaware River on the night of December 25, 1776. This daring act led to a key Patriot victory at the Battle of Trenton. German American artist Emanuel Leutze created this famous painting in 1851. A version of Leutze's *Washington Crossing the Delaware* hangs in the Metropolitan Museum of Art in New York City.

What feelings do you think Leutze wanted to inspire with this painting?

New Jersey In November 1776 the tattered Continental army was on the run. Washington's remaining 6,000 men were tired and discouraged. The one-year contract for many of them would end on December 31. Who would reenlist in this losing army, and who would replace the soldiers who left? Washington's army was in danger of vanishing.

Thinking the rebellion would end soon, Howe left New Jersey in the hands of soldiers from the German state of Hesse. The Hessians were **mercenaries**—foreign soldiers who fought not out of loyalty, but for pay.

On December 7 Washington retreated across the Delaware River into Pennsylvania. Even with 2,000 fresh troops, the Patriots were near the end. "These are the times that try men's souls," wrote Thomas Paine in *The American Crisis*, a series of pamphlets he began publishing in late 1776. Paine wrote *The American Crisis* to inspire the Patriots. He used loaded language—words that appeal to people's emotions—to help strengthen the American soldiers' morale.

Without a convincing victory, Washington knew he would lose his army. He decided to take a big chance and go on the offensive. The Americans would attack the Hessians at Trenton, New Jersey.

On Christmas night, 1776, with a winter storm lashing about them, Washington and 2,400 soldiers silently rowed across the ice-clogged Delaware River. As morning broke, the men, short on supplies and many with no shoes, marched through the snow to reach the enemy camp at Trenton.

The Hessians, having celebrated the holiday the night before, were fast asleep when the Patriots sprang upon them. The **Battle of Trenton** was an important Patriot victory. American soldiers took more than 900 prisoners.

British general Charles Cornwallis rushed to stop Washington as he marched northeast to Princeton. On the night of January 2, 1777, the Patriots left their campfires burning, then slipped into the darkness and circled behind the British troops. In the morning, Washington attacked. A local resident witnessed it:

"The battle was plainly seen from our door . . . and the guns went off
    so quick and many together that they could not be numbered . . .
    Almost as soon as the firing was over, our house was filled and
    surrounded with General Washington's men."

—Anonymous, quoted in *A Brief Narrative of the Ravages
of the British and Hessians at Princeton*

As Washington watched the Redcoats flee Princeton, he cheered, "It is a fine fox chase, my boys!" Now, new soldiers joined the chase. Others reenlisted. The army—and the Revolution—was saved.

Saratoga The two quick defeats stung the British. In the spring of 1777, they wanted a victory.

British general John Burgoyne decided to push through New York State and cut off New England from the other colonies. The <u>strategy</u> required perfect timing. According to the plan, Burgoyne's army would invade from Canada, recapture Fort Ticonderoga, and sweep south to Albany. General Howe, in New York City, would sail up the Hudson River to meet him, strangling New England.

Indeed, Burgoyne took Ticonderoga in early July and headed toward Albany. Here, the timing went wrong for the British. Unknown to Burgoyne, Howe had left New York, sailed up the Chesapeake Bay, and captured Philadelphia. Delegates to the Continental Congress were forced to flee.

Meanwhile, Burgoyne's army was bogged down in thick forests. The Patriots had chopped down large trees and dammed rivers to create obstacles. All along the route, the militia swarmed out of nowhere to attack the Redcoats. As Burgoyne neared Saratoga, New York, he found himself surrounded. On October 17, 1777, he was forced to surrender his entire army to General Horatio Gates.

The **Battle of Saratoga** in New York was the turning point of the Revolutionary War. It was the greatest victory yet for the American forces. Morale soared. Patriot James Thacher wrote, "This event will make one of the most brilliant pages of American history."

Academic
Vocabulary
strategy a plan for
fighting a battle or
war

Reading Check
Summarize Why
was the Battle of
Saratoga a turning
point in the war?

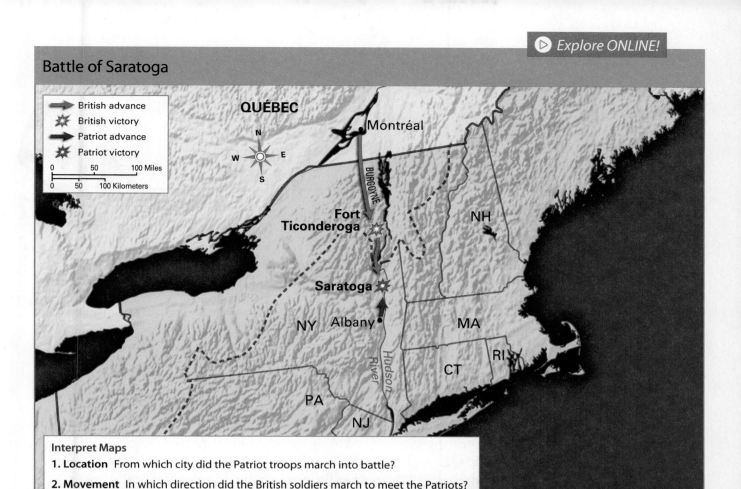

Battle of Saratoga

Explore ONLINE!

Legend:
→ British advance
✦ British victory
→ Patriot advance
✦ Patriot victory

0 50 100 Miles
0 50 100 Kilometers

QUÉBEC
Montréal
BURGOYNE
Fort Ticonderoga
NH
Saratoga
NY Albany
MA
Hudson River
CT
RI
PA
NJ

Interpret Maps

1. Location From which city did the Patriot troops march into battle?

2. Movement In which direction did the British soldiers march to meet the Patriots?

Help from Europe

The French and Indian War had drastically changed the balance of power in North America. The French and Spanish had lost a large expanse of valuable land to the British. Both countries were delighted to see their powerful rival experiencing trouble in its American colonies.

The victory at Saratoga gave the Patriots something they had been desperately seeking: foreign help. Not surprisingly, it came from Britain's enemies, France and Spain. Even Britain's old ally, Holland, joined the fight on the side of the Patriots.

Two Remarkable Europeans "The welfare of America is closely bound up with the welfare of mankind," declared a wealthy young Frenchman, the **Marquis de Lafayette**. Inspired by the ideas of the Revolution, Lafayette bought his own ship and arrived in America in 1777. He brought with him a group of well-trained soldiers and volunteered to serve in the Continental army himself without pay.

Lafayette spoke little English and had never seen battle. However, he quickly became a skillful commander, earning the title of major general. Lafayette led 2,000 Patriots to successfully pursue 6,000 Redcoats throughout Virginia during 1780–81. He gave $200,000 of his own money to support the Revolution and wrote many letters home to powerful friends and family asking their aid for the Patriot cause.

The Patriots Gain Ground

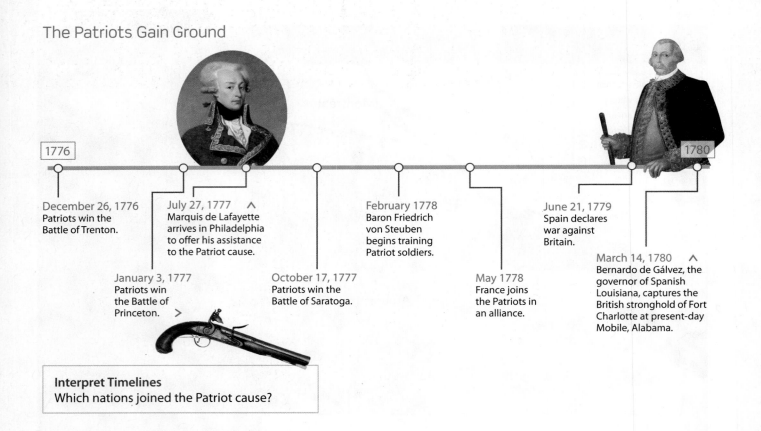

1776

December 26, 1776
Patriots win the
Battle of Trenton.

July 27, 1777
Marquis de Lafayette
arrives in Philadelphia
to offer his assistance
to the Patriot cause.

January 3, 1777
Patriots win
the Battle of
Princeton.

October 17, 1777
Patriots win the
Battle of Saratoga.

February 1778
Baron Friedrich
von Steuben
begins training
Patriot soldiers.

May 1778
France joins
the Patriots in
an alliance.

June 21, 1779
Spain declares
war against
Britain.

March 14, 1780
Bernardo de Gálvez, the
governor of Spanish
Louisiana, captures the
British stronghold of Fort
Charlotte at present-day
Mobile, Alabama.

1780

Interpret Timelines
Which nations joined the Patriot cause?

In February 1778 another European came to serve heroically under Washington. **Baron Friedrich von Steuben**, an experienced military officer from Prussia, led with a combination of respect and fear. He started training the American troops, focusing on basic military drills. Soon he turned the Continental army into a finely tuned fighting force. A historian called von Steuben's feat "perhaps the most remarkable achievement in rapid military training in the history of the world."

Help from France Benjamin Franklin, a skilled and experienced diplomat, had gone to France in 1776 to ask for support from King Louis XVI. Finally, the Battle of Saratoga in 1777 persuaded the French king that the colonists could win the war. Not until then did the king agree to an alliance with the Patriots.

In May 1778 the Continental Congress ratified the treaty of support with France. The French had been helping the Patriots all along with supplies and ammunition. After the treaty became official, the French increased the level of supplies and agreed to provide soldiers and ships. The French naval support would be a key strategic ingredient in defeating the British.

Help from Spain Spain, also a bitter enemy of Britain, joined the war in 1779. **Bernardo de Gálvez**, the governor of Spanish Louisiana, became a key ally to the Patriots. Gálvez gathered a small army of Spanish soldiers, French Americans, colonists, and Native Americans. Together they made their way east from Louisiana. Gálvez seized British posts all the way to Pensacola, Florida.

Reading Check
Summarize How did
France and Spain help
the Patriots?

Winter at Valley Forge

The entry of France and Spain into the war came at a crucial moment. The Continental army was running very low on food and clothing. In December 1777 Washington settled his 12,000 men at Valley Forge, north of Philadelphia.

To this day, the name of Valley Forge brings to mind suffering—and courage. Yet no battles took place here. The only enemy was the brutal winter of 1777–78.

Washington's men lacked even the most basic protections against shin-deep snows. In spite of the general's repeated requests for supplies, conflicts over funding between state authorities and Congress kept supplies from coming. Washington wrote in a letter:

> "To see men without clothes . . . without blankets to lie upon, without shoes . . . without a house or hut to cover them until those could be built, and submitting without a murmur, is a proof of patience and obedience which, in my opinion, can scarcely be paralleled [matched]."

> —George Washington, from *The Writings of George Washington,* edited by Worthington Chauncey Ford

As winter roared in, soldiers quickly built crude shelters that offered little protection against the weather. Some soldiers had no shirts. Others had marched the shoes off their feet. At their guard posts, they stood on their hats to keep their feet from touching the freezing ground. One soldier wrote that getting food was the "business that usually employed us."

Historical Source

Valley Forge

A surgeon at Valley Forge, Albigence Waldo kept a journal of what he saw during the winter of 1777–78.

> "*The Army which has been surprisingly healthy hitherto, now begins to grow sickly from the continued fatigues they have suffered this Campaign. Yet they still show a spirit of Alacrity [cheerful readiness] and Contentment not to be expected from so young Troops. I am Sick—discontented—and out of humour. Poor food—hard lodging—Cold Weather—fatigue—Nasty Cloaths [clothes]— nasty Cookery . . . smoke and Cold—hunger and filthyness—A pox on my bad luck.*"

> —Albigence Waldo, from *The Pennsylvania Magazine of History and Biography,* Volume 21

Analyze Historical Sources
Why did Waldo seem surprised by the soldiers' attitude?

During that terrible winter at Valley Forge, some 2,000 soldiers died of disease and malnutrition. Amazingly, those who survived not only stayed—they drilled and marched to the orders of Baron von Steuben and became better soldiers.

While the soldiers suffered through the winter at Valley Forge, the British lived a life of luxury in Philadelphia. Most of the Patriots had fled the city, leaving only Loyalists and British soldiers. Together they enjoyed the city's houses, taverns, and theaters, and held parties and balls.

War at Sea and in the West

While some Americans struggled against the British on land in the former colonies, others fought at sea and on the western frontier. Each area posed tough challenges.

War at Sea The entry of the French navy into the war greatly aided the colonists. Many people had thought that the mighty British navy would crush the much smaller American fleet. However, the British failed to use their powerful navy effectively during the war.

In the fall of 1775, the Continental Congress made plans to build four American warships. Soon afterward the Congress formally established the marines and the Continental navy. By adapting merchant vessels, the navy had eight fighting ships ready for combat by February 1776.

That month the tiny American navy launched a major offensive to damage the operating ability of the British fleet located off the Carolina coast. Rather than attack the fleet directly, the Patriots went after the British supply base on Nassau, in the Bahamas.

The American troops seized the main supply fort on the island. They then raised the newly created flag of the American Revolution over Nassau. After that campaign, the American navy focused on seizing British supply ships and weakening Britain's naval forces in the West Indies.

John Paul Jones The Patriots owed much of their success on the seas to naval hero **John Paul Jones**. Jones had once been considered an outlaw. He was born John Paul in Scotland and began working on ships at a young age. After accidentally killing the leader of a mutiny, he fled to America and added Jones to his name.

When the war broke out, Jones volunteered his services to the newly created navy. He quickly established himself as a brave and clever sailor. Considered a pirate by the British, Jones captured many British supply ships. The French greatly admired Jones. When France entered the war in 1778, French leaders presented him with a small fleet of seven vessels to command. He named his flagship *Bonhomme Richard* ("Gentleman Richard") in honor of Benjamin Franklin's *Poor Richard's Almanac*. Among the almanac's stories, jokes, and wise sayings were weather forecasts for the year and other practical scientific information.

One of Jones's most famous victories was the capture of the British warship *Serapis* on September 23, 1779. Early in the battle, the British knocked out the heaviest artillery on the *Bonhomme Richard*. Captain

On July 27, 1778, French and British fleets fought each other in the Battle of Ushant near the mouth of the English Channel. It was the first major naval battle between the two powers after France formed an alliance with the Patriots.

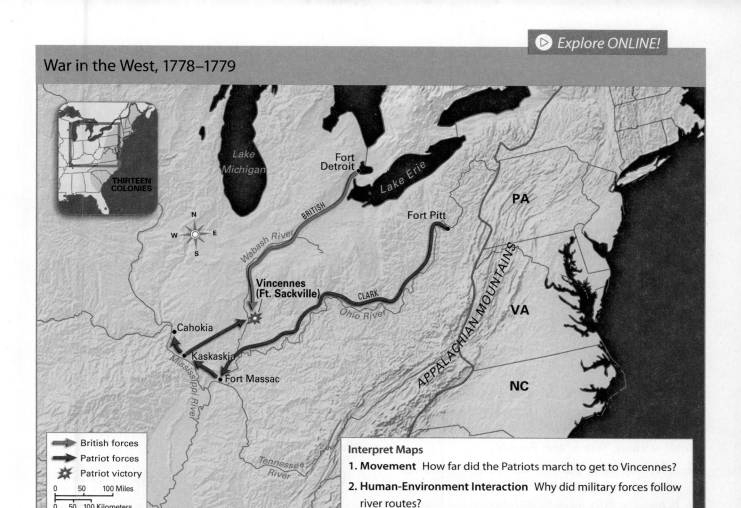

War in the West, 1778–1779

▶ Explore ONLINE!

THIRTEEN COLONIES

Lake Michigan

Fort Detroit

Lake Erie

BRITISH

Wabash River

Fort Pitt

PA

Vincennes (Ft. Sackville)

CLARK

Ohio River

VA

Cahokia

Kaskaskia

APPALACHIAN MOUNTAINS

Fort Massac

Mississippi River

NC

Tennessee River

→ British forces
→ Patriot forces
★ Patriot victory

0   50   100 Miles
0   50   100 Kilometers

Interpret Maps

1. **Movement** How far did the Patriots march to get to Vincennes?

2. **Human-Environment Interaction** Why did military forces follow river routes?

American Revolutionary war hero and frontiersman George Rogers Clark helped defeat British forces in the West.

Richard Pearson of the *Serapis* then called out to Jones, "Has your ship struck [surrendered]?" Jones replied, "I have not yet begun to fight!" The battle continued for more than two hours. Finally, the Americans wore down the British, who surrendered at 10:30 P.M.

The Continental navy used fewer than 100 ships over the course of the war. Yet the British lost more than 200 ships to the small but effective American naval force.

War in the West The lands west of the Appalachian Mountains were controlled by Native American nations. Both the British and the Patriots tried to enlist these groups in their cause.

George Rogers Clark volunteered to lead the western campaign. Clark had been a surveyor along the Ohio and Kentucky rivers. By the time the war broke out, he knew the lands of the Ohio River valley well. Clark created an army from the scattered settlements in the area. One of the best-known groups was the Over Mountain Men, a band of settlers from present-day Tennessee.

Determined to weaken British support systems, Clark targeted trading villages. Following the Ohio River to the Tennessee, Clark's force set out on a 120-mile overland trek to Kaskaskia, in present-day Illinois. The village's leaders learned of the attack and surrendered. Other Patriots took Cahokia without a fight.

In February 1779 Clark launched a surprise attack on Fort Sackville near the town of Vincennes. The attack was unexpected because the nearby Wabash River was icy and flooded. Despite overflowing riverbanks, Clark's force of 150 men endured an 18-day march through freezing water. They also managed to bring enough Patriot flags for an army of hundreds. The flags were displayed near the fort, and the skilled pioneers sustained enough musket fire to indicate a much larger army. Falling for the ruse, the commander of Fort Sackville surrendered.

In general the British were more successful at winning over the Native Americans. But Clark's many campaigns undermined British support in the West.

Summary and Preview The Patriots faced hardships as the war continued. In the next lesson you will see how they finally achieved their goal of independence.

Reading Check
Find Main Ideas
How did Jones and Clark help the Patriots' war effort?

Lesson 4 Assessment

Review Ideas, Terms, and People

1. a. Identify What groups supported the Patriot war effort? How did each group contribute?

b. Analyze Why was it difficult to find and keep soldiers in the Continental army?

2. a. Describe What early defeats did the Patriots face?

b. Elaborate Was it a mistake for the British to use mercenaries to help them fight the war? Why or why not?

c. Explain How did New Jersey's location play an important role in the American Revolution?

3. a. Elaborate Why do you think European nations supported the colonists rather than Great Britain?

b. Evaluate Do you think that the Patriots would have won the war without help from France and Spain? Why or why not?

4. a. Describe What difficulties did the Patriots face at Valley Forge?

b. Elaborate How might weather conditions affect the outcome of a battle?

5. a. Identify Who was John Paul Jones?

b. Compare In what ways was Jones's naval strategy like that of the Continental army?

Critical Thinking

6. Draw Conclusions In this lesson you learned about the war for American independence. Create a chart similar to the one below and identify the region in which major wartime events took place and how the events reflected the Patriots' successes and failures.

Region	Patriot Problems	Patriot Successes

Independence!

The Big Idea

The war spread to the southern colonies, where the British were finally defeated.

Main Ideas

- Patriot forces faced many problems in the war in the South.
- The American Patriots finally defeated the British at the Battle of Yorktown.
- The British and the Americans officially ended the war by signing the Treaty of Paris of 1783.

Key Terms and People

Francis Marion
James Armistead
Comte de Rochambeau
Battle of Yorktown
Treaty of Paris of 1783

If YOU were there . . .

You have grown up on a farm in South Carolina. You know every inch of the woods and marshes around your home. You are too young to join the Continental army, but you have heard stories about a brave group of soldiers who carry out quick raids on the British, then disappear into the woods. These fighters get no pay and live in constant danger.

Would you consider joining the fighters? Why?

War in the South

The war across the ocean was not going the way the British government in London had planned. The northern colonies, with their ragged, scrappy fighters, proved to be tough to tame. So the British switched strategies and set their sights on the South.

The British hoped to find support from the large Loyalist populations living in Georgia, the Carolinas, and Virginia. As they moved across the South, the British also planned to free enslaved Africans and enlist them as British soldiers. Under the leadership of a new commander, General Henry Clinton, the strategy paid off—for a while.

Brutal Fighting The southern war was particularly brutal. Much more than in the North, this phase of the war pitted Americans—Patriots versus Loyalists—against one another in direct combat. The British also destroyed crops, farm animals, and other property as they marched through the South. One British officer, Banastre Tarleton, sowed fear throughout the South by refusing to take prisoners and killing soldiers who tried to surrender.

Georgia, the last colony to join the Revolution, was the first to fall to the British. A force of 3,500 Redcoats easily took Savannah in 1778 and soon put in place a new colonial government.

Britain's next major target was Charleston, South Carolina. In early 1780 General Clinton landed a force of 14,000 troops around the port city. With a minimal cost of about 250 casualties, the British scored one of their biggest victories of the war. The Patriots surrendered Charleston in May, handing over four ships and some 5,400 prisoners.

A Failed Attack and an Important Victory In August 1780 Patriot forces led by Horatio Gates tried to drive the British out of Camden, South Carolina. The attack was poorly executed, however. Gates had only half as many soldiers as he had planned for, and most were tired and hungry. In the heat of battle, many panicked and ran. The Patriot attack quickly fell apart. Of some 4,000 American troops, only about 700 escaped.

General Nathanael Greene arrived to reorganize the army. As he rode through the southern countryside, he was discouraged by the devastation. He later wrote, "I have never witnessed such scenes."

On October 7, 1780, a group of Patriot militias won an important battle against a group of Loyalist militias in what is today York County, South Carolina. It became known as the Battle of Kings Mountain. The victory boosted the Patriots' morale and kept the British from further invading the Carolinas.

Guerrilla Warfare The southern Patriots switched to swift hit-and-run attacks known as guerrilla warfare. No Patriot was better at this style of fighting than **Francis Marion**. He organized Marion's Brigade, a group of guerrilla soldiers.

Marion's Brigade used surprise attacks to disrupt British communication and supply lines. Despite their great efforts, the British could not catch Marion and his men. One frustrated general claimed, "As for this . . . old fox, the devil himself could not catch him." From that point on, Marion was known as the Swamp Fox.

Reading Check
Sequence List the events of the war in the South in chronological order.

Swamp Fox

Francis Marion leads his soldiers down a river in South Carolina. Marion built a hideout on one of the river's islands. From there, he would lead lightning-fast raids against British communication and supply lines.

Which figure do you think is Francis Marion? Why?

The British scuttled, or purposely sank, dozens of their ships. This formed a barrier that kept the French ships from coming too close.

THIRTEEN COLONIES
Yorktown
ATLANTIC OCEAN

American troop positions
French troop positions
British troop positions
British defensive lines

0   0.5   1 Mile
0   0.5   1 Kilometer

Battle of Yorktown

In October 1781 American and French troops surrounded British forces and defeated them in the Battle of Yorktown.

Analyze Visuals
Human-Environment Interaction How did American and French forces trap the British at Yorktown?

Battle of Yorktown

In early 1781 the war was going badly for the Patriots. They were low on money to pay soldiers and buy supplies. The help of their foreign allies had not brought the war to a quick end as they had hoped. The British held most of the South, plus Philadelphia and New York City. The Patriots' morale took another blow when Benedict Arnold, one of America's most gifted officers, turned traitor.

Regrouped under Nathanael Greene, the Continental army began harassing British general Charles Cornwallis in the Carolinas. Hoping to stay in communication with the British naval fleet, Cornwallis moved his force of 7,200 men to Yorktown, Virginia. It was a fatal mistake.

An enslaved African named **James Armistead** worked as a spy for the Marquis de Lafayette. The information Armistead collected for Lafayette gave the Continental army an advantage over the British at Yorktown. General Washington saw a chance to trap Cornwallis there. He ordered Lafayette to block Cornwallis's escape by land. Then he combined his 2,500 troops with 4,000 French troops commanded by the **Comte de Rochambeau** (raw-shahn-BOH). Washington led the French-American force on a swift march to Virginia to cut off the other escape routes. The Patriots surrounded Cornwallis with some 16,000 soldiers. Meanwhile, a French naval fleet seized control of the Chesapeake Bay, preventing British ships from rescuing Cornwallis's stranded army.

The siege began. For weeks, the fighting steadily wore down the British defenses. Alexander Hamilton, who later became America's first secretary of the treasury, took part in the Battle of Yorktown. He commanded an infantry battalion under General Washington. In early October, Washington prepared for a major attack on the weakened British troops.

Facing near-certain defeat, on October 19, 1781, Cornwallis sent a drummer and a soldier with a white flag of surrender to Washington's camp. The Patriots took some 8,000 British prisoners—the largest British army in America.

The **Battle of Yorktown** was the last major battle of the American Revolution. Prime Minister Lord North received word of the Yorktown surrender in November. In shock he declared, "It is all over!"

The Treaty of Paris

After Yorktown, only a few small battles took place. Lacking the money to pay for a new army, Great Britain entered into peace talks with America. Benjamin Franklin had a key role in the negotiations.

Reading Check
Draw Conclusions
Why did the victory at Yorktown end the fighting?

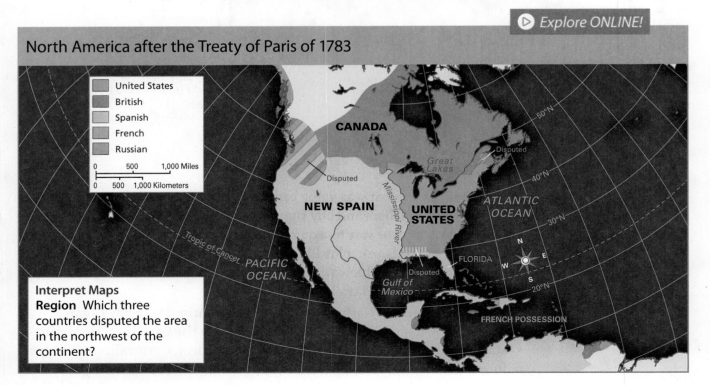

▶ *Explore ONLINE!*

North America after the Treaty of Paris of 1783

United States
British
Spanish
French
Russian

0   500   1,000 Miles
0   500   1,000 Kilometers

CANADA

Disputed

Great Lakes

Disputed

NEW SPAIN

Mississippi River

UNITED STATES

ATLANTIC OCEAN

50°N
40°N
30°N
20°N

Tropic of Cancer

PACIFIC OCEAN

FLORIDA

Disputed

Gulf of Mexico

FRENCH POSSESSION

Interpret Maps
Region Which three countries disputed the area in the northwest of the continent?

Sentiments of an American Woman

The Continental army received aid from female Patriots led by Esther DeBerdt Reed and Sarah Franklin Bache, the daughter of Benjamin Franklin. In 1780 these women organized a campaign that raised $300,000 for soldiers' clothing. The following pamphlet, written by the campaign's leaders, announced the campaign. In it, the authors used images of women helping with war efforts of the past to gain support for their cause.

The women declare that they would fight if they were allowed.

The authors list ways in which women have helped fight wars in the past.

In this phrase, the women link themselves to great women rulers of the past.

"On the **commencement**[1] of actual war, the Women of America **manifested**[2] a firm resolution to contribute . . . to the deliverance of their country. Animated by the purest patriotism they are sensible of sorrow at this day, in not offering more than barren wishes for the success of so glorious a Revolution. They aspire to **render**[3] themselves more really useful; and this sentiment is universal from the north to the south of the Thirteen United States. Our ambition is kindled by the fame of those heroines of **antiquity**[4], who . . . have proved to the universe, that . . . if opinion and manners did not forbid us to march to glory by the same paths as the Men, we should at least equal, and sometimes surpass them in our love for the public good. I glory in all that which my sex has done great and **commendable**[5]. I call to mind with enthusiasm and with admiration, all those acts of courage, of constancy and patriotism, which history has transmitted to us. . . ."

"So many famous sieges where the Women have been seen . . . building new walls, digging trenches with their feeble hands, furnishing arms to their defenders, they themselves darting the missile weapons of the enemy, resigning the ornaments of their apparel, and their fortune, to fill the public treasury, and to hasten the deliverance of their country; burying themselves under its ruins; throwing themselves into the flames rather than submit to the disgrace of humiliation before a proud enemy."

"Born for liberty, **disdaining**[6] to bear the irons of a **tyrannic**[7] Government, we associate ourselves . . . [with those rulers] who have extended the empire of liberty, and **contented**[8] to reign by sweetness and justice, have broken the chains of slavery, forged by tyrants."

Analyze Historical Sources

1. What do the writers "call to mind" in asking women to join the Patriot cause?

2. With whom do the writers associate themselves?

[1] *commencement* start
[2] *manifested* presented
[3] *render* make
[4] *antiquity* ancient times
[5] *commendable* praiseworthy
[6] *disdaining* refusing
[7] *tyrannic* unjust
[8] *contented* determined

Delegates took more than two years to come to a peace agreement. In the **Treaty of Paris of 1783**, Great Britain recognized the independence of the United States. The treaty also set America's borders. A separate treaty between Britain and Spain returned Florida to the Spanish. British leaders also accepted American rights to settle and trade west of the original thirteen colonies.

At the war's end, many members of the Iroquois nations who had fought on the side of the British moved to Canada. Those who did not were ordered to live on reservations in the northern, central, and western parts of New York. Otherwise, when the terms of the Treaty of Paris were negotiated, the concerns of Native Americans were largely ignored.

Now that the war was over, Patriot soldiers returned to their homes and families. The courage of soldiers and civilians had made America's victory possible. As they returned home, George Washington thanked his troops for their devotion. "I . . . wish that your latter days be as prosperous as your former ones have been glorious."

Summary and Preview Americans won their independence from Great Britain in 1783. In the next module you will learn how the new nation formed its first government.

Reading Check
Summarize
Explain how the War for Independence finally came to an end.

Lesson 5 Assessment

Review Ideas, Terms, and People

1. **a. Describe** What problems did the Patriots experience in the war in the South?
   b. Analyze What advantages did the southern Patriots have over the British in the South?
2. **a. Describe** What was the Patriots' strategy for defeating the British at Yorktown?
   b. Elaborate Why do you think General Cornwallis decided to surrender at the Battle of Yorktown?
3. **a. Identify** Who helped to negotiate the Treaty of Paris of 1783 for the Americans?
   b. Predict How might relations between Great Britain and its former colonies be affected by the war?

Critical Thinking

4. **Evaluate** In this lesson you learned about the events that led to the end of the war. Create a graphic organizer like the one below and then identify and describe the most important event in turning the war in the Patriots' favor.

Event	Importance to end of war

Social Studies Skills

Understand Historical Interpretation

Define the Skill

Historical interpretations are ways of explaining the past. They are based on what is known about the people, ideas, and actions that make up history. Two historians can look at the same set of facts about a person or event of the past and see things in different ways. Their explanations of the person or event, and the conclusions they reach, can be very different. The ability to recognize, understand, and evaluate historical interpretations is a valuable skill in the study of history.

Learn the Skill

When people study the past, they decide which facts are the most important in explaining why something happened. One person may believe certain facts to be important, while other people may believe other facts are more important. Therefore, their explanation of the topic, and the conclusions they draw about it, may not be the same. In addition, if new facts are uncovered about the topic, still more interpretations of it may result.

Asking the following questions will help you to understand and evaluate historical interpretations.

1. What is the main idea in the way the topic is explained? What conclusions are reached? Be aware that these may not be directly stated but only hinted at in the information provided.

2. On what facts has the writer or speaker relied? Do these facts seem to support his or her explanation and conclusions?

3. Is there important information about the topic that the writer or speaker has dismissed or ignored? If so, you should suspect that the interpretation may be inaccurate or deliberately slanted to prove a particular point of view.

Just because interpretations differ, one is not necessarily "right" and others "wrong." As long as a person considers all the evidence and draws conclusions based on a fair evaluation of that evidence, his or her interpretation is probably acceptable.

Remember, however, that trained historians let the facts *lead* them to conclusions. People who *start* with a conclusion, select only facts that support it, and ignore opposing evidence produce interpretations that have little value for understanding history.

Practice the Skill

Two widely accepted interpretations exist of the causes of the American Revolution. One holds that the Revolution was a struggle by freedom-loving Americans to be free from harsh British rule. In this view the colonists were used to self-government and resisted British efforts to take rights they claimed. The other interpretation is that a clash of economic interests caused the Revolution. In this view, the war resulted from a struggle between British and colonial merchants over control of America's economy.

Review Lessons 1, 2, and 3 of Module 4. Then answer the following questions.

1. What facts in the text support the economic interpretation of the Revolution? What evidence supports the political interpretation?

2. Which interpretation seems more convincing? Explain why.

Module 4 Assessment

Review Vocabulary, Terms, and People

1. What were American colonists who remained loyal to Great Britain called?
   a. Whigs
   b. Loyalists
   c. Royalists
   d. Democrats

2. What was the name of the battle in which the Patriots finally defeated the British?
   a. Battle of Saratoga
   b. Battle of New Jersey
   c. Battle of Yorktown
   d. Battle of Valley Forge

3. What was the name for the colonial military force created to fight the British?
   a. mercenaries
   b. Redcoats
   c. Hessians
   d. Continental army

4. Who was the French nobleman who helped the Patriots fight the British?
   a. Bernardo de Gálvez
   b. Marquis de Lafayette
   c. Baron von Steuben
   d. Lord Dunmore

Comprehension and Critical Thinking

Lesson 1

5. a. Recall Why did the British believe it was necessary to raise taxes on the American colonists?
   b. Draw Conclusions How did the Boston Massacre and the Boston Tea Party affect relations between Great Britain and the colonies?
   c. Evaluate Did the British government overreact to colonial protests by issuing the Intolerable Acts? Why or why not?

Lesson 2

6. a. Recall What actions did the First and Second Continental Congresses take?
   b. Analyze How did the events at Lexington and Concord change the conflict between Great Britain and the colonies?
   c. Elaborate Why do you think that control of Boston early in the Revolutionary War was important?

Lesson 3

7. a. Identify Why is July 4, 1776, a significant date?
   b. Draw Conclusions What effect did *Common Sense* have on colonial attitudes toward Great Britain?
   c. Predict How might the content of the Declaration of Independence lead to questions over the issue of slavery?

Lesson 4

8. a. Describe What difficulties did the Patriots experience in the early years of the war?
   b. Analyze How did the Patriots turn the tide of the war?
   c. Elaborate Could the Patriots have succeeded in the war without foreign help? Explain.

Lesson 5

9. a. Recall Why did the British think they might find support in the southern colonies?
   b. Make Inferences Why did it take more than two years for the British and the Americans to agree to the terms of the Treaty of Paris?
   c. Evaluate In your opinion, what was the most important reason for the Patriot defeat of the British?

Social Studies Skills

Understand Historical Interpretation *Use the Social Studies Skills taught in this module to answer the questions about the reading selection below.*

> In a series of battles, Howe pounded the Continental army, forcing it to retreat farther and farther. The Redcoats captured Patriots as well as supplies. Eventually, the British pushed Washington across the Hudson River into New Jersey. Howe's revenge for his defeat at Boston was complete.

10. Which statement from the passage is an interpretation of historical facts?
    a. The Redcoats captured Patriots as well as supplies.
    b. Eventually, the British pushed Washington across the Hudson River into New Jersey.
    c. Howe's revenge for his defeat at Boston was complete.

11. What might a different interpretation of the facts be?

Review Themes

12. **Politics** What are three important rights listed in the Declaration of Independence?

13. **Geography** What role did geography play in the fighting that took place in the West?

Reading Skills

Main Ideas in Social Studies *Use the Reading Skills taught at the beginning of the module to answer the question about the reading selection below.*

> (1) Native Americans were at first encouraged by both sides to remain neutral. (2) By the summer of 1776, however, both Patriots and the British were aggressively recruiting Indian fighters. (3) Many Native Americans sided with the British. (4) In northern New York, four of the six Iroquois nations fought for the British.

14. Which sentence contains the main idea of the paragraph?
    a. Sentence 1
    b. Sentence 2
    c. Sentence 3
    d. Sentence 4

Map Skills

15. **Draw a Map** Using the map of North America in Lesson 5 as reference, draw a map that shows the boundary that was set for the United States by the Treaty of Paris of 1783. Illustrate also the areas in North America that were controlled by the British, Spanish, French, and Russians.

Focus on Speaking

16. **Prepare an Oral Report** In this module you learned about great events, courageous deeds, and heroic people in the Revolutionary War. Begin preparations for an oral report by identifying one or two important ideas, events, or people for each period of the war. Next, write a one-sentence introduction to your talk. Then write a sentence or two about each period of the war. Write a concluding sentence that makes a quick connection between the Revolutionary War and our lives today. Practice your talk until you can give it with only a glance or two at your notes.

THE *American* REVOLUTION

The American Revolution led to the formation of the United States of America in 1776. Beginning in the 1760s, tensions grew between American colonists and their British rulers when Britain started passing a series of new laws and taxes for the colonies. With no representation in the British government, however, colonists had no say in these laws, which led to growing discontent. After fighting broke out in 1775, colonial leaders met to decide what to do. They approved the Declaration of Independence, announcing that the American colonies were free from British rule. In reality, however, freedom would not come until after years of fighting.

Explore some of the people and events of the American Revolution online. You can find a wealth of information, video clips, primary sources, activities, and more through your online textbook.

> "I know not what course others may take; but as for me, give me liberty or give me death!"
>
> —Patrick Henry

 "Give Me Liberty or Give Me Death!"
Read an excerpt from Patrick Henry's famous speech, which urged the colonists to fight against the British.

Seeds of Revolution
Watch the video to learn about colonial discontent in the years before the Revolutionary War.

Independence!
Watch the video to learn about the origins of the Declaration of Independence.

Victory!
Watch the video to learn how the American colonists won the Revolutionary War.

Module 5

Forming a Government

Essential Question

Did compromise make the U.S. Constitution stronger or weaker?

About the Photo: Speaker of the House Nancy Pelosi swears in the members of the 111th Congress of the United States.

▶ *Explore ONLINE!*

VIDEOS, including...
- America Gets a Constitution
- Shays's Rebellion

☑ Document-Based Investigations

☑ Graphic Organizers

☑ Interactive Games

☑ Interactive Map: Land Ordinances of 1785 and 1787

☑ Image with Hotspots: Signing the Constitution

☑ Image Carousel: Federalist Leaders

In this module you will learn about the nation's earliest government, the Articles of Confederation, and its failure to achieve national unity. You will also read about the writing of the Constitution and how it attempted to solve the problems of the Articles by creating a new system of government.

What You Will Learn ...

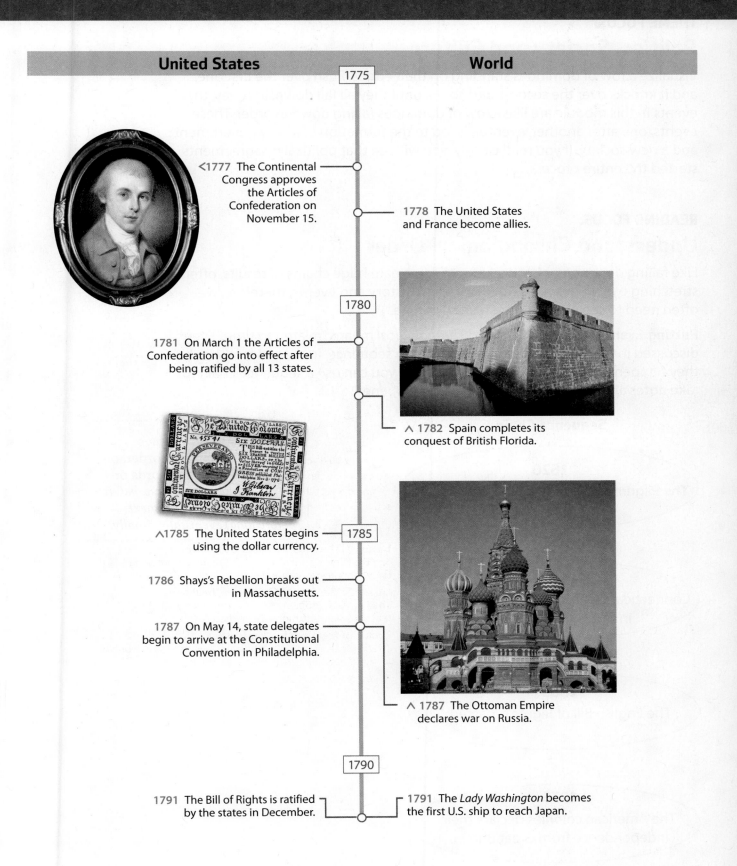

| United States | 1775 | World |

<1777 The Continental Congress approves the Articles of Confederation on November 15.

1778 The United States and France become allies.

| | 1780 | |

1781 On March 1 the Articles of Confederation go into effect after being ratified by all 13 states.

∧ **1782** Spain completes its conquest of British Florida.

∧**1785** The United States begins using the dollar currency. | 1785 |

1786 Shays's Rebellion breaks out in Massachusetts.

1787 On May 14, state delegates begin to arrive at the Constitutional Convention in Philadelphia.

∧ **1787** The Ottoman Empire declares war on Russia.

| | 1790 | |

1791 The Bill of Rights is ratified by the states in December.

1791 The *Lady Washington* becomes the first U.S. ship to reach Japan.

Reading Social Studies

THEME FOCUS:
Politics, Society and Culture

Visualize a row of dominoes standing on their edges. Push over the first one, and it knocks over the second, and so on, until they all fall down. In a way, the events in this module are like a row of dominoes falling down in order. These events, one after another, eventually led to the formation of a new government and a new society. If you read closely, you will see that political disagreements started the entire process.

READING FOCUS:
Understand Chronological Order

Like falling dominoes, historical events can create huge chains of results, often stretching over many years. To understand history and events, therefore, we often need to see how they are related in time.

Putting Events in Order The word *chronological* means "related to time." Events discussed in this history book are discussed in sequence, in the order in which they happened. To understand history better, you can use a sequence chain to take notes about events in the order they happened.

Sequence Chain

1620
The Pilgrims sign the Mayflower Compact.

↓

1639
Connecticut creates the first constitution in the English colonies.

↓

1689
The English Bill of Rights is passed.

↓

1776
The American colonies declare their independence from Great Britain.

> **Tip:** Writers sometimes signal chronological order, or sequence, by using words or phrases like these: *first, before, then, later, soon, after, next, before long, eventually, finally.*

You Try It!

Read the following passage and answer the questions that follow.

Farmers Rebel In August 1786, farmers in three western counties began a revolt. Bands of angry citizens closed down courts in western Massachusetts. Their reasoning was simple—with the courts shut down, no one's property could be taken. In September a poor farmer and Revolutionary War veteran, Daniel Shays, led hundreds of men in a forced shutdown of the Supreme Court in Springfield, Massachusetts. The state government ordered the farmers to stop the revolt under threat of capture and death. These threats only made Shays and his followers more determined. The uprising of farmers to protest high taxes and heavy debt became known as Shays's Rebellion.

Shays's forces were defeated by state troops in January 1787. By February many of the rebels were in prison. During their trials, 14 leaders were sentenced to death. However, the state soon freed most of the rebels, including Shays. State officials knew that many citizens of the state agreed with the rebels and their cause.

After you have read the passage, answer the following questions.

1. Which happened first—citizens closing courts in western Massachusetts or Shays shutting down the Supreme Court? How can you tell?

2. What happened after Shays's forces were defeated by state troops?

3. Draw a sequence chain that shows the effects of Shays's Rebellion in the order in which they occurred.

As you read Module 5, look for clues that signal the order in which events occurred.

The Articles of Confederation

The Big Idea
The Articles of Confederation provided a framework for a national government.

Main Ideas
- The American people examined many ideas about government.
- The Articles of Confederation laid the base for the first national government of the United States.
- The Confederation Congress established the Northwest Territory.

Key Terms and People
Magna Carta
constitution
Virginia Statute for Religious Freedom
suffrage
Articles of Confederation
ratification
Land Ordinance of 1785
Northwest Ordinance of 1787
Northwest Territory

If YOU were there . . .

You live in a town in New England during the 1770s. In the town meeting, people are hotly debating about who will have the right to vote. Most think that only men who own property should be able to vote. Some think that all property owners—men and women—should have that right. A few others want all free men to have the vote. Now it is time for the meeting to decide.

How would you have voted on this issue?

Ideas about Government

The American colonies had taken a bold step in declaring their independence from Great Britain in July 1776. Their next political goal was to form a new government. To do so, the American people drew from a wide range of political ideas.

English Laws and the Enlightenment England had limited the power of its kings and queens in two documents. These were the Magna Carta and the English Bill of Rights. **Magna Carta**, a document signed by King John in 1215, made the king subject to law. The English Bill of Rights, passed in 1689, declared the supremacy of Parliament. It kept the king or queen from changing laws without Parliament's consent. As a result, the people's representatives had a strong voice in England's government.

Many Americans of this period were also influenced by the Enlightenment—a philosophical movement that emphasized the use of reason to examine old ideas and traditions. Philosopher John Locke believed that a social contract existed between political rulers and the people they ruled. Baron de Montesquieu argued that the only way to achieve liberty was through the separation of governmental powers.

American Models of Government Americans had their own models of self-government to follow, like town meetings, the Virginia House of Burgesses, and the Mayflower Compact. In 1639 the people of Connecticut drew

Women's Suffrage
New Jersey allowed women to vote when it first joined the United States. This right was taken away by 1807.

up the English colonies' first written **constitution**. A constitution is a set of basic principles and laws that states the powers and duties of the government. In addition, the Declaration of Independence clearly set forth the beliefs on which Americans thought government should be based, such as the importance of laws to protect individual rights.

To keep individual leaders from gaining too much power, the new state constitutions created limited governments by restricting the power of government officials to take certain actions. The constitutions also supported the principle known as the *rule of law*, which requires that every citizen obey the laws, including political leaders. Most state constitutions had rules to protect the rights of citizens or those accused of crimes. Some banned slavery. The Massachusetts Constitution of 1780 is the oldest state constitution still in effect.

Thomas Jefferson's ideas about religious freedom were included in the **Virginia Statute for Religious Freedom**. This document declared that no person could be forced to attend a particular church or be required to pay for a church with tax money.

Right to Vote Under British rule, only free, white men who owned land could vote. Many states' constitutions expanded **suffrage**, or the right to vote, by allowing any white man who paid taxes to vote. In every state, however, only landowners could hold public office. Although some states originally allowed women and free African Americans to vote, these rights were soon taken away. Suffrage would not be restored to these groups for many decades to come.

Articles of Confederation

The Second Continental Congress was organized to create a national government. The Continental Congress appointed a Committee of Thirteen, with one member from each colony. This group was assigned to discuss and draft a national constitution.

Reading Check
Compare What two principles were common to state constitutions written during the Revolutionary War?

Under their plan, called the **Articles of Confederation**, Congress became the single branch of the national government. Congress's powers were limited to protect the individual liberties promoted in the Declaration of Independence. Each state had one vote in Congress. Congress could settle conflicts among the states, issue coins, borrow money, and make treaties with other countries and with Native Americans. Congress could also ask the states for money and soldiers. However, states had the power to refuse these requests. The government did not have a president or a national court system. Despite these limitations, the Articles provided a basis for uniting the colonies into one nation.

The Second Continental Congress passed the Articles of Confederation on November 15, 1777. Then it sent the Articles to each state legislature for **ratification**, or official approval, before the new national government could take effect.

Conflicts over claims to western lands slowed the process, but by 1779 every state except Maryland had ratified the Articles. Maryland's leaders refused to ratify until other states gave up their western land claims. Thomas Jefferson assured Maryland that western lands would be made into new states, rather than increasing territory for existing states. Satisfied with this condition, Maryland ratified the Articles in March 1781. This put the first national government of the United States into effect.

Reading Check
Summarize What were two weaknesses of the new national government?

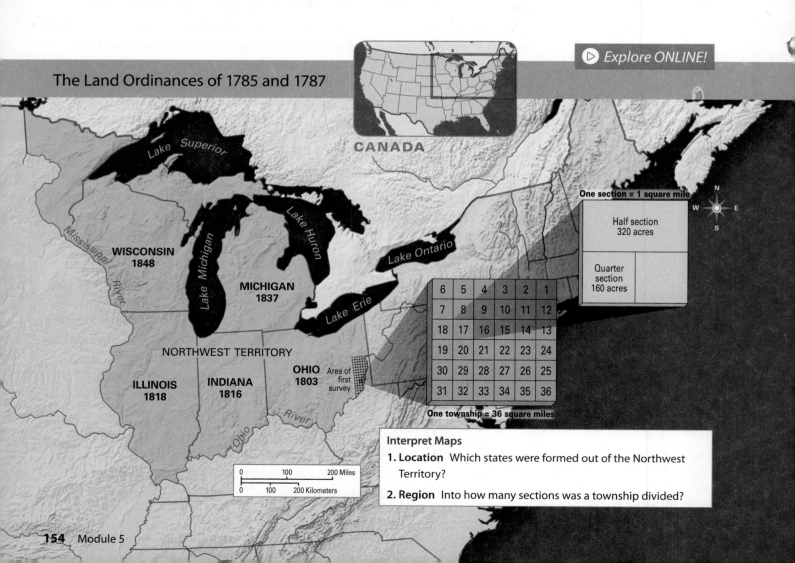

The Land Ordinances of 1785 and 1787

▶ Explore ONLINE!

CANADA

Lake Superior

Lake Michigan

Lake Huron

Lake Ontario

Lake Erie

Mississippi River

WISCONSIN
1848

MICHIGAN
1837

NORTHWEST TERRITORY

ILLINOIS
1818

INDIANA
1816

OHIO
1803

Area of first survey

Ohio River

One section = 1 square mile

Half section
320 acres

Quarter section
160 acres

6	5	4	3	2	1
7	8	9	10	11	12
18	17	16	15	14	13
19	20	21	22	23	24
30	29	28	27	26	25
31	32	33	34	35	36

One township = 36 square miles

0   100   200 Miles
0   100   200 Kilometers

Interpret Maps

1. **Location** Which states were formed out of the Northwest Territory?

2. **Region** Into how many sections was a township divided?

Northwest Territory

Congress had to decide what to do with the western lands now under its control and how to raise money to pay debts. It tried to solve both problems by selling the western lands. Congress passed the **Land Ordinance of 1785**, which set up a system for surveying and dividing western lands. The land was split into townships, which were 36 square miles divided into 36 lots of 640 acres each. One lot was reserved for a public school, and four lots were given to veterans. The remaining lots were sold to the public.

To form a political system for the region, Congress passed the **Northwest Ordinance of 1787**. The ordinance established the **Northwest Territory**, which included areas that are now in Illinois, Indiana, Michigan, Ohio, Minnesota, and Wisconsin. The Northwest Ordinance created a system for bringing new states into the Union. Congress agreed that the Northwest Territory would be divided into several smaller territories with a governor appointed by Congress. When the population of a territory reached 60,000, its settlers could draft their own constitution and ask to join the Union.

In addition, the law protected civil liberties and required that public education be provided. Finally, the ordinance stated that "there shall be neither slavery nor involuntary servitude [forced labor] in the . . . territory." This last condition banned slavery in the Territory and set the standard for future territories. However, slavery would continue to be a controversial issue.

Reading Check
Analyze Information How did the Northwest Ordinance of 1787 affect the United States?

Summary and Preview The Northwest Ordinance settled the future of the Northwest Territory. In the next lesson you will read about other challenges the new government faced.

Lesson 1 Assessment

Review Ideas, Terms, and People

1. **a. Identify** What documents influenced ideas about government in the United States?

   b. Draw Conclusions What impact did the Virginia Statute for Religious Freedom and the Declaration of Independence have on the U.S. government?

   c. Make Inferences How did the experience of living under British rule influence the attitude of Americans toward limited government and the rule of law?

   d. Identify Which groups of people were left out of the debate over the formation of a new American government?

2. **a. Identify** What was the Articles of Confederation?

   b. Summarize What powers were granted to Congress by the Articles of Confederation?

   c. Predict What are some possible problems that might result from the lack of a national court system?

3. **a. Describe** How were public lands in the West divided by the Land Ordinance of 1785?

   b. Evaluate In your opinion, what was the most important element of the Northwest Ordinance of 1787? Why?

   c. Elaborate What does the assignment of township lots reveal about values of Americans at this time?

Critical Thinking

4. **Categorize** In this lesson you learned about the Articles of Confederation. Create a chart similar to the one below and use it to show the strengths and weaknesses of the new government.

Articles of Confederation

Strengths	Weaknesses

History and Geography

Origins of the Constitution

The U.S. Constitution created a republican form of government based on the consent of the people. The framers of the Constitution blended ideas and examples from both the American colonies and England to write this lasting document.

THE MAYFLOWER COMPACT, 1620

The *Mayflower*, shown here in an illustration, sailed to America in 1620. Aboard the ship, 41 men signed the Mayflower Compact, the first document in the colonies to establish guidelines for self-government. The signers agreed that they and their families would combine to form a "civil body politic," or community.

COLONIAL ASSEMBLIES

The British Parliament's two-chamber structure also influenced colonial governments. In Article I, Section 1, of the Constitution, the framers continued the practice of a two-chamber legislature.

"All legislative powers . . . shall be vested in a Congress of the United States, which shall consist of a Senate and House of Representatives."

—Article I, Section 1, U.S. Constitution

VIRGINIA STATUTE FOR RELIGIOUS FREEDOM, 1786

Classical liberal principles, such as the written protection of citizens' personal liberties, were reflected in the addition of the Bill of Rights. The First Amendment's freedom of religion clauses were based on Thomas Jefferson's Virginia Statute for Religious Freedom. The document, which was accepted by the Virginia legislature in 1786, ensured the separation of church and state in Virginia.

"Congress shall make no law respecting an establishment of religion, or prohibiting the free exercise thereof . . . "

—First Amendment, U.S. Constitution

American colonies

MAGNA CARTA, 1215

In this painting King John of England is signing the Magna Carta, or the Great Charter, which established that the king was subject to the law just like everyone else. It also declared that people could not be deprived of their lives, liberty, or property "except by the lawful judgment of [their] peers, or by the law of the land." Compare this language to that of the Fifth Amendment to the Constitution.

"No person shall be . . . deprived of life, liberty, or property, without due process of law . . . "

—Fifth Amendment, U.S. Constitution

THE ENGLISH BILL OF RIGHTS, 1689

This painting shows King William and Queen Mary of England. Before taking the throne, William and Mary had to accept the English Bill of Rights. The English Bill of Rights took even more power away from the monarch than did the Magna Carta. It also protected the rights of English citizens. These ideas would later influence the U.S. Constitution.

"Excessive bail ought not be required, nor excessive fines imposed; nor cruel and unusual punishments inflicted."

—English Bill of Rights

THE ENLIGHTENMENT, 1700s

Enlightenment thinkers such as English philosopher John Locke supported the movement toward self-government. Locke argued in his writings that government could exist only with "the consent of the governed." The framers of the Constitution looked to Locke for inspiration when writing the Constitution, as you can see from its very first words.

"We the people of the United States, . . . "

—Preamble, U.S. Constitution

Analyze Information

1. What documents did the framers look to when writing the Constitution?

2. How did the English Parliamentary system affect the kind of government the framers created?

England

The New Nation Faces Challenges

The Big Idea

Problems faced by the young nation made it clear that a new constitution was needed.

Main Ideas

- The United States had difficulties with other nations.
- Internal economic problems plagued the new nation.
- Shays's Rebellion pointed out weaknesses in the Articles of Confederation.
- Many Americans called for changes in the national government.

Key Terms and People

tariffs
interstate commerce
inflation
depression
Daniel Shays
Shays's Rebellion

If YOU were there . . .

You own an orchard in Maryland in the 1780s. When you sell apples and apple pies in the market, people pay you with paper money. But now the tax collector says you must pay your taxes in gold or silver coins, not paper money. You and the other farmers are furious. Is this the liberty you fought a war for?

What would you do to protest these taxes?

Relations with Other Countries

Under the Articles of Confederation, Congress could not force states to provide soldiers for an army. The Continental Army had disbanded, or dissolved, soon after the signing of the Treaty of Paris of 1783. Without an army, the national government found it difficult to protect its citizens against foreign threats.

Trouble with Britain It was also difficult to enforce international treaties such as the Treaty of Paris of 1783. The United States found it especially hard to force the British to turn over "with all convenient speed" their forts on the American side of the Great Lakes. The United States wanted to gain control of these forts because they protected valuable land and fur-trade routes. Still, Britain was slow to withdraw from the area. A British official warned against the United States trying to seize the forts by force. He said that any attempt to do so would be opposed by the thousands of British soldiers who had settled in Canada after the Revolution and "are ready to fly to arms at a moment's warning."

Trade with Britain The United States also faced problems trading with Great Britain. After the signing of the Treaty of Paris, Britain closed many of its ports to American ships. Before the Revolutionary War, colonial ships had traded a

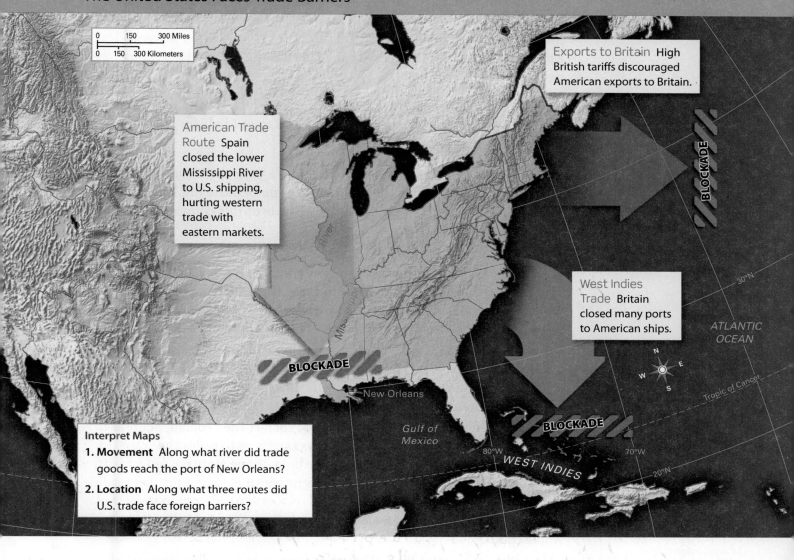

Explore ONLINE!

Exports to Britain High British tariffs discouraged American exports to Britain.

American Trade Route Spain closed the lower Mississippi River to U.S. shipping, hurting western trade with eastern markets.

West Indies Trade Britain closed many ports to American ships.

BLOCKADE

BLOCKADE

BLOCKADE

New Orleans

Gulf of Mexico

ATLANTIC OCEAN

WEST INDIES

Tropic of Cancer

30°N

20°N

80°W

70°W

Interpret Maps

1. **Movement** Along what river did trade goods reach the port of New Orleans?

2. **Location** Along what three routes did U.S. trade face foreign barriers?

great deal with the British West Indies and stopped there on their way to other destinations. This travel and trading stopped after 1783.

In addition, Britain forced American merchants to pay high **tariffs**—taxes on imports or exports. The tariffs applied to goods such as rice, tobacco, tar, and oil that were grown or mined in the United States and then sold in Britain. Merchants had to raise prices to cover the tariffs. Ultimately, the costs would be passed on to customers, who had to pay higher prices for the goods. The economic condition of the country was getting worse by the day.

Trade with Spain In 1784 Spanish officials closed the lower Mississippi River to U.S. shipping. Western farmers and merchants were furious because they used the Mississippi to send goods to eastern and foreign markets. Congress tried to work out an agreement with Spain, but the plan did not receive a majority vote in Congress. The plan could not be passed. As a result, Spain broke off the negotiations.

Many state leaders began to criticize the national government. Rhode Island's representatives wrote, "Our federal government is but a name; a mere shadow without substance [power]." Critics believed that Spain might have continued to negotiate if the United States had possessed a strong military. These leaders believed that the national government needed to be more powerful.

Impact of Closed Markets The closing of markets in the British West Indies seriously affected the U.S. economy. James Madison of Virginia wrote about the crisis.

"The Revolution has robbed us of our trade with the West Indies . . . without opening any other channels to compensate [make up for] it. In every point of view, indeed, the trade of this country is in a deplorable [terrible] condition."

—James Madison, quoted in *The Writings of James Madison*, edited by Gaillard Hunt

Farmers could no longer export their goods to the British West Indies. They also had to hire British ships to carry their goods to British markets, which was very expensive. American exports dropped while British goods flowed freely into the United States.

This unequal trade caused serious economic problems for the new nation. British merchants could sell manufactured products in the United States at much lower prices than locally made goods. This difference in prices hurt American businesses.

The Confederation Congress could not correct the problem because it did not have the authority either to pass tariffs or to order the states to pass tariffs. The states could offer little help. If one state passed a tariff, the British could simply sell their goods in another state. Most states did not cooperate in trade matters. Instead, states worked only to increase their own trade rather than working to improve the trade situation for the whole country.

In 1785 the situation led a British magazine to call the new nation the Dis-United States. As a result of the trade problems with Britain, American merchants began looking for other markets such as China, France, and the Netherlands. Despite such attempts, Britain remained the most important trading partner of the United States.

Reading Check
Analyze Information
Why was the Confederation Congress unable to solve America's international trade problems?

Economic Problems

In addition to international trade issues, other challenges soon appeared. Trade problems among the states, war debts, and a weak economy plagued the states.

Trade among States Because the Confederation Congress had no power to regulate **interstate commerce**—trade between two or more states— states followed their own trade interests. As a result, trade laws differed from state to state. The laws governing trade in one state could be very different from the laws in a neighboring state. This situation made trade difficult for merchants whose businesses crossed state lines.

This five-shilling note was issued by Rhode Island. Paper money printed by state governments helped fuel inflation.

Reading Check
Summarize What economic problems did the new nation face?

Inflation After the Revolutionary War, most states had a hard time paying off war debts and struggled to collect overdue taxes. To ease this hardship, some states began printing large amounts of paper money. The result was inflation. This money had little or no real value because states did not have gold or silver reserves to back it up. **Inflation** occurs when there are increased prices for goods and services combined with the reduced value of money. Because there was no common currency, Congress had no power to stop states from issuing more paper money and thus stop inflation.

Weak Economy In Rhode Island the state legislature printed large amounts of paper money worth very little. This made debtors—people who owe money—quite happy. They could pay back their debts with paper money worth less than the coins they had borrowed. However, creditors—people who lend money—were upset. Hundreds of creditors fled Rhode Island to avoid being paid back with worthless money.

The loss of trade with Britain combined with inflation created a **depression**. A depression is a period of low economic activity combined with a rise in unemployment.

Shays's Rebellion

Each state handled its economic problems differently. Massachusetts refused to print worthless paper money. It tried to pay its war debts by collecting taxes on land.

Heavy Debts for Farmers Massachusetts's tax policy hit farmers hard. As landowners, they had to pay the new taxes. However, farmers had trouble paying their debts. The courts began forcing them to sell their property. Some farmers had to serve terms in debtors' prison; others had to sell their labor.

Many government leaders in the state did not care about the problems of poor farmers, however. In some cases, farmers actually owed these political leaders money.

Farmers Rebel In August 1786 farmers in three western counties began a revolt. Bands of angry citizens closed down courts in western Massachusetts. Their reasoning was simple—with the courts shut down, no one's property could be taken. In September a poor farmer and Revolutionary War veteran, **Daniel Shays**, led hundreds of men in a forced shutdown of the Supreme Court in Springfield, Massachusetts. The state government ordered the farmers to stop the revolt under threat of capture and death. These threats only made Shays and his followers more determined. The uprising of farmers to protest high taxes and heavy debt became known as **Shays's Rebellion**.

Shays's Defeat Shays's forces were defeated by state troops in January 1787. By February many of the rebels were in prison. During their trials, 14 leaders were sentenced to death. However, the state soon freed most of

Daniel Shays, at the top of the steps, stands firm in the face of demands that he leave the courthouse in Springfield, Massachusetts. By shutting down the courts, farmers hoped to stop the government from selling their land.

Reading Check
Find Main Ideas What led to Shays's Rebellion?

the rebels, including Shays. State officials knew that many citizens of the state agreed with the rebels and their cause.

Calls for Change

In the end, Shays's Rebellion showed the weakness of the Confederation government. It led some Americans to admit that the Articles of Confederation had failed to protect the ideals of liberty set forth in the Declaration of Independence. When Massachusetts had asked the national government to help put down Shays's Rebellion, Congress could offer little help. More Americans began calling for a stronger central government. They wanted leaders who would be able to protect the nation in times of crisis.

Earlier in 1786 the Virginia legislature had called for a national conference. It wanted to talk about economic problems and ways to change the Articles of Confederation. The meeting took place in Annapolis, Maryland, in September 1786.

Nine states decided to send delegates to the Annapolis Convention, but some of their delegates were late and missed the meeting. Connecticut, Georgia, Maryland, and South Carolina did not respond to the request at all and sent no delegates.

Because of the poor attendance, the participants, including James Madison and Alexander Hamilton, called on all 13 states to send delegates to a Constitutional Convention in Philadelphia in May 1787. They planned to revise the Articles of Confederation to better meet the needs of the nation.

Summary and Preview Many Americans believed that Shays's Rebellion was final proof that the national government needed to be changed. In the next lesson you will read about the Constitutional Convention.

Reading Check
Find Main Ideas
Why did some people believe the national government needed to change?

Weaknesses of the Articles of Confederation

QUICK FACTS

- Most power held by states
- One branch of government
- Legislative branch has few powers
- No executive branch
- No judicial system
- No system of checks and balances

Lesson 2 Assessment

Review Ideas, Terms, and People

1. **a. Summarize** What problems did the United States experience with Spain and Great Britain after the Revolutionary War?

   b. Explain Why did Congress's inability to tax goods hurt American merchants?

   c. Predict What are some possible results of the growing problems between the United States and Great Britain? Why?

2. **a. Describe** What difficulties were involved with interstate commerce?

   b. Analyze What was the cause of inflation in the new nation, and how could it have been prevented?

3. **a. Explain** How did Massachusetts's tax policy affect poor farmers?

   b. Evaluate Defend the actions of Daniel Shays and the other rebels.

4. **a. Recall** Why did Madison and Hamilton call for a Constitutional Convention?

   b. Analyze How did Shays's Rebellion lead to a call for change in the United States?

Critical Thinking

5. **Categorize** In this lesson you learned about the problems faced by the new nation. Create a chart similar to the one below and identify those problems as either domestic or international.

Domestic Problems	International Problems

Creating the Constitution

The Big Idea

A new constitution provided a framework for a stronger national government.

Main Ideas

- The Constitutional Convention met to improve the government of the United States.

- The issue of representation led to the Great Compromise.

- Regional debate over slavery led to the Three-Fifths Compromise.

- The U.S. Constitution created federalism and a balance of power.

Key Terms and People

Constitutional Convention
James Madison
Virginia Plan
New Jersey Plan
Great Compromise
Three-Fifths Compromise
popular sovereignty
legislative branch
executive branch
judicial branch
checks and balances
federalism

Reading Check
Summarize What was the purpose of the Constitutional Convention?

If YOU were there . . .

You are a merchant in Connecticut in 1787. You have been a member of your state legislature for several years. This spring, the legislature is choosing delegates to a convention to revise the Articles of Confederation. Delegates will meet in Philadelphia. It means leaving your business in others' hands for most of the summer. Still, you hope to be chosen.

Why would you want to go to the Constitutional Convention?

Constitutional Convention

In February 1787 the Confederation Congress invited each state to send delegates to a convention in Philadelphia. The goal of the meeting was to improve the Articles of Confederation.

The **Constitutional Convention** was held in May 1787 in Philadelphia's Independence Hall to improve the Articles of Confederation. However, delegates would leave with an entirely new U.S. Constitution. This decision angered some of the participants.

Most delegates were well educated, and many had served in state legislatures or Congress. Benjamin Franklin and **James Madison** were there. Revolutionary War hero George Washington was elected president of the Convention.

Several important voices were absent. John Adams and Thomas Jefferson could not attend. Patrick Henry chose not to attend because he did not want a stronger central government. Women, African Americans, and Native Americans did not take part because they did not yet have the rights of citizens.

James Madison

Signing of the Constitution

This painting shows the signing of the Constitution on September 17, 1787. James Madison, number 4 on the diagram, became known as the "Father of the Constitution" for his ideas about government and his ability to lead the delegates to agreement.

1 Roger Sherman
2 Alexander Hamilton
3 Benjamin Franklin
4 James Madison
5 George Washington
6 James Wilson

Great Compromise

Several issues divided the delegates to the Constitutional Convention. Some members wanted only small changes to the Articles of Confederation, while others wanted to rewrite the Articles completely.

Those delegates who wanted major changes to the Articles had different goals. For example, small and large states had different ideas about representation, economic concerns such as tariffs, and slavery. In addition, delegates disagreed over how strong to make the national government.

Virginia Plan After the delegates had met for four days, Edmund Randolph of Virginia presented the **Virginia Plan**. He proposed a new federal constitution that would give sovereignty, or supreme power, to the central government. The legislature would be bicameral—made up of two houses, or groups of representatives—and chosen on the basis of state populations. Larger states would thus have more representatives than would smaller states. Delegates from the smaller states believed that it would give too much power to the larger states.

Virginia Plan	Great Compromise	New Jersey Plan
• Gave more power to national government • Bicameral legislature • Number in both houses based on population	• Bicameral legislature • Number of representatives based on state populations in lower house • Number of representatives equal from each state in upper house	• Gave more power to state governments • Unicameral legislature • Number of representatives equal from each state

New Jersey Plan The smaller states came up with a plan to stop the larger states from getting too much power. New Jersey delegate William Paterson presented the small-state or **New Jersey Plan**, which called for a unicameral, or one-house, legislature. The plan gave each state an equal number of votes, and thus an equal voice, in the federal government. The plan gave the federal government the power to tax citizens in all states, and it allowed the government to regulate commerce.

Compromise Is Reached After a month of debate, the delegates were unable to agree on how states should be represented. The convention reached a deadlock.

Finally, Roger Sherman of Connecticut proposed a compromise plan. The legislative branch would have two houses. Each state, regardless of its size, would have two representatives in the Senate, or upper house. This would give each state an equal voice, pleasing the smaller states. In the House of Representatives, or lower house, the number of representatives for each state would be determined by the state's population. This pleased the larger states. The agreement to create a two-house legislature became known as the **Great Compromise**. James Wilson, a great speaker, saw his dream of a strong national government come true.

Roger Sherman

James Wilson

Reading Check
Contrast How did the Virginia Plan and New Jersey Plan differ?

Three-Fifths Compromise

The debate over representation also involved regional differences. Southern delegates wanted enslaved Africans to be counted as part of their state populations. This way they would have more representatives, and more power, in Congress. Northerners disagreed. They wanted the number of slaves to determine taxes but not representation.

To resolve this problem, some delegates thought of a compromise. They wanted to count three-fifths of the slaves in each state as part of that state's population to decide how many representatives a state would have.

After much debate, the delegates voted to accept the proposal, called the **Three-Fifths Compromise**. Under this agreement only three-fifths of a state's slave population would count when determining representation.

Another major issue was the foreign slave trade. Some of the delegates believed slavery was wrong and wanted the federal government to ban the slave trade. Others said that the southern states' economies needed the slave trade. Many southern delegates said they would leave the Union if the Constitution immediately ended the slave trade. Also at issue was Congress's ability to tax imports and exports.

Worried delegates reached another compromise. The Commerce Compromises allowed Congress to levy tariffs on imports, but not exports, and allowed the importation of slaves until the end of 1807. The delegates omitted, or left out, the words *slavery* and *slave* in the Constitution. They referred instead to "free Persons" and "all other Persons."

Reading Check
Summarize What compromise was reached over the issue of the slave trade?

A New System of Government

Most of the delegates to the Convention wanted a stronger central government than the Articles of Confederation could provide. They believed it was necessary for the protection and administration of the group of states. But delegates also wanted to protect the individual rights that had been won in the Revolution. They wanted the new system of government to support the ideals stated in the Declaration of Independence.

The rights of citizens to "life, liberty, and the pursuit of happiness" are supported by the idea of **popular sovereignty**. This is the idea that political authority is in the hands of the people. In the new nation, people would express this power through their votes. The power of government is limited by the power of voters. In a republic, or representative democracy, the government consists of people elected by voters to represent them. This system requires government to depend on the consent of the governed. Voters can limit the actions of government by removing representatives who do not truly work for their goals.

Checks and Balances The delegates divided the power of the central government among three branches, each having specific roles. This arrangement is known as the separation of powers. The **legislative branch**, called Congress, is responsible for proposing and passing laws. It is made up of two houses, as created in the Great Compromise. The Senate and the House of Representatives have different rules governing how many members represent each state, which helps balance the power between large and small states. The **executive branch** includes the president and the departments that help run the government. The executive branch makes sure that laws are carried out. The **judicial branch** is made up of all the national courts. This branch is responsible for interpreting laws, punishing criminals, and settling disputes between states.

The framers of the Constitution created a system of **checks and balances** that keeps any branch of government from becoming too

As the home and office of the president, the White House is today a well-known symbol of the executive branch of government.

powerful. For example, Congress has the power to pass bills into law. The president has the power to veto, or reject, laws that Congress passes. However, Congress can override the president's veto with a two-thirds majority vote. The Supreme Court has the power to review laws passed by Congress and strike down any law that violates the Constitution.

Federalism Even though many of the delegates wanted a stronger central government, they did not want to destroy state governments. State governments can be more sensitive to local concerns and traditions, and they can serve as laboratories for new ideas. To balance the power between these two types of government, the delegates created the system of **federalism**. Federalism divides the powers of government between a central government and the states that make up a nation. Under the previous confederal system, states were only loosely joined together.

The Constitution requires each state to obey the authority of the federal, or national, government. States have control over government functions not specifically assigned to the federal government. These include control of local government, education, the chartering of corporations, and the supervision of religious bodies. States also have the power to create and oversee civil and criminal law. States must protect the welfare of their citizens.

Amending the Constitution One of the most important decisions the framers made was to include a method for changing or adding to the Constitution. They wanted the government to be able to adapt as changes were needed. The process for amending the Constitution was made difficult, however, so that major changes to the government would require the support of a large majority of voters. Two-thirds of each house of Congress and three-fourths of states must approve a change before it can take effect. Although many amendments, or changes to the Constitution, have been suggested, only twenty-seven have been approved. The purposes of these amendments have usually focused on protecting civil and voting rights, and on procedures for administering the government.

The Constitution Strengthens the National Government

Strengths of the Constitution
- ✓ most power held by national government
- ✓ three branches of government
- ✓ legislative branch has many powers
- ✓ executive branch led by president
- ✓ judicial branch to review the laws
- ✓ firm system of checks and balances

Weaknesses of the Articles of Confederation
- most power held by states
- one branch of government
- legislative branch has few powers
- no executive branch
- no judicial system
- no system of checks and balances

Reading Check
Explain How does the constitutional system of government prevent government power from becoming too concentrated?

Even though the final draft of the Constitution was adopted by the Convention, many disagreements still existed among the delegates. Debates continued around the power of state governments and the role of each branch. Almost as soon as the document was adopted, different interpretations of its language began to appear. Some of the disagreements affect the views of lawmakers even today, but the Constitution is still the guiding blueprint for the nation's government.

Summary and Preview The Constitution balanced power among three branches of the federal government but was only written after many compromises. In the next lesson you will read about Antifederalist and Federalist views of the Constitution, and the struggle to get it approved by the states.

Lesson 3 Assessment

Review Ideas, Terms, and People

1. **a. Recall** Why did the Confederation Congress call for a Constitutional Convention?

   b. Elaborate Why do you think it was important that most delegates had served in state legislatures?

   c. Make Inferences Why did the delegates elect Washington as president of the Convention?

2. **a. Identify** What was the Great Compromise?

   b. Draw Conclusions How did state issues lead to debate over structure of the legislature?

3. **a. Recall** How did the delegates resolve their debate on tariffs in the Commerce Compromise?

   b. Explain What was the debate between North and South over counting slave populations?

   c. Contrast How did delegates' views differ on the issue of the foreign slave trade?

4. **a. Recall** Why did the framers of the Constitution create a system of checks and balances through the separation of powers?

   b. Analyze How did federalism limit the power of the central government?

   c. Evaluate Did the Constitution resolve the weaknesses in the Articles of Confederation? Explain your answer.

Critical Thinking

5. **Evaluate** What circumstances justified the decision of the delegates to draft a new constitution instead of revising the Articles of Confederation, as was originally planned?

6. **Identify Cause and Effect** In this lesson you learned about several issues that were resolved by compromise during the Constitutional Convention. Create a graphic organizer like the one below and use it to show how the compromises affected the framework of the new government.

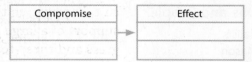

Compromise		Effect
	→	

7. **Compare and Contrast** How do the Articles of the Confederation and the Constitution each carry out democratic ideals?

8. **Draw Conclusions** Why is limited government important for maintaining popular sovereignty in a republic or representative democracy?

Ratifying the Constitution

The Big Idea

Americans carried on a
vigorous debate before
ratifying the Constitution.

Main Ideas

- Federalists and Antifederalists
  engaged in debate over the
  new Constitution.

- The *Federalist Papers* played an
  important role in the fight for
  ratification of the Constitution.

- Ten amendments were added
  to the Constitution to provide a Bill of Rights to protect
  citizens.

Key Terms and People

Antifederalists
George Mason
Federalists
Federalist Papers
amendments
Bill of Rights

If YOU were there . . .

You are a newspaper editor in Philadelphia. During
colonial rule, officials sometimes closed down your
newspaper because you had criticized the governor.
Now you are one of many Americans who want to be
sure the new Constitution will guarantee individual
rights. You are writing an editorial in your paper
explaining what you want.

**What rights would you want the
Constitution to protect?**

Federalists and Antifederalists

When the Constitution was made public, a huge debate began
among many Americans. Some **Antifederalists**—people who
opposed the Constitution—thought that the Constitutional
Convention should not have created a new government. Others,
such as James Monroe, thought the Constitution weakened
states' rights by giving too much power to the central government. For some Antifederalists, including **George Mason**, the
main problem was that the Constitution did not have a section
that guaranteed individual rights. Thomas Jefferson, who was
otherwise in favor of the Constitution, wrote to Madison from
Paris to argue that a bill of rights was needed.

Many Antifederalists were small farmers and debtors. Some
Patriots, including Samuel Adams and Patrick Henry, were also
strong Antifederalists. At the Virginia ratifying convention,
Henry spoke out against the lack of protection of individual
freedoms, saying that he valued American liberty over American union.

Antifederalists were challenged by those who believed that
the United States needed a stronger central government.
Federalists—supporters of the Constitution—included
James Madison, George Washington, Benjamin
Franklin, and Alexander Hamilton. Most Federalists
believed that through compromise, the delegates had created a

Federalists vs. Antifederalists

Alexander Hamilton
Federalist

- Supported the Constitution as an excellent plan for government
- Defended his views in the *Federalist Papers*

George Mason
Antifederalist

- Opposed the Constitution
- Believed the Constitution needed a section guaranteeing individual rights

Constitution that offered a good balance of power between various political views. Many Federalists were wealthy planters, farmers, and lawyers. However, others were workers and craftspeople.

Federalists and Antifederalists debated whether the new Constitution should be approved. They made speeches and printed pamphlets **advocating** their views. Mercy Otis Warren, an ardent Patriot during the war, wrote a pamphlet entitled *Observations on the New Constitution*, in which she criticized the lack of individual rights it provided. The Federalists had to convince people that a change in the structure of government was needed. To do this, they had to overcome people's fears that the Constitution would make the government too powerful.

Federalist Papers

One of the most important defenses of the Constitution appeared in a series of essays that became known as the *Federalist Papers*. These essays supporting the Constitution were written anonymously under the name Publius. They were actually written by Alexander Hamilton, James Madison, and John Jay.

Academic Vocabulary
advocate to plead in favor of

Reading Check
Compare and Contrast Explain the similarities and differences between the Antifederalists and the Federalists.

Federalist Papers
Nos. 10 and 51

These essays are part of a series called the Federalist Papers, *written between 1787 and 1788 to support ratification of the Constitution. They discuss how the new system of government will overcome disagreements within society and prevent abuses of power.*

> Madison believes that lawmakers are responsible for regulating the many competing concerns that make up society.

> The federal government will handle issues affecting the nation as a whole; state and local governments will handle local issues.

> The Constitution creates a national government that will be strong but limited in power.

> The federalist system provides checks and balances on the power of the national government.

"*A landed interest, a manufacturing interest, a mercantile [trading] interest, a moneyed interest, with many lesser interests, grow up of necessity in civilized nations, and divide them into different classes, actuated [moved] by different sentiments and views. The regulation of these various and interfering interests [opinions] forms the principal task of modern legislation, and involves the spirit of party and faction [group] in the necessary and ordinary operations of the government. . . .*

The federal Constitution forms a happy combination . . . the great . . . interests being referred to the national [legislature], the local and particular to the State legislatures. . . . The influence of factious leaders may kindle [start] a flame within their particular States, but will be unable to spread a general conflagration [large fire] through the other States.

—James Madison, from "Federalist No 10"

If men were angels, no government would be necessary. If angels were to govern men, neither external nor internal controls on government would be necessary. In framing a government which is to be administered by men over men, the great difficulty lies in this: you must first enable the government to control the governed; and in the next place oblige it to control itself. A dependence on the people is, no doubt, the primary control on the government; but experience has taught mankind the necessity of auxiliary precautions. . . . We see it particularly displayed in all the subordinate distributions of power, where the constant aim is to divide and arrange the several offices in such a manner as that each may be a check on the other that the private interest of every individual may be a sentinel over the public rights.

—Alexander Hamilton or James Madison, from "Federalist No 51"

Analyze Historical Sources
According to the excerpts from the essays, what will prevent the national government from becoming oppressive?

After serving a leading role in the Constitutional Convention, James Madison went on to defend the Constitution in essays he wrote for the *Federalist Papers.*

The authors of the *Federalist Papers* tried to reassure Americans that the new federal government would not overpower the newly created states. In Federalist Paper No. 10, Madison argued that the diversity of the United States would prevent any single group from dominating the government.

The *Federalist Papers* were widely reprinted in newspapers around the country as the debate over the Constitution continued. Finally, they were collected and published in book form in 1788.

The Constitution needed only nine states to pass it. However, to establish and preserve national unity, each state needed to ratify it. Every state except Rhode Island held special state conventions that gave citizens the chance to discuss and vote on the Constitution.

Paul Revere served on a committee supporting ratification. He wrote of the Constitution, "The proposed . . . government, is well calculated [planned] to secure the liberties, protect the property, and guard the rights of the citizens of America." Antifederalists also spoke out in state conventions, and wrote articles and pamphlets that became known as the Antifederalist Papers. In New York, one citizen said, "It appears that the government will fall into the hands of the few and the great."

On December 7, 1787, Delaware became the first state to ratify the Constitution. It went into effect in June 1788 after New Hampshire became the ninth state to ratify it.

Political leaders across America knew the new government needed the support of the large states of Virginia and New York, where debate still raged. Finally, Madison and fellow Virginia Federalists convinced Virginia to ratify it in mid-1788. In New York, riots had occurred when the draft of the Constitution was made public. At the state convention in Poughkeepsie to discuss ratification, Hamilton and Jay argued convincingly against the Antifederalists led by DeWitt Clinton. When news arrived of Virginia's ratification, New York ratified it as well. Rhode Island was the last state to ratify the Constitution in May 1790.

Reading Check
Draw Conclusions
Why were Virginia and New York important to the ratification of the Constitution?

Bill of Rights

Several states ratified the Constitution only after they were promised that a bill protecting individual rights would be added to it. Many Antifederalists did not think that the Constitution would protect personal freedoms.

Some Federalists said that the nation did not need a federal bill of rights because the Constitution itself was a bill of rights. It was, they argued, written to protect the liberty of all U.S. citizens.

James Madison wanted to make a bill of rights one of the new government's first priorities. In Congress's first session, Madison encouraged the legislators to put together a bill of rights. The rights would then be added to the Constitution as **amendments**, or official changes. In Article V of the Constitution, the founders had provided a way to change the document when necessary in order to reflect the will of the people. The process requires that proposed amendments must be approved by a two-thirds majority of both houses of Congress and then ratified by three-fourths of the states before taking effect.

In this document, Congress proposed 12 amendments to the U.S. Constitution. Articles III to XII became the 10 amendments known as the Bill of Rights.

Legislators took ideas from the state ratifying conventions, the Virginia Declaration of Rights, the English Bill of Rights, and the Declaration of Independence to make sure that the abuses listed in the Declaration of Independence would be illegal under the new government. In September 1789 Congress proposed 12 amendments and sent them to the states for ratification. By December 1791 the states had ratified the **Bill of Rights**—ten of the proposed amendments intended to protect citizens' rights.

These ten amendments set a clear example of how to amend the Constitution to fit the needs of a changing nation. The flexibility of the U.S. Constitution has allowed it to survive as a living document for more than two hundred years.

Summary and Preview Early disagreements over individual rights resulted in the Bill of Rights. In the next module you will learn about the structure of the Constitution.

Reading Check
Summarize Why is being able to amend the Constitution important?

Lesson 4 Assessment

Review Ideas, Terms, and People

1. **a. Identify** Who were the Federalists and the Antifederalists?

   b. Explain Why did Antifederalists such as George Mason, James Monroe, and Patrick Henry object to the Constitution?

   c. Draw Conclusions What position did Thomas Jefferson take in the debate over the Constitution?

2. **a. Recall** When did the Constitution go into effect?

   b. Draw Conclusions Why was it important that all 13 states ratify the Constitution?

   c. Elaborate Do you think that the *Federalist Papers* played an essential role in the ratification of the Constitution? Explain your answer.

3. **a. Recall** Why did Congress add the Bill of Rights?

   b. Explain From where did legislators' ideas for the Bill of Rights come?

   c. Evaluate Do you think the process for amending the Constitution is too difficult? Explain your position.

Critical Thinking

4. **Analyze** In this lesson you learned about the debate between Federalists and Antifederalists about the Constitution. Create a graphic organizer similar to the one below, and identify the outcome of the debate. Be sure to mention the Bill of Rights.

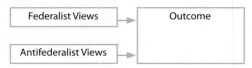

Social Studies Skills

Determine Different Points of View

Define the Skill

A *point of view* is a person's outlook or attitude. It is the way he or she looks at a topic or thing. Each person's point of view is shaped by his or her background. Because people's backgrounds are different, their points of view differ too. Since a person's point of view shapes his or her opinions, knowing that point of view helps you understand and evaluate those opinions. It also helps you understand why people in history think and act differently.

Learn the Skill

When you encounter someone's beliefs, opinions, or actions in your study of history, use the following guidelines to determine his or her point of view.

1. Look for information about the person's background.

2. Ask yourself what factors in the person's background might have influenced his or her opinion or action concerning the topic or event.

3. Be aware that sometimes the person's opinions or actions themselves will provide clues to his or her point of view.

Benjamin Lincoln led the troops that put down Shays's Rebellion in Massachusetts. He was also a state politician and a general during the Revolution. Lincoln offered this explanation of Shays's uprising.

"Among [the main causes] I rank the ease with which . . . credit was obtained . . . in the time of [the Revolution]. . . . The moment the day arrived when all discovered that things were fast returning [to normal], . . . and that the indolent [lazy persons] and improvident [unwise persons] would soon experience the evils of their idleness and sloth, many startled [panicked] . . . and . . . complained . . . of the weight of public taxes . . . and at the cruelty of . . . creditors [those to whom money is owed] to call for their just dues [rightful payment]. . . . The disaffected [unhappy people] . . . attempted . . . to stop the courts of law, and to suspend the operations of government. This they hoped to do until . . . an end should thereby be put to public and private debts."

Lincoln's background as a general, state official, and leader against the rebels likely gave him a negative point of view on the revolt. His reference to the rebels as lazy and unwise also provides clues to his attitude. You should weigh such factors when evaluating the accuracy of his statement.

Practice the Skill

The following statement about Shays's Rebellion came from a Massachusetts farmer. Read it and apply the guidelines to answer the questions.

"I've labored hard all my days. . . . I have been . . . obliged to do more than my part in the [Revolutionary] war; been loaded with . . . rates [taxes], . . . been . . . [abused] by sheriffs . . . and [debt] collectors. . . . I have lost a great deal. . . . [T]he great men are going to get all we have, and I think it is time for us to . . . put a stop to it."

1. From what point of view is this person commenting on the revolt? What is his opinion of it?

2. How does his view of himself differ from Lincoln's view of people like him?

3. Is this view of the revolt likely to be more accurate than Lincoln's view? Why or why not?

Module 5 Assessment

Review Vocabulary, Terms, and People

Match the numbered person or term with the correct lettered definition.

1. Bill of Rights
2. checks and balances
3. constitution
4. Constitutional Convention
5. *Federalist Papers*
6. inflation
7. Northwest Territory
8. George Mason
9. tariffs
10. Three-Fifths Compromise

a. agreement that stated that each slave would be counted as three-fifths of a person when determining representation

b. delegate to the Constitutional Convention who became an Antifederalist

c. increased prices for goods and services combined with the reduced value of money

d. area including present-day Illinois, Indiana, Michigan, Ohio, Wisconsin, and part of Minnesota

e. meetings held in Philadelphia at which delegates from the states attempted to improve the existing government

f. series of essays in support of the Constitution

g. set of basic principles that determines the powers and duties of a government

h. system that prevents any branch of government from becoming too powerful

i. taxes on imports or exports

j. the first 10 amendments to the Constitution

Comprehension and Critical Thinking

Lesson 1

11. a. **Describe** What powers did the Articles of Confederation give the national government?

    b. **Summarize** What did the Confederation Congress do to strengthen the United States?

    c. **Evaluate** Which document or institution do you think had the greatest influence on the development of the United States? Why?

Lesson 2

12. a. **Recall** What was Shays's Rebellion?

    b. **Draw Conclusions** What was the general attitude of foreign nations toward the new government of the United States? Why?

    c. **Evaluate** Of the problems experienced by the Confederation Congress, which do you think was the most harmful? Why?

Lesson 3

13. a. **Describe** In what ways did the Constitution strengthen the central government?

    b. **Explain** How does federalism limit the power of the central government?

    c. **Explain** How did the two compromises reached during the Constitutional Convention satisfy competing groups?

    d. **Elaborate** Which decisions made in the Constitutional Convention gave the national government greater decision-making powers than it had under the Articles of Confederation?

    e. **Evaluate** In your opinion were there any weaknesses in the Constitution? Explain your answer.

Module 5 Assessment, continued

Lesson 4

14. **a. Recall** What was the purpose of the Bill of Rights?

   b. Explain Why were some Americans opposed to the Constitution?

   c. Draw Conclusions How did the compromises in the Constitutional Convention affect the results of the ratification process?

   d. Evaluate Would you have supported the Federalists or the Antifederalists? Explain your answer.

Review Themes

15. **Politics** What political problems resulted from a weak central government under the Articles of Confederation?

16. **Politics** How did political disagreements lead to important compromises in the creation of the Constitution?

Reading Skills

Understand Chronological Order *Use the Reading Skills taught in this module to answer the question below.*

17. Organize the following events chronologically according to the module.

   a. The *Federalist Papers* are published.

   b. The Constitution is ratified.

   c. The Articles of Confederation is ratified.

   d. Shays's Rebellion occurs.

   e. The Constitutional Convention meets in Philadelphia.

Social Studies Skills

Determine Different Points of View *Use the Social Studies Skills taught in this module to answer the question below.*

18. List three differences between the Virginia Plan and the New Jersey Plan.

Focus on Writing

19. **Write an Editorial** It is 1788 and you are writing an editorial to a local newspaper. You want to convince your readers that the new Constitution will be much better than the old Articles of Confederation. You should start your editorial with a strong statement of your opinion about the Constitution. Then write two sentences about each of your main points of support—a weakness of the Articles of Confederation and/or a strength of the Constitution. End your editorial with a call to action: Ask the delegates to the Constitutional Convention to ratify the Constitution. Remember that you are trying to convince people to make a very important decision for our country—be persuasive.

Citizenship and the Constitution

Essential Question
Which ideas in the Constitution are most important for preserving freedom?

About the Photo: Citizens like these must fulfill the duties and responsibilities of citizenship.

▶ *Explore ONLINE!*

VIDEOS, including...
- Could You Pass the U.S. Citizenship Test?

HISTORY.

☑ Document-Based Investigations

☑ Graphic Organizers

☑ Interactive Games

☑ Image Carousel: The Federal Government

☑ Interactive Chart: How a Bill Becomes a Law

☑ Interactive Chart: The Pathway to Citizenship

In this module you will learn about the Constitution of the United States, the Bill of Rights, and what it means to be an American citizen. You will also be able to read the full text of the Constitution.

What You Will Learn ...

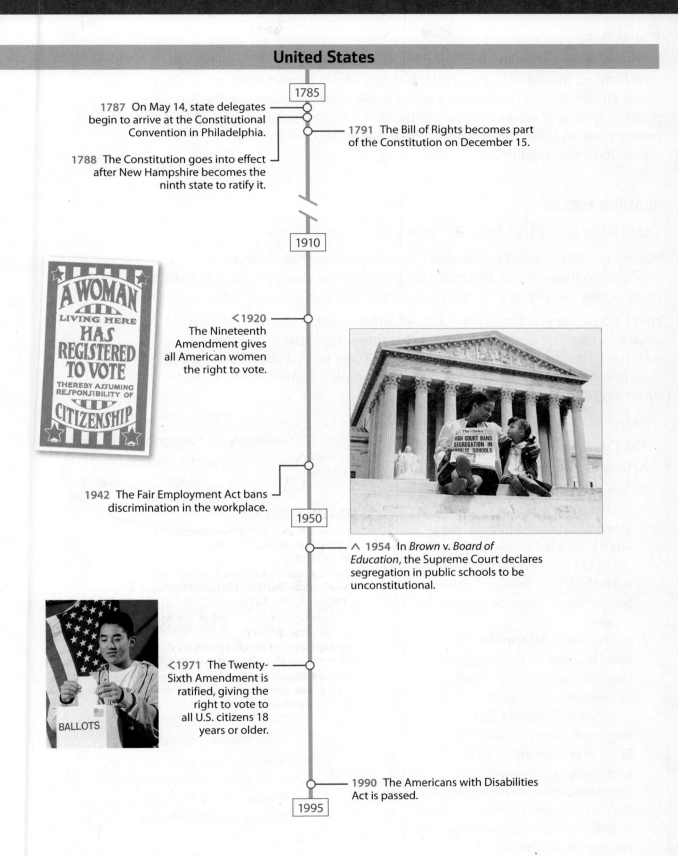

United States

1785

1787 On May 14, state delegates begin to arrive at the Constitutional Convention in Philadelphia.

1788 The Constitution goes into effect after New Hampshire becomes the ninth state to ratify it.

1791 The Bill of Rights becomes part of the Constitution on December 15.

1910

A WOMAN LIVING HERE HAS REGISTERED TO VOTE THEREBY ASSUMING RESPONSIBILITY OF CITIZENSHIP

<1920 The Nineteenth Amendment gives all American women the right to vote.

HIGH COURT BANS SEGREGATION IN PUBLIC SCHOOLS

1942 The Fair Employment Act bans discrimination in the workplace.

1950

∧ **1954** In *Brown* v. *Board of Education*, the Supreme Court declares segregation in public schools to be unconstitutional.

BALLOTS

<1971 The Twenty-Sixth Amendment is ratified, giving the right to vote to all U.S. citizens 18 years or older.

1990 The Americans with Disabilities Act is passed.

1995

Reading Social Studies

THEME FOCUS:

Politics

In this module you will read about the Constitution, the three branches of government, the Bill of Rights, and the duties and responsibilities of a United States citizen. As you read about each of these topics, you will see the American political system at work—not only in the Bill of Rights, but also through the responsibilities U.S. citizens have as they vote for leaders and work to help their communities and nation.

READING FOCUS:

Summarize Historical Texts

History books are full of information. Sometimes the sheer amount of information they contain can make processing what you read difficult. In those cases, it may be helpful to stop for a moment and summarize what you've read.

Write a Summary A summary is a short restatement of the most important ideas in a text. The example below shows three steps used in writing a summary. First, underline important details. Then, write a short summary of each paragraph. Finally, combine these paragraph summaries into a short summary of the whole passage.

The Constitution
Article II, Section 1

1. The <u>executive Power</u> shall be vested in a <u>President of the United States of America</u>. He shall hold his Office during the Term of <u>four Years</u>, and, together with the <u>Vice President</u>, chosen for the same Term, be <u>elected</u>, as follows:

2. <u>Each state shall appoint</u>, in such Manner as the Legislature thereof may direct, a Number of <u>Electors</u>, equal to the whole <u>Number of Senators and Representatives</u> to which the State may be entitled in the Congress; but no Senator or Representative, or Person holding an Office of Trust or Profit under the United States, shall be appointed an Elector.

Summary of Paragraph 1
The executive branch is headed by a president and vice president, each elected for four-year terms.

Summary of Paragraph 2
The electors who choose the president and vice president are appointed. Each state has the same number of electors as it has members of Congress.

Combined Summary
The president and vice president, who run the executive branch, are elected every four years by state-appointed electors.

You Try It!

The following passage is from the U.S. Constitution. As you read it, decide which facts you would include in a summary of the passage.

The Constitution

Article I, Section 2

1. The House of Representatives shall be composed of Members chosen every second Year by the People of the several States, and the Electors in each State shall have the Qualifications requisite for Electors of the most numerous branch of the State Legislature.

2. No person shall be a Representative who shall not have attained to the Age of twenty five years, and been seven Years a Citizen of the United States, and who shall not, when elected, be an Inhabitant of the State in which he shall be chosen.

After you read the passage, answer the following questions.

1. Which of the following statements best summarizes the first paragraph of this passage?

   a. Congress has a House of Representatives.

   b. Members of the House of Representatives are elected every two years by state electors.

2. Using the steps described on the previous page, write a summary of the second paragraph of this passage.

3. Combine the summary statement you chose in Question 1 with the summary statement you wrote in Question 2 to create a single summary of this entire passage.

As you read Module 6, think about what details you would include in a summary of each paragraph.

Establishing the Constitution

The Big Idea

A new Constitution strengthened the national government.

Main Ideas

- Delegates met at the Constitutional Convention to improve the government.

- The Great Compromise and the Three-Fifths Compromise resolved controversial issues.

- The new government was based on popular sovereignty, balance of power, and federalism.

- Federalists and Antifederalists debated the Constitution.

- The Constitution was ratified.

Key Terms and People

Constitutional Convention
James Madison
Virginia Plan
New Jersey Plan
Great Compromise
Three-Fifths Compromise
popular sovereignty
legislative branch
executive branch
judicial branch
checks and balances
federalism
amendments
Federalists
Federalist Papers
Antifederalists
Bill of Rights

If YOU were there . . .

You are representing your county at the New York Convention in 1788. You will be voting on the new Constitution. The majority of delegates oppose the new Constitution. They think it will give the national government too much power. You have read that the Constitution proposes a government that is shared between a federal government and the states. By the time you arrive in Poughkeepsie for the convention, eight states have already ratified the Constitution.

What do you want to know before you vote?

Constitutional Convention

The Confederation Congress invited each state to send delegates to a convention with the goal of improving the Articles of Confederation. The Convention opened on May 25, 1787, in Philadelphia. The first order of business was to nominate a president for the Convention. Every delegate voted for the hero of the Revolution, George Washington.

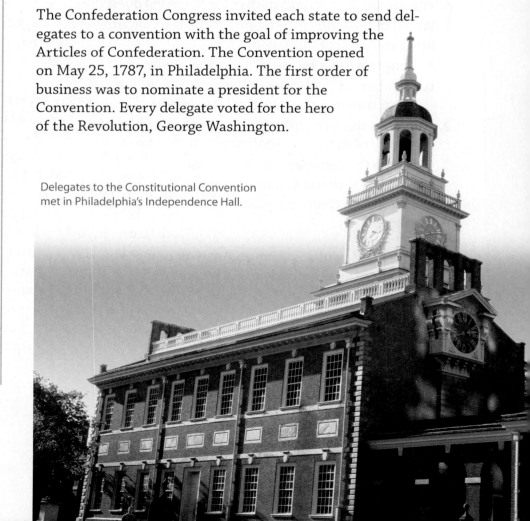

Delegates to the Constitutional Convention met in Philadelphia's Independence Hall.

The 55 delegates to the **Constitutional Convention**, as the Philadelphia meeting became known, were a very impressive group. Many had been members of their state legislatures and had helped write their state constitutions. Roger Sherman, a Connecticut delegate, was a signer of the Declaration of Independence and the Articles of Confederation. Pennsylvania's Gouverneur Morris had also signed the Articles of Confederation. Pennsylvania delegate James Wilson was known for his brilliant legal mind. Virginia delegate **James Madison** contributed many ideas that shaped the Constitution.

Some key people did not attend. Thomas Jefferson and John Adams were overseas at their diplomatic posts. Others had political objections. For example, Patrick Henry, who had been elected as a delegate from Virginia, refused to go. He said he "smelled a rat . . . tending toward monarchy."

Also, the Convention did not reflect the diverse U.S. population of the 1780s. There were no Native Americans, African Americans, or women among the delegates. These groups of people were not recognized as citizens and were not invited to attend.

Reading Check
Summarize Why did the Confederation Congress call for the Constitutional Convention?

Great Compromise

By 1787, many Americans realized that the nation needed a government that could keep order. They wanted a government that was strong enough to protect individual rights but not so strong that it would oppress them.

As the Convention began, the delegates disagreed about what form the new government would take. Edmund Randolph of Virginia presented the **Virginia Plan**. He proposed a new federal constitution that would give supreme power to the central government. The legislature would be made up of two houses of representatives. States with larger populations would have more representatives than would smaller states. Delegates from the small states feared that this plan would give large states too much power.

New Jersey delegate William Paterson presented an alternative plan. The **New Jersey Plan** called for a one-house legislature. According to this plan, each state would have an equal number of votes in the federal government. The plan gave the federal government the power to tax citizens, and it allowed the government to regulate commerce.

The delegates struggled to solve the problem of representation in the legislature. In early July, a committee led by Roger Sherman and other delegates from Connecticut offered a deal known as the **Great Compromise**. The legislative branch would have two houses. To satisfy the smaller states, each state would have an equal number of votes in the Senate. To satisfy the larger states, representation in the House of Representatives was set according to state populations.

Connecticut delegate Roger Sherman proposed the Great Compromise on June 30, 1787. The compromise combined features of the Virginia and New Jersey plans.

Reading Check
Describe What were the major challenges at the Convention in creating a stronger national government?

Compromises on Slavery

Because representation in the House of Representatives would be based on the population of each state, the delegates had to decide who would be counted in that population.

Compromise and the Slave Trade

The issue of slavery highlighted the growing division between the North and the South. Gouverneur Morris, representing Pennsylvania, spoke with much emotion against the Three-Fifths Compromise. Also, the idea of banning the foreign slave trade prompted southerners such as John Rutledge of South Carolina to defend the practice.

"If the Convention thinks that North Carolina, South Carolina, and Georgia will ever agree to the plan [to prohibit the slave trade], unless their right to import slaves be untouched, the expectation is vain [useless]."

—John Rutledge, quoted in *The Atlantic Monthly,* February 1891, by Frank Gaylord Cook

"The admission of slaves into the Representation . . . comes to this: that the inhabitant of [a state] who goes to the coast of Africa and . . . tears away his fellow creatures from their dearest connections and damns them to the most cruel bondage [slavery], shall have more votes in a Government [established] for protection of the rights of mankind."

—Gouverneur Morris, quoted in *The Constitution: A Pro-Slavery Compact,* edited by Wendell Phillips

Analyze Historical Sources
How did these two views of slavery differ?

Representation based on population raised the question of whether slaves should be counted as people. The southern states had many more slaves than the northern states. Southerners wanted the slaves to be counted as part of the population for representation but not for taxation. Northerners, whose states had few slaves, argued that slaves were not citizens and should not be counted for representation but should be counted for taxation.

The delegates reached an agreement, known as the **Three-Fifths Compromise**. Three-fifths of the slave population would be counted for both purposes: representation in the legislature and taxation.

The delegates had another point of disagreement. Some of the delegates believed slavery was wrong and wanted the federal government to ban the slave trade. Others said that the southern states' economies needed the slave trade. The delegates from South Carolina and Georgia stated that they would never accept any plan "unless their right to import slaves be untouched." Again, the delegates settled on a compromise. On August 29, they agreed that Congress could not ban the slave trade until 1808.

Reading Check
Analyze Point of View How did the Constitutional Convention compromise on the issue of slavery?

A New System of Government

Most Convention delegates wanted a strong national government. At the same time, they hoped to protect **popular sovereignty**, the idea that political authority belongs to the people. Americans had boldly declared this idea in the Declaration of Independence.

The framers of the Constitution divided the national government into three branches. The **legislative branch** is responsible for proposing and passing laws. It is made up of the Senate and the House of Representatives. The **executive branch** includes the president and the departments that help run the government. The executive branch makes sure that laws are carried out. The **judicial branch** is made up of all the national courts. This branch interprets laws, punishes criminals, and settles disputes between states.

The Constitution also includes a system of **checks and balances**, which keeps any branch of the government from becoming too powerful. For example, Congress has the power to pass bills into law. The president has the power to veto laws that Congress passes. Congress can then override the president's veto with a two-thirds majority vote. The Supreme Court has the power to review laws passed by Congress and strike down any laws that violate the Constitution.

To balance the power between the national and state governments, the delegates created the system of **federalism**. Federalism is the sharing of power between a central government and the states that make up a country. The Constitution requires each state to obey the authority of the federal, or national, government. States have control over government functions not specifically assigned to the federal government.

The framers of the Constitution also included a method for changing or adding to the Constitution. They wanted the government to be able to adapt as changes were needed. The process for amending, or adding **amendments** to, the Constitution was made difficult. Major changes to the government would require the approval of two-thirds of each house of Congress and three-fourths of states before it could take effect.

On September 17, 1787, the delegates passed the Constitution. All but three of the 42 delegates present signed the Constitution. Even though the Constitution was adopted by the Convention, delegates continued to debate the power of state governments and the role of each branch of the national government.

Federalists and Antifederalists

The framers of the Constitution knew that the document would cause controversy. At once they began to campaign for ratification, or approval, of the Constitution.

Concerns of the Federalists The framers suspected that people might be afraid that the Constitution would take too much power away from the states. To address this fear, the framers explained that the Constitution was based on federalism. Linking themselves to the idea of federalism, the people who supported the Constitution took the name **Federalists**.

The legislative branch consists of the Senate and the House of Representatives. Members of both bodies meet at the U.S. Capitol in Washington, DC, to discuss, debate, and craft national policies and laws.

Reading Check
Explain How did the concept of popular sovereignty influence the new system of government?

The Federalists promoted their views and answered their critics in a series of essays known as the ***Federalist Papers***. Three well-known politicians wrote the *Federalist Papers*—James Madison, Alexander Hamilton, and John Jay. These essays first appeared as letters in New York newspapers. Calling for ratification of the Constitution, the *Federalist Papers* appealed both to reason and emotion.

Concerns of the Antifederalists The **Antifederalists**, people who opposed the Constitution, thought the Constitution took too much power away from the states and did not guarantee rights for the people. Some feared that a strong president might be declared king. Others feared the Senate might become a powerful ruling class. In either case, they thought, the liberties fiercely won during the Revolution might be lost.

Antifederalists received support from rural areas, where people feared a strong government that might add to their tax burden. Large states and those with strong economies, such as New York, also were unsupportive of the Constitution at first.

Reading Check
Compare and Contrast Describe the disagreements between Federalists and Antifederalists.

Ratifying the Constitution

The proposed U.S. Constitution contained no guarantee that the government would protect the rights of the people or of the states. Some supporters of the Constitution, including Thomas Jefferson, wanted to add a bill of rights—a formal summary of citizens' rights and freedoms—as a set of amendments to the Constitution.

Ratification Process Antifederalists wanted written guarantees that the people would have their individual freedoms protected. In the end, Federalists yielded to the people's demands and promised to add a bill of rights if the states ratified the Constitution.

In December 1787, Delaware, New Jersey, and Pennsylvania voted for ratification. In January 1788, Georgia and Connecticut ratified the Constitution, followed by Massachusetts in early February. By late June, nine states had ratified. The Constitution was officially ratified with nine votes.

It was vital, however, to get the support of Virginia, the largest state. James Madison recommended that Virginia ratify the Constitution, with the addition of a bill of rights. After bitter debate, at the end of June, Virginia narrowly ratified the Constitution with 89 in favor and 79 opposed.

The news of Virginia's vote arrived while the New York convention was in debate. Until then, the Antifederalists had outnumbered the Federalists. But with Virginia's ratification, New Yorkers decided to join the Union. New York also called for a bill of rights. It would be another year before North Carolina ratified the Constitution, followed by Rhode Island in 1790. By then, the new Congress had already written a bill of rights and submitted it to the states for approval.

Bill of Rights Madison, who took office in the first Congress in the winter of 1789, took up the cause of the bill of rights. In September 1789 Congress

Virginian James Madison is often called the Father of the Constitution. He played a key role in writing the document, and then rallied support for its adoption along with the Bill of Rights.

proposed 12 amendments and sent them to the states for ratification. By December 1791 the states had ratified the **Bill of Rights**—ten of the proposed amendments intended to protect citizens' rights.

Of these amendments to the Constitution, the first nine guarantee basic individual freedoms, including freedom of religion, of speech, and of the press. Taken as a whole, the Bill of Rights creates an invisible but powerful shield that protects people from government abuse.

But the Bill of Rights was more than that. It was the first step in making the Constitution a living document, one that can be amended to reflect changes in society. The Constitutional Convention provided for such changes. Two-thirds of each house of Congress or two-thirds of the state legislatures can propose an amendment. To become law, an amendment then needs the approval of three-fourths of the states. By this process, the Bill of Rights became the first ten amendments.

Summary and Preview In this lesson you learned how the Constitution was created, developed, debated, and finally ratified. In the next lesson you will learn more details about the structure of the U.S. government.

Reading Check
Evaluate Explain how the lack of a bill of rights made ratification of the Constitution more difficult.

Lesson 1 Assessment

Review Ideas, Terms, and People

1. a. Summarize What was the purpose of the Constitutional Convention?

b. Describe Who attended the Constitutional Convention?

c. Explain Why did the Convention not reflect the diverse U.S. population at that time?

2. a. Contrast How did the Virginia Plan and New Jersey Plan differ?

b. Analyze Which plan appealed more to the smaller states? Explain why.

c. Summarize How did the Great Compromise resolve the issue over representation?

3. a. Recall Under the Three-Fifths Compromise, what was decided about how each state's population would be counted?

b. Describe Under what conditions did southern states agree to consider a ban on the slave trade?

c. Summarize What were the main points of disagreement on the issue of slavery?

4. a. Recall Why did the framers of the Constitution create the ability to add amendments?

b. Explain What is popular sovereignty?

c. Analyze What power did federalism give to state governments?

5. a. Recall How did Federalists get their name?

b. Summarize What arguments did the Antifederalists use to convince people to reject the Constitution?

c. Explain Why were the *Federalist Papers* important?

6. a. Recall When was the Constitution officially ratified?

b. Explain Why was the ratification of the Constitution in Virginia especially important?

c. Analyze Why did the Antifederalists demand the Bill of Rights?

Critical Thinking

7. Summarize In this lesson you learned how the Constitution was developed and established. Create a web diagram similar to the one below and use it to summarize the important achievements of the Constitution.

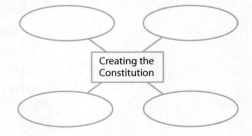

Creating the Constitution

Structure of the Government

The Big Idea

The U.S. Constitution balances the powers of the federal government among the legislative, executive, and judicial branches.

Main Ideas

- The framers of the Constitution devised the federal system.
- The legislative branch makes the nation's laws.
- The executive branch enforces the nation's laws.
- The judicial branch determines whether or not laws are constitutional.

Key Terms and People

federal system
impeach
veto
executive orders
pardons
Thurgood Marshall
Sandra Day O'Connor
Sonia Sotomayor

If YOU were there . . .

You have just been elected to the U.S. House of Representatives. You know that committees do much of the work in Congress. They deal with many different fields such as foreign policy, agriculture, national security, science, and education. You would like to ask for a spot on a committee whose work interests you.

Which committee would you ask to serve on?

The Federal System

The framers of the Constitution wanted to create a government powerful enough to protect the rights of citizens and defend the country against its enemies. To do so, they set up a **federal system** of government, a system that divides powers between the states and the federal government.

The Constitution assigns certain powers to the national government. These are called delegated powers. Among them are the right to coin and regulate money, regulate trade among the states and with other nations, make treaties with foreign nations, declare war, and make any laws necessary to carry out these powers. National powers are designed to promote the general welfare, or common good—the needs and interests of the people as a whole. For example, by regulating trade and developing a uniform monetary system, the government creates conditions that allow businesses throughout the nation to prosper.

Reserved powers are those kept by the states. These powers include creating local governments and holding elections. Concurrent powers are those shared by the federal and state governments. They include taxing, borrowing money, and enforcing laws.

Sometimes, Congress has had to stretch its delegated powers to deal with new or unexpected issues. A clause in the Constitution states that Congress may "make all

Compare Landmark Documents

Magna Carta (1215)

- set limits to the king's power
- guaranteed fair legal proceedings for all free English citizens

Declaration of Independence (1776)

- declared that citizens have natural rights that cannot be taken away
- argued that a government's power comes from the consent of the governed

Articles of Confederation (1777)

- created a democratic republic
- established a national government while preserving most state powers

U.S. Constitution (1787)

- created a federal system with a strong national government
- balanced power among three branches of the national government

Federalist Papers (1787–1788)

- defended the Constitution against critics
- explained how checks and balances and other features of the Constitution limited authority and preserved liberty

Bill of Rights (1789)

- guaranteed basic individual freedoms such as freedom of speech and the right to due process for all free Americans
- set an example of how to change the Constitution through amendments

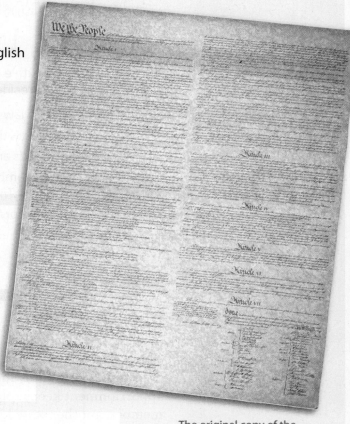

The original copy of the U.S. Constitution is housed in the National Archives in Washington, DC.

Reading Check
Summarize How is power divided between the federal and state governments?

Academic Vocabulary
distinct separate

Laws which shall be necessary and proper" for carrying out its duties. This clause, called the elastic clause—because it can be stretched (like elastic)—provides flexibility for the government. The federal government has used this clause to provide public services such as funding for the arts and humanities.

Legislative Branch

The federal government has three branches, each with <u>distinct</u> responsibilities and powers. This separation balances the branches and keeps any one of them from growing too powerful. The first branch of government

Separation of Powers

U.S. Constitution

Legislative Branch (Congress)

- Writes the laws
- Confirms presidential appointments
- Approves treaties
- Grants money
- Declares war

Executive Branch (President)

- Proposes laws
- Administers the laws
- Commands armed forces
- Appoints ambassadors and other officials
- Conducts foreign policy
- Makes treaties

Judicial Branch (Supreme Court)

- Interprets the Constitution and other laws
- Reviews lower-court decisions

is the legislative branch, or Congress. The legislators elected to Congress make the nation's laws. Article I of the Constitution divides Congress into the House of Representatives and the Senate.

With 435 members, the House of Representatives is the larger congressional house. The U.S. Census, a population count made every ten years, determines how many members represent each state. A system called apportionment keeps total membership at 435. If one state gains a member, another state loses one. Members must be at least 25 years old, live in the state where they were elected, and have been U.S. citizens for seven years. They serve two-year terms.

The Senate has two members, or senators, per state. Senators represent the interests of the whole state, not just a district. They must be at least 30 years old, have been U.S. citizens for nine years, and live in the state they represent. They serve six-year terms. The senior senator of a state is the one who has served the longer of the two. Members of Congress can serve an unlimited number of terms in office.

The political party with more members in each house is the majority party. The one with fewer members is the minority party. The leader of the House of Representatives, or Speaker of the House, is elected by House members from the majority party.

The U.S. vice president serves as president of the Senate. He takes no part in Senate debates but can vote to break ties. If the vice president is absent, the president pro tempore (pro tem for short) leads the Senate. There is no law for how the Senate must choose this position, but it traditionally goes to the majority party's senator who has served the longest.

Congress begins sessions, or meetings, each year in the first week of January. Both houses do most of their work in committees. Each committee studies certain types of bills, or suggested laws. For example, all bills about taxes begin in the House Ways and Means Committee.

Reading Check
Compare and Contrast What are the similarities in requirements for members of the House of Representatives and the Senate? What are the differences?

Executive Branch

Article II of the Constitution lists the powers of the executive branch. This branch enforces the laws passed by Congress.

President and Vice President As head of the executive branch, the president is the most powerful elected leader in the United States. To qualify for the presidency or vice presidency, one must be a native-born U.S. citizen at least 35 years old. The president must also have been a U.S. resident for 14 years.

Americans elect a president and vice president every four years. Franklin D. Roosevelt, who won four times, was the only president to serve more than two terms. Now, the Twenty-Second Amendment limits presidents to two terms. If a president dies, resigns, or is removed from office, the vice president becomes president for the rest of the term.

The House of Representatives can **impeach**, or vote to bring charges of serious crimes against, a president. Impeachment cases are tried in the Senate. If a president is found guilty, Congress can remove him from office. In 1868 Andrew Johnson was the first president to be impeached. President Bill Clinton was impeached in 1998. However, in each instance, the Senate found the president not guilty.

Quick Facts

Checks and Balances

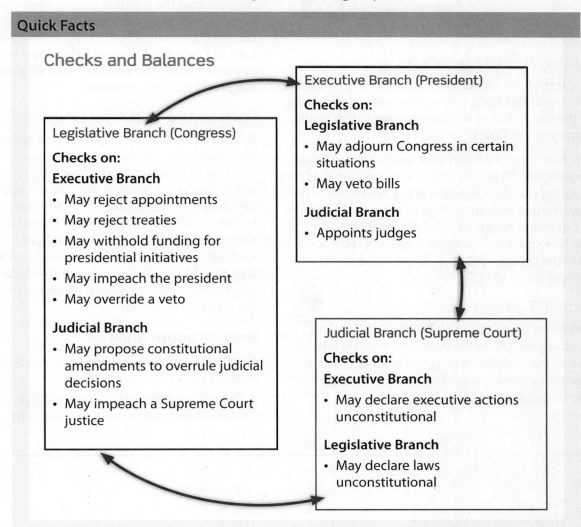

Legislative Branch (Congress)

Checks on:

Executive Branch
- May reject appointments
- May reject treaties
- May withhold funding for presidential initiatives
- May impeach the president
- May override a veto

Judicial Branch
- May propose constitutional amendments to overrule judicial decisions
- May impeach a Supreme Court justice

Executive Branch (President)

Checks on:

Legislative Branch
- May adjourn Congress in certain situations
- May veto bills

Judicial Branch
- Appoints judges

Judicial Branch (Supreme Court)

Checks on:

Executive Branch
- May declare executive actions unconstitutional

Legislative Branch
- May declare laws unconstitutional

Working with Congress The president and Congress are often on different sides of an issue. However, they must still work together.

Congress passes laws. The president, however, can ask Congress to pass or reject bills. The president also can **veto**, or cancel, laws Congress has passed. Congress can try to override, or undo, the veto. However, this is difficult since it takes a two-thirds majority vote. To carry out laws affecting the Constitution, treaties, and statutes, the president issues **executive orders**. These commands have the power of law. The president also may grant **pardons**, or freedom from punishment, to persons convicted of federal crimes or facing criminal charges.

SUPREME COURT DECISIONS

Background of the Court

The rest of the Supreme Court Decisions features you see in this book will highlight important cases of the Court. But in this first one, we'll discuss the history of the Court.

The first Supreme Court met in 1790 at the Royal Exchange in New York City. The ground floor of this building was an open-air market. When the national government moved to Philadelphia, the Court met in basement rooms in Independence Hall. Once in Washington, the Court heard cases in the Capitol until the present Supreme Court building was completed in 1932.

Circuit Riding

Today the Supreme Court holds court only in Washington, DC. In the past, however, the justices had to travel through assigned circuits, hearing cases together with a district judge in a practice known as circuit riding.

The justices complained bitterly about the inconvenience of travel, which was often over unpaved roads and in bad weather. This system was not just inconvenient to the justices, however. Some people worried about the fairness of a system that required justices who had heard cases at trial to rule on them again on appeal. Other people, however, thought that the practice helped keep the justices in touch with the needs and feelings of the average citizen. Eventually, circuit riding interfered so much with the increased amount of business of the Supreme Court that Congress passed a law ending the practice in the late 1800s.

Path to the Supreme Court

When a case is decided by a state or federal court, the losing side may have a chance to appeal the decision to a higher court. Under the federal system, this higher court is called the court of appeals. A person who loses in that court may then appeal to the Supreme Court to review the case. But the Supreme Court does not have to accept all appeals. It usually chooses to hear only cases in which there is an important legal principle to be decided or if two federal courts of appeals disagree on how an issue should be decided.

Analyze Information

1. What are two reasons why the practice of circuit riding ended?

2. Why do you think the Supreme Court does not hear every case that is appealed to it?

The president also commands the armed forces. In emergencies, the president can call on U.S. troops. Only Congress, however, can declare war. Other executive duties include conducting foreign relations and creating treaties.

Executive departments do most of the executive branch work. As of 2014 there were 15 such departments. The president chooses department heads, who are called secretaries, and the Senate approves them. The heads make up the cabinet, which advises the president. The Office of Homeland Security was established in 2002 to address the increased threat of terrorism following September 11, 2001. In 2003 the office became the Department of Homeland Security, the newest executive department.

Reading Check
Analyze How does the veto help balance power between the president and Congress?

Judicial Branch

The third branch of government, the judicial branch, is made up of a system of federal courts headed by the U.S. Supreme Court. The Constitution created the Supreme Court, but the Judiciary Act of 1789 created the system of lower district and circuit courts.

Article III generally outlines the courts' duties. Federal courts can strike down a state or federal law if the court finds a law unconstitutional. Congress can then try to revise the law to make it constitutional.

District Courts The president makes appointments to federal courts. In an effort to keep federal judges free of party influence, the judges are given life appointments. The lower federal courts are divided according to cases over which they have jurisdiction, or authority. Each state has at least one of the 94 district courts.

Courts of Appeals If someone convicted of a crime believes the trial was unfair, he or she may take the case to the court of appeals. There are 13 courts of appeals. Each has a panel of judges to decide if cases heard in the lower courts were tried appropriately. If the judges uphold, or accept, the original decision, the original outcome stands. Otherwise, the case may be retried in the lower court.

Supreme Court After a case is decided by the court of appeals, the losing side may appeal the decision to the Supreme Court. Thousands of cases go to the Supreme Court yearly in the hope of a hearing, but the Court has time to hear only about 100. Generally, the cases heard involve important constitutional or public-interest issues. If the Court declines to hear a case, the court of appeals decision is final.

Nine justices sit on the Supreme Court. The chief justice of the United States leads the Court. Unlike the president and members of Congress, there are no specific constitutional requirements for becoming a justice.

Sonia Sotomayor is the first Hispanic American and the third woman to serve on the Supreme Court.

In recent decades, the Supreme Court has become more diverse. In 1967 **Thurgood Marshall** became the first African American justice. **Sandra Day O'Connor** became the first female Court justice after her 1981 appointment by President Ronald Reagan. In 2009 President Barack Obama appointed the first Hispanic American justice, **Sonia Sotomayor**.

Summary and Preview In this lesson you learned about the balance between the different branches of the federal government. In the next lesson you will learn about the Bill of Rights.

Reading Check
Summarize
Describe the structure and responsibilities of the judicial branch.

As a lawyer, Thurgood Marshall challenged racial discrimination in the courts, arguing thirty-two cases before the Supreme Court. In 1967, he became the Court's first African American justice.

Lesson 2 Assessment

Review Ideas, Terms, and People

1. **a. Describe** What type of government did the Constitution establish for the United States?

   b. Contrast What is the difference between delegated, reserved, and concurrent (shared) powers?

   c. Draw Conclusions In what circumstances are national laws and rules better suited for promoting the common good than laws and rules of individual states?

2. **a. Compare and Contrast** In what ways are the Senate and the House of Representatives similar and different?

   b. Elaborate Why do you think the requirements for serving in the Senate are stricter than those for serving in the House of Representatives?

   c. Evaluate How important is the role of legislator in a representative democracy? Explain.

3. **a. Describe** What powers are granted to the president?

   b. Make Generalizations Why is it important that the president and Congress work together in resolving governmental issues?

   c. Evaluate What do you think is the most important power granted to the president? Why?

4. **a. Explain** What is the main power of the judicial branch?

   b. Summarize What are the roles of the different levels in the federal court system?

   c. Evaluate Which branch of government do you feel is most important? Explain your answer.

Critical Thinking

5. **Categorize** In this lesson you learned about the branches of government. Create a web diagram similar to the one below and use it to show two powers of each branch of government.

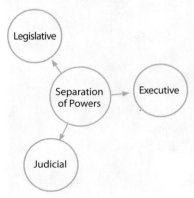

The Constitution of the United States

Preamble

The preamble states the main purposes of the new government under the Constitution. The government will strengthen the relationship between the states, create a fair legal system, maintain order within the country, defend the nation against foreign enemies, promote the public's well-being, and protect individual liberties. The phrase "We the People" emphasizes that the government's power and legitimacy come from the American people as a whole, not from the individual states.

We the People of the United States, in Order to form a more perfect Union, establish Justice, insure domestic Tranquility, provide for the common defence, promote the general Welfare, and secure the Blessings of Liberty to ourselves and our Posterity, do ordain and establish this Constitution for the United States of America.

Note: The parts of the Constitution that have been lined through are no longer in force or no longer apply because of later amendments. The titles of the sections and articles are added for easier reference.

Legislative Branch Article I explains how the legislative branch, called Congress, is organized. The chief purpose of the legislative branch is to make laws. Congress is made up of the Senate and the House of Representatives.

The House of Representatives The number of members each state has in the House is based on the population of the individual state. In 1929 Congress permanently fixed the size of the House at 435 members.

Vocabulary

[1] **those bound to Service** indentured servants

[2] **all other Persons** slaves

[3] **Enumeration** census or official population count

ARTICLE I THE LEGISLATURE

Section 1. Congress

All legislative Powers herein granted shall be vested in a Congress of the United States, which shall consist of a Senate and House of Representatives.

Section 2. The House of Representatives

1. Elections The House of Representatives shall be composed of Members chosen every second Year by the People of the several States, and the Electors in each State shall have the Qualifications requisite for Electors of the most numerous Branch of the State Legislature.

2. Qualifications No Person shall be a Representative who shall not have attained to the Age of twenty five Years, and been seven Years a Citizen of the United States, and who shall not, when elected, be an Inhabitant of that State in which he shall be chosen.

3. Number of Representatives Representatives and direct Taxes shall be apportioned among the several States which may be included within this Union, according to their respective Numbers, which shall be determined by adding to the whole Number of free Persons, including **those bound to Service**[1] for a Term of Years, and excluding Indians not taxed, three fifths of **all other Persons**.[2] The actual **Enumeration**[3] shall be made within three Years after the first Meeting of the Congress of the United States, and within every subsequent Term of ten Years, in such Manner as they shall by Law direct. The Number of Representatives shall not exceed one for every thirty Thousand, but each State shall have at Least one Representative; and until such enumeration shall be made, the State of New Hampshire shall be entitled to choose three, Massachusetts eight, Rhode Island and Providence Plantations one, Connecticut five, New York six, New Jersey four, Pennsylvania eight, Delaware one, Maryland six, Virginia ten, North Carolina five, South Carolina five, and Georgia three.

4. Vacancies When vacancies happen in the Representation from any State, the Executive Authority thereof shall issue Writs of Election to fill such Vacancies.

5. Officers and Impeachment The House of Representatives shall choose their Speaker and other Officers; and shall have the sole Power of impeachment.

Section 3. The Senate

1. Number of Senators The Senate of the United States shall be composed of two Senators from each State, chosen by the Legislature thereof, for six Years; and each Senator shall have one Vote.

2. Classifying Terms Immediately after they shall be assembled in Consequence of the first Election, they shall be divided as equally as may be into three Classes. The Seats of the Senators of the first Class shall be vacated at the Expiration of the second Year, of second Class at the Expiration of the fourth Year, and of the third Class at the Expiration of the sixth Year, so that one third may be chosen every second Year; ~~and if Vacancies happen by Resignation, or otherwise, during the Recess of the Legislature of any State, the Executive thereof may make temporary Appointments until the next Meeting of the Legislature, which shall then fill such Vacancies.~~

3. Qualifications No Person shall be a Senator who shall not have attained to the Age of thirty Years, and been nine Years a Citizen of the United States, and who shall not, when elected, be an Inhabitant of that State for which he shall be chosen.

4. Role of Vice President The Vice President of the United States shall be President of the Senate, but shall have no Vote, unless they be equally divided.

5. Officers The Senate shall choose their other Officers, and also a President **pro tempore**,[4] in the Absence of the Vice President, or when he shall exercise the Office of President of the United States.

6. Impeachment Trials The Senate shall have the sole Power to try all **Impeachments**.[5] When sitting for that Purpose, they shall be on Oath or Affirmation. When the President of the United States is tried, the Chief Justice shall preside: And no Person shall be convicted without the Concurrence of two thirds of the Members present.

7. Punishment for Impeachment Judgment in Cases of Impeachment shall not extend further than to removal from Office, and disqualification to hold and enjoy any Office of honor, Trust or Profit under the United States: but the Party convicted shall nevertheless be liable and subject to Indictment, Trial, Judgment and Punishment, according to Law.

Quick Facts

Federal Office Terms and Requirements

Position	Term	Minimum Age	Residency	Citizenship
President	4 years	35	14 years in the U.S.	natural-born
Vice President	4 years	35	14 years in the U.S.	natural-born
Supreme Court Justice	unlimited	none	none	none
Senator	6 years	30	state in which elected	9 years
Representative	2 years	25	state in which elected	7 years

Section 4. Congressional Elections

1. Regulations The Times, Places and Manner of holding Elections for Senators and Representatives, shall be prescribed in each State by the Legislature thereof; but the Congress may at any time by Law make or alter such Regulations, except as to the Places of choosing Senators.

2. Sessions ~~The Congress shall assemble at least once in every Year, and such Meeting shall be on the first Monday in December, unless they shall by Law appoint a different Day.~~

Section 5. Rules/Procedures

1. Quorum Each House shall be the Judge of the Elections, Returns and Qualifications of its own Members, and a Majority of each shall constitute a **Quorum**[6] to do Business; but a smaller Number may **adjourn**[7] from day to day, and may be authorized to compel the Attendance of absent Members, in such Manner, and under such Penalties as each House may provide.

2. Rules and Conduct Each House may determine the Rules of its Proceedings, punish its Members for disorderly Behaviour, and, with the Concurrence of two thirds, expel a Member.

3. Records Each House shall keep a Journal of its Proceedings, and from time to time publish the same, excepting such Parts as may in their Judgment require Secrecy; and the Yeas and Nays of the Members of either House on any question shall, at the Desire of one fifth of those Present, be entered on the Journal.

4. Adjournment Neither House, during the Session of Congress, shall, without the Consent of the other, adjourn for more than three days, nor to any other Place than that in which the two Houses shall be sitting.

Section 6. Payment

1. Salary The Senators and Representatives shall receive a Compensation for their Services, to be ascertained by Law, and paid out of the Treasury of the United States. They shall in all Cases, except Treason, Felony and Breach of the Peace, be privileged from Arrest during their Attendance at the Session of their respective Houses, and in going to and returning from the same; and for any Speech or Debate in either House, they shall not be questioned in any other Place.

2. Restrictions No Senator or Representative shall, during the Time for which he was elected, be appointed to any civil Office under the Authority of the United States, which shall have been created, or the **Emoluments**[8] whereof shall have been increased during such time; and no Person holding any Office under the United States, shall be a Member of either House during his **Continuance**[9] in Office.

Section 7. How a Bill Becomes a Law

EXPLORE THE DOCUMENT
The framers felt that because members of the House are elected every two years, representatives would listen to the public and seek its approval before passing taxes. *How does Section 7 address the colonial demand of "no taxation without representation"?*

1. Tax Bills All **Bills**[10] for raising Revenue shall originate in the House of Representatives; but the Senate may propose or concur with Amendments as on other Bills.

2. Lawmaking Every Bill which shall have passed the House of Representatives and the Senate, shall, before it become a Law, be presented to the President of the United States: If he approve he shall sign it, but if not he shall return it, with his Objections to that House in which it shall have originated, who shall enter the Objections at large on their Journal, and proceed to reconsider it. If after such Reconsideration two thirds of that House shall agree to pass the Bill, it shall be sent, together with the Objections, to the other House, by which it shall likewise be reconsidered, and if approved by two thirds of that House, it shall become a Law. But in all such Cases the Votes of both Houses shall be determined by Yeas and Nays, and the Names of the Persons voting for and against the Bill shall be entered on the Journal of each House respectively. If any Bill shall not be returned

How a Bill Becomes a Law

❶ A member of the House or the Senate introduces a bill and refers it to a committee.

❷ The House or Senate Committee may approve, rewrite, or kill the bill.

❸ The House or the Senate debates and votes on its version of the bill.

❹ House and Senate conference committee members work out the differences between the two versions.

❺ Both houses of Congress pass the revised bill.

❻ The president signs or vetoes the bill.

❼ Two-thirds majority vote of Congress is needed to approve a vetoed bill. Bill becomes a law.

Analyze Information
Why do you think the framers created this complex system for adopting laws?

by the President within ten Days (Sundays excepted) after it shall have been presented to him, the Same shall be a Law, in like Manner as if he had signed it, unless the Congress by their Adjournment prevent its Return, in which Case it shall not be a Law.

3. Role of the President Every Order, Resolution, or Vote to which the Concurrence of the Senate and House of Representatives may be necessary (except on a question of Adjournment) shall be presented to the President of the United States; and before the Same shall take Effect, shall be approved by him, or being disapproved by him, shall be repassed by two thirds of the Senate and House of Representatives, according to the Rules and Limitations prescribed in the Case of a Bill.

Section 8. Powers Granted to Congress

1. Taxation The Congress shall have Power To lay and collect Taxes, **Duties**,[11] **Imposts**[12] and **Excises**,[13] to pay the Debts and provide for the common Defense and general Welfare of the United States; but all Duties, Imposts and Excises shall be uniform throughout the United States;

2. Credit To borrow Money on the credit of the United States;

3. Commerce To regulate Commerce with foreign Nations, and among the several States, and with the Indian Tribes;

4. Naturalization and Bankruptcy To establish an uniform **Rule of Naturalization**,[14] and uniform Laws on the subject of Bankruptcies throughout the United States;

5. Money To coin Money, regulate the Value thereof, and of foreign Coin, and fix the Standard of Weights and Measures;

6. Counterfeiting To provide for the Punishment of counterfeiting the **Securities**[15] and current Coin of the United States;

7. Post Office To establish Post Offices and post Roads;

EXPLORE THE DOCUMENT
The veto power of the president is one of the important checks and balances in the Constitution. *Why do you think the framers included the ability of Congress to override a veto?*

Vocabulary

[11] **Duties** tariffs

[12] **Imposts** taxes

[13] **Excises** internal taxes on the manufacture, sale, or consumption of a commodity

[14] **Rule of Naturalization** a law by which a foreign-born person becomes a citizen

[15] **Securities** bonds

Link to Today

Native Americans and the Commerce Clause

The commerce clause gives Congress the power to "regulate Commerce with . . . the Indian Tribes." The clause has been interpreted to mean that the states cannot tax or interfere with businesses on Indian reservations, but that the federal government can. It also allows American Indian nations to develop their own governments and laws. These laws, however, can be challenged in federal court. Although reservation land usually belongs to the government of the Indian group, it is administered by the U.S. government.

Draw Conclusions
How would you describe the status of American Indian nations under the commerce clause?

8. Patents and Copyrights To promote the Progress of Science and useful Arts, by securing for limited Times to Authors and Inventors the exclusive Right to their respective Writings and Discoveries;

9. Courts To constitute Tribunals inferior to the supreme Court;

10. International Law To define and punish Piracies and Felonies committed on the high Seas, and Offences against the Law of Nations;

11. War To declare War, grant **Letters of Marque and Reprisal**,[16] and make Rules concerning Captures on Land and Water;

12. Army To raise and support Armies, but no Appropriation of Money to that Use shall be for a longer Term than two Years;

13. Navy To provide and maintain a Navy;

14. Regulation of the Military To make Rules for the Government and Regulation of the land and naval Forces;

15. Militia To provide for calling forth the Militia to execute the Laws of the Union, suppress Insurrections and repel Invasions;

16. Regulation of the Militia To provide for organizing, arming, and disciplining, the Militia, and for governing such Part of them as may be employed in the Service of the United States, reserving to the States respectively, the Appointment of the Officers, and the Authority of training the Militia according to the discipline prescribed by Congress;

17. District of Columbia To exercise exclusive Legislation in all Cases whatsoever, over such District (not exceeding ten Miles square) as may, by Cession of particular States, and the Acceptance of Congress, become the Seat of the Government of the United States, and to exercise like Authority over all Places purchased by the Consent of the Legislature of the State in which the Same shall be, for the Erection of Forts, Magazines, Arsenals, dock-Yards, and other needful Buildings;—And

18. Necessary and Proper Clause To make all Laws which shall be necessary and proper for carrying into Execution the foregoing Powers, and all other Powers vested by this Constitution in the Government of the United States, or in any Department or Officer thereof.

Section 9. Powers Denied Congress

1. Slave Trade ~~The Migration or Importation of such Persons as any of the States now existing shall think proper to admit, shall not be prohibited by the Congress prior to the Year one thousand eight hundred and eight, but a Tax or duty may be imposed on such Importation, not exceeding ten dollars for each Person.~~

2. Habeas Corpus The Privilege of the **Writ of Habeas Corpus**[17] shall not be suspended, unless when in Cases of Rebellion or Invasion the public Safety may require it.

3. Illegal Punishment No **Bill of Attainder**[18] or **ex post facto Law**[19] shall be passed.

4. Direct Taxes No **Capitation**,[20] or other direct, Tax shall be laid, unless in Proportion to the Census or enumeration herein before directed to be taken.

5. Export Taxes No Tax or Duty shall be laid on Articles exported from any State.

6. No Favorites No Preference shall be given by any Regulation of Commerce or Revenue to the Ports of one State over those of another; nor shall Vessels bound to, or from, one State, be obliged to enter, clear, or pay Duties in another.

7. Public Money No Money shall be drawn from the Treasury, but in Consequence of Appropriations made by Law; and a regular Statement and Account of the Receipts and Expenditures of all public Money shall be published from time to time.

8. Titles of Nobility No Title of Nobility shall be granted by the United States: And no Person holding any Office of Profit or Trust under them, shall, without the Consent of the Congress, accept of any present, Emolument, Office, or Title, of any kind whatever, from any King, Prince, or foreign State.

Section 10. Powers Denied the States

1. Restrictions No State shall enter into any Treaty, Alliance, or Confederation; grant Letters of Marque and Reprisal; coin Money; emit Bills of Credit; make any Thing but gold and silver Coin a Tender in Payment of Debts; pass any Bill of Attainder, ex post facto Law, or Law impairing the Obligation of Contracts, or grant any Title of Nobility.

2. Import and Export Taxes No State shall, without the Consent of the Congress, lay any Imposts or Duties on Imports or Exports, except what may be absolutely necessary for executing it's inspection Laws: and the net Produce of all Duties and Imposts, laid by any State on Imports or Exports, shall be for the Use of the Treasury of the United States; and all such Laws shall be subject to the Revision and Control of the Congress.

Executive Branch The president is the chief of the executive branch. It is the job of the president to enforce the laws. The framers wanted the president's and vice president's terms of office and manner of selection to be different from those of members of Congress. They decided on four-year terms, but they had a difficult time agreeing on how to select the president and vice president. The framers finally set up an electoral system, which varies greatly from our electoral process today.

Presidential Elections In 1845 Congress set the Tuesday following the first Monday in November of every fourth year as the general election date for selecting presidential electors.

3. Peacetime and War Restraints No State shall, without the Consent of Congress, lay any Duty of Tonnage, keep Troops, or Ships of War in time of Peace, enter into any Agreement or Compact with another State, or with a foreign Power, or engage in War, unless actually invaded, or in such imminent Danger as will not admit of delay.

ARTICLE II. THE EXECUTIVE

Section 1. The Presidency

1. Terms of Office The executive Power shall be vested in a President of the United States of America. He shall hold his Office during the Term of four Years, and, together with the Vice President, chosen for the same Term, be elected, as follows:

2. Electoral College Each State shall appoint, in such Manner as the Legislature thereof may direct, a Number of Electors, equal to the whole Number of Senators and Representatives to which the State may be entitled in the Congress: but no Senator or Representative, or Person holding an Office of Trust or Profit under the United States, shall be appointed an Elector.

3. Former Method of Electing President ~~The Electors shall meet in their respective States, and vote by Ballot for two Persons, of whom one at least shall not be an Inhabitant of the same State with themselves. And they shall make a List of all the Persons voted for, and of the Number~~

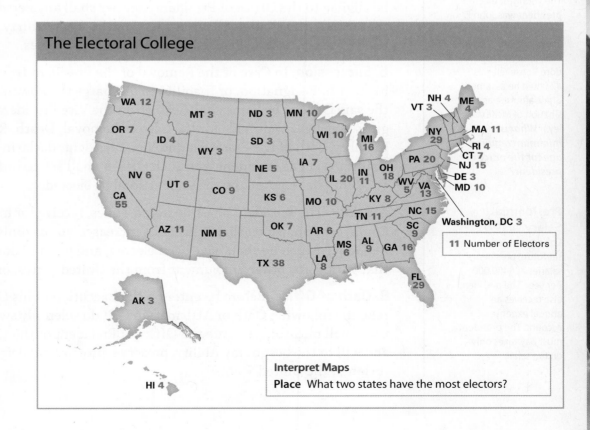

The Electoral College

Interpret Maps
Place What two states have the most electors?

of Votes for each; which List they shall sign and certify, and transmit sealed to the Seat of the Government of the United States, directed to the President of the Senate. The President of the Senate shall, in the Presence of the Senate and House of Representatives, open all the Certificates, and the Votes shall then be counted. The Person having the greatest Number of Votes shall be the President, if such Number be a Majority of the whole Number of Electors appointed; and if there be more than one who have such Majority, and have an equal Number of Votes, then the House of Representatives shall immediately choose by Ballot one of them for President; and if no Person have a Majority, then from the five highest on the List the said House shall in like Manner choose the President. But in choosing the President, the Votes shall be taken by States, the Representation from each State having one Vote; A quorum for this purpose shall consist of a Member or Members from two thirds of the States, and a Majority of all the States shall be necessary to a Choice. In every Case, after the Choice of the President, the Person having the greatest Number of Votes of the Electors shall be the Vice President. But if there should remain two or more who have equal Votes, the Senate shall choose from them by Ballot the Vice President.

4. Election Day The Congress may determine the Time of choosing the Electors, and the Day on which they shall give their Votes; which Day shall be the same throughout the United States.

5. Qualifications No Person except a natural born Citizen, or a Citizen of the United States, at the time of the Adoption of this Constitution, shall be eligible to the Office of President; neither shall any Person be eligible to that Office who shall not have attained to the Age of thirty five Years, and been fourteen Years a Resident within the United States.

6. Succession In Case of the Removal of the President from Office, or of his Death, Resignation, or Inability to discharge the Powers and Duties of the said Office, the Same shall devolve on the Vice President, and the Congress may by Law provide for the Case of Removal, Death, Resignation or Inability, both of the President and Vice President, declaring what Officer shall then act as President, and such Officer shall act accordingly, until the Disability be removed, or a President shall be elected.

7. Salary The President shall, at stated Times, receive for his Services, a Compensation, which shall neither be increased nor diminished during the Period for which he shall have been elected, and he shall not receive within that Period any other Emolument from the United States, or any of them.

8. Oath of Office Before he enter on the Execution of his Office, he shall take the following Oath or Affirmation:—"I do solemnly swear (or affirm) that I will faithfully execute the Office of President of the United States, and will to the best of my Ability, preserve, protect and defend the Constitution of the United States."

EXPLORE THE DOCUMENT

The youngest elected president was John F. Kennedy; he was 43 years old when he was inaugurated. (Theodore Roosevelt was 42 when he assumed office after the assassination of McKinley.) *What is the minimum required age for the office of president?*

Presidential Salary In 1999 Congress voted to set future presidents' salaries at $400,000 per year. The president also receives an annual expense account. The president must pay taxes only on the salary.

Section 2. Powers of Presidency

1. Military Powers The President shall be Commander in Chief of the Army and Navy of the United States, and of the Militia of the several States, when called into the actual Service of the United States; he may require the Opinion, in writing, of the principal Officer in each of the executive Departments, upon any Subject relating to the Duties of their respective Offices, and he shall have Power to grant **Reprieves**[21] and **Pardons**[22] for Offences against the United States, except in Cases of Impeachment.

2. Treaties and Appointments He shall have Power, by and with the Advice and Consent of the Senate, to make Treaties, provided two thirds of the Senators present concur; and he shall nominate, and by and with the Advice and Consent of the Senate, shall appoint Ambassadors, other public Ministers and Consuls, Judges of the supreme Court, and all other Officers of the United States, whose Appointments are not herein otherwise provided for, and which shall be established by Law: but the Congress may by Law vest the Appointment of such inferior Officers, as they think proper, in the President alone, in the Courts of Law, or in the Heads of Departments.

3. Vacancies The President shall have Power to fill up all Vacancies that may happen during the Recess of the Senate, by granting Commissions which shall expire at the End of their next Session.

Section 3. Presidential Duties

He shall from time to time give to the Congress Information of the State of the Union, and recommend to their Consideration such Measures as he shall judge necessary and expedient; he may, on extraordinary Occasions, convene both Houses, or either of them, and in Case of Disagreement between them, with Respect to the Time of Adjournment, he may adjourn them to such Time as he shall think proper; he shall receive Ambassadors and other public Ministers; he shall take Care that the Laws be faithfully executed, and shall Commission all the Officers of the United States.

Section 4. Impeachment

The President, Vice President and all civil Officers of the United States, shall be removed from Office on Impeachment for, and Conviction of, Treason, Bribery, or other high Crimes and Misdemeanors.

ARTICLE III THE JUDICIARY

Section 1. Federal Courts and Judges

The judicial Power of the United States shall be vested in one supreme Court, and in such inferior Courts as the Congress may from time to time ordain and establish. The Judges, both of the supreme and inferior Courts,

---

Commander in Chief Today the president is in charge of the army, navy, air force, marines, and coast guard. Only Congress, however, can decide if the United States will declare war.

Appointments Most of the president's appointments to office must be approved by the Senate.

Vocabulary

[21] **Reprieves** delays of punishment

[22] **Pardons** releases from the legal penalties associated with a crime

The State of the Union Every year the president presents to Congress a State of the Union message. In this message, the president introduces and explains a legislative plan for the coming year.

shall hold their Offices during good Behavior, and shall, at stated Times, receive for their Services a Compensation, which shall not be diminished during their Continuance in Office.

Section 2. Authority of the Courts

1. General Authority The judicial Power shall extend to all Cases, in Law and Equity, arising under this Constitution, the Laws of the United States, and Treaties made, or which shall be made, under their Authority;—to all Cases affecting Ambassadors, other public Ministers and Consuls;—to all Cases of admiralty and maritime Jurisdiction;—to Controversies to which the United States shall be a Party;—to Controversies between two or more States —between a State and Citizens of another State; —between Citizens of different States;—between Citizens of the same State claiming Lands under Grants of different States, and between a State, or the Citizens thereof, and foreign States, Citizens or Subjects.

2. Supreme Authority In all Cases affecting Ambassadors, other public Ministers and Consuls, and those in which a State shall be Party, the supreme Court shall have original Jurisdiction. In all the other Cases before mentioned, the supreme Court shall have appellate Jurisdiction, both as to Law and Fact, with such Exceptions, and under such Regulations as the Congress shall make.

3. Trial by Jury The Trial of all Crimes, except in Cases of Impeachment, shall be by Jury; and such Trial shall be held in the State where the said Crimes shall have been committed; but when not committed within any State, the Trial shall be at such Place or Places as the Congress may by Law have directed.

Federal Judicial System QUICK FACTS

Supreme Court
Reviews cases appealed from lower federal courts and highest state courts

Courts of Appeals
Review appeals from district courts

District Courts
Hold trials

Section 3. Treason

1. Definition Treason against the United States, shall consist only in levying War against them, or in adhering to their Enemies, giving them Aid and Comfort. No Person shall be convicted of Treason unless on the Testimony of two Witnesses to the same overt Act, or on Confession in open Court.

2. Punishment The Congress shall have Power to declare the Punishment of Treason, but no Attainder of Treason shall work **Corruption of Blood**,[23] or Forfeiture except during the Life of the Person attainted.

ARTICLE IV RELATIONS AMONG STATES

Section 1. State Acts and Records

Full Faith and Credit shall be given in each State to the public Acts, Records, and judicial Proceedings of every other State. And the Congress may by general Laws prescribe the Manner in which such Acts, Records and Proceedings shall be proved, and the Effect thereof.

Section 2. Rights of Citizens

1. Citizenship The Citizens of each State shall be entitled to all Privileges and Immunities of Citizens in the several States.

2. Extradition A Person charged in any State with Treason, Felony, or other Crime, who shall flee from Justice, and be found in another State, shall on Demand of the executive Authority of the State from which he fled, be delivered up, to be removed to the State having Jurisdiction of the Crime.

3. Fugitive Slaves ~~No Person held to Service or Labour in one State, under the Laws thereof, escaping into another, shall, in Consequence of any Law or Regulation therein, be discharged from such Service or Labour, but shall be delivered up on Claim of the Party to whom such Service or Labour may be due.~~

Section 3. New States

1. Admission New States may be admitted by the Congress into this Union; but no new State shall be formed or erected within the Jurisdiction of any other State; nor any State be formed by the Junction of two or more States, or Parts of States, without the Consent of the Legislatures of the States concerned as well as of the Congress.

2. Congressional Authority The Congress shall have Power to dispose of and make all needful Rules and Regulations respecting the Territory or other Property belonging to the United States; and nothing in this Constitution shall be so construed as to Prejudice any Claims of the United States, or of any particular State.

Federalism

National
- Declare war
- Maintain armed forces
- Regulate interstate and foreign trade
- Admit new states
- Establish post offices
- Set standard weights and measures
- Coin money
- Establish foreign policy
- Make all laws necessary and proper for carrying out delegated powers

Shared
- Maintain law and order
- Levy taxes
- Borrow money
- Charter banks
- Establish courts
- Provide for public welfare

State
- Establish and maintain schools
- Establish local governments
- Regulate business within the state
- Make marriage laws
- Provide for public safety
- Assume other powers not delegated to the national government nor prohibited to the states

Analyze Information
Why does the power to declare war belong only to the national government?

EXPLORE THE DOCUMENT
In a republic, voters elect representatives to act in their best interest. *How does Article IV protect the practice of republicanism in the United States?*

EXPLORE THE DOCUMENT
America's founders may not have realized how long the Constitution would last, but they did set up a system for changing or adding to it. They did not want to make it easy to change the Constitution. *By what methods may the Constitution be amended? Under what sorts of circumstances do you think an amendment might be necessary?*

Section 4. Guarantees to the States

The United States shall guarantee to every State in this Union a Republican Form of Government, and shall protect each of them against Invasion; and on Application of the Legislature, or of the Executive (when the Legislature cannot be convened), against domestic Violence.

ARTICLE V AMENDING THE CONSTITUTION

The Congress, whenever two thirds of both Houses shall deem it necessary, shall propose Amendments to this Constitution, or, on the Application of the Legislatures of two thirds of the several States, shall call a Convention for proposing Amendments, which, in either Case, shall be valid to all Intents and Purposes, as Part of this Constitution, when ratified by the Legislatures of three fourths of the several States, or by Conventions in three fourths thereof, as the one or the other Mode of Ratification may be proposed by the Congress; Provided that no Amendment which may be made prior to the Year One thousand eight hundred and eight shall in any Manner affect the first and fourth Clauses in the Ninth Section of the first Article; and that no State, without its Consent, shall be deprived of its equal Suffrage in the Senate.

National Supremacy
One of the biggest problems facing the delegates to the Constitutional Convention was the question of what would happen if a state law and a federal law conflicted. Which law would be followed? Who would decide? The second clause of Article VI answers those questions. When a federal law and a state law disagree, the federal law overrides the state law. The Constitution and other federal laws are the "supreme Law of the Land." This clause is often called the supremacy clause.

ARTICLE VI SUPREMACY OF NATIONAL GOVERNMENT

All Debts contracted and Engagements entered into, before the Adoption of this Constitution, shall be as valid against the United States under this Constitution, as under the Confederation.

This Constitution, and the Laws of the United States which shall be made in Pursuance thereof; and all Treaties made, or which shall be made, under the Authority of the United States, shall be the supreme Law of the Land; and the Judges in every State shall be bound thereby, any Thing in the Constitution or Laws of any State to the Contrary notwithstanding.

The Senators and Representatives before mentioned, and the Members of the several State Legislatures, and all executive and judicial Officers, both of the United States and of the several States, shall be bound by Oath or Affirmation, to support this Constitution; but no religious Test shall ever be required as a Qualification to any Office or public Trust under the United States.

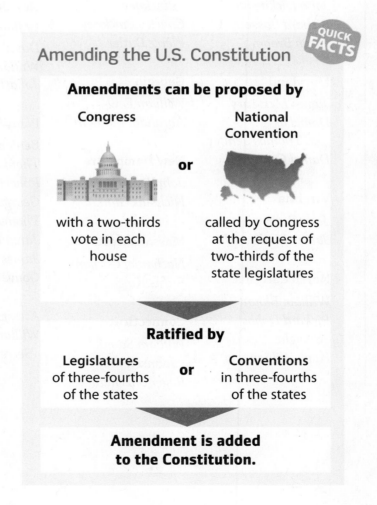

Amending the U.S. Constitution QUICK FACTS

Amendments can be proposed by

Congress

National Convention

or

with a two-thirds vote in each house

called by Congress at the request of two-thirds of the state legislatures

Ratified by

Legislatures of three-fourths of the states

or

Conventions in three-fourths of the states

Amendment is added to the Constitution.

ARTICLE VII RATIFICATION

The Ratification of the Conventions of nine States, shall be sufficient for the Establishment of this Constitution between the States so ratifying the Same.

Done in Convention by the Unanimous Consent of the States present the Seventeenth Day of September in the Year of our Lord one thousand seven hundred and Eighty seven and of the Independence of the United States of America the Twelfth In witness whereof We have hereunto subscribed our Names,

George Washington— President and deputy from Virginia

Delaware

George Read
Gunning Bedford Jr.
John Dickinson
Richard Bassett
Jacob Broom

Maryland

James McHenry
Daniel of
* St. Thomas Jenifer*
Daniel Carroll

Virginia

John Blair
James Madison Jr.

North Carolina

William Blount
Richard Dobbs
* Spaight*
Hugh Williamson

South Carolina

John Rutledge
Charles Cotesworth
* Pinckney*
Charles Pinckney
Pierce Butler

Georgia

William Few
Abraham Baldwin

New Hampshire

John Langdon
Nicholas Gilman

Massachusetts

Nathaniel Gorham
Rufus King

Connecticut

William Samuel
* Johnson*
Roger Sherman

New York

Alexander Hamilton

New Jersey

William Livingston
David Brearley
William Paterson
Jonathan Dayton

Pennsylvania

Benjamin Franklin
Thomas Mifflin
Robert Morris
George Clymer
Thomas FitzSimons
Jared Ingersoll
James Wilson
Gouverneur Morris

Attest:
William Jackson,
* Secretary*

Constitutional Amendments

Note: The first ten amendments to the Constitution were ratified on December 15, 1791, and form what is known as the Bill of Rights.

Bill of Rights

One of the conditions set by several states for ratifying the Constitution was the inclusion of a bill of rights. Many people feared that a stronger central government might take away basic rights of the people that had been guaranteed in state constitutions.

EXPLORE THE DOCUMENT

The First Amendment forbids Congress from making any "law respecting an establishment of religion" or restraining the freedom to practice religion as one chooses. *Why is freedom of religion an important right?*

Rights of the Accused

The Fifth, Sixth, and Seventh Amendments describe the procedures that courts must follow when trying people accused of crimes.

Vocabulary

[24] **quartered** housed

[25] **Warrants** written orders authorizing a person to make an arrest, a seizure, or a search

[26] **infamous** disgraceful

[27] **indictment** the act of charging with a crime

AMENDMENTS 1–10. THE BILL OF RIGHTS

Amendment I

Congress shall make no law respecting an establishment of religion, or prohibiting the free exercise thereof; or abridging the freedom of speech, or of the press; or the right of the people peaceably to assemble, and to petition the Government for a redress of grievances.

Amendment II

A well regulated Militia, being necessary to the security of a free State, the right of the people to keep and bear Arms, shall not be infringed.

Amendment III

No Soldier shall, in time of peace be **quartered**[24] in any house, without the consent of the Owner, nor in time of war, but in a manner to be prescribed by law.

Amendment IV

The right of the people to be secure in their persons, houses, papers, and effects, against unreasonable searches and seizures, shall not be violated, and no **Warrants**[25] shall issue, but upon probable cause, supported by Oath or affirmation, and particularly describing the place to be searched, and the persons or things to be seized.

Amendment V

No person shall be held to answer for a capital, or otherwise **infamous**[26] crime, unless on a presentment or **indictment**[27] of a Grand Jury, except in cases arising in the land or naval forces, or in the Militia, when in actual service in time of War or public danger; nor shall any person be subject for the same offence to be twice put in jeopardy of life or limb; nor shall be compelled in any criminal case to be a witness against himself, nor be deprived of life, liberty, or property, without due process of law; nor shall private property be taken for public use, without just compensation.

Fundamental Liberties

Freedom of Religion

Freedom of Speech

Freedom to Petition the Government

Freedom of Assembly

Freedom of the Press

Analyze Information
Which amendment guarantees these fundamental freedoms?

Trials The Sixth Amendment makes several guarantees, including a prompt trial and a trial by a jury chosen from the state and district in which the crime was committed.

Vocabulary

[28] **ascertained** found out

Amendment VI

In all criminal prosecutions, the accused shall enjoy the right to a speedy and public trial, by an impartial jury of the State and district wherein the crime shall have been committed, which district shall have been previously **ascertained**[28] by law, and to be informed of the nature and cause of the accusation; to be confronted with the witnesses against him; to have compulsory process for obtaining witnesses in his favor, and to have the Assistance of Counsel for his defence.

Amendment VII

In suits at common law, where the value in controversy shall exceed twenty dollars, the right of trial by jury shall be preserved, and no fact tried by a jury, shall be otherwise reexamined in any Court of the United States, than according to the rules of the common law.

Amendment VIII

Excessive bail shall not be required, nor excessive fines imposed, nor cruel and unusual punishments inflicted.

EXPLORE THE DOCUMENT

The Ninth and Tenth Amendments were added because not every right of the people or of the states could be listed in the Constitution. *How do the Ninth and Tenth Amendments limit the power of the federal government?*

Vocabulary

[29] **construed**
explained or interpreted

President and Vice President
The Twelfth Amendment changed the election procedure for president and vice president.

Amendment IX

The enumeration in the Constitution, of certain rights, shall not be construed to deny or disparage others retained by the people.

Amendment X

The powers not delegated to the United States by the Constitution, nor prohibited by it to the States, are reserved to the States respectively, or to the people.

AMENDMENTS 11–27

Amendment XI
PASSED BY CONGRESS MARCH 4, 1794. RATIFIED FEBRUARY 7, 1795.

The Judicial power of the United States shall not be **construed**[29] to extend to any suit in law or equity, commenced or prosecuted against one of the United States by Citizens of another State, or by Citizens or Subjects of any Foreign State.

Amendment XII
PASSED BY CONGRESS DECEMBER 9, 1803. RATIFIED JUNE 15, 1804.

The Electors shall meet in their respective states and vote by ballot for President and Vice-President, one of whom, at least, shall not be an inhabitant of the same state with themselves; they shall name in their ballots the person voted for as President, and in distinct ballots the person voted for as Vice-President, and they shall make distinct lists of all persons voted for as President, and of all persons voted for as Vice-President, and of the number of votes for each, which lists they shall sign and certify, and transmit sealed to the seat of the government of the United States, directed to the President of the Senate;—the President of the Senate shall, in the presence of the Senate and House of Representatives, open all the certificates and the votes shall then be counted;—The person having the greatest number of votes for President, shall be the President, if such number be a majority of the whole number of Electors appointed; and if no person have such majority, then from the persons having the highest numbers not exceeding three on the list of those voted for as President, the House of Representatives shall choose immediately, by ballot, the President. But in choosing the President, the votes shall be taken by states, the representation from each state having one vote; a quorum for this purpose shall consist of a member or members from two-thirds of the states, and a majority of all the states shall be necessary to a choice. And if the House of Representatives shall not choose a President whenever the right of choice shall devolve upon them, before the fourth day of March next following, then the Vice-President shall act as President, as in case of the death or other constitutional disability of the President.—The person having the greatest number of votes as Vice-President, shall be the Vice-President, if such number be a majority of the whole number of Electors appointed, and if no person have a majority, then from the two highest numbers on the list, the Senate shall choose the Vice-President; a quorum for the purpose shall consist of two-thirds of the whole number of Senators, and a majority of the whole number shall be necessary to a choice. But no person constitutionally ineligible to the office of President shall be eligible to that of Vice-President of the United States.

Amendment XIII

PASSED BY CONGRESS JANUARY 31, 1865. RATIFIED DECEMBER 6, 1865.

1. Slavery Banned Neither slavery nor **involuntary servitude**,[30] except as a punishment for crime whereof the party shall have been duly convicted, shall exist within the United States, or any place subject to their jurisdiction.

2. Enforcement Congress shall have power to enforce this article by appropriate legislation.

Amendment XIV

PASSED BY CONGRESS JUNE 13, 1866. RATIFIED JULY 9, 1868.

1. Citizenship Defined All persons born or naturalized in the United States, and subject to the jurisdiction thereof, are citizens of the United

Abolishing Slavery Although some slaves had been freed during the Civil War, slavery was not abolished until the Thirteenth Amendment took effect.

Vocabulary

[30] **involuntary servitude** being forced to work against one's will

The Reconstruction Amendments

The Thirteenth, Fourteenth, and Fifteenth Amendments are often called the Reconstruction Amendments. This is because they arose during Reconstruction, the period of American history following the Civil War. A key aspect of Reconstruction was extending the rights of citizenship to former slaves.

The Thirteenth Amendment banned slavery. The Fourteenth Amendment defined citizenship to include former slaves. It also required states to follow established rules (due process) when subjecting anyone to legal procedures and to provide all people with equal protection of their rights. The Fifteenth Amendment gave African American men the right to vote.

Analyze Information
Why was the "equal protection" clause of Section 1 of the Fourteenth Amendment important for the goals of Reconstruction?

African Americans participate in an election.

Protecting the Rights of Citizens In 1833 the Supreme Court ruled that the Bill of Rights limited the federal government but not the state governments. This ruling was interpreted to mean that states were able to keep African Americans from becoming state citizens and keep the Bill of Rights from protecting them. The Fourteenth Amendment defines citizenship and prevents states from interfering in the rights of citizens of the United States.

States and of the State wherein they reside. No State shall make or enforce any law which shall abridge the privileges or immunities of citizens of the United States; nor shall any State deprive any person of life, liberty, or property, without due process of law; nor deny to any person within its jurisdiction the equal protection of the laws.

2. Voting Rights Representatives shall be apportioned among the several States according to their respective numbers, counting the whole number of persons in each State, ~~excluding Indians not taxed~~. But when the right to vote at any election for the choice of electors for President and Vice-President of the United States, Representatives in Congress, the Executive and Judicial officers of a State, or the members of the Legislature thereof, is denied to any of the ~~male~~ inhabitants of such State, ~~being twenty-one years of age~~, and citizens of the United States, or in any way abridged, except for participation in rebellion, or other crime, the basis of representation therein shall be reduced in the proportion which the number of such ~~male~~ citizens shall bear to the whole number of ~~male~~ citizens ~~twenty-one years of age~~ in such State.

3. Rebels Banned from Government No person shall be a Senator or Representative in Congress, or elector of President and Vice-President, or hold any office, civil or military, under the United States, or under any State, who, having previously taken an oath, as a member of Congress, or as an officer of the United States, or as a member of any State legislature, or as an executive or judicial officer of any State, to support the Constitution of the United States, shall have engaged in insurrection or rebellion against the same, or given aid or comfort to the enemies thereof. But Congress may by a vote of two-thirds of each House, remove such disability.

4. Payment of Debts The validity of the public debt of the United States, authorized by law, including debts incurred for payment of pensions and bounties for services in suppressing insurrection or rebellion, shall not be questioned. But neither the United States nor any State shall assume or pay any debt or obligation incurred in aid of insurrection or rebellion against the United States, or any claim for the loss or emancipation of any slave; but all such debts, obligations and claims shall be held illegal and void.

5. Enforcement The Congress shall have the power to enforce, by appropriate legislation, the provisions of this article.

Amendment XV
PASSED BY CONGRESS FEBRUARY 26, 1869. RATIFIED FEBRUARY 3, 1870.

1. Voting Rights The right of citizens of the United States to vote shall not be denied or abridged by the United States or by any State on account of race, color, or previous condition of servitude.

2. Enforcement The Congress shall have the power to enforce this article by appropriate legislation.

Timeline: Amendments to the U.S. Constitution

The Constitution has been amended only 27 times since it was ratified more than 200 years ago. Amendments help the structure of the government change along with the values of the nation's people. Read the timeline below to learn how each amendment changed the government.

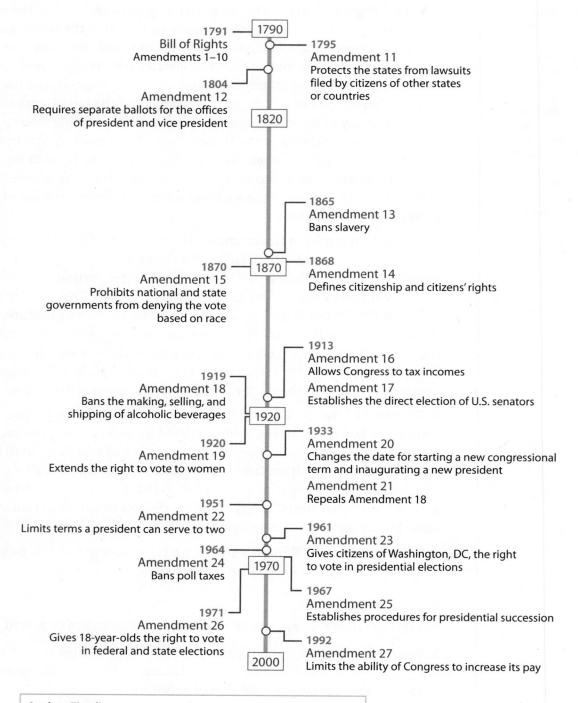

1790

1791
Bill of Rights
Amendments 1–10

1795
Amendment 11
Protects the states from lawsuits
filed by citizens of other states
or countries

1804
Amendment 12
Requires separate ballots for the offices
of president and vice president

1820

1865
Amendment 13
Bans slavery

1870

1868
Amendment 14
Defines citizenship and citizens' rights

1870
Amendment 15
Prohibits national and state
governments from denying the vote
based on race

1913
Amendment 16
Allows Congress to tax incomes

Amendment 17
Establishes the direct election of U.S. senators

1919
Amendment 18
Bans the making, selling, and
shipping of alcoholic beverages

1920

1933
Amendment 20
Changes the date for starting a new congressional
term and inaugurating a new president

1920
Amendment 19
Extends the right to vote to women

Amendment 21
Repeals Amendment 18

1951
Amendment 22
Limits terms a president can serve to two

1961
Amendment 23
Gives citizens of Washington, DC, the right
to vote in presidential elections

1964
Amendment 24
Bans poll taxes

1970

1967
Amendment 25
Establishes procedures for presidential succession

1971
Amendment 26
Gives 18-year-olds the right to vote
in federal and state elections

1992
Amendment 27
Limits the ability of Congress to increase its pay

2000

Analyze Timelines

1. How are the Eighteenth and Twenty-First Amendments related?

2. Which amendments relate to the right to vote?

Amendment XVI

PASSED BY CONGRESS JULY 2, 1909. RATIFIED FEBRUARY 3, 1913.

The Congress shall have power to lay and collect taxes on incomes, from whatever source derived, without apportionment among the several States, and without regard to any census or enumeration.

Amendment XVII

PASSED BY CONGRESS MAY 13, 1912. RATIFIED APRIL 8, 1913.

1. Senators Elected by Citizens The Senate of the United States shall be composed of two Senators from each State, elected by the people thereof, for six years; and each Senator shall have one vote. The electors in each State shall have the qualifications requisite for electors of the most numerous branch of the State legislatures.

2. Vacancies When vacancies happen in the representation of any State in the Senate, the executive authority of such State shall issue writs of election to fill such vacancies: *Provided*, That the legislature of any State may empower the executive thereof to make temporary appointments until the people fill the vacancies by election as the legislature may direct.

3. Future Elections This amendment shall not be so construed as to affect the election or term of any Senator chosen before it becomes valid as part of the Constitution.

Amendment XVIII

PASSED BY CONGRESS DECEMBER 18, 1917. RATIFIED JANUARY 16, 1919. REPEALED BY AMENDMENT XXI.

1. Liquor Banned After one year from the ratification of this article the manufacture, sale, or transportation of intoxicating liquors within, the importation thereof into, or the exportation thereof from the United States and all territory subject to the jurisdiction thereof for beverage purposes is hereby prohibited.

2. Enforcement The Congress and the several States shall have concurrent power to enforce this article by appropriate legislation.

3. Ratification This article shall be inoperative unless it shall have been ratified as an amendment to the Constitution by the legislatures of the several States, as provided in the Constitution, within seven years from the date of the submission hereof to the States by the Congress.

Amendment XIX

PASSED BY CONGRESS JUNE 4, 1919. RATIFIED AUGUST 18, 1920.

1. Voting Rights The right of citizens of the United States to vote shall not be denied or abridged by the United States or by any State on account of sex.

EXPLORE THE DOCUMENT
The Seventeenth Amendment requires that senators be elected directly by the people instead of by the state legislatures. *What principle of our government does the Seventeenth Amendment protect?*

Prohibition Although many people believed that the Eighteenth Amendment was good for the health and welfare of the American people, it was repealed 14 years later.

Women's Suffrage Abigail Adams and others were disappointed that the Declaration of Independence and the Constitution did not specifically include women. It took many years and much campaigning before suffrage for women was finally achieved.

Women Fight for the Vote

To become part of the Constitution, a proposed amendment must be ratified by three-fourths of the states. Here, suffragists witness Kentucky governor Edwin P. Morrow signing the Nineteenth Amendment in January 1920. By June of that year, enough states had ratified the amendment to make it part of the Constitution. American women, after generations of struggle, had finally won the right to vote.

Analyze Information
What right did the Nineteenth Amendment grant?

Taking Office
In the original Constitution, a newly elected president and Congress did not take office until March 4, which was four months after the November election. The officials who were leaving office were called lame ducks because they had little influence during those four months. The Twentieth Amendment changed the date that the new president and Congress take office. Members of Congress now take office during the first week of January, and the president takes office on January 20.

2. Enforcement Congress shall have power to enforce this article by appropriate legislation.

Amendment XX
PASSED BY CONGRESS MARCH 2, 1932. RATIFIED JANUARY 23, 1933.

1. Presidential Terms The terms of the President and the Vice President shall end at noon on the 20th day of January, and the terms of Senators and Representatives at noon on the 3d day of January, of the years in which such terms would have ended if this article had not been ratified; and the terms of their successors shall then begin.

2. Meeting of Congress The Congress shall assemble at least once in every year, and such meeting shall begin at noon on the 3d day of January, unless they shall by law appoint a different day.

3. Succession of Vice President If, at the time fixed for the beginning of the term of the President, the President elect shall have died, the Vice President elect shall become President. If a President shall not have been chosen before the time fixed for the beginning of his term, or if the President elect shall have failed to qualify, then the Vice President elect shall act as President until a President shall have qualified; and the Congress may by law provide for the case wherein neither a President elect nor a Vice President shall have qualified, declaring who shall then act as President, or the manner in which one who is to act shall be selected, and such person shall act accordingly until a President or Vice President shall have qualified.

4. Succession by Vote of Congress The Congress may by law provide for the case of the death of any of the persons from whom the House of Representatives may choose a President whenever the right of choice shall have devolved upon them, and for the case of the death of any of the persons from whom the Senate may choose a Vice President whenever the right of choice shall have devolved upon them.

5. Ratification ~~Sections 1 and 2 shall take effect on the 15th day of October following the ratification of this article.~~

6. Ratification ~~This article shall be inoperative unless it shall have been ratified as an amendment to the Constitution by the legislatures of three-fourths of the several States within seven years from the date of its submission.~~

Amendment XXI
PASSED BY CONGRESS FEBRUARY 20, 1933. RATIFIED DECEMBER 5, 1933.

1. 18th Amendment Repealed The eighteenth article of amendment to the Constitution of the United States is hereby repealed.

2. Liquor Allowed by Law The transportation or importation into any State, Territory, or Possession of the United States for delivery or use therein of intoxicating liquors, in violation of the laws thereof, is hereby prohibited.

3. Ratification ~~This article shall be inoperative unless it shall have been ratified as an amendment to the Constitution by conventions in the several States, as provided in the Constitution, within seven years from the date of the submission hereof to the States by the Congress.~~

Amendment XXII
PASSED BY CONGRESS MARCH 21, 1947. RATIFIED FEBRUARY 27, 1951.

1. Term Limits No person shall be elected to the office of the President more than twice, and no person who has held the office of President, or acted as President, for more than two years of a term to which some other person was elected President shall be elected to the office of President more than once. ~~But this Article shall not apply to any person holding the office of President when this Article was proposed by Congress, and shall not prevent any person who may be holding the office of President, or acting as President, during the term within which this Article becomes operative from holding the office of President or acting as President during the remainder of such term.~~

EXPLORE THE DOCUMENT
From the time of President George Washington's administration, it was a custom for presidents to serve no more than two terms in office. Franklin D. Roosevelt, however, was elected to four terms. The Twenty-Second Amendment restricted presidents to no more than two terms in office. *Why do you think citizens chose to limit the power of the president in this way?*

After Franklin D. Roosevelt was elected to four consecutive terms, limits were placed on the number of terms a president could serve.

2. Ratification ~~This article shall be inoperative unless it shall have been ratified as an amendment to the Constitution by the legislatures of three-fourths of the several States within seven years from the date of its submission to the States by the Congress.~~

Amendment XXIII
PASSED BY CONGRESS JUNE 16, 1960. RATIFIED MARCH 29, 1961.

Voting Rights
Until the ratification of the Twenty-Third Amendment, the people of Washington, DC, could not vote in presidential elections.

1. District of Columbia Represented The District constituting the seat of Government of the United States shall appoint in such manner as Congress may direct:

A number of electors of President and Vice President equal to the whole number of Senators and Representatives in Congress to which the District would be entitled if it were a State, but in no event more than the least populous State; they shall be in addition to those appointed by the States, but they shall be considered, for the purposes of the election of President and Vice President, to be electors appointed by a State; and they shall meet in the District and perform such duties as provided by the twelfth article of amendment.

2. Enforcement The Congress shall have power to enforce this article by appropriate legislation.

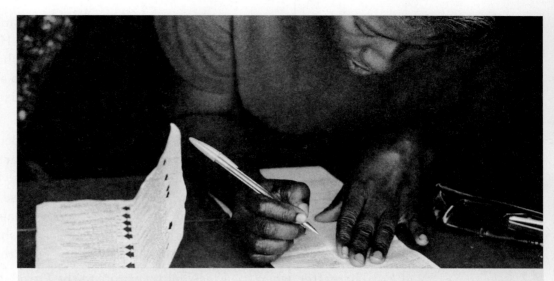

Poll Tax Amendment

Poll taxes were used to deny many poor Americans, including African Americans and Hispanic Americans, their right to vote. These taxes were made unconstitutional by the Twenty-Fourth Amendment. Above, an African American woman in Alabama votes for the first time.

Analyze Information
How did poll taxes deny poor Americans the opportunity to vote?

Presidential Disability The illness of President Eisenhower in the 1950s and the assassination of President Kennedy in 1963 were the events behind the Twenty-Fifth Amendment. The Constitution did not provide a clear-cut method for a vice president to take over for a disabled president or upon the death of a president. This amendment provides for filling the office of the vice president if a vacancy occurs, and it provides a way for the vice president—or someone else in the line of succession—to take over if the president is unable to perform the duties of that office.

Amendment XXIV

PASSED BY CONGRESS AUGUST 27, 1962. RATIFIED JANUARY 23, 1964.

1. Voting Rights The right of citizens of the United States to vote in any primary or other election for President or Vice President, for electors for President or Vice President, or for Senator or Representative in Congress, shall not be denied or abridged by the United States or any State by reason of failure to pay poll tax or other tax.

2. Enforcement The Congress shall have power to enforce this article by appropriate legislation.

Amendment XXV

PASSED BY CONGRESS JULY 6, 1965. RATIFIED FEBRUARY 10, 1967.

1. Succession of Vice President In case of the removal of the President from office or of his death or resignation, the Vice President shall become President.

2. Vacancy of Vice President Whenever there is a vacancy in the office of the Vice President, the President shall nominate a Vice President who shall take office upon confirmation by a majority vote of both Houses of Congress.

3. Written Declaration Whenever the President transmits to the President pro tempore of the Senate and the Speaker of the House of Representatives his written declaration that he is unable to discharge the powers and duties of his office, and until he transmits to them a written declaration to the contrary, such powers and duties shall be discharged by the Vice President as Acting President.

4. Removing the President Whenever the Vice President and a majority of either the principal officers of the executive departments or of such other body as Congress may by law provide, transmit to the President pro tempore of the Senate and the Speaker of the House of Representatives their written declaration that the President is unable to discharge the powers and duties of his office, the Vice President shall immediately assume the powers and duties of the office as Acting President.

Thereafter, when the President transmits to the President pro tempore of the Senate and the Speaker of the House of Representatives his written declaration that no inability exists, he shall resume the powers and duties of his office unless the Vice President and a majority of either the principal officers of the executive department or of such other body as Congress may by law provide, transmit within four days to the President pro tempore of the Senate and the Speaker of the House of Representatives their written declaration that the President is unable to discharge the powers and duties of his office. Thereupon Congress shall decide the issue, assembling within forty-eight hours for that purpose if not in session. If the Congress, within twenty-one days after receipt of the latter written declaration, or, if Congress is not in session, within twenty-one days after Congress is required to assemble, determines by two-thirds vote of both Houses that the President is unable to discharge the powers and duties of his office, the Vice President shall continue to discharge the same as Acting President; otherwise, the President shall resume the powers and duties of his office.

Amendment XXVI

PASSED BY CONGRESS MARCH 23, 1971. RATIFIED JULY 1, 1971.

1. Voting Rights The right of citizens of the United States, who are eighteen years of age or older, to vote shall not be denied or abridged by the United States or by any State on account of age.

2. Enforcement The Congress shall have power to enforce this article by appropriate legislation.

Amendment XXVII

ORIGINALLY PROPOSED SEPTEMBER 25, 1789. RATIFIED MAY 7, 1992.

No law, varying the compensation for the services of the Senators and Representatives, shall take effect, until an election of representatives shall have intervened.

Expanded Suffrage The Voting Rights Act of 1970 tried to set the voting age at 18. However, the Supreme Court ruled that the act set the voting age for national elections only, not for state or local elections. The Twenty-Sixth Amendment gave 18-year-old citizens the right to vote in all elections.

The Bill of Rights

The Big Idea

The Bill of Rights was added to the Constitution to define clearly the rights and freedoms of citizens.

Main Ideas

- The First Amendment guarantees basic freedoms to individuals.

- Other amendments focus on protecting citizens from certain abuses.

- The rights of the accused are an important part of the Bill of Rights.

- The rights of states and citizens are protected by the Bill of Rights.

Key Terms and People

majority rule
petition
search warrant
due process
indict
double jeopardy
eminent domain

If YOU were there . . .

Your father runs a bookshop in colonial Boston in 1770. Your family lives in a very small brick house. You and your sisters must share one small bedroom. One day, a red-coated British officer knocks on your front door and strides into the parlor. He says that your family will have to provide a room and meals for two British soldiers. "We're already crowded!" you protest, but he insists.

Would you support the British government's requirement that colonists provide food and shelter for troops? Why?

First Amendment

Federalist James Madison promised that a bill of rights would be added to the Constitution. This promise allowed the Constitution to pass. In 1789 Madison began writing down a huge list of proposed amendments. He then presented a shorter list to the House of Representatives. Of those, the House approved 12. The states ratified ten, which took effect December 15, 1791. Those ten amendments, called the Bill of Rights, protect U.S. citizens' individual liberties.

The protection of individual liberties is important in a representative democracy. Without safeguards, people's rights would not always be protected because of **majority rule**. This is the idea that the greatest number of people in society can make policies for everyone. While this means that most people agree on what the law should be, it also means that smaller groups, or minorities, might lose their rights. The Bill of Rights ensures that the rights of all citizens are protected.

The ideas spelled out in the First Amendment form the most basic rights of all U.S. citizens. These rights include freedom of religion, freedom of the press, freedom of speech, freedom of assembly, and the right to petition.

Amendment I

Congress shall make no law respecting an establishment of religion, or prohibiting the free exercise thereof; or abridging the freedom of speech, or of the press; or the right of the people peaceably to assemble, and to petition the Government for a redress of grievances.

Workers use the right of assembly to protest a proposed budget in New York City.

In the spirit of Thomas Jefferson's Virginia Statute for Religious Freedom, the First Amendment begins, "Congress shall make no law respecting an establishment of religion, or prohibiting the free exercise thereof." In other words, the government cannot support or interfere with the practice of a religion. This amendment keeps the government from favoring one religion over any other or establishing an official religion.

The First Amendment also guarantees freedom of speech and of the press. This means that Americans have the right to express their own ideas and views. They also have the right to hear the ideas and views of others. Former senator Margaret Chase Smith discussed why these freedoms are important. "The key to security," she once said, "is public information."

The right to free speech and a free press does not mean that people can say or print anything they want to, however. The Constitution does not protect slander—false statements meant to damage someone's reputation. Libel, or intentionally writing a lie that harms another person, is not protected, either. The Supreme Court has also ruled that speech that endangers public safety is not protected. For example, Justice Oliver Wendell Holmes declared in 1919 that falsely shouting "Fire" in a crowded theater is not protected as free speech. The government can also restrict speech or printed material that is considered obscene or poses a danger to national security.

Americans also have freedom of assembly, or of holding meetings. Any group may gather to discuss issues or conduct business. If people gather peacefully and do not engage in illegal activities, the government cannot interfere. The right to **petition**, or make a request of the government, is another right of the American people. Any American can present a petition to a government official. This right lets Americans show dissatisfaction with a law. They can also suggest new laws.

Reading Check
Summarize What rights does the First Amendment guarantee to Americans?

Protecting Citizens

The Second, Third, and Fourth Amendments relate to colonial disputes with Britain and reflect many of the ideals outlined in the Declaration of Independence. The Second Amendment deals with state militias and the right to bear arms. Colonial militias played a big role in the Revolutionary War. The framers of the Constitution thought that the states needed their militias for emergencies. Today the National Guard has largely replaced organized state militias.

Supporters of gun-control laws have generally argued that the Second Amendment was intended to protect the collective right of states to maintain well-regulated militia units. Opponents hold that the amendment was meant to protect an individual's right of self-defense. The meaning of the amendment continues to be debated.

Reading Check
Find Main Ideas Why were the Third and Fourth Amendments matters of great importance to Americans when the Bill of Rights was written?

The Third Amendment prevents the military from forcing citizens to house soldiers. Before the Revolution, the British pressured colonists to shelter and feed British soldiers. British leaders also forced colonists to submit to having their property searched for illegal goods. Anger over such actions led to the Fourth Amendment rule against "unreasonable searches and seizures." Before a citizen's property can be searched, authorities must now get a **search warrant**. This order gives authorities permission to search someone's property. A judge issues this order only when it seems likely that a search might uncover evidence relating to a crime. In emergencies, however, police can make an emergency search. This may preserve evidence needed to prove possible illegal activity.

Amendment II

A well regulated Militia, being necessary to the security of a free State, the right of the people to keep and bear Arms, shall not be infringed.

Amendment III

No Soldier shall, in time of peace be quartered in any house, without the consent of the Owner, nor in time of war, but in a manner to be prescribed by law.

Amendment IV

The right of the people to be secure in their persons, houses, papers, and effects, against unreasonable searches and seizures, shall not be violated, and no Warrants shall issue, but upon probable cause, supported by Oath or affirmation, and particularly describing the place to be searched, and the persons or things to be seized.

Rights of the Accused

The Fifth, Sixth, Seventh, and Eighth Amendments provide guidelines for protecting the rights of the accused. According to the Fifth Amendment, the government cannot punish anyone without **due process** of law. This means that the law must be fairly applied. A grand jury decides if there is enough evidence to **indict** (en–DYT), or formally accuse, a person. Without an indictment, the court cannot try anyone for a serious crime. The Fifth Amendment also protects people from having to testify at their own criminal trial. To keep from testifying, a person need only "take the Fifth." In addition, anyone found not guilty in a criminal trial cannot face **double jeopardy**. In other words, he or she cannot be tried again for the same crime.

The final clause of the Fifth Amendment states that no one can have property taken without due process of law. There is one exception: the government's power of **eminent domain**. This is the power to take personal property to benefit the public. One example would be taking private land to build a public road. However, the government must pay the owners a fair price for the property. If the property was gained illegally, then the owners are not paid.

The Sixth Amendment protects the rights of a person who has been indicted. It guarantees that person a speedy public trial. Public trials ensure that laws are being followed by allowing the public to witness the proceedings. Accused people have the right to know the charges against them and can hear and question witnesses testifying against them. Accused people

Amendment V

No person shall be held to answer for a capital, or otherwise infamous crime, unless on a presentment or indictment of a Grand Jury, except in cases arising in the land or naval forces, or in the Militia, when in actual service in time of War or public danger; nor shall any person be subject for the same offence to be twice put in jeopardy of life or limb; nor shall be compelled in any criminal case to be a witness against himself, nor be deprived of life, liberty, or property, without due process of law; nor shall private property be taken for public use, without just compensation.

A judge and jury listen to a witness in a courtroom in Orange County, California.

have the right to an attorney. If they cannot pay for legal service, the government must provide it. Sometimes accused persons refuse their Sixth Amendment rights. For example, some defendants refuse the services of an attorney, while others choose to have a trial in front of a judge alone instead of before a jury. In many cases, defendants can forgo trial and agree to a plea bargain. This means that a defendant pleads guilty to a lesser charge and avoids risking conviction for a crime with a greater sentence.

The Seventh Amendment states that juries can decide civil cases. It is possible to harm another person without committing a crime. In such cases, the injured party may sue, or seek justice, in a civil court. Civil cases usually involve disputes over money or property. For example, someone might bring a civil suit against a person who refuses to repay a debt.

A Right to Bail The Eighth Amendment allows for bail. Bail is a set amount of money that defendants promise to pay the court if they fail to appear in court at the proper time.

By posting, or paying, bail, a defendant can avoid staying in jail before and during a trial. If a defendant does not show up in court for trial, the court demands the bail money be paid and issues a warrant for arrest.

The Eighth Amendment keeps courts from setting unfairly high bail. However, in cases of very serious crimes, a judge may refuse to set bail altogether. This can be the case, for example, if the court regards a defendant as being potentially dangerous to the public by being left free. A judge can also deny bail if he or she thinks the defendant will not show up for trial. In such cases the defendant must remain in jail throughout the trial.

"Cruel and Unusual Punishments"

The Eighth Amendment also bans "cruel and unusual punishments" against a person convicted of a crime. For many years, Americans have debated the question of what exactly constitutes cruel and unusual punishment. The debate has often centered on the issue of capital punishment. In 1972 the Supreme Court ruled that the way in which most states carried out the death penalty was cruel and unusual. The Court also found that the ways in which many states sentenced people to death were unfair. However, a few years later, the Court ruled that not all executions were in themselves cruel and unusual.

Amendment IX

The enumeration in the Constitution, of certain rights, shall not be construed to deny or disparage others retained by the people.

Amendment X

The powers not delegated to the United States by the Constitution, nor prohibited by it to the States, are reserved to the States respectively, or to the people.

Students learn about the rights and responsibilities of being a U.S. citizen.

Reading Check
Summarize What is the purpose of the Eighth Amendment?

Most states still allow the death penalty. Those that do must follow the Supreme Court's rules. To do so, many states have changed the ways in which they carry out the death penalty.

Rights of States and Citizens

The final two amendments in the Bill of Rights give a general protection for other rights not addressed by the first eight amendments. These amendments also reserve some governmental powers for the states and the people.

Ninth Amendment The Ninth Amendment says that the rights listed in the Constitution are not the only rights that citizens have. This amendment has allowed the courts and Congress to decide other basic rights of citizens.

The Constitution does not address the question of education. However, most Americans believe that it is a basic and essential right. This seems especially true in view of the fact that American citizens must be able to vote for the people who represent them in government. "Education is not just another consumer item. It is the bedrock [foundation] of our democracy," explained educational leader Mary Hatwood Futrell. Today state governments offer free education from elementary through high school—to all citizens.

Tenth Amendment The Tenth Amendment recognizes that the states and the people have additional powers. These powers are any ones that the Constitution does not specifically give to Congress—the delegated powers. The Tenth Amendment makes it clear that any powers not either delegated to the federal government or prohibited to the states belong to the states and the people. Thus, the last amendment in the Bill of Rights protects citizens' rights and helps keep the balance of power between the federal and state governments.

Reading Check
Summarize How does the Tenth Amendment protect the rights of citizens?

Summary and Preview In this lesson you learned about the Bill of Rights. In the next lesson you will learn about the responsibilities of citizenship.

Lesson 3 Assessment

Review Ideas, Terms, and People

1. **a. Identify** What basic rights are protected by the First Amendment?

   b. Recall What are two ways in which the First Amendment protects the religious rights of minority groups?

   c. Explain What does the right to petition the government mean?

   d. Elaborate Why is freedom of the press an important right?

   e. Draw Conclusions Why is it important that citizens behave responsibly when using their First Amendment rights?

2. **a. Describe** How are citizens protected under the Third and Fourth Amendments?

   b. Draw Conclusions In what ways did British actions before the Revolution lead to the Second, Third, and Fourth Amendments?

3. **a. Recall** What responsibilities do the Fifth and Sixth Amendments require of the government?

   b. Identify What protections does the Eighth Amendment provide for people accused of crimes?

   c. Elaborate Why is it important that the Bill of Rights protects people accused of crimes?

4. **a. Recall** What is the purpose of the final two amendments in the Bill of Rights?

   b. Analyze How does the Tenth Amendment balance power between national and state governments?

Critical Thinking

5. **Summarize** In this lesson you learned about the Bill of Rights. Create a chart similar to the one below. Use it to summarize the rights guaranteed to citizens by each amendment in the Bill of Rights.

Amendment	Guaranteed Rights
1	
2	
3	
4	
5	
6	
7	
8	
9	
10	

On September 17, Constitution Day, Americans celebrate the signing of the United States Constitution in 1787.

Around this time, many social studies classrooms also observe Celebrate Freedom Week. This important celebration focuses on the meaning and significance of the two foundational documents in U.S. history—the Declaration of Independence and the U.S. Constitution.

The Declaration of Independence

One of the most eloquent and influential documents ever written, the Declaration of Independence gave the reasons the American colonies were willing to fight for independence. Thomas Jefferson, the main author of the document, began by explaining the purpose of government. Part of this first section, known as the Preamble, is perhaps the most famous statement from the document:

> "We hold these Truths to be self-evident, that all Men are created equal, that they are endowed by their Creator with certain unalienable Rights, that among these are Life, Liberty, and the Pursuit of Happiness. That to secure these Rights, Governments are instituted among Men, deriving their just Powers from the Consent of the Governed."
>
> —Declaration of Independence

These powerful words established the idea that governments exist to serve their citizens, and that people have basic natural rights that government cannot take away. Throughout our history, these words have inspired Americans to fight for and expand the definitions of freedom, equality, and basic rights. For example, women's rights advocates echoed the language of the Declaration of Independence in 1848 when they demanded the right to vote by declaring that "all men and women are created equal." Abolitionists and civil rights leaders also looked to the Declaration of Independence in their struggles to end slavery and ensure that African Americans were guaranteed equal rights. Even beyond America, the Declaration of Independence has inspired independence and pro-democracy movements around the world. It continues to inspire us today.

Key Facts

Declaration of Independence

Date

- Adopted July 4, 1776, by the Continental Congress

Key Author

- Thomas Jefferson

Intent

- To announce formally that the 13 American colonies considered themselves independent states no longer part of the British Empire
- To explain and justify the reasons for independence

Meaning and Importance

- Established in writing the principle that all people have certain fundamental rights that no government can take away
- Explained that the purpose of government is to serve citizens
- Influenced the U.S. Constitution and Bill of Rights
- Has inspired people throughout history in the struggle for equality, justice, and basic human rights

IN CONGRESS. JULY 4, 1776.

The unanimous Declaration of the thirteen united States of America.

The U.S. Constitution

Building on the Declaration of Independence, the U.S. Constitution established the system of government that is still in effect today. Another truly groundbreaking document, the Constitution established the rule of law and made clear that no one, including the highest government official, is above it. The document's opening words, the Preamble, elegantly state its purpose:

> "We the People of the United States, in Order to form a more perfect Union, establish Justice, insure domestic Tranquility, provide for the common defense, promote the general Welfare, and secure the Blessings of Liberty to ourselves and our Posterity, do ordain and establish this Constitution for the United States of America."

> —United States Constitution

The three opening words, *We the People*, which were written so much larger than the others, announced dramatically that in the United States the people are the source of all government power and authority.

To protect people's rights and to balance power, the Constitution set up a system that divides power among federal and state governments. Federal power is supreme, and certain powers are shared or reserved for the states. A system of checks and balances further divides power among three equal branches of government—legislative, executive, and judicial.

The Constitution also includes a process by which it can be amended, or changed. It is sometimes referred to as "a living document" for this reason; it can be added to and improved by the people to reflect changes in society. Since it was adopted in 1787, the Constitution has been amended 27 times. These amendments have abolished slavery, guaranteed women and minorities the right to vote and to receive equal treatment under the law, changed voting and election procedures, and made other improvements to our government.

One of the most important parts of the Constitution is the Bill of Rights—the first ten amendments. The Bill of Rights helps protect the rights described in the Declaration of Independence. For example, the Bill of Rights protects such basic

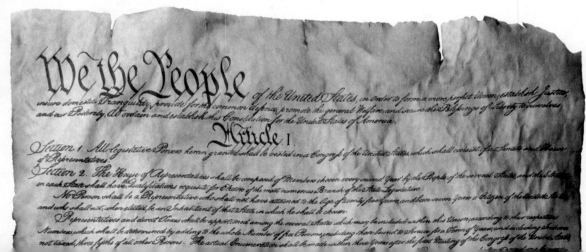

rights as freedom of speech, press, and religion as well as due process rights such as the right to a fair trial. The Bill of Rights was an important early addition to the Constitution because it stated in writing some of the specific individual rights and protections guaranteed for all Americans.

Key Facts

The Constitution

Date

- Adopted September 17, 1787, by the Constitutional Convention

Key Author

- James Madison

Intent

- To establish a new national government of the United States
- To replace the Articles of Confederation
- To safeguard the freedoms of all Americans, present and future

Meaning and Importance

- Establishes the supreme law of the land for the United States that is still in effect today
- Identifies the people as the ultimate source of government power
- Sets up a system of power sharing among the federal and state government
- Divides power into three equal branches of government
- Includes an amendment process
- Includes the Bill of Rights and other amendments that have protected and expanded individual rights and freedoms

Bill of Rights

Amendment	Description
1st Amendment	Protects freedom of religion, speech, press, assembly, petition
2nd Amendment	Protects the right to keep and bear arms
3rd Amendment	Provides restrictions on quartering soldiers in citizens' homes
4th Amendment	Bans unreasonable searches or seizures
5th Amendment	Protects citizens against self-incrimination and being tried twice for the same crime; prohibits government from depriving citizens of life, liberty, or property without due process of law
6th Amendment	Protects citizens' right to a swift and fair trial
7th Amendment	Guarantees right to trial by jury
8th Amendment	Protects citizens against cruel and unusual punishment
9th Amendment	States that citizens have rights beyond those specifically written in the Constitution
10th Amendment	States that powers not given to the government are reserved to the states or to the people

Research Activity

As part of Celebrate Freedom Week, conduct research on the two most influential documents in U.S. history. First, read the Declaration of Independence and explore how it influenced subsequent American history and has inspired people for generations. In your own words, explain how the Declaration of Independence is still relevant in our lives today. Then, review a copy of the U.S. Constitution to explore how it has been amended throughout our nation's history. Give an example of how the Constitution or Bill of Rights protects your rights and the rights of others.

Rights and Responsibilities of Citizenship

The Big Idea

American citizenship involves great privileges and serious responsibilities.

Main Ideas

- Citizenship in the United States is determined in several ways.
- Citizens are expected to fulfill a number of important duties.
- Active citizen involvement in government and the community is encouraged.

Key Terms

naturalized citizens
deport
draft
interest groups
political action committees

If YOU were there . . .

Your older brother and his friends have just turned 18. That means they must register with selective service. But it also means that they are old enough to vote in national elections. You are interested in the upcoming elections and think it would be exciting to have a real voice in politics. But your brother and his friends don't even plan to register to vote.

How would you persuade your brother that voting is important?

Gaining U.S. Citizenship

People become U.S. citizens in several ways. First, anyone born in the United States or a territory it controls is a citizen. People born in a foreign country are U.S. citizens if at least one parent is a U.S. citizen. Foreign-born people whose parents are not citizens must move to the United States to become **naturalized citizens**. Once in the United States, they go through a long process before applying for citizenship. If they succeed, they become naturalized citizens, giving them most of the rights and responsibilities of other citizens.

In the United States, legal immigrants have many of the rights and responsibilities of citizens but cannot vote or hold public office. The U.S. government can **deport**, or return to the country of origin, immigrants who break the law.

Legal immigrants over age 18 may request naturalization after living in the United States for five years. All legal immigrants have to support themselves financially. If not, someone must assume financial responsibility for them. Immigrants must be law-abiding and support the U.S. Constitution. They must demonstrate understanding of written and spoken English. They also must show basic knowledge of U.S. history and government.

When this is done, candidates go before a naturalization court and take an oath of allegiance to the United States. They then get certificates of naturalization.

Only two differences between naturalized and native-born citizens exist. Naturalized citizens can lose their citizenship, and they cannot become president or vice president. Many famous Americans have been naturalized citizens, including German Jewish scientist Albert Einstein and former secretary of state Madeleine Albright, originally from Czechoslovakia.

Responsibilities of Citizenship

For a representative democracy to work, Americans need to fulfill their civic duties. "The stakes . . . are too high for government to be a spectator sport," former Texas congresswoman Barbara Jordan once said.

Civic Duties Citizens elect officials to make laws for them. In turn, citizens must obey those laws and respect the authorities who enforce them. Obeying laws includes knowing what they are and staying informed about any changes to the law. Ignorance of a law will not prevent a person from being punished for breaking it.

Another duty is paying taxes for services such as public roads, police, and public schools. People pay sales taxes, property taxes, and tariffs. Many Americans also pay a tax on their income to the federal, and sometimes state, government.

Citizens have the duty to defend the nation. Men 18 years or older must register with selective service. In the event of a **draft**, or required military

Reading Check
Draw Conclusions
Why does U.S. law have such demanding requirements for people to become naturalized citizens?

Becoming a Citizen

For many people around the world, becoming a citizen of the United States is a lifelong dream. The highlight of the naturalization process is the ceremony, where candidates promise to "support and defend the Constitution and laws of the United States of America."

service, those able to fight are already registered. Although women do not register, many serve in the armed forces.

Americans have the right to a trial by jury under the Sixth Amendment. To protect this right, citizens should be willing to serve on a jury when they are called. Otherwise, fulfilling each person's Sixth Amendment rights would be difficult.

Civic Responsibilities In addition to duties, which are required by law, citizens also have responsibilities to fulfill. Although voluntary, these responsibilities are necessary for American democracy to work. The most important civic responsibility is voting. Representatives respond to the opinions of the voters who elect them. If only a small portion of constituents vote, the policies of a representative may not reflect the true opinions of the people he or she represents.

Military Service
By serving in the military, men and women help protect the nation from foreign threats. In addition to conducting combat and peacekeeping operations, the U.S. military may provide humanitarian assistance in overseas disasters.

Voting is closely tied to participation in political parties, because people often vote for the candidate of their own party. A majority of Americans are members of either the Democratic or the Republican Party. Others belong to smaller parties or consider themselves to be independent voters. The U.S. government has generally been dominated by two major parties, but smaller parties focused on single issues may influence public opinion. Citizens can support political parties through donations or by working on election campaigns.

Voting
A representative democracy needs its citizens to vote regularly. This responsibility involves not only casting votes in elections but also becoming educated about candidates and issues.

Reading Check
Make Inferences
Why does citizenship carry with it certain duties and responsibilities?

To make the best choices in voting, people have a responsibility to stay informed on public issues and candidates. Information is available from many sources: the Internet, newspapers, television, other media, and from attending public meetings or listening to speeches. However, voters should also be aware that some material may be deliberately biased to help or harm a particular candidate or cause. Comparing many sources of information and opinions can help voters make decisions that reflect their interests.

Citizens and Society

Participation of ordinary citizens in public groups is part of our national identity. When French writer Alexis de Tocqueville visited the United States in 1831 to study American democracy, he was amazed at the number and variety of groups that had formed to tackle problems great and small. He wrote about them:

> "What political power could ever carry on the vast multitude [large number] of lesser undertakings which the American citizens perform every day, with the assistance of the principle of association [joining a group]? . . . Nothing, in my opinion, is more deserving of our attention than the intellectual and moral associations of America."
>
> —Alexis de Tocqueville, *Democracy in America*

Academic Vocabulary
influence change or have an effect on

Influencing Government Even after an election, citizens can influence officials. The tradition of people joining together to present views to political leaders dates back to the colonial period. U.S. citizens sometimes work with **interest groups**. These groups of people share a common interest that motivates them to take political action. Interest groups organize speeches and rallies to support their cause. Sometimes they hire lobbyists, people whose job involves trying to influence the thinking of legislators or government officials. However, citizens need not join a group to influence government. They can write letters to leaders of government or attend city council meetings. Active political participation is an important responsibility for U.S. citizens and immigrants alike.

In addition to voting, many Americans choose to campaign for candidates or issues. Anyone can help a campaign, even if he or she is not eligible to vote. Many people also help campaigns by giving money directly or through **political action committees (PACs)**, groups that collect money for candidates who support certain issues.

Environmental volunteers may plant trees or clear trails in nature preserves.

Helping the Community Volunteering is another important tradition in our society. Some small communities rely on volunteer groups for essential services such as fire protection and law enforcement. In larger communities, volunteers may walk through neighborhoods and alert police if they observe criminal activity. The American Red Cross helps people cope with natural disasters and other emergencies. The Boy Scouts and Girl Scouts plan many projects such as planting trees to improve the environment. Even simple acts such as picking up trash in parks or serving food in homeless shelters will improve a community.

Community Service
Serving as a part of a volunteer group is another way to be involved in a community.

Reading Check
Summarize In what ways do volunteer groups benefit a community?

Today, social media is increasingly used to connect volunteers with organizations that can use their help. Volunteerism reduces the strain on government to provide social services, and it strengthens the bonds between members of a community.

Summary and Preview In this lesson you learned about citizens' duties toward their nation and their communities. In the next module you will learn about the first government formed under the Constitution.

Lesson 4 Assessment

Review Ideas, Terms, and People

1. **a. Identify** What are the different ways in which a person can become a U.S. citizen?
   b. Make Inferences Why do you think the law requires an immigrant to live in the United States at least five years before he or she can apply to become a naturalized citizen?

2. **a. Describe** What are three duties required of U.S. citizens?
   b. Evaluate In your opinion, which duty required of citizens is the most important? Why?

3. **a. Identify** In what ways can citizens participate in the election process?
   b. Draw Conclusions Why do you think it is important that citizens participate in the political process?

Critical Thinking

4. **Categorize** In this lesson you learned about becoming a U.S. citizen. Create a graphic organizer similar to the one below. List the ways a person becomes a citizen and then add the duties and responsibilities of citizenship.

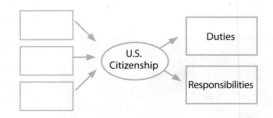

Social Studies Skills

Determine the Context of Statements

Define the Skill

A *context* is the circumstances under which something happens. *Historical context* includes values, beliefs, conditions, and practices that were common in the past. At times, some of these were quite different from what they are today. To truly understand a historical statement or event, you have to take its context into account. It is not right to judge what people in history did or said based on present-day values alone. To be fair, you must also consider the historical context of the statement or event.

Learn the Skill

To better understand something a historical figure said or wrote, use the following guidelines to determine the context of the statement.

1. Identify the speaker or writer, the date, and the topic and main idea of the statement.

2. Determine the speaker's or writer's attitude and point of view about the topic.

3. Review what you know about beliefs, conditions, or practices related to the topic that were common at the time. Find out more about the times in which the statement was made, if you need to.

4. Decide how well the statement reflects the values, attitudes, and practices of people living at that time. Then, determine how well it reflects values, attitudes, and practices related to the topic today.

Applying these guidelines will give you a better understanding of statements made by the Constitution's framers. You read in Module 6 that the Constitution created a representative democracy. However, the original Constitution gave most Americans little voice in choosing their leaders. Only the House of Representatives was elected by the voters. Alexander Hamilton, one of the Constitutional Convention's leaders, told the delegates:

"The people are turbulent and changing; they seldom judge or determine right. Give therefore to the first [upper] class a distinct, permanent share in government. They will check the unsteadiness of the second [the masses]."

By modern standards, Hamilton's remark is undemocratic. But think about the times in which it was made. Shays's Rebellion had recently occurred. In addition, in those days most Americans had little or no education. Many could not even read or write. When its historical context is considered, the statement seems less harsh and extreme.

Practice the Skill

Read the following statement made by Patrick Henry in 1788. Then answer the questions to determine its context and better understand it.

"The Constitution is said to have beautiful features, but . . . they appear to me horribly frightful. . . . Your dearest rights may be sacrificed by what may be a small minority . . . [that] . . . may continue forever unchangeably this government, although horribly defective."

1. What was Henry's opinion of the Constitution?

2. How might Americans' recent experience in the Revolution have caused him to feel that way?

Module 6 Assessment

Review Vocabulary, Terms, and People

1. What proposal for the structure of the U.S. Congress was created at the Constitutional Convention?
   a. Virginia Plan
   b. Great Compromise
   c. New Jersey Plan
   d. Three-Fifths Compromise

2. Who promised to add a bill of rights to the U.S. Constitution?
   a. Benjamin Franklin
   b. Thomas Jefferson
   c. Alexander Hamilton
   d. James Madison

3. What is the term for a person born in another country who becomes a citizen of the United States?
   a. immigrant
   b. partial citizen
   c. naturalized citizen
   d. separatist

4. What are powers granted to the states called?
   a. reserved powers
   b. concurrent powers
   c. stately powers
   d. delegated powers

5. What is the permission to look for evidence of a crime in a particular location called?
   a. petition
   b. impeachment
   c. indictment
   d. search warrant

6. Who was the first female Supreme Court justice?
   a. Abigail Adams
   b. Sonia Sotomayor
   c. Barbara Jordan
   d. Sandra Day O'Connor

Comprehension and Critical Thinking

Lesson 1

7. a. **Draw Conclusions** How was the purpose of the Constitutional Convention different from the final outcome?
   b. **Analyze** Why did the framers of the Constitution create a system of checks and balances?
   c. **Explain** What was the process for ratifying the Constitution?

Lesson 2

8. a. **Describe** Name each branch of government, and explain the duties of each.
   b. **Analyze** What checks and balances exist between the branches of government?
   c. **Evaluate** Do you think the three branches of government share their power equally? Explain your answer.

Lesson 3

9. a. **Identify** What is the Bill of Rights, and why was it added to the Constitution?
   b. **Compare and Contrast** The Bill of Rights and the Constitution both deal with issues of government power. How does their focus on this topic differ?
   c. **Analyze** In what ways does the Bill of Rights protect individuals from the power of government?
   d. **Elaborate** Which of the amendments in the Bill of Rights do you think is the most important? Why?

Lesson 4

10. a. **Describe** What are the ways in which a person can gain U.S. citizenship?
    b. **Analyze** How are citizens able to influence their government?

Reading Skills

Summarize Historical Texts *Use the Reading Skills taught in this module to answer the question about the reading selection below.*

> "The judicial power of the United States shall be vested in one supreme Court, and in such inferior Courts as the Congress may from time to time . . . establish. The Judges, both of the supreme and inferior Courts, shall hold their Offices during good Behavior, and . . . receive for their Services a Compensation. . . ."

11. Which of the following is the best summary of the selection?

    a. The U.S. judiciary consists of the Supreme Court and lower courts, and judges are paid.

    b. Congress creates lower courts.

Review Themes

12. **Politics** What important ideas has the U.S. Constitution contributed to government?

13. **Politics** Why is active political participation an important responsibility for people in the United States?

Social Studies Skills

Determine the Context of Statements *Use the Social Studies Skills taught in this module to answer the questions about the quotation below.*

> "What political power could ever carry on the vast multitude [large number] of lesser undertakings which the American citizens perform every day, with the assistance of the principle of association [joining a group]? . . . Nothing, in my opinion, is more deserving of our attention than the intellectual and moral associations of America."
>
> —Alexis de Tocqueville, *Democracy in America*

14. De Tocqueville wrote this about his trip to the United States in 1831. What is his main idea?

    a. Governments can fill every need of citizens.

    b. American organizations cannot accomplish much.

    c. American organizations get too much attention.

    d. American organizations fill important needs of citizens that government cannot.

15. Do you think that de Tocqueville's statement accurately describes modern America? Why or why not?

Focus on Writing

16. **Create a Pamphlet** Everyone in the United States benefits from our Constitution. However, many people don't know the Constitution as well as they should. Use the information you have learned about the Constitution, the Bill of Rights, and citizenship to create a four-page pamphlet. On the first page, write a title and a phrase that will get your audience's attention. On each of the following pages, you can use this format: (1) a heading and sentence at the top of the page identifying the topic of the page, and (2) the list of the most important points for that topic. Develop your pamphlet so that page 2 is on the Constitution, page 3 is on the Bill of Rights, and page 4 is on citizenship. On page 3, choose the right that you think is most important, and explain why it is important to individuals or groups. Use the Bill of Rights and modern sources to support your opinion.

Module 7

Launching the Nation

★

Essential Question

How did challenges and disagreements help shape the new nation?

About the Photo: The Washington Monument in the nation's capital is one of many tributes to George Washington.

▶ Explore ONLINE!

HISTORY.

VIDEOS, including...
• George Washington

☑ Document-Based Investigations

☑ Graphic Organizers

☑ Interactive Games

☑ Interactive Graph: Tackling the Debt

☑ Image Carousel: Battles in the Northwest Territory

☑ Image Slider: The Election of 1800

In this module you will learn about the important events of the first three presidencies and how they affected the country. You will also learn about the beginnings of many traditions that still exist today.

What You Will Learn ...

Timeline of Events 1785–1805

▶ *Explore ONLINE!*

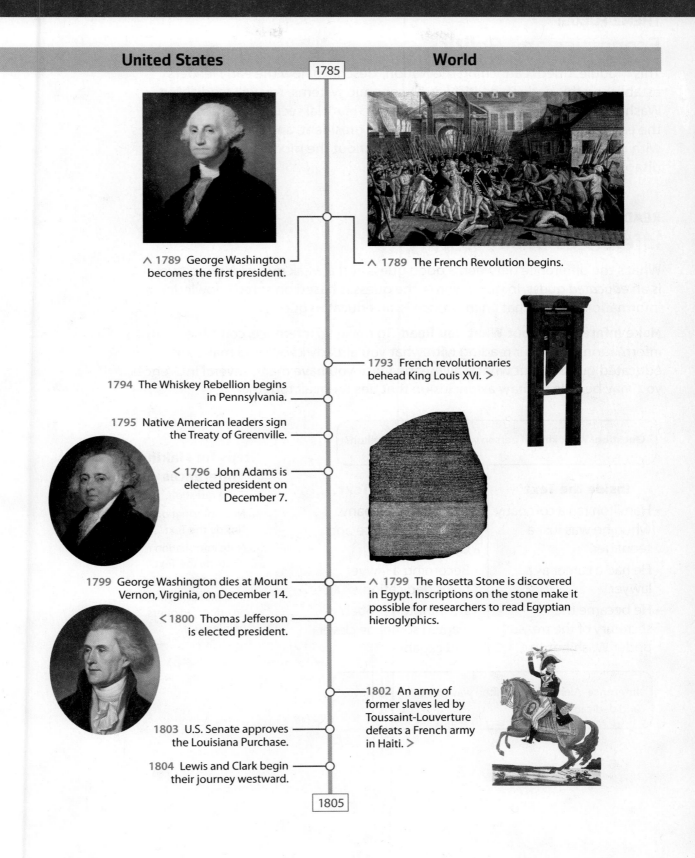

United States		World

1785

∧ **1789** George Washington becomes the first president.

∧ **1789** The French Revolution begins.

1793 French revolutionaries behead King Louis XVI. >

1794 The Whiskey Rebellion begins in Pennsylvania.

1795 Native American leaders sign the Treaty of Greenville.

< **1796** John Adams is elected president on December 7.

1799 George Washington dies at Mount Vernon, Virginia, on December 14.

∧ **1799** The Rosetta Stone is discovered in Egypt. Inscriptions on the stone make it possible for researchers to read Egyptian hieroglyphics.

< **1800** Thomas Jefferson is elected president.

1802 An army of former slaves led by Toussaint-Louverture defeats a French army in Haiti. >

1803 U.S. Senate approves the Louisiana Purchase.

1804 Lewis and Clark begin their journey westward.

1805

Reading Social Studies

THEME FOCUS:

Economics and Politics

This module, titled "Launching the Nation," describes how the early leaders established this nation's political and economic systems. You will read about Washington's presidency, Hamilton's plan for financial security for the nation, the establishment of two parties to elect the president, and Jefferson's struggles with both Washington and Hamilton. Throughout the module you will see that disagreement often defined these early days.

READING FOCUS:

Inferences about History

What's the difference between a good guess and a weak guess? A good guess is an *educated* guess. In other words, the guess is based on some knowledge or information. That's what an **inference** is, an educated guess.

Make Inferences about What You Read To make an inference, combine information from your reading with what you already know, and make an educated guess about what it all means. Once you have made several inferences, you may be able to draw a conclusion that ties them all together.

Question What kind of person was Alexander Hamilton?

Inside the Text	Outside the Text
• Hamilton ran a company when he was just a teenager.	• Running a company takes intelligence and cleverness.
• He had a career as a lawyer.	• Becoming a lawyer takes dedication.
• He became the secretary of the treasury under Washington.	• Washington probably wanted someone clever and capable.

Inference Alexander Hamilton was an intelligent, clever, and dedicated man.

Steps for Making Inferences

1. Ask a question.
2. Note information "Inside the Text."
3. Note information "Outside the Text."
4. Use both sets of information to make an educated guess, or inference.

You Try It!

Read the following passage and answer the questions that follow.

> **Economic Differences** Hamilton wanted new forms of economic growth. He wanted to promote manufacturing and business. He even suggested that the government award a prize to companies that made excellent products.
>
> In addition, Hamilton wanted to pass higher tariffs. Known as protective tariffs, these taxes would raise the prices of foreign products. Hamilton hoped this would cause Americans to buy U.S. goods. As a result, American manufacturing would be protected from foreign competition.
>
> Jefferson worried about depending too much on business and manufacturing. He believed that farmers were the most independent voters . . . Jefferson wanted to help farmers by keeping the costs of the goods they bought low. Lower tariffs would help keep prices low.

Answer these questions based on the passage you just read.

1. Which two questions can be answered directly from the text above and which one requires that you make an inference?
   a. Who wanted higher tariffs—Hamilton or Jefferson?
   b. Why do you think Hamilton and Jefferson had different views on the importance of manufacturing?
   c. Which man wanted to help the farmers?

2. To answer question b, it might help to know that Hamilton lived in New York City and Jefferson was from the more rural area of Virginia. Use that information and information in the passage to explain why one man might have valued manufacturing more than the other.

As you read Module 7, remember that you need to combine what you already know with the information in the module to make inferences.

Washington Leads a New Nation

The Big Idea

President Washington and members of Congress established a new national government.

Main Ideas

- In 1789 George Washington became the first president of the United States.

- Congress and the president organized the executive and judicial branches of government.

- Americans had high expectations for their new nation.

Key Terms and People

George Washington
electoral college
Martha Washington
precedent
Judiciary Act of 1789

If YOU were there . . .

You are a seamstress in New York City in 1789. You've joined the excited crowd in the streets for Inauguration Day. Church bells are ringing, and people are cheering. Even though you were just a young child during the Revolution, Washington is your hero. Now you watch as he takes the oath of office. You are proud to see that he is wearing a suit of American-made cloth.

What do you think America's future will be like under President Washington?

The First President

Americans believed in **George Washington**. They saw him as an honest leader and a hero of the Revolution. Many believed he should be the first U.S. president. Washington had been looking forward to retirement and a quiet life on his Virginia farm. When he hesitated at becoming a candidate for the presidency, his friends convinced him to run. Fellow politician Gouverneur Morris told him, "Should the idea prevail [win] that you would not accept the presidency, it should prove fatal . . . to the new government." Morris concluded confidently, "Of all men, you are the best fitted to fill that office."

In January 1789 each of the 11 states that had passed the Constitution sent electors to choose the first president. These delegates formed a group called the **electoral college**. The electoral college is a body of electors who represent the people's vote in choosing the president. The electoral college selected Washington unanimously, and John Adams became his vice president.

Martha Washington

Washington's wife, First Lady **Martha Washington**, entertained guests and attended social events with her husband. She described the scene to her niece: "I have not had one half-hour to myself since the day of my arrival." She ran the presidential household with style.

Other women of the time period, such as author Judith Sargent Murray, believed that women needed to play a greater role in the new nation than Martha Washington did. Murray, Abigail Adams, and others believed in Republican Motherhood, the idea that women played an important role in teaching their children to be good citizens.

Some promoters of Republican Motherhood did not expect women to participate in politics or business. Other people, however, hoped that Republican Motherhood would lead to greater opportunities for women. They hoped more women would receive an education. Only a few families were willing to provide much education for their daughters, and adult women rarely had the time or money to get an education later in life. Most women in the early republic faced long days managing their households and working hard inside or outside the home to support their families.

Reading Check

Analyze Information Why was Washington selected to be president?

Organizing the Government

Hard work also lay ahead for members of the new government. The new federal government had to create policies and procedures that would determine the future of the country. As President Washington noted in a letter to James Madison, "The first of everything in our situation will serve to establish a precedent." A **precedent** is an action or decision that later serves as an example.

The First Congress created departments in the executive branch for different areas of national policy. Washington met with the department heads, or cabinet members, who advised him.

Today we know that presidents have cabinet meetings with their top advisers. This practice started during Washington's presidency and was common by 1792.

For two of his most important cabinet positions, Washington chose carefully. He picked Alexander Hamilton as secretary of the treasury and Thomas Jefferson as secretary of state. Henry Knox served as secretary of war, and Samuel Osgood was chosen as postmaster general. Hamilton was a gifted economic planner, and Jefferson had served as ambassador to France. Knox had helped Washington run the Continental army, and Osgood had government experience.

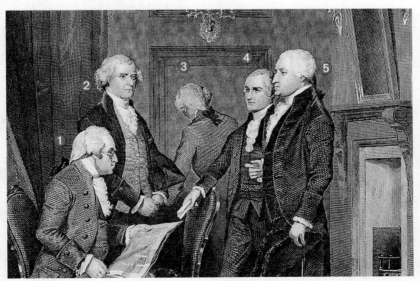

The First Cabinet

Washington's cabinet members kept him informed on political matters and debated important issues with one another. Each of the men chosen had experience that made him a wise choice to advise the nation's first president. By 1792 cabinet meetings were a common practice.

1　Henry Knox, secretary of war
2　Thomas Jefferson, secretary of state
3　Edmund Randolph, attorney general
4　Alexander Hamilton, secretary of the treasury
5　George Washington, president

To set up the federal court system and the courts' locations, Congress passed the **Judiciary Act of 1789**. This act created three levels of federal courts and defined their powers and relationship to the state courts. It set up federal district courts and circuit courts of appeals. The president nominated candidates for federal judgeships. Those candidates then had to be approved or rejected by the Senate. Washington wrote about the importance of these duties:

"I have always been persuaded that the stability and success of the national government . . . would depend in a considerable degree on the interpretation and execution of its laws. In my opinion, therefore, it is important that the judiciary system should not only be independent in its operations, but as perfect as possible in its formation."

—George Washington to the Justices of the Supreme Court, April 3, 1790

The basic parts of the federal government were now in place. Leaders began to face the challenges of the new nation. Hard work lay ahead.

Americans' Expectations for the Nation

Most Americans had high expectations for the new country. They wanted improved trade, free from too many restrictions. But they also expected the government to protect them and to keep the economy stable. However, the idea of belonging to one united nation was new to them.

In 1790 the United States was home to almost 4 million people. Most Americans lived in the countryside and worked on farms. Farmers wanted fair tax laws and the right to settle western lands. They did not want the government to interfere with their daily lives.

Other Americans worked in towns as craftspeople, laborers, or merchants. These people looked to the government to help their businesses. Most merchants wanted simpler trade laws established. Manufacturers wanted laws to protect them from foreign competitors.

Reading Check
Find Main Ideas
What two important precedents were established for the federal government?

A Rural Nation

Some Americans lived in growing cities like New York City, shown here. However, the new republic was overwhelmingly rural. Most Americans lived and worked on farms.

Why might rural Americans and urban Americans want different things from their new government?

Urban vs. Rural Population, 1790

Urban 5%
Rural 95%

Most cities were small. Only New York City and Philadelphia had populations larger than 25,000. New York City was the first capital of the United States, and it represented the spirit of the new nation. Although badly damaged during the Revolution, the city had already begun to recover. Citizens got rid of many signs of British rule.

New York City had a bustling economy. International trade and business became more active. A French visitor to New York City noted the city's energy.

"Everything in the city is in motion; everywhere the shops resound [ring out] with the noise of workers . . . one sees vessels arriving from every part of the world."

—A French visitor to New York City, quoted in *Travels Through the Two Louisianas and Among the Savage Nations of the Missouri* by Perrin du Lac and Francois Marie

Academic Vocabulary
agreement a decision reached by two or more people or groups

In 1792 some 24 stockbrokers signed an **agreement** under a buttonwood tree on Wall Street. This agreement was the foundation for what later became the New York Stock Exchange. It cemented Wall Street's image as the economic hub of the United States and eventually the world. Today, the New York Stock Exchange is the largest market for securities, or stocks, in the world.

Reading Check
Analyze Information Why was New York City chosen as the first capital of the United States?

By 1790 the city's population had topped 33,000 and was growing rapidly. To many officials, this vibrant city reflected the potential future of the new nation. It was thus a fitting place for the capital.

Summary and Preview Americans, led by President George Washington, set up their new government. In the next lesson you will read about Alexander Hamilton's economic plan.

Lesson 1 Assessment

Review Ideas, Terms, and People

1. **a. Describe** What role did the electoral college play in George Washington's election to the presidency?

   b. Summarize What were some of Martha Washington's duties as First Lady?

2. **a. Describe** What precedent did President Washington and Congress establish regarding the executive branch?

   b. Explain What was the purpose of the Judiciary Act of 1789?

   c. Evaluate What do you think was the most important element of the Judiciary Act of 1789? Why?

3. **a. Recall** What city served as the first capital of the United States? Why?

   b. Draw Conclusions What expectations did most Americans have for the new nation?

c. Make Judgments Do you think New York City should still be the capital city of the United States? Explain your answer.

Critical Thinking

4. **Compare** In this lesson you learned about the presidency of George Washington. Create a chart similar to the one below and use it to compare how Washington and Congress organized the new government.

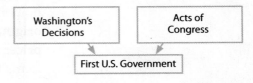

Washington's Decisions   Acts of Congress

First U.S. Government

Hamilton and National Finances

The Big Idea

Treasury secretary Alexander Hamilton developed a financial plan for the national government.

Main Ideas

- Hamilton tackled the problem of settling national and state debt.

- Thomas Jefferson opposed Hamilton's views on government and the economy.

- Hamilton created a national bank to strengthen the U.S. economy.

Key Terms and People

Alexander Hamilton
national debt
bonds
speculators
Thomas Jefferson
loose construction
strict construction
Bank of the United States

If YOU were there . . .

You live on a plantation in North Carolina in the 1790s. You have just heard that the federal government plans to pay most of the northern states' debts from the war. Your neighbors are outraged about this idea. It means more taxes and tariffs! New York and Massachusetts are far away, they say. Why should North Carolina farmers have to pay northern debts?

Would you pay other states' war debts? Why?

Settling the Debt

Alexander Hamilton seemed born with a head for economics. While still in his teens, he helped run a shipping company in his native British West Indies. Family friends then sent him to the American colonies for an education. Hamilton eventually married into a wealthy New York family and began practicing law. He served as Washington's aide and as a delegate to four Continental Congresses.

National Debt As secretary of the treasury, Hamilton's biggest challenge was paying off the **national debt**—money owed by the United States—from the Revolutionary War. The United States owed about $11.7 million to foreign countries and about $40.4 million to U.S. citizens. During the war the government raised money with bonds. **Bonds** are certificates of debt that carry a promise to buy back the bonds at a higher price. The new government could not afford to keep this promise. Bondholders who needed money sold their bonds for less than the original value to **speculators**, or people who buy items at low prices in the hope that the value will rise and they can sell the items for a profit.

Hamilton wanted to pay the foreign debt immediately and gradually repay the total value of all bonds. The second part of his plan caused disagreements because paying full value would allow speculators to make a profit. Hamilton thought

Hamilton's Economic Plan

Alexander Hamilton developed a three-point plan to solve the nation's financial problems.

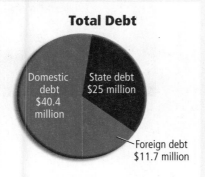

Total Debt

Domestic debt $40.4 million

State debt $25 million

Foreign debt $11.7 million

❶ **Deal with the Debt**
- Take on the foreign and domestic debt by replacing creditors' old, low-value bonds with new, interest-bearing bonds
- Take over most of the states' $25 million Revolutionary War debts

would build investor confidence in the stability of the new nation

❷ **Gain Revenue**
- Pass a tariff to both bring in revenue and help American manufacturers

would free up state money for business and trade

❸ **Stabilize the Banking System**
- Create a national bank
- Create a national mint

this was fair. He said, "He [the speculator] paid what the commodity [bond] was worth . . . and took the risks."

Thomas Jefferson disagreed. He thought the idea cheated bondholders who had sold their bonds at low prices. Jefferson wrote, "Immense sums were thus filched [stolen] from the poor and ignorant." But more politicians agreed with Hamilton. In 1790 the government exchanged old bonds for new, more reliable ones that were guaranteed.

States' Debts The states owed $25 million for Revolutionary War expenses. Hamilton wanted the federal government to pay for $21.5 million of this debt. Hamilton believed that this action would help the federal government. He thought that paying the states' debts would help the national economy. Debtor states would not have to spend so much on repayment and would have money to develop business and trade. Increased business and trade would put more money back into the national economy.

The South, however, did not want to help the federal government pay the debts of other states. States such as Virginia and North Carolina did not have many war debts. They thought Hamilton's idea was unfair. Patrick Henry said he did not believe that the Constitution gave Congress the power to pay state debts. Hamilton knew that he needed the help of southern representatives to get his plan approved.

Moving the Capital Hamilton also knew that he had something to bargain with. Officials from the southern states wanted to change the location of the nation's capital. Many southerners thought that having the capital in New York gave the northern states too much influence over national policy. Hamilton, Jefferson, and James Madison met in June 1790. Hamilton promised to convince northern members of Congress to move the capital. Jefferson and Madison then agreed to gather support in the South for Hamilton's debt plan.

Benjamin Banneker 1731–1806

Benjamin Banneker was born to a free African American family in rural Maryland. He attended a Quaker school but was largely self-educated. He was a skilled mathematician and scientist. His mathematical skills prompted Thomas Jefferson to give him a job surveying the land for the new national capital.

Draw Conclusions
How was Benjamin Banneker's life different from most African Americans' of the time?

Reading Check
Identify Points of View How did southerners feel about the federal government paying state war debts, and how did Hamilton change their minds?

The compromise worked. The national capital was moved to Philadelphia in 1791 for ten years. For the capital's permanent location, Washington chose a place on the Potomac River that included part of both Maryland and Virginia. The land was made up of swamps and farms. This site would eventually become the city of Washington, DC.

Jefferson Opposes Hamilton

Hamilton and Jefferson did not cooperate for long. Instead, they began to disagree about how to define the authority of the central government. Hamilton believed in a strong federal government. Jefferson wanted to protect the powers of the states. Their conflict reflected basic differences in their opinions about democracy. Hamilton had little faith in the average individual. He once said that "the people . . . seldom judge or determine [decide] right."

Differing Views Hamilton wanted a strong central government that balanced power between the "mass of the people" and wealthier citizens. He believed that his approach would protect everyone's liberties while keeping the people from having too much power.

Jefferson disagreed strongly with Hamilton's views of the average citizen's ability to make decisions for the country. He admitted that "the people can not be all, and always, well informed." However, Jefferson believed that it was the right of the people to rule the country.

Economic Differences Hamilton and Jefferson also fought over how the country's economy should grow. Hamilton wanted new forms of economic growth. He wanted to promote manufacturing and business. He even suggested that the government award a prize to companies that made excellent products.

In addition, Hamilton wanted to pass higher tariffs. Known as protective tariffs, these taxes would raise the prices of foreign products. Hamilton hoped this would cause Americans to buy U.S. goods. As a result, American manufacturing would be protected from foreign competition.

Role of a Citizen

Alexander Hamilton thought that the average citizen had no interest in public affairs.

Thomas Jefferson believed that each citizen could work to better society.

"We must take man as we find him, and if we expect him to serve the public, [we] must interest his passions in doing so. A reliance on pure patriotism has been the source of many of our errors."

—Alexander Hamilton, from *The Works of Alexander Hamilton*, ed. Henry Cabot Lodge

"It is my principle that the will of the Majority should always prevail [win] . . . Above all things I hope the education of the common people will be attended to; [I am] convinced that on their good sense we may rely with the most security for the preservation of a due degree of liberty."

—Thomas Jefferson, from a letter to John Adams, December 1787

Analyze Historical Sources
How did the views of Hamilton and Jefferson differ?

Reading Check
Summarize What were the main differences between Hamilton and Jefferson concerning the power of the nation's government?

Jefferson worried about depending too much on business and manufacturing. He believed that farmers were the most independent voters. They did not depend on other people's work to make a living.

Jefferson wrote, "Our governments will remain virtuous [pure] for many centuries; as long as they are chiefly agricultural." Jefferson wanted to help farmers by keeping the costs of the goods they bought low. Lower tariffs would help keep prices low.

A National Bank

Hamilton's and Jefferson's differences became more and more public in early 1791. The two men had very different opinions about how the government should approach its economic problems.

Hamilton's Plan for a National Bank Hamilton wanted to start a national bank where the government could safely deposit its money. The bank would also make loans to the government and businesses. Hamilton also thought that the United States should build a national mint, a place to make coins. Then the country could begin issuing its own currency.

Hamilton knew that people who wanted to protect states' rights might have a strong reaction to the idea of a national bank, so he suggested limiting it to a 20-year charter. After that time Congress could decide whether to extend the charter. Hamilton also asked each state to start its own bank so the national bank would not have a monopoly.

Jefferson Opposes the Bank Both Jefferson and Madison believed that Hamilton's plans for the economy gave too much power to the federal government. They also thought the U.S. Constitution did not give Congress the power to create a bank. But Hamilton quoted the elastic clause, which states that Congress can "make all laws which shall be necessary and proper" to govern the nation.

Hamilton declared that the clause allowed the government to create a national bank. Hamilton believed in **loose construction** of the Constitution. Loose construction means that the federal government can take reasonable actions that the Constitution does not specifically forbid.

Jefferson thought that the elastic clause should be used only in special cases. He wrote to President Washington, "The Constitution allows only the means which are 'necessary,' not those which are merely 'convenient.'" Jefferson believed in strict construction of the Constitution. People who favor **strict construction** think that the federal government should do only what the Constitution specifically says it can do.

President Washington and Congress agreed with Hamilton. They hoped a bank would offer stability for the U.S. economy. In February 1791 Congress enacted the charter for the **Bank of the United States**—the country's first national bank. The bank played an important role in making the U.S. economy more stable.

Reading Check
Draw Conclusions
Why did Congress and the president agree to create a national bank?

Summary and Preview Washington and Hamilton developed plans for paying the national debt. In the next lesson you will read about the U.S. neutrality policy.

Lesson 2 Assessment

Review Ideas, Terms, and People

1. **a. Describe** What economic problems did the new government face?

   b. Summarize What compromise did Alexander Hamilton, Thomas Jefferson, and James Madison reach regarding repayment of state debts?

2. **a. Identify** What disagreement did Jefferson and Hamilton have over the central government?

   b. Draw Conclusions Hamilton was a New Yorker, while Jefferson was from Virginia. How do you think that affected their views on the economy?

   c. Elaborate Do you agree with Hamilton or Jefferson regarding the average citizen's ability to make decisions for the country? Explain your answer.

3. **a. Recall** Why did Jefferson oppose the creation of the Bank of the United States?

   b. Contrast What is the difference between loose construction and strict construction of the Constitution?

   c. Elaborate Defend Alexander Hamilton's stance in favor of the creation of a national bank.

Critical Thinking

4. **Identify Solutions** In this lesson you learned about U.S. economic problems and Hamilton's solutions. Create a chart similar to the one below and use it to show how Hamilton's views on the economy differed from those of Thomas Jefferson.

	Hamilton	Jefferson
Bonds		
Economy		
Tariffs		
National Bank		

Challenges for the New Nation

The Big Idea

The United States faced significant foreign and domestic challenges under Washington.

Main Ideas

- The United States tried to remain neutral regarding events in Europe.

- The United States and Native Americans came into conflict in the Northwest Territory.

- The Whiskey Rebellion tested Washington's administration.

- In his Farewell Address, Washington advised the nation.

Key Terms and People

French Revolution
Neutrality Proclamation
privateers
Jay's Treaty
Pinckney's Treaty
Little Turtle
Battle of Fallen Timbers
Treaty of Greenville
Whiskey Rebellion

Academic
Vocabulary
neutral unbiased, not favoring either side in a conflict

If YOU were there . . .

You are the captain of an American merchant ship in the 1790s. Your ship has just picked up cargo in the French West Indies. You are headed back to your home port of Philadelphia. Suddenly, a British warship pulls alongside your ship. Marines swarm aboard. They order you into the nearest harbor and seize your goods.

How would this incident affect your views of Great Britain?

Remaining Neutral

Tensions between France and Great Britain began to build after the French people rebelled against their king. On July 14, 1789, citizens of Paris attacked and captured the Bastille, a hated fortress and prison that stood as a mighty symbol of royal power.

The storming of the Bastille was one of the first acts of the **French Revolution**—a rebellion of French people against their king in 1789. The French people overthrew their king and created a republican government.

Many French citizens had been inspired to take action by the American Revolution. Many Americans, in turn, supported the French Revolution. They thought that France was creating the same kind of democracy as the United States.

Some Americans worried about the French Revolution's violent riots and attacks on traditional authority. Revolutionaries shocked many Americans by beheading King Louis XVI in January 1793 and Queen Marie-Antoinette later that year.

A few years after the French Revolution started, France and Great Britain went to war. Some Americans supported the French, while others backed the British. Some wanted to remain **neutral**.

The Neutrality Proclamation The debate divided Congress and Washington's cabinet. Washington presented his opinion to Congress on April 22, 1793:

> "The duty and interest of the United States require that they should with sincerity and good faith adopt and pursue a conduct friendly and impartial [unbiased] towards the belligerent [fighting] powers."
>
> —George Washington, from *The Writings of George Washington*

This **Neutrality Proclamation** stated that the United States would not take sides with any European countries that were at war. Washington believed his plan was the safest for the long run, but not everyone agreed.

Some members of Congress criticized Washington's ideas. James Madison believed that the president had gone beyond his authority. He questioned Washington's right to issue the proclamation without the approval of Congress.

The French Question France's new representative to the United States, Edmond Genet (zhuh-NAY), asked American sailors to help France fight England by commanding **privateers**. Privateers were private ships hired by a country to attack its enemies. Washington told Genet that using American privateers violated U.S. neutrality. Jefferson wanted the French revolutionaries to succeed, but even he agreed that allowing France to use American privateers against England was a bad idea.

Jefferson was still upset by U.S. policy toward France. He believed that the United States should back France because France had supported the United States during the Revolutionary War. Hamilton, on the other hand, was pro-British. He hoped to strengthen trading ties with Britain—the most powerful trading nation in the world at the time. Jefferson thought

Timeline: The Struggle for Neutrality

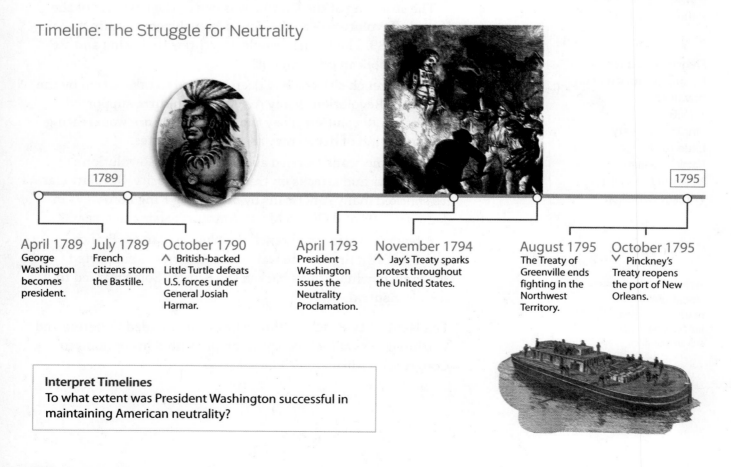

1789

1795

April 1789
George Washington becomes president.

July 1789
French citizens storm the Bastille.

October 1790
∧ British-backed Little Turtle defeats U.S. forces under General Josiah Harmar.

April 1793
President Washington issues the Neutrality Proclamation.

November 1794
∧ Jay's Treaty sparks protest throughout the United States.

August 1795
The Treaty of Greenville ends fighting in the Northwest Territory.

October 1795
∨ Pinckney's Treaty reopens the port of New Orleans.

Interpret Timelines
To what extent was President Washington successful in maintaining American neutrality?

that Hamilton had too much influence on the president's foreign policy and that Hamilton interfered with Jefferson's role as secretary of state. Jefferson decided to resign from Washington's cabinet in 1793.

Jay's Treaty There were other threats to U.S. neutrality. In late 1793 the British seized ships carrying food to the French West Indies. Hundreds of the ships were neutral American merchant ships. Also, British officers were helping Native Americans fight settlers.

Washington wanted to prevent another war with the British. He sent Chief Justice John Jay to London to work out a compromise. The British knew the United States lacked a strong navy and that U.S. businesses relied heavily on British trade. However, the British did not want to fight another war in America.

In November 1794 the two sides signed **Jay's Treaty**. Jay's Treaty settled the disputes that had arisen between the United States and Great Britain in the early 1790s. The British would pay damages on seized American ships and abandon their forts on the northwestern frontier. The United States agreed to pay debts it owed the British.

The treaty was unpopular and sparked violent protests. Citizens and congressional leaders thought the treaty hurt trade and did not punish Britain enough for some of its actions. Southerners were especially angry that the treaty did not ask Britain to repay them for slaves that Britain had set free during the Revolutionary War. Washington did not like the treaty but believed it was the most that could be done. At his urging the Senate approved the treaty.

Pinckney's Treaty American businesses faced problems as well. The Spanish disputed the border between the United States and Florida. Spain closed the port of New Orleans to U.S. trade in 1784. This hurt the American economy because all goods moving down the Mississippi to places in the East or overseas had to pass through New Orleans.

Washington asked Ambassador Thomas Pinckney to meet with Spanish officials to discuss the problem. He asked the Spaniards to reopen New Orleans to U.S. trade. Pinckney also asked for the right of deposit in New Orleans. This right would allow American boats to transfer goods in New Orleans without paying cargo fees.

Spanish minister Manuel de Godoy (goh•THOY) tried to delay reaching an agreement, hoping Pinckney would become desperate and sign a treaty that favored the Spanish. He was worried that the United States and Great Britain might join against Spain after signing Jay's Treaty. Pinckney was patient, however, and his patience was rewarded.

In October 1795 Godoy agreed to **Pinckney's Treaty**, which settled the border and trade disputes with Spain. Under the treaty Spain agreed to recognize the U.S. southern boundary as 31° north latitude. Spain's government also reopened the port at New Orleans to American ships and gave them the right of deposit. Because it opened the frontier to more expansion, Washington and most other Americans believed that Pinckney's Treaty was a successful compromise.

Reading Check
Summarize Why did President Washington want the United States to remain neutral?

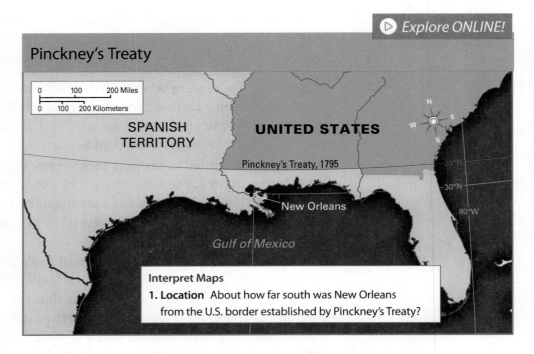

▶ Explore ONLINE!

Pinckney's Treaty

0   100   200 Miles
0   100   200 Kilometers

SPANISH TERRITORY

UNITED STATES

Pinckney's Treaty, 1795

31°N

30°N

80°W

New Orleans

Gulf of Mexico

Interpret Maps
1. **Location** About how far south was New Orleans from the U.S. border established by Pinckney's Treaty?

Conflict in the Northwest Territory

As the United States dealt with international conflicts, trouble was also brewing at home. Americans continued to settle the Northwest Territory despite Native Americans' protests. Supplied by British traders with guns, Native Americans went to war. In 1790 a Native American alliance under the command of Miami chief **Little Turtle** defeated U.S. forces under General Josiah Harmar. Then, in 1791 Native Americans defeated General Arthur St. Clair's troops.

General Wayne Takes Command In 1792 President Washington gave command of the army in the West to General Anthony Wayne. Wayne's task was to bring troops to the frontier to fight against the Indians. In 1793 General Wayne arrived in Ohio. Many of his men were ill from smallpox and influenza, so they were unable to fight well.

Wayne's troops moved north and built Fort Greenville, where they remained during the winter. They built additional forts for protection and to have supplies at hand.

As the summer of 1794 neared, several Native American groups led by Little Turtle attacked a supply train near the fort. Wayne and his men responded. They attacked Native American towns and burned crops.

The British no longer aided the Native Americans after this defeat, and Little Turtle realized that he was outmatched. He urged his people to seek peace.

"The trail has been long and bloody; it has no end. The [whites] . . . are many. They are like the leaves of the trees. When the frost comes they fall and are blown away. But when the sunshine comes again they come back more plentiful than ever before."

—Little Turtle, quoted in *The Ohio Frontier* by Douglas Hurt

Little Turtle, also known as Michikinikwa, was a Miami chief who won many battles against the United States, but eventually called for peace.

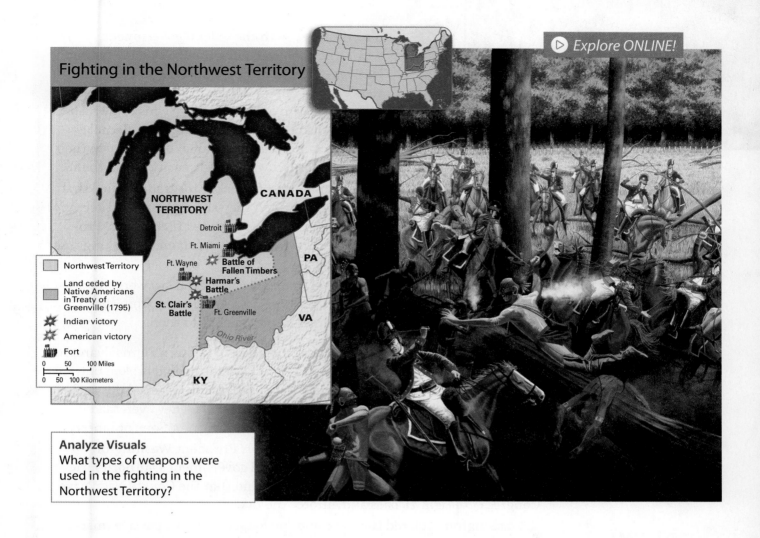

Fighting in the Northwest Territory

NORTHWEST TERRITORY

CANADA

Detroit

Ft. Miami

Ft. Wayne

Battle of Fallen Timbers

Harmar's Battle

St. Clair's Battle

Ft. Greenville

PA

VA

Ohio River

KY

Explore ONLINE!

Northwest Territory

Land ceded by Native Americans in Treaty of Greenville (1795)

Indian victory

American victory

Fort

0   50   100 Miles

0 50 100 Kilometers

Analyze Visuals
What types of weapons were used in the fighting in the Northwest Territory?

The End of Conflict On August 20, 1794, Native Americans fought Wayne's troops in the **Battle of Fallen Timbers** and were defeated. The battle was named for an area where many trees had been destroyed by a tornado. Wayne's forces burned Indians' villages and fields. The strength of Indian forces in the region was broken.

The frontier war soon ended. In August 1795 Native American leaders signed the **Treaty of Greenville**, which gave the United States claim to most Indian lands in the Northwest Territory. The treaty also guaranteed the safety of citizens there. In exchange, Native Americans received $20,000 worth of goods and an acknowledgment of their claim to the lands they still held.

Reading Check
Find Main Ideas
What conflicts did the United States face in the late 1700s?

The Whiskey Rebellion

Other conflicts were happening on the frontier. Congress passed a tax on American-made whiskey in March 1791. The tax was part of Hamilton's plan to raise money to help pay the federal debt. He was also testing the power of the federal government to control the states' actions.

Reaction in the West People in the western parts of states such as Pennsylvania, Virginia, and North Carolina were bitter about the tax. They were

Protesters tar and feather a tax collector during the Whiskey Rebellion in Pennsylvania.

already angry with the federal government, which they believed did not protect settlers from Native American attacks and did not allow settlers enough opportunities for trade. The farmers' corn crops were often made into whiskey, which was easier to transport than the corn. Because cash was rare, whiskey became like money in their region. The farmers believed that the tax was aimed specifically at them.

Farmers who produced small amounts of whiskey for trade argued that they could not afford the tax. They believed they should be able to keep the money they had made from a product they created themselves. Protests in 1792 led President Washington to issue a proclamation saying that people had to obey the law.

Westerners also disliked the fact that cases about the law were to be tried in a district court. These courts were usually far away from the people they affected and were a great inconvenience to them.

Whiskey Rebellion Is Crushed The complaints of western Pennsylvanians were at first expressed peacefully. But by 1794 fighting had broken out. In what became known as the **Whiskey Rebellion**, farmers lashed out against the tax on whiskey. Protesters refused to pay the tax. They even tarred and feathered tax collectors. Some called themselves the new Sons of Liberty.

Incidents of violence spread to other states. President Washington feared that the rebels threatened the federal government's authority. He believed he needed to make people understand that the Constitution gave Congress the right to pass and enforce the tax.

Washington declared that he could "no longer remain a passive [inactive] spectator" in the event. He personally led the army in military action against the rebellion—the first and only time an American president has done so. The army of about 13,000 men approached western Pennsylvania in November 1794. By this time most of the rebels had fled. The Whiskey Rebellion ended without a battle.

Washington Says Farewell

In 1796 Washington decided not to run for a third presidential term. He wrote that he was "tired of public life" and "devoutly [strongly] wished for retirement." He also wanted to remind Americans that the people were the country's true leaders. His decision to serve for only two terms set an example for future presidents.

With the help of Alexander Hamilton and James Madison, Washington wrote his Farewell Address. In it he spoke about what he believed were the greatest dangers to the American republic. Among these were the dangers of foreign ties and political conflicts at home. Washington warned against forming permanent ties with other countries because choosing sides could draw the United States into war.

Washington also worried about growing political conflicts within the nation. He believed that the disagreements between political groups weakened government. Political unity, he said, was a key to national success.

Reading Check
Support Points of View Defend the viewpoint of the Pennsylvania farmers who did not want to pay the whiskey tax.

Washington's Farewell Address

On September 19, 1796, President George Washington's Farewell Address first appeared in a Philadelphia newspaper. In it, Washington wrote about the nation's economy, political parties, and foreign policy.

While, then, every part of our country . . . feels an immediate and particular interest in union, all the parts combined cannot fail to find in the united mass . . . greater strength, greater resource, proportionally greater security from external danger, [and] a less frequent interruption of their peace by foreign nations; . . .

*I have already **intimated**[1] to you the danger of [political] parties in the state, with particular reference to the founding of them on geographical **discriminations**[2]. Let me now take a more **comprehensive**[3] view, and warn you in the most solemn manner against the **baneful**[4] effects of the spirit of party, generally.*

*If, in the opinion of the people, the distribution or **modification**[5] of the constitutional powers be in any particular wrong, let it be corrected by an amendment . . .*

*Promote, then, as an object of primary importance, institutions for the general **diffusion**[6] of knowledge . . . As the structure of a government gives force to public opinion, it is essential that public opinion should be enlightened . . .*

*[Avoid] likewise the accumulation of debt, . . . not ungenerously throwing upon **posterity**[7] the burden, which we ourselves ought to bear . . .*

*Observe good faith and justice toward all nations; **cultivate**[8] peace and harmony with all . . .*

The great rule of conduct for us, in regard to foreign nations, is . . . to have with them as little political connection as possible.

*It is our true policy to steer clear of permanent alliances with any portion of the foreign world . . . There can be no greater error than to expect, or **calculate**[9] upon real favors from nation to nation. It is an illusion, which experience must cure, which a just pride ought to discard.*

*The duty of holding a neutral conduct may be inferred . . . from the obligation which justice and humanity impose on every nation . . . to maintain **inviolate**[10] the relations of peace and **amity**[11] towards other nations.*

Washington lists the benefits of uniting the states under one government.

In this phrase, Washington emphasizes his warning against the dangers of political parties.

Washington points out the need for education.

This is Washington's advice to the new nation about foreign policy.

[1] *intimated:* told
[2] *discriminations:* differences
[3] *comprehensive:* complete
[4] *baneful:* destructive
[5] *modification:* change
[6] *diffusion:* spreading
[7] *posterity:* future generations
[8] *cultivate:* seek
[9] *calculate:* plan
[10] *inviolate:* unchanging
[11] *amity:* friendship

Analyze Historical Sources
1. What events happened that might have led to Washington's warning against political parties?
2. Why did Washington suggest neutrality as a foreign policy?

Reading Check
Find Main Ideas
What issues did
Washington believe
were most dangerous
to the future of the
new nation?

Washington left office warning the nation to work out its differences and protect its independence. Washington also warned against too much public debt. He thought the government should try not to borrow money. He wanted future generations to be protected from debt.

He concluded his speech by looking forward to his retirement and praising his country. "I anticipate . . . the sweet enjoyment . . . of good laws under a free government, the ever favorite object of my heart."

Summary and Preview Americans responded to foreign and domestic conflict during Washington's presidency. In the next lesson you will read about the formation of political parties in the United States and the presidency of John Adams.

Lesson 3 Assessment

Review Ideas, Terms, and People

1. a. Describe What did Washington's Neutrality Proclamation state?

    b. Compare and Contrast In what ways were Jay's Treaty and Pinckney's Treaty similar and different?

2. a. Identify Who were the leaders of American Indian and U.S. forces in the conflict in the Northwest Territory?

    b. Predict What are some possible consequences of the Treaty of Greenville for American Indians in the Northwest Territory?

3. a. Recall Why did Congress tax American-made whiskey?

    b. Explain How did the tax lead to the Whiskey Rebellion?

    c. Elaborate Why do you think that President Washington personally led the army against westerners in the Whiskey Rebellion?

4. a. Describe What warnings did Washington give the nation in his Farewell Address?

    b. Draw Conclusions Why did Washington not run for a third term as president?

Critical Thinking

5. Categorize In this lesson you learned about the challenges the young United States faced. Create a chart similar to the one below and then categorize those challenges as either foreign or domestic.

Challenges	
Foreign	
Domestic	

John Adams's Presidency

The Big Idea

The development of political parties in the United States contributed to differing ideas about the role of the federal government.

Main Ideas

- The rise of political parties created competition in the election of 1796.

- The XYZ affair caused problems for President John Adams.

- Controversy broke out over the Alien and Sedition Acts.

Key Terms and People

political parties
Federalist Party
Democratic-Republican Party
XYZ affair
Alien and Sedition Acts
Kentucky and Virginia
   Resolutions

If YOU were there . . .

You are a newspaper editor in Virginia in 1798. You've joined Jefferson's political party, which opposes the new president. In fact, your paper has printed many articles that criticize him, calling him greedy and foolish. You believe that's your right in a free country. But now Congress has passed a law that makes it illegal to criticize the government. You could be arrested for your articles!

Would you stop criticizing the government? Why?

The Election of 1796

The election of 1796 began a new era in U.S. politics. For the first time, more than one candidate ran for president. **Political parties**, groups that help elect people and shape policies, had begun to form during Washington's presidency. Despite Washington's warnings about political parties, the rivalry between two parties dominated the 1796 election.

Alexander Hamilton helped found the **Federalist Party**, which wanted a strong federal government and supported industry and trade. The Federalists chose John Adams and Thomas Pinckney as candidates. Adams knew he was not well liked in the South or the West, but he hoped people would support him after they thought about his years of loyal public service.

The Federalists, who wanted a strong federal government, were more popular in the North.

Federalists/North

Alexander Hamilton   John Adams   John Jay

The First Political Parties, 1796

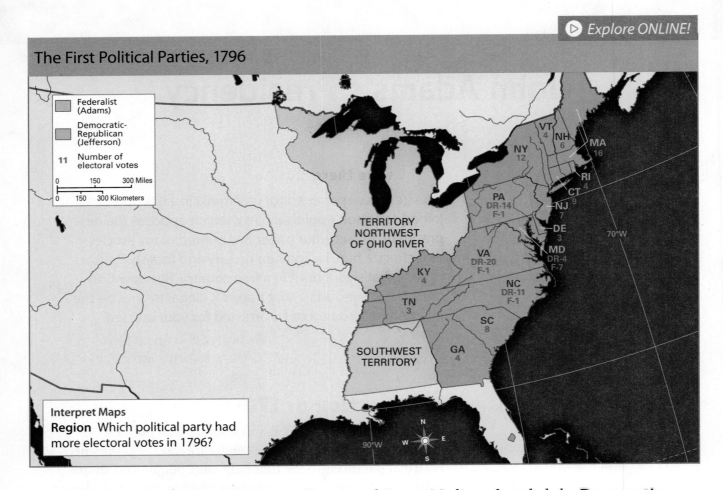

▶ Explore ONLINE!

Federalist (Adams)

Democratic-Republican (Jefferson)

11 Number of electoral votes

0   150   300 Miles

0   150   300 Kilometers

VT 4
NH 6
NY 12
MA 16
RI 4
CT 9
PA DR-14 F-1
NJ 7
DE 3
70°W
TERRITORY NORTHWEST OF OHIO RIVER
VA DR-20 F-1
MD DR-4 F-7
KY 4
NC DR-11 F-1
TN 3
SC 8
SOUTHWEST TERRITORY
GA 4
90°W

Interpret Maps

Region Which political party had more electoral votes in 1796?

Thomas Jefferson and James Madison founded the **Democratic-Republican Party**. Its members, called Republicans, wanted to limit the federal government's power. (This party is not related to today's Republican Party.) They chose Thomas Jefferson and Aaron Burr as their candidates.

Party differences were based partly on where and how people lived. Businesspeople in the cities tended to support the Federalists. Farmers in more isolated areas generally favored the Democratic-Republicans. Both sides attacked each other. Republicans called Adams a royalist—an insult to a man so involved in the Revolution. The Federalists accused the Republicans of favoring the French.

The Republicans, who wanted to limit the federal government's power, were more popular in the South.

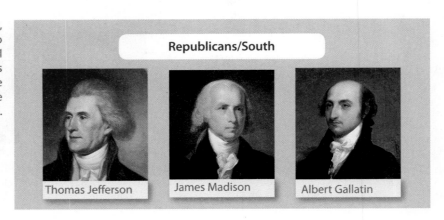

Republicans/South

Thomas Jefferson

James Madison

Albert Gallatin

Reading Check
Find Main Ideas
How did the election of 1796 change the nature of politics in the United States?

In the end, Adams defeated Jefferson. At the time, the person who came in second in a presidential election became vice president. So, after months of campaigning against one another, Adams and Jefferson took office together.

President Adams and the XYZ Affair

John Adams had the challenging task of following Washington as president. The people had adored Washington. Adams would have to work hard to win the people's trust.

A New President At first glance, John Adams did not appear well suited for the presidency. Although Adams had been a leading Patriot during the American Revolution and had later served as a foreign diplomat, he lacked Washington's dignity, and most people saw him as a cold and distant person. Still, many people—even those who opposed him—respected Adams. They recognized his hard work, honesty, and intelligence.

The United States and France One of Adams's first goals as president was to improve the relationship between the United States and France. With Great Britain and France still at war, the French had begun harassing and seizing U.S. ships. Adams sent U.S. diplomats to Paris to smooth over the conflict and to negotiate a treaty to protect U.S. shipping.

When the diplomats arrived in France, they learned that French foreign minister Talleyrand would not speak to them. Instead, they had a strange and secret visit from three French agents. Shockingly, the agents said that Talleyrand would discuss a treaty only in exchange for a $250,000 bribe. The French government also wanted a loan of $12 million. The amazed diplomats refused these demands.

In March 1798 President Adams told Congress that the peace-seeking mission had failed. He described the French terms, substituting the letters X, Y, and Z for the names of the French agents. Upon hearing the disgraceful news, Federalists in Congress called for war with France.

The **XYZ affair**, as the French demand for a bribe came to be called, outraged the American public. "Millions for defense, but not one cent for tribute!" became the rallying cry of the American people.

Preparations for War Fearing war, Adams asked Congress to expand the navy to a fleet of more than 30 ships. He thought war with France might be unavoidable. He also decided the United States should keep a peacetime army. Congress approved both measures.

Although Adams had asked Congress for military support, he did not want to go to war with France. He was worried about its cost. Therefore, he did not ask Congress to declare war. Instead, he tried to reopen peace talks with France.

Peace Efforts Adams's decision not to declare war stunned Federalists. Despite intense pressure from members of his own party, Adams refused to change his mind.

The XYZ Affair

After the XYZ affair, French ships continued to attack American ships. In this political cartoon, the United States is represented by the woman. The men, representing the French, are taking valuables from her. The people in the distance are other European nations.

Why do you think this man is encouraging the woman to look away?

These people aren't helping the woman. What do you think the cartoon is suggesting by this?

Analyze Historical Sources
How does the political cartoon show that America is being preyed upon by the French?

American and French ships, however, began fighting each other in the Caribbean. Adams sent a representative to France to engage in talks to try to end the fighting. The United States and France eventually signed a treaty. Adams then forced two members of his cabinet to resign for trying to block his peace efforts.

The Alien and Sedition Acts

Many Democratic-Republicans continued to sympathize with France. Federalists, angered by their stand, called them "democrats, mobocrats, and all other kinds of rats."

In 1798 the Federalist-controlled Congress passed four laws known together as the **Alien and Sedition Acts**. These laws were said to protect the United States, but the Federalists intended them to crush opposition to war. The most controversial of these laws was the Sedition Act, which forbade anyone from publishing or voicing criticism of the federal government. In effect, this canceled basic protections of freedom of speech and freedom of the press.

The two main Democratic-Republican leaders, Thomas Jefferson and James Madison, viewed these acts as a misuse of the government's power. Attacking the problem at the state level, they wrote resolutions passed by the Kentucky legislature in 1798 and by Virginia in 1799. Known as the

Reading Check
Identify Points of View What did Americans mean when they said "Millions for defense, but not one cent for tribute"?

Kentucky and Virginia Resolutions, these documents argued that the Alien and Sedition Acts were unconstitutional. They stated that the federal government could not pass these acts because they interfered with state government. Madison and Jefferson pressured Congress to repeal the Alien and Sedition Acts. Congress did not, although it allowed the acts to expire within a few years.

The Kentucky and Virginia Resolutions did not have the force of national law, but they supported the idea that states could challenge the federal government. This idea would grow to have a tremendous impact on American history later in the 1800s.

Summary and Preview Political parties formed to reflect different viewpoints. In the next lesson you will read about Thomas Jefferson's presidency.

Reading Check
Analyze Information How did the Kentucky and Virginia Resolutions support the rights of states?

Lesson 4 Assessment

Review Ideas, Terms, and People

1. **a. Recall** What two political parties emerged before the election of 1796? Who were the founders of each party?

   b. Analyze What effect did political parties have on the election of 1796?

   c. Elaborate Do you think it was difficult for Adams and Jefferson to serve together as president and vice president? Explain your answer.

2. **a. Recall** What was one of Adams's first goals as president?

   b. Make Inferences Why were Federalists shocked by Adams's decision to resume peace talks with the French?

3. **a. Identify** What did the Alien and Sedition Acts state?

   b. Explain What idea regarding states' rights did the Kentucky and Virginia Resolutions support?

   c. Elaborate Would you have supported the Alien and Sedition Acts? Explain your answer.

Critical Thinking

4. **Contrast** In this lesson you learned about the election of 1796 and the formation of political parties. Create a chart similar to the one below and then identify how each of the terms listed below reflected party disagreements.

XYZ Affair	
Alien and Sedition Acts	
Kentucky and Virginia Resolutions	

Jefferson Becomes President

The Big Idea

Thomas Jefferson's election began a new era in American government.

Main Ideas

- The election of 1800 marked the first peaceful transition in power from one political party to another.
- President Jefferson's beliefs about the federal government were reflected in his policies.
- *Marbury* v. *Madison* increased the power of the judicial branch of government.

Key Terms and People

John Adams
Louisiana Purchase
Meriwether Lewis
William Clark
Sacagawea
John Marshall
Marbury v. *Madison*
judicial review

If YOU were there . . .

You are a Maryland voter from a frontier district—and you are tired! For days, you and your friends have been wrangling over the presidential election. Who shall it be—John Adams or Thomas Jefferson? Your vote depends on your personal judgment.

Which candidate would you choose for president?

The Election of 1800

In the presidential election of 1800, Federalists **John Adams** and Charles C. Pinckney ran against Democratic-Republicans Thomas Jefferson and Aaron Burr. Each party believed that the American republic's survival depended upon the success of their candidates. With so much at stake, the election was hotly contested.

Unlike today, candidates did not travel around giving speeches. Instead, the candidates' supporters made their arguments in letters and newspaper editorials. Adams's supporters claimed that Jefferson was a pro-French radical. Put Jefferson in office, they warned, and the violence and chaos of the French Revolution would surely follow in the United States. In addition, Federalists argued that Jefferson's interest in science and philosophy proved that he wanted to destroy organized religion.

Democratic-Republican newspapers responded that Adams wanted to crown himself king. What else, they asked, could be the purpose of the Alien and Sedition Acts? Republicans also hinted that Adams would use the newly created permanent army to limit Americans' rights.

When the election results came in, Jefferson and Burr had won 73 electoral votes each to 65 for Adams and 64 for Pinckney. The Democratic-Republicans had won the election, but the tie between Jefferson and Burr caused a problem. Under the Constitution at that time, the two candidates with

The Election of 1800

John Adams and the Federalists
- Rule by wealthy class
- Strong federal government
- Emphasis on manufacturing
- Loose interpretation of the Constitution
- British alliance

Thomas Jefferson and the Democratic-Republicans
- Rule by the people
- Strong state governments
- Emphasis on agriculture
- Strict interpretation of the Constitution
- French alliance

| Adams receives 65 votes and Pinckney receives 64 votes. | **Election Results** | Jefferson and running mate Burr receive 73 votes each. |

- Peaceful change of political power from one party to another
- The tied race led to the Twelfth Amendment (1804), which created a separate ballot for president and vice president.

---

the most votes became president and vice-president. The decision went to the House of Representatives, as called for in the Constitution.

The House, like the electoral college, also deadlocked. Days went by as vote after vote was called, each ending in ties. Exhausted lawmakers put their heads on their desks and slept between votes. Some napped on the House floor.

Jefferson finally won on the 36th vote. The election marked the first time that one party had replaced another in power in the United States.

The problems with the voting system led Congress to propose the Twelfth Amendment. This amendment created a separate ballot for president and vice president.

Reading Check
Analyze Information What was significant about Jefferson's victory?

Jefferson in Office

When Jefferson took office, he brought with him a style and political ideas different from those of Adams and Washington. Jefferson was less formal than his predecessors, and he wanted to limit the powers of government.

Jefferson Is Inaugurated Americans looked forward with excitement to Jefferson's first speech as president. People from across the nation gathered in the new capital, Washington, DC, to hear him. Curious travelers looked with pride at the partially completed Capitol and at the executive mansion (not yet called the White House). The two buildings dominated the surrounding homes and forests.

Small businesses dotted the landscape. At one of these, a modest boardinghouse, the president-elect was putting the finishing touches on his speech. On the morning of March 4, 1801, he left the boardinghouse and walked to the Capitol. The leader of a republic, Jefferson believed, should not ride in fancy carriages.

Jefferson read his speech in a quiet voice. He wanted to make it clear that he supported the will of the majority. He also stressed the need for a limited government and the protection of civil liberties.

From these humble surroundings in which Jefferson delivered his speech, Washington eventually grew into a large and impressive city. Over the years, the Capitol and the executive mansion were joined by other state buildings and monuments. Jefferson, who had long dreamed of a new national capital that would be independent of the interests of any one state, was pleased to be a part of this process of building a federal city.

DOCUMENT-BASED INVESTIGATION   Historical Source

Jefferson's Inaugural Address

On March 4, 1801, Thomas Jefferson gave his first inaugural address. In the following excerpt, Jefferson describes his thoughts on the nation's future.

By using phrases like these, Jefferson tries to reassure his political opponents.

Here Jefferson states his opinion of what is essential to good government.

"*Let us, then, fellow citizens, unite with one heart and one mind . . . [E]very difference of opinion is not a difference of principle. We have called by different names **brethren**[1] of the same principle. We are all republicans; we are all federalists.*"

"*Still one thing more, fellow citizens, a wise and **frugal**[2] Government, which shall restrain men from injuring one another, shall leave them otherwise free to regulate their own pursuits of industry and improvement, and shall not take from the mouth of labor the bread it has earned. This is the sum of good government . . .*"

[1] *brethren:* brothers
[2] *frugal:* thrifty

This phrase shows Jefferson's determination to keep government small.

Analyze Historical Sources
What words and phrases indicate Jefferson's support for a small national government?

Jefferson Makes Changes President Jefferson faced the task of putting his Republican ideas into practice. One of his first actions was to select the members of his cabinet. His choices included James Madison as secretary of state and Albert Gallatin as secretary of the treasury.

Jefferson would also benefit from the Democratic-Republican Party's newly won control of both houses of Congress. At Jefferson's urging, Congress allowed the hated Alien and Sedition Acts to expire. Jefferson lowered military spending and reduced the size of the army. The navy was cut to seven active ships. Jefferson and Gallatin hoped that saving this money would allow the government to repay the national debt. Jefferson also asked Gallatin to find ways to get rid of domestic taxes, like the tax on whiskey. The Democratic-Republican–led Congress passed the laws needed to carry out these policies.

The entire national government in 1801 consisted of only several hundred people. Jefferson preferred to keep it that way. He believed that the primary **functions** of the federal government were to protect the nation from foreign threats, deliver the mail, and collect customs duties.

Jefferson did recognize that some of the Federalist policies—such as the creation of the Bank of the United States—should be kept. Although Jefferson had battled Hamilton over the Bank, as president, he agreed to leave it in place.

The Louisiana Purchase

Jefferson wanted to expand the borders of the United States. One problem that the young nation faced was that it had no ports on the Gulf of Mexico. Farmers in western areas had to ship their crops on boats down the Mississippi River to the port of New Orleans. The port of New Orleans was controlled by Spain. In 1801 in a secret treaty, Spain gave the Louisiana Territory back to France. The Louisiana Territory was a huge area to the west of the Mississippi that included New Orleans.

Jefferson feared that France would close New Orleans to American trade. So he sent James Monroe to Paris to try to purchase New Orleans. The French, however, offered to sell all of the Louisiana Territory to the United States for just $15 million. Monroe quickly agreed. Finalized in 1803, the **Louisiana Purchase** more than doubled the size of the United States.

The Louisiana Purchase was a remarkable bargain. However, it raised many questions. The U.S. Constitution made no mention of buying foreign lands. As a strict constructionist, Jefferson was troubled that he might be overstepping his power. However, common sense told him the purchase was a good idea. He and his advisers decided that the right to acquire territory was part of the president's constitutional power to make treaties. Some Federalists in Congress, however, called the Louisiana Purchase unconstitutional. Yet even Hamilton agreed that the purchase was good for the country. Congress quickly gave its approval.

Jefferson wanted Americans to learn more about the lands of the Louisiana Purchase. He asked his secretary, **Meriwether Lewis**, to lead an expedition to gather information about the territory. Lewis invited experienced frontiersman **William Clark** to join him as co-leader. In May 1804

Academic Vocabulary
functions uses or purposes

Reading Check
Summarize What policy changes did Democratic-Republicans introduce, and which Federalist policies did Jefferson keep?

Thomas Jefferson 1743–1826

Thomas Jefferson was born in Virginia, where he inherited a large estate from his father. At age 26 he began building his elegant lifetime home, Monticello, but he spent much of his life away from home.

Jefferson's powerful words in the Declaration of Independence have inspired people throughout the world to seek freedom, equality, and self-rule. One of his most celebrated achievements as president (1801–1809) was the purchase of the Louisiana Territory from France.

Jefferson died at Monticello on July 4, 1826, within hours of the death of President John Adams, his rival and friend. The date was also the 50th anniversary of the Declaration of Independence. Jefferson wanted only three of his accomplishments listed on his tomb: author of the Declaration of American Independence, author of the Virginia Statute for Religious Freedom, and Father of the University of Virginia. Yet, he had many other accomplishments—governor of Virginia, lawyer, Revolutionary leader, writer, inventor, architect, musician, astronomer, ambassador, secretary of state, and, of course, president of the United States.

Evaluate
Why has Thomas Jefferson been a hero to generations of Americans?

Lewis and Clark led about 30 frontier soldiers from their camp in St. Louis northwest up the Missouri River. By October the group, called the Corps of Discovery, had reached what is now North Dakota. One member of the Corps was York, an enslaved African owned by William Clark. York was a very skilled hunter.

A Shoshone Indian woman named **Sacagawea** (sak-uh-juh-WEE-uh) agreed to guide the expedition when it reached Shoshone land near the Rocky Mountains. In November 1805, after traveling more than 3,000 miles, the Corps of Discovery reached the Pacific Ocean. They finally got back to St. Louis in September 1806. Newspaper reports of their journey and the detailed journals they published made many Americans want to travel west.

Reading Check
Draw Conclusions
Why did the Louisiana Purchase trouble Jefferson?

The Supreme Court

Although Republicans controlled the presidency and Congress, Federalists dominated the federal judiciary. In an effort to continue their control over the judiciary, Federalist legislators passed the Judiciary Act of 1801 shortly before their terms of office ended. This act created 16 new federal judgeships that President Adams filled with Federalists before leaving office. The Republican press referred to these people as midnight judges.

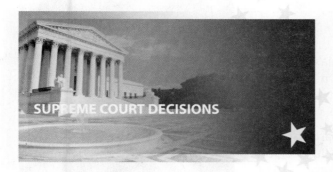

SUPREME COURT DECISIONS

Marbury v. Madison (1803)

Background of the Case

Shortly before Thomas Jefferson took office, John Adams had appointed William Marbury to be a justice of the peace. Adams had signed Marbury's commission, but it was never delivered. Marbury sued to force Madison to give him the commission.

The Court's Ruling

The Court ruled that the law Marbury based his claim on was unconstitutional.

The Court's Reasoning

The Judiciary Act of 1789 gave the Supreme Court the authority to hear a wide variety of cases, including those like Marbury's. But the Supreme Court ruled that Congress did not have the power to make such a law. Why? Because the Constitution limits the types of cases the Supreme Court can hear. Thus, the law was in conflict with the Constitution and had to be struck down.

Why It Matters

Marbury v. *Madison* was important for several reasons. It confirmed the Supreme Court's power to declare acts of Congress unconstitutional. By doing so, it established the Court as the final authority on the Constitution. This helped make the judicial branch of government equal to the other two branches. Chief Justice John Marshall and later federal judges would use this power of judicial review as a check on the legislative and executive branches.

Analyze Information
1. What do you think it means to be the final authority on the Constitution?
2. How did *Marbury* v. *Madison* affect the Constitution's system of checks and balances?

They argued that Adams had packed the judiciary with Federalists the night before he left office.

Some of these appointments were made so late that the documents that authorized them had not been delivered by the time Adams left office. This led to controversy once Jefferson took office. William Marbury, named as a justice of the peace by President Adams, did not receive his documents before Adams left office. When Jefferson took office, Marbury demanded the documents. On Jefferson's advice, however, the new secretary of state, James Madison, refused to deliver them. Jefferson argued that the appointment of the midnight judges was not valid.

Marbury brought suit, asking the Supreme Court to order Madison to deliver the appointment papers. Marbury claimed that the Judiciary Act of 1789 gave the Supreme Court the power to do so.

John Marshall, a Federalist appointed by John Adams, was the chief justice of the United States. Chief Justice Marshall and President Jefferson disagreed about many political issues. When Marshall agreed to hear Marbury's case, Jefferson protested. He said that the Federalists "have retired into the judiciary as a stronghold." Marshall wrote the Court's opinion in ***Marbury v. Madison***. This case helped establish the Supreme Court's power to check the power of the other branches of government.

John Marshall (1755–1835)

John Marshall was born, the first of 15 children, in Virginia's backcountry. He had little formal schooling. He received most of his education from his parents and a minister who lived with the family one year.

Even so, the lasting strength of the U.S. Constitution is partly due to Marshall's brilliant legal mind. In his long tenure as Chief Justice, John Marshall participated in more than 1,000 decisions and wrote 519 of them himself.

The Constitution, Chief Justice Marshall noted, gave the Supreme Court authority to hear only certain types of cases. A request like Marbury's was not one of them. The law that Marbury's case depended upon was, therefore, unconstitutional.

In denying Marbury's request in this way, the Court avoided a direct confrontation with Jefferson's administration. But more importantly, it established the Court's power of **judicial review**, the power to declare an act of Congress unconstitutional. Marshall and later federal judges would use this power of judicial review to make the judiciary a much stronger part of the national government.

Reading Check
Analyze Information Why was *Marbury* v. *Madison* an important ruling?

Summary and Preview A peaceful transfer of power took place in Washington after the election of 1800. In this module you learned about the early years of the new nation, the United States.

Lesson 5 Assessment

Review Ideas, Terms, and People

1. **a. Identify** What were the political parties in the election of 1800, and who were their candidates?

   b. Analyze Why was the election of 1800 significant?

2. **a. Describe** What ideas for government did Thomas Jefferson stress in his inaugural address?

   b. Compare and Contrast What similarities and differences did Jefferson's Republican government have with the previous Federalist one?

   c. Elaborate Defend Jefferson's preference for keeping the national government small.

3. **a. Identify** Who was John Marshall?

   b. Draw Conclusions Why is the power of judicial review important?

   c. Predict How might the *Marbury* v. *Madison* ruling affect future actions by Congress?

Critical Thinking

4. **Categorize** In this lesson you learned about Thomas Jefferson's beliefs and policies. Create a chart similar to the one below and show how Jefferson brought change through his policies.

Jefferson as President

Federalist Policies	Republican Policies

Make Group Decisions

Define the Skill

Democracy is one of the most valued principles of American society. It is based on the idea that the members of society, or representatives they choose, make the decisions that affect society. Decision making would be much more efficient if just one person decided what to do and how to do it. However, that method is not at all democratic.

Making decisions as a group is a complicated and difficult skill. However, it is an important one at all levels of society—from governing the nation to making group decisions at school, in the community, and with your friends. At every level, the skill is based on the ability of the group to interact in effective and cooperative ways.

Learn the Skill

Think about the job the first Congress faced after the Constitution was ratified. The nation was still millions of dollars in debt from the Revolutionary War. Congress had to find a way to pay these debts as well as raise money to run the government.

Leaders like Jefferson and Hamilton had ideas about how to accomplish these goals. However, neither man could act alone. In a democracy, a group such as Congress must make the decisions and take action.

This task was complicated by the fact that Jefferson and Hamilton disagreed on what to do. Each man's supporters in Congress pushed his point of view. Fortunately, its members were able to overcome their differences, compromise on goals and actions, and accept group decisions they might not have agreed with personally. Had they not possessed this ability and skill, the nation's early years might have been even more difficult than they were.

Like that first Congress, being part of an effective group requires that you behave in certain ways.

1. **Be an active member.** Take part in setting the group's goals and in making its decisions. Participate in planning and taking group action.

2. **Take a position.** State your views and work to persuade other members to accept them. However, also be open to negotiating and compromising to settle differences within the group.

3. **Be willing to take charge if leadership is needed.** But also be willing to follow the leadership of other members.

Practice the Skill

Suppose that you are a member of the first Congress. With a group of classmates, you must decide what and who should be taxed to raise the money the government needs. Remember that you are an elected official. If you do something to upset the people, you could lose your job. When your group has finished, answer the following questions.

1. Did your group have a plan for completing its task? Did it discuss what taxes to pass? Compared to other members, how much did you take part in those activities?

2. How well did your group work together? What role did you play in that? Was it a positive contribution or a negative one? Explain.

3. Was your group able to make a decision? If not, why? If so, was compromise involved? Do you support the decision? Explain why or why not.

Module 7 Assessment

Review Vocabulary, Terms, and People

Complete each sentence by filling in the blank with the correct term or person.

1. The _____ established the structure of the federal court system and its relationship to state courts.

2. Federalists angered many Republicans when they passed the _____ to protect the United States from traitors.

3. As president, Washington was able to establish several _____, or decisions that serve as examples for later action.

4. Farmers in western Pennsylvania protested taxes in the _____.

5. The _____ was created in order to strengthen the U.S. economy.

Comprehension and Critical Thinking

Lesson 1

6.
   a. **Recall** What precedents did President Washington and Congress establish for the executive and judicial branches?

   b. **Draw Conclusions** Why did Americans select George Washington as their first president?

   c. **Evaluate** Do you think the newly established government met the expectations of its citizens? Why or why not?

Lesson 2

7.
   a. **Identify** What changes did Alexander Hamilton make to the national economy?

   b. **Contrast** In what ways did Hamilton and Jefferson disagree on the economy?

   c. **Evaluate** Which of Hamilton's economic plans do you think was the most important to the new nation? Why?

Lesson 3

8.
   a. **Describe** What challenges did the nation face during Washington's presidency?

   b. **Make Inferences** Why did Washington believe that it was important for the United States to remain neutral in foreign conflicts?

   c. **Evaluate** Rate the success of Washington's presidency. Explain the reasons for your rating.

Lesson 4

9.
   a. **Describe** What role did political parties play in the election of 1796?

   b. **Analyze** How did the Alien and Sedition Acts create division among some Americans?

   c. **Predict** How might the political attacks between the Federalist and Democratic-Republican parties lead to problems in the future?

Lesson 5

10.
   a. **Recall** What were the key issues in the election of 1800?

   b. **Analyze** In what ways did *Marbury* v. *Madison* affect the power of the judicial branch?

   c. **Evaluate** Which of Jefferson's new policies do you think was most important? Why?

Module 7 Assessment, continued

Review Themes

11. Economics What economic problems troubled the nation at the beginning of Washington's presidency? How were they solved?

12. Politics How did the creation of political parties change politics in the United States?

Reading Skills

Inferences about History *Use the Reading Skills taught in this module to answer the question about the reading selection below.*

> Party differences were based partly on where and how people lived. Businesspeople in the cities tended to support the Federalists. Farmers in more isolated areas generally favored the Democratic-Republicans.

13. Which of the following statements can be inferred from the selection?
- **a.** Farmers wanted a large federal government.
- **b.** Urban Americans were usually Republicans.
- **c.** Merchants supported John Adams.
- **d.** People in the cities had different concerns than did the rural population.

Social Studies Skills

Make Group Decisions *Use the Social Studies Skills taught in this module to complete the activity below.*

Get together with a group of three or four students and discuss the Alien and Sedition Acts. Answer the following questions individually and as a group.

14. Do you think that limits should have been put on Americans' speeches and printed articles?

15. What other ideas might Congress have considered to resolve the tensions over the issue?

Focus on Writing

16. Write a Nobel Nomination The Nobel Prize is a prestigious world prize that was established in 1901, long after the four American leaders discussed in this module lived. But if the Nobel Prize had existed when Washington, Hamilton, Adams, and Jefferson were alive, which person would you choose to nominate for the Nobel Prize? Make your selection from one of these four people and write your nomination. Begin with a sentence that identifies the person you are nominating. Then give at least three reasons for your nomination. Each reason should include a specific achievement or contribution of this person. End your nomination with a sentence that sums up your reasons for nominating this person for the Nobel Prize. Be persuasive. You need to convince the Nobel Prize committee that this person deserves the prize more than anyone else in the world.

War and Expansion in the Americas

Essential Question
How should the War of 1812 be remembered?

About the Painting: General Andrew Jackson, on horseback, commands his troops against the British during the Battle of New Orleans.

In this module you will learn about events and issues surrounding the War of 1812.

What You Will Learn ...

Timeline of Events 1800–1820

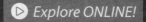

| United States | 1800 | World |

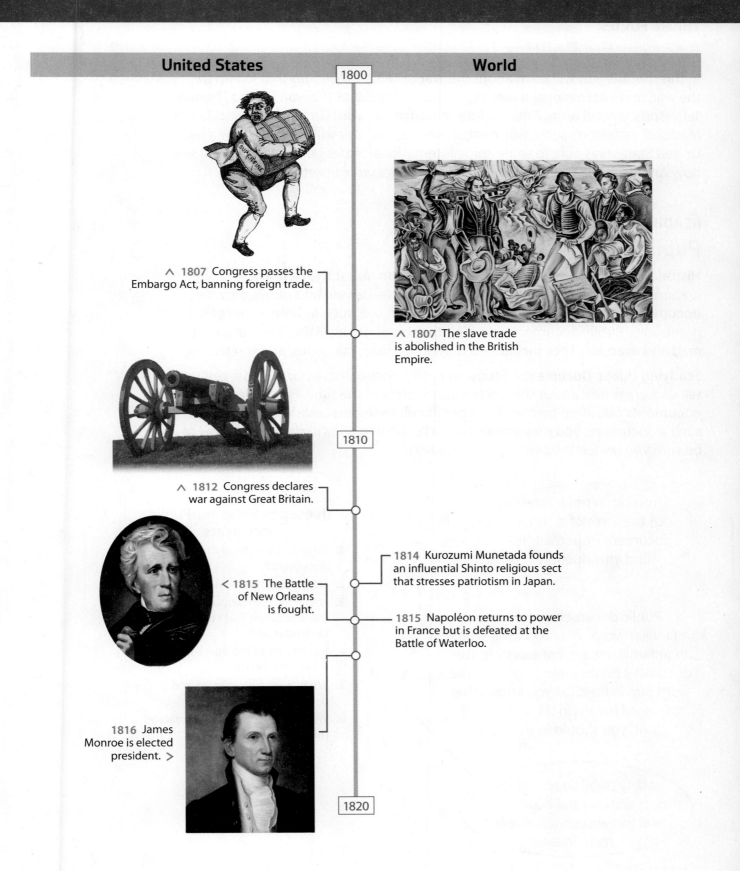

∧ **1807** Congress passes the Embargo Act, banning foreign trade.

∧ **1807** The slave trade is abolished in the British Empire.

1810

∧ **1812** Congress declares war against Great Britain.

1814 Kurozumi Munetada founds an influential Shinto religious sect that stresses patriotism in Japan.

< **1815** The Battle of New Orleans is fought.

1815 Napoléon returns to power in France but is defeated at the Battle of Waterloo.

1816 James Monroe is elected president. >

1820

Reading Social Studies

THEME FOCUS:
Geography, Politics

In this module you will learn about the War of 1812, challenges that led up to the war, and international issues that came as a result of the war. During Thomas Jefferson's second term, America found itself at war with Great Britain, and James Madison, Jefferson's successor, carried out that war. You will also learn how the United States was able to settle some international issues peacefully. You will see how America's expanding geography and politics were intertwined.

READING FOCUS:
Public Documents in History

Historians use many types of documents to learn about the past. These documents can often be divided into two types—private and public. Private documents are those written for a person's own use, such as letters, journals, or notebooks. Public documents, on the other hand, are available for everyone to read and examine. They include such things as laws, tax codes, and treaties.

Studying Public Documents Studying public documents from the past can tell us a great deal about the politics and society of the time. However, public documents can often be confusing or difficult to understand. When you read such a document, you may want to use a list of questions like the one below to be sure you understand what you're reading.

You can often figure out the topic of a public document from the title and introduction.

Public documents often use unfamiliar words or use familiar words in unfamiliar ways. For example, the document on the next page uses the word *augmented*. Do you know what the word means in this context? If not, you should look it up.

Many public documents deal with several issues and will therefore have several main ideas.

Questions Sheet for Public Documents

1. What is the topic of the document?
2. Do I understand what I'm reading?
3. Is there any vocabulary in the document that I do not understand?
4. What parts of the document should I re-read?
5. What are the main ideas and details of the document?
6. What have I learned from reading this document?

You Try It!

The passage below was taken from a Post Office notice from 1815. Read the passage and then answer the questions that follow.

Rates of Postage Postmasters will take notice, that by an act of Congress, passed on the 23d instant, the several rates of postage are augmented fifty per cent; and that after the first of February next, the Rates of Postage for single Letters will be,

For any distance not exceeding 40 miles, 12 cents
    Over 40 miles and not exceeding 90 miles, 15 cents
    Over 90 miles and not exceeding 150 miles,
      18 1/2 cents
    Over 150 miles and not exceeding 300 miles,
      25 1/2 cents
    Over 300 miles and not exceeding 500 miles, 30 cents
    Over 500 miles, 37 1/2 cents
    Double letters, or those composed of two pieces
      of paper, double those rates.
    Triple letters, or those composed of three pieces
      of paper, triple those rates.
    Packets, or letters composed of four or more
      pieces of paper, and weighing one ounce or
      more, avoirdupois, are to be rated equal to one
      single letter for each quarter ounce.

After reading the document above, answer the following questions.

1. What is this document about?

2. What was the main idea or ideas of this document? What supporting details were included?

3. Look at the word *packets* in the last paragraph of the document. The word is not used here in the same way we usually use *packets* today. What does the word mean in this case? How can you tell?

4. Are there any other words in this passage with which you are unfamiliar? How might not knowing those words hinder your understanding of the passage?

As you read Module 8, look for passages from other public documents. What can these documents teach you about the past?

Key Terms and People

Lesson 1
USS *Constitution*
impressment
embargo
Embargo Act
Non-Intercourse Act
Tecumseh
Battle of Tippecanoe
War Hawks
James Madison

Lesson 2
Oliver Hazard Perry
Battle of Lake Erie
Andrew Jackson
Treaty of Fort Jackson
Battle of New Orleans
Hartford Convention
Treaty of Ghent

Lesson 3
James Monroe
Rush-Bagot Agreement
Convention of 1818
Adams-Onís Treaty

The Coming of War

The Big Idea

Challenges at home and abroad led the United States to declare war on Great Britain.

Main Ideas

- Violations of U.S. neutrality led Congress to enact a ban on trade.
- Native Americans, Great Britain, and the United States came into conflict in the West.
- The War Hawks led a growing call for war with Great Britain.

Key Terms and People

USS *Constitution*
impressment
embargo
Embargo Act
Non-Intercourse Act
Tecumseh
Battle of Tippecanoe
War Hawks
James Madison

If YOU were there . . .

You are a tea merchant in Boston in 1807, but right now your business is at a standstill. A new law forbids trading with European nations. Now Boston Harbor is full of empty ships. It seems to you that the law is hurting American merchants more than European ones! You know that some merchants are breaking the law and smuggling goods, just to stay in business.

Would you obey the law or turn to smuggling?

Violations of Neutrality

During the late 1700s and early 1800s, American merchant ships fanned out across the oceans. The overseas trade, while profitable, was also risky. Ships had to travel vast distances, often through violent storms. Merchant ships sailing in the Mediterranean risked capture by pirates from the Barbary States of North Africa, who would steal cargo and hold ships' crews for ransom. Attacks continued until the United States sent the **USS *Constitution***, a large warship, and other ships to end them.

The Barbary pirates were a serious problem, but an even larger threat soon loomed. When Great Britain and France went to war in 1803, each country wanted to stop the United States from supplying goods to the other. Each government passed laws designed to prevent American merchants from trading with the other. In addition, the British and French navies captured many American merchant ships, searching for war supplies.

The real trouble, however, started when Britain began stopping and searching American ships for sailors who had run away from the British navy, forcing the sailors to return to British ships. Sometimes U.S. citizens were captured by accident. This **impressment**, or the practice of kidnapping and forcing people to serve in the army or navy, continued despite American protests.

The USS Constitution

Connect to Science and Technology In the early years of the republic, foreign trade was critical for the nation's survival. In 1797 Congress decided to create a navy to protect American merchant ships. The powerful warship USS *Constitution* was a key part of the new navy and was undefeated in battle. It is the oldest commissioned warship in the world.

The main mast is 220 feet high.

Copper sheathing supplied by Paul Revere protected the hull.

Most of the ship's cannons were located on the gun deck.

The crew slept and ate on the berth deck.

Boys called "powder monkeys" carried gunpowder from the orlop, or lowest deck, up to the gunners.

Analyze Visuals
Why do you think gunpowder was stored on the bottom deck?

Soon Britain was even targeting American navy ships. In June 1807, for example, the British ship *Leopard* stopped the U.S. Navy ship *Chesapeake* and tried to remove sailors. When the captain of the *Chesapeake* refused, the British took the sailors by force. The brazen attack on the *Chesapeake* stunned Americans.

The Embargo Act Great Britain's violations of U.S. neutrality sparked intense debate in America about how to respond. Some people wanted to go to war. Others favored an **embargo**, or the banning of trade, against Britain.

President Thomas Jefferson, who had easily won re-election in 1804, supported an embargo. At his urging, in late 1807 Congress passed the **Embargo Act**. The law essentially banned trade with all foreign countries. American ships could not sail to foreign ports. American ports were also closed to British ships. Congress hoped that the embargo would punish Britain and France and protect American merchant ships from capture.

The effect of the law was devastating to American merchants. Without foreign trade, they lost enormous amounts of money. Northern states that

The Embargo Act

The unpopularity of the Embargo Act prompted political cartoonists to show visually how the act was hurting American trade.

What do you think the turtle represents?

What is the turtle preventing this man from doing?

Analyze Historical Sources
How does the cartoonist emphasize the unpopularity of the Embargo Act?

What is "ograbme" spelled backward?

relied heavily on trade were especially hard hit by the embargo. Congressman Josiah Quincy of Massachusetts, in a speech before Congress, described the situation. "All the business of the nation is in disorder. All the nation's industry is at a standstill," he said.

The embargo damaged Jefferson's popularity and strengthened the Federalist Party. Angry merchants sent Jefferson hundreds of petitions demanding the Embargo Act's repeal. One New Englander said the embargo was like "cutting one's throat to stop the nose-bleed." Even worse, the embargo had little effect on Britain and France.

Non-Intercourse Act In 1809 Congress tried to revive the nation's trade by replacing the unpopular act with the **Non-Intercourse Act**. This new law banned trade only with Britain, France, and their colonies. It also stated that the United States would resume trading with the first side that stopped violating U.S. neutrality. In time, however, the law was no more successful than the Embargo Act.

Conflict in the West

Disagreements between Great Britain and the United States went beyond the neutrality issue. In the West, the British and Native Americans again clashed with American settlers over land.

The Conflict over Land In the early 1800s, Native Americans in the old Northwest Territory continued to lose land as thousands of settlers poured into the region. The United States had gained this land in the Treaty of Greenville, but American Indian leaders who had not agreed to the treaty protested the settlers' arrival. Frustrated American Indian groups considered what to do. In the meantime, Britain saw an opportunity to slow America's westward growth. British agents from Canada began to arm Native Americans who were living along the western frontier. Rumors

Reading Check
Compare and Contrast In what ways were the Embargo Act and the Non-Intercourse Act similar and different?

of British activity in the old Northwest Territory quickly spread, filling American settlers with fear and anger.

Tecumseh Resists U.S. Settlers Soon an American Indian leader emerged who seemed capable of halting the American settlers. **Tecumseh** (tuh-KUHM-suh), a Shawnee chief, had watched angrily as Native Americans were pushed off their land. A brilliant speaker, he warned other American Indians about the dangers they faced from settlers. He believed that the Native Americans had to do what white Americans had done: unite.

Tecumseh hoped to unite the Native Americans of the northwestern frontier, the South, and the eastern Mississippi Valley. He was helped by his brother, a religious leader called "the Prophet." They founded a village called Prophetstown for their followers near the Wabash and Tippecanoe rivers.

The Battle of Tippecanoe The governor of the Indiana Territory, William Henry Harrison, watched Tecumseh's activities with alarm. Harrison called him "one of those uncommon geniuses which spring up occasionally to . . . overturn the established order." The governor was convinced that Tecumseh had British backing. If true, Tecumseh could be a serious threat to American power in the West.

In 1810 Tecumseh met face to face with Harrison. The governor urged him to follow the Treaty of Greenville, which had been signed in 1795. Tecumseh replied, "The white people have no right to take the land from the Indians, because the Indians had it first." No single chief, he insisted, could sell land belonging to all American Indians who used it. In response, Harrison warned Tecumseh not to resist the power of the United States.

Tecumseh traveled south to ask the Creek nation to join his forces. In his absence, Harrison attacked. Harrison raised an army and marched his troops close to Prophetstown. Fighting broke out when the Prophet ordered an attack on Harrison's camp on November 7, 1811.

Timeline: America's Road to War

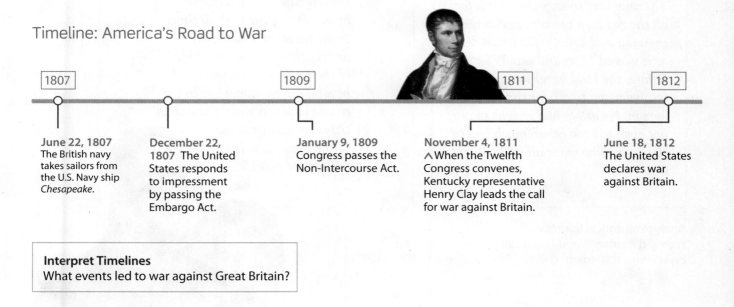

| 1807 | | 1809 | 1811 | 1812 |

June 22, 1807 The British navy takes sailors from the U.S. Navy ship *Chesapeake*.

December 22, 1807 The United States responds to impressment by passing the Embargo Act.

January 9, 1809 Congress passes the Non-Intercourse Act.

November 4, 1811 ∧ When the Twelfth Congress convenes, Kentucky representative Henry Clay leads the call for war against Britain.

June 18, 1812 The United States declares war against Britain.

Interpret Timelines
What events led to war against Great Britain?

The American Indians broke through army lines, but Harrison kept a "calm, cool, and collected" manner, according to one observer. During the all-day battle, Harrison's soldiers forced the American Indian warriors to retreat and then destroyed Tecumseh's village. Said Chief Shabbona, "With the smoke of that town and loss of that battle, I lost all hope." Although Tecumseh was safe, U.S. forces defeated Tecumseh and his followers in the **Battle of Tippecanoe**. The defeat destroyed Tecumseh's dream of a great American Indian confederation. He fled to Canada.

Reading Check
Find Main Ideas
Why were U.S. officials worried about Tecumseh's actions?

Call for War

The evidence of British support for Tecumseh further inflamed Americans. A Democratic-Republican newspaper declared, "The war on the Wabash [River] is purely BRITISH." Many Americans felt that Britain had encouraged Tecumseh to attack settlers in the West.

The War Hawks Several young members of Congress—called **War Hawks** by their opponents—took the lead in calling for war against Britain. These legislators, most of whom were from the South and West, were led by Henry Clay of Kentucky, John C. Calhoun of South Carolina, and Felix Grundy of Tennessee. They saw war as the only answer to British insults. "If we submit," Calhoun warned, "the independence of this nation is lost." Calls for war grew. Leaders wanted to put a stop to British influence among Native Americans. They also wanted to invade Canada and gain more land

---

DOCUMENT-BASED INVESTIGATION **Historical Source**

Views of War

Tecumseh urged Native Americans to unite to oppose what he called the "evil" of white settlement.

"The only way to stop this evil is for all the red men to unite in claiming a common and equal right to the land, as it was at first, and should be yet. Before, the land never was divided, but belonged to all, for the use of each person. No group had a right to sell, not even to each other, much less to strangers who want all and will not do with less."

—Tecumseh

William Henry Harrison was proud of his efforts to obtain land for settlers.

"By my own exertions in securing the friendship of the chiefs . . . by admitting them at all times to my house and table, my propositions for the purchase of their lands were successful beyond my . . . hopes . . . In the course of seven years the Indian title was extinguished to the amount of fifty millions of acres."

—William Henry Harrison

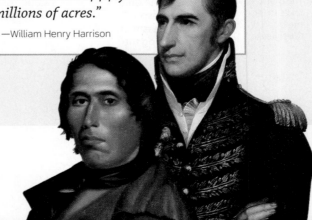

Analyze Historical Sources
How did Harrison's and Tecumseh's views on western settlement differ?

New Hampshire congressman Daniel Webster was a leading Federalist. He openly criticized war against the British and the violation of New England's shipping rights.

for settlement. Others were angered by British trade restrictions that hurt southern planters and western farmers. The War Hawks gave emotional speeches urging Americans to stand up to Great Britain.

The Opposition The strongest opponents of the War Hawks were New England Federalists. British trade restrictions and impressment had hurt New England's economy. People there wanted to renew friendly business ties with Britain instead of fighting another war.

Other politicians argued that war with Great Britain would be foolish. They feared that the United States was not yet ready to fight powerful Britain. America's army and navy were small and poorly equipped compared to Britain's military. In addition, Americans could produce only a fraction of the military supplies Britain could. Senator Obadiah German of New York pleaded with the War Hawks to be patient: "Prior to any declaration of war . . . my plan would be, and my first wish is, to prepare for it—to put the country in complete armor."

Declaring War Republican **James Madison** was elected president in 1808. He faced the difficulty of continuing an unpopular trade war begun by Jefferson. He also felt growing pressure from the War Hawks. By 1812 he decided that Congress must vote on war. Speaking to Congress, Madison blasted Great Britain's conduct. He asked Congress to decide how the nation should respond.

When Congress voted a few days later, the War Hawks won. For the first time in the nation's brief history, Congress had declared war. Months later, Americans elected Madison to a second term. He would serve as commander in chief during the War of 1812.

Summary and Preview Conflicts on the frontier and with Great Britain dominated U.S. foreign policy under Jefferson and Madison. In the next lesson you will read about the War of 1812.

Reading Check
Summarize Why did the United States declare war in 1812?

Lesson 1 Assessment

Review Ideas, Terms, and People

1. **a. Describe** In what ways did the war between France and Britain cause problems for the United States?

   b. Make Inferences What were the reasons for the failure of the Embargo Act?

   c. Elaborate Why do you think embargoes against Britain and France failed?

2. **a. Identify** What was Tecumseh's goal?

   b. Explain What role did Great Britain play in the conflict between the United States and American Indians on the western frontier?

3. **a. Identify** Who were the War Hawks? Why did they support war with Britain?

   b. Elaborate Would you have supported going to war against Great Britain? Explain your answer.

Critical Thinking

4. **Categorize** In this lesson you learned about the challenges that led to the War of 1812. Were most challenges foreign or domestic? Categorize them in a chart like the one below.

Foreign	Domestic

The War of 1812

The Big Idea

Great Britain and the United States went to battle in the War of 1812.

Main Ideas

- American forces held their own against the British in the early battles of the war.

- U.S. forces stopped British offensives in the East and South.

- The effects of the war included prosperity and national pride.

Key Terms and People

Oliver Hazard Perry
Battle of Lake Erie
Andrew Jackson
Treaty of Fort Jackson
Battle of New Orleans
Hartford Convention
Treaty of Ghent

If YOU were there . . .

It's 1812, and the United States and Great Britain are at war. You are a sailor on an American merchant ship that has been licensed as a privateer. Your ship's mission will be to chase and capture ships of the mighty British navy. Even with the help of merchant ships like yours, the American navy is badly outnumbered. You know you face danger and may not survive.

Do you think your mission will succeed?

Early Battles

In the summer of 1812, the United States was at war with one of the world's most powerful nations. Despite claims by the War Hawks, the War of 1812 would not be an easy fight.

War at Sea When the war began, the British navy had hundreds of ships. In contrast, the U.S. Navy had fewer than 20 ships. None of them was as powerful as the greatest British warships.

Most of the British navy's ships, however, were scattered around the globe. Although small, the U.S. Navy had well-trained sailors and powerful new warships such as the USS *Constitution*. American vessels defeated British ships several times in one-on-one duels. Such victories embarrassed the British and raised American morale. Eventually the British ships blockaded America's seaports.

Battles Along the Canadian Border American leaders hoped to follow up victories at sea with an overland invasion of Canada. Three attacks were planned—from Detroit, from Niagara Falls, and from up the Hudson River valley toward Montreal.

The attack from Detroit failed when British soldiers and American Indians led by Tecumseh captured Fort Detroit. The other American attacks failed when state militia troops refused to cross the Canadian border, arguing that they did not have to fight in a foreign country.

The War of 1812

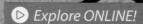 Explore ONLINE!

Disputed

BRITISH TERRITORY

Lake Superior

ME (PART OF MA)

Disputed

Montreal

St. Lawrence River

Plattsburg VT

NH

ILLINOIS TERRITORY

Lake Michigan

Lake Huron

York

Thames

Lake Ontario

Boston

MICHIGAN TERR.

Fort Niagara

NY

MA

Fort Detroit

Lake Erie

CT

RI

40°N

PERRY

HARRISON

PA

Philadelphia

NJ

New York City

Fort Dearborn

HULL

Lake Erie

INDIANA TERRITORY

OH

Baltimore

DE

MD

MISSOURI TERRITORY

Washington, D.C.

VA

KY

35°N

NC

TN

JACKSON

SC

Tallapoosa River

Horseshoe Bend

MISSISSIPPI TERRITORY

Alabama River

GA

ATLANTIC OCEAN

30°N

SPANISH TERRITORY

LA

Fort Mims

Disputed

SPANISH TERRITORY

80°W

75°W

25°N

New Orleans

Gulf of Mexico

85°W

95°W

90°W

Legend:

▬▬	American forces
✦	American victories
▬▬	British forces
✦	British victories
∥∥∥	British blockades
✦	Creek victory

0   150   300 Miles
0   150   300 Kilometers

Interpret Maps

1. **Location** According to the map, what major southern port was affected by the British blockade?

2. **Region** Which battles took place in the Great Lakes region?

In 1813 the United States went on the attack again. A key goal was to break Britain's control of Lake Erie. The navy gave the task to Commodore **Oliver Hazard Perry**. After building a small fleet, Perry sailed out to meet the British on September 10, beginning the **Battle of Lake Erie**. The battle ended when the British surrendered. Perry sent a message to General William Henry Harrison: "We have met the enemy and they are ours." Perry's brilliant victory forced the British to withdraw, giving the U.S. Army control of the lake and new hope.

With American control of Lake Erie established, General Harrison marched his army into Canada. At the Battle of the Thames River in

October 1813, he defeated a combined force of British troops and Native Americans. Harrison's victory ended British power in the Northwest. Tecumseh's death during the fighting also dealt a blow to the British alliance with Native Americans in the region.

The Creek War Meanwhile, war with American Indians erupted in the South. Creek Indians, angry at American settlers for pushing into their lands, took up arms in 1813. A large force attacked Fort Mims on the Alabama River, destroying the fort and killing close to 250 of its defenders. In response, the commander of the Tennessee militia, **Andrew Jackson**, gathered about 2,000 volunteers to move against the Creek nation.

In the spring of 1814, Jackson attacked the Creek along the Tallapoosa River in Alabama. Jackson's troops won this battle, the Battle of Horseshoe Bend. The **Treaty of Fort Jackson**, signed late in 1814, ended the Creek War and forced the Creek to give up millions of acres of their land.

Great Britain on the Offensive

Despite U.S. success on the western and southern frontiers, the situation in the East grew worse. After defeating France in April 1814, the British sent more troops to America.

British Attacks in the East Now reinforced, the British attacked Washington, DC. President Madison was forced to flee when the British broke through U.S. defenses. The British set fire to the White House, the Capitol, and other government buildings.

The British sailed on to Baltimore, Maryland, which was guarded by Fort McHenry. They shelled the fort for 25 hours. The Americans refused to surrender Fort McHenry. The British chose to retreat instead of continuing to fight.

The Battle of New Orleans After the attack on Washington, the British moved against New Orleans. British commanders hoped to capture the city and thus take control of the Mississippi River.

Reading Check
Compare What advantages did Great Britain and the United States have at the start of the war?

When the British attacked Washington, DC, First Lady Dolley Madison refused to leave until a famous portrait of George Washington was safely taken away from the White House.

Reading Check
Find Main Ideas
What happened at the Battle of New Orleans?

Andrew Jackson commanded the U.S. forces around New Orleans. His troops were a mix of regular soldiers, including two battalions of free African Americans, a group of Choctaw Indians, state militia, and pirates led by Jean Lafitte.

The battle began on the morning of January 8, 1815. Some 5,300 British troops attacked Jackson's force of about 4,500. The British began marching toward the U.S. defenses, but they were caught on an open field. The British were cut down with frightening speed. More than 2,000 British soldiers were killed or wounded. The Americans, for their part, had suffered about 70 casualties. The **Battle of New Orleans** made Andrew Jackson a hero and was the last major conflict of the War of 1812.

Effects of the War

Before the Battle of New Orleans, a group of New England Federalists gathered secretly at Hartford, Connecticut. At the **Hartford Convention**, Federalists agreed to oppose the war and send delegates to meet with Congress. Before the delegates reached Washington, however, news arrived that the war had ended. Some critics now laughed at the Federalists, and the party lost much of its political power.

Academic Vocabulary
consequences the effects of a particular event or events

Slow communications at the time meant that neither the Federalists nor Jackson knew about the **Treaty of Ghent**. The treaty, which had been signed in Belgium on December 24, 1814, ended the War of 1812.

Reading Check
Analyze Information
What were the main effects of the War of 1812?

Though each nation returned the territory it had conquered, the fighting did have several consequences. The war produced feelings of patriotism in Americans for having stood up to the mighty British. Some even called it the second war for independence. The war also broke the power of many Native American groups. Finally, a lack of goods caused by the interruption in trade boosted American manufacturing.

Summary and Preview The War of 1812 showed Americans that the nation would survive. In the next lesson you will see how the United States continued to grow.

Lesson 2 Assessment

Review Ideas, Terms, and People

1. **a. Identify** What losses did American forces face in the early battles of the War of 1812? What victories did they win?

   b. Make Generalizations What role did American Indians play in the war?

2. **a. Describe** What attacks did the British lead against American forces?

   b. Evaluate What do you think were the two most important battles of the war? Why?

3. **a. Identify** What was the purpose of the Hartford Convention?

   b. Draw Conclusions How did the War of 1812 positively affect the United States?

Critical Thinking

4. **Compare and Contrast** In this lesson you learned about the battles of the War of 1812. Compare and contrast the details of the major battles during the War of 1812 in a chart like the one below.

Battle	Details (Winner, Location, Effects)

Settling International Issues

The Big Idea

The Monroe administration secured and expanded its borders by settling issues with other nations.

Main Ideas

- The United States and Great Britain settled their disputes over boundaries and control of waterways.
- The United States gained Florida in an agreement with Spain.

Key Terms and People

James Monroe
Rush-Bagot Agreement
Convention of 1818
Adams-Onís Treaty

If YOU were there . . .

You are a Spanish settler living in West Florida in 1820. Your family has lived in Florida for many years. Only a few years ago, people in Spanish Florida were furious when American soldiers occupied the town of Pensacola. Now you hear that Spain has signed a treaty with the United States—Florida is no longer Spanish territory but rather part of the United States.

How would you feel about living under a new government?

Settling Disputes with Great Britain

In 1816 voters elected **James Monroe** to the presidency. From 1817 to 1825, Monroe's administration achieved a series of brilliant diplomatic successes. These successes settled long-standing disputes and helped secure and expand the borders of the United States.

For example, although the War of 1812 was over, there were still issues between Britain and the United States. Tensions remained high along the United States' northern border with British Canada. Both nations kept armed naval fleets in the Great Lakes to protect their interests.

On April 20, 1817, the two sides signed the **Rush-Bagot Agreement**, which limited naval power on the Great Lakes. In effect, the agreement demilitarized the border. Each nation agreed to keep only one military ship and one cannon on Lake Ontario and Lake Champlain. For the other Great Lakes, each nation was permitted two ships.

Another treaty with Britain gave the United States fishing rights off parts of the Newfoundland and Labrador coasts. This treaty, known as the **Convention of 1818**, also set the border between the United States and Canada at 49°N latitude as far west as the Rocky Mountains. Interest in the valuable fur trade in the Oregon Country was another issue resolved by this treaty. Both countries agreed to occupy the Pacific Northwest together, an agreement that would be tested in the years to come.

Reading Check
Summarize
What were the main disputes between the United States and Britain?

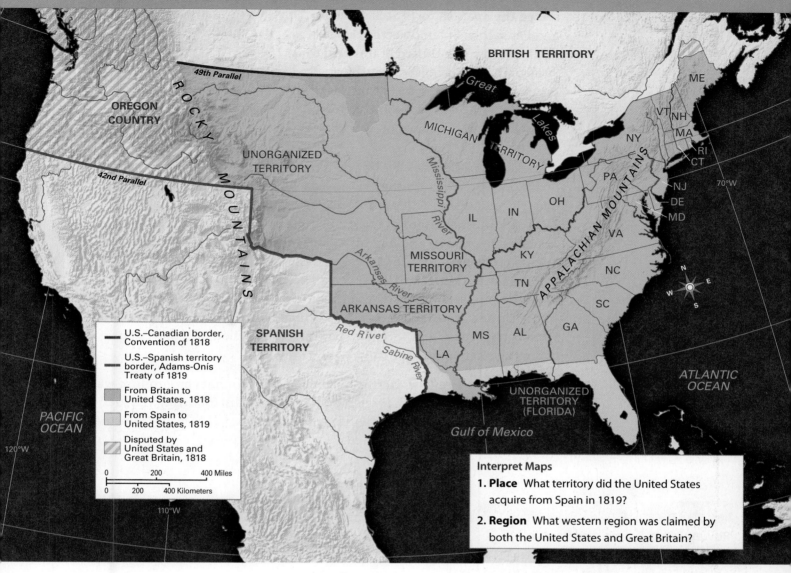

Interpret Maps

1. **Place** What territory did the United States acquire from Spain in 1819?

2. **Region** What western region was claimed by both the United States and Great Britain?

Legend:
- U.S.–Canadian border, Convention of 1818
- U.S.–Spanish territory border, Adams-Onís Treaty of 1819
- From Britain to United States, 1818
- From Spain to United States, 1819
- Disputed by United States and Great Britain, 1818

United States Gains Florida

The United States also had disputes along its southern border with Spanish Florida. After the War of 1812, the Seminoles in Florida continued to welcome runaway slaves from the United States. In turn, Americans continued to enter Florida. Some came as settlers, and others came to capture escaped slaves. Encounters between these Americans and the Seminoles were unfriendly. From 1817 to 1818, the Seminoles and their African American allies fought against Americans in a series of small battles that came to be known as the First Seminole War.

In April 1818, under General Andrew Jackson, U.S. troops invaded Florida. They drove out the Seminoles living in East Florida near the Georgia border, as well as those living west of the Suwannee River. Jackson wrote to the United States government that "the possession of Florida would be desirable [good] . . . and in sixty days it will be accomplished."

Then, believing that he had the permission of the U.S. government, Jackson seized the Spanish forts at St. Marks and Pensacola. Spain objected to Jackson's actions. The United States said that Jackson had acted without authority and returned to Spain the forts that Jackson had captured. Still, Jackson's campaign showed that Spain's hold on Florida was loosening.

Jackson's presence in Florida convinced Spain to negotiate with the United States over the ownership of Florida. On February 22, 1819, U.S. Secretary of State John Quincy Adams, son of John and Abigail Adams, and Spanish diplomat Luis de Onís signed the **Adams-Onís Treaty**, which settled all border disputes between Spain and the United States. Spain agreed to give Florida to the United States. In return, the United States gave up its claims to what is now Texas and agreed to pay up to $5 million of U.S. citizens' claims against Spain.

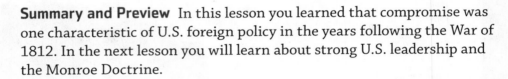

Andrew Jackson earned the nickname "Old Hickory" during the War of 1812. Soldiers called him that because he was strict. They said he was as tough as the wood of a hickory tree.

Reading Check
Summarize
How were the disagreements between the United States and Spanish Florida settled?

Summary and Preview In this lesson you learned that compromise was one characteristic of U.S. foreign policy in the years following the War of 1812. In the next lesson you will learn about strong U.S. leadership and the Monroe Doctrine.

Lesson 3 Assessment

Review Ideas, Terms, and People

1. **a. Identify** What issues were settled between the United States and Great Britain in 1817 and 1818?

   b. Make Inferences Why would the United States and Britain agree to occupy the Pacific Northwest together?

   c. Elaborate Why were the Rush-Bagot Agreement and the Convention of 1818 compromises?

2. **a. Recall** What problems existed between Spain and the United States?

   b. Analyze Why was the Adams-Onís Treaty important?

c. Evaluate Do you think that Andrew Jackson was right to act without orders? Explain your answer.

Critical Thinking

3. **Identify Cause and Effect** In this lesson you learned about U.S. foreign policy issues. Create a new chart and, for each issue, identify the nations involved, the agreement or treaty, and the effects.

Issue	Nations	Agreement/Treaty	Effects

Social Studies Skills

Work in a Group to Solve Issues

Define the Skill

You already know that the decision-making process is more complex in a group than it is if just one person makes the decisions. However, group decision-making becomes an even greater challenge when controversial issues are involved.

Group members must have additional skills for the group to function effectively when conflict exists within it. These include respect for differing views, the arts of persuasion and negotiation, and an ability to compromise. A group may not be able to find solutions to controversial problems unless its members have these skills.

Learn the Skill

Some of the biggest challenges Congress faced in the early 1800s were related to the war between Great Britain and France. Some Americans supported the British, while others favored the French. Both countries hoped for American help. When the United States would not take sides, they each began interfering with U.S. ships on the open seas.

As you read in this module, Congress tried to solve this problem by passing the Embargo Act. That solution was controversial, however. The northern states were hard hit by the law's ban on overseas trade. Their representatives in Congress demanded a less extreme action. The result was the Non-Intercourse Act. This law was a compromise between members who wanted to lift the trade ban and those who wanted to continue it. Congress was able to solve this problem because its members were able to work around their differences.

The skills Congress needed to reach its solution are valuable ones for any group that must make decisions involving controversial issues. They include the following attitudes and behaviors.

1. **Willingness to take a position.** If an issue is controversial, it is likely that group members will have differing opinions about it. You have a right to state your views and try to persuade others that you are correct.

2. **Willingness to listen to differing views.** Every other member has the same right you do. You have a duty to listen to their views, even if you do not agree. Disrespect for those whose views differ from yours makes it more difficult for the group to reach a solution.

3. **Willingness to debate.** Debate is a form of "healthy" argument because it defends and attacks ideas instead of the people who hold them. Debating the group's differences of opinion is an important step in reaching a solution.

4. **Willingness to negotiate and compromise.** If debate does not produce agreement, a compromise may be needed. Often it is better to have a solution that members may not like but can accept, than to have no agreement at all.

Practice the Skill

Check your understanding of the skill by answering the following questions.

1. Why would refusing to listen to other members make group decision-making more difficult?

2. Why is compromise often a better solution than forcing a decision on members who disagree?

Module 8 Assessment

Review Vocabulary, Terms, and People

Complete each sentence by filling in the blank with the correct term or person.

1. The British practice of capturing American sailors and forcing them to serve in the British navy, or _____, was one of the issues that led to the War of 1812.

2. After U.S. neutrality was violated, the United States issued an _____ against trade with foreign nations.

3. The War of 1812 ended soon after the U.S. victory over the British at the _____.

4. As commander of the Tennessee militia, _____ led his troops in battle against the Creek nation.

5. The border between the United States and Canada was settled in a treaty known as the _____.

6. Spain gave East Florida to the United States and the United States gave up its claims to what is now Texas when the two countries signed the _____.

Comprehension and Critical Thinking

Lesson 1

7. a. **Identify** What group, led by Congressman Henry Clay, called for war with Great Britain?

   b. **Contrast** What arguments were given in favor of war with Great Britain? What arguments were given against war with Britain?

   c. **Elaborate** In your opinion, why were the Embargo Act and the Non-Intercourse Act unsuccessful?

Lesson 2

8. a. **Identify** What roles did Andrew Jackson and William Henry Harrison play in the War of 1812?

   b. **Make Inferences** Why did the British want to capture the cities of Washington and New Orleans in the War of 1812?

   c. **Predict** In what ways might the U.S. victory over Great Britain in the War of 1812 affect the status of the United States in the world?

Lesson 3

9. a. **Identify** What issues did the Convention of 1818 resolve for the United States and Britain?

   b. **Predict** How might the decision that both countries occupy the Oregon Country be tested in the future?

   c. **Identify Cause and Effect** How did the First Seminole War begin? What effect did the war have on border disputes between Spain and the United States?

Review Themes

10. Geography In which bodies of water did the British set up blockades during the War of 1812?

11. Politics What impact did the Hartford Convention have on American politics?

Reading Skills

Public Documents in History *Use the Reading Skills taught in this module to answer the question below.*

12. Which of the following is an example of a public document?

   a. the Constitution

   b. the current president's journal

   c. a tax return

   d. an ambassador's letter to the president

Social Studies Skills

Work in a Group to Solve Issues *Use the Social Studies Skills taught in this module to answer the question below.*

13. Organize into groups of two or three students. Decide which of the following reasons for the War of 1812 you think might have been most important in Congress's decision to declare war.

   a. impressment of American sailors

   b. trade barriers with Britain and France

   c. battles with Native Americans on the frontier

   d. gaining land in Canada

Focus on Writing

14. Write a Résumé for Andrew Jackson A résumé lists a person's qualifications and work experience. It can also include a person's abilities and leadership experience. Review the information about Andrew Jackson's actions during the War of 1812 and in Florida during the First Seminole War. Choose three or four actions you think are the most important to show what kind of leader Jackson was. Write a sentence on each of those actions. Conclude with one or two sentences that summarize Andrew Jackson's leadership ability.

A New National Identity

★

Essential Question

Why did America's national identity change in the early 1800s?

About the Photo: The Erie Canal, completed in 1825, improved travel between cities and helped to unify the country.

▷ *Explore ONLINE!*

HISTORY.

VIDEOS, including...
- James Monroe
- Building the Erie Canal

☑ Document-Based Investigations

☑ Graphic Organizers

☑ Interactive Games

☑ Image with Hotspots: We Owe Allegiance to No Crown, 1814

☑ Image Carousel: Key Features of the American System

☑ Image with Hotspots: The Oxbow

☑ Image Carousel: Portraying America

In this module you will learn about the factors that contributed to the emergence of a distinctly American identity.

What You Will Learn ...

Timeline of Events 1810–1830

▶ Explore ONLINE!

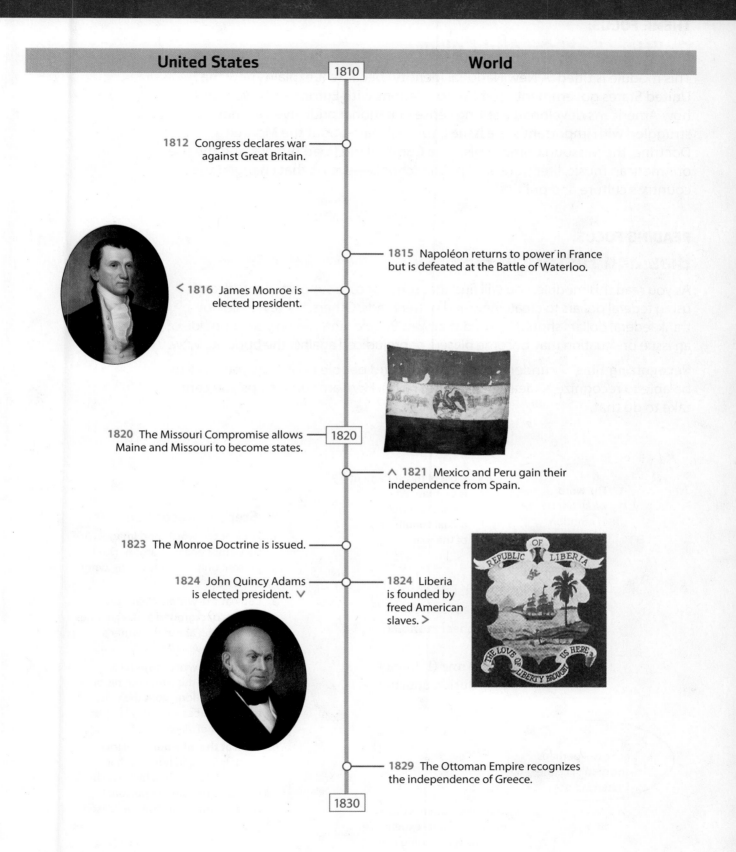

United States

World

1810

1812 Congress declares war against Great Britain.

1815 Napoléon returns to power in France but is defeated at the Battle of Waterloo.

< 1816 James Monroe is elected president.

1820 The Missouri Compromise allows Maine and Missouri to become states.

1820

∧ 1821 Mexico and Peru gain their independence from Spain.

1823 The Monroe Doctrine is issued.

1824 John Quincy Adams is elected president. **∨**

1824 Liberia is founded by freed American slaves. **>**

1829 The Ottoman Empire recognizes the independence of Greece.

1830

Reading Social Studies

Politics, Society and Culture

This module is titled "A New National Identity" because it explains how the United States government established relations with European powers and how Americans developed a strong sense of national pride even as they struggled with important state issues. You will learn about the Monroe Doctrine, the Missouri Compromise, the Cumberland Road project, and the rise of American music, literature, and public schools—events that changed the country's culture and politics.

READING FOCUS:

Bias and Historical Events

As you read this module, you will find that some people supported the idea of using federal dollars to create new and better roads. Others, however, did not think federal dollars should be used that way. People who can only see one side of an issue or situation may become biased, or prejudiced against the opposite view.

Recognizing Bias To understand the events and people in history, you have to be able to recognize a speaker's or writer's bias. Here are some steps you can take to do that.

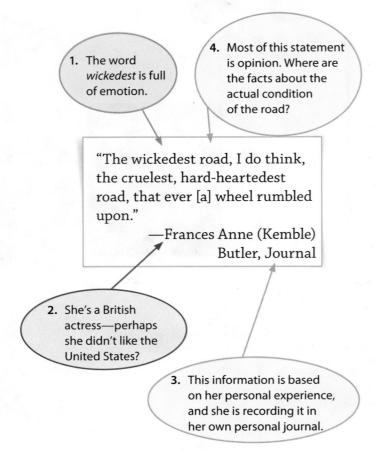

1. The word *wickedest* is full of emotion.

4. Most of this statement is opinion. Where are the facts about the actual condition of the road?

"The wickedest road, I do think, the cruelest, hard-heartedest road, that ever [a] wheel rumbled upon."

—Frances Anne (Kemble) Butler, *Journal*

2. She's a British actress—perhaps she didn't like the United States?

3. This information is based on her personal experience, and she is recording it in her own personal journal.

Steps to Recognize Bias

1. **Look at the words and images.** Are they emotionally charged? Do they present only one side or one point of view?

2. **Look at the writer.** What's the writer's background and what does that tell you about the writer's point of view?

3. **Look at the writer's sources.** Where does the writer get his or her information? Does the writer rely on sources who only support one point of view?

4. **Look at the information.** How much is fact and how much is opinion? Remember, facts can be proven. Opinions are personal beliefs—they can easily be biased.

You Try It!

The following passage is from the module you are getting ready to read. As you read the passage, think about living during the early to mid-1800s when there were no public schools.

Architecture and Education Americans also embraced educational progress. Several early American political leaders expressed a belief that democracy would only succeed in a country of educated and enlightened people. But there was no general agreement on who should provide that education.

Eventually, the idea of a state-funded public school gathered support. In 1837, Massachusetts lawmakers created a state board of education. Other states followed this example, and the number of public schools slowly grew.

After you read the passage, answer the following questions.

1. You are the editor of your town's newspaper in the year 1835. You think schools should be financed by the state government rather than the federal government. You decide to write an editorial to express your opinion. Which of the phrases below would reveal your personal bias to your readers? Why? What words in each statement create bias?

   a. overbearing federal government
   b. protecting state interests
   c. powerful federal government
   d. concerned state citizens

2. If you were going to write the editorial described in question 1, how could you avoid biased statements? How do you think this might affect people's reactions to your writing?

As you read Module 9, study the historical documents carefully. Do you see any examples of bias?

American Foreign Policy

The Big Idea

Nationalism helped guide American foreign policy in the early 1800s.

Main Ideas

- Success in foreign affairs contributed to a growing sense of American nationalism.

- The Monroe Doctrine was a major shift in American Foreign Policy.

Key Terms and People

nationalism
Era of Good Feelings
Simon Bolívar
Monroe Doctrine

If YOU were there . . .

You are a fur trader living in the Pacific Northwest in 1817. You have been extremely successful in your trade for many years. Now you hear that Great Britain and the United States have signed a treaty agreeing to occupy the Pacific Northwest together, opening the region to more settlers. Recently, you have discovered that several new fur traders are trapping on the lands you consider your hunting area.

What effect will this treaty have on your livelihood?

Growing Nationalism

American foreign policy in the early 1800s reflected a growing spirit of nationalism. **Nationalism** is a feeling of pride and loyalty to a nation. It is the belief that the interests of the nation as a whole are more important than regional interests or the interests of other countries.

In 1817 James Monroe took office as the fifth president of the United States. His presidency lasted two terms, from 1817 to 1825. During this time, the economy grew rapidly, and a spirit of nationalism and optimism prevailed. One Boston newspaper called the time the "**Era of Good Feelings**."

The good feelings at home were boosted by successes in foreign affairs. Americans were proud of their victory in the War of 1812. It made them confident in the strength of their young but growing country. Moreover, Monroe's administration achieved a series of diplomatic successes. With the Rush-Bagot Treaty and the Convention of 1818, the United States secured its northern border and convinced Britain to share territory in the Pacific Northwest. With the Adams-Onís Treaty, Monroe secured Florida for the United States.

Settled and secure at home, Americans were ready to take their place on the world stage. Nationalist feelings would soon drive a major shift in U.S. foreign policy.

Reading Check
Summarize
What events contributed to a growing sense of nationalism among Americans?

We Owe Allegiance to No Crown, 1814

After the United States won the War of 1812, American artist John Archibald Woodside painted this image.

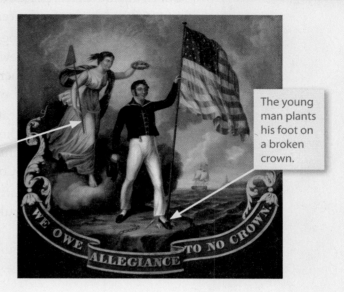

Lady Liberty carries a liberty pole and crown.

The young man plants his foot on a broken crown.

Analyze Historical Sources
How does Woodside's painting express national pride?

Academic Vocabulary
circumstances
surrounding situation

Monroe Doctrine

Despite Monroe's skillfully won agreements with Britain and Spain, the United States still faced foreign policy issues. These issues focused on the nation's neighbors to the south in Central and South America.

Spain had colonized Central and South America in the 1600s and 1700s. By the early 1820s, however, most of the Spanish colonies in the Americas had declared independence. Revolutionary fighter **Simon Bolívar**, called "the Liberator," led many of these struggles for independence. The political **circumstances** surrounding the revolutions reminded most American leaders of the American Revolution. As a result, they supported these struggles.

After Mexico broke free from Spain in 1821, President Monroe grew worried. He feared that rival European powers might try to take control of newly independent Latin American countries. He was also concerned about Russia's interest in the northwest coast of North America.

Secretary of State Adams shared President Monroe's concerns. In a Fourth of July speech before Congress, Adams said that the United States had always been friendly with European powers, and that the country did not want to be involved in wars with them. He implied that he supported the newly independent countries but said the United States would not fight their battles.

Great Britain was also interested in restraining the influence of other European nations in the Americas. This was because

President from 1817–1825, James Monroe helped shape U.S. foreign policy for the next century.

Britain had formed close trading ties with most of the independent Latin American countries. Britain wanted to issue a joint statement with the United States to warn the rest of Europe not to interfere in Latin America.

Instead, President Monroe and Secretary of State John Quincy Adams responded by declaring a new foreign policy for the United States. The policy was designed to protect American interests. In time, it would be called the Monroe Doctrine.

The **Monroe Doctrine** stated that the United States would view any European attempts to further colonize the Americas "as dangerous to our peace and safety." On December 2, 1823, Monroe issued the doctrine during his annual message to Congress.

The Monroe Doctrine had four basic points.
1. The United States would not interfere in the affairs of European nations.
2. The United States would recognize, and not interfere with, European colonies that already existed in North and South America.

DOCUMENT-BASED INVESTIGATION   Historical Source

The Monroe Doctrine

President James Monroe established the foundation for U.S. foreign policy in Latin America in the Monroe Doctrine of 1823.

In this phrase, Monroe warns European nations against trying to influence events in the Western Hemisphere.

Monroe notes here the difference between existing colonies and newly independent countries.

The occasion has been judged proper for asserting . . . that the American continents . . . are henceforth not to be considered as subjects for future colonization by any European powers . . .

The political system of the allied powers is essentially different . . . from that of America. We . . . declare that we should consider any attempt on their part to extend their system to any portion of this hemisphere as dangerous to our peace and safety . . .

With the existing colonies . . . we have not interfered and shall not interfere. But with the governments who have declared their independence and maintained it, and whose independence we have . . . acknowledged, *we could not view any* **interposition**[1] *for the purpose of oppressing them . . . by any European power in any other light than as the* **manifestation**[2] *of an unfriendly* **disposition**[3] *toward the United States.*

[1] *interposition:* interference
[2] *manifestation:* evidence
[3] *disposition:* attitude

Analyze Historical Sources
1. What warning did President Monroe give to European powers in the Monroe Doctrine?
2. How does Monroe say the United States will treat existing European colonies?

This political cartoon depicts the Monroe Doctrine, which forbade European powers from interfering with the nations of the Western Hemisphere.

How does the cartoon depict the United States in relation to the nations of Europe and Latin America?

3. The Western Hemisphere was to be off-limits to future colonization by any foreign power.
4. The United States would consider any European power's attempt to colonize or interfere with nations in the Western Hemisphere to be a hostile act.

The Monroe Doctrine was a bold statement to the great powers of Europe. It declared the Americas closed to any future European colonization. The United States would stay out of European affairs, but it would serve as leader and protector of the Americas. Some Europeans strongly criticized the Monroe Doctrine, but few European nations challenged it.

Over the next century, the Monroe Doctrine would guide American foreign policy. It was used to justify the westward expansion of the United States as well as expansionist foreign policies in Central and South America. The United States had taken its first steps toward becoming a world power.

Summary and Preview In this lesson you learned how a growing sense of nationalism guided a major shift in U.S. foreign policy. In the next lesson you will learn how national pride shaped domestic policy.

Reading Check
Analyze What effect did the revolutions in Latin America have on U.S. foreign policy?

Lesson 1 Assessment

Review Ideas, Terms, and People

1. a. Identify What is nationalism?

   b. Describe What circumstances characterized the Era of Good Feelings?

   c. Predict How might the Era of Good Feelings have been different if Americans had lost the War of 1812?

2. a. Describe What were the main points of the Monroe Doctrine?

   b. Contrast How did the Monroe Doctrine differ from Adams's Fourth of July Address?

   c. Draw Conclusions How did the Monroe Doctrine likely impact U.S. foreign policy?

   d. Elaborate What do you think the newly independent Latin American countries thought of the Monroe Doctrine?

Critical Thinking

3. Identify Cause and Effect In this lesson, you learned about nationalism and changes in U.S. foreign policy. Create a chart like the one below and use it to identify the causes and effects of foreign policy changes.

U.S. Foreign Policy

Causes	Effects

Nationalism and Sectionalism

The Big Idea

A rising sense of national unity allowed some regional differences to be set aside and national interests to be served.

Main Ideas

- Growing nationalism led to improvements in the nation's transportation systems.

- The Missouri Compromise settled an important regional conflict.

- The outcome of the election of 1824 led to controversy.

Key Terms and People

Henry Clay
American System
Cumberland Road
Erie Canal
National Road
sectionalism
Missouri Compromise
John Quincy Adams

If YOU were there . . .

You live near the western end of the newly completed Erie Canal in New York State in 1831. In fact, your older brothers helped build the canal. Every day you watch as mules pull the canal boats along the still water of the canal. Sometimes the boats carry passengers traveling from city to city. You have never been far from your home, and you are curious about their journey.

What would you like to ask the travelers on the canal boat?

Nationalism Guides Domestic Policy

The swell in nationalist feelings that arose in the early 1800s soon found its way into government policies. This new pride in the nation found a strong supporter in U.S. representative **Henry Clay** from Kentucky.

Clay believed that the nation's unity and future depended upon a strong national economy. He developed a plan eventually known as the **American System**—a series of measures intended to make the United States economically self-sufficient. The three main measures of the plan were:

1. **Establish a protective tariff,** a tax on imported goods that would protect American businesses from foreign competition. Congress passed such a tariff in 1816. By making European goods more expensive, the tariff encouraged Americans to buy less expensive American-made products.

2. **Establish a national bank** that would promote a single currency, making trade easier. At the time, most regional banks issued their own money. In 1816, Congress set up the second Bank of the United States.

3. **Improve the country's transportation systems,** which were essential for a strong economy. Poor roads, great distances, and geography slowed the movement of goods and made trade difficult and costly.

Henry Clay 1777–1852

Known as the silver-tongued Kentuckian, Henry Clay was a gifted speaker. He became involved in local politics early in his life, and by age 29 he was appointed to the U.S. Senate. Throughout his career in the Senate, he was dedicated to preserving the Union. The Missouri Compromise and a later agreement, the Compromise of 1850, helped to ease sectional tensions, at least temporarily.

Analyze
Why did Henry Clay work for compromises between regions?

Clay also proposed that the national government could spend the money it raised from a protective tariff and from selling public lands in the West to improve roads and canals. These improvements would strengthen the economy and unite North, South, East, and West.

However, some members of Congress opposed the plan. They argued that there was nothing in the Constitution granting the national government power to spend money on internal improvements. Still, Clay argued that the possible gains for the country justified federal action.

Roads and Canals In the early 1800s most roads in the United States were made of dirt, making travel difficult. British actress Frances Kemble described one New York road she had struggled along during a visit in the 1830s.

"The wickedest road, I do think, the cruellest, hard-heartedest road, that ever [a] wheel rumbled upon."

—Frances Anne (Kemble) Butler, *Journal*

Great distances and the lack of good roads made travel, trade, and communication difficult between North and South, East and West. Those settlers living in states west of the Appalachians found it especially difficult to ship goods east across the mountains.

To improve the nation's roads, Congress agreed with Clay and invested in road building. The **Cumberland Road** was the first road built by the federal government. It ran from Cumberland, Maryland, to Wheeling, a town on the Ohio River in present-day West Virginia. Construction began in 1815. Workers had to cut a 66-foot-wide band, sometimes through forest,

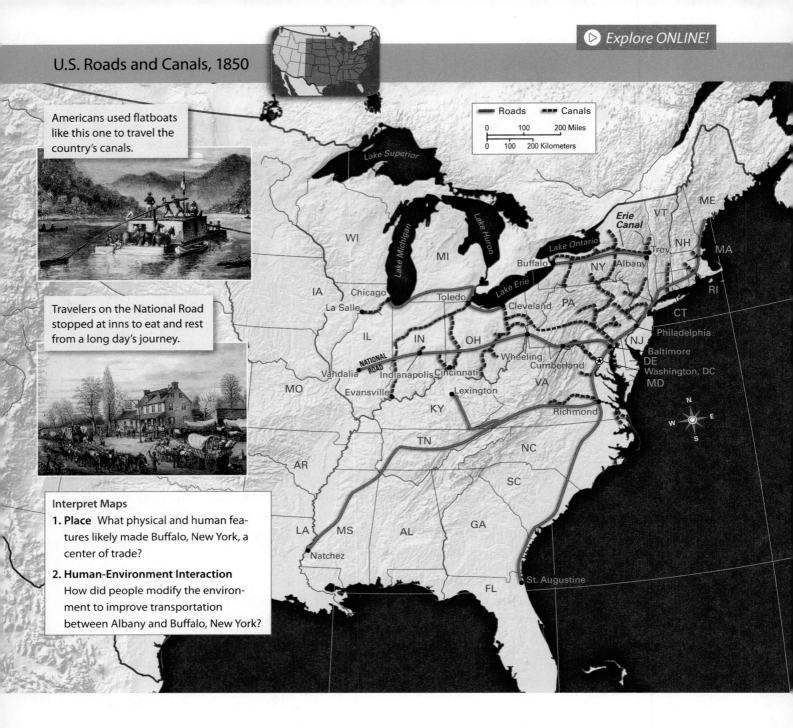

Explore ONLINE!

Americans used flatboats like this one to travel the country's canals.

Travelers on the National Road stopped at inns to eat and rest from a long day's journey.

Roads ━━ **Canals** ┅┅

0   100   200 Miles
0   100   200 Kilometers

Lake Superior

Lake Michigan

Lake Huron

Lake Ontario

Erie Canal

Lake Erie

WI

MI

IA

Chicago
La Salle

Toledo

Cleveland

PA

Buffalo

NY

Albany

Troy

VT

ME

NH

MA

RI

CT

Philadelphia

NJ

Baltimore
DE
Washington, DC
MD

IL

IN

OH

Wheeling

Cumberland

NATIONAL ROAD

Vandalia

Indianapolis

Cincinnati

VA

MO

Evansville

Lexington

KY

Richmond

TN

NC

SC

AR

LA

MS

AL

GA

Natchez

FL

St. Augustine

N
E
W
S

Interpret Maps

1. **Place** What physical and human features likely made Buffalo, New York, a center of trade?

2. **Human-Environment Interaction** How did people modify the environment to improve transportation between Albany and Buffalo, New York?

to make way for the road. Then they had to use shovels and pickaxes to dig a 12- to 18-inch roadbed, which they filled with crushed stone. All of the work had to be done without the benefit of today's bulldozers and steamrollers.

By 1818 the road reached Wheeling. By 1833 the **National Road**, as the expansion was called, stretched to Columbus, Ohio. By 1850 it reached all the way to Illinois. The National Road and smaller roads allowed people to travel and transport goods more easily, but land transportation remained slow and costly.

Boats offered faster and cheaper transportation, but geographic features could also be a challenge along water routes. Many rivers had changes

Academic
Vocabulary
incentive something
that leads people to
follow a certain course
of action

in elevation and, in some places, rapids and waterfalls made boat travel impossible. To help solve these problems, Americans built canals, human-made waterways that connected bodies of water.

In fact, the **incentive** for canal building caused so many to be built that the period from 1825 to 1850 is often called the Age of Canals. The most notable was the **Erie Canal**, a canal that created a waterway in New York between Albany and Buffalo, connecting the Hudson River with Lake Erie. Construction on the canal began in 1817 and was completed in 1825. It was 40 feet wide, 4 feet deep, and crossed 363 miles of wilderness and hilly terrain. Most of the laborers were American-born, but some were British, German, and Irish immigrants. With the help of hand tools, oxen, horses, and mules, they dug mile after mile through forests, fields, and swampland.

The opening of the Erie Canal sparked Americans' first major westward migration. It gave settlers and industries access to the fertile land and resources in the upper Ohio Valley and the Great Lakes region. People and manufactured goods moved west along the canal. In turn, farm products, timber, and other raw materials flowed east from the Great Lakes region to factories and mills in New York City.

Construction of the Erie Canal topped $7 million, but it proved a quick success and dramatically changed trade and settlement patterns. It cut the time and cost of shipping a ton of goods from Buffalo to New York City from 20 days to 6 days and from about $100 to less than $10. This helped establish New York City as a great city for industry and trade. Located where the Hudson River meets the Atlantic Ocean, New York was at the perfect geographic location to serve as a gateway between domestic and foreign trade. Smaller cities and towns sprouted up along the course of the Erie Canal and in the Great Lakes region. Trade and passenger traffic boosted local economies.

The Erie Canal also functioned as a communication highway. News and ideas travelled the waterway along with people and products. Ideas about women's rights and the abolition of slavery flourished in canal communities, as did new religious groups such as the Latter-Day Saints, or Mormons. Their ideas spread along the canal. Moreover, settlers bound for western lands brought with them different languages, customs, and religions. At a time of rising nationalist feelings, this flow of ideas helped create a bond between East and West.

Supreme Court Rulings From 1801 until 1835, John Marshall served as Chief Justice of the Supreme Court. Marshall was a firm believer in a strong national government. His Court made two key rulings that reflected nationalist feelings and strengthened the national government.

The emphasis on national unity was strengthened by two Supreme Court case decisions that reinforced the power of the federal government. In the 1819 case *McCulloch* v. *Maryland*, the Court asserted the implied powers of Congress in allowing for the creation of a national bank. In the 1824 case *Gibbons* v. *Ogden*, the Court said that the states could not interfere with the power of Congress to regulate interstate commerce.

Reading Check
Draw Inferences
How did new roads
and canals affect the
economy?

Missouri Compromise

At the same time nationalism was unifying the country, sectionalism threatened to drive it apart. **Sectionalism** is loyalty to the interests of one region of a country over the interests of the country as a whole. Regional economic and cultural differences had created some political divisions within the United States. For instance, white southerners developed an economy and culture based on cotton production and slavery. In the Northeast, wealth was based on manufacturing and trade. In the West, settlers wanted cheap land and strong transportation systems. At the level of national government, sectional interests based on regional differences often led to disagreements.

One such disagreement arose in 1819 when Congress considered Missouri's application to enter the Union as a slave state. At the time, the Union had 11 free states and 11 slave states. Adding a new slave state would have tipped the balance in the Senate in favor of the South.

To protect the power of the free states, the House passed a special amendment. It declared that the United States would accept Missouri as a slave state, but importing enslaved Africans into Missouri would be illegal. The amendment also set free the children of Missouri slaves. Southern politicians angrily opposed this plan.

North Carolina senator Nathaniel Macon wanted to continue adding slave states. "Why depart from the good old way, which has kept us in quiet, peace, and harmony?" he asked. Eventually, the Senate rejected the amendment. Missouri was still not a state.

Henry Clay convinced Congress to agree to the **Missouri Compromise**, which settled the conflict that had arisen from Missouri's application for statehood. This compromise had three main conditions:

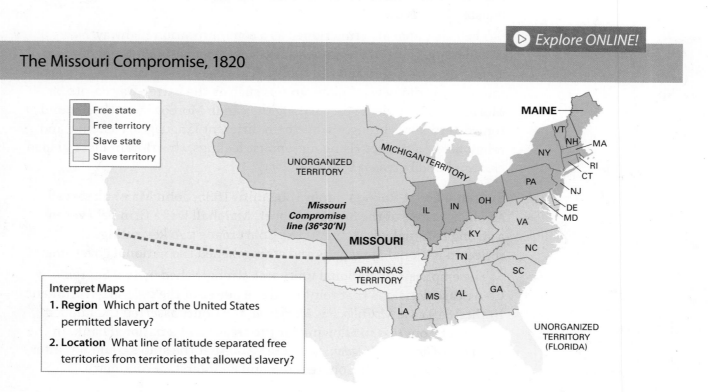

▷ *Explore ONLINE!*

The Missouri Compromise, 1820

Free state
Free territory
Slave state
Slave territory

MAINE

UNORGANIZED TERRITORY

MICHIGAN TERRITORY

VT
NH — MA
NY
RI
CT
PA
NJ
OH
DE
MD

Missouri Compromise line (36°30′N)

IL
IN
VA

MISSOURI

KY

NC

ARKANSAS TERRITORY

TN

SC

MS
AL
GA

LA

UNORGANIZED TERRITORY (FLORIDA)

Interpret Maps

1. **Region** Which part of the United States permitted slavery?

2. **Location** What line of latitude separated free territories from territories that allowed slavery?

1. Missouri would enter the Union as a slave state.
2. Maine would join the Union as a free state, keeping the number of slave and free states equal.
3. Slavery would be prohibited in any new territories or states formed north of 36°30' latitude—Missouri's southern border.

Reading Check
Draw Conclusions
Why did Henry Clay propose the Missouri Compromise to resolve the issue of Missouri statehood?

Congress passed the Missouri Compromise in 1820. Despite the success of the compromise, there were still strong disagreements between the North and South over the expansion of slavery.

The Election of 1824

Soon, a presidential election also brought controversy. Andrew Jackson won the most popular votes in 1824. However, he did not have enough electoral votes to win office. Under the Constitution, the House of Representatives had to choose the winner. When the House chose **John Quincy Adams** as president, Jackson's supporters claimed that Adams had made a corrupt bargain with Henry Clay. These accusations grew after Adams chose Clay to be secretary of state. The controversy weakened Adams's support.

Reading Check
Draw Inferences
Why did Adams have weak support during his presidency?

From 1825 to 1829, John Quincy Adams, son of John and Abigail Adams, served as the sixth president of the United States.

Summary and Preview In this lesson you learned how strong nationalistic feelings guided government policies, and how feelings of sectionalism challenged national unity. In the next lesson you will read about the development of a new national culture.

Lesson 2 Assessment

Review Ideas, Terms, and People

1. **a. Describe** How did national interests shape the policies related to regional commerce in the American System?

   b. Analyze Explain the impact the *McCulloch* v. *Maryland* and *Gibbons* v. *Ogden* decisions had on the federal government.

   c. Predict How would the National Road and the Erie Canal eventually contribute to the U.S. economy? to the westward expansion of trade and settlement?

   d. Make Inferences How did national goals, interests, and advances in transportation change perceptions of places and regions in the early 1800s?

2. **a. Describe** How was American society affected by sectionalism?

   b. Recall What role did Henry Clay play in the debate over Missouri's statehood?

   c. Explain What problem did Missouri's request for statehood cause?

   d. Elaborate Was the Missouri Compromise a good solution to the debate between free states and slave states? Explain your answer.

3. **a. Identify** Who were the candidates in the presidential election of 1824? How was the winner determined?

   b. Draw Conclusions Why did John Quincy Adams lose popular support following the election of 1824?

Critical Thinking

4. **Evaluate** In this lesson you learned about how nationalism and sectionalism affected national unity. Create a chart like the one below and use it to identify how the Missouri Compromise resolved threats to nationalism.

Sectional differences → Missouri Compromise →

Outcome
1.
2.
3.

History and Geography

The Erie Canal

In 1825 New York opened the Erie Canal, which connected Buffalo on Lake Erie to Albany on the Hudson River. With the new canal, boats and barges could travel from New York Harbor in the east to the Great Lakes region in the west. Trade boomed, new cities formed, and settlers moved farther west as the Erie Canal helped open up the Midwest region to farming and settlement.

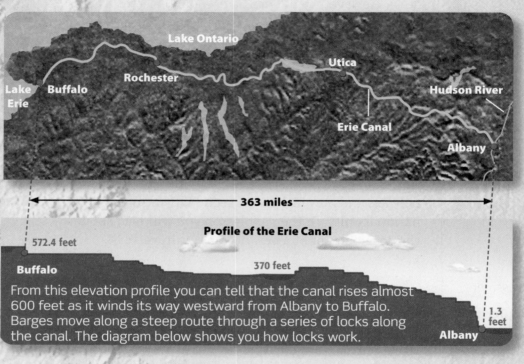

363 miles

Profile of the Erie Canal

572.4 feet

Buffalo

370 feet

From this elevation profile you can tell that the canal rises almost 600 feet as it winds its way westward from Albany to Buffalo. Barges move along a steep route through a series of locks along the canal. The diagram below shows you how locks work.

1.3 feet

Albany

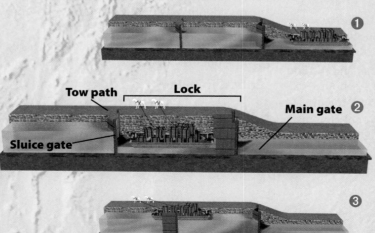

Tow path   **Lock**

Main gate

Sluice gate

How a Canal Lock Works

1. A barge enters the lock through the main gate.
2. Water flows into the lock through the sluice gate to raise the boat to the next level.
3. The barge leaves the lock as mules help pull it across the water.

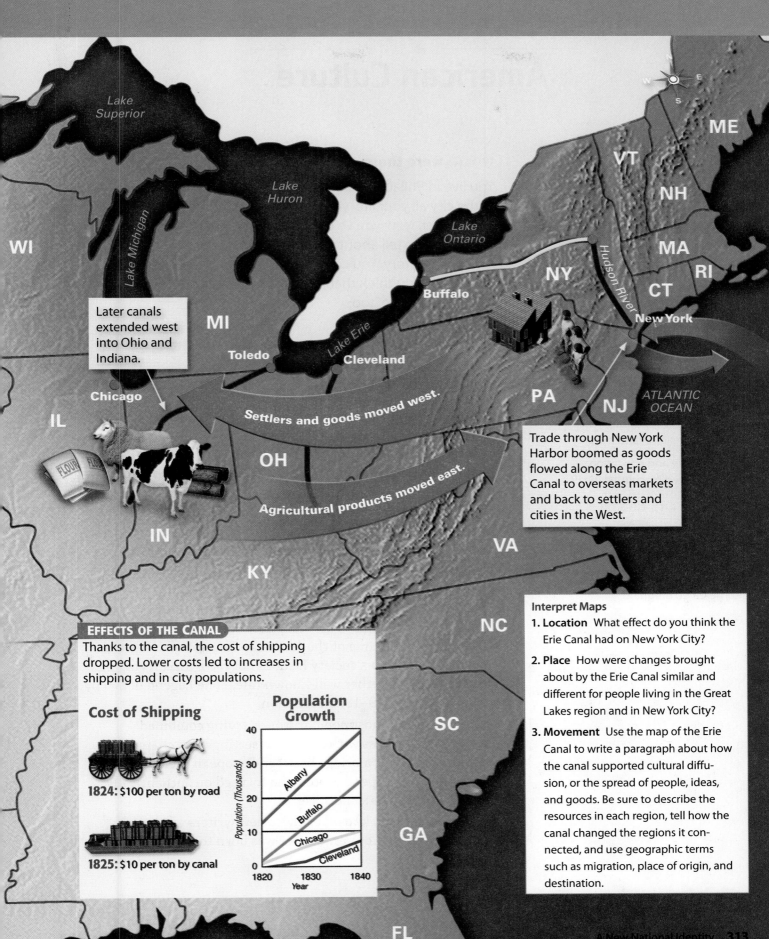

Lake Superior

Lake Huron

Lake Ontario

Lake Michigan

Lake Erie

WI

MI

Later canals extended west into Ohio and Indiana.

Chicago

IL

Toledo

Cleveland

Buffalo

NY

Hudson River

New York

ME

VT

NH

MA

RI

CT

PA

NJ

ATLANTIC OCEAN

Settlers and goods moved west.

OH

IN

KY

Agricultural products moved east.

FLOUR FLOUR

Trade through New York Harbor boomed as goods flowed along the Erie Canal to overseas markets and back to settlers and cities in the West.

VA

NC

EFFECTS OF THE CANAL

Thanks to the canal, the cost of shipping dropped. Lower costs led to increases in shipping and in city populations.

Cost of Shipping

1824: $100 per ton by road

1825: $10 per ton by canal

Population Growth

Population (Thousands)

40

30

20

10

0

Albany

Buffalo

Chicago

Cleveland

1820   1830   1840
Year

SC

GA

FL

Interpret Maps

1. **Location** What effect do you think the Erie Canal had on New York City?

2. **Place** How were changes brought about by the Erie Canal similar and different for people living in the Great Lakes region and in New York City?

3. **Movement** Use the map of the Erie Canal to write a paragraph about how the canal supported cultural diffusion, or the spread of people, ideas, and goods. Be sure to describe the resources in each region, tell how the canal changed the regions it connected, and use geographic terms such as migration, place of origin, and destination.

American Culture

The Big Idea

As the United States grew, developments in many cultural areas contributed to the creation of a new American identity.

Main Ideas

- American writers created a new style of literature.

- A new style of art showcased the beauty of America and its people.

- American ideals influenced other aspects of culture, including religion and music.

- Architecture and education were affected by cultural ideals.

Key Terms and People

Washington Irving
James Fenimore Cooper
Hudson River school
Thomas Cole
George Caleb Bingham

If YOU were there . . .

You live in Philadelphia in 1830. Though you've lived in the city all your life, you dream about the West and the frontier. Now you've discovered a wonderful writer whose stories tell about frontier life and events in American history. You can't wait to read his next exciting adventure. You think that perhaps someday you could be a frontier hero, too.

American Writers

Like many people the world over, Americans expressed their thoughts and feelings in literature and art and sought spiritual comfort in religion and music. Writers and artists were inspired by American history and the American landscape.

One of the first American writers to gain international fame was **Washington Irving**. Born in 1783, he was named after George Washington. Irving's works often told about American history. Through a humorous form of writing called satire, Irving warned that Americans should learn from the past and be cautious about the future.

Irving shared this idea in one of his best-known short stories, "Rip Van Winkle." This story describes a man who falls asleep during the time of the American Revolution. He wakes up 20 years later to a society he does not recognize. Irving published this and another well-known tale, "The Legend of Sleepy Hollow," in an 1819–1820 collection.

In some of his most popular works, Irving combined European influences with American settings and characters. His work served as a bridge between European literary traditions and a new type of writer who focused on authentically American characters and society.

Perhaps the best known of these new writers was **James Fenimore Cooper**. Cooper was born to a wealthy

New Jersey family in 1789. Stories about the West and the Native Americans who lived on the frontier fascinated him. These subjects became the focus of his best-known works.

Cooper's first book was not very successful, but his next novel, *The Spy,* was a huge success. Published in 1821, it was an adventure story set during the American Revolution. It appealed to American readers' patriotism and desire for an exciting, action-filled story.

In 1823 Cooper published *The Pioneers,* the first of five novels featuring the heroic character Natty Bumppo. Cooper's novels told of settling the western frontier and included historical events. For example, his novel *The Last of the Mohicans* takes place during the French and Indian War. By placing fictional characters in a real historical setting, Cooper popularized a type of writing called historical fiction.

Some critics said that Cooper's characters were not interesting. They particularly criticized the women in his stories; one writer labeled them "flat as a prairie." Other authors of historical fiction, such as Catharine Maria Sedgwick, wrote about interesting heroines. Sedgwick's characters were inspired by the people of the Berkshire Hills region of Massachusetts, where she lived. Her works include *A New-England Tale* and *Hope Leslie.*

Reading Check
Analyze How did American writers such as Irving and Cooper help create a new cultural identity in the United States?

A New Style of Art

The writings of Irving and Cooper inspired painters. These artists began to paint landscapes that showed the history of America and the beauty of the land. Earlier American painters had mainly painted portraits. By the 1830s, the Hudson River school had emerged. The artists of the **Hudson River school** created paintings that reflected national pride and an appreciation of the American landscape. They took their name from the subject of many of their paintings—the Hudson River valley.

Painters of the Hudson River school proved American landscapes were worthy of art. (Thomas Cole's *The Oxbow,* 1836)

In 1827 John Audubon began publishing *The Birds of America*, which was highly admired in England.

George Catlin traveled widely to paint images of Native American ways of life before they were lost.

Landscape painter **Thomas Cole** was a founder of the Hudson River school. He had moved to the United States from Britain in 1819. He soon recognized the unique qualities of the American landscape. As his work gained fame, he encouraged other American artists to show the beauty of nature. "To walk with nature as a poet is the necessary condition of a perfect artist," Cole once said.

Artists devoted themselves to other distinctly American subjects, too. John James Audubon began studying and drawing birds in the United States at the age of 18. Audubon's *The Birds of America* is a collection of 435 types of American birds.

By the 1840s the style of American painting was changing. More artists were trying to combine images of the American landscape with scenes from people's daily lives. Painters like **George Caleb Bingham** and Alfred Jacob Miller travelled west to paint scenes of the American frontier, including trappers, traders, settlers, and Native Americans.

Reading Check
Find Main Ideas
How did the style of American art change to reflect the American way of life in the early 1800s?

Religion and Music

Through the early and mid-1800s, several waves of religious revivalism swept the United States. During periods of revivalism, meetings were held for the purpose of reawakening religious faith. These meetings sometimes lasted for days and included large sing-alongs.

At many revival meetings people sang songs called spirituals. Spirituals are a type of folk hymn found in both white and African American folk-music traditions. This type of song developed from the practice of calling out text from the Bible. A leader would call out the text one line at a time, and the congregation would sing the words using a familiar tune. Each singer added his or her own style to the tune. The congregation of singers sang freely as inspiration led them.

While spirituals reflected the religious nature of some Americans, popular folk music of the period reflected the unique views of the growing nation in a different way. One of the most popular songs of the era was "Hunters of Kentucky," which celebrated the Battle of New Orleans. It became an anthem for the spirit of nationalism in the United States and was used successfully in Andrew Jackson's campaign for the presidency in 1828.

Reading Check
Summarize How did music reflect American interests in the early to mid-1800s?

Architecture and Education

American creativity extended to the ways in which people designed buildings. Before the American Revolution, most architects followed the style used in Great Britain. After the Revolution, leaders such as Thomas Jefferson called for Americans to model their architecture after the styles used in ancient Greece and Rome. Many Americans admired the ancient civilization of Greece and the Roman Republic because they contained some of the same democratic and republican ideals as the new American nation did.

As time went by, more architects followed Jefferson's ideas. Growing American cities soon had distinctive new buildings designed in the Greek and Roman styles. These buildings were usually made of marble or other stone and featured large, stately columns.

In the early to mid-1800s, American architects were inspired by ancient Greece and Rome.

Americans also embraced educational progress. Noah Webster, well known for his dictionary of American English published in 1828, spent much of his life working to provide children with a distinctly American education.

Several early American political leaders expressed a belief that democracy would only succeed in a country of educated and enlightened people. But there was no general agreement on who should provide that education.

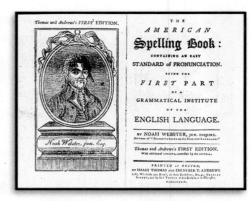

Noah Webster publishes *The American Spelling Book* in 1783 in an effort to promote American education.

Eventually, the idea of a state-funded public school gathered support. In 1837 Massachusetts lawmakers created a state board of education. Other states followed this example, and the number of public schools slowly grew.

Summary and Preview As the United States grew, so did a unique national identity. In Module 10 you will read about the changing face of American democracy.

Reading Check
Identify Points of View Why did some Americans call for new architectural styles and more education after the American Revolution?

Lesson 3 Assessment

Review Ideas, Terms, and People

1. a. **Describe** What topics interested American writers in the early 1800s?
   b. **Explain** Why is Washington Irving considered an important American writer?
2. a. **Identify** What influence did Thomas Cole have on American painters?
   b. **Describe** How did American painting styles change from the early period to the mid-1800s?
3. a. **Describe** What effect did religious revivalism have on American music?
   b. **Elaborate** Why do you think folk songs like "Hunters of Kentucky" were popular?
4. a. **Identify** On what historical examples did many American architects model their buildings? Why?
   b. **Predict** What might be some possible results of the growing interest in education in the United States?

Critical Thinking

5. **Categorize** In this lesson, you learned about new developments in American culture in the early 1800s. Create a graphic organizer similar to the one below and use it to show how cultural traits, beliefs, and characteristics reflected a new American identity.

Cultural Development ⟶	New Identity
Cultural Development ⟶	New Identity
Cultural Development ⟶	New Identity
Cultural Development ⟶	New Identity
Cultural Development ⟶	New Identity

Literature in History

Literature of the American Frontier

WORD HELP

accoutrements dress and gear

rude crude; rough

attenuated made thin

indurated hardened

unremitted ongoing

gartered fastened

ingenious clever

❶ *What do you learn about Natty Bumppo in the first paragraph?*

❷ A "girdle of wampum" is a belt strung with beads. Wampum were used by Native Americans for both money and decoration.

Make a list of the items Bumppo wears and carries. What does each item suggest about him?

About the Reading *The Last of the Mohicans* is one of five novels known as the Leatherstocking Tales. These novels follow the life and adventures of American pioneer Natty Bumppo (also known as Leatherstocking, Hawkeye, and the Deerslayer). Bumppo is the perfect woodsman: resourceful, honest, kind to both his friends and his enemies, but always a loner at heart.

As You Read Try to imagine what Natty Bumppo looks like.

From *The Last of the Mohicans*
by James Fenimore Cooper (1789–1851)

On that day, two men were lingering on the banks of a small but rapid stream . . . While one of these loiterers showed the red skin and wild accoutrements of a native of the woods, the other exhibited, through the mask of his rude and nearly savage equipments, the brighter though sunburnt and long-faded complexion of one who might claim descent from a European parentage. ❶

The frame of the white man, judging by such parts as were not concealed by his clothes, was like that of one who had known hardships and exertion from his earliest youth. His person, though muscular, was rather attenuated than full; but every nerve and muscle appeared strung and indurated by unremitted exposure and toil. He wore a hunting shirt of forest green, fringed with faded yellow, and a summer cap of skins which had been shorn of their fur. He also bore a knife in a girdle of wampum, ❷ like that which confined the scanty garments of the Indian, but no tomahawk. His moccasins were ornamented after the . . . fashion of the natives, while the only part of his underdress which appeared below the hunting frock was a pair of buckskin leggings that laced at the sides, and which were gartered above the knees with the sinews of a deer. A pouch and horn completed his personal accoutrements, though a rifle of great length, which the theory of the more ingenious whites had taught them was the most dangerous of all firearms, leaned against a neighboring sapling.

WORD HELP

dominant prevailing; ruling

apparition a ghostlike form that appears suddenly

collating comparing

spectre ghost

allege to firmly state

purport sense; gist

❶ A Hessian trooper is a German mercenary soldier from the American Revolution. *How and when is the horseman said to have died?*

❷ *Why does the horseman ride forth each night?*

❸ *What is happening "at all the country firesides"? What does this suggest about how early Americans entertained themselves?*

About the Reading "The Legend of Sleepy Hollow" has been called one of the first American short stories. Even though it is based on an old German folktale, its setting—a small village in the Hudson River valley—is American through and through. Irving's knack for capturing the look and feel of the region made the story instantly popular—as did the tale's eerie central character, a horseman without a head.

As You Read Try to picture both the ghost and the setting.

From "The Legend of Sleepy Hollow"
by Washington Irving (1783–1859)

The dominant spirit, however, that haunts this enchanted region, and seems to be commander in chief of all the powers of the air, is the apparition of a figure on horseback without a head. It is said by some to be the ghost of a Hessian trooper, ❶ whose head had been carried away by a cannon ball, in some nameless battle during the revolutionary war, and who is ever and anon seen by the country folk, hurrying along in the gloom of night, as if on the wings of the wind. His haunts are not confined to the valley, but extend at times to the adjacent roads, and especially to the vicinity of a church at no great distance. Indeed, certain of the most authentic historians of those parts, who have been careful in collecting and collating the floating facts concerning this spectre, allege, that the body of the trooper having been buried in the church yard, the ghost rides forth to the scene of battle in nightly quest of his head, ❷ and that the rushing speed with which he sometimes passes along the hollow, like a midnight blast, is owing to his being belated, and in a hurry to get back to the church yard before day break.

Such is the general purport of this legendary superstition, which has furnished materials for many a wild story in that region of shadows; and the spectre is known, at all the country firesides, by the name of The Headless Horseman of Sleepy Hollow. ❸

Connect Literature to History

1. **Draw Inferences** The writing of the period reflects a new national culture and identity. What do these passages suggest about the thoughts, feelings, or lives of early Americans?

2. **Make Predictions** *The Last of the Mohicans* takes place during the French and Indian War. Whose side do you think Natty Bumppo would most likely take—that of the French and Indians, that of the English, or neither? Explain your answer.

3. **Draw Conclusions** Both of these stories were very popular in their time. Why do you think these stories were so popular? What is it about the stories that makes them entertaining?

Social Studies Skills

Identify Central Issues

Define the Skill

The reasons for historical events are often complex and difficult to determine. An accurate understanding of them requires the ability to identify the central issues involved. A *central issue* is the main topic of concern in a discussion or dispute. In history, these issues are usually matters of public debate or concern. They generally involve political, social, moral, economic, or territorial matters.

Being able to identify central issues lets you go beyond what the participants in an event said and gain a more accurate understanding of it. The skill is also useful for understanding issues today and for evaluating the statements of those involved.

Learn the Skill

In this module you learned about the dispute that arose over Missouri's admission to the Union. Yet that was not what this controversy was really about. Recognizing the central issue in this dispute helps you understand why each side fought so hard over just one state.

Use the following steps to identify central issues when you read about historical events.

1. Identify the main subject of the information.

2. Determine the nature and purpose of what you are reading. Is it a primary source or a secondary one? Why has the information been provided?

3. Find the strongest or most forceful phrases or statements in the material. These are often clues to the issues or ideas the speaker or writer thinks most central or important.

4. Determine how the information might be connected to the major events or controversies of the time.

Practice the Skill

Soon after the Missouri Compromise passed, Secretary of State John Quincy Adams wrote:

"The impression produced upon my mind by the progress of this discussion [the dispute over Missouri] is that the bargain between freedom and slavery contained in the Constitution . . . is morally and politically vicious, . . . cruel and oppressive. . . . I have favored this Missouri Compromise, believing it to be all that can be effected [accomplished] under the present Constitution, and from an extreme unwillingness to put the Union at hazard [risk]. But perhaps it would have been a . . . bolder course to have persisted in the restriction upon Missouri till it should have terminated [ended] in a convention of the states to . . . amend the Constitution. This would have produced a new Union of thirteen or fourteen states unpolluted with slavery. . . . If the Union must be dissolved, slavery is precisely the question upon which it ought to break. For the present, however, this contest [issue] is laid to sleep."

Identify the central issues in the quote from Adams and answer the following questions:

1. What is Adams's subject? What is his reason for making these remarks?

2. What did Adams believe was the most important issue in the dispute? What strong language does he use to indicate this?

3. What evidence suggests Adams did not think the breakup of the Union was the central issue?

Module 9 Assessment

Review Vocabulary, Terms, and People

Match the word in the left column with the correct definition in the right column.

1. American System
2. George Caleb Bingham
3. Simon Bolívar
4. Henry Clay
5. Erie Canal
6. Hudson River school
7. James Monroe
8. Monroe Doctrine
9. nationalism
10. sectionalism

a. loyalty to the interests of one region of a country over the interests of the country as a whole

b. American artist known for his focus on the American landscape and people

c. sense of pride and devotion to a nation

d. a group of American artists in the mid-1800s who focused on the American landscape

e. a leader of independence movements in Latin America, known as "the Liberator"

f. the plan to raise tariffs in order to finance internal improvements such as roads and canals

g. president who promoted the acquisition of Florida, closer ties to Latin America, and presided during the Era of Good Feelings

h. project that connected the Hudson River to Lake Erie and improved trade and transportation

i. representative from Kentucky who promoted improvements in transportation and the Missouri Compromise

j. U.S. declaration that any attempt by a foreign nation to establish colonies in the Americas would be viewed as a hostile act

Comprehension and Critical Thinking

Lesson 1

11. a. **Identify** What were the four main points of the Monroe Doctrine?

    b. **Summarize** How did nationalism guide foreign policy in the early 1800s?

    c. **Draw Conclusions** Why do you think the Monroe Doctrine had such a lasting impact on U.S. foreign policy?

Lesson 2

12. a. **Recall** What developments helped strengthen national unity in this period?

    b. **Summarize** Under the American System, how did the national government use taxing and spending to influence the economy?

    c. **Analyze** How was the disagreement over Missouri's statehood an example of sectionalism? How was the disagreement resolved by Congress?

    d. **Predict** What effect might the election of 1824 have on national unity? Why?

Lesson 3

13. a. **Describe** How did popular music show the interests of Americans in the early 1800s?

    b. **Make Inferences** Why do you think new American styles of art and literature emerged?

    c. **Elaborate** Which element of American culture of the early 1800s do you find most appealing? Why?

Module 9 Assessment, continued

Review Themes

14. Politics How did the relations of the United States with foreign nations lead to a rise in nationalism?

15. Society and Culture What led to the creation of a uniquely American culture?

Reading Skills

Bias and Historical Events *Use the Reading Skills taught in this module to answer the question about the reading selection below.*

> When the House chose John Quincy Adams as president, Jackson's supporters claimed that Adams had made a corrupt bargain with Henry Clay. These accusations grew after Adams chose Clay to be secretary of state.

16. Which of the following used a biased definition, according to the above selection?

a. Andrew Jackson

b. Henry Clay

c. supporters of Jackson

d. John Quincy Adams

Social Studies Skills

Identify Central Issues *Use the Social Studies Skills taught in this module to answer the question about the reading selection below.*

> [Henry Clay] developed a plan eventually known as the American System—a series of measures intended to make the United States economically self-sufficient. To build the economy, he pushed for a national bank that would provide a single currency, making interstate trade easier. Clay wanted the money from a protective tariff to be used to improve roads and canals.

17. Which of the following is the central issue addressed by the American System?

a. economic unity

b. protective tariff

c. national bank

d. improving roads and canals

Focus on Writing

18. Write a Character Sketch Nations, like people, have characters. For example, a nation might be described as peaceful or aggressive, prosperous or struggling. Write a paragraph describing your overall impression of the nation's character. Write one sentence describing each of these aspects of the United States: its relationships with others, its feelings about itself, and its values.

Module 10

The Age of Jackson

★

Essential Question

Did Andrew Jackson advance the cause of democracy?

About the Photo: This statue of Andrew Jackson has stood in Washington, DC, for more than 150 years and captures the drive and spirit of the seventh president of the United States.

In this module you will learn about President Andrew Jackson and why historians refer to his time in office as the Age of Jackson.

What You Will Learn ...

▶ *Explore ONLINE!*

HISTORY.

VIDEOS, including...
- Jackson: Cherokees, Tariffs, and Nullification
- Jackson's Personality and Legacy
- Jackson Censured in Bank War

☑ Document-Based Investigations

☑ Graphic Organizers

☑ Interactive Games

☑ Image Slider: Dirty Politics in the 1828 Campaign

☑ Image Carousel: Regions of the United States

☑ Image Carousel: Native American Groups

Timeline of Events 1825–1845

▶ Explore ONLINE!

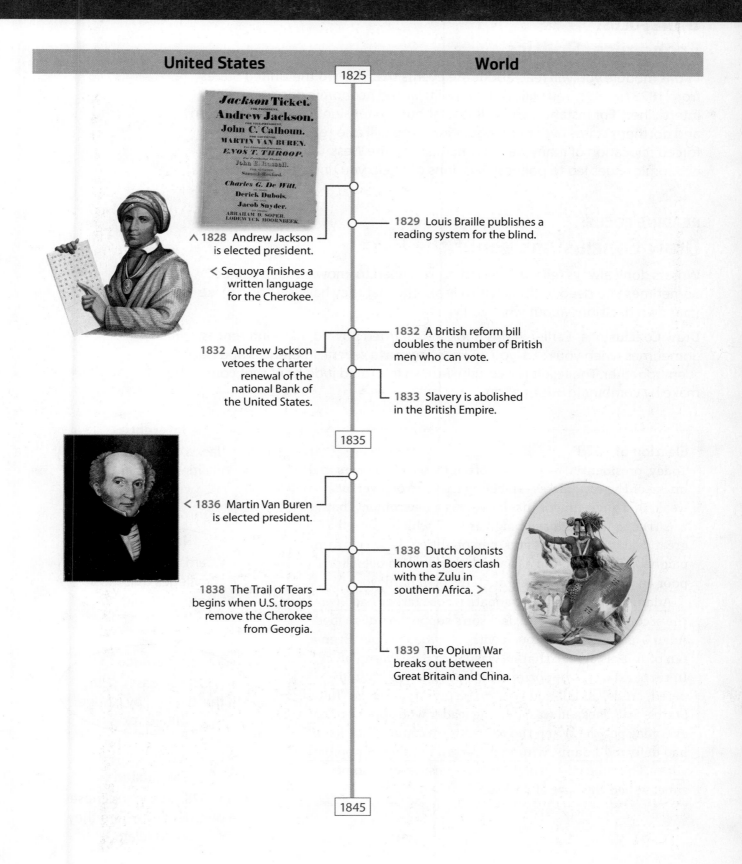

United States		World

1825

1828 Andrew Jackson is elected president.

< Sequoya finishes a written language for the Cherokee.

1829 Louis Braille publishes a reading system for the blind.

1832 Andrew Jackson vetoes the charter renewal of the national Bank of the United States.

1832 A British reform bill doubles the number of British men who can vote.

1833 Slavery is abolished in the British Empire.

1835

< **1836** Martin Van Buren is elected president.

1838 The Trail of Tears begins when U.S. troops remove the Cherokee from Georgia.

1838 Dutch colonists known as Boers clash with the Zulu in southern Africa. >

1839 The Opium War breaks out between Great Britain and China.

1845

Reading Social Studies

THEME FOCUS:
Economics, Politics

In this module you will read about the events that shaped the United States from 1828 to 1838. You will see how political and economic decisions were intertwined. For instance, you will read about the tensions between southern and northern states over tariff regulations. You will also read about the forced relocation of many Native Americans to the West. Understanding how economic issues led to political decisions will help you understand this time.

READING FOCUS:
Draw Conclusions about the Past

Writers don't always tell you everything you need to know about a subject. Sometimes you need to think critically about what they have said and make your own decisions about what you've read.

Draw Conclusions Earlier in this book, you learned how to make inferences. Sometimes when you read, you will need to make several inferences and put them together. The result is a **conclusion**, an informed judgment that you make by combining information.

Election of 1828

Today, presidential campaigns often focus on the personal image of the candidates—labeling them strong versus weak, or a government insider versus a newcomer. That was true in the 1828 campaign as well, which focused a great deal on the candidates' personalities. Jackson's campaigners described him as a war hero who had been born poor and rose to success through his own hard work.

Adams was a Harvard graduate whose father had been the second U.S. president. Jackson's supporters described Adams as being out of touch with everyday people. Even a fan of Adams agreed that he was "as cold as a lump of ice." In turn, Adams's supporters said Jackson was hot tempered, crude, and ill-equipped to be president of the United States. Still Jackson was a strong leader who appealed to everyday people. When the ballots were counted, Jackson had defeated Adams, winning a record number of popular votes. The time period of Jackson's presidency is sometimes called the "Age of Jackson."

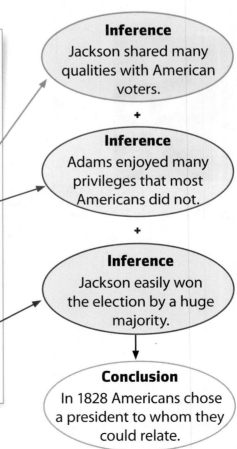

Inference
Jackson shared many qualities with American voters.

+

Inference
Adams enjoyed many privileges that most Americans did not.

+

Inference
Jackson easily won the election by a huge majority.

Conclusion
In 1828 Americans chose a president to whom they could relate.

You Try It!

The following passage is from the module you are getting ready to read. As you read the passage, look for the facts of the situation.

> **The Election of 1834** In 1834 a new political party had formed to oppose Jackson. Its members called themselves Whigs, after an English political party that opposed the monarchy, to make the point that Jackson was using his power like a king. The Whig Party favored the idea of a weak president and a strong Congress. Unable to agree on a candidate, the Whigs chose four men to run against Van Buren. Because of this indecision, and with backing from Jackson, Van Buren won the election.

After you read the passage, answer the following questions.

1. From this passage, what can you infer about President Jackson's popularity with the Whig Party?

2. The Whigs could not choose a single presidential candidate, so they nominated four men. Based on what you know about elections from your studies and your past experiences, how do you think this affected the votes each man received?

3. Jackson's backing helped Van Buren win the presidency. From this, what can you infer about Jackson's popularity with the American people as a whole?

4. Using the inferences you made answering questions 1 through 3, draw a conclusion about why Van Buren won the election of 1834.

As you read Module 10, use your personal background knowledge and experience to draw conclusions about what you are reading.

Jacksonian Democracy

The Big Idea

The expansion of voting rights and the election of Andrew Jackson signaled the growing power of the American people.

Main Ideas

- Democracy expanded in the 1820s as more Americans held the right to vote.
- Jackson's victory in the election of 1828 marked a change in American politics.

Key Terms and People

nominating conventions
Jacksonian Democracy
Democratic Party
John C. Calhoun
spoils system
Martin Van Buren
Kitchen Cabinet

If YOU were there . . .

It's 1829 and you live in Washington, D.C. You've come with a friend to the party for Andrew Jackson's inauguration as president. Your friend admires Jackson as a man of the people. You are less sure about his ability. Jackson's inauguration soon turns into a rowdy party, as mobs crowd into the White House. They break glasses and overturn the furniture.

How would you feel about having Jackson as your president?

Expansion of Democracy

America in the early 1800s was changing fast. In the North, workshops run by the craftspeople who owned them were being replaced by large-scale factories owned by businesspeople and staffed by hired workers. In the South, small family farms began to give way to large cotton plantations, owned by wealthy white people and worked by enslaved African Americans. Wealth seemed to be concentrating into fewer hands. Many ordinary Americans felt left behind.

These same people also began to believe they were losing power in their government. In the late 1700s some Americans thought that government was best managed by wealthy, property-owning men. Government policies seemed targeted to help build their power. The result was a growing belief that the wealthy were tightening their grip on power.

Hoping for change, small farmers, frontier settlers, and slaveholders rallied behind reformer Andrew Jackson, the popular hero of the War of 1812 and presidential candidate in the 1824 election. Even though he was a political leader, they believed Jackson would defend the rights of the common people and the slave states. They had been disappointed in the way Jackson had lost the 1824 election because of a decision in the House of Representatives. Jackson's supporters felt his policies and philosophies represented a move toward greater democratization.

In 1824 four men hoped to replace James Monroe as president. They were John Quincy Adams, William Crawford, Henry Clay, and Andrew Jackson. Jackson won the popular vote, but he did not receive a majority of electoral votes. According to the Constitution, if no person wins a majority of the electoral votes, the House of Representatives must choose the president. The selection was made from the top three vote-getters. Clay came in fourth and was out of the running. In the House vote, he threw his support to Adams, who then won. Because Adams later named Clay as his secretary of state, Jackson's supporters claimed that Adams gained the presidency by making a deal with Clay. Charges of a "corrupt bargain" followed Adams throughout his term. Adams had many plans for his presidency. But Congress, led by Jackson supporters, defeated his proposals.

During the time of Jackson's popularity, many democratic reforms were made. Some states changed their qualifications for voters to grant

Link to Today

Democracy in Action

Democracy spread in the early 1800s as more people became active in politics. Many of these people lived in the new western states. In these mostly rural areas, a political rally could be as simple as neighboring farmers meeting to talk about the issues of the day.

During the early 1800s democracy and demonstrations blossomed in the United States. The demonstrators of today owe much to the Americans of Andrew Jackson's time. Today, political rallies are a familiar sight in communities all over the country. The influence of Jackson is still seen in the U.S. political system today.

Analyze Information
How are the people in both pictures practicing democracy?

more white males suffrage. The revised rules, although they extended the franchise of voting to more white men, usually excluded free blacks from voting as they had been allowed under original state constitutions. Political parties began holding public **nominating conventions**, where party members choose the party's candidates instead of the party leaders. This period of expanding democracy, its ideas, and influences, in the 1820s and 1830s later became known as **Jacksonian Democracy**.

Election of 1828

Jackson supporters were determined that their candidate would win the 1828 election. They formed the **Democratic Party** to support Jackson's candidacy. Many people who backed President Adams began calling themselves National Republicans.

The 1828 presidential contest was a rematch of the 1824 election. Once again, John Quincy Adams faced Andrew Jackson. Jackson chose **John C. Calhoun** as his vice presidential running mate.

The Campaign Today, presidential campaigns often focus on the personal image of the candidates—labeling them strong versus weak,

---

BIOGRAPHY

Andrew Jackson 1767–1845

Jackson was born in Waxhaw, a region along the border of the North and South Carolina colonies. In 1788 he moved to Nashville, Tennessee, which was still a part of North Carolina. There he built a mansion called the Hermitage. He lived in Washington as president, then retired to the Hermitage, where he died.

Jackson had no formal education, but he taught himself law and became a successful lawyer. He became Tennessee's first representative to the U.S. Congress and also served in the Senate. Jackson became a national hero when his forces defeated the Creek and Seminole Indians. He went on to battle the British in the Battle of New Orleans during the War of 1812. Jackson was elected as the nation's seventh president in 1828 and served until 1837.

The power of the office became more powerful during Jackson's presidency. His belief in a strong presidency made him both loved and hated. He vetoed as many bills as the six previous presidents together. Jackson also believed in a strong Union. When South Carolina tried to nullify, or reject, a federal tariff, he threatened to send troops into the state to force it to obey.

Identify Cause and Effect
Why did Jackson gain loyal friends and fierce enemies?

People's President

Washington resident Margaret Bayard Smith was surprised by the chaos surrounding Jackson's inauguration.

"What a scene did we witness! . . . a rabble, a mob, of boys, . . . women, children, scrambling, fighting, romping. . . . Cut glass and china to the amount of several thousand dollars had been broken. . . . But it was the people's day, and the people's President, and the people would rule."

—Margaret Bayard Smith, letter to Mrs. Kirkpatrick
March 11, 1829

Analyze Historical Sources
How does the author view the people who support Jackson?

or a government insider versus a newcomer. That was true in the 1828 campaign as well, which focused a great deal on the candidates' personalities. Jackson's campaigners described him as a war hero who had been born poor and rose to success through his own hard work.

Adams was a Harvard graduate whose father had been the second U.S. president. Jackson's supporters described Adams as being out of touch with everyday people. Even a fan of Adams agreed that he was "as cold as a lump of ice." In turn, Adams's supporters said Jackson was hot-tempered, crude, and ill-equipped to be president of the United States. Still, Jackson was a strong leader who appealed to everyday people. When the ballots were counted, Jackson had defeated Adams, winning a record number of popular votes. The time period of Jackson's presidency is sometimes called the "Age of Jackson."

Quick Facts

Views of Democracy

Jackson's presidency marked a dramatic shift in American politics. Although Jackson's Democrats had grown out of Jefferson's Democratic-Republican Party, ideas of democracy had changed.

Jeffersonian Democracy	Jacksonian Democracy
Government by an educated few	More public involvement in government
Voting restricted to property owners	Voting expanded to all white males
Limited government	Limited government with a stronger executive branch

Interpret Charts
What ideas did Jeffersonians and Jacksonians share in common?

Jackson's Inauguration Jackson's supporters saw his victory as a win for the common people. A crowd cheered outside the Capitol as he took his oath of office. The massive crowd followed Jackson to a huge party on the White House lawn. The few police officers on hand had difficulty controlling the partygoers.

As president, Jackson rewarded some of his supporters with government jobs. This **spoils system**—the practice of giving government jobs to political backers—comes from the saying "to the victor belong the spoils [valued goods] of the enemy."

Secretary of State **Martin Van Buren** was one of Jackson's strongest allies in his official cabinet. President Jackson also relied a great deal on his **Kitchen Cabinet**, an informal group of trusted advisers who sometimes met in the White House kitchen.

Reading Check
Analyze Information
How might the spoils system cause disputes?

Summary and Preview The expansion of democracy swept Andrew Jackson into office. In the next lesson you will read about the increasing regional tensions that occurred during Jackson's presidency.

Lesson 1 Assessment

Review Ideas, Terms, and People

1. **a. Recall** What changes did the new western states make that allowed more people to vote?

   b. Draw Conclusions How did nominating conventions allow the people more say in politics?

   c. Explain How did the policies and philosophies of the Jacksonian Era represent a move toward greater democratization? How were voting rights expanded during the Jacksonian period?

   d. Predict How might changes to the voting process brought about by Jacksonian Democracy affect politics in the future? What were the key ideas and influences of Jacksonian Democracy?

2. **a. Recall** What two new political parties faced off in the election of 1828? Which candidate did each party support?

   b. Make Inferences Why did Andrew Jackson have more popular support than did Adams?

   c. Analyze What leadership qualities helped Andrew Jackson become president of the United States?

   d. Evaluate Do you think the spoils system was an acceptable practice? Explain your answer.

Critical Thinking

3. **Identify Effect** In this lesson you learned about the election of Andrew Jackson to the presidency. Use a cause-and-effect chart like this one to show the ways in which Jacksonian Democracy increased Americans' political power.

Jacksonian Democracy	increased Americans' political power	

Jackson's Administration

The Big Idea

Andrew Jackson's presidency was marked by political conflicts.

Main Ideas

- Regional differences grew during Jackson's presidency.
- The rights of the states were debated amid arguments about a national tariff.
- Jackson's attack on the Bank sparked controversy.
- Jackson's policies led to the Panic of 1837.

Key Terms and People

Tariff of Abominations
states' rights doctrine
nullification crisis
Daniel Webster
McCulloch v. *Maryland*
Whig Party
Panic of 1837
William Henry Harrison

If YOU were there . . .

You live on a small farm in South Carolina in 1829. Your family grows corn and cotton to sell, as well as vegetables for your own table. Although you grow your own food, you also depend on imported wool, flax, iron, and hemp to make ropes. But the government has just put new taxes on these products from Europe. Now they're too expensive for you to buy!

How would you feel about the new taxes on imports?

Sectional Differences Increase

Regional differences had a major effect on Andrew Jackson's presidency. Americans' views of Jackson's policies were based on where they lived and the economy of those regions.

Three Regions Emerge There were three main U.S. regions in the early 1800s. Different viewpoints in these regions led to debate about what was the best for the nation. The North, first of all, had an economy based on trade and on manufacturing. Northerners supported tariffs because tariffs helped them compete with British factories. Northerners also opposed the federal government's sale of public land at cheap prices. Cheap land encouraged potential laborers to move from northern factory towns to the West.

The second region was the South. Its economy was based on farming. Southern farmers raised all types of crops, but the most popular were the cash crops of cotton and tobacco. Southerners sold a large portion of their crops to foreign nations.

Southerners imported their manufactured goods. Tariffs made imported goods more expensive for southern farmers. In addition, high tariffs angered some of the South's European trading partners. These trading partners would likely raise their own tariffs in retaliation. To avoid this situation, southerners called for low tariffs.

Southerners also relied on enslaved African Americans to work the plantations. The issue of slavery would become increasingly controversial between the North and South.

Political parties also developed along these regional lines. They were influenced by the tariff policy. Tariffs, sometimes called protective tariffs, were favored by Republicans, mostly northerners, because they protected northern manufacturing. Democrats, mostly southerners, were against tariffs because they made goods they needed to import much more expensive.

In the third region, the West, the frontier economy was just emerging. Settlers favored policies that boosted their farming economy and encouraged further settlement. Western farmers grew a wide variety of crops. Their biggest priority was cheap land and internal improvements such as better roads and water transportation.

Tariff of Abominations Tariffs became one of the first issues of debate that President Jackson faced. In 1827, the year before Jackson's election, northern manufacturers began to demand a tariff on imported woolen goods. Northerners wanted the tariff to protect their industries from foreign competition, especially from Great Britain. For them the tariff helped meet economic challenges.

British companies were driving American ones out of business with their inexpensive manufactured goods. The tariff northerners supported, however, was so high that importing wool would be impossible. Southerners opposed the tariff, saying it would hurt their economy.

Before Andrew Jackson took office, Congress placed a high tariff on imports. Angry southerners called it the **Tariff of Abominations**. (An abomination is a hateful thing.) Southern voters were outraged.

President John Quincy Adams signed the tariff legislation, though he did not fully support it. In early U.S. history, presidents tended to reserve veto power for legislation that they believed violated the Constitution. Signing the tariff bill meant Adams would surely be defeated in his re-election bid. The new tariff added fuel to the growing sectional differences plaguing the young nation. Citing states' rights, some southerners said that the states could nullify laws they felt were not authorized by the Constitution. Most northerners opposed nullification.

States' Rights Debate

When Andrew Jackson took office in 1829, he was forced to respond to the growing conflict over tariffs. At the core of the dispute was the question of an individual state's right to disregard a law that had been passed by the U.S. Congress. This led to growing sectionalism, or sectional differences.

Nullification Crisis Early in his political career, Vice President John C. Calhoun had supported the **criteria** of a strong central government. But in 1828 when Congress passed the Tariff of Abominations, Calhoun joined his fellow southerners in protest. Economic depression and previous tariffs had severely damaged the economy of his home state, South Carolina. It was only beginning to recover in 1828. Some leaders in the state even

Reading Check
Summarize
Describe the sectional economic differences in the United States during the early 1800s.

Academic Vocabulary
criteria basic requirements

Regions of the United States, Early 1800s

North
- Economy based on manufacturing
- Support for tariffs— American goods could be sold at lower prices than could British goods

South
- Economy based on agriculture
- Opposition to tariffs, which increased the cost of imported goods

West
- Emerging economy
- Support for internal improvements and the sale of public lands

spoke of leaving, or secession from, the Union over the issue of tariffs. Calhoun understood the problems of South Carolina's farmers because he was one himself. But he wanted to find a way to keep South Carolina from leaving the Union. The answer he arrived at was the doctrine of nullification. A state, Calhoun said, had the right to nullify, or reject, a federal law that it considers unconstitutional.

In response to the tariff, Calhoun drafted the *South Carolina Exposition and Protest*. It said that Congress should not favor one state or region over another. Calhoun used the *Protest* to advance the **states' rights doctrine**, which said that since the states had formed the national government, state power should be greater than federal power. He believed states had the right to nullify, or reject, any federal law they judged to be unconstitutional. The debate about the importance of states' rights increased sectional tensions that would further divide the nation.

Calhoun's theory was controversial, and it drew some fierce challengers. Many of them were from the northern states that had benefited from increased tariffs. These opponents believed that the American people, not the individual states, made up the Union. Conflict between the supporters and the opponents of nullification deepened. The dispute became known as the **nullification crisis**.

Although he chose not to put his name on his *Exposition and Protest*, Calhoun did resign from the vice presidency. He was then elected to the Senate, where he continued his arguments in favor of nullification. Martin Van Buren replaced Calhoun as vice president when Jackson was re-elected president.

The Hayne-Webster Debate The debate about states' rights began, or originated, early in our nation's history. This resulted in constitutional issues arising regarding states' rights. Calhoun was not the first person to propose the doctrine of nullification. Thomas Jefferson and James Madison supported the states' power to disagree with the federal government in the Virginia and Kentucky Resolutions of 1798–99. Some of the delegates at the Hartford Convention supported states' rights. But Calhoun's theory went further. He believed that states could judge whether a law was or was not constitutional. This put the power of the Supreme Court in question.

The issue of nullification was intensely debated on the floor of the Senate in 1830. Robert Y. Hayne, senator from South Carolina, defended states' rights. He argued that nullification gave states a way to lawfully protest federal legislation. **Daniel Webster** of Massachusetts argued that the United States was one nation, not a pact among independent states. He believed that the welfare of the nation should override that of individual states.

Jackson Responds Although deeply opposed to nullification, Jackson was concerned about economic problems in the southern states. In 1832 he urged Congress to pass another tariff that lowered the previous rate. South Carolina thought the slight change was inadequate. The state legislature took a monumental step; it decided to test the doctrine of states' rights.

South Carolina's first action was to pass the Nullification Act, which declared the 1828 and 1832 tariffs "null, void . . . [and not] binding upon this State, its officers or citizens." South Carolina threatened to withdraw from the Union if federal troops were used to collect duties. The legislature also voted to form its own army. Jackson was enraged.

The president sternly condemned nullification. Jackson declared that he would enforce the law in South Carolina. At his request, Congress passed the Force Bill, approving use of the army if necessary. In light of Jackson's determined position, no other state chose to support South Carolina.

Early in 1833 Henry Clay of Kentucky had proposed a compromise that would gradually lower the tariff over several years. As Jackson's intentions became clear, both the U.S. Congress and South Carolina moved quickly to approve the compromise. The Congress would decrease the tariff, and South Carolina's leaders would enforce the law.

The tariff policy prompted sectional differences. Despite the provisions of this compromise, neither side changed its beliefs about states' rights. The argument continued for years, ending in the huge conflict known as the Civil War.

Jackson Attacks the Bank

Jackson upheld federal authority in the nullification crisis. He did not, however, always support greater federal power. For example, he opposed the Second Bank of the United States, founded by Congress in 1816.

The Second Bank of the United States was given a 20-year charter. This charter gave it the power to act exclusively as the federal government's financial agent. The Bank held federal deposits, made transfers of federal funds between states, and dealt with any payments or receipts involving the federal government. It also issued bank notes, or paper currency. Some 80 percent of the Bank was privately owned, but its operations were supervised by Congress and the president.

In the 1830 Hayne-Webster debate, Daniel Webster (above) staunchly championed the Constitution and national unity.

Reading Check
Summarize
What led to the nullification crisis, and why was it important?

States' Rights vs. the Union

The framers of the Constitution created a document that was remarkable in its scope. But a few issues were unresolved. One of the most controversial was the matter of states' rights versus the authority of the federal government. **Daniel Webster** (left) insisted that the interests of the Union should prevail. **John C. Calhoun** (right) believed that the powers of the states were greater.

Analyze Historical Sources
How did the views of Calhoun and Webster differ?

"While the Union lasts we have high, exciting, gratifying [rewarding] prospects spread out before us, for us and our children. God grant that in my day . . . my eyes shall be turned to behold the gorgeous ensign [flag] of the republic . . . bearing for its motto . . . Liberty and Union, now and forever one and inseparable."

—Daniel Webster
from the Hayne-Webster
debate, 1830

"If there be no protective power in the reserved rights of the states, they must in the end be forced to rebel. . . ."

—John C. Calhoun from a letter
to Virgil Maxcy, September 11, 1830

There was debate about the Bank. Many states, particularly in the South, had opposed the Bank. Small farmers believed that the Bank only helped wealthy businesspeople. Jackson also questioned the legality of the Bank. He believed it was an unconstitutional extension of the power of Congress. The states, he thought, should have the power to control the banking system.

Some states decided to take action. Maryland tried to pass a tax that would limit the Bank's operations. James McCulloch, cashier of the Bank's branch in Maryland, refused to pay this tax. The state took him to court, and the resulting case went all the way to the U.S. Supreme Court. In the landmark case *McCulloch* v. *Maryland*, the Court decision was that the national bank was constitutional.

Nicholas Biddle, the Bank's director, decided to push for a bill to renew the Bank's charter in 1832. Jackson campaigned for the bill's defeat. "I will kill it," he promised. True to his word, Jackson vetoed the legislation when Congress sent it to him.

Congress could not get the two-thirds majority needed to override Jackson's veto. Jackson also weakened the Bank's power by moving most of its funds to state banks. In many cases, these banks used the funds to offer easy credit terms to people buying land. While this practice helped expansion in the West, it also led to inflation.

In the summer of 1836 Jackson tried to slow this inflation. He ordered Americans to use only gold or silver—instead of paper state-bank notes—to buy government-owned land. This policy did not help the national

Jackson against the Bank

Andrew Jackson's fight with the Bank was the subject of many political cartoons, like this one.

In this scene, Jackson is shown fighting a hydra that represents the national bank. The hydra is a mythological monster whose heads grow back when cut off. The heads of the hydra are portraits of politicians who opposed Jackson's policies.

Analyze Historical Sources
How does this image show the difficulty Jackson had politically?

Andrew Jackson fights the hydra with a cane labeled "veto."

Nicholas Biddle is at the center of the hydra.

Reading Check
Analyze Information
Why did critics of the Second Bank of the United States oppose it?

economy as Jackson had hoped. Jackson did improve the economy and met economic challenges by lowering the national debt. However, his policies opened the door for approaching economic troubles.

Panic of 1837

Jackson was still very popular with voters in 1836. He chose not to run in 1836, however, and the Democrats nominated Vice President Martin Van Buren.

Timeline: The Supreme Court and Capitalism

Connect to Economics During the early 1800s, the Supreme Court made several rulings that helped define federal power over contracts and commerce. These rulings reinforced capitalism as the ruling economic system in the United States.

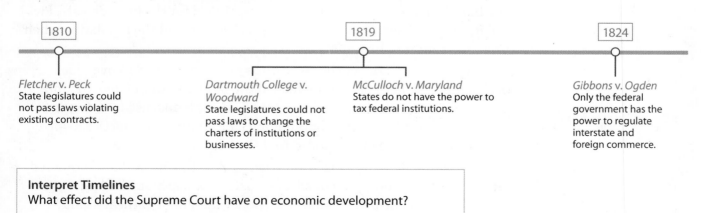

1810

Fletcher v. Peck
State legislatures could not pass laws violating existing contracts.

1819

Dartmouth College v. Woodward
State legislatures could not pass laws to change the charters of institutions or businesses.

McCulloch v. Maryland
States do not have the power to tax federal institutions.

1824

Gibbons v. Ogden
Only the federal government has the power to regulate interstate and foreign commerce.

Interpret Timelines
What effect did the Supreme Court have on economic development?

In 1834 a new political party had formed to oppose Jackson. Its members called themselves Whigs, after an English political party that opposed the monarchy, to make the point that Jackson was using his power like a king. The **Whig Party** favored the idea of a weak president and a strong Congress. Unable to agree on a candidate, the Whigs chose four men to run against Van Buren. Because of this indecision, and with backing from Jackson, Van Buren won the election.

Shortly after Van Buren took office, the country experienced the **Panic of 1837**, a severe economic depression. Jackson's banking policies and his unsuccessful plan to curb inflation contributed to the panic. But people blamed Van Buren.

In 1840 the Whigs united against the weakened Van Buren to stand behind one candidate, **William Henry Harrison**, an army general. Harrison won in an electoral landslide. The Whigs had achieved their goal of winning the presidency.

Summary and Preview The states' rights debate dominated much of Jackson's presidency. In the next lesson you will learn about the removal of American Indians from the southeastern United States.

Reading Check
Identify Cause and Effect What contributed to the Panic of 1837, and how did it affect the 1840 election?

Lesson 2 Assessment

Review Ideas, Terms, and People

1. a. Recall On what were the economies of the northern, southern, and western states, or regions, based? What were the causes and effects of their economic differences?

b. Analyze What was the impact of tariff policies on sections of the United States during this time period?

c. Summarize What were the arguments for and against protective tariffs?

d. Predict How might the sectional issues involved in the dispute over the Tariff of Abominations lead to future problems between the North and South? What issues were debated?

2. a. Describe What roles did Daniel Webster and John C. Calhoun play in the nullification crisis?

b. Summarize What idea did supporters of the states' rights doctrine promote?

c. Compare and Contrast How do the effects of congressional conflicts and compromises compare? Include examples of the roles of John C. Calhoun, Henry Clay, and Daniel Webster. Identify the provisions of these compromises.

3. a. Describe What problems resulted from weakening the Bank? Specifically, how did the absence of a national banking system affect economic stability?

b. Draw Conclusions Why did Jackson veto the bill to renew the Second Bank of the United States?

c. Analyze What different viewpoints resulted in debate about the Second Bank of the United States?

4. a. Recall What caused the Panic of 1837?

b. Summarize How did the Whig Party win the election of 1840?

c. Elaborate Why do you think Jackson chose not to run for the presidency in 1836? Do you think he made the right decision? Why?

Critical Thinking

5. Identify Cause and Effect In this lesson you learned about the political conflicts during Jackson's administration. Use a graphic organizer like the one below to show how some of Jackson's policies dealing with conflicts led to the Panic of 1837.

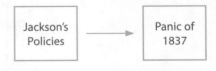

Indian Removal

If YOU were there . . .

You belong to the Cherokee nation. Your family has farmed rich lands in Georgia for as long as anyone can remember. You've learned some new ways from white settlers, too. At school you've learned to read both English and Cherokee. But now that doesn't seem important. The U.S. government is sending you and your people far away to unknown places in the West.

How would you feel about being taken away from your home?

Indian Removal Act

Native Americans had long lived in settlements stretching from Georgia to Mississippi. However, President Jackson and other political leaders wanted to open this land to settlement by American farmers. Opening new land to white settlement would also increase economic development. Under pressure from Jackson, Congress passed the **Indian Removal Act** in 1830. This policy toward American Indian nations authorized the removal of Native Americans who lived east of the Mississippi River to lands in the West.

Congress then established **Indian Territory**—U.S. land in what is now Oklahoma—and planned to move Native Americans there. Some supporters of this plan, like John C. Calhoun, argued that removal to Indian Territory would protect Indians from further conflicts with American settlers. "One of the greatest evils to which they are subject is that incessant [constant] pressure of our population," he noted. "To guard against this evil . . . there ought to be the strongest . . . assurance that the country given [to] them should be theirs." To manage Indian removal to western lands, Congress approved the creation of a new government agency, the **Bureau of Indian Affairs**.

The Choctaw were the first Indians sent to Indian Territory. The Mississippi legislature abolished the Choctaw

Indian Removal

During the Trail of Tears, thousands of Cherokee died from conditions such as disease, starvation, and harsh weather. They were forced to walk hundreds of miles to their new land in the West. Other Native Americans were also moved, with similar results.

government and then forced the Choctaw leaders to sign the Treaty of Dancing Rabbit Creek. This treaty gave more than 7.5 million acres of their land to the state. The Choctaw moved to Indian Territory during a disastrous winter trip. Federal officials did not provide enough food or supplies to the Choctaw, most of whom were on foot. About one-fourth of the Choctaw died of cold, disease, or starvation.

News of the Choctaw's hardships caused other Indians to resist removal. When the Creek resisted in 1836, federal troops resolved this conflict by moving in and capturing some 14,500 of them. They led the Creek, many in chains, to Indian Territory. One Creek woman remembered the trip being filled with "the awful silence that showed the heartaches and sorrow at being taken from the homes and even separation from loved ones." The Chickasaw, who lived in upper Mississippi, negotiated a treaty for better supplies on their trip to Indian Territory. Nevertheless, many Chickasaw lives were also lost during removal.

Cherokee Resistance

Many Cherokee had believed that they could prevent conflicts and avoid removal by adopting the **contemporary** culture of white people. In the early 1800s they invited missionaries to set up schools where Cherokee children learned how to read and write in English. The Cherokee developed their own government modeled after the U.S. Constitution with an

Reading Check
Find Main Ideas
What major changes did President Jackson make to U.S. policy regarding Native Americans?

Academic Vocabulary
contemporary existing at the same time

Trail of Tears

The Cherokee knew that they would be forced to march West, but they did not know that so many of their people would die on the way. Here is an account of the Trail of Tears, written before it started, by a Cherokee girl who made the trip.

> *"March 10, 1838*
> *Beloved Martha, I have delayed writing to you so long. . . . If we Cherokees are to be driven to the west by the cruel hand of oppression to seek a new home in the west, it will be impossible. . . . It is thus all our rights are invaded."*
>
> —Letter from Jenny, a Cherokee girl, just before her removal

Analyze Historical Sources
What is the concern of the Cherokee girl before the Trail of Tears? What do you think her concerns were after the trip?

election system, a bicameral council, and a court system. All of these were headed by a principal chief.

A Cherokee named **Sequoya** used 86 characters to represent Cherokee syllables to create a writing system for their own complex language. In 1828 his contribution led the Cherokee to begin publishing a newspaper printed in both English and Cherokee.

The adoption of white culture did not protect the Cherokee. After gold was discovered on their land in Georgia, their treaty rights were ignored. Georgia leaders began preparing for the Cherokee's removal. When they refused to move, the Georgia militia began attacking Cherokee towns. Instead of responding with force, the Cherokee fought in the American court, or judicial, system. They sued the federal government, claiming that they had sovereignty, or the right to be respected as a foreign country. The case, the *Cherokee Nation* v. *Georgia* reached the Supreme Court in 1831. Chief Justice John Marshall, however, refused to hear the case. He ruled that the Cherokee had no right to bring suit since they were neither citizens nor a foreign country.

The Cherokee, however, had another plan of attack. Samuel Austin Worcester was a white man, a teacher, and a friend to the Cherokee. The state of Georgia, carrying out the Indian Removal Act, ordered Worcester to leave Cherokee land. He refused and brought suit on behalf of himself and the Cherokee. In the suit, the Cherokee said that they were an independent, or sovereign, nation and claimed that the government of Georgia had no legal power over their lands.

In 1832 the Supreme Court, under the leadership of Chief Justice John Marshall, agreed. In **Worcester v. Georgia** the Court ruled that the Cherokee nation was a distinct community in which the laws of Georgia had no force. The Court also stated that only the federal government, not the states, had authority over Native Americans.

Georgia, however, ignored the Court's ruling, and President Jackson's response was to take no action to make Georgia follow the ruling. "John Marshall has made his decision; now let him enforce it," Jackson supposedly said. By not enforcing the Court's decision, Jackson violated his presidential oath to uphold the laws of the land. However, most members of Congress and American citizens did not protest the ways Jackson removed Native Americans. This contributed to the struggle between the Cherokee nation and the United States government.

In the spring of 1838, U.S. troops began to remove all Cherokee and resettle them in Indian Territory. A few were able to escape and hide in the mountains of North Carolina. After the Cherokee were removed, Georgia took their businesses, farms, and property.

The Cherokee's 800-mile forced march became known as the **Trail of Tears**. During the march, the Cherokee suffered from disease, hunger, and harsh weather. Almost one-fourth of the 18,000 Cherokee died on the march.

Today, members of the Cherokee nation of northeastern Oklahoma are descendants of the Cherokee who were removed to Indian Territory. The group's population is about 70,000. Members of the Eastern Band of Cherokee Indians are the descendants of the Cherokee who escaped removal. The 8,100 members of this group live mostly in western North Carolina.

Other Native Americans Resist

Other Native Americans decided to fight U.S. troops to avoid removal. Chief **Black Hawk**, a leader of the Fox and the Sauk Indians, led his people in a struggle to protect their lands in Illinois. By 1832, however, the Sauk forces

Reading Check
Find Main Ideas
What was the *Worcester* v. *Georgia* ruling, and what was Jackson's response?

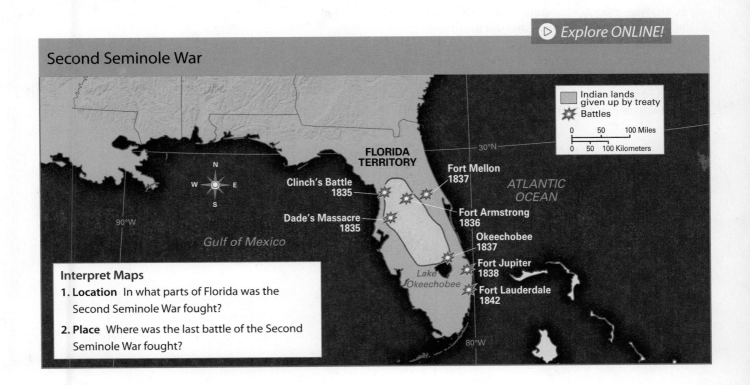

Second Seminole War

▷ Explore ONLINE!

Indian lands given up by treaty

✴ Battles

0   50   100 Miles

0   50   100 Kilometers

FLORIDA TERRITORY

30°N

ATLANTIC OCEAN

Clinch's Battle 1835

Fort Mellon 1837

Dade's Massacre 1835

Fort Armstrong 1836

90°W

Okeechobee 1837

Gulf of Mexico

Fort Jupiter 1838

Lake Okeechobee

Fort Lauderdale 1842

80°W

Interpret Maps

1. **Location** In what parts of Florida was the Second Seminole War fought?

2. **Place** Where was the last battle of the Second Seminole War fought?

were running out of food and supplies, and by 1850 they had been forced to leave.

In Florida, Seminole leaders were forced to sign a removal treaty that their followers decided to ignore. A leader named **Osceola** called upon his people to resist with force, and the Second Seminole War began. Osceola was captured and soon died in prison. His followers, however, continued to fight. Some 4,000 Seminole were removed and hundreds of others killed. Eventually, U.S. officials decided to give up the fight. Small groups of Seminole had resisted removal, and their descendants live in Florida today. In this way the conflict between the Seminoles and United States officials was resolved. Chief Black Hawk and Osceola were social leaders because they worked for better living conditions for their people.

Summary and Preview President Jackson supported the removal of thousands of Native Americans from their traditional lands to the federal territory in the West. In the next module you will learn about the westward growth of the nation as farmers, ranchers, and other settlers moved West.

Reading Check
Analyze Information
How effective was Native American resistance to removal?

Lesson 3 Assessment

Review Ideas, Terms, and People

1. a. Identify What Native American groups were affected by the Indian Removal Act? Where were they relocated?

   b. Explain Why did government officials want to relocate Native Americans to the West?

   c. Predict What are some possible effects that the Indian Removal Act might have on Native Americans already living in the West?

2. a. Identify What was the Trail of Tears?

   b. Analyze Why did the state of Georgia want to relocate the Cherokee, and what did the Cherokee do in response?

   c. Analyze Give an example of Jackson's presidential response to the Court ruling. How did he handle it?

   d. Elaborate What do you think of President Jackson's refusal to enforce the *Worcester* v. *Georgia* ruling?

3. a. Describe What led to the Second Seminole War?

   b. Compare and Contrast How were the Seminole and the Sauk resistance efforts similar and different?

Critical Thinking

4. Compare and Contrast In this lesson you learned about Indian removal. Copy the chart below and use it to identify the Native American groups and their responses to removal.

Native American Group	Response to Removal

Social Studies Skills

Solve Problems

Define the Skill

Problem solving is a process for finding workable solutions to difficult situations. The process involves asking questions, identifying and evaluating information, comparing and contrasting, and making judgments. Problem solving is useful in studying history because it helps you better understand problems people faced at certain points in time and how they dealt with those difficulties.

The ability to understand and evaluate how people solved problems in the past can help in solving similar problems today. The skill can also be applied to many other kinds of difficulties besides historical ones. It is a method for thinking through almost any situation.

Learn the Skill

Using the following steps will enable you to better understand and solve problems.

1. **Identify the problem.** Ask questions of yourself and others to make sure you know exactly what the situation is and understand why it is a problem.

2. **Gather information.** Ask questions and conduct research to learn more about the problem, such as its history, what caused it, what contributes to it, and other factors.

3. **List options.** Based on the information you have gathered, identify possible options for solving the problem that you might consider. Be aware that your final solution will probably be better and easier to reach if you have as many options as possible to consider.

4. **Evaluate the options.** Weigh each option you are considering. Think of and list the advantages it has as a solution, as well as its potential disadvantages.

5. **Choose and implement a solution.** After comparing the advantages and disadvantages of each solution, choose the one that seems best and apply it.

6. **Evaluate the solution.** Once the solution has been tried, evaluate its effectiveness in solving the problem. This step will tell you if the solution was a good one, or if another of the possible solutions should be tried instead.

Practice the Skill

One of the most challenging situations that President Jackson faced was the nullification crisis. You can use the problem-solving skills to better understand this problem and to evaluate his solution for it. Review the information about the nullification crisis in this module. Then answer the questions below.

1. What was the specific problem that Jackson faced? Why was it a problem?

2. What event led to the problem? What earlier circumstances and conditions contributed to it?

3. List possible solutions to the problem that you would have considered if you had been president, along with advantages and disadvantages.

4. Jackson threatened to send troops to South Carolina to enforce federal law. Do you think his solution was the best one? Explain why, or if not, what solution would have been better.

History and Geography

The Indian Removal Treaties

In 1830 President Andrew Jackson signed the Indian Removal Act into law. As its name implies, the purpose of the act was to remove Native Americans from land that white settlers wanted for themselves. The impact of this act was that five tribes were forced to leave their traditional lands and walk to a territory west of the Mississippi River. The land in the new Indian Territory was land white settlers did not want. It was poor and not good for farming. The poor land made life very difficult for newly arrived Indians. Many died from malnutrition and disease. Within ten years, about 60,000 Indians had been relocated.

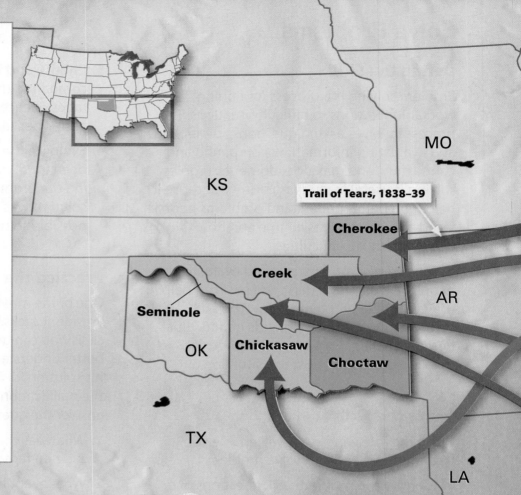

Trail of Tears, 1838–39

Treaty	Date	Indian Group	Results for United States	Results for Indian Groups	Outcome
Treaty of Greenville	1795	12 Groups	Ended battles in Northwest Territory	Payment of $20,000; acknowledgment of lands	Indian land claims disregarded by American settlers
Treaty at Holston River	1798	Cherokee	Received land promised to Cherokee	Payment of $5,000 followed by annual payments	Cherokee lands reduced
Treaty at St. Louis	1804	Sauk, Fox	Received land from the Sauk and the Fox	Annual payments of $1,000	Indians claimed their leaders acted without permission; conflicts arose as settlers moved to Sauk and Fox lands
Treaty at Fort Jackson	1814	Creek	Ended battles with Red Eagle; received 23 million acres of land in Georgia	Later receives small amount of land in Indian Territory	Conflicts between settlers and Creek led to removal of Creek to Indian Territory
Treaty of Dancing Rabbit Creek	1830	Choctaw	Received all Choctaw lands east of Mississippi River	Received land in Indian Territory	Choctaw became first tribe moved from southeast to land in Indian Territory

The Cherokee For generations, the Cherokee had called the southern Appalachian Mountain region home. But when they were forced off their land in the Trail of Tears, thousands died.

The Creek The Creek had to leave a land rich in variety. It stretched from the ridges and valleys of the Appalachian Mountains in the north, through a region of low hills and valleys, to a flat area of pine forest in the south.

The Seminole Many Seminole Indians refused to leave Florida. They hid in the swamps, battling American soldiers. Many of their descendants still live in Florida today.

The Chickasaw The Chickasaw lived in a land of rich, black prairie soil. They would find the soil west of the Mississippi much less suited for farming.

The Choctaw The Choctaw were forced to leave behind the low, rolling hills and plains of their homeland. For generations they had farmed the rich soil there.

KY

TN

Cherokee

Chickasaw

Creek

GA

AL

Choctaw

MS

FL

Seminole

ATLANTIC OCEAN

Gulf of Mexico

75°

80°W

85°W

90°W

25°N

30

N
W   E
S

Interpret Maps

1. **Place** How did land in the Indian Territory compare to the land in the Indians' homelands?

2. **Movement** How do you think being forced to leave their homelands impacted the Indians' way of life?

Module 10 Assessment

Review Vocabulary, Terms, and People

Complete each sentence by filling in the blank with the correct term or person.

1. In the Supreme Court case of _____, the Court ruled that the federal government, not the states, had authority over the Cherokee.

2. President Jackson's group of advisers was known as the _____ because of where its members met in the White House.

3. _____ served as Andrew Jackson's vice president until he resigned due to the dispute over nullification.

4. The _____ supported the power of the states over the power of the federal government.

5. The practice of rewarding supporters with positions in government is known as the _____.

Comprehension and Critical Thinking

Lesson 1

6. a. **Identify** What changes took place in the early 1800s that broadened democracy in the United States?

    b. **Analyze** How was Jackson's victory in the election of 1828 a reflection of a change in American politics?

    c. **Evaluate** Do you think the changes brought about by Jacksonian Democracy went far enough in expanding democracy? Why or why not?

Lesson 2

7. a. **Describe** What conflicts troubled the Jackson administration?

    b. **Draw Conclusions** What were the results of the conflict over the Second Bank of the United States?

    c. **Analyze** How did the Second Bank and tariffs help meet economic challenges?

    d. **Compare and Contrast** Compare and contrast how economic factors, such as tariffs, led to sectionalism. What was the impact of tariff policies on different parts of the country in this time period?

    e. **Summarize** What were the arguments for and against the banking system?

    f. **Predict** How might sectional differences and the debate over states' rights lead to future problems for the United States?

Lesson 3

8. a. **Identify** Who was Sequoya? What important contribution did he make?

    b. **Identify** What are some ways conflicts between Native Americans and government officials were solved?

    c. **Describe** What were the successes and failures of the reforms of the Age of Jackson, including Indian Removal and the Trail of Tears?

    d. **Contrast** In what different ways did the Cherokee and the Seminole attempt to resist removal to Indian Territory?

    e. **Elaborate** Do you agree with Jackson's refusal to enforce the *Worcester* v. *Georgia* ruling? Why or why not?

Module 10 Assessment, continued

Review Themes

9. **Politics** What new political party rose in opposition to President Andrew Jackson? What was the party's attitude toward the power of the president?

10. **Economics** What economic factors influenced the policy of Indian removal?

11. **Politics** Make a list of both the events and impacts of Andrew Jackson's presidency. Then write a paragraph explaining the events and their impact.

12. **Politics** What were some contributions of significant political and social leaders of this time period?

Reading Skills

Draw Conclusions about the Past *Use the Reading Skills taught in this module to answer the question about the reading selection below.*

> Native Americans had long lived in settlements stretching from Georgia to Mississippi. However, President Jackson and other political leaders wanted to open this land to settlement by American farmers.

13. Which statement below can you conclude from the passage above?
    a. Farmers moved onto the Native Americans' land after removal.
    b. Native Americans wanted to move from their lands.
    c. Native Americans resisted removal.
    d. Government officials had to use force to remove Native Americans from their land.

Social Studies Skills

Solve Problems *Use the Social Studies Skills taught in this module to answer the question about the reading selection below.*

> Northerners wanted the tariff to protect their industries from foreign competition, especially from Great Britain.
>
> British companies were driving American ones out of business with their inexpensive manufactured goods . . . Southerners opposed the tariff, saying it would hurt their economy.

14. Which of the following might be a reasonable solution to the problem discussed above?
    a. passing a low tariff
    b. passing a high tariff only in the South
    c. Britain passing a tariff
    d. selling northern and British goods for a higher price

Focus on Writing

15. **Write Interview Questions** You are a reporter for a large city newspaper in the year 1837. Andrew Jackson has just left office, and you have been given the assignment of interviewing him about his presidency and his role in American politics. Review what you have learned about Jackson's political significance, the conflicts he was involved in, and the causes and effects of his policies toward Indians. Then begin writing questions for your interview with Jackson. What will the readers of your newspaper want to learn more about? Write at least ten interview questions that your readers will want answered.

Westward Expansion

Essential Question
Was the United States truly destined to expand west in the 1800s?

About the Photo: Wagon trains carried hundreds of thousands of settlers across the Great Plains.

▶ *Explore ONLINE!*

HISTORY.

VIDEOS, including...
- The Transcontinental Railroad
- The Louisiana Purchase
- Railroads that Tamed the West
- Plains Indians
- Sitting Bull: Chief of the Lakota Nation

☑ Document-Based Investigations

☑ Graphic Organizers

☑ Interactive Games

☑ Interactive Map: Territorial Expansion of the United States, 1783–1898

☑ Image Carousel: Buffalo Bill's Wild West Show

In this module you will read about the effects of westward expansion in the United States. You will also learn about how Native Americans resisted these changes.

What You Will Learn ...

Timeline of Events 1800–1900

▶ Explore ONLINE!

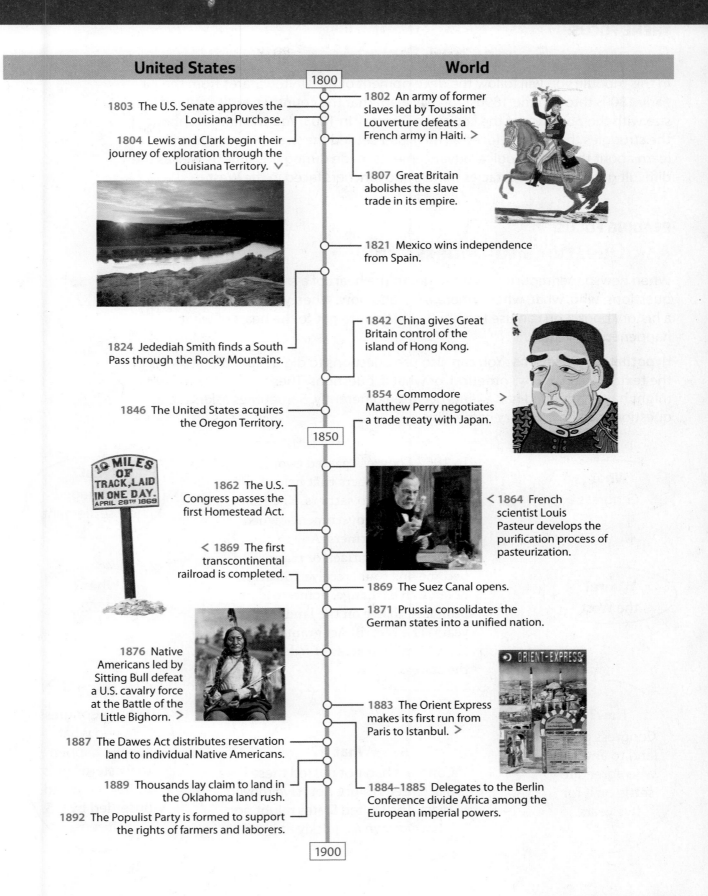

United States	World

1800

1803 The U.S. Senate approves the Louisiana Purchase.

1802 An army of former slaves led by Toussaint Louverture defeats a French army in Haiti. >

1804 Lewis and Clark begin their journey of exploration through the Louisiana Territory. ∨

1807 Great Britain abolishes the slave trade in its empire.

1821 Mexico wins independence from Spain.

1824 Jedediah Smith finds a South Pass through the Rocky Mountains.

1842 China gives Great Britain control of the island of Hong Kong.

1846 The United States acquires the Oregon Territory.

1854 Commodore Matthew Perry negotiates a trade treaty with Japan. >

1850

10 MILES OF TRACK, LAID IN ONE DAY. APRIL 28TH 1869

1862 The U.S. Congress passes the first Homestead Act.

1864 French scientist Louis Pasteur develops the purification process of pasteurization.

< 1869 The first transcontinental railroad is completed.

1869 The Suez Canal opens.

1871 Prussia consolidates the German states into a unified nation.

1876 Native Americans led by Sitting Bull defeat a U.S. cavalry force at the Battle of the Little Bighorn. >

1883 The Orient Express makes its first run from Paris to Istanbul. >

1887 The Dawes Act distributes reservation land to individual Native Americans.

1889 Thousands lay claim to land in the Oklahoma land rush.

1884–1885 Delegates to the Berlin Conference divide Africa among the European imperial powers.

1892 The Populist Party is formed to support the rights of farmers and laborers.

1900

Westward Expansion **351**

Reading Social Studies

Geography, Science and Technology

In this module you will follow the development of the United States from the early 1800s through the 1890s. You will learn that the country nearly doubled in size with the purchase of the Louisiana Territory in 1803. You will find out about the struggles that people faced as they later settled the Great Plains. You will learn about the technological advancements made during this time as well as the difficult geographical obstacles miners and ranchers faced in the West.

READING FOCUS:

Ask Questions to Understand

When newspaper reporters want to get to the heart of a story, they ask certain questions: who, what, when, where, why, and how. When you are reading a history book, you can use the same questions to get to the heart of what happened in the past.

Hypothetical Questions You can also use questions to dig deeper than what is in the text. You can ask hypothetical, or what if, questions. These questions ask what might have happened had events occurred differently. Sometimes asking such questions can help history come alive.

Who?
Congress

What?
encouraged new settlement

In 1862 Congress passed two important land acts that helped open the West to settlers. The Homestead Act gave government-owned land to small farmers. Any adult who was a U.S. citizen or planned to become one could receive 160 acres of land. In exchange, homesteaders promised to live on the land for five years. The Morrill Act granted more than 17 million acres of federal land to the states.

Where?
the West

When?
1862

How?
Congress gave land to anyone who agreed to settle on it for five years.

What if?
If Congress had not passed these laws, U.S. citizens might not have moved West. The United States might not have grown as quickly as it did.

Why?
Perhaps Congress feared what would happen to western lands if they remained unsettled by U.S. citizens.

You Try It!

Read the following passage and then answer the questions below.

Building Communities Women were an important force in the settlement of the frontier. They joined in the hard work of farming and ranching and helped build communities out of the widely spaced farms and small towns. Their role in founding communities facilitated a strong voice in public affairs. Wyoming women, for example, were granted the vote in the new state's constitution, which was approved in 1869. Annie Bidwell, one of the founders of Chico, California, used her influence to support a variety of moral and social causes such as women's suffrage and temperance.

Answer these questions based on the passage you just read.

1. Who is this passage about?
2. What did they do?
3. When did they do it?
4. How do you think they accomplished it?
5. Why do you think they were able to accomplish so much?
6. How can knowing this information help you understand the past?
7. What if women in the West had been given more rights? Fewer rights? How might the West have been different?

As you read Module 11, ask questions like *who, what, when, where, why, how,* and *what* if to help you analyze what you are reading.

Key Terms and People

Lesson 1
Daniel Boone
Louisiana Purchase
Meriwether Lewis
William Clark
Lewis and Clark expedition
Sacagawea
Zebulon Pike
John C. Frémont
John Jacob Astor
mountain men
Oregon Trail
Santa Fe Trail
Mormons
Brigham Young

Lesson 2
frontier
Comstock Lode
boomtowns
Cattle Kingdom
cattle drive
Chisholm Trail
Pony Express
transcontinental railroad
standard time

Lesson 3
Treaty of Fort Laramie
reservations
Crazy Horse
Treaty of Medicine Lodge
buffalo soldiers
George Armstrong Custer
Sitting Bull
Battle of the Little Bighorn
Massacre at Wounded Knee
Long Walk
Chief Joseph
Geronimo
Ghost Dance
Sarah Winnemucca
assimilate
Dawes General Allotment Act

Lesson 4
Homestead Act
Morrill Act
Exodusters
sodbusters
dry farming
Annie Bidwell
National Grange
deflation
William Jennings Bryan
Populist Party

A Growing Nation

The Big Idea

Americans explored and settled in the West as the nation expanded.

Main Ideas

- As American settlers moved West, control of the Mississippi River became more important to the United States.

- Expeditions led by Lewis and Clark, Pike, and Frémont increased Americans' understanding of the West.

- During the early 1800s, Americans moved west of the Rocky Mountains to settle and trade.

- Families moved into the far west and established thriving communities.

Key Terms and People

Daniel Boone
Louisiana Purchase
Meriwether Lewis
William Clark
Lewis and Clark expedition
Sacagawea
Zebulon Pike
John C. Frémont
John Jacob Astor
mountain men
Oregon Trail
Santa Fe Trail
Mormons
Brigham Young

If YOU were there . . .

You and your family live on a small farm in Kentucky in about 1800. Raised on the frontier, you are a skillful hunter and trapper. One day at the trading post, you see a poster calling for volunteers to join the Corps of Discovery. This expedition will explore the vast region west of the Mississippi River. You think it would be exciting—but dangerous. You might never come home.

Would you volunteer to join the Corps of Discovery?

The First Westerners

For centuries, the Ohio, Cumberland, and Tennessee River valleys had been the hunting grounds of many Native American tribes. By 1800, however, thousands of white settlers had set up homesteads in these areas. The land had been opened up to settlement by an intrepid group of frontier guides known as long hunters. During months-long hunting trips, they explored and surveyed the wilderness west of the Appalachian Mountains. **Daniel Boone** was one of the most famous long hunters.

Frontiersman Daniel Boone led the exploration and settlementofKentucky.

From his earliest years, Boone loved the outdoor life. In time, he became a skilled hunter, trapper, and guide. In 1769 he led a group of friends on an expedition across the Appalachian Mountains via the Cumberland Gap. They were among the first whites to venture deep into the land beyond the Appalachians. Then, in 1775 Boone and about 30 other long hunters cut a continuous road through the Cumberland Gap. By the time it was finished, this Wilderness Road stretched some 300 miles. It soon became the main thoroughfare for settlers moving West. Some used a southern route called the Natchez Trace. This was an old Native American trail that ran southwest all the way to the Mississippi River.

As the region's population grew, Kentucky, Tennessee, and Ohio were admitted to the Union. Settlers in these states depended upon the Mississippi and Ohio rivers to move their products to eastern markets. New Orleans, located at the mouth of the Mississippi, was a very important port. Its busy docks were filled with settlers' farm products and valuable furs bought from American Indians. Many of these cargoes were then sent to Europe. At the same time, manufactured goods passed through the port on their way upriver. As American dependence on the river grew, President Thomas Jefferson began to worry that a foreign power might shut down access to New Orleans.

Spain controlled both New Orleans and the Louisiana Territory. This region stretched west from the Mississippi River to the Rocky Mountains. Although Spain owned Louisiana, Spanish officials found it impossible to keep Americans out of the territory. "You can't put doors on open country," the foreign minister said in despair. Years of effort failed to improve Spain's position. Under a secret treaty, Spain agreed to trade Louisiana to France, passing the problem on to someone else. One Spanish officer expressed his relief. "I can hardly wait to leave them [the Americans] behind me," he said.

Reading Check
Analyze Information
Why was New Orleans important to settlers in the western regions of the United States?

▷ *Explore ONLINE!*

The Louisiana Purchase and Western Expeditions

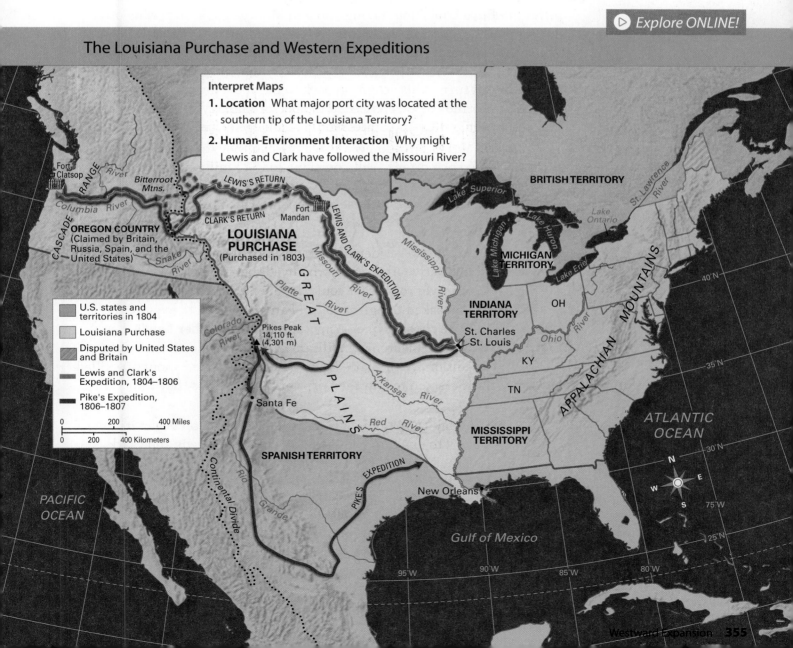

Interpret Maps

1. **Location** What major port city was located at the southern tip of the Louisiana Territory?

2. **Human-Environment Interaction** Why might Lewis and Clark have followed the Missouri River?

Fort Clatsop · Columbia River · Bitterroot Mtns. · LEWIS'S RETURN · CLARK'S RETURN · Fort Mandan · LEWIS AND CLARK'S EXPEDITION · CASCADE RANGE · **OREGON COUNTRY** (Claimed by Britain, Russia, Spain, and the United States) · Snake River · **LOUISIANA PURCHASE** (Purchased in 1803) · Missouri River · Platte River · GREAT PLAINS · Pikes Peak 14,110 ft. (4,301 m) · Colorado River · Santa Fe · Arkansas River · Red River · **SPANISH TERRITORY** · Rio Grande · Continental Divide · PIKE'S EXPEDITION · New Orleans · *Gulf of Mexico* · PACIFIC OCEAN · Lake Superior · Lake Michigan · Lake Huron · Lake Ontario · Lake Erie · St. Lawrence River · Mississippi River · **BRITISH TERRITORY** · **MICHIGAN TERRITORY** · **INDIANA TERRITORY** · OH · St. Charles · St. Louis · Ohio River · KY · TN · APPALACHIAN MOUNTAINS · **MISSISSIPPI TERRITORY** · *ATLANTIC OCEAN*

Legend:
- U.S. states and territories in 1804
- Louisiana Purchase
- Disputed by United States and Britain
- Lewis and Clark's Expedition, 1804–1806
- Pike's Expedition, 1806–1807

0 200 400 Miles
0 200 400 Kilometers

40°N · 35°N · 30°N · 25°N · 95°W · 90°W · 85°W · 80°W · 75°W

Louisiana and Western Explorers

In 1802, just before handing over Louisiana to France, Spain closed New Orleans to American shipping. Angry farmers worried about what this would do to the economy. President Jefferson asked the U.S. ambassador to France, Robert R. Livingston, to try to buy New Orleans. Jefferson sent James Monroe to help Livingston.

Napoléon and Louisiana France was led by Napoléon (nuh-POH-lay-uhn) Bonaparte, a powerful ruler who had conquered most of Europe. He wished to rebuild France's empire in North America. Napoléon's strategy was to use the French colony of Haiti, in the Caribbean, as a supply base. From there he could send troops to Louisiana. However, in the 1790s enslaved Africans, led by Toussaint Louverture (too-SAN loo-vehr-TOOR), revolted and freed themselves from French rule. Napoléon sent troops to try to regain control of the island, but they were defeated in 1802. This defeat ended his hopes of rebuilding a North American empire.

Jefferson Buys Louisiana Livingston and Monroe got a surprising offer during their negotiations with French foreign minister Charles Talleyrand. When the Americans tried to buy New Orleans, Talleyrand offered to sell all of Louisiana. With his hopes for a North American empire dashed, Napoléon had turned his attention back to Europe. France was at war with Great Britain, and Napoléon needed money for military supplies. He also hoped that a larger United States would challenge British power.

Livingston and Monroe knew a bargain when they saw one. They quickly accepted the French offer to sell Louisiana for $15 million, and Jefferson agreed to the purchase. On October 20, 1803, the Senate approved the **Louisiana Purchase** agreement, which roughly doubled the size of the United States.

Explorers Head West President Jefferson wanted to learn more about the West and the Native Americans who lived there. He also wanted to see if there was a river route that could be taken to the Pacific Ocean. So, in 1803 Jefferson asked Congress to fund an expedition to explore the West. To lead it, he chose former army captain **Meriwether Lewis**. Lewis then chose his friend Lieutenant **William Clark** to be the co-leader of the expedition. With Clark, Lewis carefully selected about 50 skilled frontiersmen to join the Corps of Discovery, as they called their group.

In May 1804 the **Lewis and Clark expedition** began its long journey to explore the Louisiana Purchase. Lewis and Clark used the Missouri River as their highway through the unknown lands. By late October the Corps of Discovery had pushed more than 1,600 miles upriver. They spent the winter among the Mandan people. At this time, the Corps also came into contact with British and Canadian trappers and traders, who were not happy to see them. The traders feared American competition in the trade in beaver fur—and they would be proved right.

The Lewis and Clark expedition followed the Missouri River for most of the journey across the Great Plains.

Meriwether Lewis's Journal Entry

On September 17, 1804, while traveling across the Great Plains, Meriwether Lewis marveled at the richness of the land.

Analyze Historical Sources
What did Lewis find so impressive about the Great Plains?

"The shortness . . . of grass gave the plain the appearance throughout its whole extent of beautiful bowling-green in fine order . . . this scenery, already rich, pleasing, and beautiful was still farther heightened by immense herds of Buffaloe, deer Elk and Antelopes which we saw in every direction feeding on the hills and plains. I do not think I exaggerate when I estimate the number of Buffalo which could be compre[hend]ed at one view to amount to 3000."

—Meriwether Lewis,
quoted in *Original Journals of the Lewis and Clark Expedition*, edited by Reuben Bold Theraites

Sacagawea, whose name is believed to mean "bird woman," contributed greatly to the success of the Lewis and Clark expedition.

In the spring of 1805, the expedition set out again. They were joined by **Sacagawea** (sak-uh-guh-WEE-uh), a Shoshone from the Rocky Mountains. Her language skills—she knew several Native American languages—and her knowledge of the geography of the region proved very useful to Lewis and Clark. Sacagawea also helped the expedition by naming plants and by gathering edible fruits and vegetables for the group. At one point, the group met with Sacagawea's brother, who provided horses and a guide to lead the expedition across the mountains.

After crossing the Rockies, Lewis and Clark followed the Columbia River. Along the way they met the powerful Nez Percé. Like the Shoshone, the Nez Percé provided the expedition with supplies. At last, in November 1805 Lewis and Clark reached the Pacific Ocean. The explorers stayed in the Pacific Northwest during the rough winter. In March 1806 Lewis and Clark set out on the long trip home.

Lewis and Clark had not found a river route across the West to the Pacific Ocean. But they had learned much about western lands and paths across the Rockies. They used this knowledge to produce the first accurate maps of the Louisiana Territory. The explorers also established contact with many Native American groups and collected much valuable information about western plants and animals.

Other Explorations In 1806 a young army officer named **Zebulon Pike** was sent on another mission to the West. He was ordered to find the starting point of the Red River. This was important because the United States considered the Red River to be a part of the Louisiana Territory's western border with New Spain.

Heading into the Rocky Mountains, in present-day Colorado, Pike tried to reach the summit of the mountain now known as Pikes Peak. In 1807 he traveled into Spanish-held lands until Spanish cavalry arrested him. They suspected Pike of being a spy. When he was finally released, he returned to the United States and reported on his trip. This report offered many Americans their first description of the Southwest. Not all of Pike's information was accurate, however. For example, he described the treeless Great Plains as a desert. This led many Americans to believe, mistakenly, that the Plains region was useless for farming.

Another explorer, **John C. Frémont**, led an expedition to the Rocky Mountains in May 1842. Upon his return, Frémont compiled a report of his journey, which became a guide for future travelers to the West. It detailed the geology, botany, and climate of the region. It also crushed the mistaken belief that the West was a vast desert, attracting more settlers as a result. Buoyed by the success of his first effort, Frémont led several more surveys of the American West in the 1840s and 1850s.

Mountain Men Go West

In the early 1800s, Americans pushed steadily westward, moving even beyond the territory of the United States. They traveled by canoe and flatboat, on horseback, and by wagon train. Some even walked much of the way.

The rush to the West occurred, in part, because of a hat. The "high hat," made of water-repellent beaver fur, was popular in the United States and Europe. While acquiring fur for the hats, French, British, and American companies gradually killed off the beaver population in the East. Companies moved West in search of more beavers. Most of the first non-Native Americans who traveled to the Rocky Mountains and the Pacific Northwest were fur traders and trappers.

American merchant **John Jacob Astor** created one of the largest fur businesses, the American Fur Company. His company bought skins from western fur traders and trappers, who became known as **mountain men**. These adventurers were among the first to explore the Rocky Mountains and lands west of them. The knowledge they acquired helped settlers who made the westward journey. Mountain men lived lonely and often dangerous lives. They trapped animals on their own, far from towns and settlements. Mountain men such as Jedediah Smith, Manuel Lisa, Jim Bridger, and Jim Beckwourth survived many hardships during their search for wealth and adventure. To survive on the frontier, mountain men adopted Native American customs and clothing. In addition, they often married Native American women. The Indian wives of trappers often worked hard to contribute to their success.

Pioneer William Ashley saw that frequently bringing furs out of the Rocky Mountains was expensive. He asked his traders to stay in the mountains and meet once a year to trade and socialize. This practice helped make the fur trade more profitable. The yearly meeting was known as the rendezvous. At the rendezvous, mountain men and Native American trappers sold their fur to fur-company agents. One trapper described the people at a typical rendezvous in 1837. He saw Americans, Canadian French, some Europeans, and "Indians, of nearly every tribe in the Rocky Mountains." The rendezvous was filled with celebrating and storytelling. At the same time, the meeting was also about conducting business.

Reading Check
Compare What did the expeditions of Lewis and Clark, Pike, and Frémont reveal about the West?

Jim Beckwourth was an African American fur trapper and explorer of the West in the early 1800s.

In 1811 John Jacob Astor founded a fur-trading post called Astoria at the mouth of the Columbia River. Astoria was one of the first American settlements in what became known as Oregon Country. American Indians occupied the region, which was rich in forests, rivers, and wildlife. However, Britain, Russia, Spain, and the United States all claimed the land. Recognizing the huge economic value of the Pacific Northwest, the United States made treaties in which Spain and Russia gave up their claims to various areas. The United States also signed treaties with Britain allowing both countries to occupy Oregon Country, the Columbia River, and its surrounding lands.

By the 1840s the era of American fur trading in the Pacific Northwest was drawing to a close. The demand for beaver furs had fallen because fashions had changed. Too much trapping had also greatly reduced the number of beavers. Some mountain men gave up their work and moved back East. Their daring stories, however, along with the treaties made by the U.S. government, fired the imagination of many Americans.

Reading Check
Draw Conclusions
How did the mountain men help to open up the West for future settlement?

Settling the West

The success of early pioneers convinced thousands of families and individuals to make the dangerous journey west. They traveled along a series of routes that led to New Mexico, Oregon, and Utah. Once in these places, the new pioneers claimed the land and established settlements.

The Oregon Trail Many settlers moving to Oregon Country and other western areas followed the 2,000-mile-long **Oregon Trail**, which stretched from places such as Independence, Missouri, and Council Bluffs, Iowa, west into Oregon Country. The trail followed the Platte and Sweetwater Rivers over the Plains. After it crossed the Rocky Mountains, the trail forked. The northern branch led to the Willamette Valley in Oregon. The other branch went to California and became known as the California Trail.

Traveling the trail challenged the strength and determination of pioneer families. The journey usually began after the rainy season ended in late spring and lasted about six months. The cost, about $600 for a family of four, was high at a time when a typical worker usually made about $1.50 per day. Young families made up most groups of settlers. They gathered in wagon trains for the trip. There could be as few as ten wagons or as many as several dozen in a wagon train. Some pioneers brought small herds of cattle with them on the trail.

Oxen, mules, or horses pulled the wagons. Pioneers often walked to save their animals' strength. They kept up a tiring pace, traveling from dawn until dusk. They faced severe hardships, including shortages of food, supplies, and water. Rough weather and geographic barriers, such as rivers and mountains, sometimes forced large numbers of pioneers to abandon their wagons. In the early days of the Oregon Trail, many Native Americans helped the pioneers, acting as guides. They also traded goods for food. Although newspapers sometimes reported Native American "massacres" of pioneers, few settlers died from Indian attacks. The settlers who arrived safely in Oregon and California found generally healthy and pleasant climates. By 1845 some 5,000 settlers occupied the Willamette Valley.

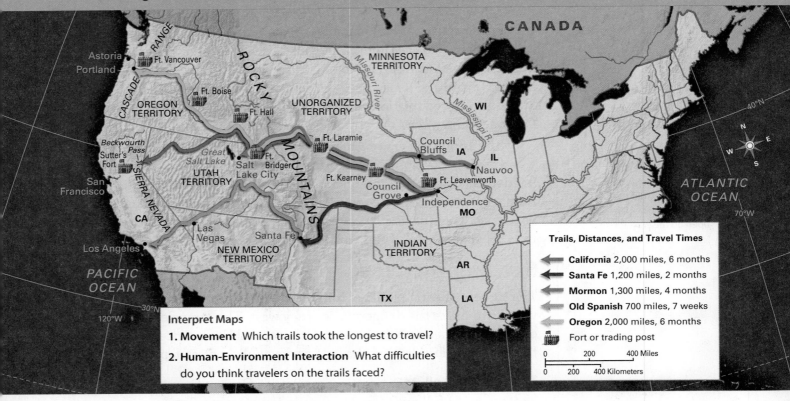

Explore ONLINE!

Interpret Maps

1. **Movement** Which trails took the longest to travel?
2. **Human-Environment Interaction** What difficulties do you think travelers on the trails faced?

Trails, Distances, and Travel Times

California 2,000 miles, 6 months
Santa Fe 1,200 miles, 2 months
Mormon 1,300 miles, 4 months
Old Spanish 700 miles, 7 weeks
Oregon 2,000 miles, 6 months
Fort or trading post

The Santa Fe Trail The **Santa Fe Trail** was another important path west. It led from Independence, Missouri, to Santa Fe, New Mexico. It followed an ancient trading route first used by Native Americans. American traders loaded their wagon trains with cloth and other manufactured goods to exchange for horses, mules, and silver from Mexican traders in Santa Fe.

The long trip across blazing deserts and rough mountains was dangerous. But the lure of high profits encouraged traders to take to the trail. One trader reported a 2,000 percent profit on his cargo. The U.S. government helped protect traders by sending troops to ensure that Native Americans were not a threat.

Mormons Travel West One large group of settlers traveled to the West in search of religious freedom. In 1830 a young man named Joseph Smith founded the Church of Jesus Christ of Latter-day Saints in western New York. The members of his church became known as **Mormons**. Smith told his followers that he had found and translated a set of golden tablets containing religious teachings. The writings were called the *Book of Mormon*.

Church membership grew rapidly, but certain beliefs and practices caused Mormons to be persecuted. For example, beginning in the 1850s some Mormon men practiced polygamy—a practice in which one man is married to several women at the same time. The church outlawed this practice in 1890.

In the early 1830s Smith and his growing number of converts left New York. Many traveled on the recently completed Erie Canal and Lake Erie to Ohio, where they set up new communities. Later, they moved on and

This Mormon family took part in an early-1900s celebration of the pioneers who made the great trek along the Mormon Trail to Utah.

established communities in Missouri and Illinois. Eventually, these communities failed. The Illinois community collapsed after an anti-Mormon mob murdered Smith in 1844. Following Smith's murder, **Brigham Young** became head of the Mormon Church. Young chose what is now Utah as the group's new home, and thousands of Mormons took the Mormon Trail to the area near the Great Salt Lake, where they prospered. By 1860 there were about 40,000 Mormons in Utah.

Summary and Preview Some of the first Americans to move West were fur traders and trappers. Settlers soon followed. In the next lesson you will learn about America's continued westward expansion.

Reading Check
Summarize How did settlers travel west, and what challenges did they face on their journey?

Lesson 1 Assessment

Review Ideas, Terms, and People

1. a. **Identify** Who helped to open up the land west of the Appalachians by building the Wilderness Road?

   b. **Explain** Why were New Orleans and the Mississippi River important to settlers in the West?

2. a. **Summarize** Why was the Louisiana Purchase important to the United States?

   b. **Describe** What areas did the Lewis and Clark expedition and the Zebulon Pike and John C. Frémont expeditions explore?

   c. **Draw Conclusions** Why were Meriwether Lewis and William Clark chosen to lead the exploration of the Louisiana Purchase?

3. a. **Identify** Who established one of the first American settlements in Oregon Country?

   b. **Describe** What were the lives of mountain men like?

4. a. **Identify** What was the Oregon Trail?

   b. **Elaborate** Would you have chosen to leave your home to travel West? Why?

c. **Summarize** What difficulties led Mormons to move to Utah?

Critical Thinking

5. **Sequence** In this lesson you learned about the westward expansion of the United States. Create a graphic organizer like the one below to rank the three most important effects of the Louisiana Purchase, from most important to least important, and explain why you chose that order.

Importance	Why
1.	
2.	
3.	

6. **Draw Conclusions** What challenges did the westward journey present for settlers?

7. **Make Predictions** What effects do you think westward migration of the mid-1800s would have on Native Americans?

History and Geography

America's Growth by 1820

In 1803 the United States made the biggest land purchase in its history—the Louisiana Purchase. With this purchase, the country stretched west all the way to the Rocky Mountains. In 1819 the United States acquired Florida from Spain, gaining even more new territory. By 1820 the young American republic had roughly doubled in size, as you can see on the map. Explorers, traders, and settlers began to pour into the new lands in search of wealth, land, and a place to call home.

50°N

British Territory

Claimed by United States, ceded to Great Britain in 1818

49th Parallel

R O C K Y   M O U N T A I N S

Oregon Country Both the United States and Great Britain claimed Oregon Country.

Oregon Country

42nd Parallel

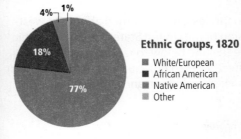

PACIFIC OCEAN

Spanish Territory

30°N

America's Population, 1820: 10.1 million

4% 1%
18%
77%

Ethnic Groups, 1820
- White/European
- African American
- Native American
- Other

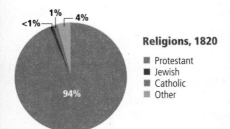

1% 4%
<1%
94%

Religions, 1820
- Protestant
- Jewish
- Catholic
- Other

- Louisiana Purchase, 1803
- Claimed by United States and Great Britain, 1818
- Convention of 1818
- From Britain to United States, 1818
- Adams-Onís Treaty of 1819
- From Spain to United States, 1819

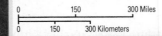
0   150   300 Miles
0   150   300 Kilometers

130°W   120°W   110°W

Early Traders Soon after Lewis and Clark explored the Louisiana Territory, American fur traders and trappers began setting up trading posts there. Many of these posts later became towns as more settlers arrived.

Through the Gaps Settlers crossed the Appalachians through valleys called gaps. In time, roads were built through the gaps, making it easier for settlers to head West.

Delaware Gap

ATLANTIC OCEAN

40°N

Unorganized Territory

Missouri River

APPALACHIAN MTS

Missouri Territory

Cumberland Gap

Arkansas Territory

Red River

Mississippi River

The Mighty Mississippi The Mississippi River was the great highway of the United States. Americans west of the Appalachians shipped farm goods and supplies up and down the Mississippi and to its major port, New Orleans.

Louisiana

New Orleans

Gulf of Mexico

Unorganized Territory (Florida)

70°W

Interpret Maps

1. **Movement** In which directions did the United States expand before 1820?

2. **Region** Based on the map, why do you think the United States was interested in claiming Oregon Country?

Boom Times in the West

The Big Idea

American settlers dramatically changed the western frontier as they began to tame the land.

Main Ideas

- Valuable deposits of gold and silver in the West created opportunities for wealth and brought more settlers to the region.
- The cattle industry thrived on the Great Plains, supplying beef to the East.
- The transcontinental railroad succeeded in linking the eastern and western United States.

Key Terms

frontier
Comstock Lode
boomtowns
Cattle Kingdom
cattle drive
Chisholm Trail
Pony Express
transcontinental railroad
standard time

Hydraulic Mining
Miners used high-powered water jets to blast earth from a hillside in order to expose the gold in the rock.

If YOU were there . . .

You are a cowboy in Texas in 1875. You love life on the open range, the quiet nights, and the freedom. You even like the hard work of the long cattle drives to Kansas. But you know that times are changing. Homesteaders are moving in and fencing off their lands. Some of the older cowboys say it's time to settle down and buy a small ranch. You hope that they're not right.

What would make you give up a cowboy's life?

Mining Boom Brings Growth

During the years surrounding the Civil War, most Americans had thought of the Great Plains and other western lands as the Great American Desert. In the years following the Civil War, Americans witnessed the rapid growth of the U.S. population and the spread of settlements throughout the West. With the admission of the state of California to the Union in 1850, the western boundary of the American **frontier**—an undeveloped area—had reached the Pacific Ocean.

The frontier changed dramatically as more and more people moved westward. Settlers built homes, fenced off land, and laid out ranches and farms. Miners, ranchers, and farmers remade the landscape of the West as they adapted to their new surroundings. The geography of the West was further changed by the development and expansion of a large and successful railroad industry that moved the West's natural resources to eastern markets. Gold and silver were the most valuable natural resources, and mining companies used the growing railroad network to bring these precious metals to the East.

Big Business Most of the precious metals were located in western Nevada. In 1859 miner Henry Comstock discovered a huge deposit of gold and silver in Nevada that became called the **Comstock Lode**. The deposit was incredibly rich

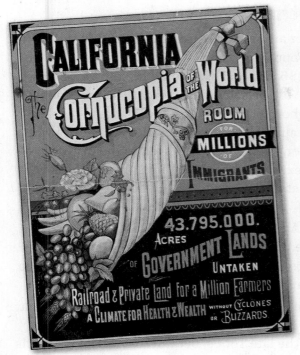

Posters like this one were designed to persuade people to move West.

and deep. In just the first year after its discovery, the Comstock Lode lured thousands of California miners to Nevada. Over the next 20 years, the Comstock Lode produced more than $500 million worth of gold and silver.

Expensive equipment was needed to remove the silver and gold that were trapped within quartz rock. Larger mining companies bought up land claims from miners who could not afford this machinery. As a result, mining became a big business in the West.

As companies dug bigger and deeper mines, the work became more dangerous. Miners had to use unsafe equipment, such as elevator platforms without protective walls. They worked in dark tunnels and breathed hot, stuffy air. They suffered from lung disease caused by dusty air. Miners often were injured or killed by poorly planned explosions or by cave-ins. Fire was also a great danger. Mining was therefore one of the most dangerous jobs in the country. In the West, worries about safety and pay led miners to form several unions in the 1860s.

Settlers People from all over the world came to work in the western mines. Some miners came from the eastern United States. Others emigrated from Europe, Central and South America, and Asia. Many Mexican immigrants and Mexican Americans were experienced miners. They were skilled in assaying, or testing, the contents of valuable ore. One newspaper reporter wrote, "Here were congregated the most varied elements of humanity . . . belonging to almost every nationality and every status of life."

New Towns Mining booms also produced **boomtowns**, communities that grew suddenly when a mine opened. They disappeared just as quickly when the mine closed. The California town of Bodie, located just southeast of Lake Tahoe, provides a vivid illustration of a mining boomtown. In the early 1870s it was a mining camp with just a handful of inhabitants. The discovery of a rich vein of gold in the late 1870s drew thousands. Within months, Bodie had become a bustling town of some 8,000 people. It had a railroad station, a school, two banks, three newspapers, two churches, and dozens of saloons. Once the gold in the mine was worked out, however, Bodie went into an equally rapid decline. By 1900 the population was less than 1,000.

Few women or families lived in even the most bustling boomtowns. "I was never so lonely and homesick in all my life," wrote one young woman. The women who did settle there washed, cooked, made clothes, and chopped wood. They also raised families, established schools, and wrote for newspapers. Their work helped turn some boomtowns into successful, permanent towns.

Reading Check
Summarize What risks did miners face?

Cattle Ranching in the West

The cattle industry was another area of rapid growth. Following the Civil War, a growing economy and population created a greater demand for beef in the East. Cattle worth $3 to $6 each in Texas could be sold for $38 each in Kansas. In New York, they could be sold for $80 each. The most popular breed of cattle was the longhorn. The longhorn breed spread quickly throughout western Texas. Because these animals needed very little water and could survive harsh weather, they were well suited to the dry, desert-like environment of western Texas. But how could Texas ranchers move the longhorns to eastern markets?

In 1867 businessman Joseph McCoy discovered a solution. He built pens for cattle in the small town of Abilene, Kansas. The Kansas Pacific Railroad line went through Abilene. As a result, cattle could be shipped by rail from there. Soon, countless Texas ranchers were making the trip north to Abilene to sell their herds of cattle.

Around the same time, cattle ranching began to expand in the Midwest. The vast open range of the Great Plains from Texas to Canada, where many ranchers raised cattle in the late 1800s, became known as the **Cattle Kingdom**. Ranchers grazed huge herds on public land called the open range. The land had once been occupied by Plains Indians and buffalo herds.

Importance of Cowboys The workers who took care of the ranchers' cattle were known as cowhands or cowboys. They adopted many techniques and tools from vaqueros (bah-KER-ohs), Mexican ranch hands who cared for cattle and horses. From vaqueros came the western saddle and the lariat, a rope used for lassoing cattle. The cowboys also borrowed the vaqueros' boot. Its narrow toe fit easily into the riding stirrup, and the high heel hooked the stirrup for stability. Cowboys adopted and changed the vaqueros' broad felt hat, turning it into the familiar high-peaked cowboy hat.

One of the cowboy's most important and dangerous duties was the **cattle drive**. On these long journeys, cowboys herded cattle to the market or to the northern Plains for grazing. These long drives usually lasted several months and covered hundreds of miles. Workdays on the drive were long—often up to 15 hours—and sometimes very dull. Excitement came with events such as stampedes. Frightened by a sudden noise such as a thunderclap, the whole herd would take off running wildly. Bringing the herd under control was dangerous and hard work. The **Chisholm Trail**, which ran from San Antonio, Texas, to the cattle town of Abilene, Kansas, was one of the earliest and most popular routes for cattle drives. It was blazed, or marked, by Texas cowboy Jesse Chisholm in the late 1860s.

At times, rowdy cowboys made life in cattle towns rough and violent. There were rarely shoot-outs in the street, but there often was disorderly behavior. Law officials such as Wyatt Earp became famous for keeping the peace in cattle towns.

End of the Open Range As the cattle business boomed, ranchers faced more competition for use of the open range. Farmers began to buy range

Myth and Reality in the Wild West

No episode in American history has given rise to as many myths as the Wild West. Writers of dime novels, popular in the East, helped create the myths in the years after the Civil War. Even today, popular books, television shows, and movies continue to portray the West in ways that are more myth than reality.

Myth: The cowboy was a free-spirited individual.

Reality: Most cowboys were employees. Many joined labor unions and even went on strike.

Myth: Western cow towns were wild places where cowboys had gunfights, and there was little law and order.

Reality: Most were orderly places with active law enforcement. Showdowns rarely, if ever, occurred.

Myth: Almost all cowboys were Anglo Americans.

Reality: About 25 percent of cowboys were African Americans, and 12 percent were Hispanic. Some Native Americans also worked as cowhands.

African American cowboy Nat Love (above); Marshal Wyatt Earp (left)

land on the Great Plains, where cattle had once grazed. Small ranchers also began competing with large ranchers for land. Then in 1874, Joseph Glidden's invention of barbed wire allowed westerners to fence off large amounts of land cheaply. The competition between farmers, large ranchers, and small ranchers increased. This competition led to range wars, or fights for access to land.

Making matters worse, in 1885 and 1886, disaster struck the Cattle Kingdom. The huge cattle herds on the Plains had eaten most of the prairie grass. Unusually severe winters in both years made the ranching situation even worse. Thousands of cattle died, and many ranchers were ruined financially. The Cattle Kingdom had come to an end.

Reading Check
Draw Conclusions
Why did the Cattle Kingdom come to an end?

The Transcontinental Railroad

As more Americans began moving West, the need to send goods and information between the East and West increased. Americans searched for ways to improve communication and travel across the country.

In 1860 a system of messengers on horseback called the **Pony Express** began to carry the mail West. The Pony Express operated from St. Joseph, Missouri, to Sacramento, California, a route of almost 2,000 miles. The business purchased over 400 horses, and riders used a relay system, switching horses at stations 10 to 15 miles apart. The Pony Express cut mail delivery time in half, from three weeks to ten days. The completion of a telegraph line to California in 1861, which sent messages much faster, quickly put the Pony Express out of business.

The Pony Express mail system helped speed up communication across the United States.

Explore ONLINE!

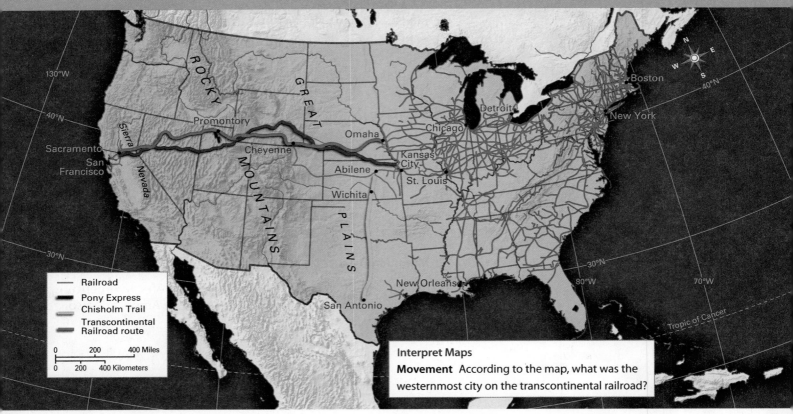

Railroad
Pony Express
Chisholm Trail
Transcontinental
Railroad route

0   200   400 Miles
0   200   400 Kilometers

Interpret Maps

Movement According to the map, what was the westernmost city on the transcontinental railroad?

Some Americans wanted to build a **transcontinental railroad**—a railroad that would cross the continent and connect the East to the West. The federal government, therefore, passed the Pacific Railway Acts in 1862 and in 1864. These acts gave railroad companies loans and large land grants that could be sold to pay for construction costs. Congress had granted more than 131 million acres of public land to railroad companies. In exchange, the government asked the railroads to carry U.S. mail and troops at a lower cost. Many railroad companies were inspired to begin laying miles of track.

Great Race Two companies, the Central Pacific and the Union Pacific, led the race to complete the transcontinental railroad. In February 1863 the Central Pacific began building east from Sacramento, California. At the end of the year, the Union Pacific started building west from Omaha, Nebraska.

The Union Pacific hired thousands of railroad workers, particularly Irish immigrants. Chinese immigrants made up some 85 percent of the Central Pacific workforce. The railroad's part-owner Leland Stanford praised them, but he paid them less than other laborers. Chinese crews also were given the most dangerous tasks and had to work longer hours than other railroad laborers. They took the job, however, because the $30 a month that the Central Pacific paid was as much as ten times what they could earn in China.

Railroad companies faced many geographic challenges. For example, workers for Central Pacific struggled to cross the Sierra Nevada mountain range in California. Breaking apart its rock formations required setting carefully controlled explosions using large amounts of blasting powder and the explosive nitroglycerin. And in the winter of 1866, snowdrifts more than 60 feet high trapped and killed dozens of workers. Faced with these obstacles, the Central Pacific took four years to lay the first 115 miles of track.

Meanwhile, Union Pacific workers faced harsh weather on the Great Plains. In addition, the company pressured them to work at a rapid pace—at times laying 250 miles of track in six months.

For both railroad companies, providing food and supplies for workers was vital. This job became more difficult in remote areas. The railroad companies consequently often relied on local resources. Professional hunters, such as William "Buffalo Bill" Cody, shot thousands of buffalo to feed Union Pacific workers.

Golden Spike Congress required the two completed rail lines to connect at Promontory, Utah. On May 10, 1869, a golden spike was used to connect the railroad tie joining the two tracks. Alexander Toponce witnessed the event.

> "Governor Stanford, president of the Central Pacific, took the sledge [hammer], and the first time he struck he missed the spike and hit the rail. What a howl went up! Irish, Chinese, Mexicans, and everybody yelled with delight. 'He missed it' . . . Then Stanford tried it again and tapped the spike."
> —Alexander Toponce, from *Reminiscences of Alexander Toponce, Written by Himself*

The railroad companies were not finished, though. Following completion of the transcontinental railroad, they continued building railroads until the West was crisscrossed with rail lines.

The Central Pacific and Union Pacific connected their tracks at Promontory, Utah, in 1869, completing the transcontinental railroad.

Results of the Railroad The transcontinental railroad increased both economic growth and the population in the West. Railroad companies provided better transportation for people and goods. They also sold land to settlers, which encouraged people to move West. The development of the West brought about the railroad; however, it also would prove to be the beginning of the end of the Plains Indians' way of life.

New railroads helped businesses. Western timber companies, miners, ranchers, and farmers shipped wood, metals, meat, and grain East by railroad. In exchange, eastern businesses shipped manufactured goods to the West. As trade between regions increased, the idea that the U.S. economy was interdependent became more widespread.

Even perceptions of time became more formal as railroad schedules began to unite areas that before had existed under different times. Before the railroads, each community determined its own time, based on calculations about the sun's travels. This system, called "solar time," caused problems for people who scheduled trains crossing a long distance. The railroad companies addressed the issue by setting up **standard time**. This system divided the United States into four time zones.

Railroad companies encouraged people to invest in the railroads, which they did—sometimes unwisely. Speculation and the collapse of railroad owner Jay Cooke's banking firm helped start the Panic of 1873. Despite such setbacks, Americans remained interested in railroad investments. By 1890 there were about 164,000 more miles of track than in 1865. Railroads had become one of the biggest industries in the United States.

Reading Check
Find Main Ideas
How did the railroad affect the development of the West?

Summary and Preview In this lesson you learned about the increased settlement of the West. In the next lesson you will learn about conflicts with Native Americans.

Lesson 2 Assessment

Review Ideas, Terms, and People

1. a. **Recall** Why did Americans move West in the years following the Civil War?

   b. **Draw Conclusions** What effect did the discovery of the Comstock Lode have on the West?

   c. **Evaluate** Do you think women were important to the success of mining towns? Why or why not?

2. a. **Recall** What led to the cattle boom in the West?

   b. **Analyze** Why was there competition between ranchers and farmers to settle in the Great Plains?

   c. **Evaluate** What played the biggest role in ending the Cattle Kingdom? Why?

3. a. **Recall** When and where did the Union Pacific and Central Pacific lines meet?

   b. **Describe** What role did Irish and Chinese immigrants play in opening up the West?

   c. **Make Generalizations** How do you think the transcontinental railroad improved people's lives?

Critical Thinking

4. **Identify Cause and Effect** In this lesson you learned about the kinds of economic opportunities that people found in the West. Create a graphic organizer similar to the one below to list these opportunities and their effects.

Opportunity	Effect

★ Wars for the West

The Big Idea

Native Americans and the U.S. government came into conflict over land in the West.

Main Ideas

- As settlers moved to the Great Plains, they encountered the Plains Indians.

- Native Americans attempted to keep their lands through treaties with the U.S. government.

- Continued pressure from white settlement and government legislation brought the Plains Indians' traditional way of life to an end.

Key Terms and People

Treaty of Fort Laramie
reservations
Crazy Horse
Treaty of Medicine Lodge
buffalo soldiers
George Armstrong Custer
Sitting Bull
Battle of the Little Bighorn
Massacre at Wounded Knee
Long Walk
Chief Joseph
Geronimo
Ghost Dance
Sarah Winnemucca
assimilate
Dawes General Allotment Act

If YOU were there . . .

You are a member of the Sioux nation, living in Dakota Territory in 1875. These lands are sacred to your people, and the U.S. government has promised them to you. But now gold has been found here, and the government has ordered you to give up your land. Some Sioux leaders want to fight. Others say that it is of no use, that the soldiers will win.

Would you fight to keep your lands? Why?

Settlers Encounter the Plains Indians

As miners and settlers began crossing the Great Plains in the mid-1800s, they pressured the federal government for more access to western lands. To protect these travelers, U.S. officials sent agents to negotiate treaties with the Plains Indians.

The Plains Indians lived in the Great Plains, which stretch north into Canada and south into Texas. Indian groups such as the Apache and the Comanche lived in and around Texas and what is now Oklahoma. The Cheyenne and the Arapaho lived in different regions across the central Plains. The Pawnee lived in parts of Nebraska. To the north were the Sioux. These groups spoke many different languages. However, they used a common sign language to communicate and they shared a similar lifestyle.

Crazy Horse (Tashunka Witco) was a Sioux chief who fought to defend his people's way of life and resisted attempts to force the Sioux onto reservations.

Hunting Buffalo For survival, the Plains Indians depended on two animals—the horse and the buffalo. The Spanish brought horses to America in the 1500s. The Plains Indians learned to ride horses, and hunters used them to follow buffalo herds year-round. While on horseback, most Plains Indian hunters used a short bow and arrows to shoot buffalo from close range.

The Plains Indians used buffalo for food, shelter, clothing, utensils, and tools. Women dried buffalo meat to make

The Plains Indians depended on two animals—the horse and the buffalo.

jerky. They made tepees and clothing from buffalo hides, and cups and tools from buffalo horns. As one Sioux explained, "When our people killed a buffalo, all of the animal was utilized [used] in some manner; nothing was wasted." The Plains Indians prospered. By 1850 some 75,000 Native Americans lived on the Plains.

Struggle to Keep Land Miners and settlers were also increasing in numbers—and they wanted the Indians' land. The U.S. government tried to avoid disputes by negotiating the **Treaty of Fort Laramie**, the first major treaty between the U.S. government and Plains Indians. Two years later, several southern Plains nations signed a treaty at Fort Atkinson in Nebraska. These treaties recognized Indian claims to most of the Great Plains. They also allowed the United States to build forts and roads and to travel across Indian homelands. The U.S. government promised to pay for any damages to Indian lands.

The treaties did not keep the peace for long. In 1858 the discovery of gold in what is now Colorado brought thousands of miners to the West. They soon clashed with the Cheyenne and the Arapaho. In 1861 the U.S. government negotiated new treaties with Plains Indians. These treaties created **reservations**, areas of federal land set aside for Native Americans. The government expected Indians to stay on the reservations, which made hunting buffalo almost impossible.

Pioneers and miners continued to cross the Great Plains. Many miners used the Bozeman Trail. To protect them, the U.S. Army built forts along the trail, which ran through favored Sioux hunting grounds. The Sioux responded with war. In late 1866 a group led by **Crazy Horse**, an Oglala Sioux chief, ambushed and killed 81 cavalry troops.

In 1868 under the Second Treaty of Fort Laramie, the U.S. government agreed to close the Bozeman Trail and abandon the forts, and forced some of the Sioux onto reservations. The U.S. government also forced

Reading Check
Summarize What was the federal policy toward the Plains Indians in the 1860s and 1870s?

some of the southern Plains Indians to move off their land. In the 1867 **Treaty of Medicine Lodge**, most southern Plains Indians agreed to live on reservations. However, many Indians did not want to give up their hunting grounds. Fighting soon broke out between the Comanche and Texans. The U.S. Army and the Texas Rangers were unable to defeat the Comanche, so they cut off the Comanche's access to food and water. In 1875 the last of the Comanche war leaders surrendered.

Fighting on the Plains

In the northern Plains, Southwest, and Far West, Native Americans continued to resist being moved to and confined on reservations. The U.S. government sent troops into the area to force the Indians to leave. These troops included African American cavalry, who the Indians called **buffalo soldiers**—a term of honor, inspired by their short, curly hair, that compared their fighting spirit to that of the buffalo.

Battles on the Northern Plains As fighting on the southern Plains came to an end, new trouble started in the north. In 1874 Lieutenant Colonel

▷ *Explore ONLINE!*

Native American Land Loss in the West, 1850–1890

Legend:
- 1850–1870
- 1870–1890
- Reservations in 1890
- UTE Native American group

0 200 400 Miles
0 200 400 Kilometers

Battles and Treaties of the Indian Wars
1. Treaties at Fort Laramie, 1851 and 1868
2. Treaty at Fort Atkinson, 1853
3. Sand Creek Massacre, 1864
4. Fetterman Massacre, 1866
5. Treaty of Medicine Lodge, 1867
6. Battle of the Little Bighorn, 1876
7. Battle of the Rosebud, 1876
8. Wounded Knee Massacre, 1890

Interpret Maps
Region In what regions did Native Americans lose land in the late 1800s?

The Native Americans are shown surrounding a small force of U.S. soldiers.

Custer is shown standing among his men as he fires.

The U.S. Army is shown on horseback in this drawing.

These horses have been captured by the Native Americans.

Two Views of a Historic Battle

Art historians have identified about 1,000 paintings of the Battle of the Little Bighorn. The painting at the top was painted in 1899. The drawing below it is one of the many colored-pencil drawings of the battle done by Amos Bad Heart Buffalo, who based his drawing on memories from Sioux warriors who participated in the battle.

Analyze Visuals
How do these paintings show the influences of different cultures?

George Armstrong Custer's soldiers discovered gold in the Black Hills of the Dakotas. **Sitting Bull**, a leader of the Lakota Sioux, protested U.S. demands for the land.

> "What treaty that the whites have kept has the red man broken? Not one. What treaty that the white man ever made with us have they kept? Not one."
>
> —Sitting Bull, quoted in *Life of Sitting Bull and the History of the Indian Wars of 1890–1891* by W. Fletcher Johnson

Apache leader Geronimo fought settlers on his land for more than 25 years—all the while avoiding permanent capture.

Other Sioux leaders listened to Sitting Bull and refused to give up land. During late 1875 and early 1876, many Sioux and Cheyenne warriors left their reservations. They united under the leadership of Sitting Bull and Crazy Horse. Their plan was to drive the intruders from the Black Hills. Custer was sent to force the Native Americans back onto their reservations.

On June 25, 1876, Custer's scouts found a large Sioux camp along the Little Bighorn River in Montana Territory. Leading about 200 of his soldiers, Custer raced ahead without waiting for any supporting forces. In the **Battle of the Little Bighorn**, Sioux and Cheyenne forces led by Crazy Horse surrounded and defeated Custer and his troops. Newspapers called the battle "Custer's Last Stand" because his entire command was killed. It was the worst defeat the U.S. Army suffered in the West. The Battle of the Little Bighorn was also the Sioux's last major victory in the Sioux Wars.

In 1881 Sitting Bull and a few followers returned from Canada where they had fled after Little Bighorn. They had run out of food during the hard winter. They joined the Sioux on Standing Rock Reservation in Dakota Territory.

Almost a decade later, in 1890, while following orders to arrest Sitting Bull, reservation police killed him. Many Sioux left the reservation in protest. Later that year, the U.S. Army shot and killed about 150 Sioux men, women, and children near Wounded Knee Creek in South Dakota. This **Massacre at Wounded Knee** was the last major military incident on the Great Plains.

Southwest The Navajo lived in what became Arizona and New Mexico. In 1863 the Navajo refused to settle on a reservation. In response, U.S. troops made raids on the Navajo's fields, homes, and livestock.

When the Navajo ran out of food and shelter, they started surrendering to the U.S. Army. In 1864 the army led Navajo captives on the **Long Walk**. On this brutal 300-mile march, the Navajo were forced to walk across the desert to a reservation in Bosque Redondo, New Mexico. Along the way, countless Navajo died.

Far West The United States had promised to let the peaceful Nez Percé keep their land in Oregon. Within a few years, however, the government ordered the Nez Percé to a reservation in what is now Idaho. A group of Nez Percé led by **Chief Joseph** resisted, and in 1877 left to seek refuge in Canada. For four months, they crossed more than 1,000 miles with army troops in pursuit. Near the border, U.S. troops overtook them and sent them to a reservation in what is now Oklahoma.

Final Battles By the 1880s, most Native Americans had stopped fighting. The Apache of the Southwest, however, continued to battle the U.S. Army. A Chiricahua Apache named **Geronimo** and his band led raids on both sides of the Arizona–Mexico border, avoiding capture for many years. In September 1886 Geronimo surrendered and was sent to an Apache internment camp in Florida. This ended the Apache armed resistance in the Southwest.

Reading Check
Contrast How did the Apache resistance differ from that of the Navajo?

A Way of Life Ends

By the 1870s many Native Americans lived on reservations, where land was usually not useful for farming or buffalo hunting. Many were starving.

A Paiute Indian named Wovoka began a religious movement, the **Ghost Dance**, that predicted the arrival of paradise for Native Americans. In this paradise, the buffalo herds would return and the settlers would disappear.

U.S. officials did not understand the meaning of the Ghost Dance. They feared it would lead to rebellion, so they tried to end the movement, which had spread to other groups, including the Sioux. After the massacre in 1890 at Wounded Knee, the Ghost Dance movement gradually died out.

In the late 1870s a Paiute Indian named **Sarah Winnemucca** called for reform—particularly of the reservation system. A writer, educator, and interpreter, she toured the country speaking on behalf of Native Americans. Her 1883 autobiography *Life Among the Paiutes* is one of the

—— BIOGRAPHY ——

Chief Joseph c. 1840–1904

Chief Joseph became leader of the Nez Percé in 1871. He led his people in an effort to hold onto their homeland and to avoid war with the United States. In 1877, when the U.S. government ordered the Nez Percé to relocate to a reservation, Chief Joseph at first agreed, but then was forced to flee. He attempted to escape into Canada with about 750 of his people. On a courageous journey across Idaho, Montana, Oregon, and Washington, they defeated pursuing troops who greatly outnumbered them. Traveling with families, and low on supplies, the Nez Percé managed to evade the U.S. Army for four months. Ultimately though, Chief Joseph saw that resistance was futile. Upon his surrender, he gave a speech that has become one of the most famous in American history.

"I am tired of fighting. Our chiefs are killed. . . . The old men are all dead. . . . It is cold, and we have no blankets. The little children are freezing to death. My people, some of them, have run away to the hills, and have no blankets, no food. No one knows where they are—perhaps freezing to death. I want to have time to look for my children, and see how many of them I can find. Maybe I shall find them among the dead. Hear me, my chiefs! I am tired. My heart is sick and sad. From where the sun now stands I will fight no more forever."

—Chief Joseph, October 5, 1877

Identify Cause and Effect
What brought suffering to Chief Joseph and his people?

Sarah Winnemucca spoke out for the fair treatment of her people.

most significant accounts of traditional Native American culture. Writer Helen Hunt Jackson published a book in 1881 that pushed for reform of U.S. Indian policy. Titled *A Century of Dishonor*, it described the mistreatment of many Native American groups in an attempt to force the government to establish fairer policies.

Some reformers believed that Native Americans should **assimilate** by giving up traditional ways and adopting Anglo-American gender and family roles, cultural and social practices, and language. The **Dawes General Allotment Act** of 1887 tried to lessen traditional influences on Indian society by making land ownership private for male-headed households rather than shared communally. The act also promised—but failed to deliver—U.S. citizenship to Native Americans. After breaking up reservation land, the government sold the acreage remaining. The act took about two-thirds of Indian land.

The U.S. government also sent many Native American children to boarding schools in an effort to "Americanize" them. The children were dressed in European-style clothes, learned English, and often spent part of the day farming or doing other work. They were discouraged from practicing their own culture or speaking their own language. Many were separated from their families for years at a time.

Reading Check
Summarize
How did reformers try to influence Native Americans' lives?

Summary and Preview In this lesson you read about conflict in the settlement of the West. In the next lesson you will learn more about Great Plains settlers.

Lesson 3 Assessment

Review Ideas, Terms, and People

1. a. Describe What animals did Plains Indians depend on, and how did they use those animals?

b. Analyze How did U.S. policy toward the Plains Indians change in the late 1850s?

c. Elaborate Would you have agreed to move to a reservation? Why or why not?

2. a. Describe What events led to the Battle of the Little Bighorn?

b. Elaborate Why do you think most Indian groups eventually stopped resisting the United States?

3. a. Describe How did the Dawes General Allotment Act affect American Indians?

b. Predict What effect do you think the Massacre at Wounded Knee would have on relations between Plains Indians and the United States?

Critical Thinking

4. Sequence In this lesson you learned about the major events surrounding the loss of land rights of Native Americans. Create a timeline similar to the one below to organize the events in sequence.

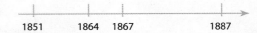

1851   1864 1867   1887

Farming and Populism

The Big Idea

Settlers on the Great Plains created new communities and a unique political movement.

Main Ideas

- Many Americans started new lives on the Great Plains.
- Economic challenges led to the creation of farmers' political groups.
- By the 1890s the western frontier had come to an end.

Key Terms and People

Homestead Act
Morrill Act
Exodusters
sodbusters
dry farming
Annie Bidwell
National Grange
deflation
William Jennings Bryan
Populist Party

If YOU were there . . .

You are a female schoolteacher in Wisconsin in 1880. You live and teach in a small town, but you grew up on a farm and are used to hard work. Now you are thinking about moving West to claim free land from the government. You could teach in a school there, too. You think it would be an exciting adventure, but your family is horrified that a single woman would move West on her own.

Would you decide to become a homesteader?

New Lives on the Plains

In 1862 Congress passed two important land grant acts that helped open the West to settlers. The **Homestead Act** gave government-owned land to small farmers. Any adult who was a U.S. citizen or planned to become one could receive 160 acres of land. In exchange, homesteaders promised to live on the land for five years. The **Morrill Act** granted more than 17 million acres of federal land to the states. The act required each state to sell this land and to use the money to build colleges to teach agriculture and engineering.

Pioneers like this family often lived in houses made of sod because there were few trees for lumber on the Plains.

This family of African Americans moved to the West in order to build new lives after the Civil War.

Settling the Plains People from all over the country moved West. Many farming families moved from areas where farmland was becoming scarce or expensive, such as New England. Many single women moved West. The Homestead Act granted land to unmarried women, which was unusual for the time.

In the late 1870s, large numbers of African Americans began to move West. Some fled the South because of violence and repression. The end of Reconstruction in 1877 led to harsh new segregation laws. Also, the withdrawal of federal troops left African Americans unprotected from attacks by such groups as the Ku Klux Klan. Benjamin "Pap" Singleton, a former slave from Tennessee, inspired others. Born in Nashville in 1809, Singleton fled slavery several times. Eventually he got to the North and settled in Detroit. There, he helped runaway slaves escape to Canada. After the Civil War, he returned to Tennessee. He wanted to help freed African Americans buy farmland. However, white landowners refused to sell. So he urged African Americans to leave the South and build their own communities in Kansas and elsewhere in the West.

By 1879 some 20,000 southern African Americans had moved to Kansas. Many others settled in Missouri, Indiana, and Illinois. These African American migrants were known as **Exodusters** because they had made a mass exodus, or departure, from the South.

The promise of free land also drew thousands of Europeans to the West. Scandinavians from Norway, Sweden, Denmark, and Finland came to the northern Great Plains in the 1870s. Many Irish who had helped to build the railroads decided to settle on the Plains. Russians also came to the Plains, bringing with them their experience of farming on the vast steppes, or grasslands, of their homeland. Germans and Czechs created many small farming communities on the Plains, especially in Texas.

Letter from the Plains, 1863

In a letter to her family in Norway, immigrant Gro Svendsen describes her new life as a farmer on the plains of Iowa.

Analyze Historical Sources
What might be some of the differences between Norway and Svendsen's new home in Iowa?

> "*I remember I used to wonder when I heard that it would be impossible to keep the milk here as we did at home. Now I have learned that it is indeed impossible because of the heat here in the summertime . . . It's difficult, too, to preserve the butter. One must pour brine [salt water] over it or salt it.*
>
> *The thunderstorms are so violent that one might think it was the end of the world . . . Quite often the lightning strikes down both cattle and people, damages property, and splinters sturdy oak trees into many pieces.*"
>
> —quoted in *Frontier Mother: The Letters of Gro Svendsen*

Laura Ingalls Wilder (right) wrote the *Little House on the Prairie* series based on her childhood in a settler family.

Academic Vocabulary
facilitate to make easier

Farming the Plains Plains farmers had many unique challenges. The seasons were extreme. Weather could be harsh. Also, the root-filled sod, or dirt, beneath the Plains grass was very tough. The hard work of breaking up the sod earned Plains farmers the nickname **sodbusters**.

In the 1890s western Plains farmers began **dry farming**, a new method of farming that shifted the focus away from water-dependent crops such as corn. Instead, farmers grew more hardy crops like red wheat. In addition, new inventions helped Plains farmers meet some of the challenges of frontier life. A steel plow invented by John Deere in 1837 and improved upon by James Oliver in 1868 sliced through the tough sod of the prairie. Windmills adapted to the Plains pumped water from deep wells to the surface. Barbed wire allowed farmers to fence in land and livestock. Reapers made the harvesting of crops much easier, and threshers helped farmers to separate grain or seed from straw.

These inventions also made farm work more efficient. During the late 1800s, farmers greatly increased their crop production. They shipped their harvest east by train. From there, crops were shipped overseas. The Great Plains soon became known as the breadbasket of the world.

Building Communities Women were an important force in the settlement of the frontier. They joined in the hard work of farming and ranching and helped build communities out of the widely spaced farms and small towns. Their role in founding communities **facilitated** a strong voice in public affairs. Wyoming women, for example, were granted the vote in the new state's constitution, which was approved in 1869. **Annie Bidwell**, one of the founders of Chico, California, used her influence to support a variety of moral and social causes such as women's suffrage and temperance.

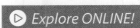

Reading Check
Compare and Contrast How were settlers' lives alike and different from their lives in the East?

Many early settlers found life on their remote farms to be extremely difficult. Farmers formed communities so that they could assist one another in times of need. One of the first things that many pioneer communities did was establish a local church and school.

Children helped with many chores around the farm. Author Laura Ingalls Wilder was one of four children in a pioneer family. Wilder's books about settlers' lives on the prairie are still popular today.

Farmers' Political Groups

From 1860 to 1900, the U.S. population more than doubled. To feed this growing population, the number of farms tripled. With modern machines, farmers in 1900 could harvest a bushel of wheat almost 20 times faster than they could in 1830.

Farm Incomes Fall The combination of more farms and greater productivity, however, led to overproduction. Overproduction resulted in lower prices for crops. As their incomes decreased, many farmers found it difficult to pay bills. Farmers who could not make their mortgage payments lost their farms and homes. Many of these homeless farmers became tenant farmers who worked land owned by others. By 1880 one-fourth of all farms were rented by tenants, and the number continued to grow.

The National Grange Many farmers blamed businesspeople—wholesalers, brokers, grain buyers, and especially railroad owners—for making money at their expense. As economic conditions worsened, farmers began to follow the example of other workers. They formed associations to protect and help their interests.

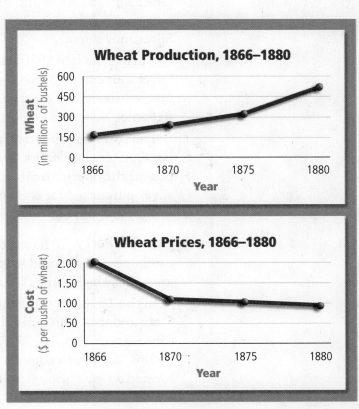

▶ *Explore ONLINE!*

Agricultural Supply and Demand

Connect to Economics The amount of goods available for sale is the supply. The willingness and ability of consumers to buy goods is called demand. The law of supply and demand says that when supply increases or demand decreases, prices fall. By contrast, when supply decreases or demand rises, prices rise.

What happened to the price of wheat as the supply increased?

After the founding of the National Grange, other groups, including the Farmers' Alliance, formed to advance the interests of farmers.

One such organization was founded by Oliver Hudson Kelley, who toured the South in 1866 for the U.S. Department of Agriculture. Kelley saw firsthand how the country's farmers suffered. Afterward, Kelley and several government clerks formed the National Grange of the Patrons of Husbandry in 1867. The **National Grange** was a social and educational organization for farmers. (*Grange* is an old word for "granary.") Local chapters were quickly founded, and membership grew rapidly.

The Grange campaigned for political candidates who supported farmers' goals. The organization also called for laws that regulated rates charged by railroads. The U.S. Supreme Court ruled in 1877 that the government could regulate railroads because they affected the public interest. In 1886 the Court said that the federal government could only regulate companies doing business across state lines. Rate regulation for railroad lines within states fell to the state governments.

In February 1887 Congress passed the Interstate Commerce Act, providing national regulations over trade between states and creating the Interstate Commerce Commission to ensure fair railroad rates. However, the commission lacked power to enforce its regulations.

Free Silver Debate Money issues also caused problems for farmers. Many farmers hoped that help would come from new laws affecting the money supply.

Since 1873 the United States had been on the gold standard, meaning that all paper money had to be backed by gold in the treasury. As a result, the money supply grew more slowly than the nation's population and led to **deflation**—a decrease in the money supply and overall lower prices. One solution was to allow the unlimited coining of silver and to back paper currency with silver. This was the position of those in the Free Silver movement.

During the late 1870s, there was a great deal of support for the Free Silver movement. Many farmers began backing political candidates who favored free silver coinage. One such candidate was **William Jennings Bryan** of Nebraska.

The two major political parties, however, largely ignored the money issue. After the election of 1888, the Republican-controlled Congress passed the Sherman Silver Purchase Act. The act increased the amount of silver purchased for coinage. However, this did not help farmers as much as they had hoped.

Populist Party To have greater power, many farmers organized to elect candidates who would help them. These political organizations became known as the Farmers' Alliances.

In the 1890 elections the Alliances were a strong political force. State and local wins raised farmers' political hopes. At a conference in Cincinnati, Ohio, in 1891, Alliance leaders met with labor and reform groups. Then, at a convention in St. Louis in February 1892, the Alliances formed a new national political party.

William Jennings Bryan
1860–1925

William Jennings Bryan was born in Illinois but moved to Nebraska when he finished law school. He was elected Nebraska's first Democratic Congress member in 1890. Through his political campaigns and work as a newspaper editor, he became one of the best-known supporters of Populist ideas. After a dramatic speech at the 1896 Democratic National Convention, Bryan was nominated for the presidency. He was the youngest presidential candidate up to that time. Although he lost the election, he continued to be an influential speaker and political leader. Many of the reforms that he fought for in the late 1800s, such as an eight-hour workday and woman suffrage, later became law.

Make Inferences
Why was Bryan's support of Populist ideas important?

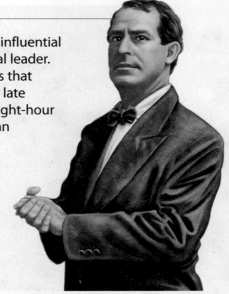

The new party was called the **Populist Party**, and it called for the government to own railroads and telephone and telegraph systems. It also favored the "free and unlimited coinage of silver." To gain the votes of workers, the Populists backed an eight-hour workday and limits on immigration.

The concerns of the Populists were soon put in the national spotlight. During the Panic of 1893, the U.S. economy experienced a crisis that some critics blamed on the shortage of gold. The failure of several major railroad companies also contributed to the economic problems.

The Panic of 1893 led more people to back the Populist call for economic reform. In 1896 the Republicans nominated William McKinley for president. McKinley was firmly against free coinage of silver. The Democrats nominated William Jennings Bryan, a strong supporter of the Free Silver movement.

The Populists had to decide between running their own candidate, and thus splitting the silver vote, or supporting Bryan. They decided to support Bryan. The Republicans had a well-financed campaign, and they won the election. McKinley's victory in 1896 marked the end of both the Populist Party and the Farmers' Alliances.

Reading Check
Summarize Why did farmers, laborers, and reformers join to form the Populist Party?

End of the Frontier

By 1870 only small portions of the Great Plains remained unsettled. For most of the next two decades, this land remained open range.

In March 1889, government officials announced that homesteaders could file claims on land in what is now the state of Oklahoma. This land had belonged to Creek and Seminole Indians. Within a month, about 50,000 people rushed to Oklahoma to stake their claims.

In all, settlers claimed more than 11 million acres of former Indian land in the famous Oklahoma land rush. This huge wave of pioneers was the

Oklahoma Land Rush

- The rush began at noon on April 22, 1889.
- Some witnesses said they could feel the ground shake as 50,000 people raced to claim land.
- Single women and widows could claim land on an equal basis with men.
- Many settlers were dismayed to find some people had claimed land before the rush legally began. These people were called *sooners*.

Guthrie, Oklahoma

Reading Check
Find Main Ideas
What event signaled the closing of the frontier?

last chapter of the westward movement. From the time it began gathering information, the U.S. Census Bureau had mapped a "frontier line" along the edge of western population. The 1890 census showed that more than 20 million people lived between the Mississippi River and the Pacific coast. "There can hardly be said to be a frontier line," a Bureau report stated. The disappearance of the "line" is considered the closing of the frontier.

Summary and Preview In this lesson you read about the challenges settlers in the West faced. Despite these difficulties, the promise of open land and a fresh start continued to lure Americans westward.

Lesson 4 Assessment

Review Ideas, Terms, and People

1. a. Describe What groups settled in the Great Plains?
   b. Explain How did the U.S. government make lands available to western settlers?
   c. Elaborate Would you have chosen to settle on the frontier? Why or why not?

2. a. Recall What was the goal of the National Grange?
   b. Make Inferences Why did the Populist Party want the government to own railroads and telegraph and telephone systems?
   c. Evaluate Do you think farmers were successful in bringing about economic and political change? Explain.

3. a. Recall What was the Oklahoma land rush?
   b. Explain Why did the frontier cease to exist in the United States?

Critical Thinking

4. Compare and Contrast In this lesson you learned about the reasons for the rise of populism in the United States. Create a table similar to the one below to explain why Populists sought the changes they did.

Change sought	Reason why

Social Studies Skills

Compare Migration Maps

Define the Skill

One of the best ways of using geography to learn history is by comparing maps. This skill allows you to see changes over time. It also helps you see relationships between one factor, such as population growth, and another factor, such as transportation routes or economic activities in an area.

Learn the Skill

Follow these steps to compare information on maps.

1. Apply basic map skills by reading the title and studying the legend and symbols for each map.

2. Note the date of each map and the area it covers. Maps compared for changes over time should include the same areas. Those used to look for relationships should have similar dates.

3. Note similarities or differences. Closely examine and compare each map's patterns and symbols.

4. Apply critical thinking skills. Make generalizations and draw conclusions about the relationships you find.

Practice the Skill

Use the maps below to answer the following questions.

1. What present-day state was unsettled by Americans in 1850 and almost completely settled in 1890?

2. Which other two present-day states show the most settlement by Americans from 1850 to 1890?

3. Why do you think the West coast was settled before the interior of the United States?

4. According to the maps, how might rivers have shaped the settlement of the West?

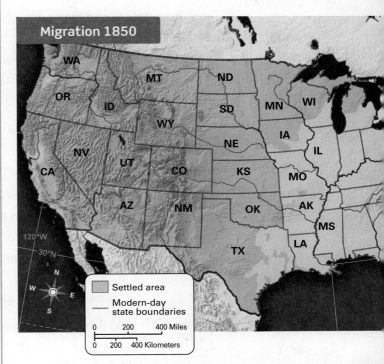

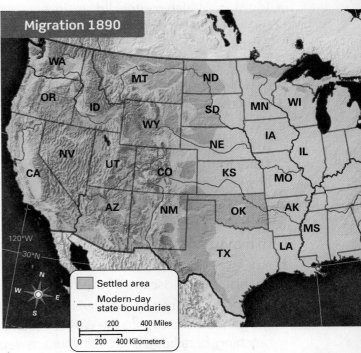

Module 11 Assessment

Review Vocabulary, Terms, and People

Complete each sentence by filling in the blank with the correct term or person.

1. In 1803 Congress approved the _____, which added former French territory in the West to the United States.

2. Members of the Church of Jesus Christ of Latter-day Saints were known as _____.

3. _____ were fur traders and trappers who lived west of the Rocky Mountains and in the Pacific Northwest.

4. The _____ Trail, which ran from Missouri to New Mexico, was an important route for trade between American and Mexican merchants

5. _____ lead the 7th Cavalry in the Battle of the Little Bighorn.

6. The _____ gave government-owned land to small farmers. In return the farmers had to live on the land for at least five years.

7. A Paiute Indian named _____ worked hard to reform the reservation system.

8. The _____ Trail was one of the most popular routes for cattle drives.

9. The huge deposit of gold and silver found in Nevada in 1859 was known as the _____.

10. Formed in 1867, the _____ was a social and educational organization for farmers.

Comprehension and Critical Thinking

Lesson 1

11. a. **Identify** Which routes did settlers use to move into the land west of the Appalachians?

    b. **Draw Conclusions** What are three ways in which the United States benefited from the Louisiana Purchase?

    c. **Evaluate** Do you think that Napoléon made a wise decision when he sold Louisiana to the United States? Explain your answer.

Lesson 2

12. a. **Recall** Why were many Americans eager to move to the western frontier?

    b. **Analyze** How did railroads and ranching change the landscape of the West?

    c. **Elaborate** In your opinion, which made the greatest changes to the West—mining, ranching, or railroads? Explain your answer.

Lesson 3

13. a. **Describe** What was life like for the Plains Indians before and after the arrival of large numbers of American settlers?

    b. **Draw Conclusions** Why did the spread of the Ghost Dance movement cause concern for U.S. officials?

    c. **Elaborate** What do you think about the reservation system established by the United States?

Lesson 4

14. a. **Identify** What political organizations did western farmers create? Why did farmers create these organizations?

    b. **Analyze** How did women participate in the settling of the American frontier?

    c. **Predict** How might the end of the frontier in the United States affect the nation?

Review Themes

15. **Geography** Through what geographic regions did the Lewis and Clark expedition travel?

16. **Geography** What geographic obstacles did miners, ranchers, and railroad workers face in the West?

17. **Science and Technology** What types of technology did farmers on the Great Plains use, and how did it benefit them?

Reading Skills

Ask Questions to Understand *Use the Reading Skills taught in this module to answer the question about the reading selection below.*

> For survival, Plains Indians depended on two animals—the horse and the buffalo. The Spanish brought horses to America in the 1500s. Plains Indians learned to ride horses, and hunters used them to follow buffalo herds year-round.

18. Write two or three questions you have about the information in the passage above. Remember to use the five Ws—Who? What? When? Where? and Why?

Social Studies Skills

Compare Migration Maps *Use the Social Studies Skills taught in this module to answer the question about the map below.*

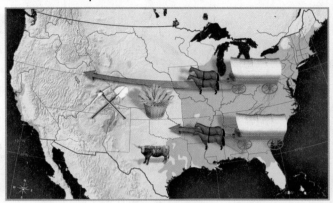

19. According to the map above, for what reasons did settlers migrate to the West?
    a. for mining, ranching, and farming
    b. for jobs in manufacturing
    c. for the homes in the major cities there
    d. for the fishing industry

Focus on Writing

20. **Write a Job Description** Write a job description for a cowboy. Note the skills required for the job and the equipment needed. Also outline a typical workday for a cowboy. To add interest to your description, include appropriate visual materials.

Lewis and Clark

In 1804, Meriwether Lewis, William Clark, and the 33-man Corps of Discovery began an 8,000-mile journey across uncharted territory. Under orders from President Thomas Jefferson, the expedition mapped a route across the Louisiana Purchase to the Pacific Ocean. From St. Louis, Missouri, they traveled west up the Missouri River, then across the Rocky Mountains, and to the Pacific. They met Native American peoples and cataloged geography,

plants, and animals. Not only was their mission one of history's greatest explorations; it also secured an American claim to the Pacific coast and helped inspire millions to migrate west.

Explore entries from Lewis's journal and other primary sources online. You can find a wealth of information, video clips, activities, and more through your online textbook.

> . . . the Indian woman recognized the point of a high plain to our right which she informed us was not very distant from the summer retreat of her nation on a river beyond the mountains which runs to the west."
>
> — Meriwether Lewis

📜 **"Lewis's Journal, Entry 1"**
Read an excerpt from Meriwether Lewis's journal that details Sacagawea's assistance during the journey.

🎥 **Underway on the Missouri**
Watch the video to see how the Corps of Discovery sailed up the Missouri River to begin their expedition.

🎥 **Making Friends Upriver**
Watch the video to see which Native American peoples the Corps met and traded with as they made their journey west.

🎥 **The Shores of the Pacific**
Watch the video to see how the Corps tried to adapt to a different climate and the new peoples that they met along the Pacific coast.

Expansion and Conflict

★

Essential Question
What was gained and lost as Americans expanded into the Southwest?

About the Photo: This Spanish mission in San Antonio was the site of the Battle of the Alamo, which was fought in March 1836 during the Texas Revolution. After losing this battle, "Remember the Alamo!" became a rallying cry for Texans during the battle that followed.

In this module you will learn about how the United States acquired lands in the Southwest.

What You Will Learn ...

▶ *Explore ONLINE!*

HISTORY

VIDEOS, including...
- Heading West
- Independence for Texas
- The Mexican-American War
- The Gold Rush
- Search for the Mother Lode
- Statehood

☑ Document-Based Investigations

☑ Graphic Organizers

☑ Interactive Games

☑ Image Carousel: Texas Settlers

☑ Image with Hotpots: Ranch Life

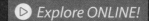
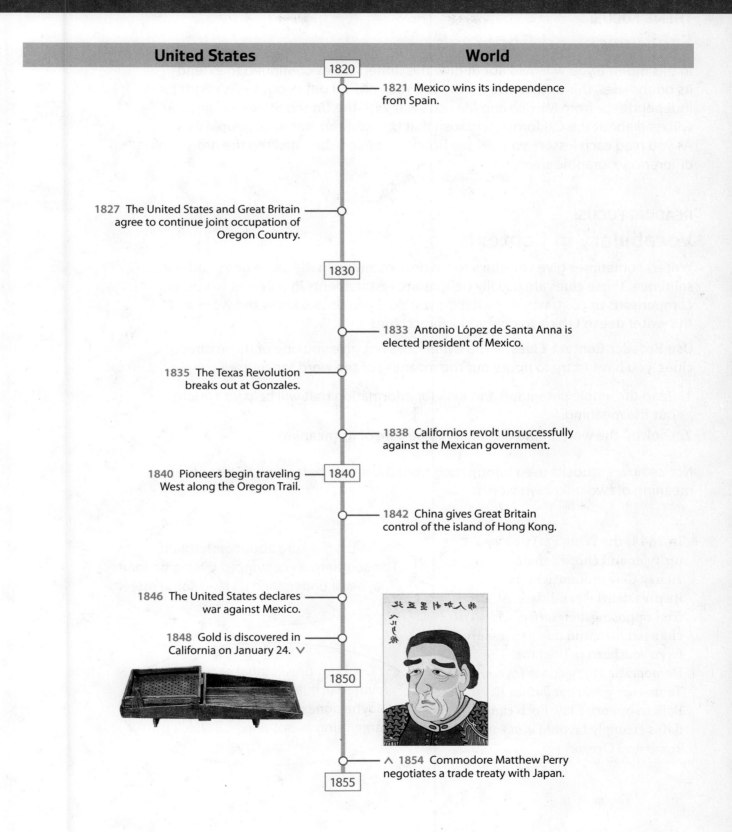

United States	World
1820	
	1821 Mexico wins its independence from Spain.
1827 The United States and Great Britain agree to continue joint occupation of Oregon Country.	
1830	
	1833 Antonio López de Santa Anna is elected president of Mexico.
1835 The Texas Revolution breaks out at Gonzales.	
	1838 Californios revolt unsuccessfully against the Mexican government.
1840 Pioneers begin traveling West along the Oregon Trail.	**1840**
	1842 China gives Great Britain control of the island of Hong Kong.
1846 The United States declares war against Mexico.	
1848 Gold is discovered in California on January 24. ∨	
1850	
	∧ **1854** Commodore Matthew Perry negotiates a trade treaty with Japan.
1855	

Reading Social Studies

THEME FOCUS:

Economics and Geography

In this module you will read about how the United States continued to extend its boundaries, this time to the southwest. You will find out about Texas's fight for independence from Mexico and Mexico's war with the United States. Finally, you will read about the California gold rush that brought thousands of people west. As you read each lesson, you will see how economic issues affected the growth of different geographic areas.

READING FOCUS:

Vocabulary in Context

Writers sometimes give you clues to a word's meaning in the same or a nearby sentence. Those clues are usually definitions, restatements in different words, or comparisons or contrasts. But what do you do if you do not know the word and the writer doesn't think to give you a direct clue?

Use Broader Context Clues If the writer does not give you one of those direct clues, you have to try to figure out the meaning of the word for yourself.

1. Read the whole paragraph and look for information that will help you figure out the meaning.
2. Look up the word in the dictionary to be sure of its meaning.

Notice how a student used information from the whole paragraph to learn the meaning of two unknown words.

In 1844, the Whig Party passed up Tyler and chose Senator Henry Clay of Kentucky as its presidential candidate. At first opposing *annexation*, Clay changed his mind due to pressure from southern politicians. The Democratic Party chose former Tennessee governor James K. Polk to oppose Clay. Both candidates strongly favored *acquiring* Texas and Oregon.

I'm not sure about *annexation*. The southerners convinced Clay to be for it. Maybe I'll understand if I read some more.

Oh, both presidential candidates favored *acquiring* Texas and Oregon. Maybe *annexation* means almost the same thing as *acquiring*. I'll check the dictionary.

You Try It!

The following passage is from the module you are about to read. Read the passage and then answer the questions.

American Settlement in the Mexican Cession The war ended after Scott took Mexico City. In February 1848, the United States and Mexico signed the Treaty of Guadalupe Hidalgo, which officially ended the war and forced Mexico to turn over much of its northern territory to the United States. Known as the Mexican Cession, this land included the present-day states of California, Nevada, and Utah. . . .

In exchange for this vast territory, the United States agreed to pay Mexico $15 million. In addition, the United States assumed claims of more than $3 million held by American citizens against the Mexican government.

Refer to the passage to answer the following questions.

1. Do you know what the word *cession* means? What clues in the first paragraph can help you figure out what the word might mean? Use those clues to write a definition of cession.

2. Look up *cession* in a dictionary. How does your definition compare to the dictionary definition?

3. In your experience, what does the word *assume* usually mean? Do you think that meaning is the one used in the second paragraph? If not, what do you think *assume* means in this case?

4. Look up *assume* in a dictionary. Does one of its meanings match the one you came up with?

As you read Module 12, use context clues to figure out the meanings of unfamiliar words. Check yourself by looking the words up in a dictionary.

Key Terms and People

Lesson 1
Father Miguel Hidalgo y Costilla
empresarios
Stephen F. Austin
Antonio López de Santa Anna
Alamo
Battle of San Jacinto

Lesson 2
manifest destiny
James K. Polk
vaqueros
Californios
Bear Flag Revolt
Treaty of Guadalupe Hidalgo
Gadsden Purchase

Lesson 3
John Sutter
Donner party
forty-niners
prospect
placer miners

The Texas Revolution

The Big Idea

In 1836 Texas gained its independence from Mexico.

Main Ideas

- Many American settlers moved to Texas after Mexico achieved independence from Spain.
- Texans revolted against Mexican rule and established an independent nation.

Key Terms and People

Father Miguel Hidalgo y Costilla
empresarios
Stephen F. Austin
Antonio López de Santa Anna
Alamo
Battle of San Jacinto

If YOU were there . . .

You are the father of a large farm family in Missouri. There is not enough land for everyone, so you're looking for another opportunity. One day, a land agent comes to town. He is looking for people to settle in Texas. The Mexican government is offering generous tracts of land to colonists. However, you have to become a citizen of Mexico and follow Mexican laws.

Would you decide to move your family to Texas? Why or why not?

American Settlers Move to Texas

By the early 1700s Spain's colony in Mexico was thriving. However, in the territories to the north—which included the modern states of California, Arizona, New Mexico, and Texas—the situation was very different. Few Spaniards lived in these largely barren territories. The Spanish government, though, feared losing territory to attacks by neighbors. They wanted to establish settlements that would secure the Spanish claim to what we now call the Southwest.

However, the Spanish did not form colonies like the English had on the East Coast. Instead, they established small individual settlements. Among them were three major types of settlements. Missions were religious settlements. Each mission housed a small number of priests and others who worked to teach local Native Americans about Christianity and the Spanish way of life. The Native Americans also grew crops to feed themselves and the priests. To protect the missions from attacks, the Spanish built presidios, or forts. The soldiers based at a presidio could ride out to defend the priests at any nearby missions. Finally, the Spanish also created towns, sometimes called pueblos, near some missions. In these towns, Spanish citizens would live, grow crops, and raise cattle. Although missions, presidios, and towns were often located near each other, each had to be able to support

Settling Texas
Stephen F. Austin (standing, in black coat) and other settlers were empresarios—they contracted with the Mexican government to bring settlers to Texas in exchange for land of their own.

itself. No one could depend entirely on support from others or from Spain to guarantee its survival.

The political situation in the Southwest changed when Mexicans moved to overthrow Spanish rule in the early 1800s. In September 1810 **Father Miguel Hidalgo y Costilla**, a Mexican priest, led a rebellion of about 80,000 poor Indians and mestizos, or people of Indian and Spanish ancestry. They hoped that if Mexico became independent from the Spanish monarchy, their lives would improve.

Hidalgo's revolt failed, but the rebellion he started grew. In 1821 Mexico became independent. In 1824 it adopted a republican constitution that declared rights for all Mexicans. The new Mexican government contracted with **empresarios**, or agents, to bring settlers to Texas. They paid the agents in land.

In 1821 one young agent, **Stephen F. Austin**, started a Texas colony on the lower Colorado River. The first 300 families became known as the Old Three Hundred. Austin's successful colony attracted other agents, and American settlers flocked to the region. These Anglo-American settlers, most of them Protestant, became known as Texians. The Mexican residents of Texas, the Tejanos, were Catholic. The two groups generally lived in separate communities. Over time, Texas developed a culture that was distinct from the rest of Mexico and from the United States.

In exchange for cheap land, settlers had to obey Mexican laws. But some settlers often **explicitly** ignored these laws. For example, despite restrictions on slavery, many brought slaves. Concerned that it was losing control of the growing American population, Mexico responded. In 1830 it banned further settlement by Americans. Angry about the new law, many Texans, as they came to be known, began to think of gaining independence from Mexico.

Academic Vocabulary
explicit fully revealed without vagueness

Reading Check
Find Main Ideas
Why did settlers
move to Texas?

By 1834 Mexico came under the rule of General **Antonio López de Santa Anna**. He soon suspended Mexico's republican constitution and gave himself more power. To the already unhappy Texans, this was too much. They felt the time had come to fight for independence.

Texans Revolt against Mexico

In October 1835 the Mexican army tried to remove a cannon from the town of Gonzales, Texas. Rebels stood next to the cannon with a flag reading "Come and take it." After a short battle, the rebels drove the Mexican force away, keeping the cannon. Within a few months, the Texas rebels formed an army and captured the key settlements of Goliad and San Antonio. The Texas Revolution, also known as the Texas War for Independence, had begun.

In 1836, when American settlers in Texas rebelled, Mexican president General Santa Anna personally marched his army into San Antonio.

Texas Independence On March 2, 1836, Texans declared their independence from Mexico. The new Republic of Texas was born. Both the declaration and the constitution that shortly followed were modeled after the U.S. documents. The Texas constitution, however, made slavery legal.

Delegates to the new Texas government chose politician David Burnet as president and Lorenzo de Zavala as vice president. Another revolutionary, Sam Houston, was named to head the Texas army. Austin went to the United States to seek money and troops.

Battle at the Alamo The Texans' actions angered Santa Anna. He began assembling a force of thousands to stop the rebellion.

A hastily created army of Texas volunteers had been clashing with Mexican troops for months. Near San Antonio, the Texans occupied and fortified the **Alamo**, a former mission that became an important battle site in the Texas Revolution. Volunteers from the United States, including frontiersman Davy Crockett, joined Texans such as Colonel Jim Bowie in the Alamo's defense.

The rebels, numbering about 200, hoped for reinforcement from other parts of Texas. For almost two weeks, from February 23 to March 6, 1836, the Texans held out. Colonel William Travis managed to get a message to other Texans through enemy lines:

> "I call on you in the name of Liberty, of patriotism, and everything dear to the American character, to come to our aid with all dispatch [speed] . . . VICTORY OR DEATH."
>
> —William Travis, from a letter written at the Alamo, 1836

Before dawn on March 6, the Mexican army attacked. Despite heavy losses, the army overcame the Texans. All the defenders of the Alamo were killed, though some civilians survived. Following a later battle at Goliad, Santa Anna ordered the execution of 350 prisoners who had surrendered. Texans were enraged by the massacres. Mexican leaders hoped that these terrible defeats would convince the Texans to stop fighting. However, the battles had the opposite effect. Outraged by the harsh treatment Texan soldiers had received, the people of Texas vowed to fight on.

Battle of San Jacinto Santa Anna now chased the untrained forces of Sam Houston. Outnumbered, the Texans fled east. Finally, they reorganized at the San Jacinto River, near Galveston Bay. There, the Texans took a stand.

Santa Anna was confident of victory, but he was careless in choosing the site for his camp. On the afternoon of April 21, 1836, while Mexican troops were resting, Houston launched a surprise attack. The Texan forces swarmed over the camp, shouting, "Remember the Alamo!" and "Remember Goliad!"

The fighting ended swiftly. In fewer than 20 minutes, Santa Anna's army was all but destroyed. In the **Battle of San Jacinto**, the Texans captured Santa Anna and forced him to sign a treaty giving Texas its independence.

An Independent Nation Sam Houston was the hero of the new independent nation of Texas. The republic created a new town named Houston and made it the capital. Voters elected Sam Houston as president. Stephen F. Austin became secretary of state, but died shortly after his election.

To increase the population, Texas offered land grants. American settlers came from nearby southern states, often bringing slaves with them to help grow and harvest cotton.

Most Texans hoped that the United States would annex, or take control of, Texas, making it a state. Some Southerners in Congress wanted to

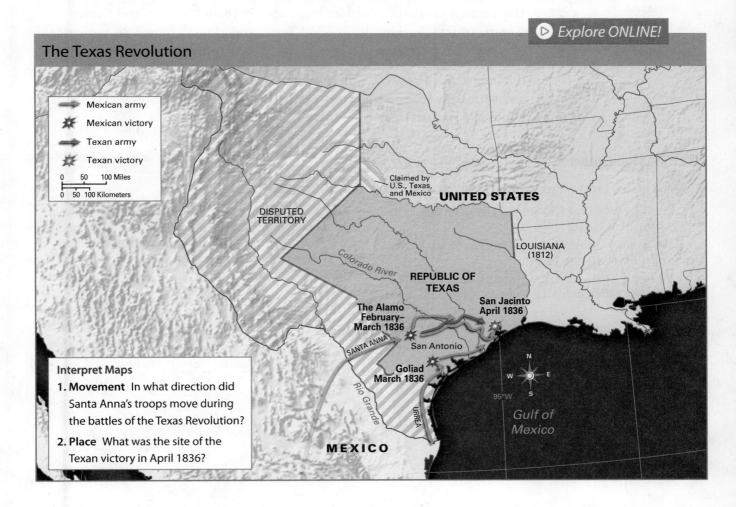

The Texas Revolution

▶ Explore ONLINE!

- → Mexican army
- ✳ Mexican victory
- → Texan army
- ✳ Texan victory

0   50   100 Miles
0   50 100 Kilometers

DISPUTED TERRITORY

Claimed by U.S., Texas, and Mexico   **UNITED STATES**

Colorado River

LOUISIANA (1812)

REPUBLIC OF TEXAS

The Alamo February–March 1836

San Jacinto April 1836

SANTA ANNA

San Antonio

Goliad March 1836

Rio Grande

URREA

N
W   E
S
95°W

Gulf of Mexico

MEXICO

Interpret Maps

1. **Movement** In what direction did Santa Anna's troops move during the battles of the Texas Revolution?

2. **Place** What was the site of the Texan victory in April 1836?

The single star of the flag represents the Republic of Texas, also called the Lone Star Republic.

annex Texas, but President Andrew Jackson did not pursue the issue. He was concerned that admitting Texas as a slave state would upset the fragile balance of free and slave states. The president also did not want to have a war with Mexico over Texas.

Finally, Jackson did recognize Texas as an independent nation. France did so in 1839. Britain, which wanted to halt U.S. expansion, recognized Texas in 1840.

The Mexican government, however, did not recognize Santa Anna's forced handover of Texas. For this reason, in 1837 the republic organized the Texas Rangers to guard its long frontier from Mexican and Native American attacks. Finally, in 1844 Texas and Mexico signed an armistice. However, Mexico refused to recognize Texas's independence.

Summary and Preview American settlers in Texas challenged the Mexican government and won their independence. In the next lesson you will learn about the war between Mexico and the United States.

Reading Check
Find Main Ideas
What issues did the new nation of Texas face?

Lesson 1 Assessment

Review Ideas, Terms, and People

1. a. Identify What role did Stephen F. Austin play in the settlement of Texas?

b. Make Inferences Why did Mexican officials want to bring more settlers to Texas?

c. Contrast How was Spanish settlement in the Southwest different from English settlement on the East Coast?

d. Evaluate Do you think Mexico's requirements for foreign immigrants were reasonable or unreasonable? Explain.

2. a. Describe What were the important battles in the Texas War for Independence? Why was each important?

b. Make Inferences Why did Texas offer land grants to settlers?

c. Predict What problems might the Republic of Texas face?

Critical Thinking

3. Sequence In this lesson you learned about American settlement in Texas. Create a chart similar to the one below and use it to show the significant events that led to the formation of the Republic of Texas.

Significant Events
1.
2.
3.
4.
5.
6. Houston is founded and made the capital.

The Mexican-American War

The Big Idea
The ideals of manifest destiny and the outcome of the Mexican-American War led to U.S. expansion to the Pacific Ocean.

Main Ideas
- Many Americans believed that the nation had a manifest destiny to claim new lands in the West.
- As a result of the Mexican-American War, the United States added territory in the Southwest.
- American settlement in the Mexican Cession produced conflict and a blending of cultures.

Key Terms and People
manifest destiny
James K. Polk
vaqueros
Californios
Bear Flag Revolt
Treaty of Guadalupe Hidalgo
Gadsden Purchase

If YOU were there . . .
Your family are Californios, Spanish settlers who have lived in California for many years. You raise horses on your ranch. So far, you have gotten along with American settlers. But it has become clear that the American government wants to take over California. You hear that fighting has already started between American and Mexican troops.

How might life change under American rule?

Manifest Destiny

"We have it in our power to start the world over again."
—Thomas Paine, from his pamphlet *Common Sense*

Americans had always believed they could build a new, better society founded on democratic principles. In 1839 writer John O'Sullivan noted, "We are the nation of human progress, and who will, what can, set limits to our onward march?"

Actually, there was one limit: land. By the 1840s the United States had a booming economy and population. Barely 70 years old, the nation already needed more room for farms, ranches, businesses, and ever-growing families. Americans looked West to what they saw as a vast wilderness, ready to be taken. With American settlers already living in Oregon, New Mexico, and Texas, many believed that the country should annex those lands to the United States, giving Americans more lands into which they could spread.

Some people believed it was America's **manifest destiny**, or obvious fate, to settle land all the way to the Pacific Ocean in order to spread American ideals. O'Sullivan coined the term in 1845. He wrote that it was America's "manifest destiny to overspread and to possess the whole continent which Providence [God] has given us for the development of the great experiment of liberty. . . ."

The woman represents America, moving west and bringing sunlight, settlers, and telegraph wires to the new lands.

The Mississippi River is in the background as settlers push farther west.

Native Americans and buffalo are pushed away by the approaching settlers.

Manifest Destiny

John Gast's 1872 painting *American Progress* shows the spirit of manifest destiny leading settlers westward.

In the 1840s and 1850s, manifest destiny was tied up with the slavery issue. If America expanded, would slavery be allowed in the new territories? Several presidents became involved in the difficult issue, including President John Tyler. A pro-slavery Whig, Tyler wanted to increase the power of the southern slave states by annexing Texas. His fellow Whigs disagreed.

In 1844 the Whig Party passed up Tyler and chose Senator Henry Clay of Kentucky as its presidential candidate. At first opposing annexation, Clay changed his mind due to pressure from southern politicians. The Democratic Party chose former Tennessee governor **James K. Polk** to oppose Clay. Both candidates strongly favored acquiring Texas and Oregon.

Southerners feared the loss of Texas, a possible new slave state. Others worried that Texas might become an ally of Britain. These concerns helped Polk narrowly defeat Clay.

Acquiring New Territory President Polk quickly set out to fulfill his campaign promise to annex Oregon and Texas. By the 1820s Russia and Spain had given up their claims to Oregon Country. Britain and the United States had agreed to occupy the territory together.

As more Americans settled there, they began to ask that Oregon become part of the United States. Polk wanted to protect these settlers' interests. Some politicians noted that Oregon Country would provide a Pacific port for the growing U.S. trade with China.

Meanwhile, Britain and the United States disagreed over how to draw the United States–Canadian border. American expansionists cried, "Fifty-four forty or fight!" This slogan referred to 54°40' north latitude, the line to which Americans wanted their northern territory to extend.

Neither side really wanted a war, though. In 1846 Great Britain and the United States signed a treaty that gave the United States all Oregon land south of the forty-ninth parallel. This treaty drew the border that still exists today. Oregon became an organized U.S. territory in February 1848.

The Texas question was also coming to a head. By March 1845 Congress had approved annexation and needed only the support of the Republic of Texas. Texas politicians hoped that joining the United States would help solve the republic's financial and military problems. The Texas Congress approved annexation in June 1845. Texas became part of the United States in December. This action angered the Mexican government, which considered Texas to be a "stolen province."

The Mexican Borderlands Though it had lost Texas, Mexico still had settlements in other areas of the present-day Southwest to govern. New Mexico was the oldest settled area, with its capital at Santa Fe. Mexico also had settlements in present-day Arizona, Nevada, and California.

During early Spanish rule, the mission system had dominated much of the present-day Southwest. Over time, it had become less important there, especially in New Mexico, where settlers lived in small villages. In California, however, missions remained the focus of everyday life. Missions under later Spanish rule carried out huge farming and ranching operations using the labor of Native Americans. Some of the Native Americans came willingly to the missions. Others were brought by force. Usually, they were not allowed to leave the mission once they had arrived. They had to adopt the clothing, food, and religion of the Spaniards.

Missions often sold their goods to local pueblos, or towns, that arose near the missions and presidios. One wealthy California settler, Mariano Guadalupe Vallejo, remembered the early days.

> "We were the pioneers of the Pacific coast, building towns and missions while General [George] Washington was carrying on the war of the Revolution."
>
> —Mariano Guadalupe Vallejo, "Ranch and Mission Days in Alta California,"
> *The Century Magazine*

After winning independence from Spain in 1821, Mexico began to change old Spanish policies toward California and Texas. In 1833, for example, Mexico ended the mission system in California. Mission lands were broken up, and huge grants were given to some of the wealthiest California settlers, including Vallejo. They created vast ranchos, or ranches, with tens of thousands of acres of land. *Vaqueros*, or cowboys, managed the large herds of cattle and sheep. Cowhides were so valuable that they were called "California banknotes." Hides were traded for household items and luxury goods from the eastern United States. Some settlers also made wine and grew citrus fruits.

Ranch Life

Spanish and Mexican *vaqueros*, or cowboys, were expert horse riders. They used their horses to herd cattle on the ranches of the Spanish Southwest.

Vaqueros were known for their specially designed hats.

Saddles like these were highly prized by *vaqueros*.

Leather chaps protected riders from dust and scrapes.

Analyze Visuals
What features of the *vaqueros'* life are shown in the painting?

Academic Vocabulary
element a basic part of an individual's surroundings

Although they had been freed from the missions, for most California Indians the **elements** of life changed very little. They continued to herd animals and do much of the hard physical labor on ranches and farms. Some, however, ran away into the wilderness or to the nearby towns of San Diego and Los Angeles.

The Californios Because of the great distance between California and the center of Mexico's government, by the early 1820s California had only around 3,200 colonists. These early California settlers, called **Californios**, felt little connection to their faraway government.

Californios developed a lasting reputation for hospitality and skilled horse riding. In *Two Years Before the Mast*, American novelist Richard Henry Dana Jr. wrote about his encounters with Californio culture. He described, for example, what happened after a Californio served a feast to Dana and a friend.

"We took out some money and asked him how much we were to pay. He shook his head and crossed himself, saying that it was charity— that the Lord gave it to us."

—Richard Henry Dana Jr., from *Two Years Before the Mast*

Reading Check
Draw Inferences
How did manifest destiny affect Mexican rule in California?

In addition to traders and travelers, a small number of settlers also arrived from the United States. They were called Anglos by the Californios. Although there were few Anglo settlers in California, their calls for independence increased tensions between Mexico and the United States.

Mexican-American War

Although diplomacy helped the United States resolve territorial disputes in the Pacific Northwest, diplomats working in the Southwest faced more challenges. Faced with an unstable and uncooperative Mexican government, the U.S. government found it necessary to become more aggressive in its diplomatic overtures. As a result, diplomatic relations between Mexico and the United States became increasingly strained. U.S. involvement in California and Texas contributed to this tension.

Conflict Breaks Out Mexico had long insisted that its northern border in Texas lay along the Nueces River and refused to accept Texas annexation as legitimate. The United States said the border was farther south, along the Rio Grande. In June 1845 President Polk ordered General Zachary Taylor to lead an army into the disputed region.

Polk sent diplomat John Slidell to Mexico City to try to settle the border dispute. Slidell came with an offer to buy New Mexico and California for $30 million. Mexican officials refused to speak to him.

In March 1846 General Taylor led his troops to the Rio Grande. He camped across from Mexican forces stationed near the town of Matamoros, Mexico. In April, the Mexican commander told Taylor to withdraw from Mexican territory. Taylor refused. The two sides clashed, and several U.S. soldiers were killed.

In response, President Polk said to Congress:

"Mexico has passed the boundary of the United States, has invaded our territory, and shed American blood upon the American soil. . . . The two nations are now at war."

—James K. Polk, from his address to Congress, May 11, 1846

Polk's war message was persuasive. Two days later, Congress declared war on Mexico.

War Begins At the beginning of the war with Mexico, the U.S. Army had better weapons and equipment. Yet it was greatly outnumbered and poorly prepared. The government put out a call for 50,000 volunteers. About 200,000 responded. Many were young men who thought the war would be a grand adventure in a foreign land.

On the home front, many Americans supported the war. However, many Whigs thought the war was unjustified and avoidable. Northern abolitionists also opposed the conflict. They feared the spread of slavery into southwestern lands.

While Americans debated the war, fighting proceeded. General Taylor's soldiers won battles south of the Nueces River. Taylor then crossed the Rio Grande and occupied Matamoros, Mexico. While Taylor waited for more men, Polk ordered General Stephen Kearny to attack New Mexico. On August 18, 1846, Kearny took Santa Fe, the capital city, without a fight. He claimed the entire province of New Mexico for the United States and marched west to California, where another conflict with Mexico was already under way.

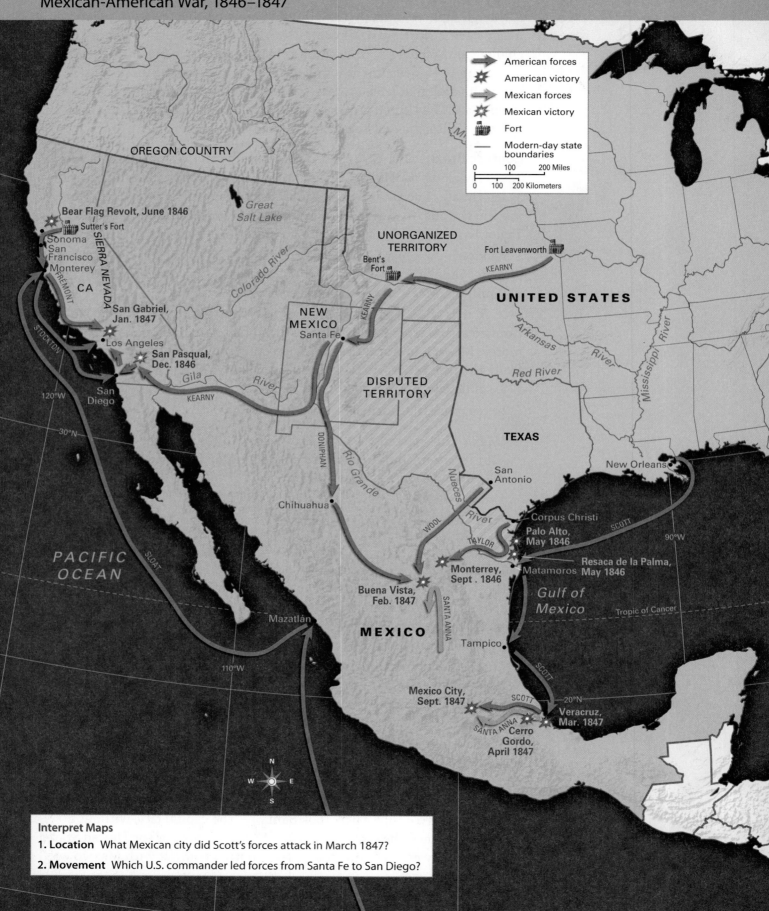

Explore ONLINE!

➡	American forces
✹	American victory
➡	Mexican forces
✸	Mexican victory
🏰	Fort
—	Modern-day state boundaries

0   100   200 Miles

0   100   200 Kilometers

OREGON COUNTRY

Great Salt Lake

UNORGANIZED TERRITORY

Bear Flag Revolt, June 1846

Sutter's Fort

Sonoma
San Francisco
Monterey

SIERRA NEVADA

CA

FRÉMONT

San Gabriel, Jan. 1847

Los Angeles

San Pasqual, Dec. 1846

STOCKTON

San Diego

KEARNY

Gila River

Colorado River

Bent's Fort

Fort Leavenworth

KEARNY

UNITED STATES

KEARNY

NEW MEXICO
Santa Fe

DISPUTED TERRITORY

Arkansas River

Red River

Mississippi River

120°W

30°N

DONIPHAN

Rio Grande

Chihuahua

Nueces River

San Antonio

TEXAS

New Orleans

PACIFIC OCEAN

SLOAT

Mazatlán

110°W

Buena Vista, Feb. 1847

MEXICO

SANTA ANNA

WOOL

TAYLOR

Monterrey, Sept. 1846

Matamoros

Palo Alto, May 1846

Corpus Christi

Resaca de la Palma, May 1846

SCOTT

90°W

Gulf of Mexico

Tropic of Cancer

Tampico

SCOTT

Mexico City, Sept. 1847

SCOTT

SANTA ANNA

Cerro Gordo, April 1847

Veracruz, Mar. 1847

20°N

N W E S

Interpret Maps

1. Location What Mexican city did Scott's forces attack in March 1847?

2. Movement Which U.S. commander led forces from Santa Fe to San Diego?

10°N

The Bear Flag Revolt
American settlers took over Sonoma, the regional headquarters of the Mexican general Mariano Vallejo, and declared California a new country: the California Republic.

The Bear Flag Revolt In 1846 only about 500 Americans lived in the huge province of California, in contrast to about 12,000 Californios. Yet, in the spirit of manifest destiny, a small group of American settlers seized the town of Sonoma, north of San Francisco, on June 14. Hostilities began between the two sides when the Americans took some horses that were intended for the Mexican militia. In what became known as the **Bear Flag Revolt**, the Americans declared California to be an independent nation. Above the town, the rebels hoisted a hastily made flag of a grizzly bear facing a red star. Californios laughed at the roughly made bear, thinking it "looked more like a pig than a bear."

John C. Frémont, a U.S. Army captain, was leading a mapping expedition across the Sierra Nevada when he heard of the possible war with Mexico. Frémont went to Sonoma and quickly joined the American settlers in their revolt against the Californios. Because war had already broken out between the United States and Mexico, Frémont's actions were seen as beneficial to the American cause in the region. His stated goal, however, was Californian independence, not to annex California to the United States. During the revolt, several important Californios were taken prisoner, including Mariano Vallejo. Governor Vallejo and his brother were held at an Anglo settlement for two months without any formal charges being brought against them. Long after his release, Vallejo wrote a history of California that included an account of his time as a bear flag prisoner.

But the bear flag was quick to fall. In July, naval forces from the United States—which never recognized Californian independence—came ashore in California and raised the stars and stripes. Kearny's army arrived from the East. The towns of San Diego, Los Angeles, and San Francisco fell rapidly. In August, U.S. Navy commodore Robert Stockton claimed California for the United States. Some Californios continued to resist until early 1847, when they surrendered.

War's End In Mexico General Taylor finally got the reinforcements he needed. He drove his forces deep into enemy lands. Santa Anna, who had been removed from office and exiled the previous year, returned to power in Mexico in September 1846. He quickly came after Taylor.

The two armies clashed at Buena Vista in February 1847. After a close battle with heavy casualties on both sides, the Mexican Army retreated. The next morning, the cry went up: "The enemy has fled! The field is ours!"

Taylor's success made him a war hero back home. The general's popularity troubled President Polk, and when Taylor's progress stalled, Polk gave the command to General Winfield Scott. A beloved leader, Scott was known by his troops as "Old Fuss and Feathers" because of his strict military discipline.

Scott sailed to the port of Veracruz, a major port and the site of the strongest fortress in Mexico. On March 29, after an 88-hour artillery attack, Veracruz fell. Scott moved on to the final goal, Mexico City, the capital. Taking a route similar to one followed by Spanish conquistador Hernán Cortés in 1519, the Americans pushed 200 or so miles inland. Santa Anna tried to stop the U.S. forces at Cerro Gordo in mid-April, but failed. By August 1847 U.S. troops were at the edge of Mexico City.

After a truce failed, Scott ordered a massive attack on Mexico City. Mexican soldiers and civilians fought fierce battles in and around the capital. At a military school atop the steep, fortified hill of Chapultepec, young Mexican cadets bravely defended their hopeless position. At least one soldier jumped to his death rather than surrender to the invading forces. Finally, on September 14, 1847, Mexico City fell. Santa Anna soon fled the country. Scott's capture of the Mexican capital led to the end of the war.

Reading Check
Sequence In chronological order, list the key battles of the Mexican-American War.

American soldier

Battle of Buena Vista

After the two-day Battle of Buena Vista, the American army gained control of northern Mexico. At the beginning of the battle, Mexican forces outnumbered the Americans. But the Mexicans suffered more than twice as many casualties.

American Settlement in the Mexican Cession

The war ended after Scott took Mexico City. In February 1848 the United States and Mexico signed the **Treaty of Guadalupe Hidalgo**, which officially ended the war and forced Mexico to turn over much of its northern territory to the United States. Known as the Mexican Cession, this land included the present-day states of California, Nevada, and Utah. In addition, it included most of Arizona and New Mexico and parts of Colorado and Wyoming. The United States also won the area claimed by Texas north of the Rio Grande. The Mexican Cession totaled more than 500,000 square miles and increased the size of the United States by almost 25 percent.

Diplomatic Agreements and Payments In exchange for this vast territory, the United States agreed to pay Mexico $15 million. In addition, the United States assumed claims of more than $3 million held by American citizens against the Mexican government. The treaty also addressed the status of Mexicans in the Mexican Cession. The treaty provided that they would be "protected in the free enjoyment of their liberty and property, and secured in the free exercise of their religion." The Senate passed the treaty in March 1848.

After the war with Mexico, some Americans wanted to guarantee that any southern railroad to California would be built completely on American soil. James Gadsden, U.S. minister to Mexico, negotiated an important diplomatic agreement with Mexico in December 1853. Under the terms of the **Gadsden Purchase**, the U.S. government paid Mexico $10 million. In exchange, the United States received the southern parts of what are now Arizona and New Mexico. With this purchase, the existing boundary with Mexico was finally fixed.

Surge of American Settlers After the Mexican-American War, a flood of Americans moved to the Southwest. Their movement sparked a new debate about slavery in the United States. Many southerners who moved west wanted to bring slaves with them into the new territories. Northerners who opposed slavery wanted to ban the practice in the new lands. Even before the war had ended, northern Senator David Wilmot proposed a policy, called the Wilmot Proviso. His policy would have banned slavery in all lands gained from Mexico. The proviso was defeated in Congress, but debates about slavery in the Mexican Cession continued for several years.

American newcomers struggled against longtime residents to control the land and other valuable resources, such as water and minerals. Most Mexicans, Mexican Americans, and Native Americans faced legal, economic, and social discrimination. As a result, they found it difficult to protect their rights.

The Treaty of Guadalupe Hidalgo promised full U.S. citizenship to all Mexicans who wished to stay in the new American lands. However, many of those who stayed faced discrimination. Even Mexican Americans who

Mexican Americans Today

Today Mexican Americans make up a little over 10 percent of the U.S. population, or about 33 million people. Mexican Americans live in all 50 states, although most live in the South and Southwest. Many Mexican Americans in these areas are descended from people who lived there long before the region became part of the United States.

Top Ten States by Mexican American Population

Rank	State	Mexican American Population
1	California	11,423,146
2	Texas	7,951,193
3	Arizona	1,657,668
4	Illinois	1,602,403
5	New Mexico	837,171
6	Colorado	757,181
7	Florida	629,718
8	Washington	601,768
9	Nevada	540,978
10	Georgia	519,502

Source: U.S. Census Bureau (2010)

were already living in Texas, some of whom had fought against Mexico, faced challenges. For example, differences between Mexican and U.S. land laws led to great confusion. The U.S. government often made Mexican American landowners go to court to prove that they had titles to their land. Landowners had to pay their own travel costs as well as those of witnesses and interpreters. They also had to pay attorneys' and interpreters' fees. These legal battles often bankrupted landowners. New settlers also tended to ignore Mexican legal concepts, such as community property or community water rights.

White settlers also battled with Native Americans over property rights. In some areas, for example, new white settlers soon outnumbered southwestern Native Americans. The Anglo settlers often tried to take control of valuable water resources and grazing lands. In addition, settlers rarely respected Native American holy places. Native American peoples such as the Navajo and the Apache tried to protect their land and livestock from the settlers. Settlers and Native Americans alike attacked one another to protect their interests.

Cultural Encounters Despite conflicts, different cultures shaped one another in the Southwest. In settlements with large Mexican populations, laws were often printed in both English and Spanish. Names of places—such as San Antonio, San Diego, and Santa Barbara—show Hispanic heritage. Other place-names, such as Taos and Tesuque, are derived from Native American words. Communities throughout the Southwest regularly celebrated both Mexican and American holidays.

Mexican and Native American knowledge and traditions also shaped many local economies. Mexican Americans taught Anglo settlers about mining in the mountains. Many ranching communities were first started by Mexican settlers. In addition, Mexican Americans introduced new types of saddles and other equipment to American ranchers. Adobe, developed by the Anasazi Indians, was adopted from the Pueblo people by the Spanish. It is still commonly used by American residents in New Mexico, Arizona, and California.

Trade also changed the Southwest. For example, the Navajo created handwoven woolen blankets to sell to Americans. Americans in turn brought manufactured goods and money to the Southwest. The city of El

Paso became an important regional trading center. As trade increased after the Mexican-American War, the economies of many Mexican American and Native American communities in the Southwest began to change.

Water Rights Eastern water-use laws commonly required owners whose land bordered streams or rivers to maintain a free flow of water. These restrictions generally prevented landowners from constructing dams because doing so would infringe upon the water rights of neighbors downstream.

In the typically dry climate of the West, large-scale agriculture was not possible without irrigation. Dams and canals were required to direct scarce water to fields. This need conflicted with the accepted eastern tradition of equal access to water.

Brigham Young established a strict code regulating water rights for the Mormon community. In any dispute over water use, the good of the community would outweigh the interests of individuals. Young's approach stood as an example for modern water laws throughout the West.

Summary and Preview America's westward expansion continued rapidly after the Mexican-American War. In the next lesson you will learn about the California gold rush.

Reading Check
Summarize What were some of the early important agreements between the United States and Mexico, and why were they significant?

Lesson 2 Assessment

Review Ideas, Terms, and People

1. a. Define What was manifest destiny?

b. Make Inferences Why was westward expansion such an important issue in the election of 1844?

c. Identify Cause and Effect How did Mexican independence affect California?

2. a. Recall Why did the United States declare war on Mexico?

b. Explain Why did American diplomacy with Mexico become more aggressive, and what was the result?

c. Summarize What was General Winfield Scott's strategy for winning the war with Mexico?

d. Elaborate Would you have sided with those who opposed the war with Mexico or with those who supported it? Why?

3. a. Describe What conflicts did American settlers, Native Americans, and Mexican Americans in the Mexican Cession experience?

b. Draw Conclusions Why were water rights so important in the American Southwest?

c. Evaluate In your opinion, what was the most important effect of the annexation of the Mexican Cession?

Critical Thinking

4. Identify Cause and Effect In this lesson you learned about manifest destiny and U.S. territorial expansion. Create a graphic organizer like the one shown below. Identify how Americans' expansion into California caused the war with Mexico as well as the effects of the war.

The California Gold Rush

The Big Idea

The California gold rush changed the future of the West.

Main Ideas

- The discovery of gold brought settlers to California.
- The gold rush had a lasting impact on California's population and economy.

Key Terms and People

John Sutter
Donner party
forty-niners
prospect
placer miners

If YOU were there . . .

You are a low-paid bank clerk in New England in early 1849. Local newspaper headlines are shouting exciting news: "Gold Is Discovered in California! Thousands Are on Their Way West." You enjoy having a steady job. However, some of your friends are planning to go west, and you are being influenced by their excitement. Your friends are even buying pickaxes and other mining equipment. They urge you to go with them.

Would you go west to seek your fortune in California? Why?

Discovery of Gold Brings Settlers

In the 1830s and 1840s, Americans who wanted to move to California started up the Oregon Trail. At the Snake River in present-day Idaho, the trail split. People bound for California took the southern route, which became known as the California Trail. This path ran through the Sierra Nevada mountain range. American emigrants and traders on the California Trail tried to cross these mountains before the season's first snows.

Although many Americans traveled along the California Trail, few actually settled in California. American merchants were usually more interested in trading goods made in factories than in establishing settlements. They traded for gold and silver coins, hides, and tallow (animal fat used to make soap and candles) from Mexico. California became a meeting ground for traders from Mexico and the United States.

Before the Mexican-American War, California's population consisted mostly of Mexicans and Native Americans. When Mexico controlled California, Mexican officials did not want many Americans to settle there. However, in 1839 they did give Swiss immigrant **John Sutter** permission to start a colony. Sutter's Fort, located near the Sacramento River, soon became a popular rest stop for many American emigrants. These new arrivals praised Sutter's hospitality and helpfulness. By the mid-1840s some Anglo Californians were publishing newspaper advertisements and guidebooks encouraging other settlers to move to the West.

The **Donner party** was a group of western-bound travelers who went to California but were stranded in the Sierra Nevada Mountains during winter. The party began its journey west in the spring of 1846. Trying to find a shortcut, the group left the main trail and got lost. When the Donner party reached the Sierra Nevada Mountains, they became trapped by heavy snows. They were stuck and had almost no food.

A rescue party found the starving and freezing group in February 1847. Of the original 87 travelers, 42 had died.

Gold in California In January 1848 Sutter sent a carpenter named James Marshall to build a sawmill beside a nearby river. While working near Sutter's Mill, Marshall glanced at the ground. "I reached my hand down and picked it up; it made my heart thump, for I was certain it was gold."

Sutter and Marshall agreed to keep the discovery a secret. However, when they examined the work site the next day, they met a Spanish-speaking Native American worker holding a nugget and shouting, "Oro [gold]! Oro! Oro!"

Sutter's workers soon quit to search for gold. Stories of the discovery rapidly spread across the country. President Polk added to the national excitement by confirming the California gold strike in his farewell message to Congress in December 1848. In 1849 about 80,000 gold-seekers came to California, hoping to strike it rich. These gold-seeking migrants to California were called **forty-niners**. As one Iowa woman who left to find gold recalled, "At that time the 'gold fever' was contagious, and few, old or young, escaped the malady [sickness]." Nearly 80 percent of the forty-niners were Americans, while the rest came from all over the world.

"Gold Fever"

"Gold fever" brought 80,000 people, like this miner, to California in 1849 alone. One California newspaper captured the excitement: "The whole country, from San Francisco to Los Angeles, and from the sea shore to the base of the Sierra Nevadas, resounds with the cry of 'gold, GOLD, GOLD!' while the field is left half planted, the house half built, and everything neglected but the manufacture of shovels and pickaxes."

Most forty-niners braved long and often dangerous journeys to reach California. Many easterners and Europeans arrived via sea routes. Midwestern gold-seekers usually traveled west in wagon trains. Most forty-niners first arrived in San Francisco. This port town became a convenient trade center and stopping point for travelers. As a result, its population increased from around 800 in March 1848 to more than 25,000 by 1850.

Staking a Claim Few of the forty-niners had any previous gold-mining experience. The work was difficult and time-consuming. The forty-niners would **prospect**, or search for gold, along the banks of streams or in shallow surface mines. The early forty-niners worked an area that ran for 70 miles along rivers in northern California.

The first person to arrive at a site would "stake a claim." Early miners frequently banded together to prospect for gold. The miners agreed that each would keep a share of whatever gold was discovered. When one group abandoned a claim, more recent arrivals often took it over, hoping for success. Sometimes two or more groups arrived in an area at the same time. In the early gold-rush days, before courts were established, this competition often led to conflict. Occasionally, violent disputes arose over competing claims.

Mining methods varied according to the location. The most popular method, placer (PLA-suhr) mining, was done along rivers and streams. **Placer miners** used pans or other devices to wash gold nuggets out of loose rock and gravel. To reach gold deposits buried in the hills, miners had to dig shafts and tunnels. These tasks were usually pursued by mining companies, rather than by individuals.

Miners came to California from around the world to make their fortune. In the photo, Anglo and Chinese miners work together in Auburn Ravine in 1852.

In 1853 California's yearly gold production peaked at more than $60 million. Individual success stories inspired many miners. One lucky man found two and a half pounds of gold after only 15 minutes of work. Two African American miners found a rich gold deposit that became known as Negro Hill in honor of their discovery. The vast majority of miners, however, did not become rich. Forty-niner Alonzo Delano commented that the "lean, meager [thin], worn-out and woebegone [sorrowful] miner . . . might daily be seen at almost every point in the upper mines."

Life in the Mining Camps Mining camps sprang up wherever enough people gathered to look for gold. These camps had colorful names, such as Hangtown or Poker Flat. The mining camps usually began as a row of tents along the streams flowing out of the Sierra Nevada. In time the tents gave way to rough wooden houses, stores, and saloons.

Miners in the camps came from many cultures and backgrounds. Most miners were young, unmarried men in search of adventure. Only around 5 percent of gold-rush immigrants were women or children. The hardworking women generally made good money by cooking meals, washing clothes, and operating boardinghouses. One such woman, Catherine Haun, recalled her first home in California—a wooden shed that was built in a day. The building next door was a saloon. However, she quite liked her new home and neighbors.

Haun's husband was a lawyer. He concluded that he could make more money practicing law than he could panning for gold. He was one of many people who made a good living supplying miners with food, clothing, equipment, and other services. Miners paid high prices for basic necessities because the large amounts of gold in circulation caused severe inflation in California. A loaf of bread, for example, might cost 5 cents in the East, but would sell for 50 to 75 cents in San Francisco. Eggs sometimes sold for $1 apiece.

Some settlers took full advantage of these conditions for free enterprise. Biddy Mason and her family, for instance, had arrived in California

A woman joins men to look for gold. Fewer women than men moved west to search for gold, but the ones who did often found greater social and economic opportunity than they had in the east.

as slaves. A Georgia slaveholder had brought them during the gold-rush years. Mason quickly discovered that most Californians opposed slavery, particularly in the gold mines. She and her family gained their freedom and moved to the small village of Los Angeles. There she saved money until she could purchase some land. Over time, Mason's property increased in value from $250 to $200,000. She became one of the wealthiest land-owners in California, a community leader, and a well-known supporter of charities.

Immigrants to California The lure of gold in California attracted miners from around the world. Many were from countries that had seen few immigrants to the United States in the past. They were drawn to California by the lure of wealth. For example, famine and economic hardship in southeastern China caused many Chinese men to leave China for America. Most hoped to find great wealth, and then return home to China. These immigrants were known in Chinese as *gam saan haak*, or "travelers to Gold Mountain." Between 1849 and 1853, about 24,000 Chinese men moved to California. "From far and near we came and were pleased," wrote merchant Lai Chun-chuen in 1855.

Chinese immigrants soon discovered that many Americans did not welcome them, however. In 1852 California placed a tax of $20 a month on all foreign miners. This was more than many of the Chinese miners could afford. However, they had no choice but to find a way to pay this tax if they wanted to prospect for gold. Some Chinese workers were the targets of violent attacks. If the Chinese miners dared to protest the attacks, the legal system favored Americans over immigrants.

Despite such treatment, many Chinese immigrants still worked in the gold mines. Some looked for other jobs. Others opened their own businesses. A newspaper reported Chinese working as "ploughmen, laundry-men, placer miners, woolen spinners and weavers, domestic servants, cigar makers, [and] shoemakers." So many Chinese owned businesses in San Francisco that their neighborhood became known as China-town, as it still is today.

In 1849 alone, about 20,000 immigrants arrived in California not only from China but also from Europe, Mexico, and South America. Like most Americans who sought gold, these new arrivals intended to return home after they had made their fortunes. However, many decided to stay. Some began businesses. For example, Levi Strauss, a German immigrant, earned a fortune by making tough denim pants for miners.

Reading Check
Categorize
What types of people came to California hoping to benefit from the gold rush?

Impact on California

During the Spanish and Mexican periods of settlement, California's population grew slowly. The arrival of the forty-niners changed this dramatically.

Population Boom By 1849 California was home to more than 100,000 people, including Americans and immigrants. Also included in this number were slaves, although a state constitution written in 1849 outlawed

Westward Movement in the United States

Causes	Effects
• Americans believe in the idea of manifest destiny.	• Native Americans are forced off lands.
• The United States acquires vast new lands in the West.	• Americans travel west to settle new areas.
• Pathfinders open trails to new territories.	• The United States stretches to the Pacific Ocean.
• Gold is discovered in California.	• California experiences a population boom.

slavery. California's population explosion made it eligible for statehood only two years after being acquired by the United States. In 1850 California became the 31st state.

However, fast population growth had negative consequences for many Californios and California Native Americans. One early observer of the gold rush described why.

> "The Yankee regarded every man but [his own kind] as an interloper [trespasser], who had no right to come to California and pick up the gold of 'free and enlightened citizens.'"
>
> —W. Kelly, *An Excursion to California*

Economic Growth In addition to rapid population growth, a flood of new businesses and industries transformed California's economy. Gold mining remained an important part of its early economy. But Californians soon discovered other ways to make a living. Farming and ranching became industries for those willing to do the necessary hard labor. The California farming industry quickly took off, with Sacramento as its business center. Soon crops from the state were being shipped to markets around the United States and the world. In addition, lumber mills and factories were established to provide for the needs of miners and city dwellers.

Perhaps the most successful industry during the gold rush, however, was retail trade. Miners wanted to spend their time looking for gold, not growing crops or making products. Instead, they chose to buy the food and supplies they needed from merchants. However, the prices they paid were often very high. California could not supply all the food and materials its new population demanded, and materials had to be imported. Food and lumber were shipped from the eastern United States and from other parts of the world in return for gold. Merchants, in turn, sold these goods for inflated prices. Many successful merchants made huge fortunes in California. Some of them took their money back east to create new companies of their own. Among the entrepreneurs who owed their fortunes to gold rush sales were railroad tycoon Leland Stanford and blue jeans manufacturer Levi Strauss.

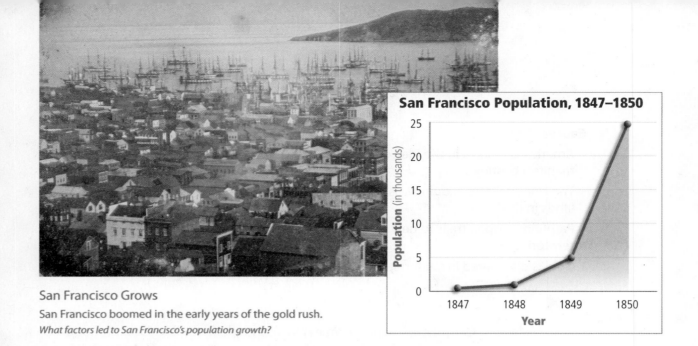

San Francisco Grows

San Francisco boomed in the early years of the gold rush.

What factors led to San Francisco's population growth?

San Francisco Population, 1847–1850

(line graph; Y-axis: Population (in thousands) from 0 to 25; X-axis: Year 1847, 1848, 1849, 1850. Values rise from near 0 in 1847 and 1848, to about 5 in 1849, to 25 in 1850.)

Reading Check

Analyze Information
What political effect resulted from California's rapid population growth?

California faced an obstacle to growth, though. The state was isolated from the rest of the country. It was difficult to bring in and ship out goods. The answer to the isolation problem was to bring the railroad all the way to California. Although Californians would have to wait almost 20 years for that, the gold rush did inspire the development of the American railroad industry. Completion of the transcontinental railroad in 1869 at last gave Californians the means to grow a stronger economy.

Summary and Preview Americans moved west to create new lives and seize new opportunities. In the next module you will learn about the Industrial Revolution in America.

Lesson 3 Assessment

Review Ideas, Terms, and People

1. **a. Recall** Why was Sutter's Mill important?

   b. Summarize What types of people participated in the California gold rush, and how did they take part in it?

   c. Elaborate What are some possible problems caused by the arrival of so many new settlers to California?

2. **a. Describe** How did some people hope to solve the problem of California's isolation from the rest of the country?

   b. Draw Inferences What effect did California's rapid population growth have on Californios and Native Americans?

   c. Evaluate Overall, do you think that the gold rush had a positive or negative effect on California? Explain.

Critical Thinking

3. **Evaluate** In this lesson you learned about the California gold rush. Create a concept web like the one shown below. Use it to show how the discovery of gold changed California.

Discovery of Gold

Social Studies Skills

Interpret Maps: Expansion

Define the Skill

Maps show features on Earth's surface. These can be physical features, such as mountains and rivers, or human features, such as roads and settlements. Historical maps show an area as it was in the past. Some show how a nation's boundaries changed over time. Interpreting maps can answer questions about history as well as geography.

Learn the Skill

Follow these steps to gain information from a map.

1. Read the title to determine what the map is about and the time period it covers.

2. Study the legend or key to understand what the colors or symbols on the map mean. Note the map scale, which is used to measure distances.

3. Note the map's other features. Maps often contain labels and other information in addition to what is explained in the legend or key.

Practice the Skill

Interpret the map below to answer the following questions about the expansion of the United States.

1. The addition of which territory almost doubled the size of the United States?

2. What was the last expansion that completed the establishment of the northern U.S. border, and when did it take place?

3. According to the map, when did California become part of the United States?

4. What choice of overland routes did a traveler have for getting to California?

5. What physical obstacles does the map show that such a traveler would face?

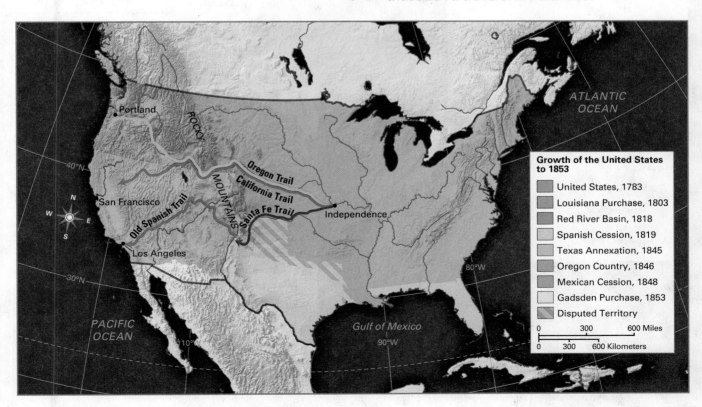

Growth of the United States to 1853

- United States, 1783
- Louisiana Purchase, 1803
- Red River Basin, 1818
- Spanish Cession, 1819
- Texas Annexation, 1845
- Oregon Country, 1846
- Mexican Cession, 1848
- Gadsden Purchase, 1853
- Disputed Territory

America's Growth by 1850

In the 1830s a new dream began to shape the American mind—manifest destiny. Manifest destiny was the belief that the United States should extend all the way to the Pacific Ocean. By 1850 that dream had become a reality. In 1845 the United States annexed Texas. In 1848 it acquired Oregon and the huge Mexican Cession. By 1853, with the Gadsden Purchase, the United States had taken the basic shape it still has today.

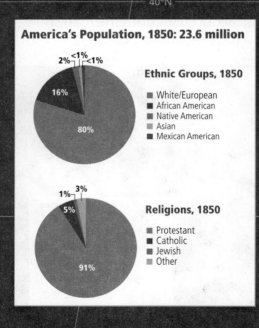

America's Population, 1850: 23.6 million

Ethnic Groups, 1850

2% <1% <1%
16%
80%

- White/European
- African American
- Native American
- Asian
- Mexican American

Religions, 1850

3%
1%
5%
91%

- Protestant
- Catholic
- Jewish
- Other

C A N A D A

Washington Territory

Oregon Territory

California

Utah Territory

San Francisco

New Mexico Territory

R O C K Y   M O U N T A I N S

M E X I C O

PACIFIC OCEAN

40°N

Tropic of Cancer

130°W   120°W   110°W

Gold Fever The discovery of gold in California in 1848 set off a massive migration. In 1849 some 80,000 forty-niners headed toward California. San Francisco, located on an excellent natural port, grew quickly as a result.

Texas annexation, 1845
Claim recognized in Oregon Treaty, 1848
Mexican Cession, 1848
Gadsden Purchase, 1853

0   150   300 Miles
0   150   300 Kilometers

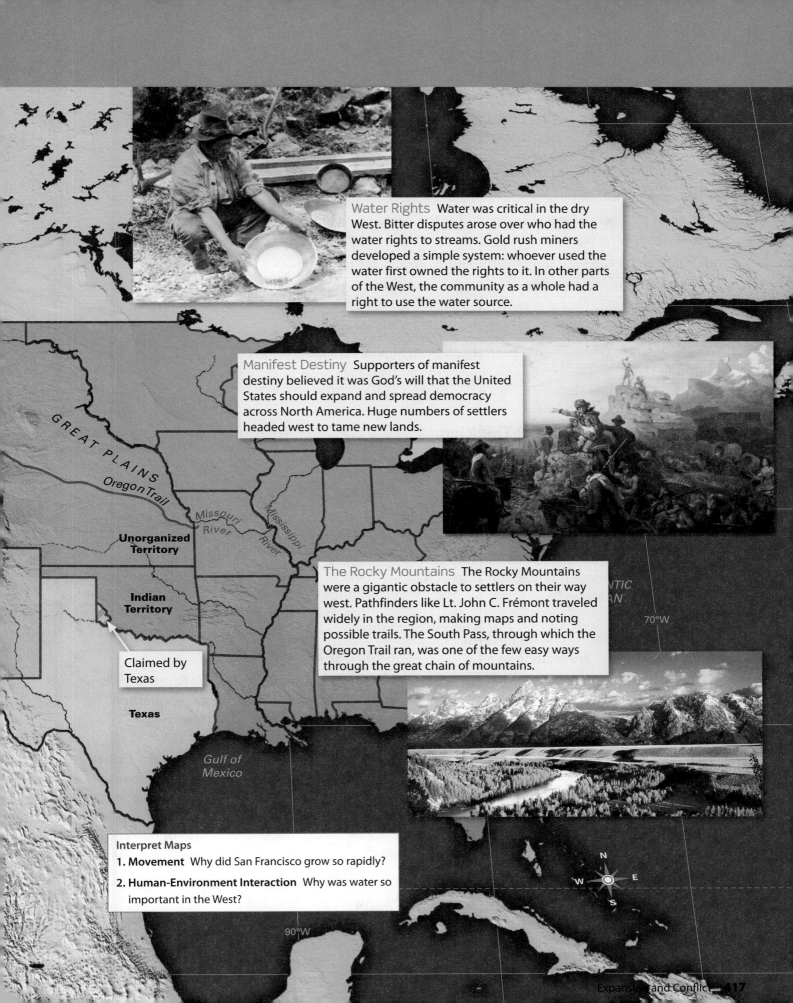

Water Rights Water was critical in the dry West. Bitter disputes arose over who had the water rights to streams. Gold rush miners developed a simple system: whoever used the water first owned the rights to it. In other parts of the West, the community as a whole had a right to use the water source.

Manifest Destiny Supporters of manifest destiny believed it was God's will that the United States should expand and spread democracy across North America. Huge numbers of settlers headed west to tame new lands.

The Rocky Mountains The Rocky Mountains were a gigantic obstacle to settlers on their way west. Pathfinders like Lt. John C. Frémont traveled widely in the region, making maps and noting possible trails. The South Pass, through which the Oregon Trail ran, was one of the few easy ways through the great chain of mountains.

GREAT PLAINS

Oregon Trail

Missouri River

Mississippi River

Unorganized Territory

Indian Territory

Claimed by Texas

Texas

Gulf of Mexico

NTIC AN

70°W

90°W

Interpret Maps

1. **Movement** Why did San Francisco grow so rapidly?

2. **Human-Environment Interaction** Why was water so important in the West?

Module 12 Assessment

Review Vocabulary, Terms, and People

Identify the correct term or person from the module that best fits each of the following descriptions.

1. Mexican priest who led a rebellion for independence from Spain

2. Early settlers in California

3. A group of pioneers who were stranded in the Sierra Nevada Mountains and struggled to survive the winter

4. Agents hired by the Mexican government to attract settlers to Texas

5. The belief that the United States was meant to expand across the continent to the Pacific Ocean

6. Mexican ruler who fought to keep Texas from gaining independence

7. Swiss immigrant who received permission from Mexico to start a colony in California

Comprehension and Critical Thinking

Lesson 1

8. a. **Identify** Who were Stephen F. Austin and Antonio López de Santa Anna?

   b. **Draw Conclusions** Why did settlers in Texas rebel against Mexican rule?

   c. **Elaborate** In what ways was the Texas struggle for independence similar to that of the United States?

Lesson 2

9. a. **Recall** Why were some Americans opposed to the annexation of new territories?

   b. **Draw Conclusions** What economic and cultural influences did Native Americans and Mexican Americans have on American settlers in the Mexican Cession?

   c. **Predict** What are some possible problems the acquisition of so much territory might cause the United States?

Lesson 3

10. a. **Identify** What roles did women and immigrants play in the California gold rush?

    b. **Make Inferences** Why were most gold-rush settlers young, unmarried men?

    c. **Predict** What long-term effects might the gold rush have on California's future?

Review Themes

11. **Economics** What impact did the gold rush have on the economy in California?

12. **Geography** Why did many Americans in the 1840s believe the United States should annex the territories of Oregon, New Mexico, and Texas?

Reading Skills

Vocabulary in Context Use the Reading Skills taught in this module to answer the question about the reading selection below.

> Texas politicians hoped that joining the United States would help solve the republic's financial and military problems. The Texas Congress approved annexation in June 1845. Texas became part of the United States in December.

13. Determine the definition of *annexation* using context clues.

Social Studies Skills

Interpret Maps: Expansion *Use the Social Studies Skills taught in this module to answer the question about the map below.*

14. Place the expansions in the order in which they were acquired by the United States, according to the map.

Focus on Writing

15. **Write an Outline for a Documentary Film** Choose one topic from this module that you think would make a good 10-minute documentary. Your outline should be organized by scene (no more than three scenes) and in chronological order. For each scene, give the following information: main idea of scene, costumes and images to be used, audio to be used, and length of scene. As you plan, remember that the audience will be students your own age.

> ▶ *Explore ONLINE!*

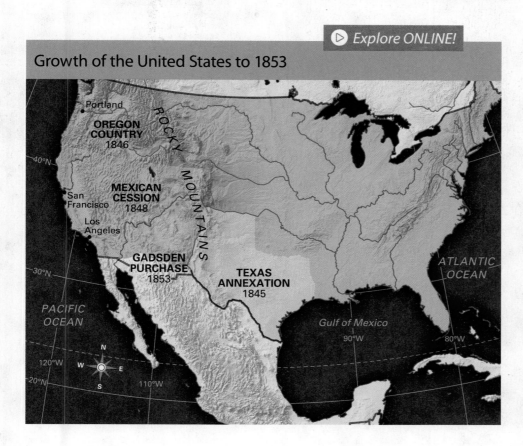

Growth of the United States to 1853

The Real West: Rush for Gold

When gold was discovered in northern California in 1848, it caused a sensation. Gold seekers from the United States and the rest of the world rushed to California to find their fortunes. The conditions of the trip were difficult, as was the labor required to extract the gold from rivers and mines. Although some people became wealthy, many more never found the riches they had expected. So many people arrived so quickly that California became a state within three years of gold being discovered.

Explore some of the history and documents of the California gold rush online. You can find a wealth of information, video clips, primary sources, activities, and more through your online textbook.

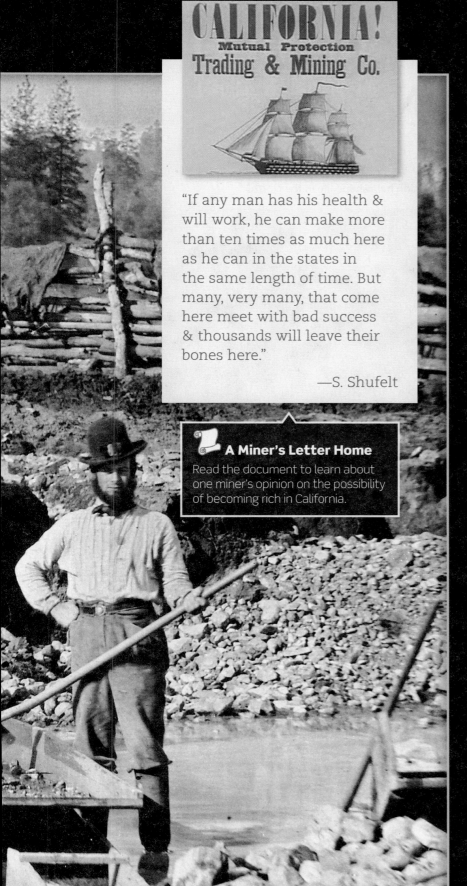

CALIFORNIA!
Mutual Protection
Trading & Mining Co.

"If any man has his health & will work, he can make more than ten times as much here as he can in the states in the same length of time. But many, very many, that come here meet with bad success & thousands will leave their bones here."

—S. Shufelt

A Miner's Letter Home
Read the document to learn about one miner's opinion on the possibility of becoming rich in California.

Heading West
Watch the video to learn about the dangers that overland travelers faced when trying to get to California from the eastern United States.

Search for the Mother Lode
Watch the video to see the various methods that forty-niners used to mine the gold in California.

Statehood
Watch the video to discover the political issues surrounding the admission of California as a free state and its implication for the rest of the nation.

The North

Essential Question

How did the Industrial Revolution help shape life in the North?

About the Photo: New machinery like this textile mill helped fuel the Industrial Revolution.

In this module you will read about the changes that occurred in the lives of Americans in the North as the result of rapid industrialization. You will also learn about some of the new inventions of the period.

What You Will Learn ...

▶ *Explore ONLINE!*

HISTORY

VIDEOS, including...
- Industrial Revolution
- Train Technology

✓ Document-Based Investigations

✓ Graphic Organizers

✓ Interactive Games

✓ Image Carousel: Elements of Mass Production

✓ Image with Hotspots: Life of a Mill Girl

✓ Image with Hotspots: The Steam Train

Timeline of Events 1785–1860

▶ Explore ONLINE!

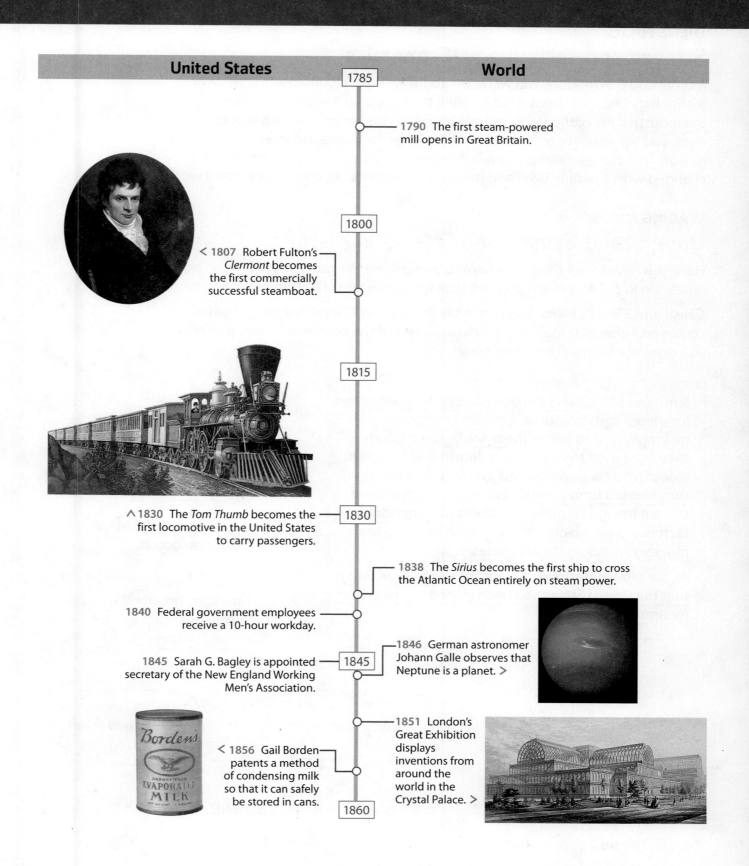

| United States | 1785 | World |

1790 The first steam-powered mill opens in Great Britain.

1800

< **1807** Robert Fulton's *Clermont* becomes the first commercially successful steamboat.

1815

∧ **1830** The *Tom Thumb* becomes the first locomotive in the United States to carry passengers.

1830

1838 The *Sirius* becomes the first ship to cross the Atlantic Ocean entirely on steam power.

1840 Federal government employees receive a 10-hour workday.

1846 German astronomer Johann Galle observes that Neptune is a planet. >

1845 Sarah G. Bagley is appointed secretary of the New England Working Men's Association.

1845

Borden's
UNSWEETENED
EVAPORATED
MILK
NET WEIGHT 1 POUND

< **1856** Gail Borden patents a method of condensing milk so that it can safely be stored in cans.

1851 London's Great Exhibition displays inventions from around the world in the Crystal Palace. >

1860

Reading Social Studies

THEME FOCUS:

Science and Technology, Economics

As you read this module, you will learn about how developments in science and technology brought about what is called the Industrial Revolution. As a result of the Industrial Revolution, you will see how American economic patterns changed. Next, you will read about how family life changed as more and more people went to work in factories. Finally, you will see how new methods of transportation changed where people lived and how new inventions affected daily life and work.

READING FOCUS:

Understand Causes and Effects in History

Have you heard the saying, "We have to understand the past to avoid repeating it."? That is one reason we look for causes and effects in history.

Cause and Effect Chains You might say that all of history is one long chain of causes and effects. It may help you to understand the course of history better if you draw out such a chain as you read.

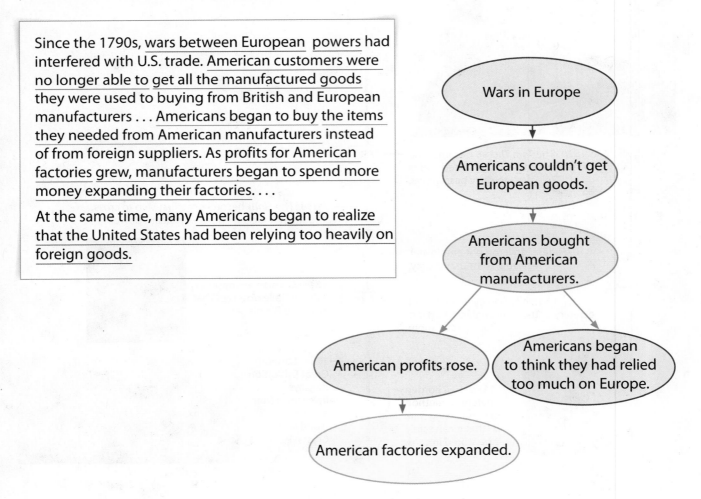

Since the 1790s, wars between European powers had interfered with U.S. trade. American customers were no longer able to get all the manufactured goods they were used to buying from British and European manufacturers . . . Americans began to buy the items they needed from American manufacturers instead of from foreign suppliers. As profits for American factories grew, manufacturers began to spend more money expanding their factories. . . .

At the same time, many Americans began to realize that the United States had been relying too heavily on foreign goods.

Wars in Europe

Americans couldn't get European goods.

Americans bought from American manufacturers.

American profits rose.

Americans began to think they had relied too much on Europe.

American factories expanded.

You Try It!

The following passage is from the module you are about to read. As you read each paragraph, ask yourself what is the cause and what is the effect of what is being discussed.

Workers Organize Factories continued to spread in the 1800s. Craftspeople, who made goods by hand, felt threatened. Factories quickly produced low-priced goods. To compete with factories, shop owners had to hire more workers and pay them less. . . .

The wages of factory workers also went down as people competed for jobs. A wave of immigration in the 1840s brought people from other, poorer countries. They were willing to work for low pay. More immigrants came to the Northeast, where the mills were located, than to the South. Competition for jobs also came from people unemployed during the financial Panic of 1837.

After you have read the passage, answer the following questions.

1. What cause is being discussed in the first paragraph? What were its effects?

2. Draw a cause and effect chain that shows the events described in the first paragraph.

3. What main effect is discussed in the second paragraph? How many causes are given for it?

4. Draw a cause and effect chain that shows the events described in the second paragraph.

As you read Module 13, look for words that signal causes or effects. Picture these causes and effects as the links in a cause and effect chain.

The Industrial Revolution in America

The Big Idea

The Industrial Revolution transformed the way goods were produced in the United States.

Main Ideas

- The invention of new machines in Great Britain led to the beginning of the Industrial Revolution.

- The development of new machines and processes brought the Industrial Revolution to the United States.

- Despite a slow start in manufacturing, the United States made rapid improvements during the War of 1812.

Key Terms and People

Industrial Revolution
textiles
Richard Arkwright
Samuel Slater
technology
Eli Whitney
interchangeable parts
mass production

Academic
Vocabulary
efficient productive
and not wasteful

If YOU were there . . .

You live in a small Pennsylvania town in the 1780s. You earn money for your family by raising sheep and spinning their wool into yarn. Your sisters knit the yarn into gloves and mittens that you sell to city merchants. But now you hear that someone has invented machines that can spin thread and make cloth.

Would you still be able to earn the same amount of money for your family? Why?

The Industrial Revolution

At the start of the 1700s, the majority of people in Europe and the United States were farmers. They made most of what they needed by hand. For example, female family members usually made clothing. First, they used a spinning wheel to spin raw materials, such as cotton or wool, into thread. Then they used a hand loom to weave the thread into cloth.

Some families produced extra cloth to sell to merchants, who sold it for a profit. In towns, a few skilled craftspeople made goods by hand in their own shops. Workers including blacksmiths, carpenters, and shoemakers specialized in their work and the goods that they produced. Their ways of life had stayed the same for generations.

A Need for Change By the mid-1700s, however, changes in Great Britain led to a greater demand for manufactured goods. As agriculture and roads improved, cities and populations grew. Overseas trade also expanded. Traditional manufacturing methods did not produce enough goods to meet everyone's needs.

People began using machines to create processes that made goods in more **efficient** ways. They also discovered new power resources to fuel the machines. These developments led to the **Industrial Revolution**, a period of rapid growth in using machines for manufacturing and production that began in the mid-1700s.

Women workers in a textile mill

Textile Industry The first important breakthrough of the Industrial Revolution took place in how **textiles**, or cloth items, were made. Before the Industrial Revolution, spinning thread took much more time than making cloth. Several skilled workers were needed to spin enough thread to supply a single weaver.

In 1769 British entrepreneur **Richard Arkwright** invented a large spinning machine called a water frame. The water frame could produce dozens of cotton threads at the same time. It lowered the cost of cotton cloth and increased the speed of textile production.

The water frame used flowing water as its source of power. Merchants began to build large textile mills, or factories, near rivers and streams. The mills were filled with spinning machines. Merchants began hiring people to work in the mills.

Additional improvements also speeded up the spinning process. Britain soon had the world's most productive textile manufacturing industry.

New Machines and Processes

New machines encouraged the rise of new processes in business and manufacturing. As the machines used to make products became more efficient, the processes involved changed dramatically.

Slater and His Secrets The new textile machines allowed Great Britain to produce cloth more quickly and inexpensively than other countries could. To protect British industry, the British Parliament had made it illegal for skilled mechanics or machine plans to leave the country. Disguised as a farmer, **Samuel Slater**, a skilled British mechanic, immigrated to the United States after carefully memorizing the designs of textile mill machines. Soon after arriving, he sent a letter to Moses Brown, who owned a textile business in New England. Slater claimed he could improve the way textiles were manufactured in the United States.

Brown had one of his workers test Slater's knowledge of machinery. Slater passed. Brown's son, Smith Brown, and son-in-law, William Almy, formed a partnership with Slater. Economic freedom in the United States allowed entrepreneurs such as Slater, Brown, and Almy to take risks by using their money and talents to launch new ventures. In 1793 they opened their first mill in Pawtucket, Rhode Island. The production of

Reading Check
Draw Conclusions
How did machines speed up textile manufacturing?

cotton thread by American machines had begun. Slater ran the mill and the machinery. He was confident that his new machines would work well.

"If I do not make as good yarn as they do in England, I will have nothing for my services, but will throw the whole of what I have attempted over the bridge."

—Samuel Slater, from *Memoir of Samuel Slater*

Slater could have lost all of his investment, but his machines worked and the Pawtucket mill became a success. Slater's wife also invented a new cotton thread for sewing. In 1798 Slater formed his own company to build a mill. By the time he died in 1835, he owned all or part of 13 textile mills.

Other Americans began building textile mills. Most were located in the Northeast. In New England, in particular, merchants had the money to invest in new mills. More importantly, the physical environment in this region was made up of many rivers and streams that provided a reliable supply of power. Fewer mills were built in the South, partly because investors in the South concentrated on expanding agriculture. There, agriculture was seen as an easier way to make money. The expansion of industrialization in the North and the South's concentration on agriculture caused the two regions to develop significant economic and cultural differences.

A Manufacturing Breakthrough Despite these great changes in machines and processes, most manufacturing was still done by hand. In the late 1790s the U.S. government worried about a possible war with France, so it wanted more muskets for the army. Skilled workers made the parts for each weapon by hand. No two parts were exactly alike, and carefully fitting all the pieces together took much time and skill.

As a result, American gunmakers could not produce the muskets quickly enough to satisfy the government's demand. Factories needed better **technology**, the tools used to produce items or to do work.

In 1798 inventor **Eli Whitney** tried to address some of these problems. Whitney gave officials a proposal for mass-producing guns for the U.S. government using water-powered machinery. Whitney explained the benefits of his ideas.

"I am persuaded that machinery moved by water [and] adapted to this business would greatly reduce the labor and facilitate [ease] the manufacture of this article."

—Eli Whitney to Secretary of the Treasury Oliver Wolcott

Eli Whitney developed the idea of using interchangeable parts. Interchangeable, or identical, parts are needed so each part does not have to be custom-made by hand.

Whitney also came up with the idea of using **interchangeable parts**—parts of a machine that are identical. Interchangeable parts became important because each part does not have to be custom-made by hand, so it saves production time. Using interchangeable parts made machines easier to assemble and broken parts easier to replace. Whitney promised to build 10,000 muskets in two years. The federal government gave him money to build his factory, and in 1801 he was called to Washington, DC, to give a demonstration.

Elements of Mass Production

Mass production requires the use of interchangeable parts, machine tools, and the division of labor. Machine tools like the one at bottom left make parts that are identical and therefore interchangeable. Mass production uses a division of labor in which the work is divided among several people. Each worker performs a specific task, like the workers below who change the spools of wire. The end result is goods that have been mass-produced. These techniques were used to build items such as the firearms at bottom right.

Why are interchangeable parts important?

Machine Tools

Division of Labor

Mass-Produced Goods

Whitney stood before President John Adams and his secretary of war. He had an assortment of parts for ten guns. He then randomly chose parts and quickly assembled them into muskets. To the audience's amazement, he repeated the process several times.

Whitney's ideas helped businesses in the manufacturing industry determine the best way to produce the goods that consumers in the American market needed. He had proven that American inventors could improve upon the new British technology. Machines that produced matching parts soon became the standard in industry. Interchangeable parts sped up **mass production**, the efficient production of large numbers of identical goods. Mass-production techniques allowed manufacturers to efficiently create more goods for the marketplace.

Reading Check
Summarize How did Eli Whitney influence American manufacturing?

Manufacturing Grows Slowly

Despite the hard work of people such as Samuel Slater and Eli Whitney, manufacturing in the United States grew slowly. In 1810 Secretary of the Treasury Albert Gallatin described some of the obstacles faced by potential factory owners in the United States.

"[The reasons include] . . . the superior attractions of agricultural pursuits [farming], . . . the abundance of land compared with the population, the high price of labor, and the want [lack] of sufficient capital [investment]."

—Albert Gallatin, from *The Writings of Albert Gallatin*

Gallatin and others believed that few people would choose to work in a factory if they could own their own farm instead. In Great Britain, on the other hand, land was more scarce and more expensive than in the United

Modern Manufacturing

The word *manufacture* comes from Latin words that mean "to make by hand." Yet in modern manufacturing, machines—not human hands—do most of the work.

A key feature of modern manufacturing is the assembly line. An assembly line is a long conveyer belt. As the product moves along the belt, or "down the line," workers assemble it. Often, the workers use machines to help them. On a growing number of assembly lines, there are no workers at all: the product is assembled by computer-controlled robots.

Although a far cry from Eli Whitney's factory, modern factories use the same elements of mass production that Whitney did more than 200 years ago.

Analyze Information
How do interchangeable parts help the modern assembly line work?

States. As a result, fewer people were able to own farms. British factory workers generally were willing to work for lower wages than factory workers in the United States were.

Because British manufacturers had plenty of factory workers with technical skills, they could produce large amounts of goods less expensively than most American businesses could. As a result, they could charge lower prices for the goods. Lower British prices made it difficult for many American manufacturers to compete with British companies. This situation in turn discouraged American investors from spending the money needed to build new factories and machinery. As a result, only a few industries had found a place to compete in the American market economy. These included cotton goods, flour milling, weapons, and iron production.

These circumstances began to change around the time of the War of 1812. Since the 1790s, conflict and wars between European powers had interfered with U.S. trade. Some goods became scarce, as American consumers were no longer able to get all the manufactured goods they were used to buying from British and European manufacturers. Then, during the War of 1812, British ships blockaded eastern seaports, preventing foreign ships from delivering goods. Americans began to buy the items they needed from American manufacturers instead of from foreign suppliers. As profits for American factories grew, manufacturers began to spend more money expanding their factories. State banks and private investors began to lend money to manufacturers for their businesses.

At the same time, many Americans began to realize that the United States had been relying too heavily on foreign goods. If the United States could not meet its own needs, it might be weak and open to attack. Former president Thomas Jefferson, who had once opposed manufacturing, changed his mind. He, too, realized that the United States was too dependent on imports.

"To be independent for the comforts of life we must fabricate [make] them ourselves. We must now place the manufacturer by the side of the agriculturalist [farmer]."

—Thomas Jefferson, from *Memoir, Correspondence, and Miscellanies from the Papers of Thomas Jefferson*

In February 1815, New Yorkers celebrated the end of the War of 1812 and the return of free trade. The streets were decorated and filled with merchants whose ships were loaded with goods. "With Peace and Commerce, America Prospers," declared one display. Eager businesspeople prepared to lead the United States into a period of industrial and economic growth. These merchants and industrialists urged northern politicians to pass higher tariffs on foreign goods to protect American companies.

Reading Check
Analyze Information
How did the War of 1812 aid the growth of American manufacturing?

Summary and Preview The Industrial Revolution started with the textile industry in England but soon spread to the United States. In the next lesson you will learn about how the spread of factories changed the working lives of many Americans.

Lesson 1 Assessment

Review Ideas, Terms, and People

1. **a. Identify** What was the first industry to begin to use machines to manufacture goods?

   b. Analyze What were some causes of the Industrial Revolution, and what effect did it have on the way products were made?

   c. Predict In what ways might life for workers change as a result of the Industrial Revolution?

2. **a. Recall** In what part of the United States were most mills located? Why?

   b. Draw Conclusions How did the ideas of Samuel Slater and Eli Whitney affect manufacturing in the United States?

   c. Evaluate Whose contributions do you think were more important—Slater's textile machines or Whitney's interchangeable parts? Why?

3. **a. Explain** How did conflict in Europe influence economic growth in America?

   b. Contrast Why was manufacturing in Great Britain in the early years more successful than that in the United States?

Critical Thinking

4. **Draw Conclusions** In this lesson you learned about the changes in manufacturing and the effect those changes had in the early 1800s. Create a chart similar to the one below and use it to show how each contribution affected manufacturing.

Invention/ Improvement	Effect on Manufacturing

Changes in Working Life

The Big Idea
The introduction of factories changed working life for many Americans.

Main Ideas

- The spread of mills in the Northeast changed workers' lives.

- The Lowell system revolutionized the textile industry in the Northeast.

- Workers organized to reform working conditions.

Key Terms and People
Rhode Island system
Francis Cabot Lowell
Lowell system
trade unions
strikes
Sarah G. Bagley

If YOU were there . . .

You live on a dairy farm in Massachusetts in about 1820. On the farm, you get up at dawn to milk the cows, and your work goes on until nighttime. But now you have a chance at a different life. A nearby textile mill is hiring young people. You would leave the farm and live with other workers. You could go to classes. Most importantly, you could earn money of your own.

Would you go to work in the textile mill? Why?

Mills Change Workers' Lives

Workers no longer needed the specific skills of craftspeople to run the machines of the new mills. The lives of workers changed along with their jobs. Resistance to these changes sometimes sparked protests.

Many mill owners in the United States could not find enough people to work in factories because other jobs were available. At first, Samuel Slater and his two partners used apprentices— young men who worked for several years to learn the trade. However, they often were given only simple work. For example, their jobs might include feeding cotton into the machines and cleaning the mill equipment. They grew tired of this work and frequently left. Apprentice James Horton, for example, ran away from Slater's mill. "Mr. Slater . . . keep me always at one thing . . . ," Horton complained. "I might have stayed there until this time and never knew nothing."

Eventually, Slater began to hire entire families who moved to Pawtucket to work in the mills. This practice allowed Slater to fill his labor needs at a low cost. Children as well as adults worked in the mills.

On most farms children worked to help their families. Therefore, few people complained about the hiring of children to work in factories. H. Humphrey, an author of books on raising children, told parents that children needed to be useful. Humphrey wrote, "If he [a child] will not study, put him on to a farm, or send him into the shop, or in some other way provide regular employment for him." The machines made many tasks in the mill simple enough for children to do. Mill owners profited because they paid children low wages. Adults usually earned as much in a day as most children did in a week.

To attract families to his mill, Slater built housing for the workers. He also provided them with a company store where they could buy necessities. In addition, he started the practice of paying workers with credit at the company store. Instead of paying the full price for an item all at once, small payments could be made over a period of time. This practice allowed Slater to reinvest his money in his business.

Slater's strategy of hiring families and dividing factory work into simple tasks became known as the **Rhode Island system**. Mill owners throughout the Northeast copied Slater's methods. Owners advertised with "Men with growing families wanted." They also sent recruiters to poor communities to find new workers. For many people, the chance to work in a factory was a welcome opportunity to earn money and to learn a new skill.

Entire families worked at Slater's mill in Pawtucket, Rhode Island. The mill's machinery was powered by the Blackstone River.

One of the earliest of the mill towns, Slatersville, was named after Samuel Slater. The town was built by Slater and his brother John. It included two houses for workers and their families, the owner's house, the company store, and the Slatersville Mill. The mill was the largest and most modern industrial building of its time.

The mills employed not only the textile workers who operated the machinery but also machine part makers and dam builders. Although the company store sold food and necessary items to workers, mill towns supported the same variety of businesses any other town needed to thrive. These included tailors and dressmakers, butchers, and other small workshops.

Reading Check
Summarize What problem did Slater have in his mills, and how did he solve it?

The Lowell System

Not all mill owners followed this system. **Francis Cabot Lowell**, an entrepreneur from New England, developed a very different approach. His ideas completely changed the textile industry in the Northeast.

The **Lowell system** was based on water-powered textile mills that employed young, unmarried women from local farms. The system included a loom that could both spin thread and weave cloth in the same mill. Lowell constructed boardinghouses for the women. Boardinghouse residents were given a room and meals along with their jobs.

With financial support from investors of the Boston Manufacturing Company, Lowell's first textile mill opened in Waltham, Massachusetts, in 1814. "From the first starting of the first power loom there was not . . . doubt about the success," wrote one investor. In 1822 the company built a larger mill in a Massachusetts town later named Lowell. Visitors to Lowell were amazed by the clean factories and neatly kept boardinghouses as well as the new machinery.

Life of a Mill Girl

No record exists today of the name of this girl, who worked in a mill around 1850. Judging from the photograph, if she were in school today, she would probably be in the seventh or eighth grade. Although hard to see in this photograph, her hands and arms are scratched and swollen—telltale signs of the hard labor required of young girls who worked up to 14 hours a day.

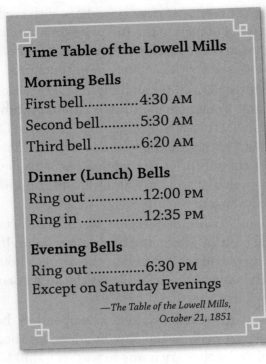

Time Table of the Lowell Mills

Morning Bells
First bell..............4:30 AM
Second bell..........5:30 AM
Third bell...........6:20 AM

Dinner (Lunch) Bells
Ring out..............12:00 PM
Ring in ....12:35 PM

Evening Bells
Ring out ....6:30 PM
Except on Saturday Evenings

—*The Table of the Lowell Mills,*
October 21, 1851

The young women working in the mills soon became known as Lowell girls. The mills paid them between $2 and $4 each week. The workers were required to pay $1.25 for room and board. These wages were much better than the wages women could earn per week in other available jobs, such as domestic work.

Many young women came to Lowell from different parts of New England. They wanted the chance to earn money instead of working on the family farm. Working in the Lowell mills gave young women the opportunity to achieve economic independence. "I must of course have something of my own before many more years have passed over my head," wrote one young woman. The typical Lowell girl worked at the mills for about four years.

The Lowell system aimed to overcome the perception that factory workers had a lower social status. Unlike other factory workers, the Lowell girls were encouraged to use their free time to take classes and form women's clubs. They even wrote their own magazine, the *Lowell Offering*. Lucy Larcom, who started working in the Lowell mills at age 11, later praised her fellow workers:

"I regard it as one of the privileges [advantages] of my youth that I . . . [grew] up among those active, interesting girls, whose lives . . . had principle [ideals] and purpose distinctly their own."

—Lucy Larcom, from *A New England Girlhood*

Reading Check
Contrast How was the Lowell system different from the Rhode Island system?

Mill life was hard, however. The workday was between 12 and 14 hours long, and daily life was carefully controlled. Ringing bells ordered workers to breakfast or lunch. Employees had to work harder and faster to keep up with new equipment. Cotton dust also began to cause health problems, such as chronic cough, for workers.

Workers Organize

Factories continued to spread in the 1800s. Craftspeople, who made goods by hand, felt threatened because factories were able to produce low-priced goods more quickly. To compete with factories, shop owners had to hire more workers and pay them less. Shoemaker William Frazier complained about the situation in the mid-1840s. "We have to sit on our seats from twelve to sixteen hours per day, to earn one dollar."

The wages of factory workers also went down as people competed for jobs. A wave of immigration in the 1840s brought people from other, poorer countries. They were willing to work for low pay. More immigrants came to the Northeast, where the mills were located, than to the South. Competition for jobs also came from people unemployed during the financial Panic of 1837. For example, about 50,000 workers in New York City alone lost their jobs.

The Beginning of Trade Unions Facing low wages and the fear of losing their jobs, skilled workers formed **trade unions**, groups that tried to improve pay and working conditions. Eventually, unskilled factory workers also formed trade unions, seeking economic equity. Most employers did not want to hire union workers. Employers believed that the higher cost of union employees prevented competition with other manufacturers.

Sometimes, labor unions staged protests called **strikes**. Workers on strike refuse to work until employers meet their demands. Most early strikes were not successful, however. Courts and police usually supported companies, not striking union members.

Labor Reform Efforts A strong voice in the union movement was that of millworker **Sarah G. Bagley**. She wrote magazine articles and made speeches about working in the mills. She organized workers to help change conditions. Bagley founded the Lowell Female Labor Reform Association in 1844 and publicized the struggles of factory laborers. The association's two main goals were to influence an investigation of working conditions by the Massachusetts state legislature and to obtain a ten-hour workday. Members of the association passed out pamphlets and circulated petitions.

President Martin Van Buren had granted a ten-hour workday in 1840 for many federal employees. Bagley wanted this rule to apply to employees of private businesses. These men and women often worked 12 to 14 hours per day, six days per week.

Many working men and women supported the ten-hour-workday campaign, despite the opposition of business owners. In 1845 Sarah G. Bagley was elected vice president of the New England Working Men's Association. She was the first woman to hold such a high-ranking position in the American labor movement.

Over time, the unions achieved some **concrete** legal victories. Connecticut, Maine, New Hampshire, Ohio, Pennsylvania, and a few other states passed ten-hour-workday laws.

For factory workers in other states, long hours remained common. One witness described how children were "summoned by the factory bell before daylight" and worked until eight o'clock at night "with nothing but [a] recess of forty-five minutes to get their dinner." Union supporters continued to fight for work reforms such as an end to child labor in factories during the 1800s.

Summary and Preview With the growth of factories, workers faced new opportunities and challenges. In the next lesson you will learn about how the Transportation Revolution brought changes to commerce and the daily lives of Americans.

Academic Vocabulary
concrete specific, real

Reading Check
Find Main Ideas
Why did workers form unions, and what were the main goals of union reformers?

Lesson 2 Assessment

Review Ideas, Terms, and People

1. **a. Identify** What problems did many mill owners have in finding workers?

   b. Analyze How did Samuel Slater's Rhode Island system change employment practices in mills?

2. **a. Describe** What was life like for mill workers in the Lowell system?

   b. Make Inferences Why would young women have wanted to go to work in the Lowell mills?

3. **a. Recall** Why did workers form trade unions?

   b. Predict What are some possible problems that might arise between factory owners and trade unions?

Critical Thinking

4. **Draw Conclusions** In this lesson you learned about mill life and the effect conditions had on workers. Create a chart similar to the one below to show how Samuel Slater, Francis Cabot Lowell, and Sarah G. Bagley affected workers' lives.

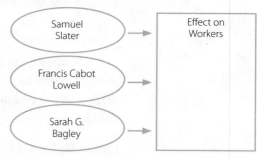

The Transportation Revolution

Reading Check
Find Main Ideas
What benefits did the Transportation Revolution bring to trade and daily life?

The Big Idea

New forms of transportation improved business, travel, and communication in the United States.

Main Ideas

- The Transportation Revolution affected trade and daily life.
- The steamboat was one of the first developments of the Transportation Revolution.
- Railroads were a vital part of the Transportation Revolution.
- The Transportation Revolution brought many changes to American life and industry.

Key Terms and People

Transportation Revolution
Robert Fulton
Clermont
Gibbons v. *Ogden*
Peter Cooper

If YOU were there . . .

You live in a small town in Iowa in the 1860s. You've never been more than 30 miles from home and have always traveled by wagon or on horseback. Now there are plans to build a railroad westward from Chicago, 200 miles to the east. The tracks will come through your town! Twice a week, trains will bring goods from the city and take people farther west.

How would the coming of the railroad change your life?

Trade and Daily Life

During the 1800s the United States was transformed by a **Transportation Revolution**—a period of rapid growth in the speed and convenience of travel because of new methods of transportation. The Transportation Revolution created a boom in business across the country, particularly by reducing shipping time and costs. As one foreign observer declared in 1835, "The Americans . . . have joined the Hudson to the Mississippi, and made the Atlantic Ocean communicate with the Gulf of Mexico."

These improvements were made possible largely by the invention of two new forms of transportation: steamboats and steam-powered trains. They enabled goods, people, and information to travel rapidly and efficiently across the United States.

Steamboats

American and European inventors had developed steam-powered boats in the late 1700s. However, they were not in wide use until the early 1800s.

Steamboat Era In 1803 American **Robert Fulton** tested his first steamboat design in France. Several years later, he tested the first full-sized commercial steamboat, called the *Clermont*, in the United States. On August 9, 1807,

Mississippi River Steamboats

Deckhands load a Mississippi River steamboat in Memphis, Tennessee. By the mid-1800s, hundreds of steamboats traveled up and down American rivers. Steamboats enabled Americans to ship more goods farther, faster, and for less money than ever before.

Upstream River Rates

Dollars (per 100 pounds)

the *Clermont* traveled against the current up the Hudson River without trouble. Demand for steamboat ferry service soon arose.

The steamboat was well suited for river travel. It could move upriver and did not rely on wind power. Steamboats and the location of rivers in the United States created new economic opportunities during the 1800s. Steamboats increased trade and profits because goods could be moved quickly and thus more cheaply. More than 500 steamboats were in use in the United States by 1840. By the 1850s steamboats were also being used to carry people and goods across the Atlantic Ocean, creating more opportunities for international trade.

Gibbons v. Ogden Increased steamboat shipping led to conflict over waterway rights. In 1819 Aaron Ogden sued Thomas Gibbons for operating steamboats in New York waters that Ogden said he owned. Gibbons did not have a license to operate in New York, but argued that his federal license gave him the right to use New York waterways.

Reading Check
Summarize Explain the effects of the *Gibbons* v. *Ogden* ruling.

In the case of **_Gibbons_ v. _Ogden_**, which reached the Supreme Court in 1824, Chief Justice John Marshall reinforced the federal government's authority to regulate trade between the states by ending monopolistic control over waterways in several states. At the same time, it strengthened the idea that national interests should be placed ahead of regional concerns. The ruling freed up waters to even greater trade and competition within the shipping industry.

American Railroads

What the steamboat did for water travel, the train did for overland travel. Steam-powered trains had first been developed in Great Britain in the early 1800s. However, they did not become popular in the United States until the 1830s. In 1830 **Peter Cooper** built a small but powerful locomotive called the *Tom Thumb*. He raced the locomotive against a horse-drawn railcar.

The *Tom Thumb* was made famous in a race against a horse-drawn carriage. The locomotive was small, but powerful for its day.

Eyewitness John Latrobe later described the race, in which *Tom Thumb* had a slow start and fell behind. Latrobe wrote, "The pace increased, the passengers shouted, the engine gained on the horse . . . then the engine passes the horse, and a great hurrah hailed the victory." Unfortunately for Cooper, victory was spoiled when *Tom Thumb* broke down and lost the race near the end.

Despite the defeat, the contest showed the power and speed of even a small locomotive. Railroad fever soon spread. By 1840 railroad companies had laid about 2,800 miles of tracks—more than existed in all of Europe. French economist Michel Chevalier described Americans as having "a perfect passion for railroads."

As more railroads were built, engineers and mechanics overcame many tough challenges. Most British railroads, for example, ran on straight tracks across flat ground. In the United States, however, many railroads had to run up and down steep mountains, around tight curves, and over swift rivers. Railroad companies also built the tracks quickly and often with the least expensive materials available. As time went on, engineers and mechanics built heavier, faster, and more powerful steam locomotives.

By 1860 about 30,000 miles of tracks linked almost every major city in the eastern United States. As a result, the economy surged forward. For example, American locomotives hauled more freight than those in any other country. The railroad companies quickly became some of the most powerful businesses in the nation. As the railroad system grew, manufacturers and farmers could send their goods to distant markets.

In addition to their tremendous economic impact, the railroads made a powerful impression on the senses of many passengers and observers. Trains were the fastest form of transportation that most people had ever experienced. While wagons often traveled less than 2 miles per hour, locomotives averaged about 20 miles per hour. Writer George Templeton Strong of New York City described the thrill of a steam train passing by in the night:

"Whizzing and rattling and panting, with its fiery furnace gleaming in front, its chimney vomiting fiery smoke above, and its long train of cars rushing along behind like the body and tail of a gigantic dragon— . . . and all darting forward at the rate of twenty miles an hour. Whew!"

—George Templeton Strong, from *The Diary of George Templeton Strong*

Riding on the early trains was often an adventure, but it could also be quite dangerous. Engineers trying to stay on time sometimes traveled too fast. English citizen Charles Richard Weld was on a railroad car that flew off the tracks. To his amazement, the other passengers did not complain about the accident. Instead, they praised the engineer for trying to keep on schedule!

Passengers accepted such risks because the railroads reduced travel time dramatically. The development of the railroads changed people's perceptions of distance. What was once considered to be a long distance to travel suddenly became just a short train ride away. Railroads also helped tie communities together. In 1847 Senator Daniel Webster spoke for many people in the United States when he declared that the railroad "towers above all other inventions of this or the preceding age."

Reading Check
Make Inferences
In what ways did railroads affect the economy of the United States?

Transportation Revolution Brings Changes

The Transportation Revolution brought many changes to America. Steamboats and railroads made getting goods to distant markets much easier and less costly. People in all areas of the nation now had access to products made and grown far away. More than ever before, there was a national economy. The wealth, however, was centered in the North.

Railroads contributed to the expansion of the borders of the nation and guided population growth. Towns sprang up at railroad junctions as people migrated from rural areas. Those towns that did not have railroads nearby suffered and began to decline. Cities grew as trains brought new residents and raw materials for industry and construction. By linking previously isolated cities, towns, and settlements, the railroads promoted trade and interdependence. The growing prosperity of the nation, especially in the North, encouraged Americans to take pride in their country.

A New Fuel The Transportation Revolution also increased the use of certain natural resources that had not been important until then. Throughout the early Transportation Revolution, wood was the primary source of fuel for trains and steamboats, as well as for cooking, light, and heat. As faster locomotives were built, new power resources were used to fuel them. Coal replaced wood as the main source of power. A half ton of coal produced as much energy as two tons of wood but at half the cost. Coal also became popular for heating homes. Railroads transported the coal from mines to towns and cities.

As the demand for coal increased, a coal-mining industry developed in many states, including Pennsylvania, western Virginia, and Illinois. Coal mining changed the landscape in a number of ways. New towns, such as

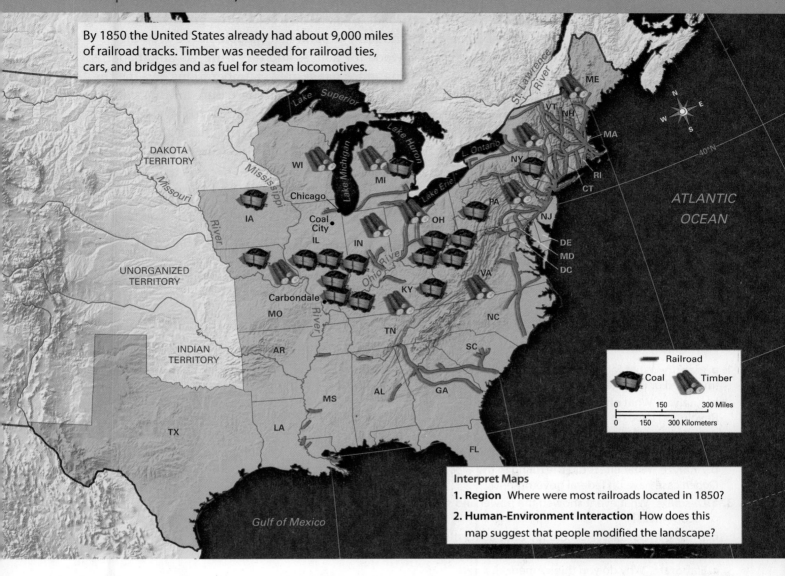

Transportation Routes, 1850

▶ Explore ONLINE!

By 1850 the United States already had about 9,000 miles of railroad tracks. Timber was needed for railroad ties, cars, and bridges and as fuel for steam locomotives.

DAKOTA TERRITORY

WI

MI

Chicago

Coal City

IA

IL

IN

UNORGANIZED TERRITORY

Carbondale

MO

INDIAN TERRITORY

AR

TX

LA

MS

AL

GA

FL

Gulf of Mexico

Lake Superior

Lake Michigan

Lake Huron

Mississippi River

Missouri River

Ohio River

St. Lawrence River

L. Ontario

Lake Erie

ME

VT

NH

MA

NY

RI

CT

PA

NJ

OH

DE

MD

DC

VA

KY

TN

NC

SC

ATLANTIC OCEAN

40°N

Legend
- Railroad
- Coal
- Timber

0   150   300 Miles
0   150   300 Kilometers

Interpret Maps

1. **Region** Where were most railroads located in 1850?

2. **Human-Environment Interaction** How does this map suggest that people modified the landscape?

Coal City and Carbondale in Illinois, sprang up in places where coal deposits could be mined. Miners made deep gashes in the earth removing the coal.

Later, in the 1870s, the demand for coal increased as the demand for steel grew. Many steel mills were built where there was an abundance of coal and iron ore. Steel is made through a smelting process—heating iron ore to very high temperatures. Coal was used to fire the furnaces. Steel, which is much stronger than iron, was increasingly used to build factories and the machines they produced.

Cooperation among the steel and railroad industries helped the economy grow. Steel was used to make the rails that trains ride on and the growing market for steel helped fuel the need for more railroads. Railroads transported steel to places where new factories were being built. Railroads also brought new steel farming tools and machines to farmers in the Midwest. Using the new equipment, farmers produced more crops. Railroads then transported their harvests to markets.

Effects of Railroads The development of railroads helped establish new markets and offered more opportunities for entrepreneurs to start their own businesses. The railroads also played a role in the growth of existing businesses. The logging industry expanded as people in the growing towns and cities needed wood for houses and furniture. As newspaper publishing increased, demand for paper grew. Lumber items became the primary product of New England. Sometimes there were unintended environmental consequences. Settlers spreading out across the Midwest cut down trees and plowed up prairies to make farmland. Deforestation, or cutting down and removing trees, took place on a large scale.

Railroads also caused cities to grow. Some cities became transportation hubs. Chicago was one such city. Its location on Lake Michigan made it an ideal transportation hub, linking the Midwest to the East and South.

Summary and Preview The Transportation Revolution changed the way business was done. In the next lesson you will learn about more technological advances.

Reading Check
Analyze Information
What role did railroads play in the growth of the coal industry?

Lesson 3 Assessment

Review Ideas, Terms, and People

1. **a.** Identify What forms of transportation were improved or invented at this time?
   b. Analyze What effect did the Transportation Revolution have on the United States?

2. **a.** Describe What were the benefits of steamboat travel?
   b. Analyze What effect did the ruling in the *Gibbons* v. *Ogden* case have on federal government?

3. **a.** Describe What event showed the power and speed of locomotives?
   b. Draw Conclusions How did railroads affect trade and business in the United States?
   c. Elaborate Why do you think Americans were fascinated by railroads?

4. **a.** Describe What physical obstacles did railroad construction in the United States face?
   b. Analyze What effects did the Transportation Revolution have on the U.S. economy?
   c. Identify What kind of changes did humans make to the environment during the Transportation Revolution?

Critical Thinking

5. **Identify Effects** In this lesson you learned about the steamboat and the locomotive. Create a chart similar to the one below and use it to show how they affected business, travel, and communication in the United States.

More Technological Advances

The Big Idea

Advances in technology led to new inventions that continued to change daily life and work.

Main Ideas

- The telegraph made swift communication possible from coast to coast.

- With the shift to steam power, businesses built new factories closer to cities and transportation centers.

- Improved farm equipment and other labor-saving devices made life easier for many Americans.

- New inventions changed lives in American homes.

Key Terms and People

Samuel F. B. Morse
telegraph
Morse code
John Deere
Cyrus McCormick
Isaac Singer

If YOU were there . . .

You own a small shop in Chicago, Illinois, in the 1850s. You sell ladies' hats and gowns. When you need more hats, you send a letter to the manufacturer in New York. Sometimes it takes weeks for the letter to get there. One day, the owner of the shop next door tells you about a wonderful new machine. It can send orders from Chicago to New York in just minutes!

How would a machine like this change your business?

Telegraph Speeds Communication

In 1832 **Samuel F. B. Morse** perfected the **telegraph**—a device that could send information over wires across great distances. To develop the telegraph, Morse studied electricity and magnetism. In time, Morse put the work of other scientists together in a practical machine.

The telegraph sent pulses, or surges, of electric current through a wire. The telegraph operator tapped a bar, called a telegraph key, that controlled the length of each pulse. At the other end of the wire, these pulses were changed into clicking sounds. A short click was called a dot. A long click was called a dash. Morse's partner, Alfred Lewis Vail, developed a system known as **Morse code**—different combinations of dots and dashes that represent each letter of the alphabet. For example, *dot dot dot, dash dash dash, dot dot dot* is the distress signal called SOS. Skilled telegraph operators could send and receive many words per minute.

Several years passed before Morse was able to connect two locations with telegraph wires. Despite that achievement, people doubted his machine. Some people did not think that he was reading messages sent from miles away. They claimed that he was making lucky guesses.

Morse's break came during the 1844 Democratic National Convention in Baltimore, Maryland. A telegraph wired news of the presidential candidate's nomination to politicians

Samuel F. B. Morse 1791–1872

Like steamboat creator Robert Fulton, Samuel F. B. Morse began his career as a painter rather than as an inventor. In 1832 Morse was a widower struggling to raise his three children alone. He became interested in the idea of sending messages electrically. Morse hoped he could invent a device that would earn him enough money to support his family. Eventually, earnings from the telegraph made Morse extremely wealthy.

Draw Conclusions
What motivated Morse to invent the telegraph?

in Washington. The waiting politicians responded, "Three cheers for the telegraph!" Telegraphs were soon sending and receiving information for businesses, the government, and newspapers. This new tool helped businesses become more efficient by speeding up their communication. Private citizens also began using the telegraph to communicate socially.

The telegraph grew with the railroad. Telegraph companies strung their wires on poles along railroads across the country. They established telegraph offices in many train stations. Thousands of miles of telegraph line were added every year in the 1850s. The first transcontinental line was finished in 1861. By the time he died in 1872, Morse was famous across the United States.

Steam Power and New Factories

At the start of the Industrial Revolution, most factories ran on water-power. In time, however, factory owners began using steam power. This shift brought major changes to the nation's industries. Water-powered factories had to be built near streams or waterfalls. In contrast, steam power allowed business owners to build factories almost anywhere. Yet the Northeast was still home to most of the nation's industries. By 1860 New England alone had as many factories as the entire South did.

Some companies decided to build their factories closer to cities and transportation centers. This provided easier access to workers, allowing businesses to lower wages. Being closer to cities also reduced shipping costs. Cities soon became the center of industrial growth. People from rural areas as well as foreign countries flocked to the cities for factory jobs.

Factory workers improved the designs of many kinds of machines. Mechanics invented tools that could cut and shape metal, stone, and wood with great precision. By the 1840s this new machinery was able to produce interchangeable parts. Within a short period of time, the growing machine-tool industry was even making customized equipment.

Reading Check
Identify Cause and Effect
What event led to the widespread use of the telegraph, and what effect did the telegraph have on cross-country communications?

Reading Check
Find Main Ideas
What changes resulted from the shift to steam power?

Timeline: American Inventions

1830

1855

1831
Cyrus McCormick invents the mechanical reaper and harvesting grain becomes much more efficient.

1832 ∨
Samuel Morse invents the telegraph making long-distance communication almost instantaneous.

1837 ∧
John Deere invents the steel plow that makes plowing the tough prairie soil easier.

1849
Walter Hunt invents the safety pin.

1851
Isaac Singer improves the sewing machine. The production and repair of clothing becomes much easier.

Improved Farm Equipment

During the 1830s technology began transforming the farm as well as the factory. In 1837 blacksmith **John Deere** saw that friends in Illinois had difficulty plowing thick soil with iron plows. He thought a steel blade might work better. His design for a steel plow was a success. By 1846 Deere was selling 1,000 plows per year.

In 1831 **Cyrus McCormick** developed a new harvesting machine, the mechanical reaper, which quickly and efficiently cut down wheat. He began mass-producing his reapers in a Chicago factory. McCormick used new methods to encourage sales. His company advertised, gave demonstrations, and provided a repair and spare parts department. He also let customers buy on credit.

The combination of Deere's plow and McCormick's reaper allowed Midwestern farmers to plant and harvest huge crop fields. By 1860 U.S. farmers were producing more than 170 million bushels of wheat and more than 800 million bushels of corn per year.

Improvements in farming technology made farming more efficient, but it also meant fewer laborers were needed to work the land. As a result, many people moved from rural areas to cities to find work.

Changing Life at Home

Many inventions of the Industrial Revolution simply made life easier. When Alexis de Tocqueville of France visited the United States in the early 1830s, he identified what he called a very American quality.

> "[Americans want] to be always making life more comfortable and convenient, to avoid trouble, and to satisfy the smallest wants [desires] without effort and almost without cost."
>
> —Alexis de Tocqueville, from *Democracy in America*

Reading Check
Summarize
What marketing methods did McCormick use to help sell his farm equipment?

The sewing machine was one of these conveniences. It was first invented by Elias Howe, a factory apprentice in Lowell, Massachusetts. **Isaac Singer** then made improvements to Howe's design. Like McCormick, Singer allowed customers to buy his machines on credit and provided a repair service. By 1860 Singer's company was the world's largest maker of sewing machines.

Other advances improved on everyday items. In the 1830s iceboxes cooled by large blocks of ice became available. Iceboxes stored fresh food safely for longer periods. Iron cookstoves began replacing cooking fires and stone hearths.

Companies also began to mass-produce earlier inventions. This allowed many families to buy household items, such as clocks, that they could not afford in the past. For example, a clock that cost $50 in 1800 was selling for only $1.50 by the 1850s. Additional useful items created during this period include matches, introduced in the 1830s, and the safety pin, invented in 1849. All of these inventions helped make life at home more convenient for an increasing number of Americans.

Reading Check
Analyze How did labor-saving inventions affect daily life?

Summary and Preview New machines and inventions changed the way Americans lived and did business in the early 1800s. A market economy developed as people began to buy and sell goods rather than making goods for their own use. In the next module you will learn how agricultural changes affected the South.

Lesson 4 Assessment

Review Ideas, Terms, and People

1. a. Describe How did the telegraph work?

   b. Predict What impact might the telegraph have on the future of the United States?

2. a. Describe How did water-powered factories differ from steam-powered factories?

   b. Explain How did the shift to steam power lead to the growth of cities?

3. a. Identify What contributions did John Deere and Cyrus McCormick make to farming?

   b. Analyze What effect did new inventions have on agriculture in the United States?

4. a. Identify What inventions improved life at home?

   b. Evaluate Which invention do you think had the greatest effect on the daily lives of Americans? Why?

Critical Thinking

5. Support a Point of View In this lesson you learned about more technological advances and their effects. Create a table like the one below that shows the three advances you think are most important and why.

Most Important	Why

Social Studies Skills

Personal Conviction and Bias

Define the Skill

Everyone has *convictions*, or firmly held beliefs. However, when we let our beliefs automatically slant or shape our point of view on topics, we may be showing bias. *Bias* is a fixed idea or opinion about someone or something. Some bias is based on a set of ideas about a group to which the person or thing belongs. This type of bias is called a *stereotype*. If the group is defined by race, religion, age, gender, or similar characteristics, the bias is known as *prejudice*.

Bias, stereotypes, and prejudice are not always negative in nature. They include favorable opinions, too. For example, the belief that a student is good at math because that person is male is a bias that shows both stereotyping and prejudice.

We should always be on guard for the presence of personal bias. Eliminating stereotyping and prejudice is particularly important. However, even "good" biases can slant how we view, judge, and communicate information. Honest and accurate communication requires that the information and ideas we express be as free of bias as possible.

Learn the Skill

Not all beliefs are biases, even if those beliefs are strongly held. Biases are beliefs that have little or no evidence to support them. The more unreasonable a person's view is in light of facts and evidence, the more likely it is that the belief is a bias.

Another characteristic of bias is the person's reluctance to question his or her belief if it is challenged by evidence. Sometimes people stubbornly cling to views that overwhelming evidence proves wrong. This is why bias is defined as a "fixed" idea or opinion. One of the most damaging effects of bias, and a good reason for trying to avoid it, is that it can prevent us from learning new things.

The following precautions can help you reduce the amount of bias you express.

1. When discussing a topic, keep in mind beliefs and experiences in your own background that might affect how you feel about the topic.

2. Try to not mix statements of fact with statements of opinion. Clearly separate and indicate what you *know* to be true from what you *believe* to be true.

3. Avoid using emotional, positive, or negative words when communicating factual information.

Practice the Skill

In 1834 Tennessee congressman Davy Crockett visited the textile mills at Lowell, Massachusetts. Read his account of the "Lowell girls" who worked in the factory and complete the activity below.

"Here are thousands [of young women], useful to others, . . . with the prospect before them of future comfort and respectability. . . . There are more than five thousand females employed in Lowell; and when you come to see the amount of labour performed by them, in superintending [operating] the different machinery, you will be astonished."

Suppose that you were a "Lowell girl" who has just read this account of Crockett's visit. Write a letter to the editor of the *Lowell Offering* reacting to the biases and stereotypes about women that Crockett shows in his account.

Module 13 Assessment

Review Vocabulary, Terms, and People

Complete each sentence below by filling in the blank with the correct term or person from the module.

1. The system of _____ was developed to represent letters of the alphabet when sending telegraph messages.

2. The first American woman to hold a high-ranking position in the labor movement was _____.

3. The _____ was a period of rapid growth in the use of machines and manufacturing.

4. The first locomotive in the United States was built by _____.

5. Workers would sometimes go on _____ to force factory owners to meet their demands for better pay and working conditions.

6. The _____ industry, which produced cloth items, was the first to use machines for manufacturing.

Comprehension and Critical Thinking

Lesson 1

7. a. Identify What ideas did Eli Whitney want to apply to the manufacture of guns?

    b. Analyze How did the War of 1812 lead to a boom in manufacturing in the United States?

    c. Elaborate Why do you think the Industrial Revolution began in Great Britain rather than in the United States?

Lesson 2

8. a. Describe What was mill life like?

    b. Draw Conclusions How did the Rhode Island system and the Lowell system change the lives of American workers?

    c. Evaluate Were reformers such as Sarah G. Bagley effective in improving labor conditions? Why?

Lesson 3

9. a. Describe How were Americans affected by the introduction of steamboats?

    b. Make Inferences How did railroad companies become some of the most powerful businesses in the country?

    c. Elaborate What was the most important result of the Transportation Revolution? Why?

Lesson 4

10. a. Recall What important change took place in how factories were powered?

    b. Draw Conclusions How did the telegraph affect communication in the United States?

    c. Evaluate Do you think moving factories close to cities helped or hurt working life? Explain.

Module 13 Assessment, continued

Review Themes

11. **Science and Technology** What are the three most important inventions of the Industrial Revolution? Why?

12. **Economics** What was the overall effect of the Industrial Revolution on the U.S. economy?

Reading Skills

Understand Causes and Effects in History *Use the Reading Skills taught in this module to answer the question about the reading selection below.*

> Many young women came to Lowell from different parts of New England. They wanted the chance to earn money instead of working on the family farm.

13. According to the passage above, what was a cause for moving to Lowell?
    - a. working long hours
    - b. earning money
    - c. meeting people
    - d. working on a farm

Social Studies Skills

Personal Conviction and Bias *Use the Social Studies Skills taught in this module to answer the question about the reading selection below.*

> "Is anyone such a fool as to suppose that out of six thousand factory girls in Lowell, sixty would be there if they could help it?"
>
> —Sarah G. Bagley, quoted in *Voice of Industry*, September 18, 1845

14. Do you think that Bagley's opposition to the Lowell system was unfairly biased? Why or why not?

Focus on Writing

15. **Write a Newspaper Advertisement** Review the inventions discussed in the module. Choose one invention for which you will create an advertisement. Then answer these questions to help you plan your advertisement: Who is your audience? Who will buy this invention? How will the invention benefit this audience? What words or phrases will best persuade this audience? Once you have answered these questions, design your advertisement. To draw readers' attention to your ad, include an illustration, a catchy heading, and a few lines of text.

Module 14

The South

★

Essential Question

How important was slavery for the economy and society of the South?

About the Photo: Slaves processing sugarcane on a Georgia plantation

In this module you will learn how the South developed an agricultural economy and how that economy was dependent on the labor of enslaved people. You will also read about the role of slavery in Southern society.

What You Will Learn ...

Timeline of Events 1790–1860

▶ *Explore ONLINE!*

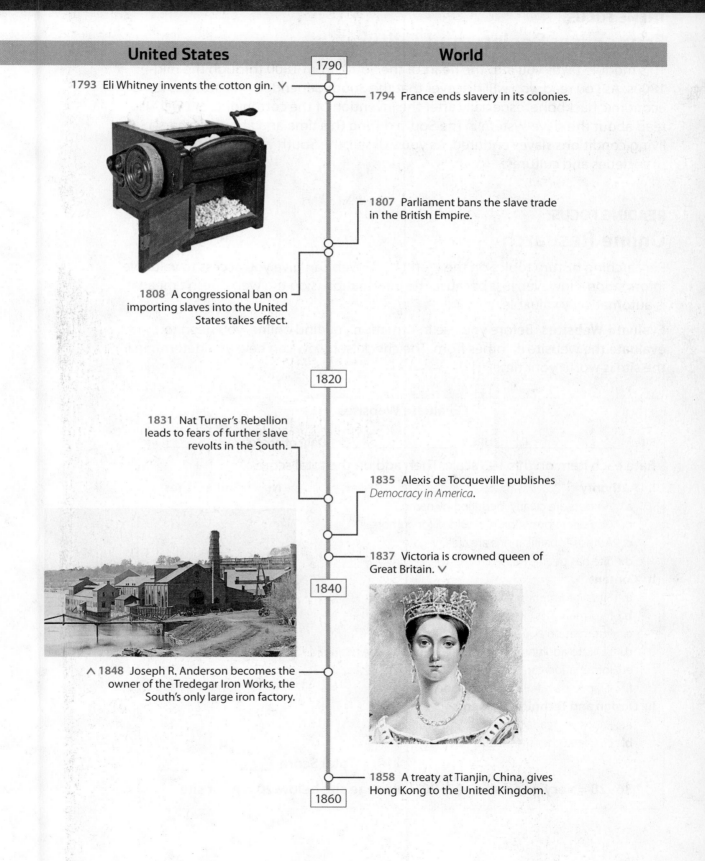

United States	World

1790

1793 Eli Whitney invents the cotton gin. ∨

1794 France ends slavery in its colonies.

1807 Parliament bans the slave trade in the British Empire.

1808 A congressional ban on importing slaves into the United States takes effect.

1820

1831 Nat Turner's Rebellion leads to fears of further slave revolts in the South.

1835 Alexis de Tocqueville publishes *Democracy in America*.

1837 Victoria is crowned queen of Great Britain. ∨

1840

∧ **1848** Joseph R. Anderson becomes the owner of the Tredegar Iron Works, the South's only large iron factory.

1858 A treaty at Tianjin, China, gives Hong Kong to the United Kingdom.

1860

Reading Social Studies

THEME FOCUS:

Economics, Society and Culture

This module takes you into the heart of the South from 1800 through the mid-1800s. As you read, you will discover that the South depended on cotton as its economic backbone, especially after the invention of the cotton gin. You will also read about the slave system in the South during this time and about the harsh living conditions slaves endured. As you will see, the South was home to a variety of societies and cultures.

READING FOCUS:

Online Research

Researching history topics on the World Wide Web can give you access to valuable information. However, just because the information is on the web doesn't mean it is automatically valuable.

Evaluate Websites Before you use information you find online, you need to evaluate the website it comes from. The checklist below can help you determine if the site is worth your time.

Evaluate Websites

Site: _____ URL: _____ Date of access: _____

Rate each item on this 1–3 scale. Then add up the total score.

	No	Some	Yes
I. Authority			
a. Authors are clearly identified by name.	1	2	3
b. Contact information is provided for authors.	1	2	3
c. Authors' qualifications are clearly stated.	1	2	3
d. Site has been updated recently.	1	2	3
II. Content			
a. Site's information is useful to your project.	1	2	3
b. Information is clear and well organized.	1	2	3
c. Information appears to be at the right level.	1	2	3
d. Links to additional important information are provided.	1	2	3
e. Information can be verified in other sources.	1	2	3
f. Graphics are helpful, not just decorative.	1	2	3
III. Design and Technical Elements			
a. Pages are readable and easy to navigate.	1	2	3
b. Links to other sites work.	1	2	3

Total Score _____

36–28 = very good site   27–20 = average site below 20 = poor site

---

You Try It!

Key Terms and People

Lesson 1
cotton gin
planters
cotton belt
factors
Tredegar Iron Works
Lesson 2
yeomen
Lesson 3
overseers
spirituals
oral tradition
folktales
Nat Turner

The passage below is from the module you are about to read.

Cotton Becomes Profitable Cotton had been grown in the New World for centuries, but it had not been a very profitable crop. Before cotton could be spun into thread for weaving into cloth, the seeds had to be removed from the cotton fibers.

Long-staple cotton, also called black-seed cotton, was fairly easy to process. Workers could pick the seeds from the cotton with relative ease. But long-staple cotton grew well in only a few places in the South. More common was short-staple cotton, which was also known as green-seed cotton. Removing the seeds from this cotton was difficult and time consuming. A worker could spend an entire day picking the seeds from a single pound of short-staple cotton.

After you read the passage, complete the following activity.

Suppose that after reading this passage you decide to do some research on cotton growing. You use a search engine that directs you to a website. At that site, you find the information described below. Using the evaluation criteria listed on the previous page, decide if this is a site you would recommend to others.

a. The authors of the site are listed as "Bob and Mack, good friends who enjoy working together."

b. The site was last updated on "the last time we got together."

c. The title of the site is "Cotton Pickin'." There are few headings.

d. This ten-page site includes nine pages about the authors' childhood on a cotton farm. No illustrations are included.

e. Pages are very long, but they load quickly, as there are no graphics. There is one link to a site selling cotton clothing.

As you read Module 14, think about what topics would be interesting to research on the web. If you do some research on the web, remember to use the evaluation list to analyze websites.

Growth of the Cotton Industry

The Big Idea

The invention of the cotton gin made the South a one-crop economy and increased the need for slave labor.

Main Ideas

- The invention of the cotton gin revived the economy of the South.

- The cotton gin created a cotton boom in which farmers grew little else.

- Some people encouraged southerners to focus on other crops and industries.

Key Terms and People

cotton gin
planters
cotton belt
factors
Tredegar Iron Works

If YOU were there . . .

You are a field-worker on a cotton farm in the South in about 1800. Your job is to separate the seeds from the cotton fibers. It is dull, tiring work because the tiny seeds are tangled in the fibers. Sometimes it takes you a whole day just to clean one pound of cotton! Now you hear that someone has invented a machine that can clean cotton 50 times faster than by hand.

How might this machine change your life?

Reviving the South's Economy

Sectional differences had always existed between different regions of the United States. The geographic features of each region contributed to the development of differing economic activities. Revolutionary changes in industry and transportation deepened the differences between North and South. While the North began to focus on industrialization, the South remained mainly agricultural.

Before the American Revolution, three crops dominated southern agriculture—tobacco, rice, and indigo. These crops played a central role in the southern economy and culture. They were produced mostly by enslaved African Americans.

After the American Revolution, however, prices for tobacco, rice, and indigo dropped. When crop prices fell, the demand for and the price of slaves also went down. In an effort to protect their incomes, many farmers tried, with little success, to grow other crops that needed less labor. Soon, however, cotton would transform the southern economy and greatly increase the demand for slave labor.

Cotton Becomes Profitable Cotton had been grown in the New World for centuries, but it had not been a very profitable crop. Before cotton could be spun into thread for weaving into cloth, the seeds had to be removed from the cotton fibers.

Cotton Gin

Connect to Science and Technology Eli Whitney's cotton gin enabled workers to easily remove seeds from cotton fibers. The result was a dramatic increase in cotton production in the South.

How did the cotton gin remove seeds from cotton fibers?

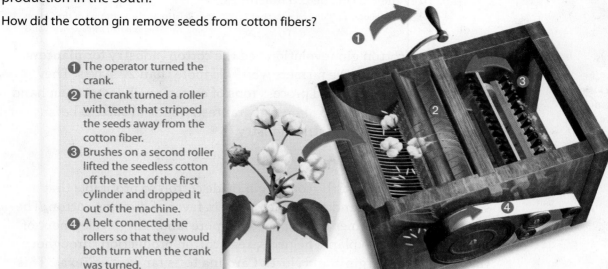

1 The operator turned the crank.

2 The crank turned a roller with teeth that stripped the seeds away from the cotton fiber.

3 Brushes on a second roller lifted the seedless cotton off the teeth of the first cylinder and dropped it out of the machine.

4 A belt connected the rollers so that they would both turn when the crank was turned.

Long-staple cotton, also called black-seed cotton, was fairly easy to process. Workers could pick the seeds from the cotton with relative ease. But long-staple cotton grew well in only a few places in the South. More common was short-staple cotton, which was also known as green-seed cotton. Removing the seeds from this cotton was difficult and time consuming. A worker could spend an entire day picking the seeds from a single pound of short-staple cotton.

By the early 1790s the demand for American cotton began increasing rapidly. For instance, in Great Britain, new textile factories needed raw cotton that could be used for making cloth. American cotton producers could not keep up with the high demand for their cotton. These producers of cotton needed a machine that could remove the seeds from the cotton more rapidly.

Eli Whitney's Cotton Gin Northerner Eli Whitney finally patented such a machine in 1793. The year before, Whitney had visited a Georgia plantation owned by Catherine Greene. Workers there were using a machine that removed seeds from long-staple cotton. This machine did not work well on short-staple cotton. Greene asked Whitney if he could improve it. By the next spring, Whitney had perfected his design for the **cotton gin**, a machine that removes seeds from short-staple cotton. (*Gin* is short for "engine.") The cotton gin used a hand-cranked cylinder with wire teeth to pull cotton fibers from the seeds.

Whitney hoped to keep the design of the gin a secret, but the machine was very useful. His patent was often ignored by other manufacturers. Whitney described how his invention would improve the cotton business.

> "One man will clean ten times as much cotton as he can in any other way before known and also clean it much better than in the usual mode [method]. This machine may be turned by water or with a horse, with the greatest ease, and one man and a horse will do more than fifty men with the old machines."
>
> —Eli Whitney, quoted in "Correspondence of Eli Whitney Relative to the Invention of the Cotton Gin," *The American Historical Review* Vol. 3

Reading Check
Draw Conclusions
What effects did the cotton gin have on the southern economy?

Whitney's cotton gin revolutionized the cotton industry for **planters**. Planters were large-scale farmers who held more than 20 slaves. They built cotton gins that could process tons of cotton much faster than hand processing. A healthy crop almost guaranteed financial success because of high demand from the textile industry.

The Cotton Boom

Whitney's invention of the cotton gin made cotton so profitable that southern farmers abandoned other crops in favor of growing cotton. The removal of Native Americans opened up more land. The development of new types of cotton plants helped spread cotton production throughout the South from Virginia and North Carolina to as far west as Texas. This area of high cotton production became known as the **cotton belt**.

Production increased rapidly—from about 2 million pounds in 1791 to roughly a billion pounds by 1860. As early as 1840, the United States was producing more than half of the cotton grown in the entire world. The economic boom attracted new settlers and built up wealth among wealthy white southerners. The cotton economy firmly put in place the institution of slavery in the South.

Cotton Belt Cotton had many advantages as a cash crop. It cost little to market. Unlike food staples, harvested cotton could be stored for a long time. Because cotton was lighter than other staple crops, it also cost less to transport long distances.

Farmers eager to profit from growing cotton headed west to find land. Farmers also began to apply scientific methods to improve crop production. Cotton had one disadvantage as a crop—it rapidly used up the nutrients in the soil. After a few years, cotton could make the land useless for growing anything. Some agricultural scientists recommended crop rotation—changing the crop grown on a particular plot of land every few years. Different crops needed different nutrients, so crop rotation would keep the land fertile longer. Other agricultural scientists began to study soil chemistry, in an effort to keep the land rich and productive.

As the cotton belt grew, farmers continued trying to improve the crop. Agricultural scientists worked at crossbreeding short-staple cotton with other varieties. As a result, new stronger types of cotton were soon growing throughout the cotton belt. This led to expansion of the cotton industry through the 1860s.

The cotton boom involved much more than growing and harvesting cotton. Harvested cotton had to be ginned, pressed into bales, and then

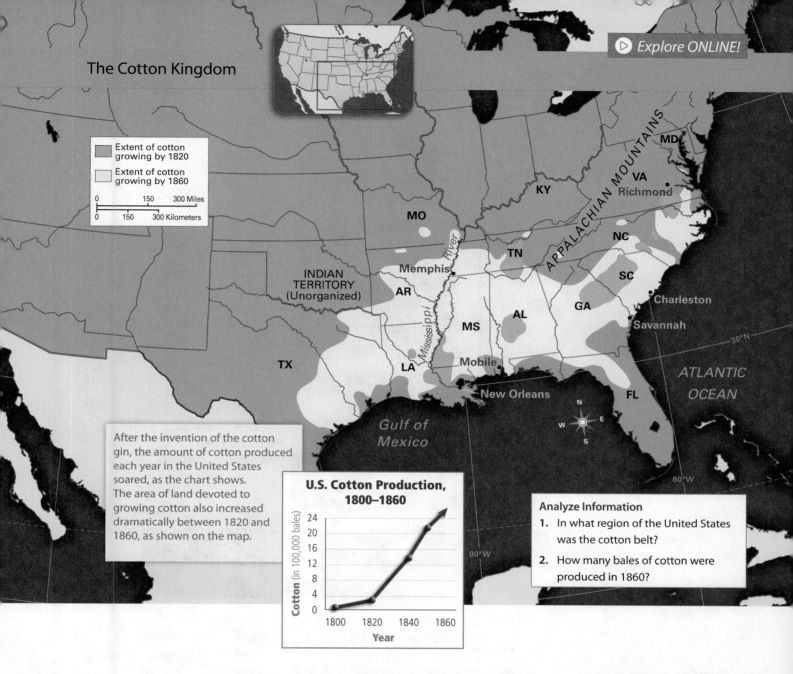

The Cotton Kingdom

Extent of cotton growing by 1820

Extent of cotton growing by 1860

0 150 300 Miles
0 150 300 Kilometers

KY
MO
INDIAN TERRITORY (Unorganized)
Memphis
TN
AR
MS
AL
TX
LA
Mobile
New Orleans
Mississippi River
APPALACHIAN MOUNTAINS
MD
VA
Richmond
NC
SC
GA
Charleston
Savannah
FL
ATLANTIC OCEAN
Gulf of Mexico
30°N
80°W
90°W

N W E S

After the invention of the cotton gin, the amount of cotton produced each year in the United States soared, as the chart shows. The area of land devoted to growing cotton also increased dramatically between 1820 and 1860, as shown on the map.

U.S. Cotton Production, 1800–1860

Cotton (in 100,000 bales)

24
20
16
12
8
4
0

1800 1820 1840 1860
Year

Analyze Information

1. In what region of the United States was the cotton belt?

2. How many bales of cotton were produced in 1860?

shipped to market or to warehouses. Special agents helped do everything. They helped market cotton to customers and also insured crops against loss or damage. Factories were built to produce items needed by cotton farmers, such as ropes to bale cotton.

Growing and harvesting cotton required many field hands. Rather than pay wages to free workers, planters began to use more slave labor. Congress had made bringing slaves into the United States illegal in 1808. However, the growing demand for slaves led to an increase in the slave trade within the United States.

Cotton Trade In an 1858 speech before the U.S. Senate, South Carolina politician James Henry Hammond declared, "Cotton is King!" Without cotton, Hammond claimed, the global economy would fail. He believed that southern cotton was one of the most valuable resources in the world.

The South's Cotton Economy

Eli Whitney's cotton gin began the cotton boom. Soon, the Cotton Kingdom stretched across the South. For the cotton planters to succeed, they had to get their cotton to market.

Enslaved African Americans did most of the planting, harvesting, and processing of cotton.

Cotton was shipped on river steamboats to major ports such as Charleston.

From southern ports, ships carried the cotton to distant textile mills.

A large amount of cotton was sold to textile mills in the northeastern United States.

Textile mills in Great Britain were the largest foreign buyers of southern cotton.

Draw Conclusions
Why do you think cotton was so important to the South's economy?

Southern cotton was used to make cloth in England and the North. Many southerners shared Hammond's viewpoints about cotton. Southerner David Christy declared, "King cotton is a profound [learned] statesman, and knows what measures will best sustain [protect] his throne."

The cotton boom made the South a major player in world trade. Great Britain became the South's most valued foreign trading partner. Southerners also sold tons of cotton to the growing textile industry in the northeastern United States. This increased trade led to the growth of major port cities in the South, including Charleston, South Carolina; Savannah, Georgia; and New Orleans, Louisiana.

In these cities, crop brokers called **factors** managed the cotton trade. Farmers sold their cotton to merchants, who then made deals with the factors. Merchants and factors also arranged loans for farmers who needed to buy supplies. They often advised farmers on how to invest profits. Once farmers got their cotton to the port cities, factors arranged for transportation aboard trading ships.

However, shipping cotton by land to port cities was very difficult in the South. The few major road projects at the time were limited to the Southeast. Most southern farmers had to ship their goods on the region's rivers. On the Ohio and Mississippi rivers, flatboats and steamboats carried cotton and other products to port. Eventually, hundreds of steamboats traveled up and down the mighty Mississippi River each day.

Other Crops and Industries

While industrialization continued to grow in the North, some leaders worried that the South was depending too much on cotton. They wanted southerners to try a variety of cash crops and investments.

Food and Cash Crops One such crop was corn, the **primary** southern food crop. By the late 1830s the top three corn-growing states in the nation were all in the South. The South's other successful food crops included rice, sweet potatoes, wheat, and sugarcane.

Production of tobacco, the South's first major cash crop, was very time consuming. Tobacco leaves had to be cured, or dried, before they could be shipped to market. In 1839 a slave discovered a way to improve the drying process by using heat from burning charcoal. This new, faster curing process increased tobacco production.

Partly as a result of the cotton boom, hemp and flax also became major cash crops. Their fibers were used to make rope and sackcloth. Farmers used the rope and sackcloth to bundle cotton into bales.

Industry Many of the first factories in the South were built to serve farmers' needs by processing crops such as sugarcane. In 1803 the nation's first steam-powered sawmill was built in Donaldsonville, Louisiana. This new technology enabled lumber companies to cut, sort, and clean wood quickly.

By the 1840s entrepreneurs in Georgia began investing in cotton mills. In 1840 there were 14 cotton mills. By the mid-1850s there were more than 50. A few mill owners followed the model established by Francis Cabot Lowell. However, most built small-scale factories on the falls of a river for waterpower. A few steam-powered mills were built in towns without enough waterpower.

Southerners such as Hinton Rowan Helper encouraged industrial growth in the South.

"We should . . . keep pace with the progress of the age. We must expand our energies, and acquire habits of enterprise and industry; we should rouse ourselves from the couch of lassitude [laziness] and inure [set] our minds to thought and our bodies to action."

—Hinton Rowan Helper, *The Impending Crisis of the South: How to Meet It*

Tredegar Iron Works
After Joseph Anderson took over the Tredegar Iron Works in 1848, it became the largest manufacturer of iron products in the South.

Joseph R. Anderson followed Helper's advice. In 1848 Anderson became the owner of the **Tredegar Iron Works** in Richmond, Virginia. It was one of the most productive ironworks in the nation. It was the only factory in the South to produce products such as cannons, steam engines, and bridge materials.

Unlike in the North, however, industry remained a small part of the southern economy. Southern industry faced stiff competition from the North and from England, both of which could produce many goods more cheaply. And as long as agricultural profits remained high, southern investors preferred to invest in land.

Reading Check
Make Inferences
Why were there fewer industries in the South?

Summary and Preview You have read about how southern farmers worked to improve farming methods. In the next lesson you will read about the structure of southern society.

Lesson 1 Assessment

Review Ideas, Terms, and People

1. **a. Describe** How did the cotton gin make processing cotton easier?

   b. Draw Conclusions Why had slavery been on the decline before the invention of the cotton gin? How did slavery change as a result of the cotton gin?

   c. Predict How might the rise of cotton production and slavery affect southern society?

2. **a. Identify** What areas of the United States made up the cotton belt?

   b. Evaluate Do you think the South should have paid more attention to its industrial growth? Why?

3. **a. Describe** What other crops and industries were encouraged in the South?

   b. Make Inferences Why were some southern leaders worried about the South's reliance on cotton?

Critical Thinking

4. **Identify Cause and Effect** In this lesson you learned about the causes of the cotton boom. Create a graphic organizer similar to the one below and add to it to identify the effects of the cotton boom on the South.

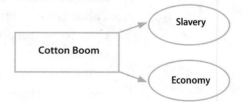

★ Southern Society

The Big Idea

Southern society centered around agriculture.

Main Ideas

- Southern society and culture consisted of four main groups.
- Free African Americans in the South faced a great deal of discrimination.

Key Terms and People

yeomen

If YOU were there . . .

Your family owns a small farm in Georgia in the 1840s. Sometimes you work in the fields, but more often you tend the vegetable garden and peach orchard. Since you have no close neighbors, you look forward to Sundays. Going to church gives you a chance to socialize with other young people. Sometimes you wonder what it would be like to live in a city like Savannah.

How would life be different if you left the farm for the city?

Southern Society and Culture

Although the South had some industry, the economy was not primarily industrial as it was in the North. Agriculture was the heart of the southern economy, and cotton was king.

Popular fiction often made it seem that all white southerners had many slaves and lived on large plantations. Many fiction writers wrote about wealthy southern families who had frequent, grand parties. The ideal image of the Antebellum (before the war) South included hospitality and well-treated slaves on beautiful plantations that almost ran themselves.

This romantic view was far from the reality. During the first half of the 1800s, only about one-third of white southern families had slaves. Fewer families had plantations. Despite their small numbers, these planters had a powerful influence over the South. Many served as political leaders. They led a society made up of many different kinds of people, including yeoman farmers, poor whites, slaves, and free African Americans. Each of these segments of society contributed to the economic success of the South.

Planters As the wealthiest members of southern society, planters also greatly influenced the economy. Some showed off their wealth by living in beautiful mansions. Many others chose to live more simply. A visitor described wealthy planter

Alexander Stephens's estate as "an old wooden house" surrounded by weeds. Some planters saved all of their money to buy more land and slaves.

Male planters were primarily concerned with raising crops and supervising slave laborers. They left the running of the plantation household to their wives. The planter's wife oversaw the raising of the children and supervised the work of all slaves within the household. Slave women typically cooked, cleaned, and helped care for the planter's children. Wives also took on the important social duties of the family. For example, many southern leaders discussed political issues at the dances and dinners hosted by their wives.

Planters often arranged their children's marriages based on business interests. Lucy Breckinridge, the daughter of a wealthy Virginia planter, was married by arrangement in 1865. Three years earlier, she had described in her journal how she dreaded the very thought of marriage. "A woman's life after she is married, unless there is an immense amount of love, is nothing but suffering and hard work." How Breckinridge's life in her own arranged marriage would have turned out cannot be known. She died of typhoid fever just months after her wedding.

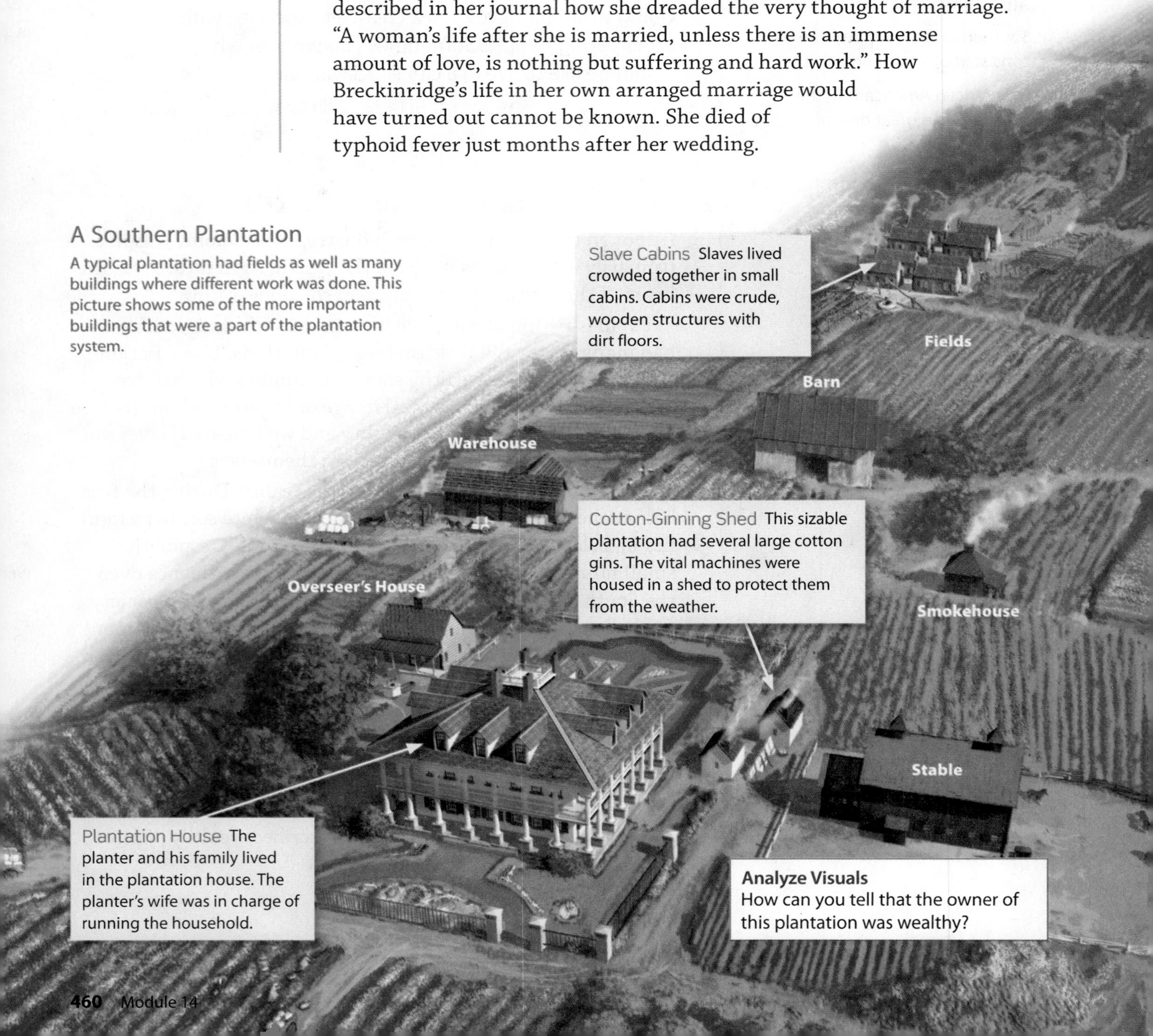

A Southern Plantation

A typical plantation had fields as well as many buildings where different work was done. This picture shows some of the more important buildings that were a part of the plantation system.

Slave Cabins Slaves lived crowded together in small cabins. Cabins were crude, wooden structures with dirt floors.

Fields

Barn

Warehouse

Cotton-Ginning Shed This sizable plantation had several large cotton gins. The vital machines were housed in a shed to protect them from the weather.

Overseer's House

Smokehouse

Stable

Plantation House The planter and his family lived in the plantation house. The planter's wife was in charge of running the household.

Analyze Visuals
How can you tell that the owner of this plantation was wealthy?

Yeomen and Poor Whites Most white southerners were **yeomen**, owners of small farms. Yeomen owned few slaves or none at all. The typical farm averaged 100 acres. Yeomen took great pride in their work. In 1849 a young Georgia man wrote, "I desire above all things to be a 'Farmer.' It is the most honest, upright, and sure way of securing all the comforts of life."

Yeoman families, including women and children, typically worked long days at a variety of tasks. Some yeomen held a few slaves but worked alongside them.

The poorest of white southerners lived on land that could not grow cash crops. They survived by hunting, fishing, raising small gardens, and doing odd jobs for money.

Religion and Society Most white southerners shared similar religious beliefs. Because of the long distances between farms, families often saw their neighbors only at church events, such as revivals or socials. Rural women often played volunteer roles in their churches. Wealthy white southerners thought that their religion justified their position in society and the institution of slavery. They argued that God created some people, like themselves, to rule others. This belief opposed many northern Christians' belief that God was against slavery.

Urban Life Many of the largest and most important cities in the South were strung along the Atlantic coast and had begun as shipping centers. Although fewer in number, the southern cities were similar to northern cities. City governments built public water systems and provided well-maintained streets. Public education was available in a few places. Wealthy residents occasionally gave large sums of money to charities, such as orphanages and public libraries. Southern urban leaders wanted their cities to appear as modern as possible.

Reading Check
Summarize
What different groups made up southern society?

As on plantations, slaves did much of the work in southern cities. Slaves worked as domestic servants, in mills, in shipyards, and at skilled jobs. Many business leaders held slaves or hired them from nearby plantations.

Free African Americans and Discrimination

Although the vast majority of African Americans in the South were enslaved, more than 250,000 free African Americans lived in the region by 1860. Some were descendants of slaves who were freed after the American Revolution. Others were descendants of refugees from the Haitian Revolution led by Toussaint Louverture in the late 1790s. Still others were former slaves who had run away, been freed by their slaveholder, or earned enough money to buy their freedom.

Free African Americans lived in both rural and urban areas. Most lived in the countryside and worked as paid laborers on plantations or farms. Free African Americans in cities often worked a variety of jobs, mostly as skilled artisans. Some, like barber William Johnson of Natchez, Mississippi, became quite successful in their businesses. Frequently, free African Americans, especially those in the cities, formed social and economic ties with one another. Churches often served as the center of their social lives.

Free African Americans in the South

In 1860 about 1 out of 50 African Americans in the South was free. Many worked in skilled trades, like this barber in Richmond, Virginia. In Charleston, South Carolina, a system of badges was set up to distinguish between free African Americans and slaves.

How would the work of the free African American in this picture be different from that of slaves in the South?

Free African Americans faced constant discrimination from white southerners. Many governments passed laws limiting the rights of free African Americans. Most free African Americans could not vote, travel freely, or hold certain jobs. In some places, free African Americans had to have a white person represent them in any business transaction. In others, laws restricted where they were allowed to live or conduct business.

Many white southerners argued that free African Americans did not have the ability to take care of themselves. Southerners used this belief to justify the institution of slavery. "The status of slavery is the only one for which the African is adapted," wrote one white Mississippian. To many white southerners, the very existence of free African Americans threatened the institution of slavery.

Reading Check
Find Main Ideas What challenges did free African Americans face in the South?

Summary and Preview Southern society was led by rich planters but included groups of small farmers, slaves, and free African Americans as well. These groups each had their own culture. In the next lesson you will read about life under slavery.

Lesson 2 Assessment

Review Ideas, Terms, and People

1. a. **Identify** What was the largest social group in the South? How did its members make a living?

   b. **Compare** In what ways were southern cities similar to northern cities?

   c. **Elaborate** Which southern social class do you think had the most difficult life? Why?

2. a. **Describe** What jobs were available to free African Americans in the South? Why were these jobs the only ones available?

   b. **Analyze** Why did many white southerners fear free African Americans?

   c. **Elaborate** Why do you think that discrimination against free African Americans was harsher in the South than in the North?

Critical Thinking

3. **Compare and Contrast** In this lesson you learned about the different groups of people who lived in the South. Create a graphic organizer similar to the one below to identify the similarities and differences of the lives of planters, yeomen, and free African Americans.

	Similarities	Differences
Planters		
Free African Americans		
Yeomen		

Slavery in the South

The Big Idea

Enslaved people faced cruel treatment and difficult lives, which led them to resist the slave system and sometimes rebel.

Main Ideas

- Slaves faced harsh living conditions in the South.

- A common African American culture developed in the South, which helped slaves to survive the cruelties of slavery.

- Slave rebellions drew a harsh response from white southerners.

Key Terms and People

overseers
spirituals
oral tradition
folktales
Nat Turner

If YOU were there . . .

You are an enslaved person living on a large cotton plantation in the South in the 1850s. You work in the hot sun all day long picking cotton. After working in the fields, your body aches from bending over, your hands hurt from picking the cotton, and you're hungry from having little to eat. To take your mind off of your harsh life and to bring you comfort, you make up stories and poems. Your family and friends love to gather round to hear you tell these stories.

What is a story you think you would tell?

Living Under Slavery

Eli Whitney's cotton gin made cotton growing very profitable. Soon, cotton farming spread across the South. Since it required a lot of labor to grow cotton, the need for enslaved people grew as the number of cotton farms increased. By the mid-1800s, enslaved African Americans accounted for about one-third of the population of the South.

Differences existed in the lives of enslaved people. Where they lived, the work they did, and how they were treated all affected their day-to-day lives.

Enslaved African American house servants often cared for the children of slaveholders.

Working Life Work was the dominant feature of the lives of enslaved people. Men, women, and children were forced to work whenever their slaveholders demanded. For most slaves this meant every day of their lives from sunrise to sunset. Even sickness and poor weather rarely served as reasons to stop working.

The majority of enslaved people lived and worked on farms or large plantations in the South, where cotton was the leading crop. The majority of slaves worked as field hands. They planted, tended, picked, and processed cotton. They also cleared land, repaired buildings and fences, and performed many of the other tasks needed to keep the farms and plantations running. Slaves who worked outside were supervised by **overseers**. These were men that farmers and planters hired to watch over and direct the work of slaves. Other slaves worked in the plantation owners' homes. They performed a wide variety of servant duties, such as cooking, cleaning, and child care. Some enslaved people had learned a trade. They worked as bricklayers, blacksmiths, and carpenters.

Not all enslaved people worked on plantations. In cities, some worked as domestic servants, skilled craftspeople, factory hands, and day laborers. Some were hired out and allowed to keep part of their earnings. But they were still enslaved—under the law, they were considered property.

Living Conditions Enslaved African Americans who worked in the fields on plantations usually lived in terrible conditions. They were housed in tiny cabins with leaky roofs and dirt floors. The food and clothing they were given were equally as poor. When they were sick, they rarely, if ever, received medical care.

Some slaveholders provided better living conditions than others. Generally, they did this to gain obedience, not out of a sense of compassion. Most slaveholders, however, treated their slaves harshly. They used a wide variety of punishments to ensure obedience, including beatings, withholding food, and threatening family members. Wes Brady recalled the punishments faced by field hands:

> "The overseer was 'straddle his big horse at three o'clock in the mornin', roustin' the hands off to the field. . . . The rows was a mile long and no matter how much grass was in them, if you [left] one sprig on your row they [beat] you nearly to death."

> —Wes Brady, quoted in *Born in Slavery: Slave Narratives from the Federal Writers' Project, 1936–1938*

Enslaved people often lived in small cabins with dirt floors.

An African American father is sold away from his family.

Perhaps the cruelest part of slavery was the sale of family members away from one another. Although some slaveholders would not separate mothers from children, many did, causing unforgettable grief. When enslaved families could manage to be together, they took comfort in family life. Enslaved people did marry each other, although their marriages were not legally recognized. They tried to raise children while knowing that their children could be taken from them and sold at any time. Abolitionist Frederick Douglass, who was born into slavery, recalled visits from his mother, who lived 12 miles away.

"I do not recollect [remember] ever seeing my mother by the light of day. She was with me in the night. She would lie down with me, and get me to sleep, but long before I waked she was gone."

—Frederick Douglass, *Narrative of the Life of Frederick Douglass, an American Slave*

Reading Check
Summarize How did slaveholders treat enslaved people?

Douglass's mother resisted slavery by the simple act of visiting her child. Douglass later rebelled by escaping to the North. By and large, the vast majority of enslaved people resisted slavery in one way or another.

A Common Culture

By the early 1800s, a distinctive African American culture had emerged in the South. This common culture was based on strong religious convictions, close personal bonds, and music that accompanied almost every part of life. It helped enslaved African Americans to endure the hardships of plantation life.

Finding Strength in Religion Religion was a cornerstone of African American culture in the South. By the early 1800s, a large number of slaves practiced Christianity. Some slaveholders tried to use religion to force enslaved people to accept mistreatment. They emphasized such Bible passages as "Servants, obey your masters." But slaves took their own messages from the Bible. They were particularly inspired by the book of Exodus, which tells of Moses leading the Hebrews out of bondage in Egypt. Many enslaved African Americans believed that this story offered a message of hope for their own people.

Slaves developed their own form of Christianity, which mixed in features of their traditional African religions. The practice of religion became a way for slaves to resist the power and control that slaveholders wielded over them. So, they worshipped in secret, often at night under the cover of darkness.

Enslaved African Americans often expressed their beliefs in **spirituals**—folk songs that mixed African and European music and were often religious in nature. Singing spirituals offered comfort for pain, eased the drudgery of daily work, and bound people together at religious meetings. Many spirituals voiced the desire for freedom:

Plantation Burial
The English artist John Antrobus painted this work in 1860. Antrobus lived in the United States for about eight years. *Plantation Burial* was part of a series of paintings he planned to create about life in rural Louisiana.

"Dear Lord! dear Lord! when slavery'll cease,
Then we poor souls can have our peace;
There's a better day coming, will you go along with me?
There's a better day coming, go sound the jubilee."

—from *The Anti-Slavery Harp*, compiled by William W. Brown

Sometimes, spirituals contained coded messages about a planned escape or a plantation owner's unexpected return. African American spirituals had a strong influence on later developments in American music, such as gospel, blues, and jazz.

An Oral Tradition Another feature of African American culture was **oral tradition**—the passing on of stories, poems, and songs by word of mouth. In this way enslaved African Americans kept their heritage alive by passing down family histories and African traditions and customs. **Folktales**, or stories with a moral, also were part of this oral tradition. These tales usually included animals with human characteristics. Most often a smaller animal, such as a rabbit, would defeat a bigger, stronger animal, such as a bear, fox, or wolf, by outwitting it.

The rabbit represented slaves. The moral of the folktales was that slaves could survive by outsmarting the slaveholder, who was represented by the more powerful animal. In some tales, however, the bigger animal outsmarted the rabbit. This reflected how slaveholders sometimes lied to and deceived slaves. Such stories served as a warning that slaves should be very careful about trusting slaveholders.

Other Challenges to Slavery In small ways, and on a daily basis, slaves resisted the slave system and tried to gain a measure of control over their lives. Some worked slowly or damaged equipment or crops to protest

Reading Check
Make Inferences
Why might slaves
be inspired by
the biblical story
of Moses?

increased hours in the fields. Others ran away for a few days to visit family members or to avoid an angry slaveholder. Sometimes, slaves tried to escape to the North. But this journey to freedom was long and difficult. If they were captured, the punishment was flogging or, sometimes, death. Even so, thousands of enslaved people succeeded in getting to the North.

Slave Rebellions

Armed rebellion by enslaved persons was the most extreme form of resistance to slavery. Gabriel Prosser planned an attack on Richmond, Virginia, in 1800. In 1822 Denmark Vesey planned a revolt in Charleston, South Carolina. Both plots were betrayed, and the leaders, as well as numerous followers, were hanged.

The most famous rebellion was led by **Nat Turner** in Southampton County, Virginia, in 1831. Turner planned to gain freedom by killing slaveholders and their families. On August 21, Turner gathered about 70 followers and encouraged them with these words:

"We do not go forth for the sake of blood and carnage; . . . Remember that ours is not a war for robbery, . . . it is a struggle for freedom."

—Nat Turner, quoted in *History of the Negro Race in America, 1619–1880*, by George Washington Williams

---

BIOGRAPHY

Nat Turner 1800–1831

Nat Turner was born into slavery in Virginia. As a child, he learned to read and write and became an enthusiastic reader of the Bible. He soon gained a reputation in the local slave community for his religious beliefs. Enslaved people regularly gathered in forest clearings to listen to his powerful sermons.

Turner believed that he had been called by God to free the slaves, by armed rebellion if necessary. When a solar eclipse took place in August 1831, he interpreted it as a sign that it was time to revolt. In an account of events that he dictated to a white lawyer before his execution, Turner defended the justice of his cause. He was a "prophet," he claimed, called by God to commit his violent acts.

Analyze Points of View
How did Turner justify his rebellion?

Nat Turner meets with a group of followers in the woods.

Turner and his followers killed about 55 white men, women, and children. The rebellion was quickly put down. Most of Turner's men were captured when their ammunition ran out, and some were killed. Dozens of innocent slaves who played no part in the uprising also were put to death. Turner managed to evade capture for six weeks. After he was caught, he was tried and hanged.

Turner's rebellion spread fear throughout the South. Whites killed hundreds of African Americans in revenge. The state of Virginia even considered ending slavery because of the upheaval, but the proposal was narrowly defeated. Most southern state legislatures, however, passed harsh laws that further restricted the limited freedoms of both enslaved and free African Americans. For African Americans in the South, the grip of slavery grew ever tighter.

Summary and Preview Enslaved African Americans adopted many ways to adapt to and resist the harsh conditions of slavery. Some attempted to end slavery by rebellion, but they failed. In the next module you will review the origins and development of slavery in the United States.

Reading Check
Find Main Ideas
How did white southerners respond to Nat Turner's Rebellion?

Lesson 3 Assessment

Review Ideas, Terms, and People

1. a. Identify What types of work did enslaved people in cities do?

   b. Summarize What challenges did enslaved families face?

2. a. Recall What forms did resistance to slavery take?

   b. Explain How were enslaved African Americans able to keep their African heritage alive?

3. a. Describe Who was Nat Turner, and how did he resist slavery?

   b. Make Inferences How do you think the actions of Nat Turner affected the lives of enslaved African Americans who did not join his cause?

Critical Thinking

4. Categorize In this lesson you learned about the hardships faced by enslaved people. Create a graphic organizer similar to the one below to identify how the following characteristics of their culture helped them respond to their conditions and endure their hardships.

Religion	
Spirituals	
Oral Tradition	

Interpret Graphs

Define the Skill

Graphs are drawings that classify and display data in a clear, visual format. There are three basic types of graphs. *Line graphs* and *bar graphs* plot changes in quantities over time. Bar graphs are also used to compare quantities within a category at a particular time. *Circle graphs*, also called *pie graphs*, have a similar use. The circle represents the whole of something, and the slices show what proportion of the whole is made by each part.

Graphs allow you to see and understand patterns and relationships more easily than you can in information delivered in tables or text. This is especially true if the information is detailed or the relationships are complicated.

Learn the Skill

The following guidelines will help you interpret data that is presented as a graph.

1. Read the title to identify the subject and purpose of the graph. Note the type of graph, remembering what each type is designed to indicate. Also note how the graph's subject relates to any printed material that accompanies it.

2. Study the graph's parts. Pay close attention to the labels that define each axis. Note the units of measure. Identify the categories used. If there are different colors on bars or lines in the graph, determine what those differences mean.

3. Analyze the data in the graph. Note any increases or decreases in quantities. Look for trends, changes, and other relationships in the data.

4. Apply the information in the graph. Use the results of your analysis to draw conclusions. Ask yourself what generalizations can be made about the trends, changes, or relationships shown in the graph.

Practice the Skill

The graph below is a double-line graph. It shows both changes and relationships over time. This type of graph allows you to see how changes in one thing compare with changes in something else. Apply the guidelines to interpret the graph and answer the questions that follow.

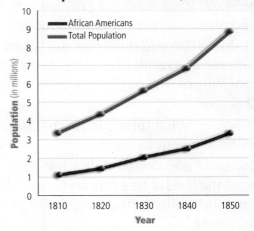

Population of the South, 1810–1850

1. What is shown on each axis of this graph? What are the units of measure on each axis?

2. What does each of the lines represent?

3. What was the total population of the South in 1810? in 1850? By how much did the African American population grow during that period?

4. Was the white population or the African American population growing faster? Explain how you know.

Module 14 Assessment

Review Vocabulary, Terms, and People

Match the definition in the left column with the correct term in the right column.

1. A region of cotton-producing areas that stretched from South Carolina to Texas

2. Emotional songs that mixed African and European music and expressed religious beliefs

3. Owners of small farms who made up the largest social class in the South

4. Crop brokers who often managed the cotton trade in the South

5. Wealthy farmers and plantation owners

a. cotton belt
b. factors
c. planters
d. spirituals
e. yeomen

Comprehension and Critical Thinking

Lesson 1

6. a. Describe How did the cotton gin lead to a cotton boom in the South?

    b. Analyze What were the positive and negative results of the cotton boom?

    c. Evaluate Do you think that the South suffered as a result of its reliance on cotton? Why or why not?

Lesson 2

7. a. Describe What three groups made up white southern society?

    b. Compare and Contrast In what ways were the lives of free African Americans and white southerners similar and different?

    c. Predict What might have been the attitude of yeomen and poor white southerners toward slavery? Why?

Lesson 3

8. a. Identify What are some small ways in which enslaved people tried to challenge the slave system?

    b. Analyze Information What were some ways that enslaved people sent messages or warnings to one another?

    c. Make Inferences How did religion and family help enslaved people cope with their lives?

Reading Skills

Online Research *Use the Reading Skills taught in this module to answer the question below.*

9. Which of the following would be the best website to find information about life in the South before the Civil War?

    a. a Civil War historian's homepage

    b. a collection of autobiographies written by slaves

    c. a site with information about how to grow cotton

    d. a collection of biographies of inventors

Review Themes

10. Society and Culture How were the different social classes in the South affected by the cotton boom?

11. Economics How did the cotton boom affect the economy of the South?

Module 14 Assessment, continued

Social Studies Skills

Interpret Graphs *Use the Social Studies Skills taught in this module to answer the questions about the graph below.*

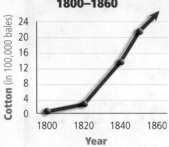

U.S. Cotton Production, 1800–1860

12. What span of time saw the largest increase in cotton production?
   a. 1800 to 1820
   b. 1820 to 1840
   c. 1840 to 1860
   d. after 1860

13. About what year did cotton production reach 1.2 million bales per year?
   a. 1800
   b. 1820
   c. 1840
   d. 1860

Focus on Writing

14. **Write a Biographical Sketch** In this module you learned about life in the South during the first half of the 1800s. List what you learned about living on a large cotton farm in the South and then choose an imaginary person to write about. Think about what life would have been like for this person. What might he or she have looked like? How might he or she have spoken? What might a typical day have been like? Once you have answered these questions, write two paragraphs about a day in the life of this person.

Module 15
Slavery in the United States

---★---

Essential Question
How did slavery shape life in the United States?

In this module you will read about slavery in the United States. You will learn about how it began, what life as a slave was like, and how the issue of slavery affected American politics and society.

About the Painting: In the painting *A Ride for Liberty—The Fugitive Slaves*, artist Eastman Johnson depicts a family of slaves attempting an escape toward freedom.

▶ *Explore ONLINE!*

VIDEOS, including...
- Freedom's Road: Slavery and the Opposition
- The Sale of Josiah Henson

☑ Document-Based Investigations

☑ Graphic Organizers

☑ Interactive Games

☑ Image Carousel: Plantation Work

☑ Interactive Map: Growth of the United States to 1848

☑ Image Carousel: Resistance to the Fugitive Slave Act

What You Will Learn ...

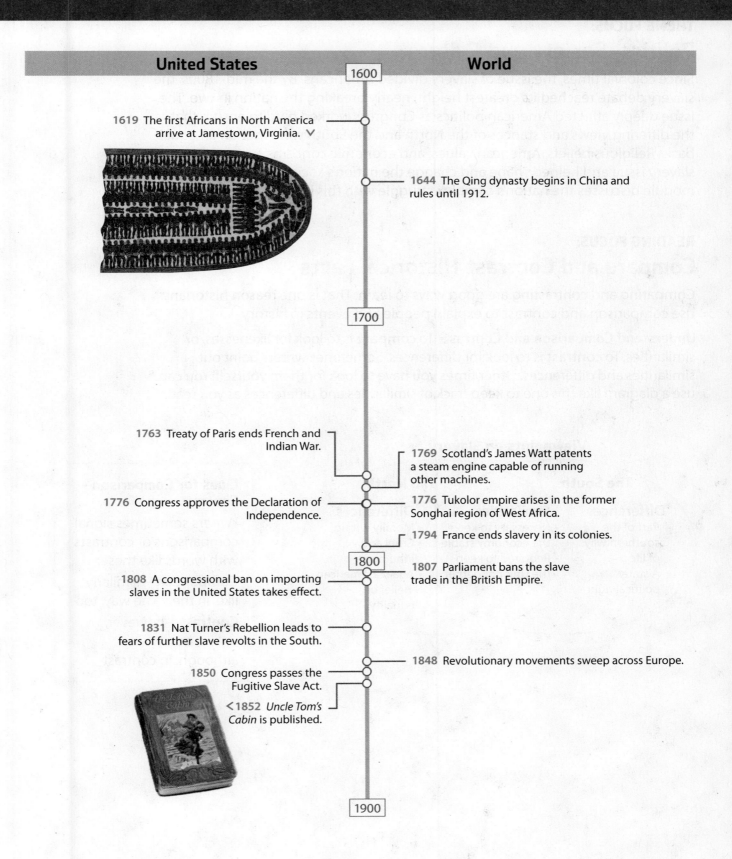

United States	1600	World

1619 The first Africans in North America arrive at Jamestown, Virginia. ⌄

1644 The Qing dynasty begins in China and rules until 1912.

1700

1763 Treaty of Paris ends French and Indian War.

1769 Scotland's James Watt patents a steam engine capable of running other machines.

1776 Congress approves the Declaration of Independence.

1776 Tukolor empire arises in the former Songhai region of West Africa.

1794 France ends slavery in its colonies.

1800

1808 A congressional ban on importing slaves in the United States takes effect.

1807 Parliament bans the slave trade in the British Empire.

1831 Nat Turner's Rebellion leads to fears of further slave revolts in the South.

1848 Revolutionary movements sweep across Europe.

1850 Congress passes the Fugitive Slave Act.

◁1852 *Uncle Tom's Cabin* is published.

1900

Reading Social Studies

THEME FOCUS:

Politics, Society and Culture

Since colonial times, the issue of slavery divided Americans. By the mid-1800s, the slavery debate reached its greatest height, nearly breaking the nation in two. The issue deeply affected American politics as Congress worked hard to ensure that the differing views and stances of the North and the South were met on an equal basis. Religious beliefs, American values, and economic concerns surrounded the slavery issue and helped shape and change the nation's society and culture. This module discusses the nation's complex struggle with this issue.

READING FOCUS:

Compare and Contrast Historical Facts

Comparing and contrasting are good ways to learn. That is one reason historians use comparison and contrast to explain people and events in history.

Understand Comparison and Contrast To **compare** is to look for likenesses, or similarities. To **contrast** is to look for differences. Sometimes writers point out similarities and differences. Other times you have to look for them yourself. You can use a diagram like this one to keep track of similarities and differences as you read.

Viewpoints on Slavery

The South

Differences
- Part of the southern way of life
- A state's political right

Similarities
- Necessary to keep the economy stable
- Required to keep the Union together

The North

Differences
- Morally wrong
- Cruel and inhumane
- Against American belief of equality

Clues for Comparison—Contrast

Writers sometimes signal comparisons or contrasts with words like these:

Comparison—similarly, like, in the same way, too

Contrast—however, unlike, but, while, although, in contrast

You Try It!

The following passage is from the module you are getting ready to read. As you read the passage, look for word clues about similarities and differences.

Abolitionists came from many different backgrounds and opposed slavery for various reasons. The Quakers were among the first groups to challenge slavery on religious grounds. Elihu Embree, the son of a Quaker minister, published the first newspapers in the country devoted to the abolitionist cause.

Other religious leaders gave speeches and published pamphlets that moved many Americans to support abolition. In one of these, abolitionist Theodore Weld wrote that "everyman knows that slavery is a curse." Other abolitionists referred to the Declaration of Independence. They reminded people that the American Revolution had been fought in the name of liberty.

Antislavery reformers did not always agree on the details, however. They differed over how much equality they thought African Americans should have. Some believed that African Americans should receive the same treatment as white Americans, whereas other abolitionists were against full political and social equality.

After you read the passage, answer the following questions.

1. What does the word *whereas* (in the last sentence of the passage) compare or contrast?

2. On what issue did abolitionists disagree? What comparison or contrast signal word helped you answer this question?

3. What other comparison or contrast words do you find in the passage? How do these words or phrases help you understand the passage?

As you read Module 15, keep an eye out for compare and contrast signal words. How do they help you understand the content?

Key Terms and People

Lesson 1
immune
Middle Passage
African Diaspora

Lesson 2
folktales
spirituals
Nat Turner's Rebellion
Nat Turner

Lesson 3
abolition
Elihu Embree
William Lloyd Garrison
American Anti-Slavery Society
Angelina and Sarah Grimké
Frederick Douglass
Sojourner Truth
Underground Railroad
Harriet Tubman

Lesson 4
Wilmot Proviso
sectionalism
Free-Soil Party
secede
Compromise of 1850
Fugitive Slave Act
Anthony Burns
Harriet Beecher Stowe
Uncle Tom's Cabin

★
Beginnings of Slavery in the Americas

The Big Idea
Europeans forced millions of African slaves to work in their colonies.

Main Ideas
- European diseases wiped out much of the Native American population, causing colonists to look for a new labor force.
- Europeans enslaved millions of Africans and sent them to work in their colonies.
- Slaves in the Americas created distinct cultures.

Key Terms and People
immune
Middle Passage
African Diaspora

Academic Vocabulary
structure the way something is set up or organized

If YOU were there . . .

You are an enslaved African living in North America. Your family is all that you have. You help each other, and your family provides some relief from the forced labor and harsh life on the plantation. Still, you long for your freedom. A fellow slave has told you of a plan to escape.

Will you stay with your family or try to flee?

The Need for a New Labor Force

European diseases had a devastating effect on the Native American population. Measles, smallpox, and typhus were common in Europe. As a result, most adult Europeans were **immune**, or had a natural resistance, to them. Native Americans, however, had never been exposed to such diseases and had no immunity to them. As a result, many Native Americans became terribly sick after their first encounters with Europeans. Millions of them died in the years after Columbus reached the New World.

No one knows exactly how many Native Americans died from European diseases, but the loss of life was staggering. Spanish author Fernández de Oviedo reported in 1548 about the destruction of the Native Americans of Hispaniola. He reported that, of the estimated 1 million Indians who had lived on the island in 1492, "there are not now believed to be at the present time . . . five hundred persons [left]." In North America the Native American population north of Mexico was about 10 million when Columbus arrived. This number would drop to less than a million. The drop in the native population played a major role in the emerging need for an alternative labor force.

Plantation agriculture was a mainstay of the colonial economic **structure**. Spain and Portugal established sugar plantations that relied on large numbers of native laborers.

In the 1600s English tobacco farmers in North America also needed workers for their plantations. With a lack of Native American workers, they, too, needed another source of labor. Plantation owners in both North and South America wanted a cheap work force.

Some colonists, including Spanish priest Bartolomé de Las Casas, suggested using enslaved Africans as workers. Africans had already developed immunity to European diseases. The colonists soon agreed that slaves from West Africa could be the solution to their labor needs.

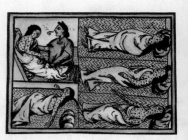

Native Americans had no resistance to European diseases. As a result, throughout the Americas, millions suffered and died. This illustration from a Spanish missionary account of 16th-century Mexico shows victims of smallpox.

Reading Check
Analyze
How did disease contribute to the slave trade?

The Slave Trade

The practice of slavery had existed in Africa and in many parts of the world for centuries. Traditionally, slavery in West Africa mostly involved only black Africans, who were both slaveholders and slaves. This changed in the 600s when Arab Muslims, and later Europeans, became slave traders. Though Europeans had long traded resources with Africa, they became more interested in the growing slave trade.

In 1510 the Spanish government legalized the sale of slaves in its colonies. The first full cargo ship of Africans arrived in the Americas eight years later. Over the next century, more than a million enslaved Africans were brought to the Spanish and Portuguese colonies in the New World. The Dutch and English also became active in the slave trade.

Middle Passage Enslavement was a horrible experience for the slaves. Most enslaved people had been captured in the interior of Africa, often by Africans who profited from selling slaves to Europeans. The captives were chained around the neck and then marched to the coast. This journey could be as long as 1,000 miles.

The **Middle Passage** was the voyage across the Atlantic Ocean that enslaved Africans were forced to endure. Africans were packed like cargo in the lower decks of the slave ships. The slaves were chained together and crammed into spaces about the size of coffins. The height between the decks was sometimes only 18 inches.

In this confinement, disease spread quickly, killing many Africans. Others suffocated or died from malnutrition. Some slaves took their own lives to end their suffering. It is estimated that one out of every six Africans died during the Middle Passage.

African Diaspora Between the 1520s and 1860s, about 12 million Africans were shipped across the Atlantic as slaves. More than 10 million of these captives survived the voyage and reached the Americas. The slave trade led to the **African Diaspora**. (A diaspora is the scattering of a people.) Enslaved Africans were sent all across the New World.

More than a third of the enslaved Africans, nearly 4 million people, were sent to work in Brazil. Most of these people were forced to labor on Portuguese sugar plantations. Nearly 2 million enslaved people were sent to the colonies of New Spain. Some worked on plantations in the Caribbean, while others were taken to toil in the mines of Peru and Mexico.

King Afonso of Kongo (seated) wrote the king of Portugal in 1526 asking him to do what he could to stop the practice of taking African slaves from his kingdom.

Some 3 million slaves worked in British and French colonies in the Caribbean and Latin America. More than 600,000 slaves went to Britain's North American colonies, which later became the United States.

Colonial leaders across the Americas developed laws that regulated slave treatment and behavior. Slaves were given few rights in the colonies. The law considered enslaved Africans to be property. In some colonies, a slaveholder was not charged with murder if he killed a slave while punishing him. Enslaved Africans, on the other hand, received harsh penalties for minor offenses, such as breaking a tool. Runaways were often tortured and sometimes killed.

The treatment of enslaved Africans varied from slaveholder to slaveholder. To protect their investment, some slaveholders provided adequate food, clothing, and shelter for their slaves. However, severe treatment was more common. Whippings, brandings, and even worse torture were all part of American slavery.

The Enslaved Fight Back Although they were in bondage, people of African origin found ways to resist their enslavement. They sometimes worked slowly, damaged goods, or deliberately carried out orders the wrong way.

In South Carolina, enslaved people vastly outnumbered whites, who lived in fear of slave rebellions. Their fears came true in the late 1730s when a revolt occurred in South Carolina. In September 1739, an uprising known as the Stono Rebellion took place. The revolt began when about 20 slaves gathered at the Stono River just southwest of Charles Town. Wielding weapons, they killed whites and marched south, beating drums and chanting "Liberty!" They called out for others to join them in their plan to seek freedom in Spanish-held Florida. Many joined, and their numbers grew until there were perhaps 100 in open rebellion. Seven plantations were burned along their route and 20 whites were killed. By late that afternoon, however, a white militia had surrounded the escaping slaves. The two sides clashed, and many slaves died in the fighting. Those captured were executed.

Stono and similar revolts led planters to make slave codes even stricter. Slaves were now forbidden from leaving plantations without written permission. The laws also made it illegal for slaves to meet with free blacks. Such laws made the conditions of slavery even more inhumane.

Reading Check
Generalize
How were enslaved Africans treated in the Americas?

Slave Culture in the Americas

Slaves in the Americas came from many different parts of Africa. They spoke different languages and had different cultural backgrounds. But enslaved Africans also shared many customs and viewpoints. They built upon what they had in common to create new African American cultures.

Families were a vital part of slave culture. Families provided a refuge— a relationship not fully under the slaveholders' control. However, slave families faced many challenges. Families were often broken apart when a family member was sold to another owner. In Latin America, there were many more enslaved males than females. This made it difficult for slaves there to form stable families.

Religion was a second refuge for slaves. It gave enslaved Africans a form of expression that was partially free from their slaveholders' control. Slave religion was primarily Christian, but it included traditional elements from African religions as well. Religion gave slaves a sense of self-worth and a hope for salvation in this life and the next. Spirituals were a common form of religious expression among slaves. Slaves also used songs and folktales to tell their stories of sorrow, hope, agony, and joy.

Reading Check
Identify Points of View Why was religion important to slaves in the Americas?

Many slaves expressed themselves through art and dance. Dances were important social events in slave communities. Like most elements of slave culture, art and dance were heavily influenced by African traditions.

Summary and Preview After disease wiped out much of the Native American population, colonists turned to African slave labor. In the next lesson you will learn what life was like under slavery and how some tried to rebel against it.

Lesson 1 Assessment

Review Ideas, Terms, and People

1. a. **Recall** Why did so many Native Americans die after coming into contact with Europeans?

   b. **Summarize** Why did plantation owners turn to enslaved Africans as a labor force?

2. a. **Identify** What was the Middle Passage?

   b. **Describe** Explain how enslaved Africans were treated after they reached the colonies in the Americas.

3. a. **Explain** What are spirituals?

   b. **Analyze** How did religion and family provide a refuge from the harsh life enslaved Africans were forced to endure?

Critical Thinking

4. **Identify Cause and Effect** In this lesson you learned about the slave trade. Create a chart similar to the one below and identify the causes and effects of the slave trade.

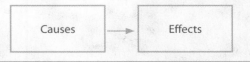

History and Geography

The Atlantic Slave Trade

The slave system that arose in the American colonies was strongly influenced by geographic forces. The climate of the southern colonies was suited to growing certain crops, like cotton, tobacco, and sugarcane. These crops required a great deal of labor to grow and to process. To meet this great demand for labor, the colonists looked to one main source—enslaved Africans.

Colonial Slave Ports Slave ships sailed to slave ports, where they unloaded their human cargo. Slave ports like Boston, Newport, and Charleston were located near farming areas and the mouths of rivers.

NORTH AMERICA

Boston
Newport

Charleston

ATLANTIC OCEAN

40°N

Tropic of Cancer

20°N

WEST INDIES

MIDDLE PASSAGE

SOUTH AMERICA

Equator

20°S

Tropic of Capricorn

40°S

60°S

The Middle Passage The terrifying and deadly voyage across the Atlantic was known as the Middle Passage. Enslaved Africans were chained and crowded together under ships' decks on this long voyage, as the drawing shows.

The West Indies Africans were brought to the West Indies to work on large sugar plantations. Sugarcane thrived in the West Indies, but it required huge amounts of labor to grow.

60°W   140°W   120°W   100°W   80°W   0°

Slave forts began as trading posts. They were built near river mouths to provide easy access to both the sea and inland areas.

AFRICA

St. Luis de Senegal

James Fort

Accra

Elmina

Whydah

Assinie

Elmina slave fort, Ghana

New England traders exchanged goods for slaves on the West African coast and then transported the slaves to the American colonies or to the West Indies.

20°N

AFRICA

Kidnapped and Taken to a Slave Ship

Mahommah G. Baquaqua was captured and sold into slavery as a young man. In this 1854 account, he recalls being taken to the African coast to board a slave ship.

"I was taken down to the river and placed on board a boat; the river was very large and branched off in two different directions, previous to emptying itself into the sea. . . . We were two nights and one day on this river, when we came to a . . . place . . . [where] the slaves were all put into a pen, and placed with our backs to the fire. . . . When all were ready to go aboard, we were chained together, and tied with ropes round about our necks, and were thus drawn down to the sea shore."

Slaves Brought to the Americas, 1493–1810

Number of slaves (in millions)

7
6
5
4
3
2
1
0

1493–1600 1601–1700 1701–1810

Years

40°S

Interpret Maps
Human-Environment Interaction What geographic factors influenced the development of the Atlantic slave trade?

20°E 40°E 60°E 80°E 100°E

60°S

The Slave System

The Big Idea

The slave system in the South produced harsh living conditions and occasional rebellions.

Main Ideas

- Slaves worked at a variety of jobs on plantations.
- Life under slavery was difficult and dehumanizing.
- Slave culture centered around family, community, and religion.
- Slave uprisings led to stricter slave codes in many states.

Key Terms and People

folktales
spirituals
Nat Turner's Rebellion
Nat Turner

If YOU were there . . .

You are a reporter for a newspaper in Philadelphia in the 1850s. You are writing a series of articles about the slave system in the South. To get background for your stories, you are planning to interview some former slaves who now live in Philadelphia. Some have bought their freedom, while others have successfully escaped from slavery.

What questions will you ask in your interviews?

Slaves and Work

Most enslaved African Americans lived in rural areas where they worked on farms and plantations. Enslaved people on small farms usually did a variety of jobs. On large plantations, most slaves were assigned to specific jobs, and most worked in the fields. Most slaveholders demanded that slaves work as much as possible. Supervisors known as drivers, who were sometimes slaves themselves, made sure that slaves followed orders. Drivers also carried out punishments.

Working in the Field Most plantation owners used the gang-labor system. In this system, all field hands worked on the same task at the same time. They usually worked from sunup to sundown. Former slave Harry McMillan had worked on a plantation in South Carolina. He recalled that the field hands usually did not even get a break to eat lunch. "You had to get your victuals [food] standing at your hoe," he remembered.

Men, women, and even children older than about 10 usually did the same tasks. Sickness and poor weather rarely stopped the work. "The times I hated most was picking cotton when the frost was on the bolls [seed pods]," recalled former Louisiana slave Mary Reynolds. "My hands git sore and crack open and bleed."

Working in the Planter's Home Some slaves worked as butlers, cooks, or nurses in the planter's home. These slaves

Typical Daily Schedule:

3:00 a.m.	*Out of bed, tend animals*
6:00 a.m.	*Prayers*
7:00 a.m.	*Start work*
12:00 p.m.	*Lunch*
1:00 p.m.	*Return to work*
7:00 p.m.	*Dinner*
8:00 p.m.	*Return to work*
11:00 p.m.	*Lights out*

A Slave's Daily Life
The lives of slaves revolved around the work required of them. Although created in 1874, the illustration above shows the backbreaking work of harvesting cotton. The schedule at left details how a slave might have spent his or her day.

often had better food, clothing, and shelter than field hands did, but they often worked longer hours. They had to serve the planter's family 24 hours a day.

Working at Skilled Jobs On larger plantations, some enslaved African Americans worked at skilled jobs, such as blacksmithing or carpentry. Sometimes planters let these slaves sell their services to other people. Often planters collected a portion of what was earned but allowed slaves to keep the rest. In this way, some skilled slaves earned enough money to buy their freedom from their slaveholders. For example, William Ellison earned his freedom in South Carolina by working for wages as a cotton gin maker. For years he worked late at night and on Sundays. He bought his freedom with the money he earned. Eventually he was also able to buy the freedom of his wife and daughter.

Life Under Slavery

Generally, slaveholders viewed slaves as property, not as people. Slaveholders bought and sold slaves to make a profit. The most common method of sale was at an auction. The auction itself determined whether families would be kept together or separated. Sometimes a buyer wanted a slave to

Reading Check
Summarize
What were some types of work done by enslaved people on plantations?

A Nurse's Work
Slaveholders' children were often cared for by enslaved women. At the time, women who looked after children were called nurses. This nurse is posing with her slaveholder's child in about 1850.

fill a specific position, such as heavy laborer, carpenter, or blacksmith. The buyer might be willing to pay for the slave who could do the work, but not for that slave's family. Families would then be separated, with little hope of ever getting back together.

Slave traders sometimes even kidnapped free African Americans and then sold them into slavery. For example, Solomon Northup, a free African American, was kidnapped in Washington, DC. He spent 12 years as a slave until he finally proved his identity and gained his release.

Living Conditions Enslaved people often endured poor living conditions. Planters housed them in dirt-floor cabins with few furnishings and often leaky roofs. The clothing given to them was usually simple and made of cheap, coarse fabric. Some slaves tried to brighten up their clothing by sewing on designs from discarded scraps of material. In this way, they expressed their individuality and personalized the clothing assigned to them by the planters.

Likewise, many slaves did what they could to improve their small food rations. Some planters allowed slaves to keep their own gardens for vegetables and chickens for eggs. Other slaves were able to add a little variety to their diet by fishing or picking wild berries.

Punishment and Slave Codes Some planters offered more food or better living conditions to encourage slaves' obedience. However, most slaveholders used punishment instead. Some would punish one slave in front of others as a warning to them all. Harry McMillan recalled some of the punishments he had witnessed.

> "The punishments were whipping, putting you in the stocks [wooden frames to lock people in] and making you wear irons and a chain at work. Then they had a collar to put round your neck with two horns, like cows' horns, so that you could not lie down. . . . Sometimes they dug a hole like a well with a door on top. This they called a dungeon keeping you in it two or three weeks or a month, or sometimes till you died in there."
>
> —Harry McMillan, quoted in *Major Problems in the History of the American South, Volume I*, edited by Paul D. Escott and David R. Goldfield

To further control slaves' actions, many states passed strict laws called slave codes. Some laws prohibited slaves from traveling far from their homes. Literacy laws in most southern states prohibited the education of slaves. Alabama, Virginia, and Georgia had laws that allowed the fining and whipping of anyone caught teaching enslaved people to read and write.

Reading Check
Summarize
How did slaveholders control slaves?

Slave Culture

Many enslaved Africans found comfort in their community and culture. They made time for social activity, even after exhausting workdays, in order to relieve the hardship of their lives.

Academic Vocabulary
aspect part

Family and Community Family was the most important **aspect** of slave communities, and many slaves feared separation more than they feared punishment. Josiah Henson never forgot the day that he and his family were auctioned. His mother begged the slaveholder who bought her to buy Josiah, too. The slaveholder refused, and Henson's entire family was separated. "I must have been then between five or six years old," he recalled years later. "I seem to see and hear my poor weeping mother now."

Enslaved parents kept their heritage alive by passing down family histories as well as African customs and traditions. They also told **folktales**, or traditional stories that often had a moral, to teach lessons about how to survive under slavery. These folktales often included a clever animal character called a trickster. The trickster—which often represented slaves—defeated a stronger animal by outwitting it. Folktales reassured slaves that they could survive by outsmarting more powerful slaveholders.

Religion Religion also played an important part in slave culture. By the early 1800s, many slaves were Christians. They came to see themselves, like the slaves in the Old Testament, as God's chosen people, much like the Hebrew slaves in ancient Egypt who had faith that they would someday live in freedom.

Some slaves sang **spirituals**, emotional Christian songs that blended African and European music, to express their deeply held religious beliefs.

Most slaves found hope and a short escape from their daily misery in Sunday church services. Others sought to escape permanently and ran away, hoping to reach the freedom of the North. A failed escape attempt, however, could result in a cruel whipping—or worse.

For example, "The Heavenly Road" reflected slaves' belief in their equality in the eyes of God.

"Come, my brother, if you never did pray,
    I hope you pray tonight;
    For I really believe I am a child of God
    As I walk on the heavenly road."

—Anonymous, quoted in *Afro-American Religious History*, edited by Milton C. Sernett

Slaves blended some aspects of their traditional African religions with those of the Christianity that the slaveholders followed. They worshipped in secret, out of sight of slaveholders. Some historians have called slave religion the invisible institution.

Seeds of Rebellion Maintaining their own religious beliefs and practices was only one way in which enslaved people resisted slaveholders' attempts to control them completely. In small ways, slaves rebelled against the system daily. Sometimes they worked slower to protest long hours in the fields. Other times they ran away for a few days to avoid an angry slave-holder. Some slaves tried to escape permanently, but most left only for short periods, often to go and visit relatives.

Gaining freedom by escaping to the North was hard. If discovered, slaves were captured and sent back to their slaveholders, where they faced certain punishment or death. However, thousands of enslaved people succeeded in escaping.

Slave Uprisings

Although violent slave revolts were relatively rare, white southerners lived in fear of them. Two planned rebellions were stopped before they began. Gabriel Prosser planned a rebellion near Richmond, Virginia, in 1800. Denmark Vesey planned one in Charleston, South Carolina, in 1822. Local authorities executed most of those involved in planning these rebellions. Though Vesey was executed as the leader of the Charleston conspiracy, several accounts written after his death by antislavery writers claimed he was a hero.

Reading Check
Summarize
How did slaves' religious beliefs affect their attitudes toward slavery?

The most violent slave revolt in the country occurred in 1831 and is known as **Nat Turner's Rebellion**. **Nat Turner**, a slave from Southampton County, Virginia, believed that God had told him to end slavery. On an August night in 1831, Turner led a group of slaves in a plan to kill all of the slaveholders and their families in the county. First they attacked the family who held Turner as a slave. Soon they had killed about 60 white people in the community.

More than 100 innocent slaves who were not part of Turner's group were killed in an attempt to stop the rebellion. Turner himself led authorities on a chase around the countryside for six weeks. He hid in caves and in the woods before he was caught and brought to trial. Before his trial, Turner made a confession. He expressed his belief that the revolt was justified and

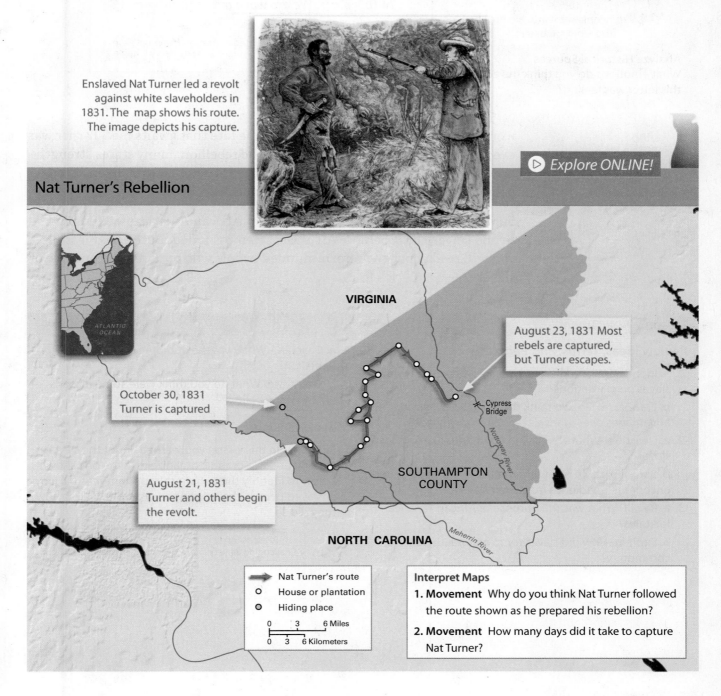

Enslaved Nat Turner led a revolt against white slaveholders in 1831. The map shows his route. The image depicts his capture.

▶ Explore ONLINE!

Nat Turner's Rebellion

ATLANTIC OCEAN

VIRGINIA

August 23, 1831 Most rebels are captured, but Turner escapes.

October 30, 1831 Turner is captured

Cypress Bridge

Nottoway River

August 21, 1831 Turner and others begin the revolt.

SOUTHAMPTON COUNTY

NORTH CAROLINA

Meherrin River

→ Nat Turner's route
○ House or plantation
◉ Hiding place

0   3   6 Miles
0   3   6 Kilometers

Interpret Maps
1. **Movement** Why do you think Nat Turner followed the route shown as he prepared his rebellion?
2. **Movement** How many days did it take to capture Nat Turner?

Nat Turner's Rebellion

In 1831 a white southerner who had escaped the rebellion wrote a letter describing the mood of the area where Nat Turner's group had killed slaveholders and their families.

> The author believes no one in the county has been through a worse event.

> The author says that many people went into hiding when the rebellion began.

"The oldest inhabitants of our county have never experienced such a distressing [terrible] time, as we have had since Sunday night last. The [slaves], about fifteen miles from this place, have massacred from 50 to 75 women and children, and some 8 or 10 men. Every house, room and corner in this place is full of women and children, driven from home, who had to take to the woods, until they could get to this place. We are worn out with fatigue [tiredness]."

—*Richmond Enquirer*, quoted in *The Southampton Slave Revolt of 1831* by Henry I. Tragle

Analyze Historical Sources
What emotions do you think the author of this letter was feeling?

Reading Check
Find Main Ideas
What was Nat Turner's Rebellion, and what happened as a result?

worth his death: "I am willing to suffer the fate that awaits me." Turner was executed on November 11, 1831. After the rebellion, many states strengthened their slave codes. The new codes placed stricter control on enslaved people. Despite resistance, slavery continued to spread.

Summary and Preview Several groups of African Americans attempted to end slavery by rebellion. All of the attempts failed. In the next lesson, you will read about the reform-minded people who opposed the practice of slavery.

Lesson 2 Assessment

Review Ideas, Terms, and People

1. **a. Identify** What different types of work were done by slaves on plantations?

   b. Elaborate Do you think that skilled slaves had advantages over other slaves? Why or why not?

2. **a. Describe** What were living conditions like for most slaves?

   b. Summarize In what different ways did slaveholders encourage obedience from their slaves?

3. **a. Recall** What was the purpose of African American folktales?

   b. Explain How did slaves try to maintain a sense of community?

4. **a. Describe** What was the outcome of Nat Turner's Rebellion?

   b. Elaborate What do you think were some reasons why slaves rebelled?

Critical Thinking

5. **Evaluate** In this lesson you learned about the slavery system. Create a graphic organizer like the one shown below to identify the two most important reasons why enslaved people challenged the system as well as how they did so.

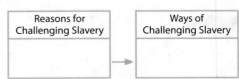

Reasons for Challenging Slavery	→	Ways of Challenging Slavery

The Movement to End Slavery

The Big Idea

In the mid-1800s, debate over slavery increased as abolitionists organized to challenge slavery in the United States.

Main Ideas

- Americans from a variety of backgrounds actively opposed slavery.

- Abolitionists organized the Underground Railroad to help enslaved Africans escape.

- Despite efforts of abolitionists, many Americans remained opposed to ending slavery.

Key Terms and People

abolition
Elihu Embree
William Lloyd Garrison
American Anti-Slavery Society
Angelina and Sarah Grimké
Frederick Douglass
Sojourner Truth
Underground Railroad
Harriet Tubman

If YOU were there . . .

You live in southern Ohio in the 1850s. A friend who lives across the river in Kentucky has asked you to join a network that helps escaping slaves. She reminds you that your house has a secret cellar where you could easily hide fugitives for a few days. You are opposed to slavery. But you know this might get you in trouble with your neighbors—and with the law.

Would you become an agent for the Underground Railroad? Why?

Americans Oppose Slavery

Some Americans had opposed slavery since before the country was founded. Benjamin Franklin was the president of the first antislavery society in America, the Pennsylvania Society for Promoting the Abolition of Slavery. In the 1830s Americans took more organized action to support **abolition**, or a complete end to slavery.

Differences among Abolitionists Abolitionists came from many different backgrounds and opposed slavery for various reasons. The Quakers were among the first groups to challenge slavery on religious grounds. **Elihu Embree**, the son of a Quaker minister, published the first newspapers in the country devoted to the abolitionist cause. One newspaper was called *The Emancipator*. Embree proclaimed that "freedom is the inalienable right of *all men*."

Other religious leaders gave speeches and published pamphlets that moved many Americans to support abolition. In one of these, abolitionist Theodore Weld wrote that "everyman knows that slavery is a curse." Other abolitionists referred to the Declaration of Independence. They reminded people that the American Revolution had been fought in the name of liberty.

Antislavery reformers did not always agree on the details, however. They differed over how much equality they thought

African Americans should have. Some believed that African Americans should receive the same treatment as white Americans. In contrast, other abolitionists were against full political and social equality.

Some abolitionists wanted to send freed African Americans to Africa to start new colonies. They thought that this would prevent conflicts between the races in the United States. In 1817 a minister named Robert Finley started the American Colonization Society, an organization dedicated to establishing colonies of freed slaves in Africa. Five years later, the society founded the colony of Liberia on the west coast of Africa. About 12,000 African Americans eventually settled in Liberia. However, many abolitionists who once favored colonization later opposed it. Some African Americans also opposed it. David Walker was one such person. In his 1829 essay, "Appeal to the Colored Citizens of the World," Walker explained his opposition to colonization.

> "The greatest riches in all America have arisen from our blood and tears: and they [whites] will drive us from our property and homes, which we have earned with our blood."
>
> —David Walker, quoted in *From Slavery to Freedom* by John Hope Franklin and Alfred A. Moss Jr.

Spreading the Abolitionist Message Abolitionists found many ways to further their cause. Some went on speaking tours or wrote pamphlets and newspaper articles. John Greenleaf Whittier wrote abolitionist poetry and literature. **William Lloyd Garrison** published an abolitionist newspaper, the *Liberator,* beginning in 1831. In 1833 he also helped found the **American Anti-Slavery Society**. Its members wanted immediate emancipation and racial equality for African Americans. Garrison later became its president.

Both the *Liberator* and the Anti-Slavery Society relied on support from free African Americans. Society members distributed antislavery literature and petitioned Congress to end federal support of slavery. In 1840 the American Anti-Slavery Society split. One group wanted immediate freedom for enslaved African Americans and a bigger role for women. The others wanted gradual emancipation and for women to play only minor roles in the movement.

Angelina and Sarah Grimké, two white southern women, were prominent antislavery activists of the 1830s. They came from a South Carolina slaveholding family but disagreed with their parents' support of slavery. Angelina Grimké tried to recruit other white southern women in a pamphlet called *Appeal to the Christian Women of the South* in 1836.

William Lloyd Garrison proclaimed in 1853, "Wherever there is a human being, I see God-given rights. . . ."

"I know you do not make the laws, but . . . if you really suppose you can do nothing to overthrow slavery, you are greatly mistaken. . . . Try to persuade your husband, father, brothers, and sons that slavery is a crime against God and man."

—Angelina Grimké, quoted in *The Grimké Sisters from South Carolina*, edited by Gerda Lerner

This essay was very popular in the North. In 1839 the Grimké sisters wrote *American Slavery As It Is*. The book was one of the most important antislavery works of its time.

African American Abolitionists Many former slaves were active in the antislavery cause. **Frederick Douglass** escaped from slavery when he was 20 and went on to become one of the most important African American leaders of the 1800s. Douglass secretly learned to read and write as a boy, despite a law against it. His public-speaking skills impressed members of the Anti-Slavery Society. In 1841 they asked him to give regular lectures.

At a Fourth of July celebration in 1852, he captured the audience's attention with his powerful voice.

"The blessings in which you, this day, rejoice, are not enjoyed in common. . . . This Fourth of July is *yours*, not *mine*. You may rejoice, I must mourn."

—Frederick Douglass, quoted in *From Slavery to Freedom* by John Hope Franklin and Alfred A. Moss Jr.

BIOGRAPHY

Frederick Douglass 1817–1895

Frederick Douglass was born in rural Maryland. At age six he was sent to live in Baltimore, and at age 20 he escaped to New York City. For most of his life, Douglass lived in Rochester, New York, making his home into a stop along the Underground Railroad. Douglass became the most famous African American in the 1800s.

After hearing the abolitionist William Lloyd Garrison speak in 1841, Douglass began his own speaking tours about his experiences as a slave. He traveled often, giving powerful antislavery speeches to audiences throughout the North and in Europe. His personal stories and elegant speaking style helped the abolitionist movement to grow.

In midlife he wrote an autobiography and started an abolitionist newspaper called the *North Star*. During the Civil War, Douglass persuaded black soldiers to fight for the North. His words remain an inspiration to this day.

Draw Conclusions
What made Frederick Douglass's speeches and writings so powerful?

Sojourner Truth was a former slave who became a leading abolitionist as well as an active supporter of women's rights.

In addition to his many speaking tours in the United States and Europe, Douglass published a newspaper called the *North Star* and wrote several autobiographies. His autobiographies were intended to show the injustices of slavery.

Another former slave, **Sojourner Truth**, also contributed to the abolitionist cause. She claimed God had called her to travel through the United States and preach the truth about slavery and women's rights. With her deep voice and quick wit, Truth became legendary in the antislavery movement for her fiery and dramatic speeches.

Other African Americans wrote narratives about their experiences as slaves to expose the cruelties that many slaves faced. In 1861 Harriet Jacobs published *Incidents in the Life of a Slave Girl*, one of the few slave narratives by a woman. William Wells Brown wrote an antislavery play as well as a personal narrative in the form of a novel called *Clotel*.

Reading Check
Find Main Ideas In what ways did African Americans participate in the abolition movement?

The Underground Railroad

By the 1830s, a loosely organized group had begun helping slaves escape from the South. Free African Americans, former slaves, and a few white abolitionists worked together. They created what became known as the **Underground Railroad**. The organization was not an actual railroad but was a network of people who arranged transportation and hiding places for fugitives, or escaped slaves.

Fugitives would travel along "freedom trails" that led them to northern states or sometimes into Canada. At no time did the Railroad have a central leadership. No one person, or group of people, was ever officially in charge. Despite the lack of any real structure, the Underground Railroad managed to achieve dramatic results.

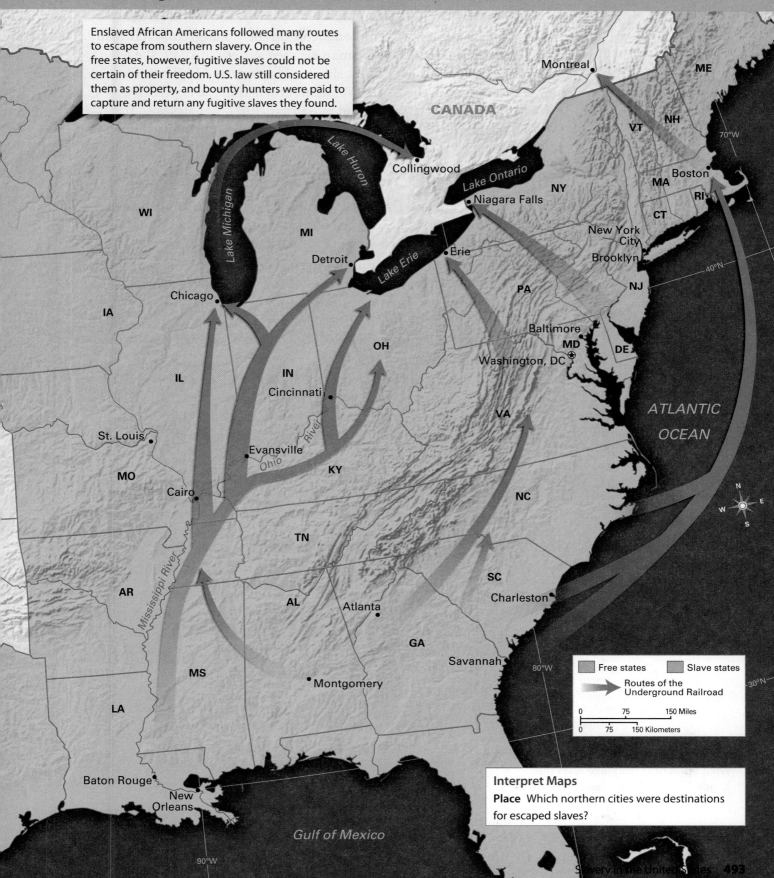

The Underground Railroad

Enslaved African Americans followed many routes to escape from southern slavery. Once in the free states, however, fugitive slaves could not be certain of their freedom. U.S. law still considered them as property, and bounty hunters were paid to capture and return any fugitive slaves they found.

CANADA

Montreal

ME

VT
NH

Collingwood

MA
Boston

Lake Huron

Lake Ontario

NY

RI

Niagara Falls

CT

New York City

WI

Lake Michigan

MI

Detroit

Lake Erie

Erie

Brooklyn

PA

NJ

Chicago

IA

Baltimore

MD

DE

OH

Washington, DC

IL

IN

Cincinnati

VA

ATLANTIC OCEAN

St. Louis

Ohio River

Evansville

KY

MO

Cairo

NC

TN

N
W E
S

AR

AL

Atlanta

SC

Charleston

Mississippi River

GA

MS

Savannah

Montgomery

LA

Free states **Slave states**

→ Routes of the Underground Railroad

| 0 | 75 | 150 Miles |

| 0 | 75 | 150 Kilometers |

Baton Rouge

New Orleans

Gulf of Mexico

Interpret Maps

Place Which northern cities were destinations for escaped slaves?

Often wearing disguises, fugitives moved along the "railroad" at night, led by people known as conductors. Many times, the fugitives had no other guideposts but the stars. They stopped to rest during the day at "stations," often barns, attics, or other places on property owned by abolitionists known as station masters. The station masters hid and fed the fugitives.

The most famous and daring conductor on the Underground Railroad was **Harriet Tubman**. When Tubman escaped slavery in 1849, she left behind her family. She swore that she would return and lead her whole family to freedom in the North. Tubman returned to the South 19 times, successfully leading her family and more than 300 other slaves to freedom. At one time, the reward for Tubman's capture reportedly climbed to $40,000, a huge amount of money at that time.

Opposition to Ending Slavery

Although the North was the center of the abolitionist movement, many white northerners agreed with the South and supported slavery. Others disliked slavery but opposed equality for African Americans.

Newspaper editors and politicians warned that freed slaves would move north and take jobs from white workers. Some workers feared losing jobs to newly freed African Americans, whom they believed would accept lower wages. Abolitionist leaders were threatened with violence as some northerners joined mobs. Such a mob killed abolitionist Elijah Lovejoy in 1837 in Alton, Illinois.

The federal government also obstructed abolitionists. Between 1836 and 1844, the U.S. House of Representatives used what was called a gag rule. Congress had received thousands of antislavery petitions. Yet the gag rule forbade members of Congress from discussing them. This rule

Reading Check
Draw Inferences
Why were the operations of the Underground Railroad kept secret?

DOCUMENT-BASED INVESTIGATION   Historical Source

Anti-Abolitionist Rally

Members of an anti-abolitionist group used this flyer to call people together in order to disrupt a meeting of abolitionists in 1837.

Seditious means "guilty of rebelling against lawful authority."

The group believes abolition violates the Constitution.

Analyze Historical Sources
What emotional language does this handbill use to get its message across?

OUTRAGE.

Fellow Citizens,

AN

ABOLITIONIST,

of the most revolting character is among you, exciting the feelings of the North against the South. A seditious Lecture is to be delivered

THIS EVENING,

at 7 o'clock, at the Presbyterian Church in Cannon-street. You are requested to attend and unite in putting down and silencing by peaceable means this tool of evil and fanaticism. Let the rights of the States guaranteed by the Constitution be protected.

Feb. 27, 1837.   *The Union forever!*

violated the First Amendment right of citizens to petition the government. But southern members of Congress did not want to debate slavery. Many northern members of Congress preferred to avoid the issue.

Eventually, representative and former president John Quincy Adams was able to get the gag rule overturned. His resolution to enact a constitutional amendment halting the expansion of slavery never passed, however.

Many white southerners saw slavery as vital to the South's economy and culture. They also felt that outsiders should not interfere with their way of life. After Nat Turner's Rebellion in 1831, when Turner led some slaves to kill slaveholders, open talk about slavery disappeared in the South. It became dangerous to voice antislavery sentiments in southern states. Abolitionists like the Grimké sisters left rather than air unpopular views to hostile neighbors. Racism, fear, and economic dependence on slavery made emancipation all but impossible in the South.

Reading Check
Draw Conclusions
Why did many northern workers oppose the abolition movement?

Summary and Preview The issue of slavery grew more controversial in the United States during the first half of the nineteenth century. In the next lesson you will learn how slavery affected politics in the United States.

Lesson 3 Assessment

Review Ideas, Terms, and People

1. a. Identify What contributions did William Lloyd Garrison make to the abolition movement?

b. Draw Conclusions In what ways did contributions from African Americans aid the struggle for abolition?

c. Elaborate What do you think about the American Colonization Society's plan to send free African Americans to Liberia?

2. a. Describe How did the Underground Railroad work?

b. Explain Why did Harriet Tubman first become involved with the Underground Railroad?

c. Evaluate Do you think the Underground Railroad was a success? Why or why not?

3. a. Describe What action did Congress take to block abolitionists?

b. Analyze Why did some Americans oppose equality for African Americans?

c. Predict How might the debate over slavery lead to conflict in the future?

Critical Thinking

4. Identify Cause and Effect In this lesson, you learned about the abolitionist movement of the early and mid-1800s. Create a graphic organizer similar to the one below to show the reasons for opposition to the movement and the effects of that opposition.

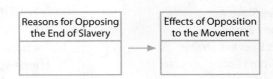

| Reasons for Opposing the End of Slavery | | Effects of Opposition to the Movement |

The Politics of Slavery

The Big Idea

The acquisition of new lands and antislavery writings intensified the debate over slavery.

Main Ideas

- The gaining of new territory in the West renewed disputes over the issue of slavery.
- The Compromise of 1850 tried to solve the disputes over slavery.
- The Fugitive Slave Act caused controversy and led to the growth of antislavery leanings.

Key Terms and People

Wilmot Proviso
sectionalism
Free-Soil Party
secede
Compromise of 1850
Fugitive Slave Act
Anthony Burns
Harriet Beecher Stowe
Uncle Tom's Cabin

If YOU were there . . .

You are a member of Congress from the North in 1850. You have just taken part in a heated floor debate about whether or not California should be accepted into the Union as a free or slave state. Several members from the South have threatened that their states will leave the Union if California enters as a free state. The nation is on the verge of splitting up.

What can you do to keep the nation united?

Slavery and Territorial Expansion

By the mid-1800s the nation was divided into two societies—the North, where workers labored for wages, and the South, where a large number of workers were enslaved. The developing debate over slavery was largely one of property rights versus human rights. Many Americans at the time thought that the property rights of slaveholders were more important that the human rights of slaves.

After winning the Mexican-American War, the United States added more than 500,000 square miles of new territory through the Mexican Cession. Eventually, new states would be formed out of this vast area. The key question became whether these states would ban or allow slavery. The Missouri Compromise of 1820 had banned slavery in most of the northern part of the Louisiana Purchase. Antislavery supporters wanted to do something similar with this new territory. On the other hand, some Americans wanted to allow slavery in the new lands.

During the Mexican-American War, Representative David Wilmot offered the **Wilmot Proviso**, a document stating that "neither slavery nor involuntary servitude shall ever exist in any part of [the] territory." Although the document was passed in the northern-controlled House, it was not passed by the southern-dominated Senate. Politicians formerly supported their party's ideas, but the Wilmot Proviso spurred a

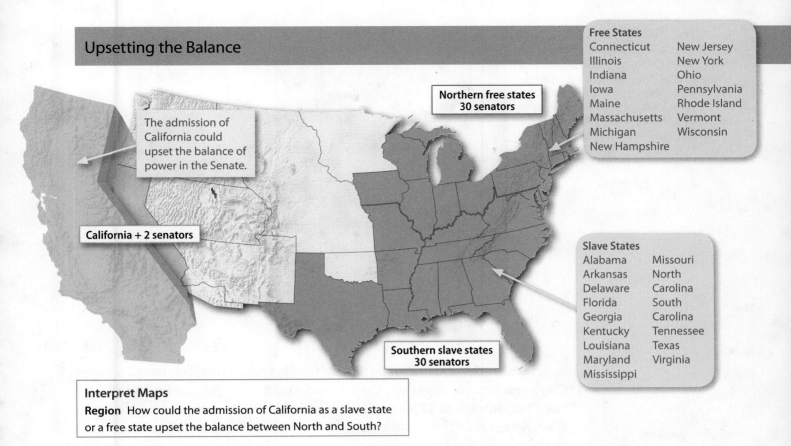

Free States
Connecticut   New Jersey
Illinois   New York
Indiana   Ohio
Iowa   Pennsylvania
Maine   Rhode Island
Massachusetts Vermont
Michigan   Wisconsin
New Hampshire

Northern free states
30 senators

The admission of California could upset the balance of power in the Senate.

California + 2 senators

Slave States
Alabama   Missouri
Arkansas   North
Delaware   Carolina
Florida   South
Georgia   Carolina
Kentucky   Tennessee
Louisiana   Texas
Maryland   Virginia
Mississippi

Southern slave states
30 senators

Interpret Maps

Region How could the admission of California as a slave state or a free state upset the balance between North and South?

debate that showed growing **sectionalism**, or favoring the interests of one section or region over the interests of the entire country.

In response to the unwillingness of the Democrats and Whigs to take a clear position on slavery, a new political party developed during the presidential campaign of 1848. Antislavery northerners formed the **Free-Soil Party**, which supported the Wilmot Proviso. They chose former president Martin Van Buren as their candidate. Their candidate did not win, but the votes he received helped Democrat Lewis Cass, who opposed the Wilmot Proviso, to lose to Whig candidate Zachary Taylor. The Wilmot Proviso, however, never was passed.

Another Attempt at Compromise

By 1850 the population in California had grown so much because of the gold rush that it applied to join the Union as a state instead of as a territory. This request brought the issue of slavery to the surface. If California entered the Union as a free state, the balance between free and slave states would change, favoring the free states. This was unacceptable to the South.

Kentucky Senator Henry Clay introduced a plan that proposed several compromises on the slavery issue. Clay's plan drew attack from representatives from the North and the South. Senator John C. Calhoun of South Carolina argued that letting California enter as a free state would destroy the nation's balance. He asked that the slave states be allowed to **secede**, or formally withdraw, from the Union.

Reading Check
Draw Inferences
How did the mixed results of the passage of the Wilmot Proviso illustrate the growth of sectionalism?

The Great Compromiser
Henry Clay was nicknamed "the Great Compromiser" for his success in negotiating agreements that balanced the interests of slave-owning states and the rest of the country. He was instrumental in achieving the Compromise of 1820, the Compromise Tariff of 1833, and the Compromise of 1850.

Reading Check
Analyze
Which element of the Compromise of 1850 could be considered a "win" by both northerners and southerners?

After months of debate, the Senate finally passed five laws based on Clay's resolutions. Together, these laws formed what became known as the **Compromise of 1850**. California was able to enter the Union as a free state. The rest of the Mexican Cession was divided into two territories—Utah and New Mexico—where the question of whether to allow slavery would be decided by popular sovereignty. Texas agreed to give up its land claims in New Mexico in exchange for financial aid from the federal government. Lastly, the compromise outlawed the slave trade in the District of Columbia and established a new fugitive slave law.

The Crisis Deepens

The issues the Compromise of 1850 seemed to solve were soon replaced by others. One part of the compromise itself was very controversial.

The Fugitive Slave Act The **Fugitive Slave Act** made it a crime to help runaway slaves and allowed officials to arrest those slaves in free areas. People accused of being escaped slaves had to prove that they were not, which was often difficult or impossible. Also, escaped slaves who had lived in the North for years were returned to slavery if caught.

The law was openly resisted by people in the North. Many northerners who had previously been quiet on slavery issues were now furious. Mobs rescued enslaved people from northern police stations. They threatened slave catchers. In 1854 **Anthony Burns**, a fugitive slave from Virginia, was arrested in Boston. Abolitionists used force while trying to rescue him from jail, killing a deputy marshal. A federal ship was ordered to return Burns to Virginia after his trial. Many people in the North, particularly in Massachusetts, were outraged.

The event persuaded many to join the abolitionist cause. At the same time, angered by these reactions of the northerners, some southern leaders began again to talk of seceding from the Union.

Outrage over the Act Abolitionists in the North used the stories of fugitive slaves like Anthony Burns to gain sympathy for their cause. These slave narratives also educated people about their hardships.

Harriet Beecher Stowe, a magazine writer in Maine, had once lived in Cincinnati, Ohio, an important stop on the Underground Railroad. There she heard tales of slavery's cruelty and horror. Angered by the Fugitive Slave Act, she wrote a series of short stories about slave life for an antislavery newspaper in 1851. A year later these stories were published as an antislavery novel entitled *Uncle Tom's Cabin*.

Uncle Tom's Cabin was published by Harriet Beecher Stowe in 1852.

Although Stowe had little firsthand knowledge of slavery or the South, her novel became an enormous success, selling more than two million copies around the United States. Its popularity caused one northerner to claim that the book had created "two millions of abolitionists." However, the book outraged many southerners. They accused Stowe of writing lies about plantation life. *Uncle Tom's Cabin* raised tensions over slavery to new heights.

Reading Check
Identify Cause and Effect What effect did the Fugitive Slave Act have on the antislavery movement?

Summary and Preview The United States experienced increasing disagreement over the issue of slavery. The Compromise of 1850 and the Fugitive Slave Act tried to address these disagreements with legislation. In the next module you will read about several reform movements in the United States that arose from issues, including that of slavery.

Lesson 4 Assessment

Reviewing Ideas, Terms, and People

1. a. **Recall** What caused the creation of the Free-Soil Party?

   b. **Predict** What do you think might result from the growing sectionalism in Congress?

2. a. **Make Inferences** Why might the Compromise of 1850 have been controversial in both the North and the South?

   b. **Evaluate** Was the Compromise of 1850 a good solution to the conflict over slavery?

3. a. **Identify** What were the effects of the Fugitive Slave Act?

   b. **Elaborate** Do you think slave narratives such as *Uncle Tom's Cabin* were an effective tool in the fight against slavery? Why or why not?

Critical Thinking

4. **Sequence** In this lesson, you learned about the sequence of events surrounding the debate over slavery during the mid-1800s. Create a graphic organizer like the one below to illustrate the chain of events explaining how each event led to the next. Add boxes as necessary.

Literature in History

Antislavery Literature

WORD HELP

conceive imagine

desolate alone

forlorn unhappy

slacking slowing
down

thither there

❶ *What detail tells
you how long Eliza has
walked up to this point?*

❷ *Why do you think
she chooses that escape
route?*

About the Reading Harriet Beecher Stowe came from a family of abolitionists. While Stowe and her family were living in Cincinnati, Ohio, they bravely sheltered slaves fleeing from the neighboring slave state of Kentucky. Outrage at the Fugitive Slave Act of 1850 led Stowe to write *Uncle Tom's Cabin*. This novel, published in 1852, revealed the cruelties of slavery. But it also went a step further—and showed the evil effects that slavery had on slaveholders themselves.

Uncle Tom's Cabin made Stowe famous. It was translated into more than 20 languages. Because of its popularity, it drew the world's attention to the injustice of slavery in the South. Published nine years before the outbreak of the Civil War, *Uncle Tom's Cabin* focused the nation's attention on the cruelties of slavery. In the following section, Stowe describes how a slave named Eliza is trying to escape to save her son from being sold.

As You Read Look for details that appeal to your feelings.

From *Uncle Tom's Cabin*
by Harriet Beecher Stowe (1811–1896)

It is impossible to conceive of a human creature more wholly desolate and forlorn than Eliza when she turned her footsteps from Uncle Tom's cabin. . . .

The boundaries of the farm, the grove, the wood lot passed by her dizzily as she walked on; and still she went, leaving one familiar object after another, slacking not, pausing not, till reddening daylight found her many a long mile from all traces of any familiar objects upon the open highway. ❶

She had often been, with her mistress, to visit some connections in the little town of T—, not far from the Ohio River, and knew the road well. ❷ To go thither, to escape across the Ohio River, were the first hurried outlines of her plan of escape; beyond that she could only hope in God. . . .

Connect Literature to History

1. **Analyze** Slaves had no legal rights. They were considered to be property, not human beings. How do the actions and description in this passage contradict these ideas about slaves?

2. **Compare and Contrast** Frederick Douglass, Sojourner Truth, and other former slaves wrote narratives about their experiences. Yet these true stories did not have as much impact as Stowe's novel. Why do you think this fictional story about slavery had more impact than true slave narratives?

Conduct Internet Research

Define the Skill

The Internet is a huge network of computers that are linked together. You can connect to this network from a personal computer or from a computer at a public library or school. Once connected, you can go to places called websites, which consist of one or more web pages. Each page contains information that you can view on the computer screen. Governments, businesses, individuals, and many different types of organizations, such as universities, news organizations, and libraries, have websites.

The Internet can be a very good reference source. It allows you to gather information on almost any topic without ever having to leave your chair. However, finding the information you need can sometimes be difficult. Having the skill to use the Internet efficiently increases its usefulness.

Learn the Skill

There are millions of websites on the Internet. This can make it hard to locate specific information. The following steps will help you in doing research on the Internet.

1. **Use a search engine.** This is a website that searches other sites. Type a word or phrase related to your topic into the search engine. It will list web pages that might contain information on your topic. Clicking on an entry in this list will bring that page to your screen.

2. **Study the web page.** Read the information to see if it is useful. You can print the page on the computer's printer or take notes. If you take notes, be sure to include the page's URL. This is its location or "address" on the Internet. You need this as the source of the information.

3. **Use hyperlinks.** Many web pages have connections, called hyperlinks, to related information on the site or on other websites. Clicking on these links will take you to those pages. You can follow their links to even more pages, collecting information as you go.

4. **Return to your results list.** If the information or a hyperlink on a web page is not useful, return to the list of pages that your search engine produced and repeat the process.

The Internet is a useful tool. But remember that information on the Internet is no different than printed resources. It must be evaluated with the same care and critical thinking as other sources.

Practice the Skill

Apply the guidelines to explore slavery in the United States during the 1800s and answer the following questions.

1. How would you begin if you wanted information about the abolition movement from the Internet?

2. What words might you type into a search engine to find out about life as a plantation slave?

3. Use a computer to research the Fugitive Slave Act. What kinds of pages did your research produce? Evaluate the usefulness of each type.

Module 15 Assessment

Review Vocabulary, Terms, and People

Match the word in the left column with the correct definition in the right column.

1. Middle Passage
2. Frederick Douglass
3. secede
4. Free-Soil Party
5. sectionalism
6. Fugitive Slave Act
7. Harriet Beecher Stowe
8. Nat Turner
9. Underground Railroad
10. abolition

a. a network of people who arranged transportation and hiding places for escaped slaves
b. leader of the most violent slave revolt in the country
c. group formed by antislavery northerners to promote and support the Wilmot Proviso
d. author of the antislavery novel, *Uncle Tom's Cabin*
e. favoring the interests of one region over the interests of the entire country
f. provision within the Compromise of 1850 that made it a crime to help runaway slaves
g. the complete end to slavery
h. the voyage across the Atlantic Ocean that enslaved Africans were forced to endure
i. formally withdraw
j. an escaped slave who became an important leader in the abolition movement

Comprehension and Critical Thinking

Lesson 1

11. a. **Identify** What was the main reason the Spanish could not continue to use Native Americans for slave labor?
    b. **Make Inferences** How might the African Diaspora have affected the societies and cultures within Africa?
    c. **Analyze** What role did religion play in the American slave culture?

Lesson 2

12. a. **Recall** How were slaves viewed in the South?
    b. **Make Inferences** What types of jobs were assigned to slaves, and why do you think this was the case?
    c. **Analyze** How might the slave codes have helped prevent revolts by slaves?

Lesson 3

13. a. **Identify** What were the methods use by members of the abolition movement to gain support for their cause?
    b. **Describe** How did the Underground Railroad work?
    c. **Draw Conclusions** Why do you think members of Congress refused to address petitions from abolitionists?

Lesson 4

14. a. **Identify** What was the main reason members of Congress were concerned about accepting California as a free state?
    b. **Analyze** Why was the Fugitive Slave Act so controversial for northerners?
    c. **Draw Conclusions** Why might slave narratives and other forms of literature have helped the abolitionists' cause?

Module 15 Assessment, continued

Review Themes

15. Politics How did the issue of slavery affect the actions of Congress during the 1800s?

16. Society and Culture What effect did their belief in abolition have on southern abolitionists?

Reading Skills

Compare and Contrast Historical Facts *Use the Reading Skills taught in this module to answer the question about the reading selection below.*

> The Missouri Compromise of 1820 had banned slavery in most of the northern part of the Louisiana Purchase. Antislavery supporters wanted to do something similar with this new territory. On the other hand, some Americans wanted to allow slavery in the new lands.

17. Based on the reading selection above, which of the following phrases signals a contrast?
a. banned slavery
b. on the other hand
c. antislavery supporters
d. something similar

Social Studies Skills

Conduct Internet Research *Use the Social Studies Skills taught in this module to answer the question below.*

18. Which of the following terms would be a useful search term when researching the Compromise of 1850?
a. Wilmot Proviso
b. Anthony Burns
c. *Uncle Tom's Cabin*
d. Henry Clay

Focus on Writing

19. Write a Biographical Sketch Review the content in the text relating to what life was like for slaves who worked on plantations. Then choose an imaginary person to write about. Think about what their life was like. Who were they and what did they look like? What did they wear? What job did they perform? How difficult was it to perform? Where did they live? Who did they interact with? What might a typical day have been like? Take your answers to these questions and write two paragraphs about a day in the life of this person from their perspective.

Reform Movements in the United States

Essential Question

How successful were reformers at improving living conditions for Americans in the early 1800s?

About the Photo: Busy port cities brought goods and people across the Atlantic.

Explore ONLINE!

HISTORY.

VIDEOS, including...
- Abolitionists and the Underground Railroad
- Frederick Douglass

✓ Document-Based Investigations

✓ Graphic Organizers

✓ Interactive Games

✓ Image with Hotspots: New York City, Mid-1800s

✓ Image Carousel: Transcendentalists

✓ Image Carousel: Abolitionist Leaders

In this module you will read about changes in American society and the goals of social reformers. You will also learn about the leaders of social reform movements.

What You Will Learn ...

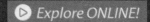

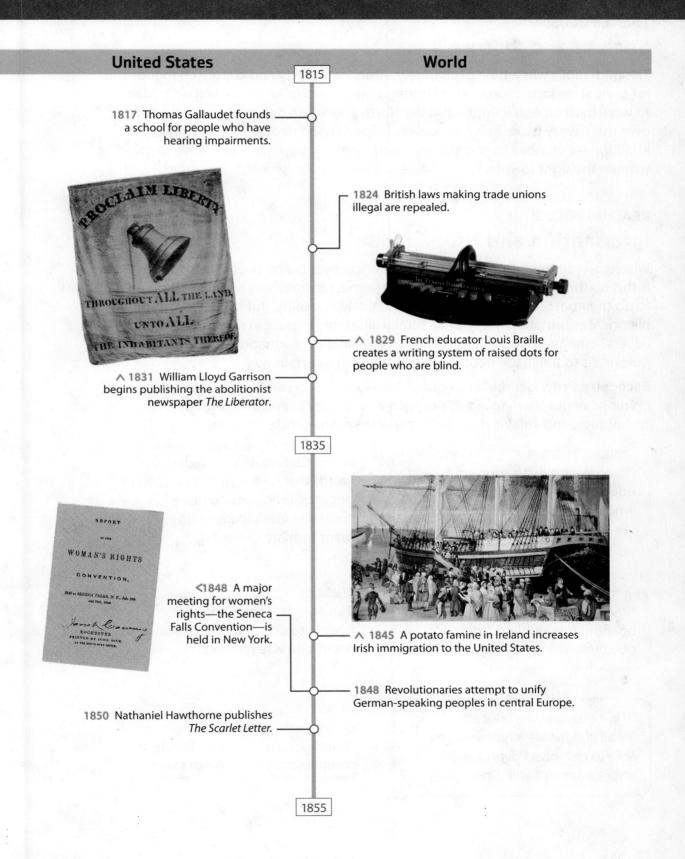

United States		World
	1815	

1817 Thomas Gallaudet founds a school for people who have hearing impairments.

1824 British laws making trade unions illegal are repealed.

1829 French educator Louis Braille creates a writing system of raised dots for people who are blind.

1831 William Lloyd Garrison begins publishing the abolitionist newspaper *The Liberator*.

1835

1848 A major meeting for women's rights—the Seneca Falls Convention—is held in New York.

1845 A potato famine in Ireland increases Irish immigration to the United States.

1848 Revolutionaries attempt to unify German-speaking peoples in central Europe.

1850 Nathaniel Hawthorne publishes *The Scarlet Letter.*

1855

Reading Social Studies

THEME FOCUS:

Society and Culture

The mid-1800s was a time of change in America. Society and culture changed for several reasons: thousands of immigrants arrived in America; women began to work hard for equal rights; and the North and South debated more and more over the slavery issue. Religious beliefs helped shape people's views toward abolition—the move to end slavery—and women's suffrage—the move to give women the right to vote. This module discusses these issues.

READING FOCUS:

Information and Propaganda

Where do you get information about historical events and people? One source is this textbook and others like it. You can expect the authors of your textbook to do their best to present the facts objectively and fairly. But some sources of historical information may have a totally different purpose in mind. For example, advertisements in political campaigns may contain information, but their main purpose is to persuade people to act or think in a certain way.

Recognize Propaganda Techniques Propaganda is created to change people's opinions or get them to act in a certain way. Learn to recognize propaganda techniques, and you will be able to separate propaganda from the facts.

"People who don't support public education are greedy monsters who don't care about children!"	**Name Calling** Using loaded words, words that create strong positive or negative emotions, to make someone else's ideas seem inappropriate or wrong
"People all around the country are opening free public schools. It's obviously the right thing to do."	**Bandwagon** Encouraging people to do something because "everyone else is doing it"
"If we provide free education for all children, everyone will be able to get jobs. Poverty and unemployment will disappear."	**Oversimplification** Making a complex situation seem simple; a complex problem easy to solve

You Try It!

The flyer below was published in 1837.

Flyer from 1837

> **OUTRAGE.**
>
> **Fellow Citizens,**
>
> AN
>
> **ABOLITIONIST,**
>
> of the most revolting character is among you, exciting the feelings of the North against the South. A seditious Lecture is to be delivered
>
> **THIS EVENING,**
>
> at 7 o'clock, at the Presbyterian Church in Cannon-street. You are requested to attend and unite in putting down and silencing by peaceable means this tool of evil and fanaticism. Let the rights of the States guaranteed by the Constitution be protected.
>
> **Feb. 27, 1837.** *The Union forever!*

After studying the flyer, answer the following questions.

1. What is the purpose of this flyer?

2. Who do you think distributed this flyer?

3. Do you think this flyer is an example of propaganda? Why or why not? If you think it is propaganda, what kind is it?

4. If you were the subject of this flyer, how would you feel? How might you respond to it?

As you read Module 16, look carefully at all the primary sources. Do any of them include examples of propaganda?

Immigrants and Urban Challenges

The Big Idea

The population of the United States grew rapidly in the early 1800s with the arrival of millions of immigrants.

Main Ideas

- Millions of immigrants, mostly German and Irish, arrived in the United States despite anti-immigrant movements.

- Industrialization led to the growth of cities.

- American cities experienced urban problems due to rapid growth.

Key Terms

nativists
Know-Nothing Party
middle class
tenements

If YOU were there . . .

It is 1850, and you are a German immigrant standing on the deck of a steamboat, crossing Lake Erie. Other immigrants are on board, but they are strangers to you. Soon, you will arrive at your new home in Cleveland, Ohio. You've been told that other Germans have settled there. You hope to find friends and work as a baker. Right now, America seems very big and very strange.

What would you expect from your new life in America?

Millions of Immigrants Arrive

In the mid-1800s, large numbers of immigrants crossed the Atlantic Ocean to begin new lives in the United States. More than 4 million of them settled in the United States between 1840 and 1860, most from Europe. More than 3 million of these immigrants arrived from Ireland and Germany. Many of them were fleeing economic troubles in their native countries. Some were seeking political or religious freedom.

Fleeing the Irish Potato Famine Most immigrants from the British Isles during that period were Irish. In the mid-1840s, potato blight, a disease that causes rot in potatoes, left many families in Ireland with little food. More than a million Irish people died of starvation and disease. Even more fled to the United States.

Most Irish immigrants were very poor and settled in northeastern cities to look for work. By 1850 the Irish made up one-fifth of the population in seven major cities, including New York, Philadelphia, and Boston. They worked at unskilled jobs in the cities or on building canals and railroads. Irish women often worked as domestic servants for wealthy families, laboring 16 or more hours per day. In 1849 a Boston health committee reported that low wages forced most Irish immigrants to live in poor housing.

An Irish immigrant family could expect hardships in their adopted country, but they could also find greater opportunities for a new and better life.

Still, many immigrants enjoyed a new feeling of equality. Patrick Dunny wrote home to his family about this situation.

> "People that cuts a great dash [style] at home . . . think it strange [in the United States] for the humble class of people to get as much respect as themselves."
>
> —Patrick Dunny, quoted in *Who Built America?* by Bruce Levine et al.

A Failed German Revolution Many Germans also came to the United States during this time. In the early 1800s, many Germans were attracted by the First Amendment protection of religious freedom and came to the United States to escape religious persecution. In 1848 some Germans had staged a revolution against harsh rule. Some educated Germans fled to the United States to escape persecution caused by their political activities. Most German immigrants, however, were working class, and they came for economic reasons. The United States seemed to offer both greater economic opportunity and more freedom from government control. While most Irish immigrants were Catholics, German immigrant groups included Catholics, Jews, and Protestants.

German immigrants were more likely than the Irish to become farmers and live in rural areas. They moved to midwestern states where more land was available. Unlike the Irish, a high percentage of German immigrants arrived in the United States with money. Despite their funds and skills, German immigrants often had to take low-paying jobs. Many German immigrants worked as tailors, seamstresses, bricklayers, servants, clerks, cabinetmakers, bakers, and food merchants.

Anti-Immigration Movements Industrialization and the waves of people from Europe greatly changed the American labor force. While many immigrants went to the Midwest to get farmland, other immigrants filled the need for cheap labor in towns and cities. Industrial jobs in the Northeast attracted many people.

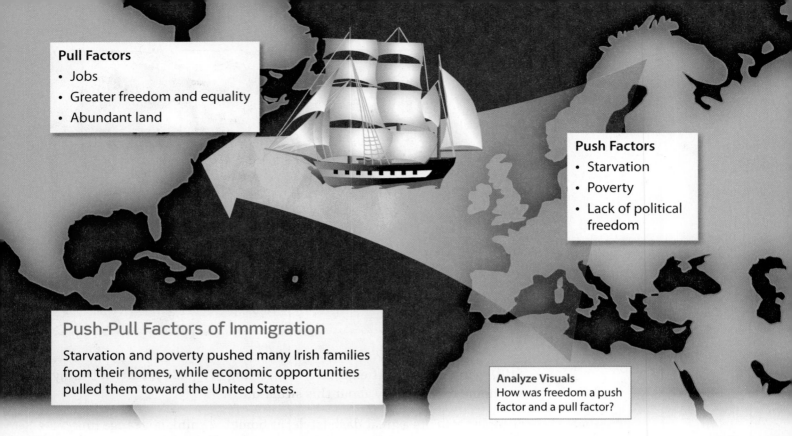

Pull Factors
- Jobs
- Greater freedom and equality
- Abundant land

Push Factors
- Starvation
- Poverty
- Lack of political freedom

Push-Pull Factors of Immigration
Starvation and poverty pushed many Irish families from their homes, while economic opportunities pulled them toward the United States.

Analyze Visuals
How was freedom a push factor and a pull factor?

Academic Vocabulary
implicit understood though not clearly put into words

Yet a great deal of native-born Americans feared losing their jobs to immigrants who might work for lower wages. Some felt **implicitly** threatened by the new immigrants' cultures and religions. For example, before Catholic immigrants arrived, most Americans were Protestants. Conflicts between Catholics and Protestants in Europe caused American Protestants to mistrust Catholic immigrants. Some Protestants believed that Catholics threatened democracy. Those Protestants feared that the pope, the head of the Roman Catholic Church, was plotting to overthrow democracy in America. Those Americans and others who opposed immigration were called **nativists**. In cities such as New York and Boston, nativists formed a secret society. Members promised not to vote for Catholics or immigrants running for political office.

In the 1840s and 1850s some nativists became politically active. An 1844 election flyer gave Americans this warning.

"Look at the . . . thieves and vagabonds [tramps] roaming our streets . . . monopolizing [taking] the business which properly belongs to our own native and true-born citizens."
—Election flyer, quoted in *Who Built America?*, by Bruce Levine et al.

In 1849 nativists founded a political organization, the **Know-Nothing Party**, that supported measures making it difficult for foreigners to become citizens or hold office. Its members wanted to keep Catholics and immigrants out of public office. They also wanted to require immigrants to live in the United States for 21 years before becoming citizens. Know-Nothing politicians had some success getting elected during the 1850s. Later, disagreements over the issue of slavery caused the party to fall apart. Immigrants continued to come to the United States, and the resulting mix of ethnicities and religions continued to influence American society and culture.

Reading Check
Identify Cause and Effect Why did the Know-Nothing Party try to limit the rights of immigrants?

Rapid Growth of Cities

The Industrial Revolution led to the creation of many new jobs in American cities. These city jobs drew immigrants from many nations as well as migrants from rural parts of the United States. The Transportation Revolution helped connect cities and made it easier for people to move to them. As a result of these two trends, American cities grew rapidly in number and population during the mid-1800s. Cities in the northeastern and Middle Atlantic states grew the most. By the mid-1800s, three-quarters of the country's manufacturing jobs were in these areas.

The rise of industry and the growth of cities changed American life. Those who owned their own businesses or worked in skilled jobs benefited most from those changes. The families of these merchants, manufacturers, professionals, and master craftspeople made up a growing social class. This new **middle class** was a social and economic level between the wealthy and the poor. Those in the new middle class built large, dignified homes that demonstrated their place in society.

In the growing cities, people found entertainment and an enriched cultural life. Many enjoyed visiting places such as libraries and clubs or attending concerts or lectures. In the mid-1800s people also attended urban theaters. Favorite pastimes included bowling, boxing, and playing cards. The rules of baseball were formalized in 1845, and the game became increasingly popular.

Cities during this time were compact and crowded. Many people lived close enough to their jobs that they could walk to work. Wagons carried goods down streets paved with stones, making a noisy, busy scene. One observer noted that the professionals in New York City always had a "hurried walk."

Reading Check
Summarize
How did the Industrial Revolution affect life in American cities?

Urban Problems

American cities in the mid-1800s faced many challenges due to rapid growth. Because public and private transportation was limited, city residents had to live near their workplaces. In addition, there was a lack of safe housing. Many city dwellers, particularly immigrants, could afford to live only in **tenements**—poorly designed apartment buildings that housed large numbers of people. These structures were often dirty, overcrowded, and unsafe.

Public services were also poor. The majority of cities did not have clean water, public health regulations, or healthful ways to get rid of garbage and human and animal waste. Under these conditions, diseases spread easily and epidemics were common. In 1832 and 1849, for example, New York City suffered cholera epidemics that killed thousands.

City life held other dangers. As urban areas grew, they became centers of criminal activity. Most cities—including New York, Boston, and Philadelphia—had no permanent or organized force to fight crime and violence. Instead, they relied on volunteer night watches, which offered little protection. The violence was often between various ethnic or racial groups, who had different economic and social goals. Immigrants often

In the mid-1800s, cities such as New York City lured thousands of people in search of jobs and a better life. Many city dwellers found living in crowded urban conditions difficult.

came from a mix of social classes, which led to cultural conflicts among groups. Differences in political goals and opinions also led to disagreements between groups.

Fire was another constant and serious danger in crowded cities. There was little organized fire protection. Most cities were served by volunteer fire companies. Firefighters used hand pumps and buckets to put out fires. In addition, there were not enough sanitation workers and road maintenance crews. These shortages and flaws caused health and safety problems for many city residents.

Summary and Preview Immigrants expected a better life in America, but not all Americans welcomed newcomers. The rapid growth of cities caused many problems. In the next lesson you will read about how America developed its own style of art and literature.

Reading Check
**Analyze
Information**
Why did so many American cities have problems in the mid-1800s?

Lesson 1 Assessment

Review Ideas, Terms, and People

1. a. **Identify** Who were the nativists?

   b. **Identify** What were the most common religious groups among the Irish and German immigrants?

   c. **Compare and Contrast** In what ways were Irish and German immigrants to the United States similar and different?

   d. **Analyze** How did the First Amendment's guarantee of religious freedom help change the ethnic and religious makeup of the United States?

   e. **Predict** How might the rise of anti-immigrant groups lead to problems in the United States?

2. a. **Describe** What led to the growth of cities?

   b. **Analyze** How did the rise of industrialization and the growth of cities change American society?

3. a. **Describe** What were tenements?

   b. **Summarize** What problems affected American cities in the mid-1800s?

   c. **Explain** How did religion, social class, and political beliefs cause conflicts between immigrant groups? How were these conflicts resolved?

   d. **Evaluate** What do you think was the biggest problem facing cities in the United States? Why?

Critical Thinking

4. **Identify Cause and Effect** In this lesson you learned about the causes and effects of immigration and urban growth. Create a graphic organizer similar to the ones below, identifying the causes and effects of each.

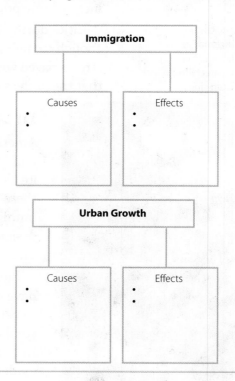

American Arts

The Big Idea

New movements in art and literature influenced many Americans in the early 1800s.

Main Ideas

- Transcendentalists and utopian communities withdrew from American society.
- American Romantic painters and writers made important contributions to art and literature.

Key Terms and People

transcendentalism
Ralph Waldo Emerson
Margaret Fuller
Henry David Thoreau
utopian communities
Nathaniel Hawthorne
Edgar Allan Poe
Emily Dickinson
Henry Wadsworth Longfellow
Walt Whitman

If YOU were there . . .

You are a teacher living in Massachusetts in the 1840s. Some of your neighbors have started an experimental community. They want to live more simply than present-day society allows. They hope to have time to write and think, while still sharing the work. Some people will teach; others will raise food. You think this might be an interesting place to live.

What would you ask the leaders of the community?

Transcendentalists

Some New England writers and philosophers found spiritual wisdom in **transcendentalism**, the belief that people could transcend, or rise above, material things in life. Transcendentalists also believed that people should depend on themselves and their own insights, rather than on outside authorities. Important transcendentalists included **Ralph Waldo Emerson**, **Margaret Fuller**, and **Henry David Thoreau**.

Walden Pond, where Thoreau lived for two years

The First Harvest in the Wilderness painted by Asher Durand is an example of how artists of the Romantic movement celebrated nature in their dramatic paintings.

Academic Vocabulary
abstract expressing a quality or idea without reference to an actual thing

Reading Check
Make Inferences
Why did utopian communities only last a short time?

Emerson was a popular writer and thinker who argued that Americans should disregard institutions and follow their own beliefs. "What I must do is all that concerns me, not what the people think," he wrote in an essay called "Self-Reliance." Fuller edited the famous transcendentalist publication *The Dial*. Thoreau advised even stronger self-reliance and simple living away from society in natural settings. He wrote his book *Walden* after he lived for two years at Walden Pond.

Some transcendentalists formed a community at Brook Farm, Massachusetts, in the 1840s. It was one of many experiments with **utopian communities**, groups of people who tried to form a perfect society. People in utopian communities pursued **abstract** spirituality and cooperative lifestyles. Communities sprang up in New Harmony, Oneida, and many other places. However, few communities lasted for long.

American Romanticism

Ideas about the simple life and nature also inspired painters and writers in the early and mid-1800s. Some joined the Romantic movement that had begun in Europe. Romanticism involved a great interest in nature, an emphasis on individual expression, and a rejection of many established rules. These painters and writers felt that each person brings a unique view to the world. They believed in using emotion to guide their creative output. Some Romantic artists, like Thomas Cole, painted the American landscape. Their works showed the beauty and wonder of nature in the United States.

Nathaniel Hawthorne was born in Salem, Massachusetts. Much of his writing is set in New England and expresses themes of evil and sin.

Reading Check
Summarize
Who were some American Romantic authors, and why were they important?

Their images contrasted with the huge cities and corruption of nature that many Americans saw as typical of Europe.

Many female writers, like Ann Sophia Stephens, wrote historical fiction that was popular in the mid-1800s. New England writer **Nathaniel Hawthorne** wrote *The Scarlet Letter* during that period. One of the greatest classics of Romantic literature, it explored Puritan life in the 1600s. Hawthorne's friend Herman Melville, a writer and former sailor, wrote novels about the sea, such as *Moby-Dick* and *Billy Budd*. Many people believe that *Moby-Dick* is one of the finest American novels ever written.

American Romantic authors also wrote a great deal of poetry. The poet **Edgar Allan Poe**, also a short-story writer, became famous for a haunting poem called "The Raven." Other gifted American poets included **Emily Dickinson**, **Henry Wadsworth Longfellow**, and **Walt Whitman**. Most of Dickinson's short, thoughtful poems were not published until after her death. Longfellow, the best-known poet of the mid-1800s, wrote popular story-poems, like *The Song of Hiawatha*. Whitman praised American individualism and democracy in his simple, unrhymed poetry. In his poetry collection *Leaves of Grass*, he wrote, "The United States themselves are essentially the greatest poem."

Summary and Preview American Romantic artists and authors were inspired by ideas about the simple life, nature, and spirituality. In the next lesson you will learn about ideas that changed American society.

Lesson 2 Assessment

Review Ideas, Terms, and People

1. **a. Identify** What were the main teachings of transcendentalism?

   b. Summarize What was one of the utopian communities established in the United States, and what was its goal?

   c. Elaborate Do you agree with transcendentalists that Americans put too much emphasis on institutions and traditions? Explain your answer.

2. **a. Recall** Who were some important American authors and poets at this time?

   b. Explain What ideas did artists in the Romantic movement express?

   c. Evaluate Do you think the Romantic movement was important to American culture? Explain.

Critical Thinking

3. **Compare and Contrast** In this lesson you learned about new movements in art and literature in the mid-1800s. Create a graphic organizer similar to the one below and use it to show the similarities and differences between the two movements.

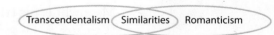

Transcendentalism | Similarities | Romanticism

Literature in History

Literature of the Young Nation: Romanticism and Realism

Word Help

belfry bell tower

muster gathering

barrack building where soldiers meet

grenadiers soldiers who belong to a special regiment

❶ When the poem was written, there were still a few people alive who had lived during the Revolution.

❷ Longfellow uses poetic language to make Revere's story more dramatic.

❸ The sounds of the night are described to help the reader feel the excitement.

About the Reading "Paul Revere's Ride" was published in a book called *Tales of a Wayside Inn*. The book is a collection of poems that tell well-known stories from history and mythology. By including the story of Paul Revere with other famous stories, Longfellow helped increase the importance of Paul Revere's ride.

As You Read Notice how Longfellow describes Revere as a hero.

From "Paul Revere's Ride" from *Tales of a Wayside Inn*
by Henry Wadsworth Longfellow (1807–1882)

Listen my children and you shall hear
Of the midnight ride of Paul Revere,
On the eighteenth of April, in Seventy-five;
Hardly a man is now alive
Who remembers that famous day and year. ❶

He said to his friend, "If the British march
By land or sea from the town to-night,
Hang a lantern aloft in the belfry arch
Of the North Church tower as a signal light,—
One if by land, and two if by sea;
And I on the opposite shore will be,
Ready to ride and spread the alarm
Through every . . . village and farm,
For the country folk to be up and to arm." ❷

Meanwhile, his friend, through alley and street
Wanders and watches with eager ears,
Till in the silence around him he hears
The muster of men at the barrack door,
The sound of arms, and the tramp of feet,
And the measured tread of the grenadiers,
Marching down to their boats on the shore. ❸

Word Help

lame disabled

irascible difficult

bliss happiness

ambition hope for the future

affliction problem

pathetic very sad

perpetual constant

❶ Some women kept companions to help entertain them and perform small chores. *Why might Jo not want to be a companion?*

❷ How was Jo different from most women in the 1880s?

❸ What might Jo be able to do for work in the 1800s?

About the Reading *Little Women* is a novel about four sisters living in a small New England town before the Civil War. Still popular with young people today, *Little Women* describes a family much like the one Louisa May Alcott grew up in. Alcott based the main character, Jo March, on herself. Like Alcott, Jo was different from most women of her time. She was outspoken, eager for adventure, and in conflict with the role her society expected her to play.

As You Read Try to understand how Jo is different from Aunt March.

From *Little Women*
by Louisa May Alcott (1832–1888)

Jo happened to suit Aunt March, who was lame and needed an active person to wait upon her. The childless old lady had offered to adopt one of the girls when the troubles came, and was much offended because her offer was declined . . .

The old lady wouldn't speak to them for a time, but happening to meet Jo at a friend's, . . . she proposed to take her for a companion. ❶ This did not suit Jo at all, but she accepted the place since nothing better appeared, and to everyone's surprise, got on remarkably well with her irascible relative . . .

I suspect that the real attraction was a large library of fine books, which was left to dust and spiders since Uncle March died . . . The dim, dusty room, with the busts staring down from the tall bookcases, the cozy chairs, the globes, and, best of all, the wilderness of books, in which she could wander where she liked, made the library a region of bliss to her . . . ❷

Jo's ambition was to do something very splendid. What it was she had no idea, as yet, but left it for time to tell her, and, meanwhile, found her greatest affliction in the fact that she couldn't read, run, and ride as much as she liked. ❸ A quick temper, sharp tongue, and restless spirit were always getting her into scrapes, and her life was a series of ups and downs, which were both comic and pathetic. But the training she received at Aunt March's was just what she needed, and the thought that she was doing something to support herself made her happy in spite of the perpetual "Josy-phine!"

Connect Literature to History

1. **Draw Conclusions** Henry Wadsworth Longfellow was the most popular American poet of his time. How does his version of Paul Revere's ride increase the importance of the story?

2. **Compare and Contrast** The lives of women in the 1800s were very different from the lives of women today. How does this excerpt of *Little Women* show some similarities and differences between now and then?

Reforming Society

The Big Idea

Reform movements in the early 1800s affected religion, education, and society.

Main Ideas

- The Second Great Awakening sparked interest in religion.

- Social reformers began to speak out about temperance and prison reform.

- Improvements in education reform affected many segments of the population.

- Northern African American communities became involved in reform efforts.

Key Terms and People

Second Great Awakening
Charles Grandison Finney
Lyman Beecher
temperance movement
Dorothea Dix
common-school movement
Horace Mann
Catharine Beecher
Thomas Gallaudet

If YOU were there . . .

You live in New York State in the 1850s. You are the oldest daughter in your family. Since childhood you have loved mathematics, which puzzles your family. Your sisters are happy learning to sew and cook and run a household. You want more. You know that there is a female seminary nearby, where you could study and learn much more. But your parents are undecided.

How might you persuade your parents to send you to the school?

Second Great Awakening

During the 1790s and early 1800s, some Americans felt there was a strong need for religious reform and took part in a Christian renewal movement called the **Second Great Awakening**. It swept through towns across upstate New York and through the frontier regions of Kentucky, Ohio, Tennessee, and South Carolina. By the 1820s and 1830s, this new interest in religion had spread to New England and the South.

Charles Grandison Finney was one of the most important leaders of the Second Great Awakening. After experiencing a dramatic religious conversion in 1821, Finney left his career as a lawyer and began preaching. He challenged some traditional Protestant beliefs, telling congregations that each individual was responsible for his or her own salvation. He also believed that sin was avoidable. Finney held revivals, emotional prayer meetings that lasted for days. Many people converted to Christianity during these revivals. Finney told new converts to prove their faith by doing good deeds.

Finney's style of preaching and his ideas angered some traditional ministers, like Boston's **Lyman Beecher**. Beecher wanted to prevent Finney from holding revivals in his city. "You mean to carry a streak of fire to Boston. If you attempt it, as the Lord liveth, I'll meet you . . . and fight every inch of the way." Despite the opposition of Beecher and other traditional

The Second Great Awakening saw the growth of revivals such as the one shown here. Revivals were designed to reawaken religious feelings.

ministers, Finney's appeal remained powerful. Also, the First Amendment guarantee of freedom of religion prevented the government from passing laws banning the new religious practices. Ministers were therefore free to spread their message of faith and salvation to whoever wished to listen.

Due to the efforts of Finney and his followers, church membership across the country grew a great deal during the Second Great Awakening. Many new church members were women and African Americans. The African Methodist Episcopal Church was formed and spread across the Middle Atlantic states. Although the movement had begun in the Northeast and on the frontier, the Second Great Awakening renewed some people's religious faith throughout America.

Reading Check
Draw Conclusions
What impact did the Second Great Awakening have on religion in America?

Social Reformers Speak Out

Renewed religious faith often led to involvement in movements to fix the problems created by urban growth. One solution was political action. For example, in 1844 New York City created the first city police force.

Members of the growing middle class, especially women, often led the efforts. Many of the women did not work outside the home and had servants to care for their households. This gave them time to work in reform groups.

Temperance Movement Many social reformers worked to prevent alcohol abuse. They believed that Americans drank too much. In the 1830s, on average, an American consumed seven gallons of alcohol per year. Countless Americans thought that alcohol abuse caused social problems, such as family violence, poverty, and criminal behavior.

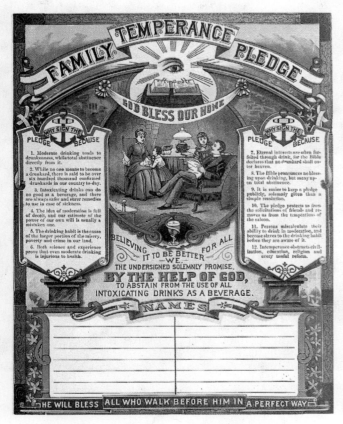

The temperance movement, an effort to convince people to avoid drinking alcohol, promoted abstinence with posters like the one shown here.

Americans' worries about the effects of alcohol on people led to the growth of a **temperance movement**. This reform effort urged people to use self-discipline to stop drinking hard liquor.

Reformers asked people to limit themselves to beer and wine in small amounts. Groups like the American Temperance Society and the American Temperance Union helped to spread the message. Minister Lyman Beecher spoke widely about the evils of alcohol. He claimed that people who drank alcohol were "neglecting the education of their families—and corrupting their morals." As a result of the temperance movement, the legislators of the state of Maine outlawed alcohol in 1851. Over the next several years, the legislators of 12 other states outlawed it as well.

Prison Reform Another target of reform was the prison system. **Dorothea Dix** was a middle-class reformer who visited prisons throughout Massachusetts beginning in 1841. Dix reported that mentally ill people frequently were jailed with criminals. They were sometimes left in dark cells without clothes or heat and were chained to the walls and beaten. Dix spoke of what she saw to the state legislature.

In response, the Massachusetts government built facilities for the mentally ill. Dix's work had a nationwide effect. Eventually, more than 100 state hospitals were built to give mentally ill people professional care.

Prisons also held runaway children and orphans. Some had survived only by begging or stealing, and they got the same punishment as adult criminals. Boston mayor Josiah Quincy asked that young offenders receive different punishments than adults. In the 1820s several state and local governments founded reform schools for children who had been housed in prisons. There, children lived under strict rules and learned useful skills.

Some reformers also tried to end the overcrowding and cruel conditions in prisons. Their efforts led to the creation of houses of correction. These institutions did not use punishment alone to change behavior. They also offered prisoners education.

Improvements in Education

Another challenge facing America in the early 1800s was poor public education. During this era, childhood was beginning to be viewed as a separate stage of life in which education was of the utmost importance in creating responsible citizens. However, many children worked in factories or on farms to help support their families. If children could read the Bible, write, and do simple math, that was often considered to be enough.

Reading Check
Summarize How did reformers change the punishment of criminals?

Education in the Early 1800s The availability of education varied widely. New England had the most schools, while the South and the West had the fewest. Few teachers were trained. Schoolhouses were small, and students of all ages and levels worked in one room.

McGuffey's Readers were the most popular textbooks. William Holmes McGuffey, an educator and minister, put selections from British and American literature in them as well as instruction in moral and social values.

Social background and wealth affected the quality of education. Rich families sent children to private schools or hired tutors. However, poor children had only public schools. Girls could go to school, but parents usually thought that girls needed little education and kept them home. Therefore, few girls learned to read.

This photograph shows a Washington, DC, classroom inspired by the ideas of Horace Mann.

Common-School Movement People in the **common-school movement** wanted all children taught in a common place, regardless of background. **Horace Mann** was a leader of this movement.

In 1837 Mann became Massachusetts's first secretary of education. He convinced the state to double its school budget and raise teachers' salaries. He lengthened the school year and began the first school for teacher training. Mann's success set a standard for education reform throughout the country.

Women's Education Education reform created greater opportunities for women. **Catharine Beecher** started an all-female academy in Hartford, Connecticut. The first college-level educational institution available to women was the Troy Female Seminary, opened by Emma Willard in 1821. Several other women's colleges opened during the 1830s, including Mount Holyoke College. The first medical college for women, who were barred from men's medical schools, opened in Boston in 1848.

BIOGRAPHY

Horace Mann 1796–1859

Born in Franklin, Massachusetts, Mann had little schooling, but he educated himself well enough at the local library to get into Brown University and attend law school. Despite a busy law practice, he served in the Massachusetts legislature for ten years. He was also an outspoken advocate for public education. In 1837 the state created the post of secretary of education for him. His achievements in that office made him famous. He later served in the U.S. House of Representatives and as president of Antioch College in Ohio.

His influence on education is reflected by the fact that many American schools are named for him.

Analyze Information
How do you think Mann's own education influenced his desire for public schools?

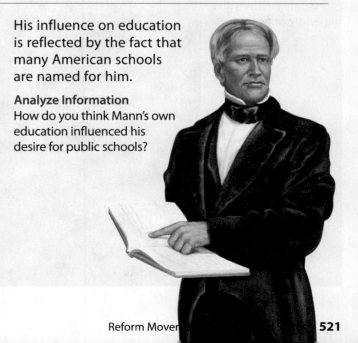

Reading Check
Summarize
What were Horace
Mann's achievements?

Teaching People with Special Needs Efforts to improve education also helped people with special needs. In 1831 Samuel Gridley Howe opened the Perkins School for the Blind in Massachusetts. Howe traveled widely, talking about teaching people with visual impairment. **Thomas Gallaudet** improved the education and lives of people with hearing impairments. He founded the first free American school for hearing-impaired people in 1817.

African American Communities

Free African Americans usually lived in segregated, or separate, communities in the North. Most of them lived in cities such as New York, Boston, and Philadelphia. Community leaders were often influenced by the Second Great Awakening and its spirit of reform.

Founded by former slave Richard Allen, the Free African Religious Society became a model for other groups that pressed for racial equality and the education of blacks. In 1816 Allen became the first bishop of the African Methodist Episcopal Church, or AME Church. This church broke away from white Methodist churches after African Americans were treated poorly in some white congregations.

Other influential African Americans of the time, such as Alexander Crummel, pushed for the creation of schools for black Americans. The New York African Free School in New York City educated hundreds of children, many of whom became brilliant scholars and important African American leaders. Philadelphia also had a long history of educating African Americans. This was largely because Philadelphia was a center of Quaker influence, and the Quakers believed strongly in equality. The city ran seven schools for African American students by the year 1800. In 1820 Boston followed Philadelphia's lead and opened a separate

This photograph of the Oberlin College class of 1855 shows the expansion of education for women as well as the slow integration of African Americans into previously white colleges.

elementary school for African American children. The city began allowing them to attend school with whites in 1855.

African Americans rarely attended college because few colleges would accept them. In 1835 Oberlin College became the first to do so. Harvard University soon admitted African Americans, too. Several African American colleges were founded beginning in the 1840s. In 1842 the Institute for Colored Youth opened in Philadelphia. Avery College, also in Pennsylvania, was founded in 1849.

While free African Americans had some opportunities to attend school in the North and Midwest, few had this chance in the South. Laws in the South barred most enslaved people from getting any education, even at the primary school level. While some slaves learned to read on their own, they almost always did so in secret. Slaveholders were fearful that education and knowledge in general might encourage a spirit of revolt among enslaved African Americans.

Reading Check
Draw Conclusions
Why was it difficult for African Americans to get an education in the South in the early 1800s?

Summary and Preview The efforts of reformers led to improvements in many aspects of American life in the early to mid-1800s. In the next lesson you will learn about reform-minded people who opposed the practice of slavery.

Lesson 3 Assessment

Review Ideas, Terms, and People

1. **a. Identify** What was the Second Great Awakening, and who was one of its leaders?

   b. Identify What was one cause of the Second Great Awakening?

   c. Summarize What effects did the Second Great Awakening have on religion in the United States?

2. **a. Identify** What role did Dorothea Dix play in social reforms of the early 1800s?

   b. Summarize What different reforms helped improve the U.S. prison system?

   c. Elaborate How might the Second Great Awakening have led to the growth of social reform movements?

3. **a. Identify** What was the common-school movement, and who was one of its leaders?

   b. Analyze Why did reformers set out to improve education in the United States?

   c. Evaluate Do you think Horace Mann's ideas for educational reform were good ones? Explain.

4. **a. Recall** In what cities were the first public schools for African Americans located?

   b. Draw Conclusions How did free African Americans benefit from educational reforms?

Critical Thinking

5. **Categorize** In this lesson you learned about key reform movements in the early to mid-1800s. Create a chart similar to the one below to identify the leaders and accomplishments of each reform movement.

Movement	Leaders	Accomplishments
Prison and Mental Health Reform		
Temperance		
Education		

Abolition

If YOU were there . . .

You live in South Carolina in the 1850s. You are invited by a friend to hear Angelina and Sarah Grimké, two southerners fighting to abolish slavery, speak at your friend's house. Your father is a slaveholder, and you know he disapproves of abolition and the Grimké sisters. You are interested in hearing what they have to say. But you know this might get you in trouble with your father and other family members.

Would you attend the meeting? Why?

Demanding an End to Slavery

Since the beginning of slavery in the United States, enslaved people made efforts to escape their difficult lives. However, the number of escape attempts increased sharply during the 1830s. These courageous slaves may have been encouraged by a small movement that was gaining support in the North. The **abolition movement** was a campaign to abolish, or end, slavery. This movement grew into one of the largest reform movements of the mid-1800s. No other movement attracted as many followers or had such an impact on the history of the United States. Supporters of the abolition movement were called abolitionists, and they included men and women as well as blacks and whites from both the North and the South.

Religious Roots The abolition movement had deep roots in religion. Since the colonial period, the Quakers were among the first groups to challenge slavery on religious grounds, believing it to be immoral. Pennsylvania, with many Quaker residents, was a center of activity, with the Pennsylvania Abolition Society established in 1775. Other religious leaders published pamphlets and gave speeches that encouraged many Americans to support the cause.

The rebirth of religious fervor in the Second Great Awakening also contributed to the rise of the abolition movement.

'Am I not a Woman and a Sister?'

This engraving highlighted the connections between the antislavery movement and the women's rights movement in the mid-1800s.

Many religious people in the North saw slavery as a clear moral wrong that went directly against their beliefs. Many joined reform societies to campaign against slavery. By 1836 more than 500 of these groups existed.

However, antislavery reformers did not always agree on the details. They differed over how much equality they thought African Americans should have. Some believed that African Americans should be treated as equal to white Americans, while others were against full political and social equality. **Lucretia Mott** founded the Philadelphia Female Anti-Slavery Society in 1833, when women were prohibited from joining the American Anti-Slavery Society. This organization, unlike some others, had both white and black members from its beginnings.

Abolitionist Leaders One of the most outspoken abolitionists was a Philadelphia journalist named **William Lloyd Garrison**. In 1828 he was convinced by a Quaker friend to join the abolition movement and soon became its leading spokesperson. Although many abolitionists favored a gradual abolition of slavery, Garrison demanded that it be abolished immediately. In 1831 he began publishing an abolitionist newspaper called the *Liberator*. He continued to publish the paper until slavery was abolished 35 years later.

In 1833 he helped found the **American Anti-Slavery Society**, the most influential abolitionist group to call for the immediate end to slavery in the United States. By 1840 the society's membership was almost 200,000. In the same year, however, the society split into two groups. One wanted immediate freedom for enslaved African Americans and a bigger role for women. The other wanted gradual emancipation and for women to play a minor role in the movement.

As in other reform movements of the time, however, women played a major role in the abolition campaign. Two outspoken campaigners for the movement were **Angelina and Sarah Grimké**. Daughters of a South Carolina plantation owner, the Grimké sisters witnessed the suffering of slaves firsthand. Angelina Grimké wrote a pamphlet trying to recruit other white southern women to the cause. Their vocal and public support of the movement earned them the disapproval of their community. They eventually moved to the North, where they not only fought against slavery but also for the rights of women. After moving to Philadelphia, the sisters wrote *American Slavery As It Is*. This book was considered to be one of the most important antislavery works of its time.

Like the Grimkés, **Frederick Douglass** supported women's rights. He was a featured speaker at the Seneca Falls Convention. But he is most remembered for his work as an abolitionist. Born into slavery in Maryland, Douglass escaped when he was 20. His intelligence and speech-making skills eventually earned him a place as a popular speaker to antislavery audiences. In 1845 he published his autobiography, *Narrative of the Life of Frederick Douglass*. In writing about his quest to escape slavery, Douglass stated, "You have seen how a man was made a slave, you shall now see how a slave was made a man." Douglass went on to publish an abolitionist newspaper called *The North Star*. His firsthand experience, his writings, and his powerful speeches made Douglass one of the most influential abolitionists in the United States.

Another former slave, **Sojourner Truth**, also contributed to the abolitionist cause. She believed God had called her to travel around the United States and preach the truth about slavery as well as about women's rights. With her deep voice and quick wit, Truth became legendary in the antislavery movement for her fiery and dramatic speeches, especially her "Ain't I a Woman" speech given in 1851.

Escape to the North

In their attempt to escape their enslavement, many enslaved people tried to reach the free states of the North or get as far as Canada or Mexico, where slavery was illegal. Over the years an informal, constantly changing network of escape routes developed. By the 1830s a loosely organized group had begun helping slaves escape from the South. Known as the **Underground Railroad**, the organization was not an actual railroad but a network of people who arranged transportation and hiding places for fugitives, or escaped slaves.

Reading Check
Find Main Ideas
What methods did abolitionists use to gain support for their cause?

Frederick Douglass began publishing *The North Star,* an abolitionist newspaper, in 1847.

Harriet Tubman was a courageous conductor on the Underground Railroad.

Reading Check
Make Inferences
Why do you think
the routes of the
Underground Railroad
constantly changed?

Sympathetic white people and free blacks provided escapees with food, hiding places, and directions to their next destination, closer to free territory. Despite the lack of any real structure, the Underground Railroad managed to achieve dramatic results. The most famous conductor on the Underground Railroad was **Harriet Tubman**. Tubman had escaped slavery herself, and she helped many others on their journey to freedom. She returned to the South nearly 20 times, successfully leading her family and more than 300 other slaves to freedom.

Opposing Abolition

The majority of white southerners did not own slaves. To those who were slaveholders, the abolition movement was an outrage. They viewed the movement as an attack on their livelihood, their way of life, and even their religion.

Southern ministers built arguments attempting to justify slavery in biblical terms. Slaveholders and politicians argued that slavery was essential to the production of cotton and the health of the economy. Even in the North, to many this was a powerful argument.

Reading Check
Summarize
What arguments
were used against
the abolishment
of slavery?

In fact, there was support for, and toleration of, slavery in the North. To northern workers, freedom for slaves meant more competition for jobs. Even Congress obstructed the efforts of abolitionists by establishing a gag rule that forbade members of Congress from discussing antislavery petitions. Still the pressure to abolish slavery was undeniable. Frederick Douglass said the issue of slavery was "the great, paramount, imperative, and all-commanding question for this age and nation to solve." This proved all too true, as the tensions regarding slavery soon would rip the nation apart.

Summary and Preview The abolition movement led to increased tensions and conflict among Americans during the mid-1800s. In the next lesson you will learn about women's rights.

Lesson 4 Assessment

Review Ideas, Terms, and People

1. a. Identify Who was William Lloyd Garrison?

   b. Draw Conclusions Why do you think it was necessary for Angelina and Sarah Grimké to move to the North?

   c. Elaborate What do you think made Frederick Douglass such an effective abolitionist?

2. a. Describe What was the Underground Railroad, and how did it work?

   b. Draw Conclusions Why do you think Harriet Tubman was willing to risk her freedom by helping others escape on the Underground Railroad?

   c. Evaluate What words would best describe the experiences of traveling on the Underground Railroad?

3. a. Describe How did Congress restrict progress of the abolition movement?

   b. Analyze Why did some Americans oppose equality for African Americans?

   c. Predict How might the conflicting opinions over slavery lead to conflict in the future?

Critical Thinking

4. Identify Cause and Effect In this lesson you learned about the abolition movement and its leaders. Create a graphic organizer similar to the one below to list each key individual of the movement and their contribution.

Individual	Contribution to Abolition

★ Women's Rights

The Big Idea

Reformers sought to improve women's rights in American society.

Main Ideas

- Influenced by the abolition movement, many women struggled to gain equal rights for themselves.

- Calls for women's rights met opposition from men and women.

- The Seneca Falls Convention launched the first organized women's rights movement in the United States.

Key Terms and People

Elizabeth Cady Stanton
Seneca Falls Convention
Declaration of Sentiments
Lucy Stone
Susan B. Anthony
Matilda Joslyn Gage

If YOU were there . . .

You are a schoolteacher in New York State in 1848. Although you earn a small salary, you still live at home. Your father does not believe that unmarried women should live alone or look after their own money. One day in a shop, you see a poster about a public meeting to discuss women's rights. You know your father will be angry if you go to the meeting. But you are very curious.

Would you attend the meeting? Why?

Women's Struggle for Equal Rights

Fighting for the rights of African Americans led many female abolitionists to fight for women's rights. In the mid-1800s, these women found that they had to defend their right to speak in public, particularly when a woman addressed both men and women. For example, members of the press, the clergy, and even some male abolitionists criticized the Grimké sisters. These critics thought that the sisters should not give public speeches. They did not want women to leave their traditional female roles. The Grimkés protested that women had a moral duty to lead the antislavery movement.

The Grimké sisters, Sarah and Angelina, fought for rights for African Americans and women.

Early Writings for Women's Rights In 1838 Sarah Grimké published a pamphlet arguing for equal rights for women. She titled it *Letters on the Equality of the Sexes and the Condition of Women*.

> "I ask no favors for my sex . . . All I ask our brethren [brothers] is that they will take their feet from off our necks, and permit us to stand upright on that ground which God designed us to occupy."
>
> —Sarah Grimké, *Letter on the Equality of the Sexes and the Condition of Women*
> Addressed to Mary S. Parker

Sarah Grimké also argued for equal educational opportunities. She pointed out laws that negatively affected women. In addition, she demanded equal pay for equal work.

Sarah Grimké never married. She explained that the government did not protect the rights of women. The laws of the day gave a husband complete control of his wife's property. Therefore, she feared that by marrying, she would become more like a slave than a wife. Her sister, Angelina, did marry, but she refused to promise to obey her husband during their marriage ceremony. She married Theodore Weld, an abolitionist. Weld agreed to give up his legal right to control her property after they married. For the Grimkés, the abolitionist principles and women's rights principles were identical.

In 1845 the famous transcendentalist Margaret Fuller published *Woman in the Nineteenth Century*. This book used well-known sayings to explain the role of women in American society. Fuller used democratic and transcendentalist principles to stress the importance of individualism to all people, especially women. The book influenced many leaders of the women's rights movement.

Sojourner Truth Sojourner Truth was another powerful supporter of both abolition and women's rights. She had been born into slavery in about 1797. Her birth name was Isabella Baumfree. She took the name Sojourner Truth because she felt that her mission was to be a sojourner, or traveler, and spread the truth. Though she never learned to read or write, she impressed many well-educated people. One person who thought highly of her was the author Harriet Beecher Stowe. Stowe said that she had never spoken "with anyone who had more . . . personal presence than this woman." Truth stood six feet tall and was a confident speaker.

In 1851 Truth gave a speech that is often quoted to this day.

> "That man over here says that women need to be helped into carriages and lifted over ditches, and to have the best place everywhere. Nobody ever helps me into carriages or over mud puddles, or gives me any best place . . . Look at me! I have ploughed and planted and . . . no man could head [outwork] me. And ain't I a woman?"
>
> —Sojourner Truth, Delivered at the 1851 Women's Convention, Akron, Ohio

Truth, the Grimké sisters, and other supporters of the women's movement were determined to be heard.

Reading Check
Make Inferences
Why would reformers link the issues of abolition and women's rights?

Antisuffragists
As the suffrage movement picked up speed, opponents to women's suffrage also began to organize. Antisuffragists argued that women's suffrage would distract women from building strong families and improving communities.

Opposing the Call for Women's Rights

Publications about women's rights first appeared in the United States shortly after the American Revolution. However, women's concerns did not become a national issue with strong opposition for many more years.

The Movement Grows The change took place when women took a more active and leading role in reform and abolition. Other social changes also led to the rise of the women's movement. Women took advantage of better educational opportunities in the early 1800s. Their efforts on behalf of reform groups helped them learn how to organize more effectively and to work together.

Another benefit of reform-group work was that some men began to fight for women's rights. Many activists, both men and women, found it unacceptable that women were denied the democratic right to vote or sit on juries. They were also upset that married women in many states had little or no control over their own property.

Opposition to Women's Rights Like the abolitionist movement, the struggle for women's rights faced opposition. Many people did not agree with some of the goals of the women's rights movement. Some women believed that they did not need new rights. They said that women were not unequal to men, only different. Some critics believed that women should not try to work in public for social changes. Women were welcome to work for social change, but only from within their homes. "Let her not look away from her own little family circle for the means of producing moral and social reforms," wrote T. S. Arthur. His advice appeared in a popular women's magazine called *The Lady at Home.*

Reading Check
Draw Conclusions
Why did some men and women think that the women's rights movement was misguided?

Some people also thought that women lacked the physical or mental strength to survive without men's protection. They believed that a woman should go from the protection of her father's home to that of her husband's. They also thought that women could not cope with the outside world; therefore, a husband should control his wife's property. Despite opposition, women continued to pursue their goal of greater rights.

Seneca Falls Convention

In 1840 **Elizabeth Cady Stanton** attended the World's Anti-Slavery Convention in London, England, while on her honeymoon. She discovered that, unlike her husband, she was not allowed to participate. All women in attendance had to sit behind a curtain in a separate gallery of the convention hall. William Lloyd Garrison, who had helped found the American Anti-Slavery Society, sat with them in protest.

The treatment of women abolitionists at the convention angered Stanton and her new friend, Lucretia Mott, a Quaker, abolitionist, and women's rights advocate from Massachusetts. Apparently, even many abolitionists did not think that women were equal to men. Stanton and Mott wanted to change this, so they planned to "form a society to advance the rights of

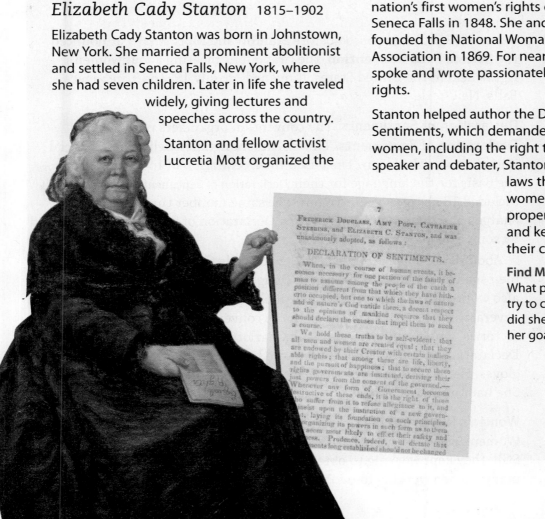

BIOGRAPHY

Elizabeth Cady Stanton 1815–1902

Elizabeth Cady Stanton was born in Johnstown, New York. She married a prominent abolitionist and settled in Seneca Falls, New York, where she had seven children. Later in life she traveled widely, giving lectures and speeches across the country.

Stanton and fellow activist Lucretia Mott organized the nation's first women's rights convention, at Seneca Falls in 1848. She and Susan B. Anthony founded the National Woman Suffrage Association in 1869. For nearly six decades, she spoke and wrote passionately about women's rights.

Stanton helped author the Declaration of Sentiments, which demanded equal rights for women, including the right to vote. A brilliant speaker and debater, Stanton spoke out against laws that kept married women from owning property, earning wages, and keeping custody of their children.

Find Main Ideas
What problems did Stanton try to correct? What problems did she face in accomplishing her goals?

Declaration of Sentiments

At the 1848 Seneca Falls Convention, 100 people signed the Declaration of Sentiments, a document declaring the rights of women. The wording of the document purposely echoed the Declaration of Independence.

> The authors use the same words that are in the Declaration of Independence, but include women.

> Here the women demand that they become a part of government.

*We hold these truths to be self-evident: that all men and women are created equal; that they are endowed by their Creator with certain **inalienable**[1] rights; that among these are life, liberty, and the pursuit of happiness; that to secure these rights governments are instituted, deriving their just powers from the consent of the governed. Whenever any form of government becomes destructive of these ends, it is the right of those who suffer from it to refuse **allegiance**[2] to it, and to insist upon the institution of a new government, laying its foundation on such principles, and organizing its powers in such form, as to them shall seem most likely to effect their safety and happiness.*

[1] *inalienable* not able to be taken away   [2] *allegiance* loyalty

Analyze Historical Sources
Why would women want to use the Declaration of Independence as a source for their own declaration?

women." Eight years passed before Stanton and Mott finally announced the **Seneca Falls Convention**, the first public meeting about women's rights held in the United States. It opened on July 19, 1848, in Seneca Falls, New York.

Declaration of Sentiments The convention organizers wrote a **Declaration of Sentiments**. This document detailed beliefs about social injustice toward women. They used the Declaration of Independence as the basis for the language for their Declaration of Sentiments. The authors included 18 charges against men—the same number that had been charged against King George III. The Declaration of Sentiments was signed by some 100 people.

About 240 people attended the Seneca Falls Convention, including men such as abolitionist Frederick Douglass. Many other reformers who also worked in the temperance and abolitionist movements were present. Several women who participated in the convention worked in nearby factories. One of them, 19-year-old Charlotte Woodward, signed the Declaration of Sentiments. She worked long hours in a factory, making gloves. Her wages were very low, and she could not even keep her earnings. She had to turn her wages over to her father.

Women's Rights Leaders After the convention, the struggle continued. Women's rights activists battled many difficulties and much opposition. Still, they kept working to obtain greater equality for women. Among the many women working for women's rights, four became important leaders:

Lucy Stone, Susan B. Anthony, Matilda Joslyn Gage, and Elizabeth Cady Stanton. Each brought different strengths to the fight for women's rights.

Lucy Stone was a well-known spokesperson for the Anti-Slavery Society. In the early years of the women's rights movement, Stone became known as a gifted speaker. Elizabeth Cady Stanton called her "the first who really stirred the nation's heart on the subject of women's wrongs."

Susan B. Anthony brought strong organizational skills to the women's rights movement. She did much to turn the fight for women's rights into a political movement. Anthony argued that women and men should receive equal pay for equal work. She also believed that women should be allowed to enter traditionally male professions, such as religion and law. Anthony was especially concerned with laws that affected women's control of money and property.

Anthony led a campaign to change laws regarding the property rights of women. She wrote in her diary that no woman could ever be free without "a purse of her own." After forming a network to cover the entire state of New York, she collected more than 6,000 signatures to petition

Lucy Stone worked for equal rights for women and African Americans.

Timeline: Women's Rights

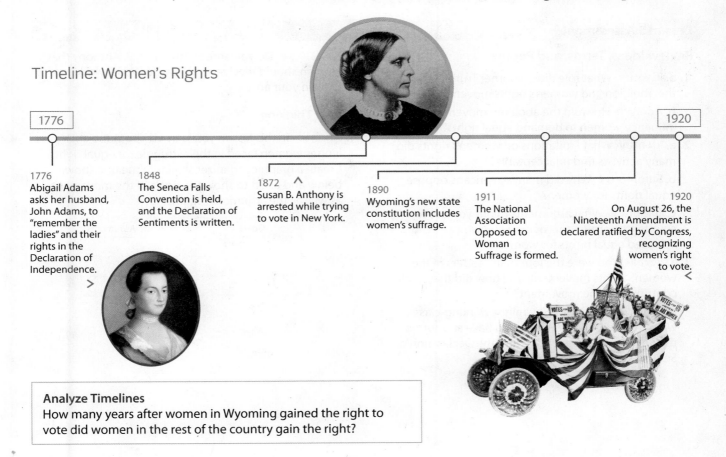

1776

1920

1776
Abigail Adams asks her husband, John Adams, to "remember the ladies" and their rights in the Declaration of Independence.

1848
The Seneca Falls Convention is held, and the Declaration of Sentiments is written.

1872
Susan B. Anthony is arrested while trying to vote in New York.

1890
Wyoming's new state constitution includes women's suffrage.

1911
The National Association Opposed to Woman Suffrage is formed.

1920
On August 26, the Nineteenth Amendment is declared ratified by Congress, recognizing women's right to vote.

Analyze Timelines
How many years after women in Wyoming gained the right to vote did women in the rest of the country gain the right?

for a new property-rights law. In 1860, due largely to the efforts of Anthony, New York finally gave married women ownership of their wages and property. Other states in the Northeast and Midwest soon created similar laws.

Elizabeth Cady Stanton wrote many of the documents and speeches of the movement, which were often delivered by Anthony. Along with Lucy Stone and **Matilda Joslyn Gage**, Stanton founded the National Woman Suffrage Association (NWSA) in 1869. This organization was considered one of the more radical groups because of its position that abolition was not a more important cause than women's rights.

Matilda Joslyn Gage was a writer and an advocate in New York. After cofounding the NWSA, she became the publisher of its official newspaper, the *National Citizen and Ballot Box*. She also worked with Stanton and Anthony to write and edit *History of Woman Suffrage*.

Not every battle was won. Other major reforms, such as women's right to vote, were not achieved at this time. Still, more women than ever before became actively involved in women's rights issues. Leaders such as Stanton, Anthony, Stone, and Gage continued to fight for equal treatment and recognition. This increased activity was one of the movement's greatest accomplishments.

Summary and Preview Women's rights became a major issue in the mid-1800s, as women began to demand a greater degree of equality. In the next module you will read about western expansion.

Reading Check
Draw Conclusions
What did Susan B. Anthony mean when she said that no woman could be free without "a purse of her own"?

Lesson 5 Assessment

Review Ideas, Terms, and People

1. a. Identify What role did Sojourner Truth play in both the abolition and women's rights movements?

   b. Analyze How did the abolition movement influence women to demand equal rights?

2. a. Identify What limitations on women's rights did many activists find unacceptable?

   b. Summarize Why did many Americans oppose equal rights for women?

   c. Elaborate What arguments might you use to counter the arguments of men and women who opposed equal rights for women?

3. a. Recall Who were the four main leaders of the women's rights movement, and how did they each contribute to the movement?

   b. Draw Conclusions Why might working-class women like Charlotte Woodward have supported the Seneca Falls Convention and the Declaration of Sentiments?

   c. Evaluate Do you agree with Susan B. Anthony that women should receive equal pay for equal work? Explain your answer.

Critical Thinking

4. Analyze In this lesson you learned about the challenges women faced in their struggle for equal rights. Create a graphic organizer similar to the one shown below and use it to show the goals of the movement, as well as the arguments against it.

Goals	Opponents' Arguments

Social Studies Skills

Accept Social Responsibility

Define the Skill

A *society* is an organized group of people who share a common set of activities, traditions, and goals. You are part of many societies— your school, community, and nation are just three. Every society's strength depends on the support and contributions of its members. *Social responsibility* is the obligation that every person has to the societies of which he or she is a member.

Learn the Skill

As a part of your school, community, and nation, you have obligations to the people around you. The most obvious is to do nothing to harm your society. You also have a duty to take part in it. At the very least, this means exercising the rights and responsibilities of membership. These include being informed about issues in your society.

Another level of social responsibility is support of change to benefit society. This level of involvement goes beyond being informed about issues to trying to do something about them. If you take this important step, here are some points to consider.

1. Few efforts to change society have everyone's support. Some people will want things to stay the same. They may treat you badly if you work for change. You must be prepared for this possibility.

2. Sometimes, efforts to improve things involve opposing laws or rules that need to be changed. No matter how just your cause is, if you break laws or rules, you must be willing to accept the consequences of your behavior.

3. Remember that violence is *never* an acceptable method for change. People who use force in seeking change are not behaving in a socially responsible manner, even if their cause is good.

This module was filled with the stories of socially responsible people. Many of them devoted their lives to changing society for the better. Some did so at great personal risk. Boston abolitionist William Lloyd Garrison barely escaped with his life from a local mob that tried to lynch him because of his views.

Garrison and the other reformers you read about demonstrated the highest level of social responsibility. They saw an issue they believed to be a problem in society, and they worked tirelessly to make changes.

Practice the Skill

Review the "If you were there" scene in Lesson 4. Imagine yourself as that South Carolinian. You believe slavery to be wrong. However, you also respect your father. In addition, you know that most of your neighbors do not feel as you do about slavery. They might harm you or your property if you take this stand against it.

1. Would listening to the Grimké sisters' speak help benefit society? Explain why or why not.

2. Are you willing to risk the anger of your neighbors? Why or why not?

3. Would helping the Grimké sisters be a socially responsible thing to do? Explain why or why not.

Review Vocabulary, Terms, and People

1. Which of the following authors wrote about Puritan life in *The Scarlet Letter*?
   a. Emily Dickinson
   b. Herman Melville
   c. Thomas Gallaudet
   d. Nathaniel Hawthorne

2. Which document expressed the complaints of supporters of women's rights?
   a. Declaration of the Rights of Women
   b. Declaration of Sentiments
   c. Letters on Women's Rights
   d. Seneca Falls Convention

3. As leader of the common-school movement, who worked to improve free public education?
   a. Walt Whitman
   b. Horace Mann
   c. Lyman Beecher
   d. Sojourner Truth

Comprehension and Critical Thinking

Lesson 1

4. a. Identify What political party was founded by nativists, and what policies did it support?
   b. Analyze What factors caused U.S. cities to grow so fast?
   c. Evaluate Do you think that the benefits of city life outweighed its drawbacks? Explain.

Lesson 2

5. a. Describe Who were some important transcendentalists, and what ideas did they promote?
   b. Compare and Contrast In what ways were transcendentalists and Romantics similar and different?
   c. Elaborate Which movement appeals to you more—American transcendentalism or Romanticism? Why?

Lesson 3

6. a. Identify What important reform movements became popular in the early 1800s?
   b. Analyze Why did education become an important topic for reformers in the 1800s?

   c. Evaluate Which reform movement do you think had the greatest effect on the United States? Why?

Lesson 4

7. a. Recall What caused some Americans to support the abolition movement?
   b. Make Inferences How did northerners and southerners use the economy to support their reason for opposing abolition?
   c. Evaluate Which of the methods used by leaders of the abolition movement do you think was most successful? Why?

Lesson 5

8. a. Recall What led many women to question their place in American society?
   b. Make Inferences Why did female factory workers like Charlotte Woodward support the women's rights movement?
   c. Evaluate Do you think the women's movement was successful by 1860? Explain your answer.

Module 16 Assessment, continued

Review Themes

9. **Society and Culture** What social and cultural changes took place from 1800 to the mid-1800s?

Reading Skills

Information and Propaganda *Use the Reading Skills taught in this module to answer the question below.*

10. Which of the following is *not* an example of propaganda?

    a. a flyer protesting new tax laws

    b. an ad about a political candidate

    c. a radio announcement sponsored by an interest group

    d. a list of camping rules from a park

Social Studies Skills

Accept Social Responsibility *Use the Social Studies Skills taught in this module to fill in the chart below.*

11.

Action	Is it socially responsible?	Why or why not?
Remove litter from a park		
Vote		
Read a political magazine		
Run a red light		

Focus on Writing

12. **Write a Persuasive Letter** In this module you have learned about a number of important events and political, religious, and artistic movements of the early 1800s. Choose the one you consider most important. Think about how it changed life for people in the United States. Then write a two-paragraph persuasive letter to the newspaper, arguing for the event or movement you chose. In the first paragraph, identify the event or movement you chose as well as a thesis explaining why it is important. In the second paragraph, include details about the event or movement that support your thesis. Close with one or two sentences that sum up your points.

A Divided Nation

Essential Question

Could the Civil War have been avoided?

About the Photo: Historical photos and artifacts, such as these in the Charles H. Wright Museum of African American History, allow us to explore our nation's history.

In this module you will learn about how the debate over slavery increasingly divided Americans during the mid-1800s. You will also read about the major events that preceded the Civil War.

What You Will Learn ...

Timeline of Events 1845–1865

▶ Explore ONLINE!

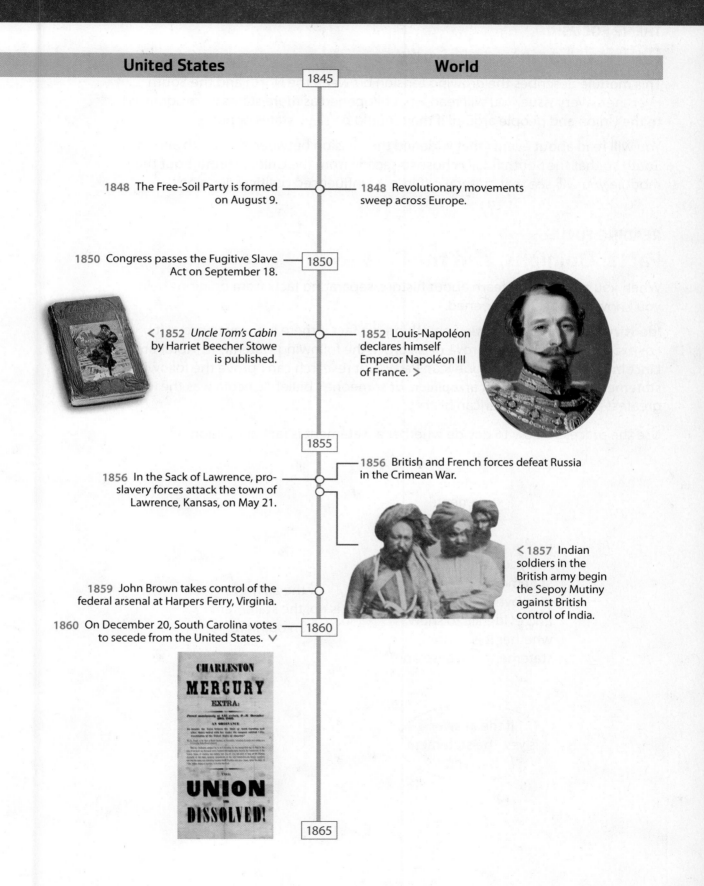

United States		World
	1845	
1848 The Free-Soil Party is formed on August 9.		**1848** Revolutionary movements sweep across Europe.
1850 Congress passes the Fugitive Slave Act on September 18.	**1850**	
< **1852** *Uncle Tom's Cabin* by Harriet Beecher Stowe is published.		**1852** Louis-Napoléon declares himself Emperor Napoléon III of France. >
	1855	
1856 In the Sack of Lawrence, pro-slavery forces attack the town of Lawrence, Kansas, on May 21.		**1856** British and French forces defeat Russia in the Crimean War.
		< **1857** Indian soldiers in the British army begin the Sepoy Mutiny against British control of India.
1859 John Brown takes control of the federal arsenal at Harpers Ferry, Virginia.		
1860 On December 20, South Carolina votes to secede from the United States. ∨	**1860**	
	1865	

CHARLESTON
MERCURY
EXTRA:

AN ORDINANCE

THE
UNION
DISSOLVED!

Reading Social Studies

Politics, Society and Culture

This module describes the growing tension between the North and the South over the slavery issue. You will read what happened as more states were admitted to the Union and people argued if they should be slave states or not.

You will read about events that widened the division between the North and the South so that the South finally chose to secede from the Union. Throughout the module you will see that cultural differences influenced political decisions.

READING FOCUS:

Facts, Opinions, and the Past

When you are trying to learn about history, separating facts from opinions helps you know what really happened.

Identify Facts and Opinions Something is a **fact** if there is a way to prove it. For example, research can prove or disprove the following statement: "Abraham Lincoln belonged to the Republican Party." But research can't prove the following statement because it is just an **opinion**, or someone's belief: "Lincoln was the greatest president in American history."

Use the process below to decide whether a statement is fact or opinion.

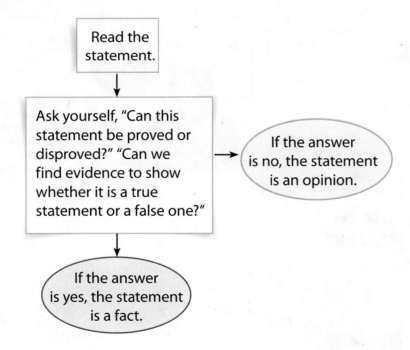

You Try It!

The following passage tells about the debates that Abraham Lincoln had with Stephen Douglas. All the statements in this passage are facts. What makes them facts and not opinions?

The Lincoln-Douglas Debates In 1858 Illinois Republicans nominated Abraham Lincoln for the U.S. Senate. His opponent was Democrat Stephen Douglas, who had represented Illinois in the Senate since 1847. Lincoln challenged Douglas in what became the historic Lincoln-Douglas debates.

In each debate, Lincoln stressed that the central issue of the campaign was the spread of slavery in the West. He said that the Democrats were trying to spread slavery across the nation.

Lincoln talked about the *Dred Scott* decision. He said that African Americans were "entitled to all the natural rights" listed in the Declaration of Independence, specifically mentioning "the right to life, liberty, and the pursuit of happiness."

Identify each of the following as a fact or an opinion and then explain your choice.

1. Lincoln accused the Democrats of trying to spread slavery across the nation.
2. The Lincoln-Douglas debates were the most important debates in the history of the nation.
3. Stephen Douglas was a U.S. senator from Illinois.
4. Abraham Lincoln ran against Douglas in the 1858 Senate election.
5. Most Americans believed that the *Dred Scott* decision was a good one.
6. Lincoln was the best debater people from Illinois had ever heard.

As you read Module 17, look closely at quotes from historical figures. Are these quotes showing you facts or opinions?

Key Terms and People

Lesson 1
popular sovereignty
Wilmot Proviso
sectionalism
Free-Soil Party
secede
Compromise of 1850
Fugitive Slave Act
Anthony Burns
Uncle Tom's Cabin
Harriet Beecher Stowe

Lesson 2
Franklin Pierce
Stephen Douglas
Kansas-Nebraska Act
Pottawatomie Massacre
Charles Sumner
Preston Brooks

Lesson 3
Republican Party
James Buchanan
John C. Frémont
Dred Scott
Roger B. Taney
Abraham Lincoln
Lincoln-Douglas debates
Freeport Doctrine

Lesson 4
John Brown's raid
John C. Breckinridge
Constitutional Union Party
John Bell
John J. Crittenden
Confederate States of America
Jefferson Davis

The Debate over Slavery

The Big Idea

Antislavery literature and the annexation of new lands intensified the debate over slavery.

Main Ideas

- The addition of new land in the West renewed disputes over the expansion of slavery.

- The Compromise of 1850 tried to solve the disputes over slavery.

- The Fugitive Slave Act caused more controversy.

- Abolitionists used antislavery literature to promote opposition.

Key Terms and People

popular sovereignty
Wilmot Proviso
sectionalism
Free-Soil Party
secede
Compromise of 1850
Fugitive Slave Act
Anthony Burns
Uncle Tom's Cabin
Harriet Beecher Stowe

If YOU were there . . .

You live in a crowded neighborhood in New York City in 1854. Your apartment building is home to a variety of people—long-time residents, Irish immigrants, and free African Americans. One day federal marshals knock on your door. They claim that one of your neighbors is a fugitive slave. The marshals say you must help them find her. If you don't, you will be fined or even sent to jail.

What would you tell the federal marshals?

New Land Renews Slavery Disputes

The United States added more than 500,000 square miles of land as a result of winning the Mexican-American War in 1848. The additional land caused bitter debate about slavery. The Missouri Compromise of 1820 had divided the Louisiana Purchase into either free or slave regions. It prohibited slavery north of latitude 36°30' but let Missouri become a slave state. In the 1840s President James K. Polk wanted to extend the 36°30' line to the West coast, dividing the Mexican Cession into two parts—one free and one enslaved. Some leaders, including Senator Lewis Cass of Michigan, encouraged **popular sovereignty**, the idea that political power belongs to the people, who should decide on banning or allowing slavery.

Regional Differences about Slavery Some northerners wanted to outlaw slavery in all parts of the Mexican Cession. During the war, Representative David Wilmot offered the **Wilmot Proviso**, a document stating that "neither slavery nor involuntary servitude shall ever exist in any part of [the] territory."

The northern-controlled House passed the document, but in the Senate, the South had more power. The Wilmot

Whig candidate Zachary Taylor is shown here on an 1848 presidential campaign banner with his running mate, Millard Fillmore.

Reading Check
Make Inferences
Why did sectionalism in the United States increase in the late 1840s?

Proviso did not pass. Before this time, politicians had usually supported the ideas of their political parties. However, the Wilmot Proviso spurred a debate that showed growing **sectionalism**, or favoring the interests of one section or region over the interests of the entire country.

To attract voters, the Democrats and the Whigs did not take a clear position on slavery in the presidential campaign of 1848. In response, antislavery northerners formed a new party, the **Free-Soil Party**, which supported the Wilmot Proviso. They worried that slave labor would mean fewer jobs for white workers. Party members chose former president Martin Van Buren as their candidate. The new party won 10 percent of the popular vote, drawing away votes from Democrat Lewis Cass. Whig candidate Zachary Taylor won a narrow victory.

The California Question The California gold rush caused such rapid population growth that California applied to join the Union as a state instead of as a territory. But would California enter the Union as a free state or a slave state?

Most Californians opposed slavery, which had been illegal when the state was part of Mexico. Also, many forty-niners had come from free states. But if California became a free state, the balance between free and slave states would change, favoring the free states.

In the South, an imbalance was unacceptable. "We are about permanently to destroy the balance of power between the sections," said Senator Jefferson Davis of Mississippi. He and many other southerners did not want California to enter the Union as a free state.

Compromise of 1850

Senator Henry Clay of Kentucky had helped to settle the Missouri crisis of 1819–20 and the nullification crisis of 1832–33 by proposing compromises. He now had another plan to help the nation maintain peace. His ideas were designed to give both sides things that they wanted:

1. California would enter the Union as a free state.
2. The rest of the Mexican Cession would be federal land. In this territory, popular sovereignty would decide on slavery.
3. Texas would give up land east of the upper Rio Grande. In return, the government would pay Texas's debts from when it was an independent republic.
4. The slave trade—but not slavery—would end in the nation's capital.
5. A more effective fugitive slave law would be passed.

Clay's plan drew attack, especially regarding California. Senator William Seward of New York defended antislavery views and wanted California admitted "directly, without conditions, without qualifications, and without compromise." However, Senator John C. Calhoun of South Carolina argued that letting California enter as a free state would destroy the nation's balance. He warned people of issues that would later start the Civil War. Calhoun asked that the slave states be allowed to **secede**—formally withdraw—from the Union.

In contrast, Senator Daniel Webster of Massachusetts favored Clay's plan:

> "I wish to speak today, not as a Massachusetts man, nor as a Northern man, but as an American . . . I speak today for the preservation of the Union. Hear me for my cause."
>
> —from the Seventh of March Speech, March 7, 1850

Webster criticized northern abolitionists and southerners who talked of secession.

A compromise was enacted that year and seemed to settle most disputes between free and slave states. It achieved the majority of Clay's proposals. With the **Compromise of 1850**, California was able to enter the Union

Historical Source

The Seventh of March Speech

On March 7, 1850, Daniel Webster spoke on the floor of the Senate in favor of the Compromise of 1850.

Webster is upset by talk of secession.

Webster is saying that just as it is impossible to move water in the ocean without making waves, it is impossible for states to peacefully secede.

> I hear with pain and anguish, and distress, the word secession. . . . Secession! Peaceable secession! Sir, your eyes and mine are never destined to see that miracle. The dismemberment [taking apart] of this vast country without convulsion! The breaking up of the fountains of the great deep without ruffling the surface! Who is so foolish— I beg everybody's pardon—as to expect to see any such thing? . . . There can be no such thing as a peaceable secession.
>
> —from the Seventh of March Speech, March 7, 1850

Analyze Historical Sources
Why did Webster support the Compromise of 1850?

Southern View of the Compromise of 1850

John C. Calhoun from South Carolina wrote a speech saying that the proposed compromise did not go far enough to satisfy the South.

> I have, senators, believed from the first that the agitation [unrest] of the subject of slavery would, if not prevented by some timely and effective measure, end in disunion. . . . The South asks for justice, simple justice, and less she ought not to take. She has no compromise to offer but the Constitution, and no concession or surrender to make."
>
> —from Speech on the Slavery Question, delivered in the Senate, March 4, 1850

Analyze Historical Sources
Why did Calhoun urge southern senators to vote against the compromise?

Calhoun believes the South's position was supported by the Constitution.

Henry Clay introduced the Compromise of 1850 on the Senate floor.

Daniel Webster spoke eloquently in support of the compromise.

John C. Calhoun was weak and near death. He had his speech in support of slavery read to the Senate for him.

as a free state. The rest of the Mexican Cession was divided into two territories—Utah and New Mexico—where the question of whether to allow slavery would be decided by popular sovereignty.

Texas agreed to give up its land claims in New Mexico in exchange for financial aid from the federal government. The compromise outlawed the slave trade in the District of Columbia and established a new fugitive slave law.

Reading Check
Analyze Information
How was Texas affected by the Compromise of 1850?

Fugitive Slave Act

The newly passed **Fugitive Slave Act** made it a crime to help runaway slaves and allowed officials to arrest those slaves in free areas. Slaveholders were permitted to take suspected fugitives to U.S. commissioners, who decided their fate.

Details of the Fugitive Slave Act Slaveholders could use testimony from white witnesses, but enslaved African Americans accused of being fugitives could not testify. Nor could people who hid or helped a runaway slave—they faced six months in jail and a $1,000 fine. Commissioners who rejected a slaveholder's claim earned $5, while those who returned suspected fugitives to slaveholders earned $10. Clearly, the commissioners benefited from helping slaveholders.

Reactions to the Fugitive Slave Act Enforcement of the Fugitive Slave Act began immediately. In September 1850—the same month the law was passed—federal marshals arrested African American James Hamlet.

Public rallies denouncing the Fugitive Slave Act often included speeches from key abolitionists such as Frederick Douglass (seated at the table on the left).

They returned him to a slaveholder in Maryland, although he had lived in New York City for three years.

Thousands of northern African Americans fled to Canada in fear. In the ten years after Congress passed the Fugitive Slave Act, some 343 fugitive slave cases were reviewed. The accused fugitives were declared free in only 11 cases.

The Fugitive Slave Act upset northerners, who were uncomfortable with the commissioners' power. Northerners disliked the idea of a trial without a jury. They also disapproved of commissioners' higher fees for returning slaves. Most were horrified that some free African Americans had been captured and sent to the South.

Most northerners opposed to the act peacefully resisted, but violence did erupt. In 1854 **Anthony Burns**, a fugitive slave from Virginia, was arrested in Boston. Abolitionists used force while trying to rescue him from jail, killing a deputy marshal. A federal ship was ordered to return Burns to Virginia after his trial. Many people in the North, particularly in Massachusetts, were outraged. The event persuaded many to join the abolitionist cause.

Antislavery Literature

Abolitionists in the North used the stories of fugitive slaves like James Hamlet and Anthony Burns to gain sympathy for their cause. Slave narratives also educated people about their hardships.

Fiction also informed people about the evils of slavery. *Uncle Tom's Cabin*, the antislavery novel written by **Harriet Beecher Stowe**, spoke out powerfully against slavery. Stowe, the daughter of Connecticut minister

Reading Check
Draw Conclusions
What concerns did northerners have about the Fugitive Slave Act?

Lyman Beecher, moved to Ohio when she was 21. There she met fugitive slaves and learned about the cruelties of slavery. The Fugitive Slave Act greatly angered Stowe. She decided to write a book that would educate northerners about the realities of slavery.

Uncle Tom's Cabin was published in 1852. The main character, a kindly enslaved African American named Tom, is taken from his wife and sold "down the river" in Louisiana. Tom becomes the slave of cruel Simon Legree. In a rage, Legree has Tom beaten to death.

The novel electrified the nation and sparked outrage in the South. Louisa McCord, a famous southern writer, questioned the "foul imagination which could invent such scenes."

Within a decade, more than 2 million copies of *Uncle Tom's Cabin* had been sold in the United States. The book's popularity caused one northerner to remark that Stowe and her book had created "two millions of abolitionists." Stowe later wrote *A Key to Uncle Tom's Cabin* to answer those who had criticized her book.

The impact of Stowe's book is suggested by her reported meeting with Abraham Lincoln in 1862, a year after the start of the Civil War. Lincoln supposedly said to Stowe that she was "the little lady who made this big war." Her book is still widely read today as a source of information about the harsh realities of slavery.

Summary and Preview The United States experienced increasing disagreement over the issue of slavery. The Compromise of 1850 and the Fugitive Slave Act tried to address these disagreements with legislation. In the next lesson you will read about another disputed law concerning slavery—the Kansas-Nebraska Act—and the violence it sparked.

Reading Check
Identify Cause and Effect Why did abolitionists use antislavery literature to promote their cause, and what effect did it have on the slavery debate?

Lesson 1 Assessment

Review Ideas, Terms, and People

1. a. **Describe** What ideas did the Free-Soil Party promote?
   b. **Predict** What are some possible results of the growing sectional debate over slavery?
2. a. **Describe** What were the major points of the Compromise of 1850?
   b. **Contrast** What differing opinions emerged toward Henry Clay's proposed compromise?
3. a. **Identify** What were the effects of the Fugitive Slave Act?
   b. **Draw Conclusions** Why did some Americans believe the Fugitive Slave Act was unfair?
4. a. **Identify** What are three examples of antislavery literature?
   b. **Elaborate** Do you think literature was an effective tool against slavery? Why or why not?

Critical Thinking

5. **Evaluate** In this lesson you learned about the sequence of events in the debate over slavery and the effects of each. Create a graphic organizer similar to the one below to evaluate how the Compromise of 1850, the Fugitive Slave Act, and antislavery literature affected the slavery debate.

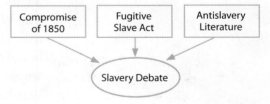

| Compromise of 1850 | Fugitive Slave Act | Antislavery Literature |

Slavery Debate

Trouble in Kansas

The Big Idea

The Kansas-Nebraska Act heightened tensions in the conflict over slavery.

Main Ideas

- The debate over the expansion of slavery influenced the election of 1852.

- The Kansas-Nebraska Act gave voters the choice to allow or prohibit slavery.

- Pro-slavery and antislavery groups clashed violently in what became known as "Bleeding Kansas."

Key Terms and People

Franklin Pierce
Stephen Douglas
Kansas-Nebraska Act
Pottawatomie Massacre
Charles Sumner
Preston Brooks

Reading Check
Draw Conclusions
What issues determined the outcome of the presidential election of 1852?

If YOU were there . . .

You live on a New England farm in 1855. You often think about moving West. But the last few harvests have been bad, and you can't afford to have another bad harvest. Now the Emigrant Aid Society offers to help you move to Kansas. To bring in antislavery voters like you, they'll give you a wagon, livestock, and farm machines. Still, you know that Kansas might be dangerous.

Would you decide to risk settling in Kansas?

Election of 1852

Four leading candidates for the Democratic presidential nomination emerged in 1852. It became clear that none of them would win a majority of votes. Frustrated delegates at the Democratic National Convention turned to **Franklin Pierce**, a little-known politician from New Hampshire. Pierce promised to honor the Compromise of 1850 and the Fugitive Slave Act. Therefore, southerners trusted Pierce on the issue of slavery.

Franklin Pierce

The opposing Whigs also held their convention in 1852. In other presidential elections, they had nominated well-known former generals such as William Henry Harrison and Zachary Taylor. This had been a good strategy, as both men had won. The Whigs decided to choose another war hero. They passed over the current president, Millard Fillmore, because they believed that his strict enforcement of the Fugitive Slave Act would cost votes. Instead, they chose Winfield Scott, a Mexican War hero. Southerners did not trust Scott, however, because he had not fully supported the Compromise of 1850.

Pierce won the election of 1852 by a large margin. Many Whigs viewed the election as a painful defeat not just for their candidate but also for their party.

The Kansas-Nebraska Act

In his inaugural address, President Pierce expressed his hope that the slavery issue had been put to rest "and that no sectional . . . excitement may again threaten the durability [stability] of our institutions." Less than a year later, however, a proposal to build a railroad to the West coast helped revive the slavery controversy and opened a new period of sectional conflict.

Douglas and the Railroad Ever since entering Congress in the mid-1840s, **Stephen Douglas** had supported the idea of building a railroad to the Pacific Ocean. Douglas favored a line running from Chicago. The first step toward building such a railroad would be organizing what remained of the Louisiana Purchase into a federal territory. The Missouri Compromise required that this land be free territory and eventually free states.

Southerners in Congress did not support Douglas's plan, recommending a southern route for the railroad. Their preferred line ran from New Orleans, across Texas and New Mexico Territory, to southern California. Determined to have the railroad start in Chicago, Douglas asked a few key southern senators to support his plan. They agreed to do so if the new territory west of Missouri was opened to slavery.

Two New Territories In January 1854 Douglas introduced what became the **Kansas-Nebraska Act**, a plan that would divide the remainder of the Louisiana Purchase into two territories—Kansas and Nebraska—and allow the people in each territory to decide on the question of slavery. The act would eliminate the Missouri Compromise's restriction on slavery north of the 36°30' line.

Antislavery northerners were outraged by the **implications**. Some believed the proposal was part of a terrible plot to turn free territory into a "dreary region . . . inhabited by masters and slaves." All across the North, citizens attended protest meetings and sent anti-Nebraska petitions to Congress.

Even so, with strong southern support—and with Douglas and President Pierce pressuring their fellow Democrats to vote for it—the measure passed both houses of Congress and was signed into law on May 30, 1854. Lost amid all the controversy over the territorial bill was Douglas's proposed railroad to the Pacific Ocean. Congress would not approve the construction of such a railroad until 1862.

Kansas Divided Antislavery and pro-slavery groups rushed their supporters to Kansas. One of the people who spoke out strongly against slavery in Kansas was Senator Seward.

> "Gentlemen of the Slave States . . . I accept [your challenge] in . . . the cause of freedom. We will engage in competition for . . . Kansas, and God give the victory to the side which is stronger in numbers as it is in right."

> —from Speech of William Henry Seward on the Kansas and Nebraska Bill, delivered in the Senate, May 26, 1854

Academic Vocabulary
implications things that are inferred or deduced

▷ Explore ONLINE!

The Missouri Compromise, 1820

Under the Missouri Compromise of 1820, there are an equal number of free states (orange) and slave states (green).

The Compromise of 1850

The Compromise of 1850 allowed for one more free state (California) than slave state, but also passed a strict fugitive slave law.

	Free state
	Free territory
	Slave state
	Slave territory
	Popular sovereignty

The Kansas-Nebraska Act

As a result of the Kansas-Nebraska Act, the question of slavery is to be decided by popular sovereignty—by the people who vote in the elections there—in the newly organized territories of Kansas and Nebraska. The act sparked violent conflict between pro-slavery and antislavery groups.

Interpret Maps

1. **Region** In what part of the United States were the slave states located?

2. **Place** What free state was added with the Compromise of 1850?

Reading Check
Analyze Information
Why did northerners dislike the Kansas-Nebraska Act?

Elections for the Kansas territorial legislature were held in March 1855. Almost 5,000 pro-slavery voters crossed the border from Missouri, voted in Kansas, and then returned home. As a result, the new legislature had a huge pro-slavery majority. The members of the legislature passed strict laws that made it a crime to question slaveholders' rights and said that those who helped fugitive slaves could be put to death. In protest, antislavery Kansans formed their own legislature 25 miles away in Topeka. President Pierce, however, only recognized the pro-slavery legislature.

Bleeding Kansas

By early 1856 Kansas had two opposing governments, and the population was angry. Settlers had moved to Kansas to homestead in peace, but the controversy over slavery began to affect everyone.

In April 1856 a congressional committee arrived in Kansas to decide which government was legitimate. Although committee members declared the election of the pro-slavery legislature to be unfair, the federal government did not agree.

Attack on Lawrence The new pro-slavery settlers owned guns, and anti-slavery settlers received weapons shipments from friends in the East. Then, violence broke out. In May 1856 a pro-slavery grand jury in Kansas charged leaders of the antislavery government with treason. About 800 men rode to the city of Lawrence to arrest the antislavery leaders, but they had fled. The posse took its anger out on Lawrence by setting fires, looting buildings, and destroying presses used to print antislavery newspapers. One man was killed in the pro-slavery attack that became known as the Sack of Lawrence.

John Brown's Response Abolitionist John Brown was from New England, but he and some of his sons had moved to Kansas in 1855. The Sack of Lawrence made him determined to "fight fire with fire" and to "strike terror in the hearts of the pro-slavery people." On the night of May 24, 1856, along Pottawatomie Creek, Brown and his men killed five pro-slavery men in Kansas in what became known as the **Pottawatomie Massacre**. Brown and his men dragged the pro-slavery men out of their cabins and killed them with swords. The abolitionist band managed to escape capture. Brown declared that his actions had been ordered by God.

Kansas collapsed into civil war, and about 200 people were killed. The events in "Bleeding Kansas" became national front-page news stories. In September 1856 a new territorial governor arrived and began to restore order.

This group of abolitionists took the law into their own hands to free one of their comrades from prison.

This cartoon shows Preston Brooks beating Charles Sumner with his cane. Sumner's only protection is a quill pen, symbolically representing the law.

Brooks Attacks Sumner Congress also reacted to the violence of the Sack of Lawrence. Senator **Charles Sumner** of Massachusetts criticized pro-slavery people in Kansas and personally insulted Andrew Pickens Butler, a pro-slavery senator from South Carolina. Representative **Preston Brooks**, a relative of Butler's, responded strongly.

On May 22, 1856, Brooks used a walking cane to beat Sumner unconscious in the Senate chambers. Dozens of southerners sent Brooks new canes, but northerners were outraged and called the attacker "Bully Brooks." Brooks only had to pay a $300 fine to the federal court. It took Sumner three years before he was well enough to return to the Senate.

Summary and Preview The Kansas-Nebraska Act produced a national uproar. In the next lesson you will read about divisions in political parties.

Reading Check
Summarize
What were some of the results of the intense division in Kansas?

Lesson 2 Assessment

Review Ideas, Terms, and People

1. a. Identify What issues influenced the outcome of the election of 1852?

b. Draw Conclusions Why did northern and southern Democrats support Franklin Pierce?

2. a. Recall What did the Kansas-Nebraska Act do?

b. Explain Why did antislavery and pro-slavery groups encourage people to move to Kansas?

c. Evaluate Would you have supported or opposed the Kansas-Nebraska Act? Why?

3. a. Describe What was the Pottawatomie Massacre?

b. Analyze How did Charles Sumner's views on "Bleeding Kansas" lead to conflict?

c. Elaborate Do you think Preston Brooks's punishment was reasonable? Why or why not?

Critical Thinking

4. Sequence In this lesson you learned about the railroad construction plan of Stephen Douglas and how it led to the Kansas-Nebraska Act. Create a graphic organizer like the one shown below and use it to show the sequence of events that led to violence in Kansas.

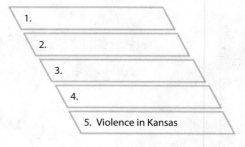

1.
2.
3.
4.
5. Violence in Kansas

Political Divisions

The Big Idea

The split over the issue of slavery intensified due to political division and judicial decisions.

Main Ideas

- Political parties in the United States underwent change due to the movement to expand slavery.

- The *Dred Scott* decision created further division over the issue of slavery.

- The Lincoln-Douglas debates brought much attention to the conflict over slavery.

Key Terms and People

Republican Party
James Buchanan
John C. Frémont
Dred Scott
Roger B. Taney
Abraham Lincoln
Lincoln-Douglas debates
Freeport Doctrine

If YOU were there . . .

You are traveling through Michigan in July 1854. As you pass through the town of Jackson, you see a crowd of several hundred people gathered under the trees. You join them and find that it is a political rally. Antislavery supporters from different parties are meeting to form a new political party. Speakers promise to fight slavery "until the contest be terminated."

How do you think this new party will affect American politics?

Political Parties Undergo Change

Democrat Stephen Douglas had predicted that the Kansas-Nebraska Act would "raise a . . . storm." He was right. The Kansas-Nebraska Act brought the slavery issue back into the national spotlight. Some Whigs, Democrats, Free-Soilers, and abolitionists joined in 1854 to form the **Republican Party**, a political party united against the spread of slavery in the West.

Democrats were in trouble. Those who supported the Kansas-Nebraska Act were not re-elected. The Whig Party also fell apart when northern and southern Whigs refused to work together. A senator from Connecticut complained, "The Whig Party has been killed off . . . by that miserable Nebraska business." Some Whigs and Democrats joined the American Party, also known as the Know-Nothing Party. At the party's convention, delegates argued over slavery, then chose former president Millard Fillmore as their candidate for the election of 1856.

The Democrats knew they could not choose a strong supporter of the Kansas-Nebraska Act, such as President Pierce or Senator Douglas. They nominated **James Buchanan** of Pennsylvania. Buchanan had a great deal of political experience as Polk's secretary of state. Most importantly, he had been in Great Britain as ambassador during the Kansas-Nebraska Act dispute and had not been involved in the debate.

At their first nominating convention, the Republicans chose explorer **John C. Frémont** as their candidate. He had little political experience, but he stood against the spread of slavery. The public saw Republicans as a single-issue party. They had almost no supporters outside of the free states.

On election day, Buchanan won 14 of the 15 slave states and became the new president. Frémont won 11 of the 16 free states. Fillmore won only one state—Maryland. Buchanan had won the election.

Reading Check
Summarize
What were the major political parties in the election of 1856, and who was the candidate for each party?

Dred Scott Decision

Just two days after Buchanan became president, the Supreme Court issued a historic ruling about slavery. News of the decision threw the country back into crisis. The Court reviewed and decided the **complex** case involving an enslaved man named **Dred Scott**.

Academic Vocabulary
complex difficult, not simple

Dred Scott Sues for Freedom Dred Scott was the slave of Dr. John Emerson, an army surgeon who lived in St. Louis, Missouri. In the 1830s Emerson had taken Scott on tours of duty in Illinois and the Wisconsin Territory. After they returned to Missouri, the doctor died, and Scott became the slave of Emerson's widow. In 1846 Scott sued for his freedom in the Missouri state courts, arguing that he had become free when he lived in free territory. Though a lower court ruled in his favor, the Missouri Supreme Court overturned this ruling.

Scott's case reached the U.S. Supreme Court 11 years later, in 1857. The justices—a majority of whom were from the South—had three key issues before them. First, the Court had to rule on whether Scott was a citizen. Only citizens could sue in federal court. Second, the Court had to decide if his time living on free soil made him free. Third, the Court had to determine the constitutionality of prohibiting slavery in parts of the Louisiana Purchase.

The Supreme Court's decision against Dred Scott (seen here) was a severe setback for abolitionists.

The Supreme Court's Ruling Chief Justice **Roger B. Taney** (TAW•nee), himself from a slaveholding family in Maryland, wrote the majority opinion in the *Dred Scott* decision in March 1857. First, he addressed the issue of Dred Scott's citizenship. Taney said the nation's founders believed that African Americans "had no rights which a white man was bound to respect." He therefore concluded that all African Americans, whether slave or free, were not citizens under the U.S. Constitution. Thus, Dred Scott did not have the right to file suit in federal court.

Taney also ruled on the other issues before the Court. As to whether Scott's residence on free soil made him free, Taney flatly said it did not. Because Scott had returned to the slave state of Missouri, the chief justice said, "his *status*, as free or slave, depended on the laws of Missouri."

Finally, Taney declared the Missouri Compromise restriction on slavery north of 36°30' to be unconstitutional. He pointed out that the Fifth Amendment said no one could "be deprived of life, liberty, or property without due process of law." Because slaves were considered property, Congress could not prohibit someone from taking slaves into a federal territory. Under this ruling, Congress had no right to ban slavery in any federal territory.

Most white southerners cheered this decision. It "covers every question regarding slavery and settles it in favor of the South," reported a Georgia newspaper. Another newspaper, the New Orleans *Picayune*, assured its readers that the ruling put "the whole basis of the . . . Republican organization under the ban of law."

The ruling stunned many northerners. The Republicans were particularly upset because their platform in 1856 had argued that Congress held the right to ban slavery in the federal territories. Now the nation's highest court had ruled that Congress did not have this right.

Indeed, some northerners feared that the spread of slavery would not stop with the federal territories. Illinois lawyer **Abraham Lincoln** warned that a future Court ruling, or what he called "the next *Dred Scott* decision," would prohibit states from banning slavery.

> "We shall *lie down* pleasantly dreaming that the people of *Missouri* are on the verge of [close to] making their state *free*; and we shall *awake* to the *reality*, instead, that the Supreme Court has made *Illinois* a *slave state*."
>
> —Abraham Lincoln, quoted in *Speeches and Letters of Abraham Lincoln 1832–1865*, edited by Merwin Roe

Reading Check
Summarize
What were the major rulings of the *Dred Scott* decision?

Lincoln-Douglas Debates

In 1858 Illinois Republicans nominated Abraham Lincoln for the U.S. Senate. His opponent was Democrat Stephen Douglas, who had represented Illinois in the Senate since 1847. Lincoln challenged Douglas in what became the historic **Lincoln-Douglas debates**.

In each debate, Lincoln stressed that the central issue of the campaign was the spread of slavery in the West. He said that the Democrats were trying to spread slavery across the nation.

Lincoln talked about the *Dred Scott* decision. He said that African Americans were "entitled to all the natural rights" listed in the Declaration of Independence, specifically mentioning "the right to life, liberty, and the pursuit of happiness." However, Lincoln believed that African Americans were not necessarily the social or political equals of whites. Hoping to cost Lincoln votes, Douglas charged that Lincoln "thinks that the Negro is his brother . . ."

A House Divided

In 1858 Abraham Lincoln gave a passionate speech to Illinois Republicans about the dangers of the disagreement over slavery. Some considered it a call for war.

> *"In my opinion, it [disagreement over slavery] will not cease [stop], until a crisis shall have been reached and passed. "A house divided against itself cannot stand." I believe this government cannot endure permanently half slave and half free. I do not expect the Union to be dissolved—I do not expect the house to fall—but I do expect it will cease to be divided."*
>
> —Abraham Lincoln, quoted in *Speeches and Letters of Abraham Lincoln 1832–1865*, edited by Merwin Roe

This line is a paraphrase of a line in the Bible.

Lincoln expresses confidence that the Union will survive.

Analyze Historical Sources
What do you think Lincoln meant by "crisis"?

Quick Facts

A Growing Conflict

Causes of Conflict
- Failure of Missouri Compromise
- Failure of Compromise of 1850
- Kansas-Nebraska Act
- *Dred Scott* decision

▼

Short-Term Effects
- Political battles
- Sectional differences
- "Bleeding Kansas"
- Lincoln-Douglas debates

▼

Long-Term Effect
- Civil War

Douglas also criticized Lincoln for saying that the nation could not remain "half slave and half free." Douglas said that the statement revealed a Republican desire to make every state a free state. This, he warned, would only lead to "a dissolution [destruction] of the Union" and "warfare between the North and the South."

At the second debate, in the northern Illinois town of Freeport, Lincoln pressed Douglas on the apparent contradiction between the Democrats' belief in popular sovereignty and the *Dred Scott* decision. Lincoln asked Douglas to explain how, if Congress could not ban slavery from a federal territory, Congress could allow the citizens of that territory to ban it.

Douglas responded that it did not matter what the Supreme Court decided about slavery. He argued that "the people have the lawful means to introduce it or exclude it as they please, for the reason that slavery cannot exist a day or an hour anywhere, unless it is supported by local police regulations."

This notion that the police would enforce the voters' decision if it contradicted the Supreme Court's decision in the *Dred Scott* case became known as the **Freeport Doctrine**.

Reading Check
Make Inferences
Why did Abraham Lincoln make slavery's expansion the central issue of the Lincoln-Douglas debates?

The Freeport Doctrine put the slavery question back in the hands of American citizens. It helped Douglas win the Senate seat. Lincoln, while not victorious, became a strong, important leader of the Republican Party.

Stephen Douglas (seen here) debated with Abraham Lincoln seven times during their 1858 election campaign.

Summary and Preview The *Dred Scott* decision and the Lincoln-Douglas debates dealt with the conflict over slavery in the western territories. In the next lesson you will read about how the conflict broke apart the Union.

Lesson 3 Assessment

Review Ideas, Terms, and People

1. **a. Identify** What was the major issue of the newly formed Republican Party?

   b. Draw Conclusions How did the Kansas-Nebraska Act affect political parties?

   c. Elaborate Why do you think James Buchanan won the election of 1856?

2. **a. Identify** Who was Roger B. Taney, and why was he important?

   b. Draw Conclusions How did the *Dred Scott* decision affect the Missouri Compromise and the expansion of slavery?

   c. Predict What problems might result from the Supreme Court's ruling in the *Dred Scott* case?

3. **a. Recall** What was the major issue of the Lincoln-Douglas debates?

   b. Make Inferences Despite his loss in the election, how did Lincoln become the leader of the Republican Party?

Critical Thinking

4. **Identify Points of View** In this lesson you learned about the effects the political divisions and the *Dred Scott* decision had on the slavery debate. Create a graphic organizer like the one below and identify the views of Abraham Lincoln and Stephen Douglas on the issue of slavery.

Lincoln	vs.	Douglas

★ The Nation Divides

The Big Idea

The United States broke apart due to the growing conflict over slavery.

Main Ideas

- John Brown's raid on Harpers Ferry intensified the disagreement between free states and slave states.

- The outcome of the election of 1860 divided the United States.

- The dispute over slavery led the South to secede.

Key Terms and People

John Brown's raid
John C. Breckinridge
Constitutional Union Party
John Bell
John J. Crittenden
Confederate States of America
Jefferson Davis

If YOU were there . . .

You work for the weekly newspaper in Harpers Ferry, Virginia. You strongly oppose slavery, but you think the question ought to be resolved by laws, not bloodshed. Now your newspaper has sent you to interview the famous abolitionist John Brown in prison. His raids in "Bleeding Kansas" killed several people. Now he is in jail for attacking a federal arsenal and taking weapons.

What questions would you ask John Brown?

Raid on Harpers Ferry

In 1858 John Brown tried to start an uprising. He wanted to attack the federal arsenal in Virginia and seize weapons there. He planned to arm local slaves. Brown expected to kill or take hostage white southerners who stood in his way. He urged abolitionists to give him money so that he could support a small army. But after nearly two years, Brown's army had only about 20 men.

On the night of October 16, 1859, **John Brown's raid** began when he and his men took over the arsenal in Harpers Ferry, Virginia, in hopes of starting a slave rebellion. He sent several of his men into the countryside to get slaves to join him. However, enslaved African Americans did not come to Harpers Ferry, fearing punishment if they took part. Instead, local white southerners attacked Brown. Eight of his men and three local men were killed. Brown and some followers retreated to a firehouse.

Federal troops arrived in Harpers Ferry the following night. The next morning, Colonel Robert E. Lee ordered a squad of marines to storm the firehouse. In a matter of seconds, the marines killed two more of Brown's men and captured the rest—including Brown.

Brown was quickly convicted of treason, murder, and conspiracy. Some of his men received death sentences. John A. Copeland, a fugitive slave, defended his actions:

"If I am dying for freedom, I could not die for a better cause." Convinced that he also would be sentenced to death, Brown delivered a memorable speech.

> "Now, if it is deemed [thought] necessary that I should forfeit [give up] my life for the furtherance of the ends of justice, and mingle [mix] my blood . . . with the blood of millions in this slave country whose rights are disregarded by wicked, cruel, and unjust enactments, I say, let it be done."
>
> —John Brown, quoted in *John Brown, 1800–1859* by Oswald Garrison Villard

As expected, the judge ordered Brown to be hanged. The sentence was carried out one month later on December 2, 1859.

Many northerners mourned John Brown's death, but some abolitionists criticized his extreme actions. Abraham Lincoln said Brown "agreed with us in thinking slavery wrong." However, Lincoln continued, "That cannot excuse violence, bloodshed, and treason."

Most southern whites—both slaveholders and non-slaveholders—felt threatened by the actions of John Brown. They worried that a "John Brown the Second" might attack. One South Carolina newspaper voiced these fears: "We are convinced the safety of the South lies only outside the present Union." Another newspaper stated that "the sooner we get out of the Union, the better."

Reading Check
Draw Conclusions
Why did John Brown's raid lead some southerners to talk about leaving the Union?

DOCUMENT-BASED INVESTIGATION   Historical Source

John Brown's Last Speech

At his trial, after being pronounced guilty, John Brown spoke in his own defense about his plan to free slaves.

Brown says he never meant to start a rebellion.

By *His*, Brown means "God's."

> "*I intended certainly to have made a clean thing of that matter [freeing slaves]. . . . I never did intend murder or treason, or the destruction of property, or to excite or incite the slaves to rebellion, or to make insurrection [revolt]. . . . Had I interfered in the manner which I admit . . . in behalf of the rich, the powerful, the intelligent, the so-called great . . . it would have been all right, and every man in this Court would have deemed it an act worthy of reward rather than punishment. . . . I believe that to have interfered as I have done . . . in behalf of His despised poor, is no wrong, but right.*"
>
> —John Brown, quoted in *The Life, Trial and Execution of Captain John Brown*

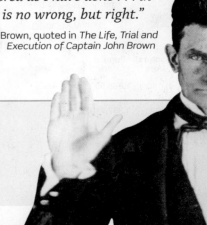

Analyze Historical Sources
How does Brown contrast his ideas with the Court's ideas?

Election of 1860

In this climate of distrust, Americans prepared for another presidential election in 1860. The northern and southern Democrats could not agree on a candidate. Northern Democrats chose Senator Stephen Douglas. Southern Democrats backed the current vice president, **John C. Breckinridge** of Kentucky, who supported slavery in the territories.

Meanwhile, a new political party emerged. The **Constitutional Union Party** recognized "no political principle other than the Constitution of the country, the Union of the states, and the enforcement of the laws." Members of this new party met in Baltimore, Maryland, and selected **John Bell** of Tennessee as their candidate. Bell was a slaveholder, but he had opposed the Kansas-Nebraska Act in 1854.

Senator William Seward of New York was the Republicans' leading candidate at the start of their convention. But it turned out that Lincoln appealed to more party members. A moderate who was against the spread of slavery, Lincoln promised not to abolish slavery where it already existed.

Douglas, Breckinridge, and Bell each knew he might not win the election. They hoped to win enough electoral votes to prevent Lincoln from winning in the electoral college. But with a unified Republican Party behind him, Lincoln won. Although he received the highest number of votes, he won only about 40 percent of the overall popular vote.

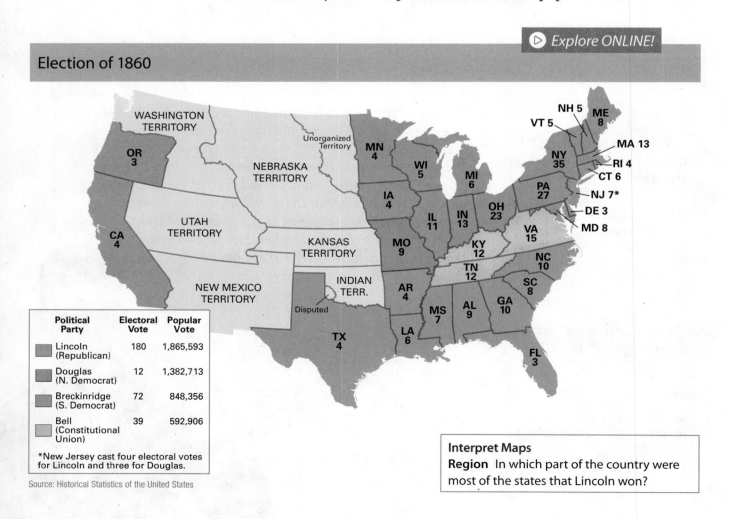

Explore ONLINE!

Election of 1860

Political Party	Electoral Vote	Popular Vote
Lincoln (Republican)	180	1,865,593
Douglas (N. Democrat)	12	1,382,713
Breckinridge (S. Democrat)	72	848,356
Bell (Constitutional Union)	39	592,906

*New Jersey cast four electoral votes for Lincoln and three for Douglas.

Source: Historical Statistics of the United States

Interpret Maps
Region In which part of the country were most of the states that Lincoln won?

Reading Check
Analyze
Information Why
was Lincoln viewed by
many as a moderate
candidate during
his campaign for the
presidency?

Lincoln won 180 of 183 electoral votes in free states. Douglas had the second-highest number of popular votes, but he won only one state. He earned just 12 electoral votes. Breckinridge and Bell split electoral votes in other slave states.

The election results angered southerners. Lincoln did not campaign in their region and did not carry any southern states, but he became the next president. The election signaled that the South was losing its national political power.

The South Secedes

Lincoln insisted that he would not change slavery in the South. However, he said that slavery could not expand and thus would eventually die out completely. That idea angered many southerners.

Southerners' Reactions People in the South believed their economy and way of life would be destroyed without slave labor. They reacted immediately. Within a week of Lincoln's election, South Carolina's legislature called for a special convention. The delegates considered secession. Southern secessionists believed that they had a right to leave the Union. They pointed out that each of the original states had voluntarily joined the Union by holding a special convention that had ratified the Constitution. Surely, they reasoned, states could leave the Union by the same process.

Critics of secession thought this argument was ridiculous. President Buchanan said the Union was not "a mere voluntary association of States, to be dissolved at pleasure by any one of the contracting parties." President-elect Abraham Lincoln agreed, saying, "No State, upon its own mere motion, can lawfully get out of the Union." Lincoln added, "They can only do so against [the] law, and by revolution."

While South Carolina representatives were meeting in Charleston to discuss secession, Congress examined a plan to save the Union. Senator **John J. Crittenden** of Kentucky proposed a series of constitutional amendments that he believed would satisfy the South by protecting slavery. Crittenden hoped the country could avoid secession and a civil war.

Lincoln disagreed with Crittenden's plan. He believed there could be no compromise about the extension of slavery. Lincoln wrote, "The tug has to come and better now than later." A Senate committee voted on Crittenden's plan, and every Republican rejected it, as Lincoln had requested.

Rebel Government
This photograph shows a crowd gathered at the inauguration of Jefferson Davis. The ceremony took place on February 18, 1861 on the steps of the state capitol in Montgomery, Alabama.

The Confederate States of America South Carolina elected to dissolve "the union now subsisting [existing] between South Carolina and other States" on December 20, 1860. Mississippi, Florida, Alabama, Georgia, Louisiana, and Texas also seceded to form the **Confederate States of America**, also called the Confederacy. Its new constitution guaranteed citizens the right to own slaves.

Delegates from seceded states elected **Jefferson Davis** of Mississippi as president of the Confederacy. Davis had hoped to be the commanding general of Mississippi's troops. He responded to the news of his election with reluctance.

When the southern states seceded, the question of who owned federal property in the South arose. For instance, the forts in the harbor of Charleston, South Carolina, were federal property. However, Confederate president Davis and the Confederacy were ready to prevent the federal army from controlling the property.

Lincoln Takes Office President Lincoln was inaugurated on March 4, 1861. In writing his inaugural address, Lincoln looked to many of the nation's founding documents. Referring to the idea that governments receive "their just powers from the consent of the governed," a line from the Declaration of Independence, Lincoln stated, "This country, with its institutions, belongs to the people who inhabit it. Whenever they shall grow weary of the existing Government, they can exercise their *constitutional* right of amending it or their *revolutionary* right to dismember [take apart] or overthrow it. I can not be ignorant of the fact that many worthy and patriotic citizens are desirous [wanting] of having the National Constitution amended . . . "

While he believed that U.S. citizens had the power to change their government through majority consent, he opposed the idea that southern states could leave the Union because they were unhappy with the government's position on slavery.

He announced in his inaugural address that he would keep all government property in the seceding states. However, he also tried to convince southerners that his government would not provoke a war. He hoped that, given time, southern states would return to the Union.

Summary and Preview The secession of the southern states hinted at the violence to come. In the next module you will read about the Civil War.

Reading Check
Draw Conclusions
Why did some southern states secede from the Union?

Lesson 4 Assessment

Review Ideas, Terms, and People

1. **a. Recall** Why did John Brown want to seize the federal arsenal at Harpers Ferry?

   b. Explain Why did some abolitionists disagree with Brown's actions?

2. **a. Identify** List the candidates in the presidential election of 1860, and identify what party each supported.

   b. Predict How might Abraham Lincoln's victory in the election of 1860 lead to future problems?

3. **a. Identify** What states made up the Confederate States of America?

   b. Explain Why did Lincoln disagree with John J. Crittenden's plan to keep the Union together?

   c. Elaborate Do you believe that the southern states had the right to secede? Why or why not?

Critical Thinking

4. **Summarize** In this lesson you learned about key people and events that led to secession. Create a graphic organizer similar to the one below and use it to summarize the causes of secession.

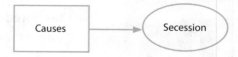

Social Studies Skills

Assess Primary and Secondary Sources

Define the Skill

All historical information comes from primary and secondary sources. *Primary sources* are documents written by someone who witnessed or took part in an event. They include diaries, letters, autobiographies, and newspaper reports. *Secondary sources* are accounts of events written after the events have occurred by someone who did not witness or take part in them. They retell, interpret, and summarize information from primary sources. History books and biographies are examples of secondary sources.

Historical sources often disagree. One writer's version of an event may be different from another writer's version. You must assess the reliability of a primary or secondary source in order to weigh its value to you as a source of accurate information.

Learn the Skill

Use these guidelines to analyze and evaluate primary and secondary sources.

1. Identify the nature of the material. Is it a first-hand, eyewitness account or is it based on information provided by others?

2. Evaluate the author. If the material is a secondary source, what qualifications does the author have to interpret the sources from which it came? If the material is a primary source, what was the author's connection to the event he or she is writing about?

3. Determine the audience. Was the source meant to be seen by the public? Was it meant for a friend, or for the writer alone? The intended audience can influence a source's content.

4. Determine the purpose. Even authors of primary sources can have reasons to distort the truth to suit their own purposes. Look for evidence of emotion, exaggeration, opinion, or bias that may have influenced the account.

5. Look for documentation. Look for other information or evidence that supports the source's account. Compare sources whenever possible.

Practice the Skill

The passage below concerns the attack on Lawrence, Kansas, that you read about in this module. The passage contains both a primary and a secondary source. The secondary account was written by John A. Garraty, a well-known historian. Review the information on the attack, analyze the passage, and answer the questions that follow.

"Sheriff Jones, at the head of an army of Missourians, marched into Lawrence. In broad daylight they threw the printing presses of two newspapers into a river. They burned down the Free State Hotel and other buildings. Antislavery Kansans seethed with rage. Here is how one eyewitness described the attack:

'Sheriff Jones, after looking at the flames rising from the hotel and saying that it was 'the happiest day of his life,' dismissed the troops and they began their lawless destruction.'"

1. Did the author of the primary source likely support the attackers or the people of Lawrence? What clues in the passage suggest this?

2. For whom was the primary source likely written?

3. Which source is more reliable for information about this incident? Explain why.

Module 17 Assessment

Review Vocabulary, Terms, and People

Identify the correct term or person from the module that best fits each of the following descriptions.

1. belief that voters should be given the right to decide if slavery would be permitted or banned

2. chief justice of the Supreme Court who wrote the majority opinion for the *Dred Scott* decision

3. Democratic candidate for president in 1852 who promised to enforce the Compromise of 1850 and the Fugitive Slave Act

4. a fugitive slave whose arrest led to violence between government officials and abolitionists

5. Republican candidate for the presidency in 1856 who opposed the spread of slavery in the West

6. slave who sued for freedom, claiming that by living in free territory, he had earned his freedom

7. Stephen Douglas's bill leaving states and territories to determine the issue of slavery through popular sovereignty

Comprehension and Critical Thinking

Lesson 1

8. a. **Describe** How did literature aid the anti-slavery movement?

    b. **Draw Conclusions** How did the issue of slavery promote sectionalism?

    c. **Evaluate** Do you think the Compromise of 1850 was a good solution? Explain your answer.

Lesson 2

9. a. **Identify** Who were the candidates in the presidential election of 1852, and what issues did each support?

    b. **Analyze** How did the Kansas-Nebraska Act lead to growing hostility between pro-slavery and antislavery supporters?

    c. **Elaborate** Why do you think "Bleeding Kansas" produced intense controversy among many Americans?

Lesson 3

10. a. **Identify** Who was Dred Scott, and why was his case important?

    b. **Analyze** How were political parties affected by the debate over slavery?

    c. **Elaborate** Why do you think Republicans challenged Stephen Douglas's run for the Senate?

Lesson 4

11. a. **Recall** Why did John Brown's raid on Harpers Ferry fail?

    b. **Explain** Why did the results of the election of 1860 anger southerners?

    c. **Draw Conclusions** Do you think that Lincoln could have avoided losing southern states to the Confederacy after he was elected in 1861? Explain why or why not.

Review Themes

12. **Politics** Copy the graphic organizer below. List the five most important events that led to the Civil War, and explain how each event increased conflict between the North and the South.

Events	Effect on Conflict

13. **Politics** How did sectionalism affect American politics?

14. **Society and Culture** What effect did Harriet Beecher Stowe's book *Uncle Tom's Cabin* have on the debate over slavery?

Reading Skills

Facts, Opinions, and the Past *Use the Reading Skills taught in this module to answer the question about the reading selection below.*

> In 1858 John Brown tried to start an uprising. He wanted to attack the federal arsenal in Virginia and seize weapons there. He planned to arm local slaves. Brown expected to kill or take hostage white southerners who stood in his way.

15. Based on the reading selection above, which of the following statements is an opinion?

   a. John Brown's raid was in 1858.

   b. John Brown hated all slaveholders.

   c. John Brown's raid took place in Virginia.

   d. Local slaves helped John Brown.

Social Studies Skills

Assess Primary and Secondary Sources *Use the Social Studies Skills taught in this module to answer the question below.*

16. Which of the following is *not* an example of a primary source used in this module?

   a. *A People's History of the United States* by Howard Zinn

   b. the "Seventh of March" speech by Daniel Webster

   c. Abraham Lincoln's "A House Divided" speech

   d. John Brown's last speech

Focus on Writing

17. **Write an Autobiography** When you read about history, it can be difficult to imagine how events you read about affected ordinary people. Write an autobiography of a fictional character, telling how the events covered in this module affected him or her. As you write the autobiography, be sure to mention each of the events and how your character heard about them, what he or she was doing at the time, how he or she felt about the event, and how it affected him or her. What are your character's hopes and fears for the future?

Module 18

The Civil War

★

Essential Question

How did the Civil War transform the nation?

About the Photo: Among those who marched off to war were these drummer boys of the Union army.

▶ *Explore ONLINE!*

HISTORY.

VIDEOS, including...

• Emancipation Proclamation
• Battle of Antietam
• Indian Warriors
• 54th Regiment
• The Civil War: Gettysburg
• Sherman's March to the Sea

☑ Document-Based Investigations

☑ Graphic Organizers

☑ Interactive Games

☑ Animation: Ironclad Technology

☑ Image with Hotspots: Copperhead Political Cartoon

☑ Image Carousel: Civil War Families

In this module you will learn how the resources of the North enabled it to defeat the South in the Civil War.

What You Will Learn ...

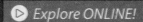
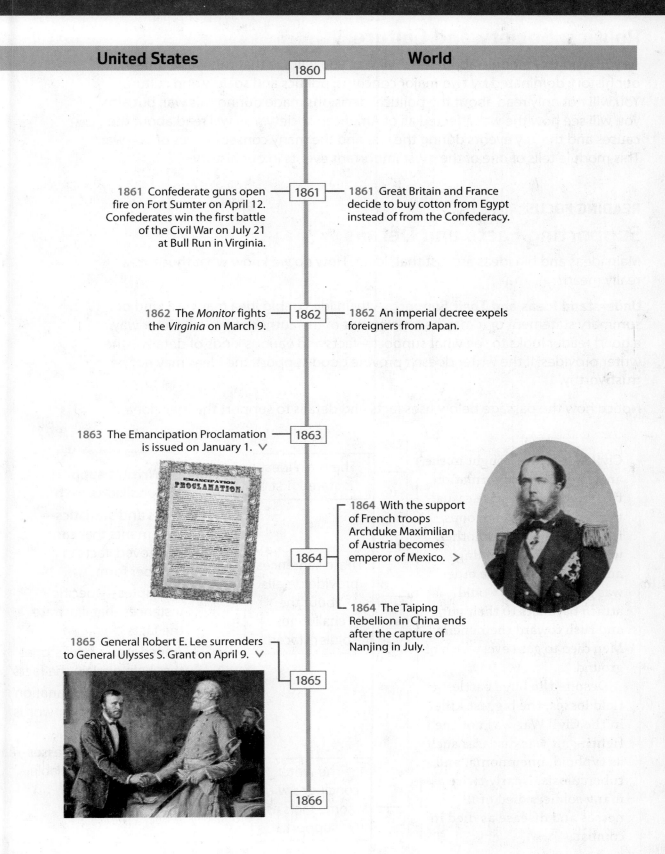

United States

World

1860

1861 Confederate guns open fire on Fort Sumter on April 12. Confederates win the first battle of the Civil War on July 21 at Bull Run in Virginia.

1861

1861 Great Britain and France decide to buy cotton from Egypt instead of from the Confederacy.

1862 The *Monitor* fights the *Virginia* on March 9.

1862

1862 An imperial decree expels foreigners from Japan.

1863 The Emancipation Proclamation is issued on January 1. ∨

1863

1864 With the support of French troops Archduke Maximilian of Austria becomes emperor of Mexico. >

1864

1864 The Taiping Rebellion in China ends after the capture of Nanjing in July.

1865 General Robert E. Lee surrenders to General Ulysses S. Grant on April 9. ∨

1865

1866

Reading Social Studies

Politics, Society and Culture

As you read this module about the Civil War, you will see that this was a time in our history dominated by two major concerns: politics and society and culture. You will not only read about the political decisions made during this war, but also you will see how the war affected all of American society. You will read about the causes and the key events during the war and the many consequences of this war. This module tells of one of the most important events in our history.

READING FOCUS:

Supporting Facts and Details

Main ideas and big ideas are just that, ideas. How do we know what those ideas really mean?

Understand Ideas and Their Support A main idea or big idea may be a kind of summary statement or it may be a statement of the author's opinion. Either way, a good reader looks to see what support—facts and various kinds of details—the writer provides. If the writer doesn't provide good support, the ideas may not be trustworthy.

Notice how the passage below uses facts and details to support the main idea.

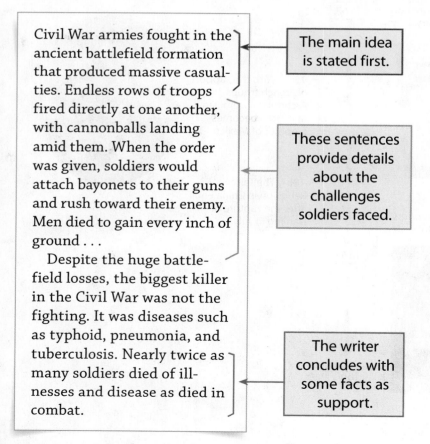

Civil War armies fought in the ancient battlefield formation that produced massive casualties. Endless rows of troops fired directly at one another, with cannonballs landing amid them. When the order was given, soldiers would attach bayonets to their guns and rush toward their enemy. Men died to gain every inch of ground . . .

Despite the huge battlefield losses, the biggest killer in the Civil War was not the fighting. It was diseases such as typhoid, pneumonia, and tuberculosis. Nearly twice as many soldiers died of illnesses and disease as died in combat.

The main idea is stated first.

These sentences provide details about the challenges soldiers faced.

The writer concludes with some facts as support.

Writers support propositions with . . .

1. **Facts and statistics**—statements that can be proved; facts in number form
2. **Examples**—specific instances that illustrate the facts
3. **Anecdotes**—brief stories that help explain the facts
4. **Definitions**—explanation of unusual terms or words
5. **Comments from the experts or eyewitnesses**—statements from reliable sources

You Try It!

The following passage is from the module you are about to read. As you read it, look for the writer's main idea and support.

> In February 1862 Grant led an assault force into Tennessee. With help from navy gunboats, Grant's Army of the Tennessee took two outposts on key rivers in the West. On February 6 he captured Fort Henry on the Tennessee River. Several days later he took Fort Donelson on the Cumberland River.
>
> Fort Donelson's commander asked for the terms of surrender. Grant replied, "No terms except an unconditional and immediate surrender can be accepted." The fort surrendered. The North gave a new name to Grant's initials: "Unconditional Surrender" Grant.

After you read the passage, answer the following questions.

1. Which sentence best states the writer's main idea?
   a. The fort surrendered.
   b. In February 1862 Grant led an assault force into Tennessee.
   c. Fort Donelson's commander asked for the terms of surrender.

2. Which method of support is not used to support the main idea?
   a. facts
   b. comments from experts or eyewitnesses
   c. anecdotes

3. Which sentence in this passage provides a comment from an expert or eyewitness?

As you read Module 18, pay attention to the details that the writers have chosen to support their main ideas.

The War Begins

The Big Idea

Civil war broke out between the North and the South in 1861.

Main Ideas

- Following the outbreak of war at Fort Sumter, Americans chose sides.
- The Union and the Confederacy prepared for war.

Key Terms and People

Fort Sumter
border states
Winfield Scott
cotton diplomacy

If YOU were there . . .

You are a college student in Charleston in early 1861. Seven southern states have left the Union and formed their own government. All-out war seems unavoidable. Your friends have begun to volunteer for either the Union or the Confederate forces. You are torn between loyalty to your home state and to the United States.

Would you join the Union or the Confederate army?

Americans Choose Sides

Furious at Lincoln's election and fearing a federal invasion, seven southern states had seceded. The new Commander in Chief tried desperately to save the Union.

In his inaugural address, Lincoln promised not to end slavery where it existed. The federal government "will not assail [attack] you. You can have no conflict without being yourselves the aggressors," he said, trying to calm southerners' fears. However, Lincoln also stated his intention to preserve the Union. He believed that saving the Union would help to save democracy. If the Union and its government failed, then monarchs could say that people were unable to rule themselves. As a result, Lincoln refused to recognize secession, declaring the Union to be "unbroken."

In fact, after decades of painful compromises, the Union was badly broken. From the Lower South, a battle cry was arising, born out of fear, rage—and excitement. Confederate officials began seizing branches of the federal mint, arsenals, and military outposts. In a last-ditch effort to avoid war between the states, Secretary of State Seward suggested a united effort of threatening war against Spain and France for interfering in Mexico and the Caribbean. In the highly charged atmosphere, it would take only a spark to unleash the heat of war.

In 1861 that spark occurred at **Fort Sumter**, a federal outpost in Charleston, South Carolina, that was attacked by

In Charleston all activity came to a complete stop. Citizens crowded rooftops to watch the battle.

Charleston

Castle Pinckney

Charleston Harbor

The first shot fired on Fort Sumter was fired from Fort Johnson.

Shots fired at the ironclad battery did little damage.

Fort Johnson

Fort Sumter

Fort Sumter was strategically placed to control Charleston Harbor.

Fort Moultrie

Cummings Point

Atlantic Ocean

Charleston

Fort Sumter

The first shots of the Civil War were fired at Fort Sumter, South Carolina. Although no one was killed there, the bloodiest war in the country's history had begun.

Interpret Maps

1. **Human-Environment Interaction** Why would the Union army need to resupply Fort Sumter?

2. **Place** What advantages would a floating battery have?

Confederate troops, beginning the Civil War. Determined to seize the fortress—which controlled the entrance to Charleston Harbor—the Confederates ringed the harbor with heavy guns. Instead of surrendering the fort, Lincoln decided to send in ships to provide badly needed supplies to defend the fort. Confederate officials demanded that the federal troops evacuate. The fort's commander, Major Robert Anderson, refused.

Now it was Jefferson Davis who faced a dilemma. If he did nothing, he would damage the image of the Confederacy as a sovereign, independent nation. On the other hand, if Davis ordered an attack on Fort Sumter, he would turn peaceful secession into war. Davis chose war. Before sunrise on April 12, 1861, Confederate guns opened fire on Fort Sumter. A witness wrote that the first shots brought "every soldier in the harbor to his feet, and every man, woman, and child in the city of Charleston from their beds." The Civil War had begun.

The fort, although massive, stood little chance. Its heavy guns faced the Atlantic Ocean, not the shore. After 34 hours of cannon blasts, Fort Sumter surrendered. "The last ray of hope for preserving the Union has expired at the assault upon Fort Sumter . . ." Lincoln wrote.

Reaction to Lincoln's Call The fall of Fort Sumter stunned the North. Lincoln declared the South to be in a state of rebellion and asked state governors for 75,000 militiamen to put down the rebellion. States now had to choose: Would they secede, or would they stay in the Union? Democratic senator Stephen Douglas, speaking in support of Lincoln's call for troops, declared, "There can be no neutrals in this war, *only patriots—or traitors.*"

Pennsylvania, New Jersey, and the states north of them rallied to the president's call. The crucial slave states of the Upper South— North Carolina, Tennessee, Virginia, and Arkansas—seceded and joined the Confederate States of Texas, Louisiana, Mississippi, Alabama, Georgia, Florida, and South Carolina. The slave states of the Upper South provided soldiers and supplies to the rest of the South. The western territories were disputed between the Union and the Confederacy. Mary Boykin Chesnut, whose husband became a Confederate congressman, wrote in her diary:

"I did not know that one could live in such days of excitement. . . . Everybody tells you half of something, and then rushes off . . . to hear the last news."

—Mary Boykin Chesnut, quoted in *Mary Chesnut's Civil War*, edited by C. Vann Woodward

Recruitment posters like this one made use of eye-catching symbols and colors to entice Pennsylvanians to fight for the Union.

Wedged between the North and the South were the key **border states** of Delaware, Kentucky, Maryland, and Missouri—slave states that did not join the Confederacy. Kentucky and Missouri controlled parts of important rivers. Maryland separated the Union capital, Washington, DC, from the North.

People in the border states were deeply divided on the war. The president's own wife, Mary Todd Lincoln, had four brothers from Kentucky who fought for the Confederacy. Lincoln sent federal troops into the border states to help keep them in the Union. He also sent soldiers into western Virginia, where Union loyalties were strong. West Virginia set up its own state government in 1863.

Northern Resources Numbers tell an important story about the Civil War. Consider the North's advantages. It could draw soldiers and workers from a population of 22 million. The South had only 5.5 million people to draw from. One of the greatest advantages in the North was the region's network of roads, canals, and railroads. Some 22,000 miles of railroad track could move soldiers and supplies throughout the North. The South had only about 9,000 miles of track.

In the North, the Civil War stimulated economic growth. To supply the military, the production of coal, iron, wheat, and wool increased. Also, the export of corn, wheat, beef, and pork to Europe doubled. In the South, the export of resources decreased because of the Union blockade.

QUICK FACTS

▶ Explore ONLINE!

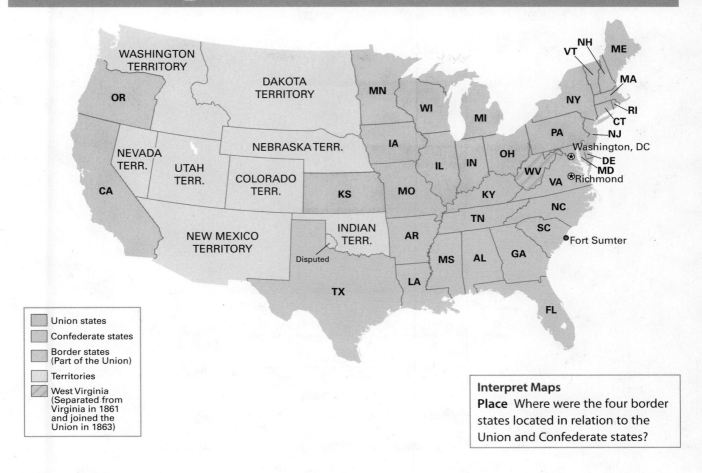

Legend:
- Union states
- Confederate states
- Border states (Part of the Union)
- Territories
- West Virginia (Separated from Virginia in 1861 and joined the Union in 1863)

Interpret Maps
Place Where were the four border states located in relation to the Union and Confederate states?

Finally, the Union had money. It had a more developed economy, banking system, and a currency called greenbacks. The South had to start printing its own Confederate dollars. Some states printed their own money, too. This led to financial chaos.

Taking advantage of the Union's strengths, General **Winfield Scott** developed a two-part strategy: (1) destroy the South's economy with a naval blockade of southern ports; (2) gain control of the Mississippi River to divide the South. Other leaders urged an attack on Richmond, Virginia, the Confederate capital.

Southern Resources The Confederacy had advantages as well. With its strong military tradition, the South put many brilliant officers into battle. Southern farms provided food for its armies. The South's best advantage, however, was strategic. It needed only to defend itself until the North grew tired of fighting.

The North had to invade and control the South. To accomplish this, the Union army had to travel huge distances. For example, the distance from northern Virginia to central Georgia is about the length of Scotland and England combined. Because of distances such as this, the North had to maintain long supply lines.

Resources of the North and South

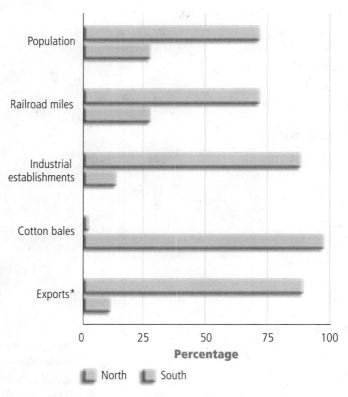

*Southern exports do not include Tennessee, Arkansas, and Mississippi.

Analyze Visuals

1. Do you think the North or the South could maintain better supply lines for their troops? Explain.

2. Do you think the North or the South could provide more weapons for their troops? Explain.

In addition, wilderness covered much of the South. Armies found this land difficult to cross. Also, in Virginia many of the rivers ran from east to west. Because of this, they formed a natural defense against an army that attacked from the north to the south. As a result, northern generals were often forced to attack Confederate troops from the side rather than from the front. Furthermore, because southerners fought mostly on their home soil, they were often familiar with the area.

The South hoped to wear down the North and to capture Washington, DC. Confederate president Jefferson Davis also tried to win foreign allies through **cotton diplomacy**. This was the idea that Great Britain would support the Confederacy because it needed the South's raw cotton to supply its booming textile industry. Cotton diplomacy did not work as the South had hoped. Britain had large supplies of cotton, and it got more from India and Egypt.

Reading Check
Compare What advantages did the North and South have leading up to the war?

Union and Confederate Soldiers

Early in the war, uniforms differed greatly, especially in the Confederate army. Uniforms became simpler and more standard as the war dragged on.

The soldiers carried food, extra ammunition, and other items in their haversacks.

Each soldier was armed with a bayonet, a knife that can be attached to the barrel of a rifle. The bayonets were stored in scabbards on their belts.

Confederate Soldier

Both soldiers were also armed with single-shot, muzzle-loading rifles.

Union Soldier

Analyze Visuals
How are the Union and Confederate uniforms and equipment similar and different?

Preparing for War

The North and the South now rushed to war. Neither side was prepared for the tragedy to come.

Volunteer Armies Volunteer militias had sparked the revolution that created the United States. Now they would battle for its future. At the start of the war, the Union army had only 16,000 soldiers. Within months that number had swelled to a half million soldiers. Southern men rose up to defend their land and their ways of life. Virginian Thomas Webber came to fight "against the invading foe [enemy] who now pollute the sacred soil of my beloved native state." When Union soldiers asked one captured rebel why he was fighting, he replied, "I'm fighting because you're down here."

Helping the Troops Civilians on both sides helped those in uniform. They raised money, provided aid for soldiers and their families, and ran emergency hospitals. Dr. Elizabeth Blackwell, the first woman to receive a license to practice medicine, organized a group that pressured President Lincoln to form the U.S. Sanitary Commission in June 1861. The Sanitary, as it was called, was run by clergyman Henry Bellows. Tens of thousands of volunteers worked with the U.S. Sanitary Commission to send bandages, medicines, and food to Union army camps and hospitals. Some 3,000 women served as nurses in the Union army.

Training the Soldiers Both the Union and Confederate armies faced shortages of clothing, food, and even rifles. While the U.S. Army troops had standard issue uniforms, volunteer militias frequently had their own uniforms and individual volunteers often simply wore their own clothes. Eventually, each side chose a color for their uniforms. The Union chose blue. The Confederates wore gray.

The problem with volunteers was that many of them had no idea how to fight. Schoolteachers, farmers, and laborers all had to learn the combat basics of marching, shooting, and using bayonets.

Days in camp were long and boring. They typically began at 5 a.m. in summer and 6 a.m. in winter. After breakfast, the men took part in up to five daily drills. During these two-hour sessions they learned and practiced battlefield maneuvers. Between drills, the troops cleaned the camp, gathered firewood, wrote letters home, and played games. With visions of glory and action, many young soldiers were eager to fight. They would not have to wait long.

Discipline and drill were used to turn raw volunteers into an efficient fighting machine. During a battle, the success or failure of a regiment often depended on its discipline—how well it responded to orders.

Volunteers also learned how to use rifles. Eventually, soldiers were expected to be able to load, aim, and fire their rifles three times in one minute. The quality of the weapons provided varied greatly. Most soldiers favored the Springfield and Enfield rifles for their accuracy. On the other hand, soldiers often complained about their Austrian and Belgian rifles. A soldier remarked, "I don't believe one could hit the broadside of a barn with them."

On average, soldiers spent about 75 percent of their time in camp. In wet weather, camps were a sea of mud. In dry weather, they were filled with clouds of dust. The Union army provided the infantry with two-person tents. However, soldiers often discarded these tents in favor of more portable ones. The Confederate army did not usually issue tents. Instead, Confederates often used tents that were captured from the Union army.

Reading Check
Summarize
How did soldiers and civilians prepare for war?

Summary and Preview As citizens chose sides in the Civil War, civilians and soldiers alike became involved in the war effort. In the next lesson you will learn about some early battles in the war, both on land and at sea.

Lesson 1 Assessment

Review Ideas, Terms, and People

1. a. Identify What event triggered the war between the Union and the Confederacy?

   b. Contrast How did the Union's strategy differ from that of the Confederacy?

   c. Evaluate Which side do you believe was better prepared for war? Explain your answer.

2. a. Describe How did women take part in the war?

   b. Summarize In what ways were the armies of the North and South unprepared for war?

   c. Elaborate Why did men volunteer to fight in the war?

Critical Thinking

3. Compare and Contrast In this lesson you learned about the preparations for war by the North and the South. Create a chart similar to the one below and use it to show the strengths and weaknesses of each side in the war.

	Union	Confederacy
Strengths		
Weaknesses		

The War in the East

The Big Idea

Confederate and Union forces faced off in Virginia and at sea.

Main Ideas

- Union and Confederate forces fought for control of the war in Virginia.
- The Battle of Antietam gave the North a slight advantage.
- The Confederacy attempted to break the Union naval blockade.

Key Terms and People

Thomas "Stonewall" Jackson
First Battle of Bull Run
George B. McClellan
Robert E. Lee
Seven Days' Battles
Second Battle of Bull Run
Battle of Antietam
ironclads

If YOU were there . . .

You live in Washington, DC, in July 1861. You and your friends are on your way to Manassas, near Washington, to watch the battle there. Everyone expects a quick Union victory. Your wagon is loaded with food for a picnic, and people are in a holiday mood. You see some members of Congress riding toward Manassas, too. Maybe this battle will end the war!

Why would you want to watch this battle?

War in Virginia

The troops that met in the first major battle of the Civil War found that it was no picnic. In July 1861 Lincoln ordered General Irvin McDowell to lead his 35,000-man army from the Union capital, Washington, to the Confederate capital, Richmond. The soldiers were barely trained. McDowell complained that they "stopped every moment to pick blackberries or get water; they would not keep in the ranks." The first day's march covered only five miles.

Bull Run/Manassas McDowell's army was headed to Manassas, Virginia, an important railroad junction. If McDowell could seize Manassas, he would control the best route to the Confederate capital. Some 22,000 Confederate troops under the command of General Pierre G. T. Beauregard were waiting for McDowell and his troops along a creek called Bull Run. For two days Union troops tried to find a way around the Confederates. During that time, Beauregard requested assistance, and General Joseph E. Johnston headed toward Manassas with another 10,000 Confederate troops. By July 21, 1861, they had all arrived.

In this painting of the First Battle of Bull Run, Confederate general Thomas "Stonewall" Jackson looks over the battlefield.

That morning, Union troops managed to cross the creek and drive back the left side of the Confederate line. Yet one unit held firmly in place.

"There is Jackson standing like a stone wall!" cried one southern officer. "Rally behind the Virginians!" At that moment General **Thomas "Stonewall" Jackson** earned his famous nickname.

A steady stream of Virginia volunteers arrived to counter the attack. The Confederates surged forward. One eyewitness described the scene.

> "There is smoke, dust, wild talking, shouting; hissings, howlings, explosions. It is a new, strange, unanticipated experience to the soldiers of both armies, far different from what they thought it would be."
>
> —Charles Coffin, quoted in *Voices of the Civil War* by Richard Wheeler

The battle raged through the day, with rebel soldiers still arriving. Finally, the weary Union troops gave out. They tried to make an orderly retreat back across the creek, but the roads were clogged with the fancy carriages of panicked spectators. The Union army scattered in the chaos.

The Confederates lacked the strength to push north and capture Washington, DC. But clearly, the rebels had won the day. The **First Battle of Bull Run** was the first major battle of the Civil War and the Confederates' victory. The battle is also known as the First Battle of Manassas. It shattered the North's hopes of winning the war quickly.

More Battles in Virginia The shock at Bull Run persuaded Lincoln of the need for a better-trained army. He put his hopes in General **George B. McClellan**. The general assembled a highly disciplined force of 100,000 soldiers called the Army of the Potomac. The careful McClellan spent

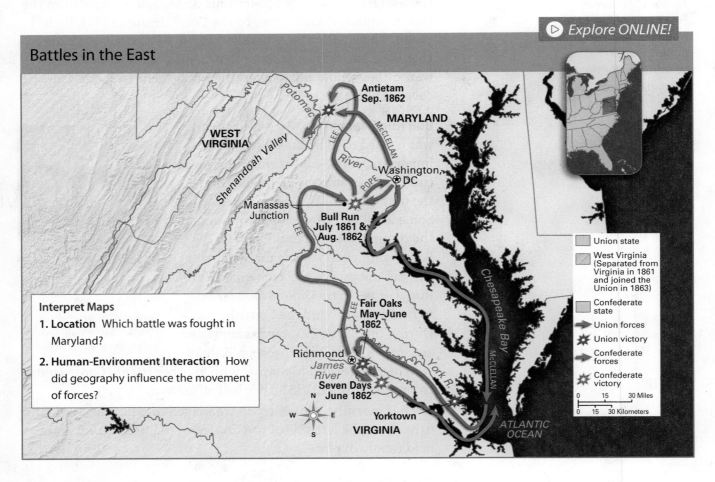

Explore ONLINE!

Battles in the East

Interpret Maps

1. **Location** Which battle was fought in Maryland?

2. **Human-Environment Interaction** How did geography influence the movement of forces?

Union state

West Virginia (Separated from Virginia in 1861 and joined the Union in 1863)

Confederate state

Union forces

Union victory

Confederate forces

Confederate victory

0   15   30 Miles

0   15   30 Kilometers

Robert E. Lee 1807–1870

Robert E. Lee was born into a wealthy Virginia family and graduated second in his class from West Point, the U.S. military academy. He fought in the Mexican-American War of 1846, helping to capture Veracruz. When the Civil War began, President Lincoln asked Lee to lead the Union army. Although Lee opposed secession, he declined Lincoln's offer and resigned from the U.S. Army to become a general in the Confederate army. As a general, Lee was brilliant, but a lack of supplies from civilian leaders weakened his position. His soldiers—some of whom called him

Uncle Robert—almost worshiped him because he insisted on sharing their hardships. After the war ended, Lee became president of Washington College in Virginia, now known as Washington and Lee University. Lee swore renewed allegiance to the United States, but Congress accidentally neglected to restore his citizenship. Still, Lee never spoke bitterly of northerners or the Union, and many southerners saw Lee as a war hero.

Draw Conclusions
How did Lee's choice reflect the division of the states?

months training. However, because he overestimated the size of the Confederate army, McClellan hesitated to attack. Lincoln grew impatient. Finally, in the spring of 1862 McClellan launched an effort to capture Richmond, called the "Peninsular Campaign." Instead of marching south for a direct assault, McClellan slowly brought his force through the peninsula between the James and York rivers. More time slipped away.

The South feared that McClellan would receive reinforcements from Washington. To prevent this, Stonewall Jackson launched an attack toward Washington. Although the attack was pushed back, it prevented the Union from sending reinforcements to McClellan.

In June 1862, with McClellan's force poised outside Richmond, the Confederate army in Virginia came under the command of General **Robert E. Lee**. A graduate of the U.S. Military Academy at West Point, Lee had served in the Mexican War and had led federal troops at Harpers Ferry. Lee was willing to take risks and make unpredictable moves to throw Union forces off balance.

During the summer of 1862, Lee strengthened his positions. On June 26 he launched a series of clashes known as the **Seven Days' Battles** that forced the Union army to retreat from near Richmond. Confederate general D. H. Hill described one failed attack. "It was not war—it was murder," he said. Lee saved Richmond and forced McClellan to retreat. A frustrated Lincoln ordered General John Pope to march directly on Richmond.

Jackson wanted to defeat Pope's army before it could join up with McClellan's larger Army of the Potomac. Jackson's troops met Pope's Union forces on the battlefield in August 1862. The three-day battle became known as the **Second Battle of Bull Run**, or the Second Battle of Manassas.

The first day's fighting was savage. Captain George Fairfield of the 7th Wisconsin regiment later recalled, "What a slaughter! No one appeared to know the object of the fight, and there we stood for one hour, the men falling all around." The fighting ended in a stalemate.

On the second day, Pope found Jackson's troops along an unfinished railroad grade. Pope hurled his men against the Confederates. But the attacks were pushed back with heavy casualties on both sides.

On the third day, the Confederates crushed the Union army's assault and forced it to retreat in defeat. The Confederates had won a major victory, and General Robert E. Lee decided it was time to take the war to the North.

Reading Check
Sequence List in order the events that forced Union troops out of Virginia.

Battle of Antietam

Confederate leaders hoped to follow up Lee's successes in Virginia with a major victory on northern soil. On September 4, 1862, some 40,000 Confederate soldiers began crossing into Maryland. General Robert E. Lee decided to divide his army. He sent about half of his troops, under the command of Stonewall Jackson, to Harpers Ferry. There they defeated a Union force and captured the town. Meanwhile, Lee arrived in the town of Frederick and issued a Proclamation to the People of Maryland, urging them to join the Confederates. However, his words would not be enough to convince Marylanders to abandon the Union. Union soldiers, however, found a copy of Lee's battle plan, which had been left at an abandoned Confederate camp. General McClellan learned that Lee had divided his army in order to attack Harpers Ferry. However, McClellan hesitated to attack. As a result, the Confederates had time to reunite.

The two armies met along Antietam Creek in Maryland on September 17, 1862. The battle lasted for hours. By the end of the day, the Union had

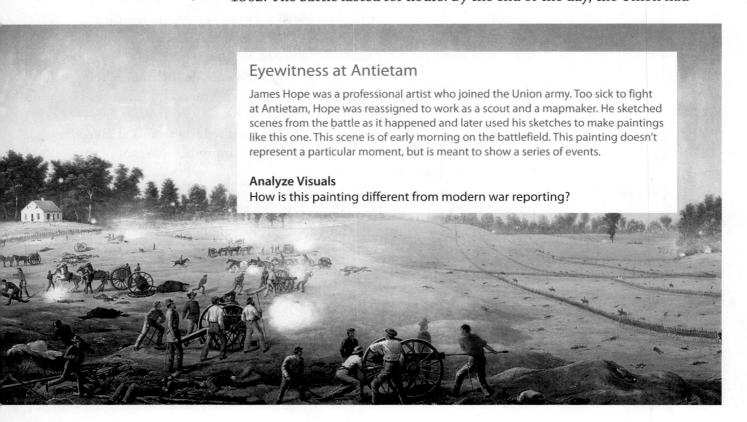

Eyewitness at Antietam

James Hope was a professional artist who joined the Union army. Too sick to fight at Antietam, Hope was reassigned to work as a scout and a mapmaker. He sketched scenes from the battle as it happened and later used his sketches to make paintings like this one. This scene is of early morning on the battlefield. This painting doesn't represent a particular moment, but is meant to show a series of events.

Analyze Visuals
How is this painting different from modern war reporting?

suffered more than 12,000 casualties. The Confederates endured more than 13,000 casualties. Union officer A. H. Nickerson later recalled, "It seemed that everybody near me was killed." The **Battle of Antietam**, also known as the Battle of Sharpsburg, was the bloodiest single-day battle of the Civil War—and of U.S. history. More soldiers were killed and wounded at the Battle of Antietam than the deaths of all Americans in the American Revolution, War of 1812, and Mexican-American War combined.

During the battle, McClellan kept four divisions of soldiers in reserve and refused to use them to attack Lee's devastated army. McClellan was convinced that Lee was massing reserves for a counterattack. Those reserves did not exist. Despite this blunder, Antietam was an important victory. Lee's northward advance had been stopped.

Reading Check
Analyze Why was the Battle of Antietam significant?

Breaking the Union's Blockade

While the two armies fought for control of the land, the Union navy controlled the sea. The North had most of the U.S. Navy's small fleet, and many experienced naval officers had remained loyal to the Union. The North also had enough industry to build more ships. The Confederacy turned to British companies for new ships.

The Union's Naval Strategy The Union navy quickly mobilized to set up a blockade of southern ports. The blockade largely prevented the South from selling or receiving goods, and it seriously damaged the southern economy.

The blockade was hard to maintain because the Union navy had to patrol thousands of miles of coastline from Virginia to Texas. The South used small, fast ships to outrun the larger Union warships. Most of these blockade runners traveled to the Bahamas or Nassau to buy supplies for the Confederacy. These ships, however, could not make up for the South's

Historical Source

Anaconda Plan

This cartoon shows visually the North's plan to cut off supplies to the South through naval blockades, a strategy called the Anaconda Plan.

Why is the snake's head red, white, and blue?

How does the cartoonist show what the snake represents?

Analyze Historical Sources
Why do you think the plan was called the Anaconda Plan?

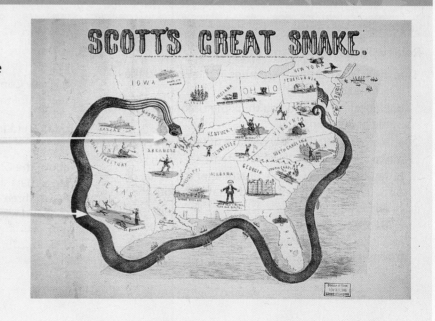

loss of trade. The Union blockade reduced the number of ships entering southern ports from 6,000 to 800 per year.

Clash of the Ironclads Hoping to take away the Union's advantage at sea, the Confederacy turned to a new type of warship—**ironclads**, or ships heavily armored with iron. The British government neglected to stop these ships from being delivered, in violation of its pledge of neutrality. The Confederates had captured a Union steamship, the *Merrimack*, and turned it into an ironclad, renamed the *Virginia*. One Union sailor described the **innovation** as "a huge half-submerged crocodile." In early March 1862 the ironclad sailed into Hampton Roads, Virginia, an important waterway guarded by Union ships. Before nightfall, the *Virginia* easily sank two of the Union's wooden warships, while it received minor damage.

Academic Vocabulary
innovation a new idea or way of doing something

The Union navy had already built its own ironclad, the *Monitor*, designed by Swedish-born engineer John Ericsson. Ericsson's ship had unusual new features, such as a revolving gun tower. One Confederate soldier called the *Monitor* "a tin can on a shingle!" Although small, the *Monitor* carried powerful guns and had thick plating.

When the *Virginia* returned to Hampton Roads later that month, the *Monitor* was waiting. After several hours of fighting, neither ship was seriously damaged, but the *Monitor* forced the *Virginia* to withdraw. This success saved the Union fleet and continued the blockade. The clash of the ironclads also signaled a revolution in naval warfare. The days of wooden warships powered by wind and sails were drawing to a close.

Reading Check
Evaluate How effective was the Union blockade?

The *Monitor* sank in North Carolina in the winter of 1862. Scientists located the shipwreck in 1973, and remains of the ship are part of the exhibit at the USS *Monitor* Center, which opened in 2007.

Summary and Preview The early battles of the Civil War were centered in the East. In the next lesson you will read about battles in the West.

Lesson 2 Assessment

Review Ideas, Terms, and People

1. a. **Identify** List the early battles in the East and the outcome of each battle.

   b. **Elaborate** Why do you think the Union lost the First Battle of Bull Run?

2. a. **Describe** What costly mistake did the Confederacy make before the Battle of Antietam?

   b. **Analyze** What was the outcome of the Battle of Antietam, and what effect did it have on both the North and the South?

   c. **Elaborate** Why do you think General George B. McClellan did not finish off General Robert E. Lee's troops when he had the chance?

3. a. **Describe** What was the Union's strategy in the war at sea?

   b. **Draw Conclusions** Why were ironclads more successful than older, wooden ships?

Critical Thinking

4. **Support a Point of View** In this lesson you learned about the Civil War battles in the East and at sea. Create a chart similar to the one below and use it to show which three conflicts you think were the most significant and why.

Most Significant	Why

The War in the West

The Big Idea

Fighting in the Civil War spread to the western United States.

Main Ideas

- Union strategy in the West centered on control of the Mississippi River.

- Confederate and Union troops struggled for dominance in the Far West.

Key Terms and People

Ulysses S. Grant
Battle of Shiloh
David Farragut
Siege of Vicksburg

If YOU were there . . .

You live in the city of Vicksburg, set on high bluffs above the Mississippi River. Vicksburg is vital to the control of the river, and Confederate defenses are strong. But the Union general is determined to take the town. For weeks you have been surrounded and besieged. Cannon shells burst overhead, day and night. Some have fallen on nearby homes. Supplies of food are running low.

How would you survive this siege?

Union Strategy in the West

While Lincoln fumed over the cautious, hesitant General McClellan, he had no such problems with **Ulysses S. Grant**. Bold and restless, Grant grew impatient when he was asked to lead defensive military maneuvers. He wanted to be on the attack. As a commander of forces in the Union's western campaign, he would get his wish.

The western campaign focused on taking control of the Mississippi River. This strategy would cut off the eastern part of the Confederacy from sources of food production in Arkansas, Louisiana, and Texas. From bases on the Mississippi, the Union army could attack southern communication and transportation networks.

In February 1862 Grant led an assault force into Tennessee. With help from navy gunboats, Grant's Army of the Tennessee took two outposts on key rivers in the West. On February 6 he captured Fort Henry on the Tennessee River. Several days later he took Fort Donelson on the Cumberland River.

Fort Donelson's commander asked for the terms of surrender. Grant replied, "No terms except an unconditional and immediate surrender can be accepted." The fort surrendered. The North gave a new name to Grant's initials: "Unconditional Surrender" Grant.

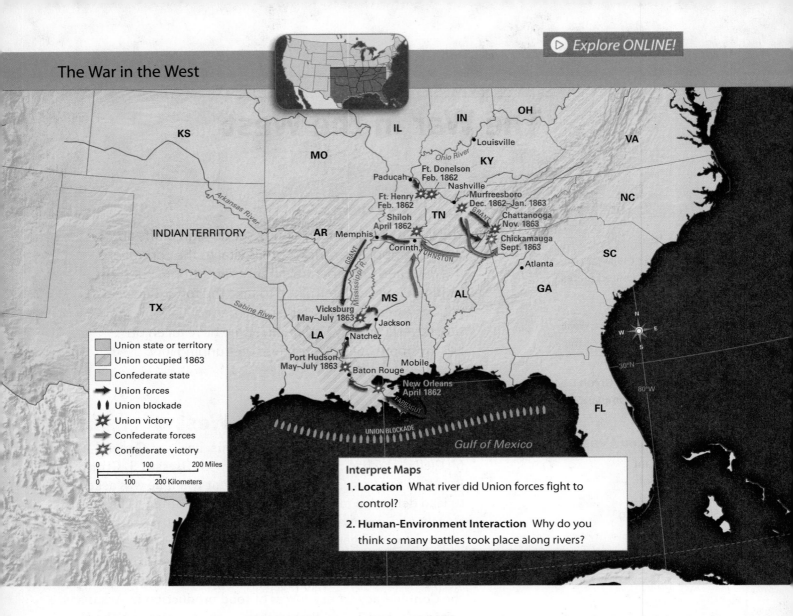

Explore ONLINE!

KS

MO

IL

IN

OH

Ohio River

Louisville

KY

VA

NC

Paducah

Ft. Donelson
Feb. 1862

Nashville

Murfreesboro
Dec. 1862–Jan. 1863

Ft. Henry
Feb. 1862

Shiloh
April 1862

TN

GRANT

Chattanooga
Nov. 1863

Arkansas River

INDIAN TERRITORY

AR

Memphis

Corinth

JOHNSTON

Chickamauga
Sept. 1863

SC

Atlanta

GRANT

AL

GA

TX

Sabine River

Mississippi R.

MS

Vicksburg
May–July 1863

Jackson

LA

Natchez

Port Hudson
May–July 1863

Baton Rouge

Mobile

New Orleans
April 1862

FARRAGUT

FL

UNION BLOCKADE

Gulf of Mexico

30°N

80°W

N
W   E
S

	Union state or territory
	Union occupied 1863
	Confederate state
→	Union forces
▮▮	Union blockade
✶	Union victory
→	Confederate forces
✶	Confederate victory

0   100   200 Miles
0   100   200 Kilometers

Interpret Maps

1. **Location** What river did Union forces fight to control?

2. **Human-Environment Interaction** Why do you think so many battles took place along rivers?

Advancing south in Tennessee, General Grant paused near Shiloh Church to await the arrival of the Army of the Ohio. Grant knew that the large rebel army of General A. S. Johnston was nearby in Corinth, Mississippi, but he did not expect an attack. Instead of setting up defenses, he worked on drilling his new recruits.

In the early morning of April 6, 1862, the rebels sprang on Grant's sleepy camp. This began the **Battle of Shiloh**, in which the Union army gained greater control of the Mississippi River valley.

During the bloody two-day battle, each side gained and lost ground. Johnston was killed on the first day. The arrival of the Ohio force helped Grant regain territory and push the enemy back into Mississippi. The armies finally gave out, each with about 10,000 casualties. Both sides claimed victory, but, in fact, the victor was Grant.

The Fall of New Orleans As Grant battled his way down the Mississippi, the Union navy prepared to blast its way upriver to meet him. The first obstacle was the port of New Orleans, the largest city in the Confederacy and the gateway to the Mississippi River.

David Farragut 1801–1870

David Farragut was born in Tennessee to a Spanish father and an American mother. At age seven Farragut was adopted by a family friend who agreed to train the young boy for the navy. Farragut received his first navy position—midshipman at large—at age nine and commanded his first vessel at 12. He spent the rest of his life in the U.S. Navy. Farragut helped the war effort of the North by leading key attacks on the southern ports of Vicksburg and New Orleans.

Draw Inferences
How did Farragut help the war effort of the North?

With 18 ships and 700 men, Admiral **David Farragut** approached the two forts that guarded the entrance to New Orleans from the Gulf of Mexico. Unable to destroy the forts, Farragut decided to race past them.

The risky operation would take place at night. Farragut had his wooden ships wrapped in heavy chains to protect them like ironclads. Sailors slapped Mississippi mud on the ships' hulls to make them hard to see. Trees were tied to the masts to make the ships look like the forested shore.

Before dawn on April 24, 1862, the warships made their daring dash. The Confederates fired at Farragut's ships from the shore and from gunboats. They launched burning rafts, one of which scorched Farragut's own ship. But his fleet slipped by the twin forts and made it to New Orleans. The city fell on April 29.

Farragut sailed up the Mississippi River, taking Baton Rouge, Louisiana, and Natchez, Mississippi. He then approached the city of Vicksburg, Mississippi.

The Siege of Vicksburg Vicksburg's geography made invasion all but impossible. Perched on 200-foot-high cliffs above the Mississippi River, the city could rain down firepower on enemy ships or on soldiers trying to scale the cliffs. Deep gorges surrounded the city, turning back land assaults. Nevertheless, Farragut ordered Vicksburg to surrender.

"Mississippians don't know, and refuse to learn, how to surrender . . . If Commodore Farragut . . . can teach them, let [him] come and try."
—Colonel James L. Autry, military commander of Vicksburg

Farragut's guns had trouble reaching the city above. It was up to General Grant. His solution was to starve the city into surrender.

General Grant's troops began the **Siege of Vicksburg** in mid-May 1863, cutting off the city and shelling it repeatedly. As food ran out, residents and soldiers survived by eating horses, dogs, and rats. "We are utterly cut off from the world, surrounded by a circle of fire," wrote one woman. "People do nothing but eat what they can get, sleep when they can, and dodge the shells."

The Confederate soldiers were also sick and hungry. In late June a group of soldiers sent their commander a warning.

"If you can't feed us, you had better surrender us, horrible as the idea is. . . . This army is now ripe for mutiny [rebellion], unless it can be fed."
—Confederate soldiers at Vicksburg to General John C. Pemberton, 1863

Reading Check
Summarize
How did the Union gain control of the Mississippi River?

On July 4 Pemberton surrendered. Grant immediately sent food to the soldiers and civilians. He later claimed that "the fate of the Confederacy was sealed when Vicksburg fell."

Struggle for the Far West

Early on in the war, the Union halted several attempts by Confederate armies to control lands west of the Mississippi. In August 1861 a Union detachment from Colorado turned back a Confederate force at Glorieta Pass. Union volunteers also defeated rebel forces at Arizona's Pichaco Pass.

Confederate attempts to take the border state of Missouri also collapsed. Failing to seize the federal arsenal at St. Louis in mid-1861, the rebels fell back to Pea Ridge in northwest Arkansas. There, in March 1862 they attacked again, aided by some 800 Cherokee. The Union defense of Missouri held.

The Union navy played an important part in the Civil War. Besides blockading and raiding southern ports, the navy joined battles along the Mississippi River, as in this painting of Vicksburg.

DOCUMENT-BASED INVESTIGATION
Historical Source

Response to Farragut

The mayor of New Orleans considered the surrender of the city to the Union navy:

"*We yield to physical force alone and maintain allegiance to the Confederate States; beyond this, a due respect for our dignity, our rights and the flag of our country does not, I think, permit us to go.*"
—Mayor John T. Monroe quoted in *Confederate Military History*, Vol. 10

Analyze Historical Sources
How does Monroe's statement reveal his attitude about surrender?

Although the Union army won the battle, Indian troops commanded by Cherokee leader Stand Watie fought bravely. Watie was later promoted to general, the only Native American on either side to hold this rank in the war.

More than 10,000 Native Americans took part in the Civil War. Many Cherokee fought for the Confederacy, but the war bitterly divided the Cherokee—and other nations as well—over issues of loyalty and slavery.

Some nations saw the transfer of soldiers from western forts to eastern battlefields as a chance to take back land they had lost. The Indians also hoped the Confederates would give them greater freedom. In addition, slavery was legal in Indian Territory, and some Native Americans who were slaveholders supported the Confederacy. Pro-Confederate forces remained active in the region throughout the war. They attacked Union forts and raided towns in Missouri and Kansas, forcing Union commanders to keep valuable troops stationed in the area.

Summary and Preview The North and the South continued their struggle with battles in the West. A number of key battles took place in the Western theater, and several important Union leaders emerged from these battles. One, Ulysses S. Grant, would soon become even more important to the Union army. In the next lesson you will learn about the lives of civilians, enslaved African Americans, and soldiers during the war.

Reading Check
Analyze What was the importance of the fighting in the Far West?

Lesson 3 Assessment

Review Ideas, Terms, and People

1. **a. Identify** What role did Ulysses S. Grant play in the war in the West?

   b. Explain Why was the Battle of Shiloh important?

   c. Elaborate Do you think President Lincoln would have approved of Grant's actions in the West? Why or why not?

2. **a. Describe** How did the Union take New Orleans, and why was it an important victory?

   b. Draw Conclusions How were civilians affected by the Siege of Vicksburg?

   c. Predict What might be some possible results of the Union victory at Vicksburg?

Critical Thinking

3. **Identify Cause and Effect** In this lesson you learned about the Union's military strategy in the West. Create a graphic organizer similar to the one below and use it to show the causes and effects of each battle.

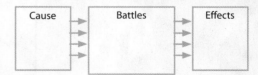

Cause → Battles → Effects

The Vicksburg Strategy

"Vicksburg is the key!"

President Abraham Lincoln declared. "The war can never be brought to a close until that key is in our pocket." Vicksburg was so important because of its location on the Mississippi River, a vital trade route and supply line. Union ships couldn't get past the Confederate guns mounted on the high bluffs of Vicksburg. Capturing Vicksburg would give the Union control of the Mississippi, stealing a vital supply line and splitting the Confederacy in two. The task fell to General Ulysses S. Grant.

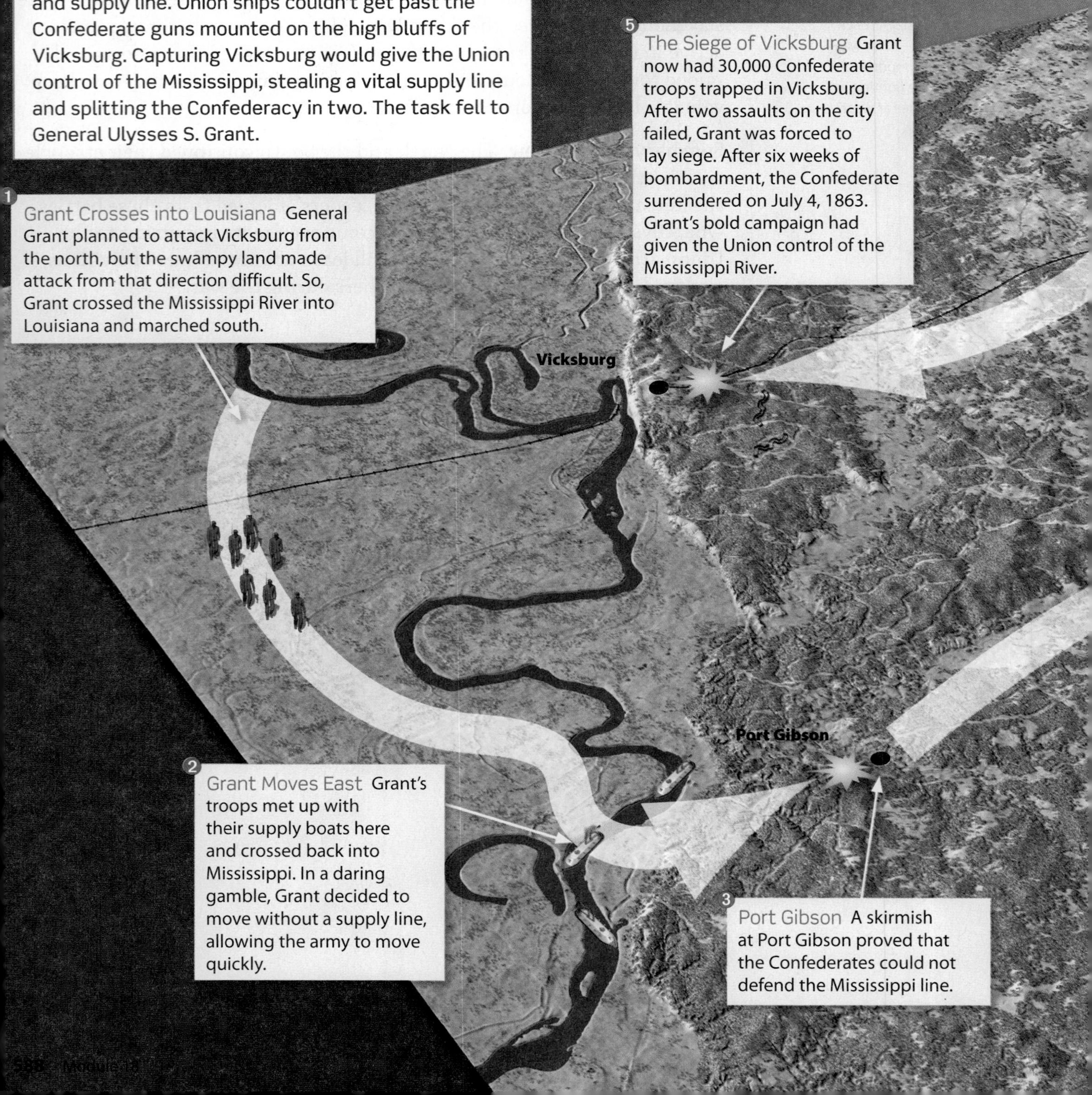

5 The Siege of Vicksburg Grant now had 30,000 Confederate troops trapped in Vicksburg. After two assaults on the city failed, Grant was forced to lay siege. After six weeks of bombardment, the Confederate surrendered on July 4, 1863. Grant's bold campaign had given the Union control of the Mississippi River.

1 Grant Crosses into Louisiana General Grant planned to attack Vicksburg from the north, but the swampy land made attack from that direction difficult. So, Grant crossed the Mississippi River into Louisiana and marched south.

Vicksburg

Port Gibson

2 Grant Moves East Grant's troops met up with their supply boats here and crossed back into Mississippi. In a daring gamble, Grant decided to move without a supply line, allowing the army to move quickly.

3 Port Gibson A skirmish at Port Gibson proved that the Confederates could not defend the Mississippi line.

UNION CONTROL

CONFEDERATE CONTROL

GULF OF MEXICO

Missouri · Kentucky · Virginia · Arkansas · Tennessee · North Carolina · South Carolina · Alabama · Georgia · Mississippi · Louisiana · VICKSBURG

Jackson

4 **The Battle of Jackson** Grant defeated a Confederate army at Jackson and then moved on to Vicksburg. This prevented Confederate forces from reinforcing Vicksburg.

Ironclads Union ironclads were vital to the Vicksburg campaign. These gunboats protected Grant's troops when they crossed the Mississippi. Later, they bombarded Vicksburg during the siege of the city.

─── BIOGRAPHY ───

Ulysses S. Grant 1822–1885

Ulysses S. Grant was born in April 1822 in Ohio. Grant attended West Point in New York and fought in the Mexican-American War. He resigned in 1854 and worked at various jobs in farming, real estate, and retail. When the Civil War started, he joined the Union army and was quickly promoted to general. After the Civil War, Grant rode a wave of popularity to become president of the United States.

Interpret Maps

1. **Location** Why was Vicksburg's location so important?

2. **Place** What natural features made Vicksburg difficult to attack?

Daily Life during the War

The Big Idea

The lives of many Americans were affected by the Civil War.

Main Ideas

- The Emancipation Proclamation freed slaves in Confederate states.

- African Americans participated in the war in a variety of ways.

- President Lincoln faced opposition to the war.

- Life was difficult for soldiers and civilians alike.

Key Terms and People

emancipation
Emancipation Proclamation
contrabands
54th Massachusetts Infantry
Copperheads
habeas corpus
Clara Barton

If YOU were there . . .

You live in Maryland in 1864. Your father and brothers are in the Union army, and you want to do your part in the war. You hear that a woman in Washington, DC, is supplying medicines and caring for wounded soldiers on the battlefield. She is looking for volunteers. You know the work will be dangerous, for you'll be in the line of fire. You might be shot or even killed.

Would you join the nurses on the battlefield?

Emancipation Proclamation

At the heart of the nation's bloody struggle were millions of enslaved African Americans. Abolitionists urged President Lincoln to free them.

In an 1858 speech, Lincoln declared, "There is no reason in the world why the negro is not entitled to all the natural rights numerated in the Declaration of Independence—the right to life, liberty, and the pursuit of happiness." Yet as president, Lincoln found **emancipation**, or the freeing of slaves, to be a difficult issue. He did not believe he had the constitutional power. He also worried about the effects of emancipation.

Lincoln Issues the Proclamation Northerners had a range of opinions about abolishing slavery.

- The Democratic Party, which included many laborers, opposed emancipation. Laborers feared that freed slaves would come north and take their jobs at lower wages.
- Abolitionists argued that the war was pointless if it did not win freedom for African Americans. They warned that the Union would remain divided until the problem was resolved.

- Lincoln worried about losing support for the war. Previous wartime Confiscation Acts that had attempted to free the slaves had been unpopular in the border states.
- Others, including Secretary of War Edwin Stanton, agreed with Lincoln that the use of slave labor was helping the Confederacy make war. Therefore, as commander in chief, the president could free the slaves in all rebellious states. Freed African Americans could then be recruited into the Union army.

For several weeks in 1862, Lincoln worked intensely, thinking, writing, and rewriting. He finally wrote the **Emancipation Proclamation**, the order to free the Confederate slaves. The proclamation declared that:

". . . all persons held as slaves within any State or designated part of a State the people whereof shall then be in rebellion against the United States shall be then, thenceforward, and forever free."

—Emancipation Proclamation, 1862

Confederates reacted to the Proclamation with outrage. Jefferson Davis called it the "most execrable [hateful] measure recorded in the history of guilty man." As some northern Democrats had predicted, the Proclamation had made the Confederacy more determined than ever to fight to preserve its way of life.

The Emancipation Proclamation was a military order that freed slaves only in areas controlled by the Confederacy. In fact, the proclamation had little immediate effect. It was impossible for the federal government to enforce the proclamation in the areas where it actually applied—the states in rebellion that were not under federal control. The proclamation did not

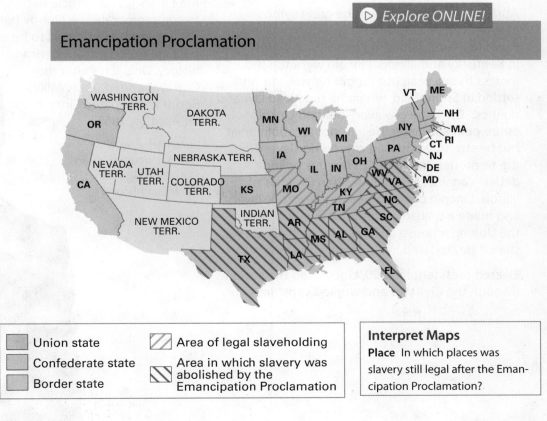

▶ Explore ONLINE!

Emancipation Proclamation

Legend:
- Union state
- Confederate state
- Border state
- Area of legal slaveholding
- Area in which slavery was abolished by the Emancipation Proclamation

Interpret Maps
Place In which places was slavery still legal after the Emancipation Proclamation?

stop slavery in the border states, where the federal government would have had the power to enforce it. The words written in the Emancipation Proclamation were powerful, but the impact of the document was more symbolic than real. It defined what the Union was fighting against and discouraged Britain from aiding the Confederacy.

Lincoln wanted to be in a strong position in the war before announcing his plan. The Battle of Antietam gave him the victory he needed. He issued the Emancipation Proclamation on September 22, 1862. The proclamation went into effect on January 1, 1863. As one of the first civil rights documents in United States history, the Emancipation Proclamation continues to impact Americans today as a symbol of equal rights for all Americans. The historic document paved the way for future civil rights legislation, which gave minorities and women more equal rights.

Reaction to the Proclamation New Year's Eve, December 31, 1862: In "night watch" meetings at many African American churches, worshippers prayed, sang, and gave thanks. When the clocks struck midnight, millions were free. Abolitionists rejoiced. Frederick Douglass called January 1, 1863, "the great day which is to determine the destiny not only of the American Republic, but that of the American Continent."

William Lloyd Garrison was quick to note, however, that "slavery, as a system" continued to exist in the loyal slave states. Yet where slavery

---

Abraham Lincoln 1809–1865

Abraham Lincoln is one of the great symbols of American democracy. He was born in a log cabin to a poor family in Kentucky and grew-up in Kentucky and Illinois. Lincoln went to school for less than a year, but taught himself law and settled in Springfield, where he practiced law and politics. The issue of slavery defined Lincoln's entire political career. He was not an abolitionist, but he strongly opposed extending slavery into the territories. In a series of famous political debates against Senator Stephen Douglas of Illinois, Lincoln championed his views on slavery and made a brilliant defense of democracy and the Union. "A house divided against itself cannot stand," he declared in a debate with Douglas.

Elected president in 1860, Lincoln led the nation through the Civil War and worked constantly to preserve a unified nation. In 1863, he issued the Emancipation Proclamation. His address to commemorate the bloody battlefield at Gettysburg is considered to be one of the best political speeches in American history. Only days after the Civil War ended, John Wilkes Booth assassinated Lincoln on April 14, 1865.

Summarize
Why is Lincoln such an important figure in American history?

remained, the proclamation encouraged many enslaved African Americans to escape when the Union troops came near. They flocked to the Union camps and followed them for protection. The loss of slaves crippled the South's ability to wage war.

African Americans Participate in the War

As the war casualties climbed, the Union needed even more troops. African Americans were ready to volunteer. Not all white northerners were ready to accept them, but eventually they had to. Frederick Douglass believed that military service would help African Americans gain rights.

> "Once let the black man get upon his person the brass letters, U.S.; . . . and a musket on his shoulder and bullets in his pocket, and there is no power on earth which can deny that he has earned the right to citizenship."
>
> —Frederick Douglass, quoted in *The Life and Writings of Frederick Douglass, Vol. 3*

Congress began allowing the army to sign up African American volunteers as laborers in July 1862. The War Department also gave **contrabands**, or escaped slaves, the right to join the Union army in South Carolina. Free African Americans in Louisiana and Kansas also formed their own units in the Union army. By the spring of 1863, African American army units were proving themselves in combat. They took part in a Union attack on Port Hudson, Louisiana, in May.

One unit stood out above the others. The **54th Massachusetts Infantry** consisted mostly of free African Americans. In July 1863 this regiment led a heroic charge on South Carolina's Fort Wagner. The 54th took heavy fire and suffered huge casualties in the failed operation. About half the regiment was killed, wounded, or captured. Edward L. Pierce, a

Reading Check
Find Main Ideas
How did northerners view the Emancipation Proclamation?

DOCUMENT-BASED INVESTIGATION   Historical Source

Letter from a Union Soldier

On June 23, 1863, Joseph E. Williams, an African American soldier and recruiter from Pennsylvania, wrote this letter describing why African Americans fought for the Union.

"We are now determined to hold every step that has been offered to us as citizens of the United States for our elevation [benefit], which represent justice, the purity, the truth, the aspiration [hope] of heaven. We must learn deeply to realize the duty, the moral and practical necessity for the benefit of our race . . . Every consideration of honor, of interest, and of duty to God and man, requires that we should be true to our trust."

—quoted in *A Grand Army of Black Men*, edited by Edwin S. Redkey

Analyze Historical Sources
Why did Williams think being soldiers was so important for African Americans?

New Soldiers

African American soldiers, such as the 54th Massachusetts Infantry and Company E of the 4th U.S. Colored Infantry, shown here, fought proudly and bravely in the Civil War. At right is a flyer used to recruit African American soldiers.

NOW IN CAMP AT READVILLE!
54th REGIMENT!
MASS. VOLUNTEERS, composed of men of
AFRICAN DESCENT
Col. ROBERT G. SHAW.
Colored Men, Rally 'Round the Flag of Freedom!
BOUNTY $100!
AT THE EXPIRATION OF THE TERM OF SERVICE.
Pay, $13 a Month!
Good Food & Clothing!
State Aid to Families!
RECRUITING OFFICE,
COR. CAMBRIDGE & NORTH RUSSELL STS.,
BOSTON.
Lieut. J. W. M. APPLETON, Recruiting Officer.
EWALL & CO., Steam Job Printers, No. 47 Congress Street, Boston.

correspondent for the *New York Tribune,* wrote, "The Fifty-fourth did well and nobly . . . They moved up as gallantly as any troops could, and with their enthusiasm they deserved a better fate." The bravery of the 54th regiment made it the most celebrated African American unit of the war.

About 180,000 African Americans served with the Union army. They initially received $10 a month, while white soldiers got $13. In June 1864 Congress passed a bill granting African American soldiers equal pay.

African Americans faced special horrors on the battlefield. Confederates often killed their black captives or sold them into slavery. In the 1864 election, Lincoln suggested rewarding African American soldiers by giving them the right to vote.

Reading Check
Analyze Information How did African Americans support the Union?

Growing Opposition

The deepening shadows in Lincoln's face reflected the huge responsibilities he carried. Besides running the war, he had to deal with growing tensions in the North.

Copperheads As the months rolled on and the number of dead continued to increase, a group of northern Democrats began speaking out against

The Copperheads
This political cartoon pokes fun at Copperhead northerners who want peace. The cartoon implies that the Copperheads plan is to bore the Confederate states into rejoining the Union.

Reading Check
Identify Cause and Effect Who opposed the war, and how did Lincoln respond to the conflict?

the war. Led by U.S. representative Clement L. Vallandigham of Ohio, they called themselves Peace Democrats. Their enemies called them Copperheads, comparing them to a poisonous snake. The name stuck.

Many **Copperheads** were midwesterners who sympathized with the South and opposed abolition. They believed the war was not necessary and called for its end. Vallandigham asked what the war had gained and then said, "Let the dead at Fredericksburg and Vicksburg answer."

Lincoln saw the Copperheads as a threat to support of the war effort. To silence them, he suspended the right of habeas corpus. **Habeas corpus** is a constitutional protection against unlawful imprisonment. Ignoring this protection, Union officials jailed their enemies, including some Copperheads, without evidence or trial. Lincoln's action greatly angered Democrats and some Republicans.

Northern Draft In March 1863 war critics erupted again when Congress approved a draft, or forced military service. For $300, men were allowed to buy their way out of military service. For an unskilled laborer, however, that was nearly a year's wages. Critics of the draft called the Civil War a "rich man's war and a poor man's fight."

In July 1863 riots broke out when African Americans were brought into New York City to replace striking Irish dockworkers. The city happened to be holding a war draft at the same time. The two events enraged rioters, who attacked African Americans and draft offices. More than 100 people died.

In this tense situation, the northern Democrats nominated former general George McClellan for president in 1864. They called for an immediate end to the war. Lincoln defeated McClellan in the popular vote, winning by about 400,000 votes out of 4 million cast. The electoral vote was not even close. Lincoln won 212 to 21.

Life for Soldiers and Civilians

Young, fresh recruits in both armies were generally eager to fight. Experienced troops, however, knew better.

On the Battlefield Civil War armies fought in the ancient battlefield formation that produced massive casualties. Endless rows of troops fired directly at one another, with cannonballs landing amid them. When the order was given, soldiers would attach bayonets to their guns and rush toward their enemy. Men died to gain every inch of ground.

Doctors and nurses in the field saved many lives. Yet they had no medicines to stop infections that developed after soldiers were wounded. Many soldiers endured the horror of having infected legs and arms amputated without painkillers. Infections from minor injuries caused many deaths.

Despite the huge battlefield losses, the biggest killer in the Civil War was not the fighting. It was diseases such as typhoid, pneumonia, and tuberculosis. Nearly twice as many soldiers died of illnesses and disease as died in combat.

Infantry Family
While wealthy civilians could avoid military service, poorer men were drafted to serve in the Union army. This member of the 31st Pennsylvania Infantry brought his family along with him. His wife probably helped the soldier with many of the daily chores such as cooking and laundry.

Why would soldiers bring their families to live with them in camp?

Prisoners of War As hard as army life was, conditions for prisoners of war were much worse. At first, neither North nor South kept large numbers of captured soldiers. Many prisoners were released if they promised to go home instead of back to their army. Others were exchanged for prisoners held by the other side. Military prisoners on both sides lived in unimaginable misery. In prison camps, such as Andersonville, Georgia, and Elmira, New York, soldiers were packed into camps designed to hold only a fraction of their number. Soldiers had little shelter, food, or clothing. Starvation and disease killed thousands of prisoners.

Life as a Civilian The war effort involved all levels of society. Women as well as people too young or too old for military service worked in factories and on farms. Economy in the North boomed as production and prices soared. The lack of workers caused wages to rise by 43 percent between 1860 and 1865.

Women were the backbone of civilian life and took over farms, plantations, stores, and other businesses while their fathers, husbands, and sons served in armies. On the farms, women and children performed the daily chores usually done by men. One visitor to Iowa in 1862 reported that he "met more women . . . at work in the fields than men." Southern women also managed farms and plantations.

The need for clothes, shoes, and other supplies created about 100,000 jobs for women in northern factories. Women also worked in the South's few factories, and women on both sides performed dangerous work making ammunition for the troops.

Many women found new occupations. Hundreds were hired by the Union government as clerks. They became the first women to hold federal government jobs. Women also staffed government offices in the South. Like clerical work, nursing was a man's job before the war. During the war, however, about 3,000 women served the Union army as paid nurses.

One woman brought strength and comfort to countless wounded Union soldiers. Volunteer **Clara Barton** organized the collection of medicine and supplies for delivery to the battlefield. At the field hospitals, the "angel of the battlefield" soothed the wounded and dying and assisted doctors as bullets flew around her. Barton's work formed the basis for the future American Red Cross.

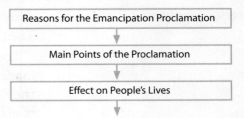

Clara Barton founded the American Red Cross.

In the South, Sally Louisa Tompkins established a small hospital in Richmond, Virginia. By the end of the war, it had grown into a major army hospital. Jefferson Davis recognized her value to the war effort by making her a captain in the Confederate army.

Reading Check
Analyze How did women help the war effort on both sides?

Summary and Preview Many lives were changed by the war. In the next lesson you will learn about the end of the war.

Lesson 4 Assessment

Review Ideas, Terms, and People

1. **a. Recall** Why did some Americans want to end slavery?

   b. Contrast How did reactions to the Emancipation Proclamation differ?

   c. Elaborate How and why does the Emancipation Proclamation continue to impact American life? Explain your answer.

2. **a. Recall** Why did some northerners want to recruit African Americans into the Union army?

   b. Contrast In what ways did African American soldiers face more difficulties than white soldiers did?

3. **a. Identify** Who were Copperheads, and why did they oppose the war?

   b. Evaluate Should President Lincoln have suspended the right to habeas corpus? Why?

4. **a. Describe** What were conditions like in military camps?

   b. Draw Conclusions How did the war change life on the home front?

Critical Thinking

5. **Identify Effects** In this lesson you learned about the Emancipation Proclamation. Create a chart similar to the one below and use it to summarize the reasons for the Emancipation Proclamation, its main points, and its effects on different people.

Reasons for the Emancipation Proclamation

   ↓

Main Points of the Proclamation

   ↓

Effect on People's Lives

   ↓

The Tide of War Turns

The Big Idea
Union victories in 1863, 1864, and 1865 ended the Civil War.

Main Ideas
- The Union tried to divide the Confederate army at Fredericksburg, but the attempt failed.
- The Battle of Gettysburg in 1863 was a major turning point in the war.
- During 1864, Union campaigns in the East and South dealt crippling blows to the Confederacy.
- Union troops forced the South to surrender in 1865, ending the Civil War.

Key Terms and People
Battle of Gettysburg
George Pickett
Pickett's Charge
Gettysburg Address
Wilderness Campaign
William Tecumseh Sherman
total war
Appomattox Courthouse

If YOU were there . . .

You live in southern Pennsylvania in 1863, near a battlefield where thousands died. Now people have come from miles around to dedicate a cemetery here. You are near the front of the crowd. The first speaker impresses everyone with two hours of dramatic words and gestures. Then President Lincoln speaks—just a few minutes of simple words. Many people are disappointed.

Why do you think the president's speech was so short?

Fredericksburg and Chancellorsville

Frustrated by McClellan's lack of aggression, Lincoln replaced him with General Ambrose E. Burnside as leader of the Army of the Potomac. Burnside favored a swift, decisive attack on Richmond by way of Fredericksburg. In November 1862 he set out with 120,000 troops.

Burnside's tactics surprised General Lee. The Confederate commander had divided his force of 78,000 men. Neither section of the Confederate army was in a good position to defend Fredericksburg. However, Burnside's army experienced delays in crossing the Rappahannock River. These delays allowed Lee's army to reunite and entrench themselves around Fredericksburg. Finally, the Union army crossed the Rappahannock and launched a series of charges. These attacks had heavy casualties and failed to break the Confederate line. Eventually, after suffering about 12,600 casualties, Burnside ordered a retreat. The Confederates had about 5,300 casualties.

Soon Burnside stepped down from his position. Lincoln made General Joseph Hooker the commander of the Army of the Potomac. At the end of April 1863, Hooker and his army of about 138,000 men launched a frontal attack on Fredericksburg. Then Hooker ordered about 115,000 of his troops to split off and approach the Confederate's flank, or side. Hooker's strategy seemed about to work. But for some reason he hesitated and had his flanking troops take a defensive position at Chancellorsville. This town was located a few miles west of Fredericksburg.

The following day, Lee used most of his army (about 60,000 men) to attack Hooker's troops at Chancellorsville. Stonewall Jackson led an attack on Hooker's flank while Lee commanded an assault on the Union front. The Union army was almost cut in two. They managed to form a defensive line, which they held for three days. Then Hooker ordered a retreat.

Lee's army won a major victory. But this victory had severe casualties. During the battle, Lee's trusted general, Stonewall Jackson, was accidentally shot by his own troops. He died a few days later.

Reading Check
Compare What did generals McClellan, Burnside, and Hooker have in common?

Battle of Gettysburg

General Lee launched more attacks within Union territory. As before, his goal was to break the North's will to fight. He also hoped that a victory would convince other nations to recognize the Confederacy. The three-day battle at Gettysburg was the largest and bloodiest battle of the Civil War. In three days, more than 51,000 soldiers were killed, wounded, captured, or went missing. It was an important victory for the Union, and it stopped Lee's plan of invading the North.

First Day In early June 1863 Lee cut across northern Maryland into southern Pennsylvania. His forces gathered west of a small town called Gettysburg. Lee was unaware that Union soldiers were encamped closer to town. He had been suffering from a lack of enemy information for three days because his cavalry chief "Jeb" Stuart was not performing his duties. Stuart and his cavalry had gone off on their own raiding party, disobeying Lee's orders.

Day One:
July 1, 1863
Artillery played a key role in the Battle of Gettysburg on July 1, 1863.

Another Confederate raiding party went to Gettysburg for boots and other supplies. There, Lee's troops ran right into Union general George G. Meade's cavalry, triggering the **Battle of Gettysburg**, a key battle that finally turned the tide against the Confederates. The battle began on July 1, 1863, when the Confederate raiding party and the Union forces began exchanging fire. The larger Confederate forces began to push the Union troops back through Gettysburg.

The Union soldiers regrouped along the high ground of Cemetery Ridge and Culp's Hill. General Lee wanted to prevent the Union forces from entrenching themselves. He therefore ordered General Ewell to attack immediately. However, Ewell hesitated and thereby gave the Federals time to establish an excellent defensive position.

In fact, Confederate general James Longstreet thought that the Union position was almost impossible to overrun. Instead of attacking, he felt that the Confederate army should move east, take a strong defensive position, and wait for the Union forces to attack them. However, General Lee was not convinced. He believed that his troops were invincible.

The Confederates camped at Seminary Ridge, which ran parallel to the Union forces. Both camps called for their main forces to reinforce them and prepare for combat the next day.

Second Day On July 2, Lee ordered an attack on the left side of the Union line. Lee knew that he could win the battle if his troops captured Little Round Top from the Union forces. From this hill, Lee's troops could easily fire down on the line of Union forces. Union forces and Confederate troops fought viciously for control of Little Round Top. The fighting was particularly fierce on the south side of the hill. There, the 20th Maine led by Colonel Joshua Chamberlain battled the 15th Alabama led by Colonel

Day Two: July 2, 1863, 10 a.m.

Union soldiers desperately defended Little Round Top from a fierce Confederate charge.

William Oates. Later, when describing the conflict, Oates said, "The blood stood in puddles in some places in the rocks." Eventually, the Union soldiers forced the Confederates to pull back from Little Round Top.

Then, the Confederates attacked Cemetery Hill and Culp's Hill. The fighting lasted until nightfall. The assault on Cemetery Hill was unsuccessful. The Confederates did manage to take a few trenches on Culp's Hill. Even so, the Union forces still held a strong defensive position by the day's end.

Pickett's Charge On the third day of battle, Longstreet again tried to convince Lee not to attack. But Lee thought that the Union forces were severely battered and ready to break. Because of this, he planned to attack the center of the Union line on Cemetery Ridge. Such a tactic, he felt, would not be expected. Indeed, General Meade left only about 5,750 troops to defend the center.

For over an hour, the Confederates shelled Cemetery Ridge with cannon fire. For a while, the Union cannons fired back. Then they slacked off. The Confederates assumed that they had seriously damaged the Union artillery. In reality, the Confederate barrage did little damage.

The task of charging the Union center fell to three divisions of Confederate soldiers. General **George Pickett** commanded the largest unit. In late afternoon nearly 15,000 men took part in **Pickett's Charge**. For one mile the Confederates marched slowly up toward Cemetery Ridge.

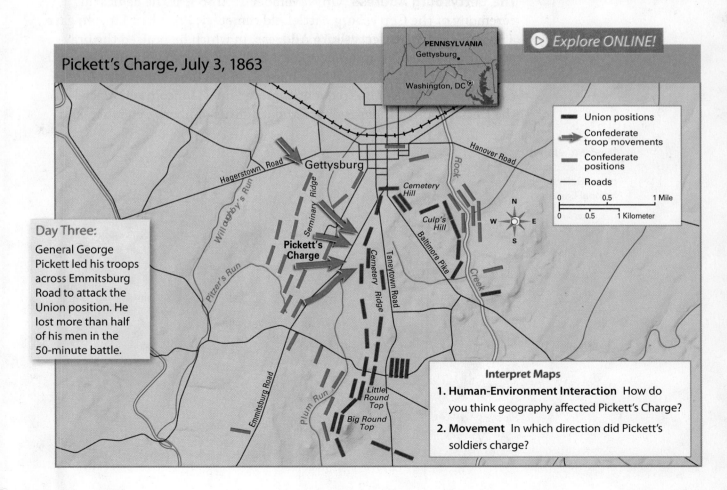

Pickett's Charge, July 3, 1863

PENNSYLVANIA
Gettysburg
Washington, DC

Explore ONLINE!

Day Three:
General George Pickett led his troops across Emmitsburg Road to attack the Union position. He lost more than half of his men in the 50-minute battle.

Union positions
Confederate troop movements
Confederate positions
Roads

Interpret Maps
1. **Human-Environment Interaction** How do you think geography affected Pickett's Charge?
2. **Movement** In which direction did Pickett's soldiers charge?

Showered with cannon and rifle fire, they suffered severe losses. But eventually, some of them almost reached their destination. Then Union reinforcements added to the barrage on the rebels. Soon the Confederates retreated, leaving about 7,500 casualties on the field of battle. Distressed by this defeat, General Lee rode among the survivors and told them, "It is all my fault."

On the fourth day, Lee began to retreat to Virginia. In all, nearly 75,000 Confederate soldiers and 90,000 Union troops had fought during the Battle of Gettysburg.

General Meade decided not to follow Lee's army. This decision angered Lincoln. He felt that Meade had missed an opportunity to crush the Confederates and possibly end the war.

Aftermath of Gettysburg Gettysburg was a turning point in the war. Lee's troops would never again launch an attack in the North. The Union victory at Gettysburg took place on the day before Grant's capture of Vicksburg, Mississippi. These victories made northerners believe that the war could be won.

In addition, the Union win at Gettysburg helped to end the South's search for foreign influence in the war. After Gettysburg, Great Britain and France refused to provide aid to the Confederacy. The South's attempt at cotton diplomacy failed.

The Gettysburg Address On November 19, 1863, at the dedicating ceremony of the Gettysburg battlefield cemetery, President Lincoln gave a speech called the **Gettysburg Address**, in which he praised the bravery of Union soldiers and renewed his commitment to winning the Civil War. This short but moving speech is one of the most famous in American history. In one of its frequently quoted lines, Lincoln referenced the Declaration of Independence and its ideals of liberty, equality, and

Lincoln's address at the dedication of the Gettysburg National Cemetery

Reading Check
Analyze Why was Gettysburg a turning point?

democracy—ideals that still impact Americans today. He reminded listeners that the war was being fought for those reasons.

Lincoln rededicated himself to winning the war and preserving the Union. A difficult road still lay ahead.

Union Campaigns Cripple the Confederacy

Lincoln had been impressed with General Grant's successes in capturing Vicksburg. He transferred Grant to the East and gave him command of the Union army. In early 1864 Grant forced Lee to fight a series of battles in Virginia that stretched Confederate soldiers and supplies to their limits.

Wilderness Campaign in the East From May through June, the armies fought in northern and central Virginia. Union troops launched the **Wilderness Campaign**—a series of battles designed to capture the Confederate capital at Richmond, Virginia. The first battle took place in early May, in woods about 50 miles outside of Richmond. Grant then ordered General Meade to Spotsylvania, where the fighting raged for five days.

Over the next month Union soldiers moved the Confederate troops back toward Richmond. However, Grant experienced his worst defeat at the Battle of Cold Harbor in early June, just 10 miles northeast of Richmond. In only a few hours the Union army suffered 7,000 casualties. The battle delayed Grant's plans to take the Confederate capital.

Union forces had suffered twice as many casualties as the Confederates had, yet Grant continued his strategy. He knew he would be getting additional soldiers, and Lee could not. Grant slowly but surely advanced his troops through Virginia. He told another officer, "I propose to fight it out on this line if it takes all summer."

Academic Vocabulary
execute to perform, carry out

After Cold Harbor, General Grant moved south of Richmond. He had hoped to take control of the key railroad junction at Petersburg, Virginia. Lee's army, however, formed a solid defense, and Grant could not **execute** his attack. Grant was winning the war, but he still had not captured Richmond. Facing re-election, Lincoln was especially discouraged by this failure.

Sherman Strikes the South Lincoln needed a victory for the Union army to help him win re-election in 1864. The bold campaign of General **William Tecumseh Sherman** provided this key victory. Sherman carried out the Union plan to destroy southern railroads and industries.

In the spring of 1864 Sherman marched south from Tennessee with 100,000 troops. His goal was to take Atlanta, Georgia, and knock out an important railroad link. From May through August, Sherman's army moved steadily through the Appalachians toward Atlanta. Several times, Sherman avoided defenses set up by Confederate general Joseph Johnston.

In July Sherman was within sight of Atlanta. Confederate president Jefferson Davis gave General John Hood command of Confederate forces in the region. Hood repeatedly attacked Sherman in a final attempt to save Atlanta, but the Union troops proved stronger. The Confederate troops retreated as Sherman held Atlanta under siege.

Explore ONLINE!

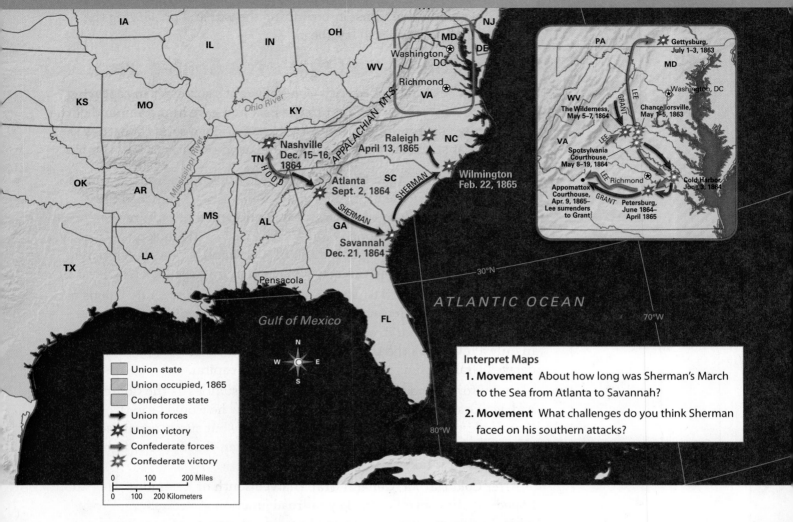

Interpret Maps

1. **Movement** About how long was Sherman's March to the Sea from Atlanta to Savannah?

2. **Movement** What challenges do you think Sherman faced on his southern attacks?

Atlanta fell to Sherman's troops on September 2, 1864. Much of the city was destroyed by artillery and fire. Sherman ordered the residents who still remained to leave. Responding to his critics, Sherman later wrote, "War is war, and not popularity-seeking." The loss of Atlanta cost the South an important railroad link and its center of industry.

Many people in the North had been upset with the length of the war. However, the capture of Atlanta showed that progress was being made in defeating the South. This success helped to convince Union voters to re-elect Lincoln in a landslide.

Sherman did not wait long to begin his next campaign. His goal was the port city of Savannah, Georgia. In mid-November 1864, Sherman left Atlanta with a force of about 60,000 men. He said he would "make Georgia howl!"

During his March to the Sea, Sherman practiced **total war**—destroying civilian and economic resources. Sherman believed that total war would ruin the South's economy and its ability to fight. He ordered his troops to destroy railways, bridges, crops, livestock, and other resources. They burned plantations and freed slaves.

Reading Check
Draw Conclusions
How did Sherman hope to help the Union with his total-war strategy?

Sherman's army reached Savannah on December 10, 1864. They left behind a path of destruction 60 miles wide. Sherman believed that this march would speed the end of the war. He wanted to break the South's will to fight by marching Union troops through the heart of the Confederacy. In the end Sherman's destruction of the South led to anger and resentment toward the people of the North that would last for generations.

The South Surrenders

In early April Sherman closed in on the last Confederate defenders in North Carolina. At the same time, Grant finally broke through the Confederate defenses at Petersburg. On April 2 Lee was forced to retreat from Richmond.

Fighting Ends By the second week of April 1865, Grant had surrounded Lee's army and demanded the soldiers' surrender. Lee hoped to join other Confederates in fighting in North Carolina, but Grant cut off his escape just west of Richmond. Lee tried some last-minute attacks but could not break the Union line. Lee's forces were running low on supplies. General James Longstreet told about the condition of Confederate troops. "Many weary soldiers were picked up . . . some with, many without, arms [weapons],—all asking for food."

Trapped by the Union army, Lee recognized that the situation was hopeless. "There is nothing left for me to do but go and see General Grant," Lee said, "and I would rather die a thousand deaths."

On April 9, 1865, the Union and Confederate leaders met at a home in the small town of **Appomattox Courthouse** where Lee surrendered to Grant, thus ending the Civil War.

During the meeting, Grant assured Lee that his troops would be fed and allowed to keep their horses, and they would not be tried for treason. Then

Surrender at Appomattox
Union general Grant rose to shake hands with Confederate general Lee after the surrender. Grant allowed Lee to keep his sword and Lee's men to keep their horses.

Was it important for Grant and Lee to shake hands? Why or why not?

Causes and Effects of the Civil War

Causes
- Disagreement over the institution of slavery
- Economic differences
- Political differences

▼

Effects
- Slavery ends
- 620,000 Americans killed
- Military districts created
- Southern economy in ruins

Interpret Charts
How important was slavery to the Civil War?

Lee signed the surrender documents. The long, bloody war had finally ended. Grant later wrote that he found the scene at Appomattox Courthouse more tragic than joyful.

"I felt . . . sad and depressed at the downfall of a foe [enemy] who had fought so long and valiantly [bravely], and had suffered so much for a cause, though that cause was, I believe, one of the worst for which a people ever fought."

—Ulysses S. Grant, *Battle Cry of Freedom*

As General Lee returned to his troops, General Grant stopped Union forces from cheering their victory. "The war is over," Grant said with relief. "The rebels are our countrymen again."

The Civil War had deep and long-lasting effects. Almost 620,000 Americans lost their lives during the four years of fighting.

The defeat of the South ended slavery there. The majority of former slaves, however, had no homes or jobs. The southern economy was in ruins.

A tremendous amount of hostility remained, even after the fighting had ceased. The war was over, but the question remained: How could the United States be united once more?

Summary and Preview After four long years of battles, the Civil War ended with General Lee's surrender at Appomattox Courthouse. In the next module you will read about the consequences of the war in the South.

Reading Check
Predict What problems might the Union face following the Civil War?

Lesson 5 Assessment

Review Ideas, Terms, and People

1. **a. Identify** What Confederate general died from his wounds at Chancellorsville?
   b. Draw Conclusions Why was the Union army defeated at Chancellorsville?
2. **a. Identify** What was the Gettysburg Address?
   b. Analyze Why was geography important to the outcome of the Battle of Gettysburg?
3. **a. Recall** What was the purpose of the Wilderness Campaign?
   b. Draw Conclusions In what way was the capture of Atlanta an important victory for President Lincoln?

4. **a. Identify** What events led to Lee's surrender at Appomattox Courthouse?
   b. Summarize How did the military conflict of the Civil War impact the United States?

Critical Thinking

5. **Support a Point of View** In this lesson you learned about the end of the Civil War. Create a similar triangle to the one below and use it to show the three events in this lesson that you think contributed most to the end of the Civil War and explain why.

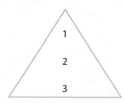

Interpret Political Cartoons

Define the Skill

Political cartoons are drawings that express views on important issues. They have been used throughout history to influence public opinion. The ability to interpret political cartoons will help you understand issues and people's attitudes about them.

Learn the Skill

Political cartoons use both words and images to convey their message. They often contain caricatures or symbolism. A caricature is a drawing that exaggerates the features of a person or object. Symbolism is the use of one thing to represent something else. Cartoonists use these techniques to help make their point clear. They also use titles, labels, and captions to get their message across.

Use these steps to interpret political cartoons.

1. Read any title, labels, and caption to identify the cartoon's general topic.

2. Identify the people and objects. Determine if they are exaggerated and, if so, why. Identify any symbols and analyze their meaning.

3. Draw conclusions about the message the cartoonist is trying to convey.

The following cartoon was published in the North in 1863. The cartoonist has used symbols to make his point. Lady Liberty, representing the Union, is being threatened by the Copperheads. The cartoonist has expressed his opinion of these people by drawing them as the poisonous snake for which they were named. This cartoon clearly supports the Union's continuing to fight the war.

Practice the Skill

Apply the guidelines to interpret the cartoon below and answer the questions that follow.

1. What do the two men on either side of Lincoln represent?

2. What message do you think the artist was trying to convey?

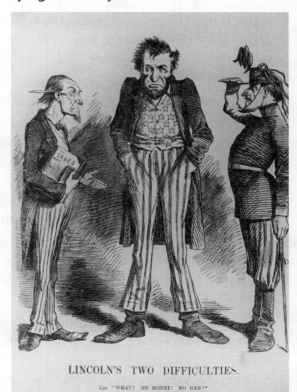

LINCOLN'S TWO DIFFICULTIES.

Lin. "WHAT? NO MONEY! NO MEN!"

Module 18 Assessment

Review Vocabulary, Terms, and People

Match the numbered definitions with the correct terms from the list below.

a. contrabands
b. cotton diplomacy
c. Second Battle of Bull Run
d. Siege of Vicksburg
e. Thomas "Stonewall" Jackson

1. Attack by Union general Ulysses S. Grant that gave the North control of the Mississippi River
2. Confederate general who held off Union attacks and helped the South win the First Battle of Bull Run
3. Important Confederate victory in which General Robert E. Lee defeated Union troops and pushed into Union territory for the first time
4. Southern strategy of using cotton exports to gain Britain's support in the Civil War
5. Term given to escaped slaves from the South

Comprehension and Critical Thinking

Lesson 1

6. a. **Identify** When and where did fighting in the U.S. Civil War begin?
   b. **Analyze** How did civilians help the war effort in both the North and the South?
   c. **Elaborate** Why do you think the border states chose to remain in the Union despite their support of slavery?

Lesson 2

7. a. **Identify** What was the first major battle of the war? What was the outcome of the battle?
   b. **Analyze** What was the Union army hoping to accomplish when it marched into Virginia at the start of the war?
   c. **Evaluate** Was the Union's naval blockade of the South successful? Why or why not?

Lesson 3

8. a. **Identify** Which side did the Cherokee support in the fighting at Pea Ridge? Why?
   b. **Draw Conclusions** What progress did Union leaders make in the war in the West?
   c. **Evaluate** Which victory in the West was most valuable to the Union? Why?

Lesson 4

9. a. **Describe** What responsibilities did women take on during the war?
   b. **Analyze** What opposition to the war did President Lincoln face, and how did he deal with that opposition?
   c. **Predict** What might be some possible problems that the newly freed slaves in the South might face?

Lesson 5

10. a. **Recall** When and where did the war finally end?
    b. **Compare and Contrast** How were the efforts of generals Grant and Sherman at the end of the war similar and different?
    c. **Elaborate** What do you think led to the South's defeat in the Civil War? Explain.

Social Studies Skills

Interpret Political Cartoons *Use the Social Studies Skills taught in this module to answer the question about the political cartoon below.*

11. What do you think the artist is saying about politicians with this cartoon?

Reading Skills

Supporting Facts and Details *Use the Reading Skills taught in this module to answer the question about the reading selection below.*

> Lee was unaware that Union soldiers were encamped closer to town. He had been suffering from a lack of enemy information for three days because his cavalry chief "Jeb" Stuart was not performing his duties. Stuart and his cavalry had gone off on their own raiding party, disobeying Lee's orders.

12. What is the main idea of the reading selection?
   a. "Jeb" Stuart was not performing his duties.
   b. Stuart and his cavalry had gone off on their own.
   c. Stuart and his cavalry disobeyed Lee's orders.
   d. Lee was suffering from a lack of enemy information.

Review Themes

13. **Society and Culture** What effects did the Civil War have on American society?
14. **Politics** What political difficulties did the Emancipation Proclamation cause for President Lincoln?

Focus on Writing

15. **Write a Newspaper Article** Consider all the Civil War events discussed in this module. Then choose one of those events to write about in a newspaper article. Write an attention-grabbing headline. Then write the news article, describing the event and giving as many facts as possible about the event. Be sure to use proper grammar, punctuation, spelling, and capitalization.

DAYS OF DARKNESS:
THE GETTYSBURG CIVILIANS

Gettysburg, Pennsylvania, was a sleepy agricultural town of about 2,400 residents when the Civil War arrived on its doorstep in the early summer of 1863. Many of the town's men were elsewhere, either fighting in the war or guarding their livestock in the countryside. This left mostly women and children to endure the battle. For three terrifying days, they hid in basements or in tightly shuttered houses. Even after the battle finally ended, the horrors continued, as the Gettysburg civilians emerged to find a scene of unimaginable death and destruction.

Explore some of the personal stories and recollections of the Gettysburg civilians online. You can find a wealth of information, video clips, primary sources, activities, and more through your online textbook.

> "I had scarcely reached the front door, when, on looking up the street, I saw some of the men on horseback. . . . What a horrible sight! . . .
> I was fully persuaded that the Rebels had actually come at last. What they would do with us was a fearful question to my young mind. . . ."
>
> —Tillie Pierce, age 15

A Young Woman's Account

Read the document to witness the arrival of Confederate troops through the eyes of a Gettysburg teenager.

HISTORY

Go online to view these and other **HISTORY**® resources.

A Citizen-Soldier

Watch the video to meet John Burns, the man who would come to be called the "Citizen Hero of Gettysburg."

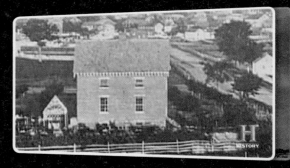

A Family's Story

Watch the video to discover the story of courage and commitment exhibited by one Gettysburg family.

The National Cemetery

Watch the video to learn about the Soldiers' National Cemetery and the speech President Lincoln gave there.

Module 19
Reconstruction

★

Essential Question
To what extent did Reconstruction achieve its goals?

About the Photo: The ruins of this southern plantation stand as a bleak reminder of the changes brought to the South by the Civil War.

▶ Explore ONLINE!

VIDEOS, including...
- Lincoln's Legacy
- The Fall of Richmond
- After the Assassination
- Johnson's Impeachment

☑ Document-Based Investigations

☑ Graphic Organizers

☑ Interactive Games

☑ Image Carousel: Testing Freedoms

☑ Image with Hotspots: *The First Vote*

In this module you will learn about the challenges that faced the nation after the Civil War and the attempts to meet those challenges.

What You Will Learn ...

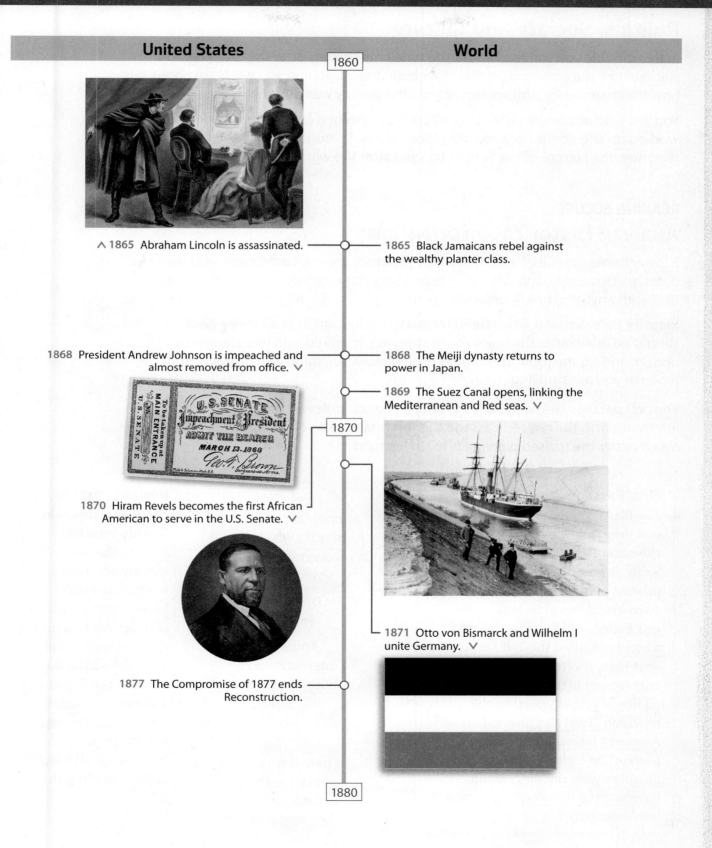

United States

1860

▲ **1865** Abraham Lincoln is assassinated.

1865 Black Jamaicans rebel against the wealthy planter class.

1868 President Andrew Johnson is impeached and almost removed from office. ∨

1868 The Meiji dynasty returns to power in Japan.

1869 The Suez Canal opens, linking the Mediterranean and Red seas. ∨

1870

1870 Hiram Revels becomes the first African American to serve in the U.S. Senate. ∨

1871 Otto von Bismarck and Wilhelm I unite Germany. ∨

1877 The Compromise of 1877 ends Reconstruction.

World

1880

Reading Social Studies

Politics, Society and Culture

In this module you will read about the time immediately after the Civil War. You will see how the government tried to rebuild the South and you will learn about how life changed for African Americans after slavery was declared illegal.

You will read about the political conflicts that emerged as southern leadership worked to gain control of Reconstruction efforts. Throughout the module you will read how the culture of the South changed after the war.

READING FOCUS:

Analyze Historical Information

History books are full of information. As you read, you are confronted with names, dates, places, terms, and descriptions on every page. You don't want to have to deal with anything unimportant or untrue.

Identify Relevant and Essential Information Information in a history book should be relevant to the topic you're studying. It should also be essential to understanding the topic and should be verifiable. Anything else distracts from the material you are studying.

The first passage below includes several pieces of irrelevant and nonessential information. In the revised passage this information has been removed. Note how much easier the revised passage is to understand.

First Passage

President Abraham Lincoln, who was very tall, wanted to reunite the nation as quickly and painlessly as possible. He had proposed a plan for readmitting the southern states even before the war ended, which happened on a Sunday. Called the Ten Percent Plan, it offered southerners amnesty, or official pardon, for all illegal acts supporting the rebellion. Today a group called Amnesty International works to protect the rights of prisoners. Lincoln's plan certainly would have worked if it would have been implemented.

Lincoln's appearance and the day on which the war ended are not essential facts.

Amnesty International is not relevant to this topic.

There is no way to prove the accuracy of the last sentence.

Revised Passage

President Abraham Lincoln wanted to reunite the nation as quickly and painlessly as possible. He had proposed a plan for readmitting the southern states even before the war ended. Called the Ten Percent Plan, it offered southerners amnesty, or official pardon, for all illegal acts supporting the rebellion.

You Try It!

The following passage is adapted from the module you are about to read. As you read the passage, look for irrelevant, nonessential, or unverifiable information.

Freedmen's Bureau In 1865 Congress established the Freedmen's Bureau, an agency providing relief for freedpeople and certain poor people in the South. The Bureau had a difficult job. It may have been one of the most difficult jobs ever. At its high point, about 900 agents served the entire South. All 900 people could fit into one hotel ballroom today. Bureau commissioner Oliver O. Howard eventually decided to use the Bureau's limited budget to distribute food to the poor and to provide education and legal help for freedpeople. One common food in the South at that time was salted meat. The Bureau also helped African American war veterans. Today the Department of Veterans' Affairs assists American war veterans.

After you read the passage, answer the following questions.

1. Which sentence in this passage is unverifiable and should be cut?

2. Find two sentences in this passage that are irrelevant to the discussion of the Freedmen's Bureau. What makes those sentences irrelevant?

3. Look at the last sentence of the passage. Do you think this sentence is essential to the discussion? Why or why not?

As you read Module 19, ask yourself what makes the information you are reading essential to a study of Reconstruction.

Rebuilding the South

The Big Idea

The nation faced many problems in rebuilding the Union.

Main Ideas

- President Lincoln and Congress differed in their views as Reconstruction began.
- The end of the Civil War meant freedom for African Americans in the South.
- President Johnson's plan began the process of Reconstruction.

Key Terms and People

Reconstruction
Ten Percent Plan
Thirteenth Amendment
Freedmen's Bureau
Andrew Johnson

If YOU were there . . .

You are a young soldier who has been fighting in the Civil War for many months. Now that the war is over, you are on your way home. During your journey, you pass plantation manor homes, houses, and barns that have been burned down. No one is doing spring planting in the fields. As you near your family's farm, you see that fences and sheds have been destroyed. You wonder what is left of your home and family.

What would you think your future on the farm would be like?

Reconstruction Begins

After the Civil War ended in 1865, the U.S. government faced the problem of dealing with the defeated southern states. The challenges of **Reconstruction**, the process of readmitting the former Confederate states to the Union, lasted from 1865 to 1877.

Damaged South Tired southern soldiers returned home to find that the world they had known before the war was gone. Cities, towns, and farms had been ruined. Because of high food prices and widespread crop failures, many southerners faced starvation. The Confederate money most southerners held was now worthless. Banks failed, and merchants had gone bankrupt because people could not pay their debts.

Former Confederate general Braxton Bragg was one of many southerners who faced economic hardship. He found that "*all, all* was lost, except my debts." In South Carolina, Mary Boykin Chesnut wrote in her diary about the isolation she experienced after the war. "We are shut in here. . . . All RR's [railroads] destroyed—bridges gone. We are cut off from the world."

Lincoln's Plan President Abraham Lincoln wanted to reunite the nation as quickly and painlessly as possible. He had proposed a plan for readmitting the southern states even before the war ended. Called the **Ten Percent Plan**, it offered southerners amnesty, or official pardon, for all illegal acts supporting the rebellion. To receive amnesty, southerners had to do two things. They had to swear an oath of loyalty to the United States. They also had to agree that slavery was illegal. Once 10 percent of voters in a state made these pledges, they could form a new government. The state then could be readmitted to the Union.

Louisiana quickly elected a new state legislature under the Ten Percent Plan. Other southern states that had been occupied by Union troops soon followed Louisiana back into the United States.

Wade-Davis Bill Some politicians argued that Congress, not the president, should control the southern states' return to the Union. They believed that Congress had the power to admit new states. Also, many Republican members of Congress thought the Ten Percent Plan did not go far enough. A senator from Michigan expressed their views.

> "The people of the North are not such fools as to . . . turn around and say to the traitors, 'all you have to do [to return] is . . . take an oath that henceforth you will be true to the Government.'"
>
> —Senator Jacob Howard, quoted in *Reconstruction: America's Unfinished Revolution, 1863–1877*, by Eric Foner

Academic Vocabulary
procedure a series of steps taken to accomplish a task

Two Republicans—Senator Benjamin Wade and Representative Henry Davis—had an alternative to Lincoln's plan. Following **procedures** of the Wade-Davis bill, a state had to meet two conditions before it could rejoin the Union. First, it had to ban slavery. Second, a majority of adult males in the state had to take the loyalty oath.

Under the Wade-Davis bill, only southerners who swore that they had never supported the Confederacy could vote or hold office. In general, the bill was much stricter than the Ten Percent Plan. Its provisions would make it harder for southern states to rejoin the Union quickly.

President Lincoln therefore refused to sign the bill into law. He thought that few southern states would agree to meet its requirements. He believed that his plan would help restore order more quickly.

Reading Check
Contrast How was the Ten Percent Plan different from the Wade-Davis bill?

Freedom for African Americans

One thing Republicans agreed on was abolishing slavery. The Emancipation Proclamation had freed slaves only in areas that had not been occupied by Union forces, not in the border states. Many people feared that the federal courts might someday declare the proclamation unconstitutional.

Slavery Ends On January 31, 1865, at President Lincoln's urging, Congress proposed the **Thirteenth Amendment**. This amendment made slavery illegal throughout the United States.

The amendment was ratified and took effect on December 18, 1865. When abolitionist William Lloyd Garrison heard the news, he declared that his work was now finished. He called for the American Anti-Slavery Society to break up. Not all abolitionists agreed that their work was done,

These freedpeople have packed their household belongings and are leaving Richmond. Many people traveled in search of relatives. Others placed newspaper advertisements looking for long-lost relatives.

In what ways did former slaves react to freedom?

however. Frederick Douglass insisted that "slavery is not abolished until the black man has the ballot [vote]."

Freedom brought important changes to newly freed slaves. Many couples held ceremonies to legalize marriages that had not been recognized under slavery. Many freedpeople searched for relatives who had been sold away from their families years earlier. Others placed newspaper ads seeking information about their children. Many women began to work at home instead of in the fields. Still others adopted children of dead relatives to keep families together. Church members established voluntary associations and mutual-aid societies to help those in need.

Now that they could travel without a pass, many freedpeople moved from mostly white counties to places with more African Americans. Other freedpeople traveled simply to test their new freedom of movement. Northern migration, while not as extensive as the coming World War I Great Migration beginning in 1910, significantly increased the urban black population of the North. Detroit's African American population, for instance, more than doubled during the 1860s with the vast majority of its new arrivals coming from the South. A South Carolina woman explained this need. "I must go, if I stay here I'll never know I'm free."

For this couple, freedom brought the right to marry.

For most former slaves, freedom to travel was just the first step on a long road toward equal rights and new ways of life. Adults took new last names and began to insist on being called Mr. or Mrs. as a sign of respect, rather than by their first names or by nicknames. Freedpeople began to demand the same economic and political rights as white citizens. Henry Adams, a former slave, argued that "if I cannot do like a white man I am not free."

Forty Acres to Farm? Many former slaves wanted their own land to farm. Near the end of the Civil War, Union general William Tecumseh Sherman had issued an order to break up plantations in coastal South Carolina and Georgia. He wanted to divide the land into 40-acre plots and give them to former slaves as compensation for their forced labor before the war.

Many white planters refused to surrender their land. Some freedpeople pointed out that it was only fair that they receive some of this land because their labor had made the plantations prosper. In the end, the U.S. government returned the land to its original owners. At this time, many freedpeople were unsure about where they would live, what kind of work they would do, and what rights they had. Freedoms that were theirs by law were difficult to enforce.

Freedmen's Bureau In 1865 Congress established the **Freedmen's Bureau**, an agency providing relief for freedpeople and certain poor people in the South. The Bureau had a difficult job. At its high point, about 900 agents served the entire South. Bureau commissioner Oliver O. Howard eventually decided to use the Bureau's limited budget to distribute food to the poor and to provide education and legal help for freedpeople. The Bureau also helped African American war veterans.

The Freedmen's Bureau played an important role in establishing more schools in the South. Laws against educating slaves meant that most freedpeople had never learned to read or write. Before the war ended, however, northern groups, such as the American Missionary Association, began providing books and teachers to African Americans. The teachers were mostly women who were committed to helping freedpeople. One teacher said of her students, "I never before saw children so eager to learn. . . . It is wonderful how [they] . . . can have so great a desire for knowledge, and such a capacity for attaining [reaching] it."

After the war, some freedpeople organized their own education efforts. For example, Freedmen's Bureau agents found that some African Americans had opened schools in abandoned buildings. Many white southerners continued to believe that African Americans should not be educated. Despite

African American students and teachers outside the Freedmen's Bureau school in Beaufort, South Carolina

Helping the Freedpeople

Congress created the Freedmen's Bureau to help freedpeople and poor southerners recover from the Civil War. The Bureau assisted people by:

- providing supplies and medical services.
- establishing schools.
- supervising contracts between freedpeople and employers.
- taking care of lands abandoned or captured during the war.

What role did the Freedmen's Bureau play during Reconstruction?

opposition, by 1869 more than 150,000 African American students were attending more than 3,000 schools. The Freedmen's Bureau also helped establish a number of universities for African Americans, including Howard and Fisk universities.

Students quickly filled the new classrooms. Working adults attended classes in the evening. African Americans hoped that education would help them to understand and protect their rights and to enable them to find better jobs. Both black and white southerners benefited from the effort to provide greater access to education in the South.

Reading Check
Analyze How did the Freedmen's Bureau help reform education in the South?

President Johnson's Reconstruction Plan

While the Freedmen's Bureau was helping African Americans, the issue of how the South would politically rejoin the Union remained unresolved. Soon, however, a tragic event ended Lincoln's dream of peacefully reuniting the country.

A New President On the evening of April 14, 1865, President Lincoln and his wife attended a play at Ford's Theater in Washington, DC. During the play, John Wilkes Booth, a southerner who opposed Lincoln's policies, sneaked into the president's theater box and shot him. Lincoln was rushed to a boardinghouse across the street, where he died early the next morning. Lincoln, his leadership remembered for its honesty, deep intelligence, and high morals, became a symbol for the nation of the struggle of the Civil War.

Vice President **Andrew Johnson** was sworn into office quickly. Reconstruction had now become his responsibility. He would have to win the trust of a nation shocked at its leader's death. Johnson's plan for bringing southern states back into the Union was similar to Lincoln's plan. However, he decided that wealthy southerners and former Confederate officials would need a presidential pardon to receive amnesty. Johnson shocked Radical Republicans by eventually pardoning more than 7,000 people by 1866.

New State Governments Johnson was a Democrat whom Republicans had put on the ticket in 1864 to appeal to the border states. A former slaveholder, he was a stubborn man who would soon face a hostile Congress.

Johnson offered a mild program for setting up new southern state governments. First, he appointed a temporary governor for each state. Then, he required that the states revise their constitutions. Next, voters elected state and federal representatives. The new state government had to declare that secession was illegal. It also had to ratify the Thirteenth Amendment and refuse to pay Confederate debts.

By the end of 1865, all the southern states except Texas had created new governments. Johnson approved them all and declared that the United States was restored. Newly elected representatives came to Washington from each reconstructed southern state. However, Republicans complained that many new representatives had been leaders of the Confederacy. Congress therefore refused to readmit the southern states into the Union. Clearly, the nation was still divided.

Summary and Preview In this lesson you learned about early plans for Reconstruction. In the next lesson you will learn that disagreements about Reconstruction became so serious that the president was almost removed from office.

Reading Check
Summarize What was President Johnson's plan for Reconstruction?

Lesson 1 Assessment

Review Ideas, Terms, and People

1. **a. Identify** What does Reconstruction mean?
   b. Summarize What was President Lincoln's plan for Reconstruction?
2. **a. Recall** What is the Thirteenth Amendment?
   b. Elaborate In your opinion, what was the most important accomplishment of the Freedmen's Bureau? Explain.
3. **a. Recall** Why was President Lincoln killed?
   b. Analyze Why did some Americans oppose President Johnson's Reconstruction plan?

Critical Thinking

4. **Summarize** In this lesson you learned about Reconstruction. Create a graphic organizer similar to the one below and show how African Americans were affected by the end of the war.

African Americans and Reconstruction — Marriages are legalized.

The Fight over Reconstruction

The Big Idea

The return to power of the pre-war southern leadership led Republicans in Congress to take control of Reconstruction.

Main Ideas

- Black Codes led to opposition to President Johnson's plan for Reconstruction.

- The Fourteenth Amendment ensured citizenship for African Americans.

- Radical Republicans in Congress took charge of Reconstruction.

- The Fifteenth Amendment gave African Americans the right to vote.

Key Terms and People

Black Codes
Radical Republicans
Civil Rights Act of 1866
Fourteenth Amendment
Reconstruction Acts
impeachment
Fifteenth Amendment

If YOU were there . . .

A member of Congress, you belong to the same political party as the president. But you strongly disagree with his ideas about Reconstruction and civil rights for African Americans. Now some of the president's opponents are trying to remove him from office. You do not think he is a good president. On the other hand, you think removing him would be bad for the unity of the country.

Will you vote to remove the president?

Opposition to President Johnson

In 1866 Congress continued to debate the rules for restoring the Union. Meanwhile, new state legislatures approved by President Johnson had already begun passing laws to deny African Americans' civil rights. "This is a white man's government, and intended for white men only," declared Governor Benjamin F. Perry of South Carolina.

Black Codes Soon, every southern state passed **Black Codes**, or laws that greatly limited the freedom of African Americans. They required African Americans to sign work contracts, creating working conditions similar to those under slavery. In most southern states, any African Americans who could not prove they were employed could be arrested. Their punishment might be one year of work without pay. African Americans were also prevented from owning guns. In addition, they were not allowed to rent property except in cities.

Black Codes in Mississippi and South Carolina also included Apprentice Laws. These laws required law enforcement officials to semiannually report to the Probate Court orphaned children or children of parents deemed unfit. The Probate Court was then required to find work for the minor as an apprentice. The former owner had priority in choosing the minor as his apprentice.

"Provided, that said apprentice shall be bound by indenture, in case of males until they are twenty-one years old, and in case of females until they are eighteen years old."

—Laws of the State of Mississippi, Passed at a Regular Session of the Mississippi Legislature, Jackson, 1865

Masters had the right to inflict moderate punishment on their apprentices and to recapture runaways. But the codes also required masters to provide food and clothing to their apprentices, teach them a trade, and send them to school.

The Black Codes alarmed many Americans. As one Civil War veteran asked, "If you call this freedom, what do you call slavery?" African Americans organized to oppose the codes. One group sent a petition to officials in South Carolina.

"We simply ask . . . that the same laws which govern *white men* shall govern *black men* . . . that, in short, we be dealt with as others are— in equity [equality] and justice."

—Petition from an African American convention held in South Carolina, quoted in *There Is a River: The Black Struggle for Freedom in America* by Vincent Harding

Radical Republicans The Black Codes angered many Republicans. They thought the South was returning to its old ways. Most Republicans were moderates who wanted the South to have loyal state governments. They also believed that African Americans should have rights as citizens. They

DOCUMENT-BASED INVESTIGATION Historical Source

Johnson vs. Stevens

President **Andrew Johnson**, a southern Democrat from Tennessee and former slaveholder, argued that the South should not be placed under military control.

Thaddeus Stevens, a Pennsylvanian Radical Republican and champion of equal rights for African Americans, believed that Congress had the power to treat the South as conquered territory.

Analyze Historical Sources
How did Johnson's and Stevens's views on the South differ? What role do you think their personal backgrounds played in shaping their views?

"*Military governments . . . established for an indefinite period, would have divided the people into the vanquishers and the vanquished, and would have envenomed [made poisonous] hatred rather than have restored affection.*"

—Andrew Johnson

"*The future condition of the conquered power depends on the will of the conqueror. They must come in as new states or remain as conquered provinces. Congress . . . is the only power that can act in the matter.*"

—Thaddeus Stevens

hoped that the government would not have to force the South to follow federal laws.

Radical Republicans, on the other hand, took a harsher stance. They wanted the federal government to force change in the South. Like the moderates, they thought the Black Codes were cruel and unjust. The Radicals, however, wanted the federal government to be much more involved in Reconstruction. They feared that too many southern leaders remained loyal to the former Confederacy and would not enforce the new laws. Thaddeus Stevens of Pennsylvania and Charles Sumner of Massachusetts were the leaders of the Radical Republicans.

A harsh critic of President Johnson, Stevens was known for his honesty and sharp tongue. He wanted economic and political justice for both African Americans and poor white southerners. Sumner had been a strong opponent of slavery before the Civil War. He continued to argue tirelessly for African Americans' civil rights, including the right to vote and the right to fair laws.

Both Stevens and Sumner believed that, like Lincoln's proposed Ten Percent Plan, President Johnson's Reconstruction plan was too lenient toward the South, thereby making it a failure. Although the Radicals did not control Congress, they began to gain support among moderates when President Johnson ignored criticism of the Black Codes. Stevens believed the federal government could not allow racial inequality to survive.

Reading Check
Compare and Contrast How were Radical Republicans and moderate Republicans similar and different?

Fourteenth Amendment

Urged on by the Radicals in 1866, Congress proposed a new bill. It would give the Freedmen's Bureau more powers. The law would allow the Freedmen's Bureau to use military courts to try people accused of violating African Americans' rights. The bill's supporters hoped that these courts would be fairer than local courts in the South.

Johnson versus Congress Surprising many members of Congress, Johnson vetoed the Freedmen's Bureau bill. He insisted that Congress could not pass any new laws until the southern states were represented in Congress. Johnson also argued that the Freedmen's Bureau was unconstitutional.

Republicans responded with the **Civil Rights Act of 1866**. This act provided African Americans with the same legal rights as white Americans. President Johnson once again used his veto power. He argued that the act gave too much power to the federal government. He also rejected the **principle** of equal rights for African Americans. Congress, however, overrode Johnson's veto.

Many Republicans worried about what would happen when the southern states were readmitted. Fearing that the Civil Rights Act might be overturned, the Republicans proposed the **Fourteenth Amendment** in the summer of 1866. The Fourteenth Amendment included the following provisions:

1. It defined all people born or naturalized within the United States, except Native Americans, as citizens.

Academic Vocabulary
principle basic belief, rule, or law

2. It guaranteed citizens the equal protection of the laws.
3. It said that states could not "deprive any person of life, liberty, or property, without due process of law."
4. It banned many former Confederate officials from holding state or federal offices.
5. It made state laws subject to federal court review.
6. It gave Congress the power to pass any laws needed to enforce it.

1866 Elections President Johnson and most Democrats opposed the Fourteenth Amendment. As a result, civil rights for African Americans became a key issue in the 1866 congressional elections. To help the Democrats, Johnson traveled around the country defending his Reconstruction plan. Johnson's speaking tour was a disaster. It did little to win votes for the Democratic Party. Johnson even got into arguments with people in the audiences of some of his speaking engagements.

Two major riots in the South also hurt Johnson's campaign. On May 1, 1866, a dispute in Memphis, Tennessee, took place between local police and black Union soldiers. The dispute turned into a three-day wave of violence against African Americans. About three months later, another riot took place during a political demonstration in New Orleans. During that dispute, 34 African Americans and three white Republicans were killed.

Reading Check
Summarize What issue did the Fourteenth Amendment address, and how did it affect the congressional elections of 1866?

Congress Takes Control of Reconstruction

The 1866 elections gave the Republican Party a commanding two-thirds majority in both the House and the Senate. This majority gave the Republicans the power to override any presidential veto. In addition, the Republicans became united as the moderates joined with the Radicals. Together, they called for a new form of Reconstruction.

Reconstruction Acts In March 1867, Congress passed the first of several **Reconstruction Acts**. These laws divided the South into five districts. A U.S. military commander controlled each district.

The military would remain in control of the South until the southern states rejoined the Union. To be readmitted, a state had to write a new state constitution supporting the Fourteenth Amendment. Finally, the state had to give African American men the right to vote.

Thaddeus Stevens was one of the new Reconstruction Acts' most enthusiastic supporters. He spoke in Congress to defend the acts.

"Have not loyal blacks quite as good a right to choose rulers and make laws as rebel whites? Every man, no matter what his race or color . . . has an equal right to justice, honesty, and fair play with every other man; and the law should secure him those rights."

–Thaddeus Stevens, quoted in *Sources of the American Republic*, edited by Marvin Meyers et al.

President on Trial President Johnson strongly disagreed with Stevens. He argued that African Americans did not deserve the same treatment as white people. The Reconstruction Acts, he said, used "powers not granted

The Reconstruction Amendments

Thirteenth Amendment (1865)

"Neither slavery nor involuntary servitude, except as a punishment for crime whereof the party shall have been duly convicted, shall exist within the United States, or any place subject to their jurisdiction."

This amendment legally banned slavery throughout the United States but it was not without fault. A loophole, or an ambiguity of a law, existed. "Involuntary servitude," according to this amendment, could be enforced as punishment for a crime. The amendment also failed to specify what the legal status of freedpeople would be or if they would be fully entitled to the rights of American citizens.

How might the loophole in the Thirteenth Amendment have been exploited by opponents of the amendment's ratification?

Fourteenth Amendment (1868)

"All persons born or naturalized in the United States, and subject to the jurisdiction thereof, are citizens of the United States and the State wherein they reside. No State shall make or enforce any law which shall abridge the privileges or immunities of citizens of the United States; nor shall any State deprive any person of life, liberty, or property, without due process of law; nor deny to any person within its jurisdiction the equal protection of the laws."

Most notably, this amendment overturned the *Dred Scott* case by granting citizenship to all people born in the United States (except for Native Americans).

What role do you think Black Codes played in the drafting of this amendment?

Fifteenth Amendment (1870)

"The right of citizens of the United States to vote shall not be denied or abridged by the United States or by any State on account of race, color, or previous condition of servitude."

This amendment, for all intents and purposes, gave African American men the right to vote.

According to the language of this amendment, what group of citizens was not granted voting rights? How would you change the language to include all citizens?

---

to the federal government or any one of its branches." Knowing that Johnson did not support its Reconstruction policies, Congress passed a law limiting his power. This law prevented the president from removing cabinet officials without Senate approval. Johnson quickly broke the law by firing Edwin Stanton, the secretary of war.

For the first time in United States history, the House of Representatives responded by voting to impeach the president. **Impeachment** is the process used by a legislative body to bring charges of wrongdoing against a public official. The next step, under Article I of the Constitution, was a trial in the Senate. A two-thirds majority was required to find Johnson guilty and remove him from office.

Although Johnson was unpopular with Republicans, some of them believed he was being judged unfairly. Others did not trust the president

This Reconstruction-era painting shows African American men voting after passage of the Fifteenth Amendment.

What right did the Fifteenth Amendment protect?

pro tempore of the Senate, Benjamin Wade. He would become president if Johnson were removed from office. By a single vote, Senate Republicans failed to convict Johnson. Even so, the trial weakened his power as president.

Election of 1868 Johnson did not run for another term in 1868. The Democrats chose former New York governor Horatio Seymour as their presidential candidate. The Republicans chose Ulysses S. Grant. As a war hero, Grant appealed to many northern voters. He had no political experience but supported the congressional Reconstruction plan. He ran under the slogan "Let Us Have Peace."

Shortly after Grant was nominated, Congress readmitted seven southern states—Alabama, Arkansas, Florida, Georgia, Louisiana, North Carolina, and South Carolina. (Tennessee had already been readmitted in 1866.) Under the terms of readmission, these seven states approved the Fourteenth Amendment. They also agreed to let African American men vote. However, white southerners used violence to try to keep African Americans away from the polls.

Despite such tactics, thousands of African Americans voted for Grant and the "party of Lincoln." The *New Orleans Tribune* reported that many former slaves "see clearly enough that the Republican party [is] their political life boat." African American votes helped Grant to win a narrow victory.

Reading Check
Analyze Information
To which voters did Grant appeal in the presidential election of 1868?

Fifteenth Amendment

After Grant's victory, Congressional Republicans wanted to protect their Reconstruction plan. They worried that the southern states might try to keep black voters from the polls in future elections. Also, some Radical Republicans argued that it was not fair that many northern states still had laws preventing African Americans from voting. After all, every southern state was required to grant suffrage to African American men.

In 1869 Congress proposed the **Fifteenth Amendment**, which gave African American men the right to vote. Abolitionist William Lloyd Garrison praised what he saw as "this wonderful, quiet, sudden transformation of four millions of human beings from . . . the auction block to the ballot-box." The amendment went into effect in 1870 as one of the last Reconstruction laws passed at the federal level.

The Fifteenth Amendment did not please every reformer, however. Many women were angry because the amendment did not also grant them the right to vote.

Summary and Preview In this lesson you learned that Congress took control of Reconstruction and took steps to protect the rights of African Americans. In the next lesson you will learn about increasing opposition to Reconstruction.

Reading Check
Find Main Ideas
How did Radical Republicans take control of Reconstruction?

Lesson 2 Assessment

Review Ideas, Terms, and People

1. a. Describe What were Black Codes?
   b. Make Inferences Why did Republicans think Johnson's Reconstruction plan was a failure?
2. a. Recall What was the Civil Rights Act of 1866?
   b. Summarize Why was the Fourteenth Amendment important?
3. a. Recall Why was President Johnson impeached?
   b. Evaluate Which element of the Reconstruction Acts do you believe was most important? Why?
4. a. Recall What does the Fifteenth Amendment state?
   b. Elaborate Do you think that women should have been included in the Fifteenth Amendment? Explain.

Critical Thinking

5. Identify In this lesson you learned about the issues that led Republicans to take over Reconstruction. Create a graphic organizer similar to the one below and identify the main provisions of the Fourteenth Amendment and their effects.

Provisions	Effects

★
Reconstruction in the South

The Big Idea

As Reconstruction ended, African Americans faced new hurdles and the South attempted to rebuild.

Main Ideas

- Reconstruction governments helped reform the South.

- The Ku Klux Klan was organized as African Americans moved into positions of power.

- As Reconstruction ended, the rights of African Americans were restricted.

- Southern business leaders relied on industry to rebuild the South.

Key Terms and People

Hiram Revels
Ku Klux Klan
Enforcement Acts
Compromise of 1877
poll tax
segregation
Jim Crow laws
Plessy v. *Ferguson*
sharecropping

If YOU were there . . .

You live on a farm in the South in the 1870s. Times are hard because you do not own your farm. Instead, you and your family work in a landowner's cotton fields. You never seem to earn enough to buy land of your own. Some of your neighbors have decided to give up farming and move to the city. Others are going to work in the textile mills. But you have always been a farmer.

Will you decide to change your way of life?

Reconstruction Governments

After Grant became president in 1869, the Republicans seemed stronger than ever. They controlled most southern governments, partly because of the support of African American voters. However, most of the Republican officeholders were unpopular with white southerners.

Carpetbaggers and Scalawags Some of these office-holders were northern-born Republicans who had moved to the South after the war. Many white southerners called them carpetbaggers. Supposedly, they had rushed there carrying all their possessions in bags made from carpeting. Many southerners resented these northerners, accusing them—often unfairly—of trying to profit from Reconstruction. Because the South needed both physical and economic rebuilding, there were many business opportunities. Northerners who had not been devastated by the war had more money to invest and could therefore profit from these opportunities.

Southern Democrats cared even less for white southern Republicans. They referred to them as scalawags, or greedy rascals. Democrats believed that these southerners had betrayed the South by voting for the Republican Party. Many southern Republicans were small farmers who had supported the Union during the war. Others, like Mississippi governor James Alcorn, were former members of the Whig Party. They preferred to become Republicans rather than join the Democrats.

Clergyman and educator Hiram Revels was the first African American elected to the U.S. Senate in 1870.

African American Leaders African Americans were the largest group of southern Republican voters. During Reconstruction, more than 600 African Americans won election to state legislatures. Some 16 of these politicians were elected to Congress. Other African Americans held local offices in counties throughout the South.

African American politicians came from many backgrounds. **Hiram Revels** was born free in North Carolina and went to college in Illinois. He became a Methodist minister and served as a chaplain in the Union army. In 1870 Revels became the first African American in the U.S. Senate. He took over the seat previously held by Confederate president Jefferson Davis. Revels held a moderate view of the readmission of former Confederates. Education and employment for African Americans were two of his top priorities. Revels exemplified the ability of African Americans to take part in governing. After completing his term, he became the first president of Alcorn University.

Unlike Revels, Blanche K. Bruce grew up in slavery in Virginia. Bruce became an important Republican in Mississippi and served one term as a U.S. senator. He worked to integrate the military while in office.

State Governments Change Direction The new Reconstruction state governments made policies that increased civil and voting rights for African Americans. They passed laws that ensured African Americans were allowed to vote in every community. In many places, however, there was still resistance by whites. Because former Confederates usually could not vote, they struggled to maintain political influence.

Reconstruction governments provided money for many new programs and organizations in the South. They helped to establish some of the first state-funded public school systems in the South. They also built new hospitals, prisons, and orphanages and passed laws prohibiting discrimination against African Americans. Many of these programs improved the lives of African Americans and whites in the South and gave people economic opportunities and access to political offices. However, racism and the dramatically different culture of groups led to conflicting expectations, and sometimes tensions led to violence.

Southern states under Republican control spent large amounts of money. They aided the construction of railroads, bridges, and public buildings. These improvements were intended to help the southern economy recover from the war. To get the money for these projects, the Reconstruction governments raised taxes and issued bonds. Although some people protested the increased taxes, the improved infrastructure helped the South to increase its trade and production capabilities.

Ku Klux Klan

As more African Americans took office, resistance to Reconstruction increased among white southerners. Democrats claimed that the Reconstruction governments were corrupt, illegal, and unjust. They also disliked having federal soldiers stationed in their states. Many white southerners disapproved of African American officeholders. One Democrat

Reading Check
Summarize What reforms did Reconstruction state governments carry out?

The Ku Klux Klan

Members of the Ku Klux Klan often attacked under cover of darkness to hide their identities. This Klan member, shown on the left, even disguised his horse.

Why do you think Klan members disguised themselves?

noted, "'A white man's government' [is] the most popular rallying cry we have." In 1866 a group of white southerners in Tennessee created the **Ku Klux Klan**. This secret society opposed civil rights, particularly suffrage, for African Americans. The Klan used violence and terror against African Americans. The group's membership grew rapidly as it spread throughout the South. Klan members wore robes and disguises to hide their identities. They attacked—and even murdered—African Americans, white Republican voters, and public officials, usually at night.

Local governments did little to stop the violence. Many officials feared the Klan or were sympathetic to its activities. In 1870 and 1871 the federal government took action. In an affirmation of federal authority, Congress passed laws, called the **Enforcement Acts**, that made it a federal crime to interfere with elections or to deny citizens equal protection under the law.

Within a few years, the Klan was no longer an organized threat. But groups of white vigilantes, including the White League in Louisiana and the Red Shirts in Mississippi, North and South Carolina, continued to assault African Americans and Republicans throughout the 1870s. Unlike the Ku Klux Klan, the White League and the Red Shirts operated openly.

Reading Check
Draw Conclusions
Why did southerners join the Ku Klux Klan or other vigilante groups?

Reconstruction Ends

The violence of the Ku Klux Klan was not the only challenge to Reconstruction. Republicans slowly lost control of southern state governments to the Democratic Party. The General Amnesty Act of 1872 allowed former Confederates, except those who had held high ranks, to serve in public office. Many of these former Confederates, most of whom were Democrats, were soon elected to southern governments.

The Republican Party also began losing its power in the North. Although President Grant was re-elected in 1872, financial and political scandals in his administration upset voters. In his first term, a gold-buying scheme involving Grant's cousin led to a brief crisis on the stock market called Black Friday. During his second term, his personal secretary was involved in the Whiskey Ring scandal, in which whiskey distillers and public officials worked together to steal liquor taxes from the federal government. Also, people blamed Republican policies for the Panic of 1873.

Panic of 1873 This severe economic downturn began in September 1873 when Jay Cooke and Company, a major investor in railroads and the largest financier of the Union's Civil War effort, declared bankruptcy. The company had lied about the value of land along the side of the Northern Pacific Railroad that it owned and was trying to sell. When the truth leaked out, the company failed.

The failure of such an important business sent panic through the stock market, and investors began selling shares of stock more rapidly than people wanted to buy them. Soon, 89 of the nation's 364 railroads had failed as well. The failure of almost 18,000 other businesses followed within two years. By 1876 unemployment had risen to 14 percent, with an estimated two million people out of work. The high unemployment rate set off numerous strikes and protests, many involving railroad workers. In 1874 the Democrats gained control of the House of Representatives. Northerners were becoming less concerned about southern racism and more concerned about their financial well-being.

Election of 1876 Republicans could tell that northern support for Reconstruction was fading. Voters' attention was shifting to economic problems. In 1874 the Republican Party lost control of the House of Representatives to the Democrats. The Republicans in Congress managed to pass one last civil rights law. The Civil Rights Act of 1875 guaranteed African Americans equal rights in public places, such as theaters and public transportation. But as Americans became increasingly worried about economic problems and government corruption, the Republican Party began to abandon Reconstruction.

Republicans selected Ohio governor Rutherford B. Hayes as their 1876 presidential candidate. He believed in ending federal support of the Reconstruction governments. The Democrats nominated New York governor Samuel J. Tilden. During the election, Democrats in the South again used violence at the polls to keep Republican voters away.

The election between Hayes and Tilden was close. Tilden appeared to have won. Republicans challenged the electoral votes in Oregon and three southern states. A special commission of members of Congress and Supreme Court justices was appointed to settle the issue.

The commission narrowly decided to give all the disputed votes to Hayes. Hayes thus won the presidency by one electoral vote. In the **Compromise of 1877**, the Democrats agreed to accept Hayes's victory. In return, they wanted all remaining federal troops removed from the South. They also asked for funding for internal improvements in the South and the appointment of a southern Democrat to the president's cabinet. Shortly after he took office in 1877, President Hayes removed the last of the federal troops from the South.

Redeemers Gradually, Democrats regained control of state governments in the South. In each state, they moved quickly to get rid of the Reconstruction reforms.

Democrats who brought their party back to power in the South were called Redeemers. They came from a variety of backgrounds. For instance, U.S. senator John T. Morgan of Alabama was a former general in the Confederate army. Newspaper editor Henry Grady of Georgia was interested in promoting southern industry.

Redeemers wanted to reduce the size of state government and limit the rights of African Americans. They lowered state budgets and got rid of a variety of social programs. The Redeemers cut property taxes and cut public funding for schools. They also succeeded in limiting African Americans' civil rights.

Jim Crow Laws
This 1913 illustration shows the segregation of society caused by Jim Crow laws. After Reconstruction ended, the U.S. court system upheld legalized segregation for nearly eighty years. The Civil Rights Act of 1964 finally put an end to all state and local laws requiring segregation.

African Americans' Rights Restricted Redeemers set up the poll tax in an effort to deny the vote to African Americans. The **poll tax** was a special tax people had to pay before they could vote.

Some states also targeted African American voters by requiring them to pass a literacy test. A so-called grandfather clause written into law affected men whose fathers or grandfathers could vote before 1867. In those cases, a voter did not have to pay a poll tax or pass a literacy test. As a result, almost every white man could escape the voting restrictions.

Redeemer governments also introduced legal **segregation**, the forced separation of whites and African Americans in public places. **Jim Crow laws**—laws that enforced segregation—became common in southern states in the 1880s.

African Americans challenged Jim Crow laws in court. In 1883, however, the U.S. Supreme Court ruled that the Civil Rights Act of 1875 was unconstitutional. The Court also ruled that the Fourteenth Amendment applied only to the actions of state governments. This ruling allowed private individuals and businesses to practice segregation.

Plessy **v.** *Ferguson* In 1896 the U.S. Supreme Court returned to the issue of segregation. When Homer Plessy, an African American, refused to leave the whites-only Louisiana train car he was riding on, he was arrested and accused of breaking Louisiana's Separate Car Act of 1890. This Jim Crow law stated that:

> "all railway companies carrying passengers in their coaches in this state, shall provide equal but separate accommodations for the white, and colored races, by providing two or more passenger coaches for each passenger train, or by dividing the passenger coaches by a partition so as to secure separate accommodations. . . ."
> —Separate Car Act of 1890, Louisiana state law

Plessy sued the railroad company and lost. His lawyers argued that the law violated his right to equal treatment under the Fourteenth Amendment. He then appealed to the U.S. Supreme Court. The Supreme Court ruled against Plessy in ***Plessy v. Ferguson.*** Segregation was allowed, said the Court, if "separate-but-equal" facilities were provided. Among the justices, only John Marshall Harlan disagreed with the Court's decision.

Segregation became widespread across the country. African Americans were forced to use separate public schools, libraries, and parks. When they existed, these facilities were usually of poorer quality than those created for whites. In practice, these so-called separate-but-equal facilities were separate and unequal. Neither Congress nor the president would make significant actions to overturn the doctrine until the 1900s.

Farming in the South Few African Americans in the South could afford to buy or even rent farms. Many African Americans therefore remained on plantations. Others tried to make a living in the cities.

African Americans who stayed on plantations often became part of a system known as **sharecropping**, or sharing the crop. Landowners provided the land, tools, and supplies, and sharecroppers provided the labor. At harvest time, the sharecropper usually had to give most of the crop to the landowner. Whatever remained belonged to the sharecropper. In theory, "croppers" who saved a little might even rent land for cash and keep their full harvest in a system known as tenant farming.

Instead, most sharecroppers lived in a cycle of debt. When they needed food, clothing, or supplies, most families had to buy goods on credit because they had little cash. When sharecroppers sold their crops, they hoped to be able to pay off these debts. However, bad weather, poor harvests, or low crop prices often made this dream impossible.

Sharecroppers usually grew cotton, one of the South's most important cash crops. When too many farmers planted cotton, however, the supply became excessive. As a result, the price per bale of cotton dropped. Many farmers understood the drawbacks of planting cotton. However, farmers felt pressure from banks and others to keep raising cotton.

Reading Check
Find Main Ideas How were African Americans' rights restricted?

Rebuilding Southern Industry

The southern economy suffered through cycles of good and bad years as cotton prices went up and down. Some business leaders hoped industry would strengthen the southern economy and create a New South.

Southern Industry Henry Grady, an Atlanta newspaper editor, was a leader of the New South movement. Grady and his supporters felt that with its cheap and abundant labor, the South could build factories and provide a workforce for them.

The most successful industrial development in the South involved textile production. Businesspeople built textile mills in many small towns to produce cotton fabric. Many people from rural areas came to work in the mills, but African Americans were not allowed to work in most of them.

Southern Mill Life Work in the cotton mills appealed to farm families who had trouble making ends meet. Recruiters sent out by the mills promised good wages and steady work. Mills employed large numbers of women and children. Women did most of the spinning and were valued workers. However, few women had the opportunity to advance within the company.

The New South

Atlanta rebuilt quickly after the war, becoming a leading railroad and industrial center. Newspaper editor Henry Grady gave stirring speeches about the need for industry in the South. He became one of the best-known spokesmen of the "New South."

Why might Grady point to Atlanta as a model for economic change?

"The New South . . . is stirred with the breath of a new life."

—Henry Grady

Many mill workers were proud of the skills they used, but they did not enjoy their work. Workers often labored 12 hours a day, six days a week. Cotton dust and lint filled the air, causing asthma and an illness known as brown-lung disease. Fast-moving machinery caused injuries and even deaths. Despite the long hours and dangerous working conditions, wages remained low. However, mill work did offer an alternative to farming.

Reading Check
Find Main Ideas
What did southern business leaders hope industry would do?

Reconstruction in the North

Although most federal Reconstruction policies were designed to reform the South, they affected groups in the North as well. There were many groups that worked to advance their own rights and interests during this time.

Women and Northern African Americans The Radical Republicans passed many federal laws that required southern states to allow African American men to vote. They based their cause on the ideal of equality found in the Declaration of Independence and the Constitution. Women's suffragists began using these same arguments to support their own suffrage. Wyoming and Utah granted women the vote in 1869, but their motivations were not just to ensure equal rights for women. Wyoming leaders hoped to attract more women residents, while Utahans hoped to counteract the rising number of non-Mormon voters.

African Americans in the North faced less social discrimination than they did in the South but still faced racism and segregation. In response, some state governments passed laws that made segregation illegal. Some integrated their school systems. Still, most states upheld the principle of separate-but-equal facilities.

A Changing Economy During the war and Reconstruction, the economy of the North and the West grew rapidly. Manufacturing, commerce, and rail transportation generated tremendous fortunes. Large companies grew by buying smaller companies, and railroads made huge profits transporting goods and people. Tax revenue increased as well, and governments were able to provide more services and make more investments.

Between 1865 and 1873, more than 2 million immigrants arrived in the United States. They provided a new pool of labor for the growing industrial economy. The number of labor unions increased, and they began to push for policies that protected workers. Reformers pressed for eight-hour-workday and fair-pay laws. In addition, the increase in commercial and trading businesses led to a shift in the makeup of the working class. It now included a majority of professionals and white-collar workers.

Eventually the focus of the Republican Party began to move away from civil rights for African Americans and toward reducing government corruption. The acceptance of the Compromise of 1877 signaled the end of the Republican focus on reforming racial politics in the South.

Summary and Preview In this lesson you learned about the end of Reconstruction. In the years that followed, the South continued to rebuild, but the gains made by African Americans were reversed.

Reading Check
Compare and Contrast How was Reconstruction in the North similar to and different from Reconstruction in the South?

Lesson 3 Assessment

Review Ideas, Terms, and People

1. a. Identify Who were some prominent African American leaders during Reconstruction? Why was the election of Hiram Revels significant?

b. Evaluate What do you think was the most important change made by Reconstruction state governments? Explain your answer.

2. a. Recall For what reasons did some local governments not stop the Ku Klux Klan?

b. Draw Conclusions How did the Ku Klux Klan's use of terror interfere with elections in the South?

3. a. Summarize What was the Compromise of 1877?

b. Evaluate How did *Plessy* v. *Ferguson* affect life in the United States?

c. Explain What was the relationship between Jim Crow laws and segregation?

4. a. Identify Who was Henry Grady, and why was he important?

b. Predict What are some possible results of the rise of the "New South"?

Critical Thinking

5. Identify Causes and Effects In this lesson you learned about Reconstruction governments. Create a graphic organizer similar to the one below and show why Reconstruction ended, as well as the results of its end.

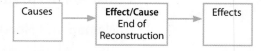

| Causes | Effect/Cause End of Reconstruction | Effects |

Social Studies Skills

Chance, Oversight, and Error in History

Understand the Skill

Sometimes, history can seem very routine. One event leads to others which, in turn, lead to still others. You learn to look for cause-and-effect relationships among events. You learn how point of view and bias can influence decisions and actions. These approaches to the study of history imply that the events of the past are orderly and predictable.

In fact, many of the events of the past *are* orderly and predictable. They may seem even more so since they're over and done with, and we know how things turned out. Yet, predictable patterns of behavior *do* exist throughout history. Recognizing them is one of the great values and rewards of studying the past. As the philosopher George Santayana once famously said, "Those who cannot remember the past are condemned to repeat it."

At its most basic level, however, history is people, and people are "human." They make mistakes. Unexpected things happen to them, both good things and bad. This is the unpredictable element of history. The current phrase "stuff happens" is just as true of the past as it is today. Mistakes, oversights, and just plain "dumb luck" have shaped the course of history—and have helped to make the study of it so exciting.

Learn the Skill

California merchant John Sutter decided to build a sawmill along a nearby American river in 1848. He planned to sell the lumber it produced to settlers who were moving into the area. Sutter put James W. Marshall to work building the mill. To install the large waterwheel that would power the saw, Marshall first had to deepen the riverbed next to the mill. During his digging, he noticed some shiny bits of yellow metal in the water. The result of this accidental find was the California gold rush, which sent thousands of Americans to California, and speeded settlement of the West.

In 1863 the army of Confederate general Robert E. Lee invaded Maryland. The Civil War had been going well for the South. Lee hoped a southern victory on Union soil would convince the British to aid the South in the war. However, a Confederate officer forgot his cigars as his unit left its camp in the Maryland countryside. Wrapped around the cigars was a copy of Lee's battle plans. When a Union soldier came upon the abandoned camp, he spotted the cigars. This chance discovery enabled the Union army to defeat Lee at the Battle of Antietam. The Union victory helped keep the British out of the war. More importantly, it allowed President Lincoln to issue the Emancipation Proclamation and begin the process of ending slavery in the United States.

Practice the Skill

In April 1865 President Lincoln was assassinated while attending the theater in Washington, DC. Bodyguard John Parker was stationed outside the door of the president's box. However, Parker left his post to find a seat from which he could watch the play. This allowed the killer to enter the box and shoot the unprotected president.

Write an essay about how this chance event altered the course of history. How might Reconstruction, North–South relations, and African Americans' struggle for equality have been different had Lincoln lived?

Module 19 Assessment

Review Vocabulary, Terms, and People

Complete each sentence by filling in the blank with the correct term or person from the module.

1. _____ were laws that allowed racial segregation in public places.
2. The Radical Republicans were led by _____, a member of Congress from Pennsylvania.
3. The period from 1865 to 1877 that focused on reuniting the nation is known as _____.
4. Following the Civil War, many African Americans in the South made a living by participating in the _____ system.
5. After opposing Congress, Andrew Johnson became the first president to face _____ proceedings.
6. The _____ Amendment made slavery in the United States illegal.
7. In 1870 _____ became the first African American to serve in the U.S. Senate.

Comprehension and Critical Thinking

Lesson 1

8. a. **Describe** How did the lives of African Americans change after the Civil War?
   b. **Compare and Contrast** How was President Johnson's Reconstruction plan similar and different from President Lincoln's Ten Percent Plan?
   c. **Evaluate** Which of the three Reconstruction plans that were originally proposed do you think would have been the most successful? Why?

Lesson 2

9. a. **Identify** Who were the Radical Republicans, and how did they change Reconstruction?
   b. **Analyze** How did the debate over the Fourteenth Amendment affect the election of 1866?
   c. **Elaborate** Do you think Congress was right to impeach President Andrew Johnson? Explain.

Lesson 3

10. a. **Describe** What reforms did Reconstruction governments in the South support?
    b. **Draw Conclusions** In what ways did southern governments attempt to reverse the accomplishments of Reconstruction?
    c. **Evaluate** Do you think the South was successful or unsuccessful in its rebuilding efforts? Explain your answer.

Review Themes

11. Politics Explain the political struggles that took place during Reconstruction.

12. Society and Culture How were the lives of ordinary southerners affected in the years after Reconstruction?

Reading Skills

Analyze Historical Information *Use the Reading Skills taught in this module to answer the question about the reading selection below.*

> Radical Republicans, on the other hand, took a harsher stance. They wanted the federal government to force change in the South. Like the moderates, they thought the Black Codes were cruel and unjust.

13. Which of the following is relevant information for the passage above?

   a. Thaddeus Stevens was a Radical Republican.

   b. Andrew Johnson was a Democrat.

   c. Radical Republicans wanted the federal government to make major changes in the South.

   d. Radical Republicans were eventually removed from power.

Social Studies Skills

Chance, Oversight, and Error in History *Use the Social Studies Skills taught in this module to answer the question about the reading selection below.*

> Johnson's speaking tour was a disaster. It did little to win votes for the Democratic Party. Johnson even got into arguments with people in the audiences of some of his speaking engagements.

14. Which of the following is an example of chance, oversight, or error that affected history?

   a. Johnson got into arguments with audiences.

   b. The tour was a disaster.

   c. The tour did not win votes.

   d. Johnson spoke for the Democratic Party.

Focus on Writing

15. Write a Job History In this module you read about the changing job scene during Reconstruction. Put yourself in the shoes of a person living then. It could be anyone—a returning soldier, a shopkeeper, a schoolteacher, or a politician. What jobs would that person seek? Why would he or she leave one job for another? Write a brief job history for that person during Reconstruction. Include at least four jobs. Make each job description two to four sentences long. End each one with a sentence or two about why the person left that job. Add one sentence explaining why he or she took the next job. Be sure to include specific historical details.

Linking Past to Present

The United States since 1877

The United States is a very different place today than it was in 1877. The nation is now bigger, more powerful, and more involved in world affairs. It has changed from a nation where most people lived in small towns to one in which most people live in cities, many with populations of more than 1 million people. The nation is also a more democratic place today—more Americans have access to the privileges and responsibilities of citizenship than at any other time in the country's history.

Still, the United States grapples with many challenges that are similar to those faced by the nation in 1877. For example, Americans still debate questions about civil rights, religion, taxes, and the role of government in their lives.

They also worry about the health of the environment, children, and the poor. Americans do not always agree on these issues. But they do believe strongly in their right to debate and to disagree. The freedom to do so—in peaceful and productive ways—is an indication of the fundamental health of the nation.

The United States as a Global Power

After the Civil War, the United States increasingly came into conflict with Native Americans. After the last major battle at Wounded Knee in 1890, American settlers began moving west in even greater numbers. The United States and Spain went to war in 1898. The two countries battled each other in the Caribbean and the Philippines. The Spanish-American War began a period of American expansionism during which U.S. influence spread throughout Latin America and the world.

In the first half of the 20th century, the United States solidified its role as a global power by fighting in World War I and World War II.

Martin Luther King Jr. (center) helped lead the fight for civil rights in the United States.

In 1914 World War I began in Europe. By 1917 the United States had entered the war, and American soldiers fought and died on the battlefields of Europe. That experience forever changed the United States. America had stepped onto the world stage with its military and industrial might. War tore Europe apart again in the 1930s and 1940s during World War II. When Japan attacked the United States at Pearl Harbor in late 1941, the United States entered the global struggle.

The Civil Rights Era

The U.S. victory in World War II had other consequences as well. Millions of World War II veterans returned home ready to start new lives in peacetime. These veterans enrolled in college in record numbers, settled into the nation's cities and new suburbs, and started families.

Soldiers who had fought on the side of democracy abroad also fought for democracy at home. This was especially true of the nation's African American and Mexican American soldiers. Their efforts to seek greater access to the rights of citizenship helped invigorate the civil rights movement. They were joined in these efforts by Americans from all walks of life—people who believed that America worked best when the promises of freedom were open to all.

By the 1960s the push for greater civil rights had become a true social movement in the United States. It was a grassroots effort on the part of ordinary Americans to change both people's attitudes and federal laws. César Chávez, for example, led the fight to win more rights for migrant workers. This movement for greater civil, educational, and political rights among racial and ethnic groups helped spur the women's rights movement of the 1960s and 1970s as well.

Refrigerator-Freezers!

THE FINAL FROST BARRIER!

IT'S HERE!
A FROST-PROOF
FOOD FREEZER!
NO FROST!
NO FROST-LOCKED
FOODS!
NO DEFROSTING!

Following World War II, the U.S. economy boomed, transforming the way middle-class Americans lived. Many bought new homes, cars, and consumer goods like refrigerators and televisions.

Economic Changes and Challenges

The U.S. economy has also changed dramatically since 1877. Changes in technology led to a second industrial revolution in which manufacturing processes became more focused on machinery than on workers. In the 1930s, millions of Americans were affected by the huge economic collapse known as the Great Depression. After World War II, the U.S. economy recovered, and the nation enjoyed a long period of prosperity. Many Americans joined the middle class for the first time, buying homes, televisions and appliances, and cars in record numbers.

Since the 1970s, the U.S. economy has had more ups and downs. Many American companies have moved their factories overseas where wages are lower, causing hardship for many American workers. Technology and housing booms during the 1990s and early 2000s created prosperity. In the late 2000s, however, a severe economic crisis emerged. The banking system nearly collapsed, houses and stocks plummeted in value, and millions of people lost their jobs. Many economists think it may take a decade or more for the U.S. economy to fully recover.

Immigration and Democracy

Immigration has always been important to the United States. Since 1877 this strong tradition of immigration has continued. During the 1900s immigrants came to the United States from all corners of the world—Latin America, Africa, Asia, and Europe. In addition to representing various cultures, they also represented different religious traditions, including Buddhism, Islam, Christianity, and Sikhism. As with the immigrants

Since the end of the Vietnam War in 1975, relations between the United States and Vietnam have slowly improved. In 1995 the U.S. and Vietnam officially established diplomatic relations. Today, about 1.7 million Americans trace their ancestry to Vietnam.

SỐ
KHOA HỌC
VÀ CÔNG NGHỆ

Following terrorist attacks on September 11, 2001, the United States faced a new global challenge—a war against terrorism.

who came before them, they came in search of a brighter future, greater freedom, and a chance to start their lives over again—and they came to become Americans.

Immigrants also came to the United States to enjoy the benefits of democracy. The United States was the world's first modern democracy, and many people around the world today look to America as an example of a democratic, free, and open society. Since 1877 American democracy has grown even stronger. More people participate in the democratic process than ever before, and there is a healthy debate over the many issues the country faces now and will face in the coming years.

The United States Then and Now

In the years since 1877, the United States has faced challenges and experienced triumphs. The threat of terrorism—made clear by the terrorist attacks of September 11, 2001—remains an ongoing challenge. And for many Americans, especially those who toiled to achieve the gains of the civil rights movement, a triumph came with the election of Barack Obama, our nation's first African American president, in 2008.

Challenges and triumphs alike highlight the importance of our nation's founding principles. More than 200 years ago, the Founders insisted that the United States was an experiment—a new nation devoted to the possibility that the ideals of equality and freedom could be supported by democracy, justice, and the rule of law. Today, just as then, this experiment works best when Americans exercise their rights seriously.

The United States today is connected to its past through the enduring principles expressed in its founding documents, the Declaration of Independence and the Constitution. These documents remain as important today as when they were created. They express what Americans stand for and where their nation is going.

References

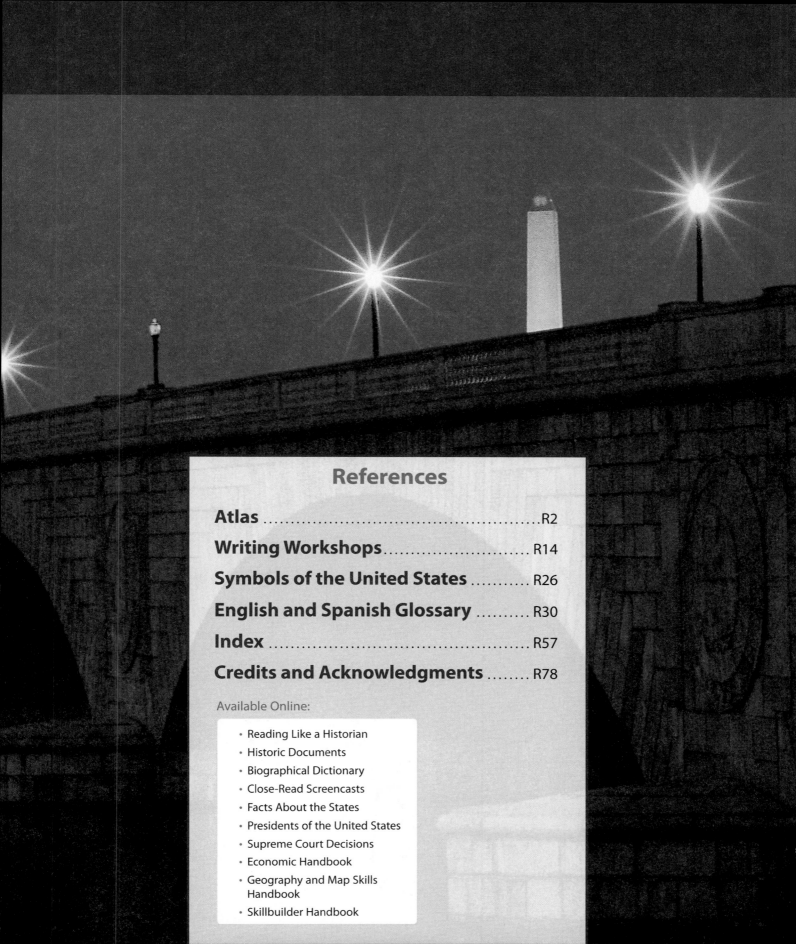

References

Available Online:

- Reading Like a Historian
- Historic Documents
- Biographical Dictionary
- Close-Read Screencasts
- Facts About the States
- Presidents of the United States
- Supreme Court Decisions
- Economic Handbook
- Geography and Map Skills Handbook
- Skillbuilder Handbook

Atlas

United States: Political

To understand the relative locations of Alaska and Hawaii, as well as the vast distances separating them from the rest of the United States, see the world map.

CANADA

MINNESOTA
Duluth
Superior
Marquette
Sault Ste. Marie
Lake Superior

WISCONSIN
Minneapolis
St. Paul
Green Bay
Madison
Milwaukee
Lansing
Grand Rapids
Saginaw
Detroit
Ann Arbor
MICHIGAN
Lake Michigan
Lake Huron

Sioux Falls
Sioux City
IOWA
Cedar Rapids
Davenport
Des Moines
Rockford
Chicago
Gary
South Bend
Fort Wayne
Toledo
Cleveland
Youngstown
Akron
Peoria
Illinois River

MISSOURI
Kansas City
Kansas City
St. Louis
East St. Louis
Springfield
ILLINOIS
INDIANA
Indianapolis
Dayton
Cincinnati
OHIO
Columbus

eka
Jefferson City
Lake of the Ozarks
Springfield
Louisville
Evansville
Frankfort
Lexington
KENTUCKY
Ohio River
Lake Barkley

ita
Keystone Lake
Tulsa
Fayetteville
Kentucky Lake
Nashville
Knoxville
Asheville
TENNESSEE
Chattanooga
Memphis
Mississippi River

ula ke
ARKANSAS
Little Rock
Pine Bluff
Huntsville
Birmingham
Greenville
Winston-Salem
Greensboro
Durham
Raleigh
Charlotte
NORTH CAROLINA
Cape Hatteras

MISSISSIPPI
ALABAMA
Atlanta
Columbus
Macon
GEORGIA
Columbia
SOUTH CAROLINA
Charleston
Vicksburg
Meridian
Jackson
Montgomery
Savannah
Savannah River
Sea Islands

las
co
LOUISIANA
Shreveport
Red River
Toledo Bend Reservoir
Beaumont
Houston
Galveston
Baton Rouge
New Orleans
Biloxi
Mobile
Pensacola
Chandeleur Islands
Tallahassee
Jacksonville
Gainesville
FLORIDA
Chattahoochee R.

MAINE
Augusta
Burlington
Montpelier
Portland
Lake Champlain
VT
NH
Concord
Manchester
Hudson R.
Connecticut R.
Lake Ontario
Rochester
Syracuse
Albany
Springfield
Boston
Worcester
Providence
MA
CT
RI
Cape Cod
Buffalo
Lake Erie
NEW YORK
Hartford
Bridgeport
New Haven
Long Island Sound
Long Island
Jersey City
Yonkers
Newark
New York City
Susquehanna River
PENNSYLVANIA
Allentown
Trenton
Harrisburg
Philadelphia
Camden
Pittsburgh
NJ
Atlantic City
Baltimore
DE
Dover
MD
Washington, D.C.
Annapolis
Delaware Bay
WEST VIRGINIA
Charleston
VIRGINIA
Richmond
Chesapeake Bay
Newport News
Virginia Beach
Norfolk

ATLANTIC OCEAN

Orlando
Tampa
St. Petersburg
Lake Okeechobee
Fort Myers
Fort Lauderdale
Miami
Cape Canaveral
Cape Sable
Florida Keys
Straits of Florida

BAHAMAS

Gulf of Mexico

N
W E
S

☉	National capital
★	State capitals
•	Other cities

0 — 100 — 200 Miles
0 — 100 — 200 Kilometers
Projection: Albers Equal Area

40°N
35°N
25°N
70°W
75°W
80°W
85°W
90°W
95°W

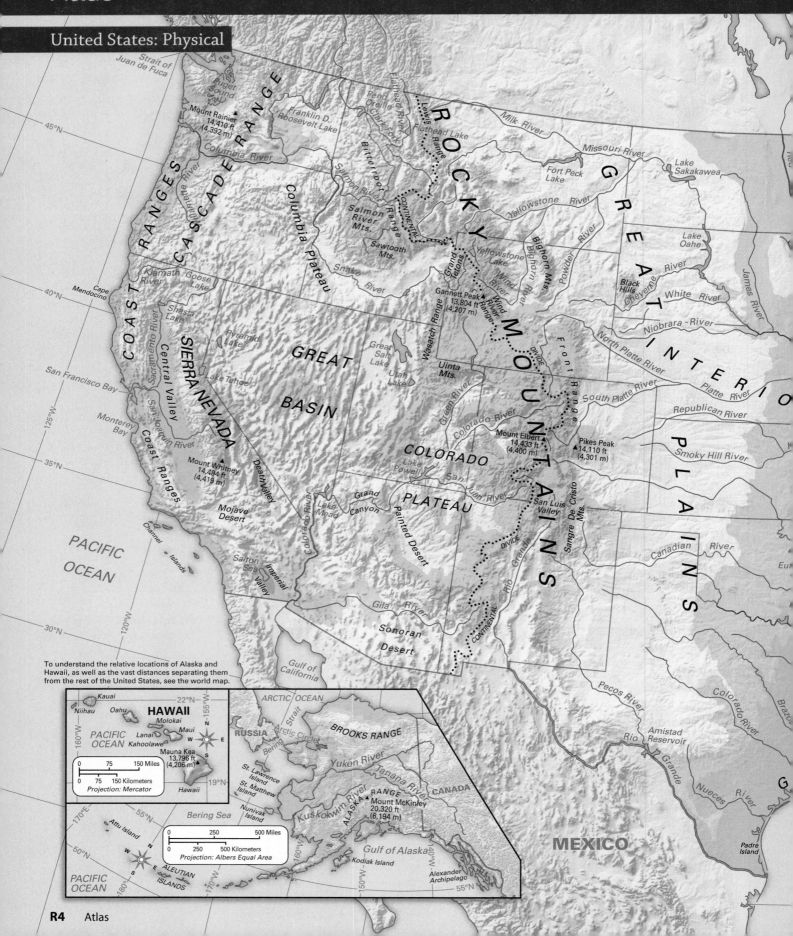

Strait of Juan de Fuca

45°N

Puget Sound

▲ Mount Rainier
14,410 ft
(4,392 m)

COAST RANGES

CASCADE RANGE

Columbia River

Willamette River

Franklin D. Roosevelt Lake

Pend Oreille River

Clark Fork

Bitterroot Range

Flathead Lake

Lewis Range

ROCKY

Milk River

Missouri River

Fort Peck Lake

Lake Sakakawea

GREAT

Cape Mendocino

40°N

Klamath River

Goose Lake

Shasta Lake

Columbia River

Columbia Plateau

Salmon River

Salmon River Mts.

Sawtooth Mts.

Snake River

CONTINENTAL

Grand Tetons

Yellowstone Lake

Yellowstone River

Wind River

Bighorn Mts.

Bighorn River

Powder River

Lake Oahe

Black Hills

Cheyenne River

White River

INTERIOR

San Francisco Bay

Monterey Bay

125°W

120°W

35°N

Pyramid Lake

Lake Tahoe

SIERRA NEVADA

Sacramento River

Central Valley

San Joaquin River

Coast Ranges

Gannett Peak
13,804 ft
(4,207 m)

Wasatch Range

Great Salt Lake

Utah Lake

Uinta Mts.

GREAT

BASIN

Green River

Wind River Range

Mount Elbert
14,433 ft
(4,400 m)

Front Range

DIVIDE

South Platte River

North Platte River

Platte River

Pikes Peak ▲
14,110 ft
(4,301 m)

Niobrara River

Republican River

PLAINS

Smoky Hill River

▲ Mount Whitney
14,494 ft
(4,419 m)

Death Valley

Mojave Desert

Colorado River

Lake Mead

Grand Canyon

Lake Powell

San Juan River

COLORADO

PLATEAU

Painted Desert

Colorado River

DIVIDE

Rio Grande

San Luis Valley

Sangre De Cristo Mts.

Canadian River

PACIFIC

OCEAN

Channel Islands

Salton Sea

Imperial Valley

30°N

Gila River

Sonoran Desert

Gulf of California

CONTINENTAL

Pecos River

Colorado River

Amistad Reservoir

Rio Grande

MEXICO

Nueces River

Padre Island

To understand the relative locations of Alaska and Hawaii, as well as the vast distances separating them from the rest of the United States, see the world map.

Kauai

Niihau

Oahu

22°N

HAWAII

Molokai

Lanai

Maui

PACIFIC OCEAN

Kahoolawe

160°W

155°W

Mauna Kea
13,796 ft
(4,206 m)

Hawaii

19°N

N
W   E
S

0   75   150 Miles
0   75   150 Kilometers
Projection: Mercator

ARCTIC OCEAN

RUSSIA

Arctic Circle

Bering Strait

BROOKS RANGE

N
W   E
S

St. Lawrence Island

St. Matthew Island

Nunivak Island

Yukon River

Kuskokwim River

Tanana River

ALASKA

RANGE

▲ Mount McKinley
20,320 ft
(6,194 m)

CANADA

170°E

Attu Island

55°N

50°N

ALEUTIAN

ISLANDS

180°

170°W

160°W

150°W

Bering Sea

0   250   500 Miles
0   250   500 Kilometers
Projection: Albers Equal Area

Gulf of Alaska

Kodiak Island

Alexander Archipelago

60°W

40°W

55°N

PACIFIC OCEAN

CANADA

Isle
Royale

Mesabi Range

Lake Superior

Minnesota River

Mississippi River

Wisconsin River

Lake Michigan

Lake Huron

St. Lawrence River

St. Lawrence Seaway

Longfellow Mts.

Penobscot River

St. John River

Lake Champlain

Green Mts.

White Mts.

Adirondack Mts.

Hudson R.

Connecticut River

Cape Cod

Lake Ontario

Lake Erie

Catskill Mts.

PLATEAU

Allegheny R.

Susquehanna River

Delaware River

Long Island Sound

Long Island

40°N

Des Moines River

Missouri River

P L A I N S

Illinois River

Wabash River

Scioto River

Ohio River

ALLEGHENY

Monongahela R.

Potomac River

APPALACHIAN MOUNTAINS

Delaware Bay

Chesapeake Bay

ATLANTIC
OCEAN

70°W

Arkansas R.

Lake of the Ozarks

OZARK PLATEAU

Keystone Lake

Lake Barkley

Kentucky Lake

Cumberland River

Cumberland Plateau

Great Smoky Mts.

BLUE RIDGE MOUNTAINS

Kanawha River

James River

Roanoke River

Pamlico Sound

Cape Hatteras

35°N

ula

ake xoma

Ouachita Mts.

White River

Tennessee River

ELEVATION

Feet   Meters

13,120   4,000

6,560   2,000

1,640   500

656   200

(Sea level) 0   0 (Sea level)

Below   Below
sea level   sea level

0   100   200 Miles

0   100   200 Kilometers

Projection: Albers Equal Area

Trinity River

Saline River

Red River

Mississippi River

Pearl River

Tombigbee River

Alabama R.

Coosa River

Chattahoochee River

Oconee River

Savannah River

P I E D M O N T

C O A S T A L   P L A I N

Altamaha River

Sea Islands

Okefenokee Swamp

Toledo Bend Reservoir

G U L F

Chandeleur Islands

Mississippi Delta

FLORIDA PENINSULA

Cape Canaveral

80°W

N
W   E
S

85°W

Gulf of Mexico

Lake Okeechobee

BAHAMAS

25°N

The Everglades

Cape Sable

Straits of Florida

75°W

Florida Keys

95°W   90°W

Atlas

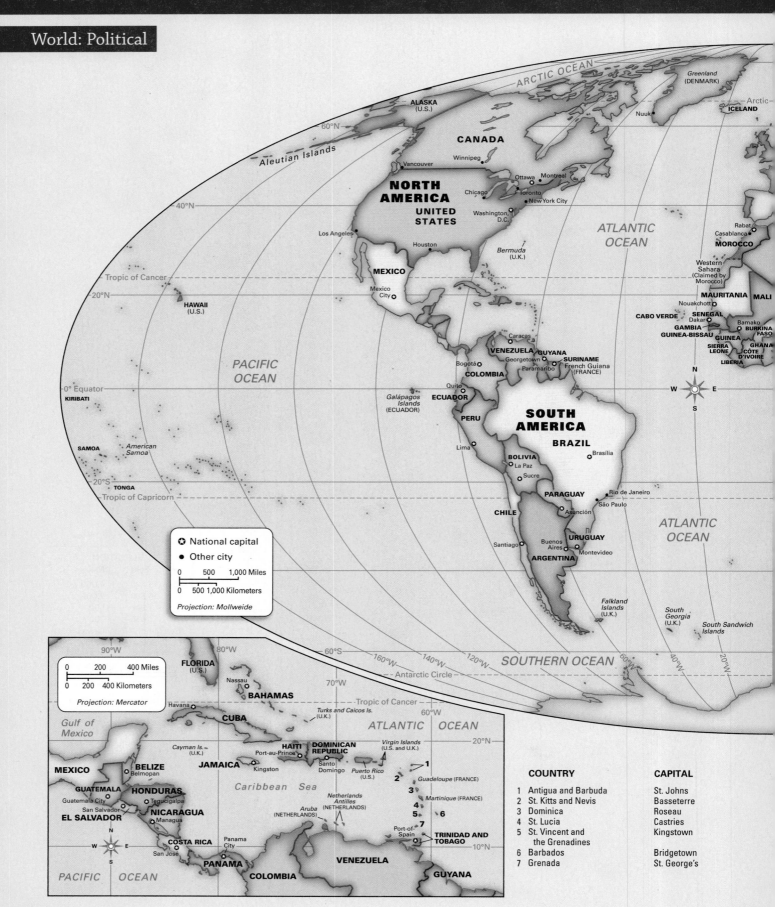

ARCTIC OCEAN

Greenland
(DENMARK)

Arctic
ICELAND

ALASKA
(U.S.)

Nuuk

CANADA

60°N

Vancouver   Winnipeg

Ottawa   Montreal

**NORTH
AMERICA**

Chicago   Toronto

40°N   **UNITED
STATES**   New York City

Washington,
D.C.

**ATLANTIC
OCEAN**

Rabat
Casablanca
MOROCCO

Los Angeles

Houston

Bermuda
(U.K.)

Western
Sahara
(Claimed by
Morocco)

Tropic of Cancer   **MEXICO**

Mexico
City

MAURITANIA   **MALI**

20°N

Nouakchott

HAWAII
(U.S.)

CABO VERDE   **SENEGAL**
Dakar

GAMBIA   Bamako   **BURKINA
FASO**

GUINEA-BISSAU   **GUINEA**   **GHANA**

SIERRA   **CÔTE**
LEONE   **D'IVOIRE**

LIBERIA

Caracas

VENEZUELA   **GUYANA**

**PACIFIC
OCEAN**

Bogotá   Georgetown   **SURINAME**

COLOMBIA   Paramaribo   French Guiana
(FRANCE)

N

0° Equator

Quito   **ECUADOR**

W   E

KIRIBATI

Galápagos
Islands
(ECUADOR)

PERU

S

**SOUTH
AMERICA**

SAMOA   American
Samoa

Lima   **BRAZIL**

BOLIVIA   Brasília

La Paz

20°S   **TONGA**   Sucre

Tropic of Capricorn   Rio de Janeiro

PARAGUAY

**ATLANTIC
OCEAN**

CHILE   São Paulo

Asunción

URUGUAY

Santiago   Buenos   Montevideo
Aires

✪ National capital   **ARGENTINA**

● Other city

0   500   1,000 Miles

Falkland
Islands
(U.K.)

South
Georgia
(U.K.)

South Sandwich
Islands

0   500 1,000 Kilometers

Projection: Mollweide

60°S   160°W   140°W   120°W   **SOUTHERN OCEAN**   60°W   40°W   20°W

Antarctic Circle

90°W   80°W   **FLORIDA**   70°W   Tropic of Cancer   60°W

(U.S.)

0   200   400 Miles

Nassau

0   200   400 Kilometers   **BAHAMAS**   20°N

Projection: Mercator   Havana   Turks and Caicos Is.
(U.K.)   **ATLANTIC   OCEAN**

CUBA

Gulf of
Mexico   Cayman Is.
(U.K.)   **HAITI**   **DOMINICAN
REPUBLIC**   Virgin Islands
(U.S. and U.K.)

Port-au-Prince   Santo   **1**

MEXICO   **BELIZE**   **JAMAICA**   Domingo   Puerto Rico
(U.S.)   **2**   Guadeloupe (FRANCE)

Belmopan   Kingston

GUATEMALA   **HONDURAS**   *Caribbean Sea*   **3**   Martinique (FRANCE)

Guatemala City   Tegucigalpa   Netherlands   **4**

San Salvador   **NICARAGUA**   Antilles   **6**

EL SALVADOR   Managua   Aruba   (NETHERLANDS)   **5**

(NETHERLANDS)   **7**

N   Port-of-
Spain   **TRINIDAD AND
TOBAGO**

W   E   **COSTA RICA**   Panama
City

S   San José   **PANAMA**   10°N

PACIFIC   OCEAN   **VENEZUELA**

COLOMBIA   **GUYANA**

COUNTRY	CAPITAL
1 Antigua and Barbuda	St. Johns
2 St. Kitts and Nevis	Basseterre
3 Dominica	Roseau
4 St. Lucia	Castries
5 St. Vincent and the Grenadines	Kingstown
6 Barbados	Bridgetown
7 Grenada	St. George's

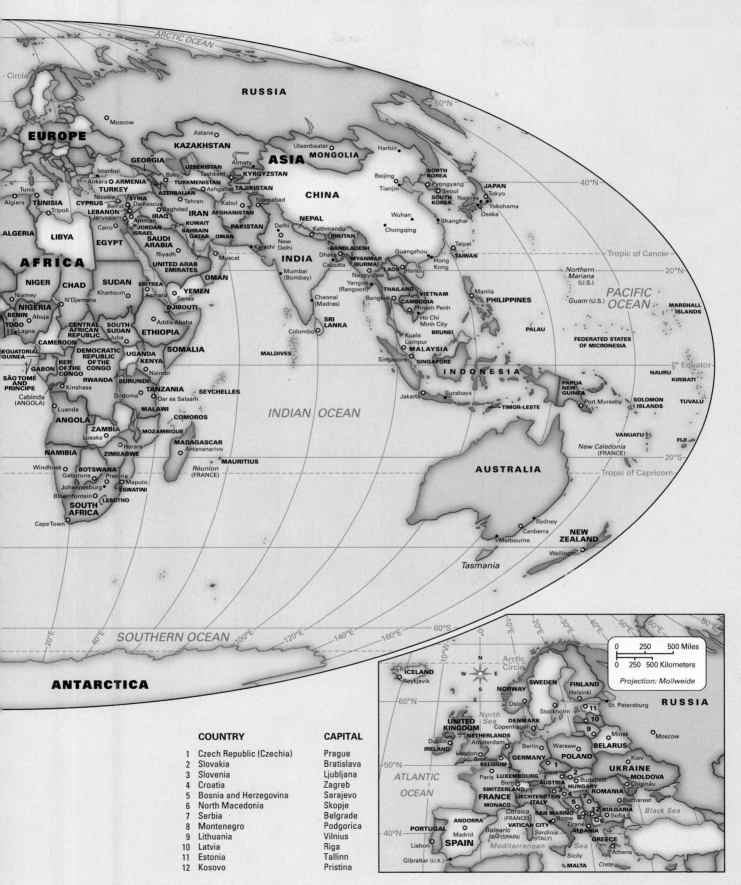

ARCTIC OCEAN

Circle

RUSSIA

EUROPE

Moscow

60°N

KAZAKHSTAN

Astana

Ulaanbaatar

Harbin

GEORGIA

Almaty

ASIA **MONGOLIA**

ARMENIA Baku **UZBEKISTAN** Tashkent **KYRGYZSTAN**

Istanbul

Ankara

TURKEY **TURKMENISTAN** **TAJIKISTAN**

Beijing

NORTH
KOREA

Pyongyang

JAPAN

40°N

Nicosia

AZERBAIJAN

Ashgabat

CHINA

Tianjin

Seoul SOUTH
KOREA

Nagoya

Tokyo

Tunis

CYPRUS **SYRIA**

Tehran

Islamabad

Osaka

Yokohama

Algiers

TUNISIA

LEBANON Beirut Damascus

IRAN **AFGHANISTAN**

Kabul

NEPAL

Wuhan

Shanghai

ISRAEL **IRAQ** Baghdad

Jerusalem Amman **JORDAN** **KUWAIT**

ALGERIA

Cairo

BAHRAIN **QATAR**

PAKISTAN

LIBYA

EGYPT

SAUDI ARABIA

Riyadh

UNITED ARAB EMIRATES

AFRICA

OMAN

Muscat

Delhi

Kathmandu

BHUTAN

Chongqing

Guangzhou

Taipei

Hong Kong

TAIWAN

Tropic of Cancer

Northern Mariana (U.S.)

20°N

Karachi

New Delhi

INDIA

Dhaka

BANGLADESH

Calcutta

MYANMAR (BURMA)

LAOS

Hanoi

Naypyidaw

PACIFIC OCEAN

Guam (U.S.)

NIGER

CHAD

SUDAN

ERITREA

Khartoum

YEMEN

Asmara

Sanaa

Mumbai (Bombay)

Yangon (Rangoon)

THAILAND

Bangkok

VIETNAM

CAMBODIA

Chennai (Madras)

MARSHALL ISLANDS

Niamey

NIGERIA Abuja

BENIN

TOGO

Lagos

DJIBOUTI

Addis Ababa

Colombo

SRI LANKA

Phnom Penh

Ho Chi Minh City

PHILIPPINES

Manila

PALAU

CENTRAL AFRICAN REPUBLIC

SOUTH SUDAN

Juba

ETHIOPIA

BRUNEI

FEDERATED STATES OF MICRONESIA

CAMEROON

MALDIVES

Kuala Lumpur

MALAYSIA

EQUATORIAL GUINEA

DEMOCRATIC REPUBLIC OF THE CONGO

UGANDA

KENYA

Singapore **SINGAPORE**

0° Equator

GABON

REP. OF THE CONGO

RWANDA

Nairobi

INDONESIA

NAURU

KIRIBATI

SÃO TOMÉ AND PRINCIPE

Kinshasa

BURUNDI

Dodoma

SEYCHELLES

Jakarta

Surabaya

PAPUA NEW GUINEA

Cabinda (ANGOLA)

Luanda

TANZANIA Dar es Salaam

Port Moresby

SOLOMON ISLANDS

TUVALU

MALAWI

COMOROS

ANGOLA

INDIAN OCEAN

VANUATU

FIJI

ZAMBIA

MOZAMBIQUE

MADAGASCAR

Lusaka

Antananarivo

New Caledonia (FRANCE)

20°S

Harare

NAMIBIA

ZIMBABWE

MAURITIUS

Windhoek

BOTSWANA

Gaborone Pretoria

Réunion (FRANCE)

AUSTRALIA

Tropic of Capricorn

Johannesburg

Maputo **ESWATINI**

Bloemfontein **LESOTHO**

SOUTH AFRICA

Cape Town

Sydney

Canberra

Melbourne

NEW ZEALAND

Wellington

Tasmania

20°E

40°E

SOUTHERN OCEAN

100°E

120°E

140°E

160°E

60°S

ANTARCTICA

0   250   500 Miles

0   250   500 Kilometers

Projection: Mollweide

ICELAND

Reykjavik

Arctic Circle

SWEDEN

FINLAND

Helsinki

St. Petersburg

RUSSIA

60°N

Oslo

Stockholm

11

NORWAY

10

North Sea

UNITED KINGDOM

DENMARK

Copenhagen

9

Minsk

Moscow

Dublin

NETHERLANDS

Amsterdam

Berlin

Warsaw

BELARUS

IRELAND

London

Brussels

GERMANY

POLAND

Kiev

50°N

Paris

BELGIUM

LUXEMBOURG

1

Vienna

2

Budapest

UKRAINE

MOLDOVA

Chişinău

ATLANTIC OCEAN

Bern

SWITZERLAND

AUSTRIA

HUNGARY

ROMANIA

FRANCE

LIECHTENSTEIN

3 **4**

7

Bucharest

MONACO

ITALY

5

12

BULGARIA

SAN MARINO

Rome

8

Sofia

VATICAN CITY

Corsica (FRANCE)

6

Tirane

ALBANIA

ANDORRA

Sardinia (ITALY)

GREECE

PORTUGAL

Madrid

Balearic Is. (SPAIN)

Black Sea

40°N

Lisbon

SPAIN

Athens

Gibraltar (U.K.)

Mediterranean

Sicily

Sea

MALTA

Crete

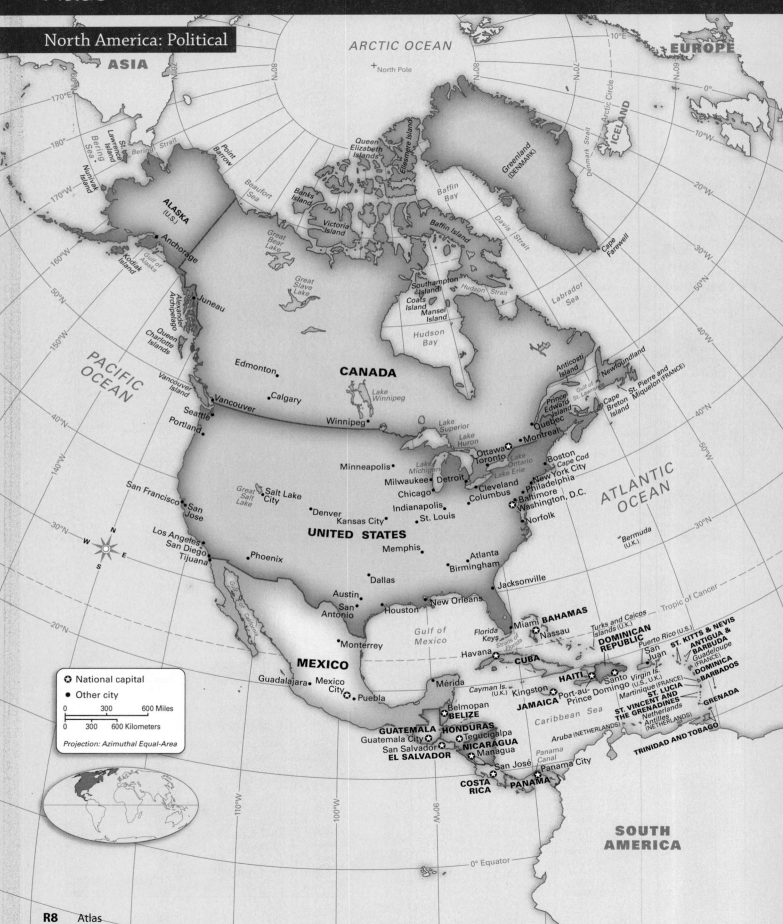

North America: Political

ASIA

ARCTIC OCEAN

+ North Pole

EUROPE

ICELAND

Bering Strait

St. Lawrence Island

Bering Sea

Nunivak Island

Point Barrow

Beaufort Sea

Banks Island

Queen Elizabeth Islands

Ellesmere Island

Greenland (DENMARK)

Denmark Strait

Arctic Circle

ALASKA (U.S.)

Anchorage

Kodiak Island

Gulf of Alaska

Great Bear Lake

Victoria Island

Baffin Bay

Davis Strait

Cape Farewell

Juneau

Alexander Archipelago

Great Slave Lake

Baffin Island

Southampton Island

Hudson Strait

Labrador Sea

Queen Charlotte Islands

Coats Island

Mansel Island

Hudson Bay

PACIFIC OCEAN

Vancouver Island

Edmonton

CANADA

Lake Winnipeg

Anticosti Island

Newfoundland

St. Pierre and Miquelon (FRANCE)

Seattle

Vancouver

Calgary

Winnipeg

Lake Superior

Prince Edward Island

Gulf of St. Lawrence

Cape Breton Island

Portland

Lake Huron

Lake Michigan

Quebec

Montreal

San Francisco

Minneapolis

Milwaukee

Detroit

Lake Ontario

Lake Erie

Ottawa

Toronto

Boston

Cape Cod

New York City

ATLANTIC OCEAN

San Jose

Salt Lake City

Great Salt Lake

Chicago

Cleveland

Columbus

Philadelphia

Baltimore

Washington, D.C.

Denver

Indianapolis

St. Louis

Norfolk

Los Angeles

San Diego

Kansas City

UNITED STATES

Tijuana

Phoenix

Memphis

Atlanta

Bermuda (U.K.)

Dallas

Birmingham

Austin

San Antonio

Houston

New Orleans

Jacksonville

Tropic of Cancer

Monterrey

Gulf of Mexico

Miami

BAHAMAS

Turks and Caicos Islands (U.K.)

Gulf of California

Florida Keys

Nassau

DOMINICAN REPUBLIC

Puerto Rico (U.S.)

ST. KITTS & NEVIS

MEXICO

Havana

Straits of Florida

CUBA

San Juan

ANTIGUA & BARBUDA

Guadeloupe (FRANCE)

Guadalajara

Mexico City

Mérida

Cayman Is. (U.K.)

Kingston

HAITI

Port-au-Prince

Santo Domingo

Virgin Is. (U.S., U.K.)

DOMINICA

Martinique (FRANCE)

BARBADOS

Puebla

JAMAICA

ST. LUCIA

Belmopan

Caribbean Sea

ST. VINCENT AND THE GRENADINES

Netherlands Antilles (NETHERLANDS)

GRENADA

BELIZE

GUATEMALA

HONDURAS

Tegucigalpa

Guatemala City

NICARAGUA

Aruba (NETHERLANDS)

San Salvador

Managua

Panama Canal

TRINIDAD AND TOBAGO

EL SALVADOR

San José

Panama City

COSTA RICA

PANAMA

SOUTH AMERICA

0° Equator

National capital
Other city

0   300   600 Miles
0   300   600 Kilometers

Projection: Azimuthal Equal-Area

South America: Political

CENTRAL AMERICA

Caribbean Sea

Barranquilla
Cartagena

Caracas

Lake Maracaibo

VENEZUELA

Georgetown
Paramaribo

GUYANA

Cayenne

SURINAME

French Guiana (FRANCE)

ATLANTIC OCEAN

Medellín

Bogotá

COLOMBIA

Cali

Malpelo Island (COLOMBIA)

Quito

ECUADOR

Guayaquil

0° Equator

Galápagos Islands (ECUADOR)

Belém

PERU

Trujillo

Recife

Callao Lima

PACIFIC OCEAN

Lake Titicaca

Arequipa

La Paz

Lake Poopó

BOLIVIA

Sucre

BRAZIL

Brasília

Salvador

Belo Horizonte

Campinas
São Paulo

Rio de Janeiro

Tropic of Capricorn

PARAGUAY

Asunción

Curitiba

Tropic of Capricorn

San Ambrosio Island (CHILE)

San Félix Island (CHILE)

CHILE

Pôrto Alegre

Córdoba

Juan Fernández Islands (CHILE)

Valparaíso
Santiago

Rosario

URUGUAY

Buenos Aires

Montevideo

ATLANTIC OCEAN

ARGENTINA

○✚ National capital
● Other city

| 0 | 250 | 500 Miles |
| 0 | 250 | 500 Kilometers |

Projection: Azimuthal Equal-Area

Strait of Magellan

Falkland Islands (U.K.)

Tierra del Fuego

South Georgia Island (U.K.)

Europe: Political

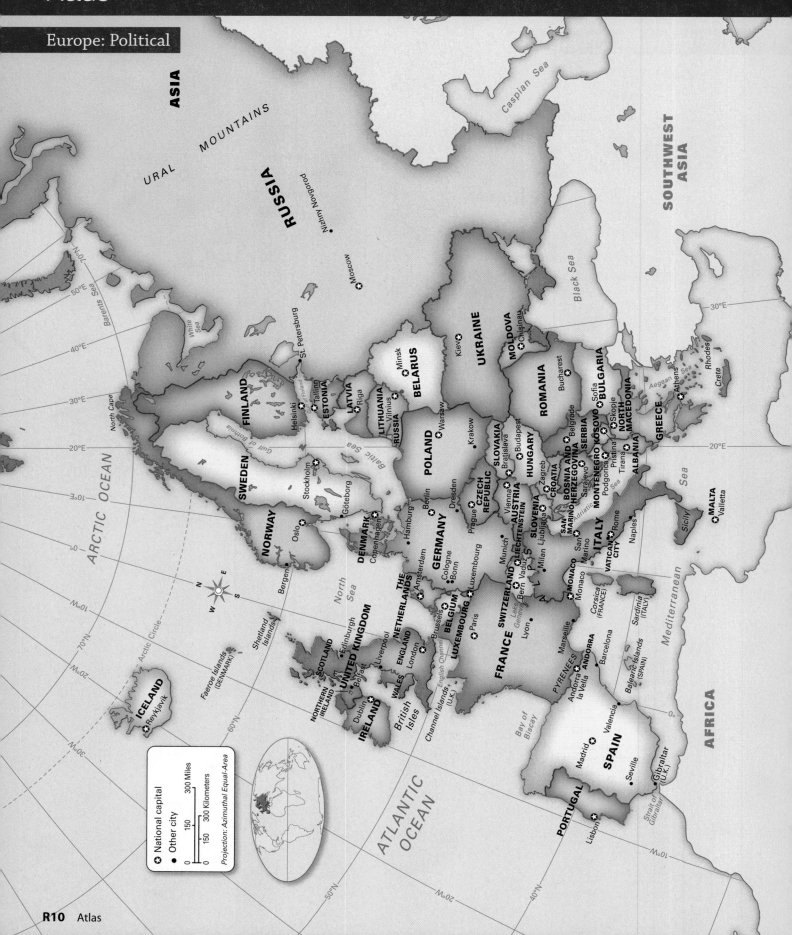

ASIA

URAL MOUNTAINS

ASIA

RUSSIA

Nizhny Novgorod •

SOUTHWEST ASIA

Caspian Sea

Barents Sea

North Cape

70°N

50°E

40°E

White Sea

Moscow ✪

St. Petersburg •

Black Sea

30°E

ARCTIC OCEAN

North Pole

30°E

FINLAND

Helsinki •

Gulf of Bothnia

Gulf of Finland

Tallinn • ESTONIA

Riga • LATVIA

Vilnius • LITHUANIA

RUSSIA

Minsk ✪ BELARUS

Kiev ✪

UKRAINE

MOLDOVA Chişinău ✪

Bucharest •

ROMANIA

BULGARIA Sofia ✪

Aegean Sea

Rhodes

20°E

30°E

20°E

SWEDEN

Stockholm •

Göteborg •

Baltic Sea

POLAND

Warsaw ✪

Krakow •

SLOVAKIA Bratislava •

Budapest •

HUNGARY

Belgrade •

CROATIA Zagreb •

SERBIA

BOSNIA AND HERZEGOVINA Sarajevo •

MONTENEGRO

KOSOVO Priština •

NORTH MACEDONIA Skopje ✪

ALBANIA Tirana ✪

GREECE

Athens ✪

Crete

NORWAY

Oslo ✪

Bergen •

DENMARK Copenhagen ✪

Hamburg •

Berlin ✪

Dresden •

GERMANY

Prague • CZECH REPUBLIC

Vienna • AUSTRIA

SLOVENIA Ljubljana •

SAN MARINO

San Marino

ITALY

Rome ✪

Naples •

Podgorica •

Adriatic Sea

Sicily

MALTA Valletta ✪

North Sea

Amsterdam ✪

THE NETHERLANDS

Cologne • Bonn •

Luxembourg ✪

Munich •

LIECHTENSTEIN Vaduz •

SWITZERLAND Bern •

Lake Geneva

Milan •

MONACO Monaco •

Marino

VATICAN CITY

Mediterranean Sea

Corsica (FRANCE)

Sardinia (ITALY)

ICELAND

Reykjavik ✪

Faeroe Islands (DENMARK)

Shetland Islands

SCOTLAND

Edinburgh •

UNITED KINGDOM

Belfast •

NORTHERN IRELAND

Dublin ✪ IRELAND

Liverpool •

ENGLAND

WALES

London ✪

English Channel

Channel Islands (U.K.)

British Isles

BELGIUM

Brussels ✪

LUXEMBOURG

Paris ✪

FRANCE

Lyon •

Marseille •

PYRENEES

Andorra la Vella • ANDORRA

Barcelona •

Balearic Islands (SPAIN)

Bay of Biscay

SPAIN

Madrid ✪

Valencia •

Seville •

Gibraltar (U.K.)

Strait of Gibraltar

AFRICA

PORTUGAL

Lisbon •

ATLANTIC OCEAN

70°N

60°N

50°N

40°N

10°W

20°W

30°W

20°W

10°W

0°

10°E

10°E

20°W

Arctic Circle

✪ National capital

• Other city

300 Miles

150

0

300 Kilometers

150

0

Projection: Azimuthal Equal-Area

Atlas

Asia: Political

National capitals ✪
Other cities •

750 Miles
750 Kilometers

Projection: Two-Point Equidistant

RUSSIA

EUROPE

AFRICA

AUSTRALIA

CHINA

INDIA

MONGOLIA

KAZAKHSTAN

RUSSIA

North Pole

Aleutian Islands

Bering Sea

Sea of Okhotsk

Sakhalin Island

Kuril Islands (RUSSIA)

Vladivostok

JAPAN

Tokyo
Yokohama
Sapporo
Osaka
Kyoto
Hiroshima

NORTH KOREA
SOUTH KOREA

Seoul
Pusan
Pyongyang

Dalian
Qingdao

Yellow Sea

East China Sea

Shanghai
Nanjing
Nagasaki

Ryukyu Islands (JAPAN)

TAIWAN
Taipei

Harbin
Fushun
Beijing
Wuhan
Chongqing
Chengdu

Guangzhou
Macao
Hong Kong
Hainan (CHINA)

South China Sea

PHILIPPINES
Manila

PACIFIC OCEAN

New Guinea

TIMOR-LESTE
Dili

INDONESIA

Celebes Sea

Ujung Pandang

Surabaya

Java Sea
Jakarta
Bandung

Medan

BRUNEI
Bandar Seri Begawan

MALAYSIA
Kuala Lumpur
SINGAPORE
Singapore

Arafura Sea

VIETNAM
Hanoi
Ho Chi Minh City

LAOS
Vientiane

CAMBODIA
Phnom Penh

THAILAND
Bangkok

Gulf of Thailand

MYANMAR (BURMA)
Naypyidaw
Yangon (Rangoon)

Andaman Islands (INDIA)

Andaman Sea

Nicobar Islands (INDIA)

Bay of Bengal

BANGLADESH
Dhaka

BHUTAN
Thimphu

NEPAL
Kathmandu

Kolkata (Calcutta)

Chennai (Madras)

SRI LANKA
Colombo

MALDIVES
Male

INDIAN OCEAN

Lakshadweep Islands (INDIA)

Bangalore

Mumbai (Bombay)

Ahmadabad

Arabian Sea

Karachi

PAKISTAN
Islamabad
Lahore
Delhi
New Delhi
Jaipur

AFGHANISTAN
Kabul

TAJIKISTAN
Dushanbe

KYRGYZSTAN
Bishkek

UZBEKISTAN
Tashkent

TURKMENISTAN
Ashgabat

Almaty

Astana

Aral Sea

Lake Balkhash

Novosibirsk

Omsk

Yekaterinburg
Chelyabinsk

URAL MOUNTAINS

Moscow

Arctic Circle

Barents Sea

Kara Sea

Yakutsk

Irkutsk

Lake Baykal

Ulaanbaatar

Caspian Sea

GEORGIA
Tbilisi

ARMENIA
Yerevan

AZERBAIJAN
Baku

IRAN
Tehran
Shiraz

TURKEY
Ankara
Istanbul
Izmir

Black Sea

CYPRUS
Nicosia

LEBANON
Beirut

ISRAEL
Tel Aviv
Jerusalem

SYRIA
Damascus

JORDAN
Amman

IRAQ
Baghdad
Mosul
Basra

KUWAIT
Kuwait City

SAUDI ARABIA
Riyadh
Mecca
Jidda

BAHRAIN
Manama

QATAR
Doha

UNITED ARAB EMIRATES
Abu Dhabi

OMAN
Masqat (Muscat)

YEMEN
Sanaa

Socotra (YEMEN)

Gulf of Aden

Red Sea

Persian Gulf

Mediterranean Sea

Tropic of Cancer

Equator

Atlas **R11**

Africa: Political

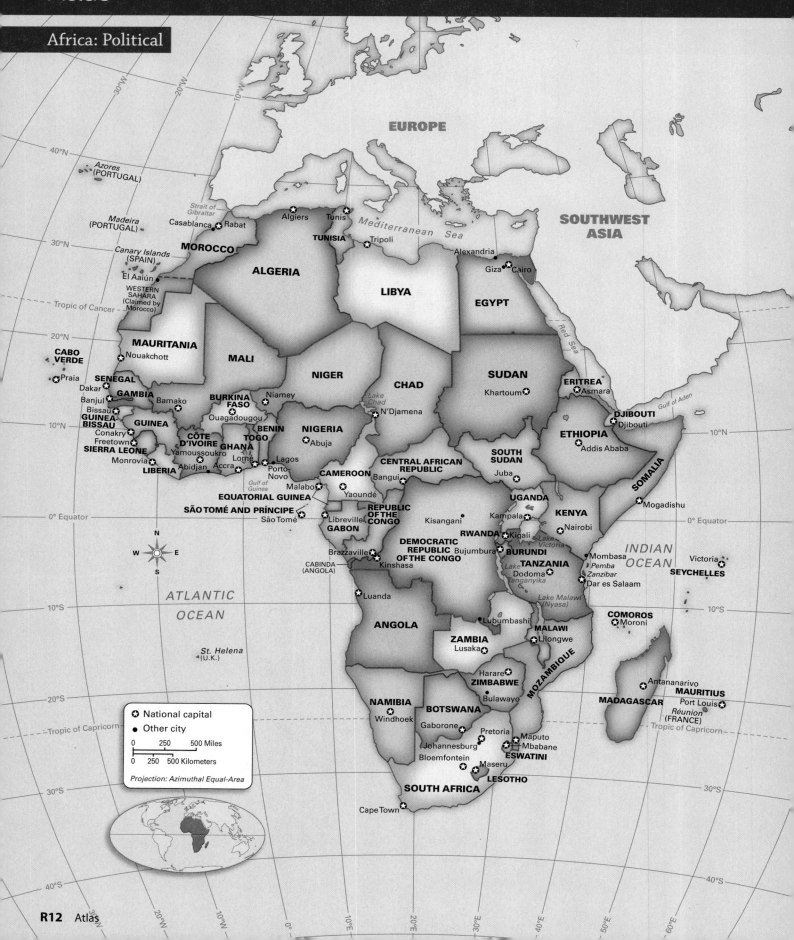

EUROPE

SOUTHWEST ASIA

Azores (PORTUGAL)

Madeira (PORTUGAL)

Strait of Gibraltar

Casablanca · Rabat

Algiers · Tunis

Mediterranean Sea

MOROCCO

TUNISIA

Tripoli

Canary Islands (SPAIN)

El Aaiún

Tropic of Cancer

WESTERN SAHARA (Claimed by Morocco)

ALGERIA

LIBYA

EGYPT

Alexandria

Giza · Cairo

Red Sea

MAURITANIA

CABO VERDE

Nouakchott

MALI

NIGER

CHAD

SUDAN

ERITREA

Asmara

Gulf of Aden

Praia

SENEGAL

Dakar

GAMBIA

Banjul

Bamako

Niamey

Khartoum

DJIBOUTI

Djibouti

Bissau

GUINEA-BISSAU

BURKINA FASO

Ouagadougou

Lake Chad

N'Djamena

GUINEA

Conakry

Freetown

SIERRA LEONE

Monrovia

LIBERIA

CÔTE D'IVOIRE

Yamoussoukro

Abidjan

GHANA

Accra

BENIN

TOGO

Lomé

NIGERIA

Abuja

Lagos

Porto-Novo

Malabo

CAMEROON

Bangui

CENTRAL AFRICAN REPUBLIC

SOUTH SUDAN

Juba

ETHIOPIA

Addis Ababa

SOMALIA

Mogadishu

EQUATORIAL GUINEA

Yaoundé

Gulf of Guinea

SÃO TOMÉ AND PRÍNCIPE

São Tomé

Libreville

GABON

REPUBLIC OF THE CONGO

Kisangani

UGANDA

Kampala

KENYA

Nairobi

0° Equator

INDIAN OCEAN

Victoria

SEYCHELLES

Brazzaville

DEMOCRATIC REPUBLIC OF THE CONGO

RWANDA

Kigali

BURUNDI

Bujumbura

Lake Victoria

CABINDA (ANGOLA)

Kinshasa

TANZANIA

Dodoma

Mombasa

Pemba

Zanzibar

Dar es Salaam

Lake Tanganyika

ATLANTIC OCEAN

Luanda

Lubumbashi

Lake Malawi (Nyasa)

COMOROS

Moroni

St. Helena (U.K.)

ANGOLA

ZAMBIA

Lusaka

MALAWI

Lilongwe

Antananarivo

MAURITIUS

Harare

ZIMBABWE

MOZAMBIQUE

Bulawayo

MADAGASCAR

Port Louis

Réunion (FRANCE)

Tropic of Capricorn

NAMIBIA

Windhoek

BOTSWANA

Gaborone

Pretoria

Maputo

Mbabane

ESWATINI

Johannesburg

Bloemfontein

Maseru

LESOTHO

SOUTH AFRICA

Cape Town

Legend
- ⊛ National capital
- • Other city

0 — 250 — 500 Miles

0 — 250 — 500 Kilometers

Projection: Azimuthal Equal-Area

The Pacific: Political

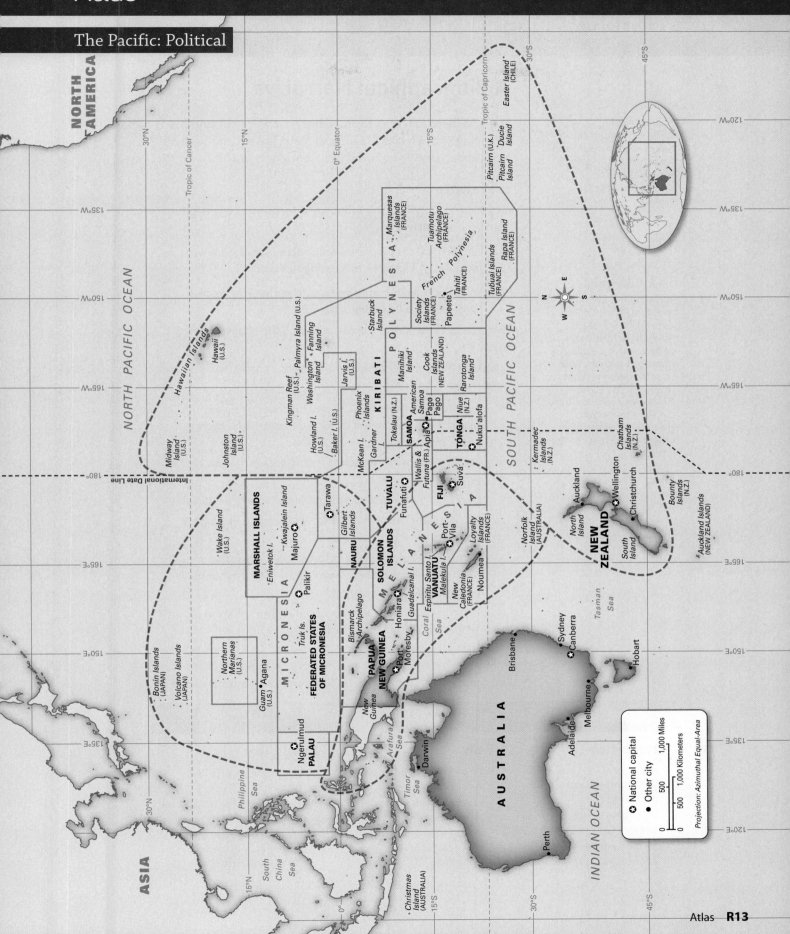

NORTH AMERICA

NORTH PACIFIC OCEAN

ASIA

Tropic of Cancer

Tropic of Capricorn

0° Equator

International Date Line

Midway Island (U.S.)

Johnston Island (U.S.)

Hawaiian Islands

Hawaii (U.S.)

Palmyra Island (U.S.)

Fanning Island

Kingman Reef (U.S.)

Washington Island

Jarvis I. (U.S.)

Howland I. (U.S.)

Baker I. (U.S.)

McKean I.

Phoenix Islands

Gardner

KIRIBATI

Starbuck Island

Manihiki Island

Tokelau (N.Z.)

Marquesas Islands (FRANCE)

Tuamotu Archipelago (FRANCE)

Rapa Island (FRANCE)

French Polynesia

Society Islands (FRANCE)

Tahiti (FRANCE)

Papeete

Tubuai Islands (FRANCE)

Easter Island (CHILE)

Ducie Island

Pitcairn (U.K.)

Pitcairn Island (U.K.)

POLYNESIA

Cook Islands (NEW ZEALAND)

Rarotonga Island

American Samoa

Pago Pago

SAMOA

Apia

Niue (N.Z.)

Nuku'alofa

TONGA

Kermadec Islands (N.Z.)

SOUTH PACIFIC OCEAN

Chatham Islands (N.Z.)

Wallis & Futuna (FR.)

Suva

FIJI

TUVALU

Funafuti

Wake Island (U.S.)

MARSHALL ISLANDS

Eniwetok I.

Kwajalein Island

Majuro

Palikir

Tarawa

Gilbert Islands

NAURU

SOLOMON ISLANDS

Honiara

Guadalcanal I.

MELANESIA

VANUATU

Espiritu Santo I.

Malekula I.

Port-Vila

Loyalty Islands (FRANCE)

New Caledonia (FRANCE)

Noumea

Norfolk Island (AUSTRALIA)

Auckland

North Island

Wellington

Christchurch

South Island

NEW ZEALAND

Bounty Islands (N.Z.)

Auckland Islands (NEW ZEALAND)

MICRONESIA

Truk Is.

FEDERATED STATES OF MICRONESIA

Bismarck Archipelago

PAPUA NEW GUINEA

Port Moresby

New Guinea

Bonin Islands (JAPAN)

Volcano Islands (JAPAN)

Northern Marianas (U.S.)

Guam (U.S.)

Agana

Ngerulmud

PALAU

Coral Sea

Arafura Sea

Timor Sea

Tasman Sea

Darwin

AUSTRALIA

Brisbane

Sydney

Canberra

Melbourne

Hobart

Adelaide

Perth

INDIAN OCEAN

Philippine Sea

South China Sea

Christmas Island (AUSTRALIA)

N E W

Legend:
- ✪ National capital
- ● Other city

1,000 Miles
1,000 Kilometers
500

Projection: Azimuthal Equal-Area

A Biographical Narrative

ASSIGNMENT
Write a biographical narrative about a person who lived in the early Americas before or during the colonial period.

TIP: ASK QUESTIONS
Try using the *5W-How?* questions (*Who? What? When? Where? Why? How?*) to help you think of descriptive details. Ask questions such as, **Who** was this person? **What** was he or she doing? Exactly **where** and **when** did the event occur? **How** did the person or other people react to the event?

You have been listening to and telling narratives all your life. A biographical narrative, a form of historical writing, is a true story about an event or brief period in a person's life.

1. Prewrite

Get Started Consider the following questions as you begin to plan your narrative:

> *Think of all the people you read about in the first few modules. Which ones interested you most?*

> *What particular events and situations in these people's lives seem most exciting or significant?*

Pick one of these events or situations as the subject of your narrative.

Create an Interesting Narrative Make your narrative lively and interesting by including

physical descriptions *of people, places, and things, using details that appeal to the five senses (sight, hearing, touch, smell, taste).*

specific actions *that relate directly to the story you are telling.*

dialogue *between the people involved or direct quotations.*

background information *about the place, customs, and setting.*

all relevant details and information *needed to relate the events of the story and how they affected the person (and perhaps history).*

Organize the events in your narrative in chronological order, the order in which they occurred.

2. Write

You can use this framework to help you draft your narrative.

A WRITER'S FRAMEWORK

Introduction	**Body**	**Conclusion**
• Grab your reader's attention with a striking detail or bit of dialogue.	• Present actions and details in the order in which they occurred.	• Wrap up the action of the narrative.
• Introduce the historical person and setting, using specific details.	• Connect actions with transition words like *first, then, next,* and *finally.*	• Tell how the person was affected by what happened.
• Set the scene by telling how the event or situation began.	• Provide specific details to make the person and the situation come alive.	• Explain how the event or situation was important in the person's life and how it affected history.

---

3. Evaluate and Revise

Evaluate Read through your completed draft to make sure your narrative is complete, coherent, and clear. Then look for ways to improve it.

EVALUATION QUESTIONS FOR A BIOGRAPHICAL NARRATIVE

- Does your introduction grab the reader's attention? Do you introduce the historical person and tell how the event or situation began?
- Do you include details to make the person, place, and event seem real?

- Are the actions in the story in the order in which they occurred? Have you included all of the actions and details a reader would need to understand what happened?
- Does the conclusion tell how the event or situation affected the person and history?

Revise When you revise your narrative, you may need to add transition words. Transition words help you link ideas between sentences and paragraphs. Notice the words in bold in the following sentences.

> **After** Cabeza de Vaca and the other adventurers left the beach and started inland, they separated into different groups. **Later**, Cabeza de Vaca heard that many of the others had died. **Still**, he never lost faith that he would reach his fellow Spaniards in Mexico.

4. Proofread and Publish

Proofread Throughout your narrative, you used transition words to link events. Make sure that you have spelled the words correctly and have not confused them with other words. For example, be sure to use two *l*'s in *finally* and not to mistake the transition word *then* for the comparative word *than*.

Publish One good way to share your biographical narrative is to exchange it with one or more classmates who have written about the same person you have. After reading each other's narratives, you can compare and contrast them. How are your stories similar? How do they differ?

5. Practice and Apply

Use the steps and strategies outlined in this workshop to write your biographical narrative.

TIP: SHOW SEQUENCE
A clear sense of the sequence of events is important in any narrative. Here is a list of words that show those relationships.

after	next
before	now
finally	soon
first	still
(second, etc.)	then
last	when
later	while

Explaining a Political Process

ASSIGNMENT
Write a paper explaining how the federal system balances power among the legislative, executive, and judicial branches of government.

How do you register to vote? What is the difference between a civil court and a federal court? When we want to know about a process or system of our government, we often turn to written explanations.

1. Prewrite

Consider Purpose and Audience   In this assignment, you will be writing for an audience of middle school students. You'll need to

- identify questions they might have about the process or system.
- identify factors or details that might confuse them.

As you plan your paper, keep your audience in mind.

Collect and Organize the Information The big idea, or thesis, of your explanation will be that the federal system balances the power among the three branches of government. To collect information about each branch and its powers, you can use a chart like the one shown here. Be sure to note the relationships among the parts. Also, note the important characteristics of each part. When you have completed the chart, you will have the basic organization of your paper.

TIP: USE A GRAPHIC ORGANIZER
A chart like the following can help you organize the body of your explanation.

Legislative	Executive	Judicial

2. Write

You can use this framework to help you write your first draft.

A WRITER'S FRAMEWORK

Introduction
- State the big idea of your paper.
- Explain briefly why this topic is important to the reader.

Body
- Identify the important characteristics of each part of the process or system.
- Explain any relationships between or among the parts.
- Define terms your readers might not know.
- Where appropriate, include graphics to illustrate your explanation.

Conclusion
- Restate your big idea in different words.
- Summarize your main points.

3. Evaluate and Revise

Evaluate Clear, straightforward language is important when explaining how things work. Use the following questions to discover ways to improve your paper.

EVALUATION QUESTIONS FOR AN EXPLANATION OF A PROCESS OR SYSTEM	
• Does your big-idea statement accurately reflect your explanation of the process or system? • Do you discuss each part of the process or system in logical order? • Do you include details and information to explain each part of the process or system?	• If you used bulleted or numbered lists, are the items parallel— that is, do they have the same grammatical forms or structures? • Does your conclusion restate your big idea and explain the importance of your topic?

TIP: USE BULLETED LISTS
The items in a bulleted list should be in the same grammatical forms or structures.

Not the same:
Duties of the judicial branch include

- interpret laws.
- overseeing lower courts.

The same:
Duties of the judicial branch include

- interpreting laws.
- overseeing lower courts.

Revise Sometimes a complex explanation sounds even more complex when you try to explain it in a paragraph. In those cases, a bulleted list of facts or examples may make it easier for your readers to understand the information you are presenting. As you revise your paper, consider whether you have any information you should put in a bulleted list.

4. Proofread and Publish

Proofread If you use special formatting in your paper, it is important to make sure that it is consistent. Here are some things to check:

- If you have used boldface or italic type, have you always used it in the same way—for important information, for a heading, for a technical term?
- If you have used a list of items, have you consistently used numbers or bullets?

Publish Since you are writing this paper for students, you might find a student in the sixth or seventh grade to read it. Find out whether your explanation seems clear and interesting.

5. Practice and Apply

Use the steps and strategies outlined in this workshop to write your explanation of a process or system.

Writing Workshop 3

Cause and Effect in History

ASSIGNMENT
Write a paper explaining the causes or the effects of the War of 1812.

Historians try to make sense of an event by considering why the event happened and what resulted from it. Exploring causes and effects can provide a deeper understanding of historical events and how they are connected to one another.

1. Prewrite

Identify Causes and Effects A **cause** is an action or a situation that makes something else happen. What happens is called an **effect**. For example, if you stay up too late watching TV (cause), you might find yourself nodding off in class (effect). Often an event or situation will have several causes as well as several effects. In those cases, we may look at the order in which the causes or effects occurred, or we may look at their relative importance.

TIP: USE A GRAPHIC ORGANIZER
Use a graphic organizer like this to organize your research.

Cause 1
↓
Cause 2
↓
Event or situation
↓
Effect
↓
Effect

Research and Organize For this paper, you will write about the causes or the effects of the event—the War of 1812. Gather information from the module in this textbook, an encyclopedia, or another source recommended by your teacher.

- Look for two or three reasons (causes) why the War of 1812 (the event or situation) occurred.
- At the same time, consider the war as a cause. Look for two or three effects of the war.

Then choose whether to write about the causes or the effects.

2. Write

You can use this framework to help you write your first draft.

A WRITER'S FRAMEWORK

Introduction

- Begin with a quote or interesting fact about the event.
- Identify the event you will discuss. [The War of 1812]
- Identify whether you will be discussing the causes or the effects.

Body

- Present the causes or effects in chronological (time) order or order of importance.
- Explain each cause or effect in its own paragraph, providing support with facts and examples.

Conclusion

- Summarize your ideas about the causes or the effects of the event [the war].

3. Evaluate and Revise

Evaluate Drawing clear, logical connections is the key to writing about causes and effects. Use these questions to evaluate and revise your paper.

> ### EVALUATION QUESTIONS FOR AN EXPLANATION OF CAUSES OR EFFECTS
>
> - Does your introduction begin with an interesting quotation or fact?
> - Does the introduction identify the event [the war] and the causes or events to be discussed?
> - Is each cause or effect explained in its own paragraph?
> - Do facts and examples help to explain each cause or effect and connect it to the event [the war]?
> - Are the causes or effects organized clearly—by chronological order or order of importance?
> - Does the conclusion summarize the causes or effects and their importance?

TIP: RECOGNIZE FALSE CAUSE-AND-EFFECT
In planning your essay, be careful to avoid false cause-and-effect relationships. The fact that one thing happened before or after another doesn't mean one caused the other. For example, the fact that James Madison was elected in 1808, just four years before the War of 1812, does not mean his election caused the War of 1812.

Revise Make sure the connections between the war and its causes or effects are clear by sharing your paper with a classmate. If your classmate is confused, add background information. If he or she disagrees with your conclusions, add evidence or rethink your reasoning.

4. Proofread and Publish

Proofread Some transitional words and phrases need to be set off from the sentence with commas. Here are two examples:

TIP: USE TRANSITIONS
Here are some transitional words and phrases that show cause or effect relationships: *because, as a result, therefore, for, since, so, consequently, for this reason.*

- The Louisiana Territory was a huge region of land. *As a result*, the size of the United States almost doubled when the land was purchased.

- Jefferson wanted to know more about the land he had purchased. *Therefore*, he asked Congress to fund an expedition.

Check your paper to see if you need to add commas after or around any transitional words or phrases.

Publish Get together with a classmate and share causes and/or effects. Compare your lists to see whether you have identified different causes or effects. Share your findings with your class.

5. Practice and Apply

Use the steps and strategies outlined in this workshop to write your explanation of the causes or effects of the War of 1812.

Comparing People or Events

ASSIGNMENT
Write a paper comparing and contrasting one of the following: (1) America before and after the Industrial Revolution, (2) the lives of free blacks in the North with the lives of free blacks in the South.

TIP: USE GRAPHIC ORGANIZERS
Venn diagrams help you focus on similarities and differences. Write details the subjects have in common in the overlapping area. Write details that make each subject different in the sections that do not overlap.

Differences (Similarities) Differences

One way to learn more about historical figures or events is to compare and contrast them. By studying how the figures or events are alike and different, you can begin to see each one more clearly.

1. Prewrite

Get Started "How are they alike?" "How are they different?" Jot down answers to these questions as you research the lives of free blacks or the Industrial Revolution. Group your answers into points of comparison. For example, points of comparison for the lives of free blacks might be work, education, etc. Points of comparison for the Industrial Revolution might be factories or farming.

Organize Your Information There are two ways to organize a compare-and-contrast paper.

> **Block Style** *Say everything you have to say about one subject. Then say everything you have to say about the second subject. Discuss the points of comparison in the same order for each subject.*

> **Point-by-Point Style** *Discuss the points of comparison one at a time. Explain how the subjects are alike and different on one point of comparison, then another, and so on. Discuss the subjects in the same order for each point of comparison.*

2. Write

You can use this framework with your notes to help you write your first draft.

A WRITER'S FRAMEWORK

Introduction
- Identify the two subjects and give background information to help readers understand your comparisons.
- State your big idea, or main purpose, in comparing and contrasting them.

Body
- Use block or point-by-point organization.
- Use three points of comparison.
- Support your points with specific historical facts, details, and examples.

Conclusion
- Restate your big idea.
- Summarize the points you made.
- Expand on your big idea, perhaps by relating it to later historical events or other historical figures.

3. Evaluate and Revise

Evaluate Use these questions to discover ways to improve your paper.

> ### EVALUATION QUESTIONS FOR A COMPARISON/ CONTRAST PAPER
>
> - Do you introduce both subjects in the first paragraph?
> - Do you provide relevant background information in a clear and concise manner?
> - Do you state your big idea in the introduction?
> - Do you include three points of comparison between the subjects?
> - Do you use either the block style or point-by-point style to organize your points of comparison?
> - Do you support your points of comparison with appropriate historical facts, details, and examples?
> - Do you restate your big idea and summarize your points?

TIP: MAKE MEANING CLEAR

One way to make relationships between ideas clear is to repeat key or similar words and phrases in your writing. For example, you can use similar wording when comparing two historical figures on the same point of comparison.

EXAMPLE

Samuel Slater filled his labor needs by hiring entire families to work in the mills. Francis Lowell filled his labor needs by hiring young, unmarried women to work in the mills.

Revise As you reread your paper, look for sentences that start with *There was* or *There were*. Sentences beginning with *There was/There were* tend to be weak: The verbs *was* and *were* do not convey any action.

> **Weak**
> There was a decline in southern agriculture after the American Revolution.
>
> **Stronger**
> Southern agriculture declined after the American Revolution.

4. Proofread and Publish

Proofread In a research report, you may be referring to the titles of your sources of information. Check to see whether you have punctuated any titles according to these guidelines.

- Underlining (if you are writing) or italics (if you are using a computer) for books, movies, TV programs, Internet sites, and magazines or newspapers
- Quotation marks for magazine articles, newspaper articles, chapters in a book

Publish Share your paper with one or more classmates. After reading each other's papers, you can compare and contrast them.

5. Practice and Apply

Use the steps and strategies outlined in this workshop to write your paper comparing and contrasting two people or events.

Writing Workshop **R21**

A Social Studies Report

ASSIGNMENT
Collect information and write an informative report on a topic related to the Civil War.

All research begins with a question. Why did the North win the Civil War? Why did Abraham Lincoln choose Ulysses S. Grant? In a research report, you find answers to questions like these and share what you learn with your reader.

1. Prewrite

Choose a Subject Since you will spend a lot of time researching and writing about your topic, pick one that interests you. First, think of several topics related to the Civil War. Narrow your list to one topic by thinking about what interests you and where you can find information about the topic.

TIP: NARROW THE TASK
The key to a successful research report is picking a topic that is broad enough that you can find information, but narrow enough that you can cover it in detail. To narrow a subject, focus on one aspect of the larger subject. Then think about whether that one aspect can be broken down into smaller parts. Here's an example of how to narrow a topic:

Too Broad: Civil War Leaders

Less Broad: Civil War Generals

Narrower: Robert E. Lee's Role in the Civil War

Develop a Research Question A guiding question related to your topic will help focus your research. For example, here is a research question for the topic "Robert E. Lee's Role in the Civil War": How did Lee's decision to turn down the leadership of the Union army affect the Civil War? The answer to this question becomes the thesis, or the big idea of your report.

Find Historical Information Use at least three sources of historical information besides your textbook. Good sources include

- books, maps, magazines, and newspapers.
- television programs, movies, Internet sites, and CD-ROMs.

For each source, write down the kinds of information shown below. When taking notes, put a circled number next to each source.

Encyclopedia article
① "Title of Article." <u>Name of Encyclopedia</u>. Edition or year published.
Book
② Author. <u>Title</u>. City of Publication: Publisher, year published.
Magazine or newspaper article
③ Author. "Title of Article." <u>Publication name</u>. Date: page number(s).
Internet site
④ Author (if known). "Document title." <u>Website</u>. Date of electronic publication. Date information was accessed \<url\>.

TIP: SEE DIFFERENT VIEWPOINTS
Consult a variety of sources, including those with different points of view on the topic. Reading sources with different opinions will give you a more complete picture of your subject. For example, reading articles about Robert E. Lee written by a southern writer as well as a northern writer may give you a more balanced view of Lee.

TIP: RECORD OTHERS' IDEAS
You will be taking three types of notes:

Paraphrases Restatements of all the ideas in your own words

Summaries Brief restatements of only the most important parts

Direct quotations The writer's exact words inside quotation marks

Take Notes As you read the sources, take thorough notes. Take special care to spell names correctly and to record dates and facts accurately. If you use a direct quotation from a source, copy it word for word and enclose it in quotation marks. Along with each note, include the number of its source and its page number.

Organize Your Ideas and Information Informative research reports are usually organized in one of these ways:

- chronological order (the order in which events occurred)
- order of importance
- causes (actions that make something else happen) and effects (results of something else)

Use one of these orders to organize your notes in an outline. Here is a partial outline for a paper on Robert E. Lee.

The Thesis/Big Idea: Robert E. Lee's decision to decline the leadership of the Union army had serious consequences for the path of the Civil War.

I. Lee's Military Expertise
   A. Achievements at the U.S. Military Academy
   B. Achievements during the Mexican War

II. Lee's Personality and Character
   A. Intelligence and strength
   B. Honesty and fairness
   C. Daring and courage

III. Lee's Military Victories
   A. Battle of Fredericksburg
   B. Battle of Chancellorsville

---

2. Write

You can use this framework to help you write your first draft.

A WRITER'S FRAMEWORK

Introduction

- Start with a quote or an interesting historical detail to grab your reader's attention.
- State the main idea of your report.
- Provide any historical background readers need to understand your main idea.

Body

- Present your information under at least three main ideas, using logical order.
- Write at least one paragraph for each of these main ideas.
- Add supporting details, facts, or examples to each paragraph.

Conclusion

- Restate your main idea, using slightly different words.
- Include a general comment about your topic.
- You might comment on how the historical information in your report relates to later historical events.

Study a Model Here is a model of a research report. Study it to see how one student developed a paper. The first and the concluding paragraphs are shown in full. The paragraphs in the body of the paper are summarized.

INTRODUCTORY PARAGRAPH
Attention grabber

Statement of thesis

"I cannot raise my hand against my birthplace, my home, my children." With these words, Robert E. Lee changed the course of the Civil War. Abraham Lincoln had turned to Lee as his first choice for commander of the Union army. However, Lee turned Lincoln down, choosing instead to side with his home state of Virginia and take command of the Confederate army. Lee's decision to turn Lincoln down weakened the North and strengthened the Confederates, turning what might have been an easy victory for the North into a long, costly war.

BODY PARAGRAPHS

In the first part of the body of the report, the student points out that Lee graduated from the U.S. Military Academy at West Point, served in the Mexican War, and was a member of the Union army. She goes on to explain that he would have been a strong leader for the North, and his absence made the North weaker.

In the middle of the report, the writer discusses Lee's personality and character. She includes information about the strength of character he showed while in the military academy and while leading the Confederate army. She discusses and gives examples of his intelligence, his daring, his courage, and his honesty.

In the last part of the body of the report, the student provides examples of Lee leading the outnumbered Confederate army to a series of victories. The student provides details of the battles of Fredericksburg and Chancellorsville and explains how a lesser general than Lee may have lost both battles.

CONCLUDING PARAGRAPH
Summary of main points
Restatement of big idea

Lee's brilliant and resourceful leadership bedeviled a series of Union generals. He won battles that most generals would have lost. If Lee had used these skills to lead the larger and more powerful Union army, the Civil War might have ended in months instead of years.

3. Evaluate and Revise

Evaluate and Revise Your Draft Evaluate your first draft by carefully reading it twice. Ask the questions below to decide which parts of your first draft should be revised.

EVALUATION QUESTIONS FOR AN INFORMATIVE REPORT

- Does the introduction attract the readers' interest and state the big idea/thesis of your report?
- Does the body have at least three paragraphs that develop your big idea? Is the main idea in each paragraph clearly stated?
- Have you included enough information to support each of your main ideas? Are all facts, details, and examples accurate? Are all of them clearly related to the main ideas they support?

- Is the report clearly organized? Does it use chronological order, order of importance, or cause and effect?
- Does the conclusion restate the big idea of your report? Does it end with a general comment about the importance or significance of your topic?
- Have you included at least three sources in the bibliography? Have you included all the sources you used and not any you did not use?

TIP: ORGANIZE YOUR TIME

By creating a schedule and following it, you can avoid that panicky moment when the due date is near and you haven't even started your research. To create your schedule and manage your time, include these six steps:

1. Develop a question and research your topic (10% of your total time).
2. Research and take notes (25%).
3. Write your main idea statement and create an outline (15%).
4. Write a first draft (25%).
5. Evaluate and revise your first draft (15%).
6. Proofread and publish your report (10%).

4. Proofread and Publish

Proofread To improve your report before sharing it, check the following:

- The spelling and capitalization of all proper names for people, places, things, and events.
- Punctuation marks around any direct quotation.
- Your list of sources (Works Cited or Bibliography) against a guide to writing research papers. Make sure you follow the examples in the guide when punctuating and capitalizing your source listings.

Publish Choose one or more of these ideas to publish your report:

- Share your report with your classmates by turning it into an informative speech.
- Submit your report to an online discussion group that focuses on the Civil War and ask for feedback.
- With your classmates, create a magazine that includes reports on several different topics or post the reports on your school website.

5. Practice and Apply

Use the steps and strategies outlined in this workshop to research and write an informative report on the Civil War.

The American flag is a symbol of the nation. It is recognized instantly, whether as a big banner waving in the wind or a tiny emblem worn on a lapel. The flag is so important that it is a major theme of the national anthem, "The Star-Spangled Banner." One of the most popular names for the flag is the Stars and Stripes. It is also known as Old Glory.

The Meaning of the Flag

The American flag has 13 stripes—7 red and 6 white. In the upper-left corner of the flag is the union—50 white five-pointed stars against a blue background.

The 13 stripes stand for the original 13 American states, and the 50 stars represent the states of the nation today. According to the U.S. Department of State, the colors of the flag also are symbolic:

Red stands for courage.

White symbolizes purity.

Blue is the color of vigilance, perseverance, and justice.

Displaying the Flag

It is customary not to display the American flag in bad weather. It is also customary for the flag to be displayed outdoors only from sunrise to sunset, except on certain occasions. In a few special places, however, the flag is always flown day and night. When flown at night, the flag should be illuminated.

Near a speaker's platform, the flag should occupy the place of honor at the speaker's right. When carried in a parade with other flags, the American flag should be on the marching right or in front at the center. When flying with the flags of the 50 states, the national flag must be at the center and the highest point. In a group of national flags, all should be of equal size and all should be flown from staffs, or flagpoles, of equal height.

The flag should never touch the ground or the floor. It should not be marked with any insignia, pictures, or words. Nor should it be used in any disrespectful way—as an advertising decoration, for instance. The flag should never be dipped to honor any person or thing.

Saluting the Flag

The United States, like other countries, has a flag code, or rules for displaying and honoring the flag. For example, all those present should stand at attention facing the flag and salute it when it is being raised or lowered or when it is carried past them in a parade or procession. A man wearing a hat should take it off and hold it with his right hand over his heart. All women and hatless men should stand with their right hands over their hearts to show their respect for the flag. The flag should also receive these honors during the playing of the national anthem and the reciting of the Pledge of Allegiance.

The Pledge of Allegiance

The Pledge of Allegiance was written in 1892 by Massachusetts magazine (*Youth's Companion*) editor Francis Bellamy. (Congress added the words "under God" in 1954.)

> *I pledge allegiance to the flag of the United States of America and to the republic for which it stands, one nation under God, indivisible, with liberty and justice for all.*

Civilians should say the Pledge of Allegiance with their right hands placed over their hearts. People in the armed forces give the military salute. By saying the Pledge of Allegiance, we promise loyalty ("pledge allegiance") to the United States and its ideals.

"The Star-Spangled Banner"

"The Star-Spangled Banner" is the national anthem of the United States. It was written by Francis Scott Key during the War of 1812. While being detained by the British aboard a ship on September 13–14, 1814, Key watched the British bombardment of Fort McHenry at Baltimore. The attack lasted 25 hours. The smoke was so thick that Key could not tell who had won. When the air cleared, Key saw the American flag that was still flying over the fort. "The Star-Spangled Banner" is sung to music written by British composer John Stafford Smith. In 1931 Congress designated "The Star-Spangled Banner" as the national anthem.

I

Oh, say, can you see, by the dawn's early light,
What so proudly we hailed at the twilight's last gleaming,
Whose broad stripes and bright stars through the perilous fight, O'er the ramparts we watched were so gallantly streaming? And the rockets' red glare, the bombs bursting in air, Gave proof through the night that our flag was still there. Oh, say, does that star-spangled banner yet wave O'er the land of the free, and the home of the brave?

II

On the shore, dimly seen through the mists of the deep,
Where the foe's haughty host in dread silence reposes,
What is that which the breeze, o'er the towering steep,
As it fitfully blows, half conceals, half discloses?
Now it catches the gleam of the morning's first beam,
In full glory reflected, now shines on the stream.
'Tis the star-spangled banner; oh, long may it wave
O'er the land of the free, and the home of the brave!

III

And where is that band who so vauntingly swore
That the havoc of war and the battle's confusion
A home and a country should leave us no more?
Their blood has washed out their foul footsteps' pollution.
No refuge could save the hireling and slave
From the terror of flight, or the gloom of the grave:
And the star-spangled banner in triumph doth wave
O'er the land of the free, and the home of the brave!

IV

Oh! thus be it ever when freemen shall stand
Between their loved homes and the war's desolation!
Blest with victory and peace, may the heaven-rescued land
Praise the Power that hath made and preserved us a nation!
Then conquer we must, for our cause it is just,
And this be our motto: "In God is our trust!"
And the star-spangled banner in triumph shall wave,
O'er the land of the free, and the home of the brave!

Sheet music to the national anthem

"America the Beautiful"

One of the most beloved songs celebrating our nation is "America, the Beautiful." Katharine Lee Bates first wrote the lyrics to the song in 1893 after visiting Colorado. The version of the song we know today is set to music by Samuel A. Ward. The first and last stanzas of "America, the Beautiful" are shown below.

O beautiful for spacious skies,
For amber waves of grain,
For purple mountain majesties
Above the fruited plain!
America! America!
God shed his grace on thee
And crown thy good with brotherhood
From sea to shining sea!

O beautiful for patriot dream
That sees beyond the years
Thine alabaster cities gleam
Undimmed by human tears!
America! America!
God shed his grace on thee
And crown thy good with brotherhood
From sea to shining sea!

Mount Rushmore

Mount Rushmore, located in the Black Hills of South Dakota, is the world's largest sculpture. Known as the "Shrine of Democracy," it features the heads of four of the nation's greatest presidents—George Washington, Thomas Jefferson, Theodore Roosevelt, and Abraham Lincoln.

The original idea to carve massive figures into the mountainside came from South Dakota historian Doane Robinson. He thought that a giant sculpture of notable people in the history of the West would draw thousands of tourists to the Black Hills. Robinson chose sculptor Gutzon Borglum, who had worked on similar projects, to do the work. Borglum wanted to change the focus of the sculpture. He suggested that it should show four presidents who had played a major role in the country's development.

- George Washington—the commander of the Continental army during the American Revolution and the nation's first president
- Thomas Jefferson—the author of the Declaration of Independence who, as president, expanded the nation with the Louisiana Purchase
- Theodore Roosevelt—the president who oversaw the nation's rise to a world power
- Abraham Lincoln—the president who preserved the Union during the Civil War

After exploring the Black Hills, Borglum chose Mount Rushmore as the best site for the sculpture, and work began in 1927. A team of workers first used dynamite to blast away the rock. Then they used jackhammers to create facial features. Finally, they planed the surfaces smooth with hand tools.

Borglum's death in 1941 soon brought work on the sculpture to an end. During the 14 years of the project, his team had blasted some 450,000 tons of rock from the mountainside and created a monument of majestic proportions.

- The presidents' heads are some 60 feet high—about the distance from the pitcher's mound to home plate on a major league baseball diamond.
- The presidents' noses measure about 20 feet long.
- The presidents' eyes are 11 feet wide.
- The presidents' mouths are about 18 feet wide.

The 1927 Act of Congress that provided the initial funds for Borglum's sculpture declared Mount Rushmore a national memorial. Since the late 1930s, the National Park Service has managed the Mount Rushmore National Memorial, which hosts some 3 million visitors each year.

George Washington, Thomas Jefferson, Theodore Roosevelt, and Abraham Lincoln look down from the heights of Mount Rushmore.

James Montgomery Flagg's Uncle Sam proved to be a powerful recruiting tool.

Uncle Sam

One of the most recognizable symbols of the United States government is the character known as Uncle Sam. The origins of this symbol go back to the early 1800s. Samuel Wilson, a merchant from New York State, provided food for the army during the War of 1812. He marked the barrels of food "U.S." to indicate that they were government property. Over time, however, many soldiers began saying that the food was provided by "Uncle Sam."

During the mid-1800s, Uncle Sam began to take on a very distinct and recognizable appearance. This was largely due to the work of Thomas Nast, a cartoonist for the magazine *Harper's Weekly*. In his cartoons, Nast portrayed Sam as a tall, thin man with chin whiskers wearing a top hat, frock coat, and striped pants. Over the years, other artists adopted Nast's image of Uncle Sam, adding such features as a stars and stripes waistcoat.

Perhaps the most famous image of Uncle Sam was produced by artist James Montgomery Flagg during World War I. Originally drawn for a magazine cover warning Americans to be prepared for war, it was quickly adopted by the U.S. Army as a recruiting poster. More than 4 million copies of the poster were produced during 1917 and 1918. It was considered such a powerful recruiting tool that it was also used in the early years of World War II.

Flagg's stern-faced, finger-pointing Uncle Sam was a long way from Samuel Wilson, the food merchant from New York. Wilson, however, was not forgotten. In 1961 Congress recognized him as the origin of "America's national symbol of Uncle Sam."

Political Party Symbols

The symbols of the two major U.S. political parties—the Democratic donkey and the Republican elephant—are recognizable to many Americans. Both symbols have a colorful origin.

The use of the donkey as a symbol for Democrats dates to the presidential election of 1828. Supporters of John Quincy Adams declared that Democrat Andrew Jackson, Adams's opponent, was like a donkey—slow and not very bright. Jackson seized on this charge. He used the donkey on his campaign posters, noting that it was a simple, loyal, and hard-working animal. However, this image did not gain popularity until the mid-1800s—again through the work of Thomas Nast.

In his cartoons, Nast often used a donkey to represent supporters of the Democratic Party. In an 1874 cartoon, Nast showed the donkey, dressed in a lion skin, terrorizing other animals in a zoo. The elephant in the cartoon was labeled "The Republican Vote." In very short order, the two animals became the political party symbols.

This 1874 Thomas Nast cartoon is the first use of the Democratic donkey and the Republican elephant together.

Today, these animals remain the symbols of the two political parties. Images of the donkey and the elephant are used in campaign materials, usually decorated with stars and stripes.

English and Spanish Glossary

Phonetic Respelling and Pronunciation Guide

Many of the key terms in this textbook have been respelled to help you pronounce them. The letter combinations used in the respelling throughout the narrative are explained in the following phonetic respelling and pronunciation guide. The guide is adapted from *Merriam-Webster's Collegiate Dictionary, 11th Edition; Merriam-Webster's Geographical Dictionary;* and *Merriam-Webster's Biographical Dictionary.*

MARK	AS IN	RESPELLING	EXAMPLE
a	alphabet	a	*AL-fuh-bet
ā	Asia	ay	AY-zhuh
ä	cart, top	ah	KAHRT, TAHP
e	let, ten	e	LET, TEN
ē	even, leaf	ee	EE-vuhn, LEEF
i	it, tip, British	i	IT, TIP, BRIT-ish
ī	site, buy, Ohio	y	SYT, BY, oh-HY-oh
	iris	eye	EYE-ris
k	card	k	KAHRD
ō	over, rainbow	oh	OH-vuhr, RAYN-boh
ù	book, wood	ooh	BOOHK, WOOHD
ò	all, orchid	aw	AWL, AWR-kid
òi	foil, coin	oy	FOYL, KOYN
aù	out	ow	OWT
ə	cup, butter	uh	KUHP, BUHT-uhr
ü	rule, food	oo	ROOL, FOOD
yü	few	yoo	FYOO
zh	vision	zh	VIZH-uhn

*A syllable printed in small capital letters receives heavier emphasis than the other syllable(s) in a word.

A

abolition an end to slavery (p. 489)
  abolición fin de la esclavitud (pág. 489)

abolition movement a campaign to end slavery (p. 524)
  movimiento abolicionista una campaña para poner fin a la esclavitud (pág. 524)

Adams-Onís Treaty (1819) an agreement in which Spain gave East Florida to the United States (p. 294)
  Tratado de Adams y Onís (1819) acuerdo en el que España le dio el territorio del este de Florida a Estados Unidos (pág. 294)

African Diaspora the population of displaced Africans and their descendants around the world (p. 477)

diáspora africana población de africanos desplazados y sus descendientes en todo el mundo (pág. 477)

Alamo Spanish mission in San Antonio, Texas, that was the site of a famous battle of the Texas Revolution in 1836 (p. 394)
  El Álamo misión española en San Antonio, Texas; escenario de una famosa batalla durante la Revolución Texana de 1836 (pág. 394)

Alien and Sedition Acts (1798) laws passed by a Federalist-dominated Congress aimed at protecting the government from treasonous ideas, actions, and people (p. 266)
  Leyes de Extranjeros y Sedición (1798) leyes aprobadas por un Congreso mayormente federalist para proteger al gobierno de la influencia de ideas, acciones y personas desleales (pág. 266)

amendment official change, correction, or addition to a law or constitution (pp. 173, 185)
enmienda cambio, corrección o adición oficial a una ley o constitución (pág. 173, 185)

American Anti-Slavery Society an organization started by William Lloyd Garrison whose members wanted immediate emancipation and racial equality for African Americans (pp. 490, 525)
Sociedad Americana contra la Esclavitud organización fundada por William Lloyd Garrison cuyos miembros pedían la emancipación inmediata y la igualdad racial de los afroamericanos (pág. 490, 525)

American System Henry Clay's plan for raising tariffs to pay for internal improvements such as better roads and canals (p. 306)
Sistema Estadounidense plan de alza de aranceles creado por Henry Clay para hacer mejoras internas como la reparación de caminos y canales (pág. 306)

Antifederalists people who opposed ratification of the Constitution (pp. 170, 186)
antifederalistas personas que se oponían a la aprobación de la Constitución (pág. 170, 186)

Appomattox Courthouse the location where General Robert E. Lee was forced to surrender, thus ending the Civil War (p. 605)
Appomattox Courthouse poblado de Virginia donde el general Robert E. Lee fue obligado a rendirse, dando fi n a la Guerra Civil (pág. 605)

Articles of Confederation (1777) the document that created the first central government for the United States; was replaced by the Constitution in 1789 (p. 154)
Artículos de Confederación (1777) documento que creó el primer gobierno central en Estados Unidos; fue reemplazado por la Constitución en 1789 (pág. 154)

assimilate to give up traditional ways in favor of mainstream practices (p. 377)
asimilar renunciar a las formas tradicionales en favor de las prácticas generales (pág. 377)

astrolabe a device that enabled navigators to learn their ship's location by charting the position of the stars (p. 38)
astrolabio aparato que permitía a los navegantes saber la ubicación de su barco al trazar la posición de las estrellas (pág. 38)

B

Bacon's Rebellion (1676) an atttack led by Nathaniel Bacon against American Indians and the colonial government in Virginia (p. 71)
Rebelión de Bacon (1676) ataque encabezado por Nathaniel Bacon contra los indígenas norteamericanos y el gobierno colonial en Virginia (pág. 71)

Bank of the United States a national bank chartered by Congress in 1791 to provide security for the U.S. economy (p. 254)
Banco de los Estados Unidos banco nacional formado por el Congreso en 1791 para dar seguridad a la economía de Estados Unidos (pág. 254)

Battle of Antietam (1862) a Union victory in the Civil War that marked the bloodiest single-day battle in U.S. military history (p. 581)
batalla de Antieta (1862) victoria del ejército de la Unión durante la Guerra Civil en la batalla de un solo día más sangrienta de la historia militar de Estados Unidos (pág. 581)

Battle of Bunker Hill (1775) a Revolutionary War battle in Boston that demonstrated that the colonists could fight well against the British army (p. 117)
batalla de Bunker Hill (1775) batalla de la Guerra de Independencia estadounidense en Boston; en ésta se demostró que los colonos podían luchar bien contra el ejército británico (pág. 117)

Battle of Fallen Timbers (1794) a battle between U.S. troops and an American Indian confederation that ended Indian efforts to halt white settlement in the Northwest Territory (p. 259)
batalla de Fallen Timbers (1794) batalla entre las tropas estadounidenses y una confederación de indígenasnorteamericanos que puso fin a los intentos de los indígenas para detener la emigración de personas de raza blanca al Territorio del Noroeste (pág. 259)

English and Spanish Glossary

Battle of Gettysburg (1863) a Union Civil War victory that turned the tide against the Confederates at Gettysburg, Pennsylvania (p. 600)

batalla de Gettysburg (1863) victoria del ejército de la Unión durante la Guerra Civil que cambió el curso de la guerra en contra de los confederados en Gettysburg, Pensilvania (pág. 600)

Battle of Lake Erie (1813) U.S. victory in the War of 1812, led by Oliver Hazard Perry; broke Britain's control of Lake Erie (p. 289)

batalla del lago Erie (1813) victoria en la Guerra de 1812 en la que el ejército estadounidense, comandado por Oliver Hazard Perry, puso fin al control británico del lago Erie (pág. 289)

Battle of New Orleans (1815) the greatest U.S. victory in the War of 1812; actually took place two weeks after a peace treaty had been signed ending the war (p. 291)

batalla de Nueva Orleáns (1815) la mayor victoria del ejército estadounidense en la Guerra de 1812; tuvo lugar dos semanas después de la firma de un tratado de paz en el que se declaraba el fi nal de la Guerra (pág. 291)

Battle of San Jacinto (1836) the final battle of the Texas Revolution; resulted in the defeat of the Mexican army and independence for Texas (p. 395)

batalla de San Jacinto (1836) batalla final de la Revolución Texana en la que el ejército mexicano fue derrotado y Texas obtuvo su independencia (pág. 395)

Battle of Saratoga (1777) a Revolutionary War battle in New York that resulted in a major defeat of British troops; marked the Patriots' greatest victory up to that point in the war (p. 132)

batalla de Saratoga (1777) batalla de la Guerra de Independencia estadounidense que tuvo lugar en Nueva York y en la que las fuerzas británicas sufrieron una de sus mayores derrotas; los patriotas obtuvieron su mayor victoria hasta ese momento (pág. 132)

Battle of Shiloh (1862) a Civil War battle in Tennessee in which the Union army gained greater control over the Mississippi River valley (p. 584)

batalla de Shiloh (1862) batalla de la Guerra Civil en Tennessee en la que el ejército de la Unión adquirió mayor control sobre el valle del río Mississippi (pág. 584)

Battle of the Little Big Horn (1876) "Custer's Last Stand"; battle between U.S. soldiers, led by George Armstrong Custer, and Sioux warriors, led by Crazy Horse and Sitting Bull, that resulted in the worst defeat for the U.S. Army in the West (p. 375)

batalla de Little Big Horn (1876) última batalla del general Custer; esta batalla entre las tropas de George Armstrong Custer y los guerreros siux al mando de Caballo Loco y Toro Sentado produjo la mayor derrota del ejército estadounidense en el Oeste (pág. 375)

Battle of Tippecanoe (1811) U.S. victory over an Indian confederation that wanted to stop white settlement in the Northwest Territory; increased tensions between Great Britain and the United States (p. 286)

batalla de Tippecanoe (1811) victoria del ejército estadounidense sobre la confederación indígena que intentaba evitar el establecimiento de poblaciones de blancos en el Territorio del Noroeste; esta batalla aumentó las hostilidades entre Gran Bretaña y Estados Unidos (pág. 286)

Battle of Trenton (1776) a Revolutionary War battle in New Jersey in which Patriot forces captured more than 900 Hessian troops (p. 132)

batalla de Trenton (1776) batalla de la Guerra de Independencia estadounidense que tuvo lugar en Nueva Jersey; en esta batalla las fuerzas de los patriotas capturaron a más de 900 soldados hessianos (pág. 132)

Battle of Yorktown (1781) the last major battle of the Revolutionary War; site of British general Charles Cornwallis's surrender to the Patriots in Virginia (p. 142)

batalla de Yorktown (1781) la última batalla importante de la Guerra de Independencia estadounidense; lugar donde se rindió el general británico Charles Cornwallis ante los patriotas en Virginia (pág. 142)

Bear Flag Revolt (1846) a revolt against Mexico by American settlers in California who declared the territory an independent republic (p. 403)

Revuelta de Bear Flag (1846) rebelión iniciada por colonos estadounidenses en contra de México para declarar al territorio de California una república independiente (pág. 403)

Berbers a group of people from northern Africa (p. 19)

bereberes grupo de habitantes del norte de África (pág. 19)

Bering Land Bridge a strip of land connecting Alaska with Russia that emerged from underwater around 38,000 BC (p. 6)

Puente de Tierra de Bering franja de tierra que conecta Alaska con Rusia y que surgió del agua alrededor del año 38,000 a.C. (pág. 6)

Bill of Rights the first 10 amendments to the Constitution; ratified in 1791 (pp. 174, 187)

Declaración de Derechos primeras 10 enmiendas a la Constitución; aprobada en 1791 (pág. 174, 187)

Black Codes laws passed in the southern states during Reconstruction that greatly limited the freedom and rights of African Americans (p. 620)

Códigos Negros decretos aprobados en los estados sureños en la época de la Reconstrucción que limitaron en gran medida la libertad y los derechos de los afroamericanos (pág. 620)

Black Death a series of plagues that killed about 25 million people in Europe starting in 1347 (p. 26)

Peste Negra serie de plagas que mataron a unos 25 millones de personas en Europa a partir de 1347 (pág. 26)

bond a certificate that represents money the government has borrowed from private citizens (p. 250)

bono certificado que representa dinero que el gobierno toma prestado de los ciudadanos (pág. 250)

boomtown a Western community that grew quickly because of the mining boom and often disappeared when the boom ended (p. 365)

pueblo de rápido crecimiento comunidad del Oeste que se desarrolló con gran rapidez debido a la fiebre del oro, pero que desapareció cuando la fiebre terminó (pág. 365)

border states Delaware, Kentucky, Maryland, and Missouri; slave states that lay between the North and the South and did not join the Confederacy during the Civil War (p. 572)

estados fronterizos Delaware, Kentucky, Maryland y Missouri; estados esclavistas ubicados entre el Norte y el Sur y que no se unieron a la Confederación durante la Guerra Civil (pág. 572)

Boston Massacre (1770) an incident in which British soldiers fired into a crowd of colonists, killing five people (p. 109)

masacre de Boston (1770) incidente en el que los soldados británicos le dispararon a una multitud de colonos, dando muerte a cinco personas (pág. 109)

Boston Tea Party (1773) a protest against the Tea Act in which a group of colonists boarded British tea ships and dumped more than 340 chests of tea into Boston Harbor (p. 111)

Motín del Té de Boston (1773) protesta en contra de la Ley del Té en la que un grupo de colonos abordó barcos británicos que transportaban té y arrojó al mar alrededor de 340 baúles de té en el puerto de Boston (pág. 111)

buffalo soldiers African American soldiers who served in the cavalry during the wars for the west (p. 373)

soldados búfalo soldados afroamericanos que sirvieron en la caballería durante las guerras del oeste (pág. 373)

Bureau of Indian Affairs a government agency created in the 1800s to oversee federal policy toward Native Americans (p. 340)

Oficina de Asuntos Indígenas agencia creada por el gobierno en el siglo XIX para supervisar las políticas federales en cuanto a los indígenas norteamericanos (pág. 340)

C

Californios Spanish colonists in California in the 1800s (p. 400)

californios colonos españoles que vivían en California en el siglo XIX (pág. 400)

English and Spanish Glossary

caravels ships that used triangular sails to sail against the wind, and had rudders to improve steering (p. 38)

carabelas barcos con velas triangulares usadas para navegar contra el viento y que tenían timones para mejorar la dirección (pág. 38)

cattle drive a long journey on which cowboys herded cattle to northern markets or better grazing lands (p. 366)

arreo de ganado viaje largo en el que los vaqueros arreaban ganado para llevarlo a los mercados del Norte o a mejores pastos (pág. 366)

Cattle Kingdom an area of the Great Plains on which many ranchers raised cattle in the late 1800s (p. 366)

Reino del Ganado área de las Grandes Planicies en la que muchos rancheros criaban ganado a fi nales de siglo XIX (pág. 366)

charter an official document that gives a person the right to establish a colony (p. 56)

carta de constitución documento oficial que da a una persona el derecho de establecer una colonia (pág. 56)

checks and balances a system established by the Constitution that prevents any branch of government from becoming too powerful (pp. 167, 185)

equilibrio de poderes sistema establecido por la Constitución para evitar que cualquier poder del gobierno adquiera demasiada autoridad (pág. 167, 185)

Chisholm Trail a trail from San Antonio, Texas, to Abilene, Kansas, established by Jesse Chisholm in the late 1860s for cattle drives (p. 366)

Camino de Chisholm camino creado por Jesse Chisholm a finales de la década de 1860 que iba desde San Antonio, Texas hasta Abilene, Kansas, para arreos de ganado (pág. 366)

circumnavigate to travel all the way around the globe (p. 44)

circunnavegar darle la vuelta al planeta (pág. 44)

Civil Rights Act of 1866 a law that gave African Americans legal rights equal to those of white Americans (p. 622)

Ley de Derechos Civiles de 1866 ley que dio a los afroamericanos los mismos derechos legales que tenían los estadounidenses blancos (pág. 622)

Clermont the first full-sized U.S. commercial steamboat; developed by Robert Fulton and tested in 1807 (p. 435)

Clermont primer barco comercial de vapor de gran tamaño, diseñado por Robert Fulton y probado en 1807 (pág. 435)

Columbian Exchange the transfer of plants, animals, and diseases between the Americas and Europe, Asia, and Africa (p. 44)

intercambio colombino intercambio de plantas, animales y enfermedades entre las Américas y Europa, Asia y África (pág. 44)

Committees of Correspondence committees created by the Massachusetts House of Representatives in the 1760s to help towns and colonies share information about resisting British laws (p. 107)

comités de correspondencia comités creados por la Cámara de Representantes de Massachusetts en la década de 1760 para que lospueblos y colonias compartieran información sobra la resistencia a las leyes británicas (pág. 107)

common-school movement a social reform effort that began in the mid-1800s and promoted the idea of having all children educated in a common place regardless of social class or background (p. 521)

movimiento de escuelas comunes reforma social iniciada a mediados del siglo XIX para fomentar la idea de que todos los niños debían recibir educación en un mismo lugar sin importar su origen o clase social (pág. 521)

Common Sense (1776) a pamphlet written by Thomas Paine that criticized monarchies and convinced many American colonists of the need to break away from Britain (p. 119)

Sentido común (1776) escrito por Thomas Paine en el que criticaba a las monarquías y convenció a muchos colonos norteamericanos de la necesidad de independizarse de Gran Bretaña (pág. 119)

Compromise of 1850 Henry Clay's proposed agreement that allowed California to enter the Union as a free state and divided the rest of the Mexican Cession into two territories where slavery would be decided by popular sovereignty (pp. 498, 544)

Compromiso de 1850 acuerdo propuesto por Henry Clay en que se permitía a California entrar en la Unión como estado libre y se proponía la division del resto del territorio de la Cesión Mexicana en dos partes donde la esclavitud sería reglamentada por soberanía popular (pág. 498, 544)

Compromise of 1877 an agreement to settle the disputed presidential election of 1876; Democrats agreed to accept Republican Rutherford B. Hayes as president in return for the removal of federal troops from the South (p. 630)

Compromiso de 1877 acuerdo en el que se resolvieron las disputadas elecciones presidenciales de 1876; los demócratas aceptaron al republican Rutherford B. Hayes como presidente a cambio del retiro de las tropas federales del Sur (pág. 630)

Comstock Lode Nevada gold and silver mine discovered by Henry Comstock in 1859 (p. 364)

veta de Comstock mina de oro y plata descubierta en Nevada por Henry Comstock en 1859 (pág. 364)

Confederate States of America the nation formed by the southern states when they seceded from the Union; also known as the Confederacy (p. 561)

Estados Confederados de América nación formada por los estados del Sur cuando se separaron de la Unión; también conocida como Confederación (pág. 561)

conquistador a Spanish soldier and explorer who led military expeditions in the Americas and captured land for Spain (p. 46)

conquistador soldado y explorador español que encabezó expediciones militares en América y capturó territorios en nombre de España (pág. 46)

constitution a set of basic principles that determines the powers and duties of a government (p. 153)

constitución conjunto de principios básicos que determina los poderes y las obligaciones de un gobierno (pág. 153)

Constitutional Convention (1787) a meeting held in Philadelphia at which delegates from the states wrote the Constitution (pp. 164, 183)

Convención Constitucional (1787) reunión en Filadelfia en la que delegados de los estados redactaron la Constitución (pág. 164, 183)

Constitutional Union Party a political party formed in 1860 by a group of northerners and southerners who supported the Union, its laws, and the Constitution (p. 560)

Partido Constitucional por la Unión partido politico formado en 1860 por habitantes del Norte y del Sur en apoyo de la Unión, sus leyes y la Constitución (pág. 560)

Continental army the army created by the Second Continental Congress in 1775 to defend the American colonies from Britain (p. 116)

Ejército Continental ejército creado por el Segundo Congreso Continental en 1775 para defender a las colonias norteamericanas del dominio británico (pág. 116)

contraband an escaped slave who joined the Union army during the Civil War (p. 593)

contrabando esclavo que escapó y se unió al ejército de la Unión durante la Guerra Civil (pág. 593)

Convention of 1818 an agreement between the United States and Great Britain that settled fishing rights and established new North American borders (p. 292)

Convención de 1818 acuerdo entre Estados Unidos y Gran Bretaña para definir los derechos de pesca y establecer las nuevas fronteras norteamericanas (pág. 292)

Copperheads a group of northern Democrats who opposed abolition and sympathized with the South during the Civil War (p. 595)

copperheads grupo de demócratas del Norte que se oponían a la abolición de la esclavitud y simpatizaban con las creencias sureñas durante la Guerra Civil (pág. 595)

cotton belt a region stretching from South Carolina to east Texas where most U.S. cotton was produced during the mid-1800s (p. 454)

región algodonera zona que se extendía desde Carolina del Sur hasta el este de Texas, en la que se producía la mayor parte del algodón cosechado en Estados Unidos a mediados del siglo XIX (pág. 454)

cotton diplomacy Confederate efforts to use the importance of southern cotton to Britain's textile industry to persuade the British to support the Confederacy in the Civil War (p. 574)

diplomacia del algodón esfuerzos de la Confederación por aprovechar la importancia del algodón del Sur en la industria textil británica para convencer a Gran Bretaña de apoyar a la Confederación en la Guerra Civil (pág. 574)

cotton gin a machine invented by Eli Whitney in 1793 to remove seeds from short-staple cotton; revolutionized the cotton industry (p. 453)

desmotadora de algodón máquina inventada por Eli Whitney en 1793 para separar las fi bras de algodón de las semillas; revolucionó la industria del algodón (pág. 453)

culture the common values and traditions of a society, such as language, government, and family relationships (p. 7)

cultura valores y tradiciones comunes de una sociedad, como el lenguaje, la forma de gobierno y las relaciones familiares (pág. 7)

Cumberland Road the first federal road project, construction of which began in 1815; ran from Cumberland, Maryland, to present-day Wheeling, West Virginia (p. 307)

camino de Cumberland primer proyecto federal de construcción de carreteras, iniciado en 1815 para crear un camino entre Cumberland, Maryland y el poblado que actualmente lleva el nombre de Wheeling, en Virginia Occidental (pág. 307)

D

Dawes General Allotment Act (1887) legislation passed by Congress that split up Indian reservation lands among individual Indians and promised them citizenship (p. 377)

Ley de Adjudicación General de Dawes (1887) ley aprobada por el Congreso que dividía el terreno de las reservas indígenas entre sus habitantes y les prometía la ciudadanía (pág. 377)

Declaration of Independence (1776) the document written to declare the colonies free from British rule (p. 120)

Declaración de Independencia (1776) document redactado para declarar la independencia de las colonias del dominio británico (pág. 120)

Declaration of Sentiments (1848) a statement written and signed by women's rights supporters at the Seneca Falls Convention; detailed their beliefs about social injustice against women (p. 532)

Declaración de Sentimientos (1848) declaración redactada y fi rmada por partidarios de los derechos de la mujer durante la Convención de Seneca Falls; se describía con detalle su punto de vista sobre las injusticias sociales que afectaban a las mujeres (pág. 532)

deflation a decrease in money supply and overall lower prices (p. 382)

deflación reducción de la disponibilidad del dinero y baja general en los precios (pág. 382)

democracy a government in which people rule themselves (p. 24)

democracia gobierno en el que el pueblo se gobierna a sí mismo (pág. 24)

Democratic Party a political party formed by supporters of Andrew Jackson after the presidential election of 1824 (p. 330)

Partido Demócrata partido político formado por partidarios de Andrew Jackson después de las elecciones presidenciales de 1824 (pág. 330)

Democratic-Republican Party a political party founded in the 1790s by Thomas Jefferson, James Madison, and other leaders who wanted to preserve the power of the state governments and promote agriculture (p. 264)

Partido Demócrata Republicano partido politico formado en la década de 1790 por Thomas Jefferson, James Madison y otros líderes políticos para preserver el poder de los gobiernos estatales y promover la agricultura (pág. 264)

deport to send an immigrant back to his or her country of origin (p. 234)
deportar enviar a un inmigrante de regreso a su país de origen (pág. 234)

depression a steep drop in economic activity combined with rising unemployment (p. 161)
depresión bajón considerable en la actividad económica, combinado con un alza en el desempleo (pág. 161)

Donner party a group of western travelers who were stranded in the Sierra Nevada during the winter of 1846–47; only 45 of the party's 87 members survived (p. 409)
grupo Donner grupo de viajeros del Oeste perdidos en la Sierra Nevada durante el invierno de 1846–47; sólo 45 de los 87 viajeros sobrevivieron (pág. 409)

double jeopardy the act of trying a person twice for the same crime (p. 226)
doble riesgo acto de juzgar a una persona dos veces por el mismo delito (pág. 226)

draft a system of required service in the armed forces (p. 235)
conscripción sistema de servicio obligatorio en las fuerzas armadas (pág. 235)

dry farming a method of farming used by Plains farmers in the 1890s that shifted focus from water-dependent crops to more hardy crops (p. 380)
agricultura de secano método de cultivo que usaban los agricultores de las Planicies en la década de 1890 que provocó un cambio de los cultivos que dependían del agua a otros más resistentes (pág. 380)

due process the fair application of the law (p. 226)
debido proceso aplicación justa de la ley (pág. 226)

E

electoral college a group of people selected from each of the states to cast votes in presidential elections (p. 246)
colegio electoral grupo de personas seleccionado en cada estado para votar en las elecciones presidenciales (pág. 246)

emancipation freeing of the slaves (p. 590)
emancipación liberación de los esclavos (pág. 590)

Emancipation Proclamation (1862) an order issued by President Abraham Lincoln freeing the slaves in areas rebelling against the Union; took effect January 1, 1863 (p. 591)
Proclamación de Emancipación (1862) orden emitida por el presidente Abraham Lincoln para liberar a los esclavos en las áreas que se rebelaban contra la Unión; entró en vigor el primero de enero de 1863 (pág. 591)

embargo the banning of trade with a country (p. 283)
embargo prohibición del comercio con un país (pág. 283)

Embargo Act (1807) a law that prohibited American merchants from trading with other countries (p. 283)
Ley de Embargo (1807) ley que prohibía a los comerciantes norteamericanos comerciar con otros países (pág. 283)

eminent domain the government's power to take personal property to benefit the public (p. 226)
derecho de expropiación poder otorgado al gobierno para tomar propiedades personales en beneficio del público (pág. 226)

empresarios agents who were contracted by the Mexican republic to bring settlers to Texas in the early 1800s (p. 393)
empresarios agentes contratados por la República Mexicana para traer pobladores a Texas a principios del siglo XIX (pág. 393)

encomienda system a system in Spanish America that gave settlers the right to tax local Indians or to demand their labor in exchange for protecting them and converting them to Christianity (p. 51)
sistema de encomienda sistema adoptado en la América española que permitía a los colonos cobrar impuestos a los indígenas o exigirles trabajo a cambio de su protección y de convertirlos al cristianismo (pág. 51)

Enforcement Acts (1870-1871) laws passed by Congress that made it a crime to interfere with elections or deny citizens equal protection under the law (p. 629)
Actos de ejecución (1870-1871) leyes aprobadas por el Congreso que determinaron que era un crimen interferir con las elecciones o negar a los ciudadanos la igualdad ante la ley (pág. 629)

English Bill of Rights (1689) a shift of political power from the British monarchy to Parliament (p. 91)
Declaración de Derechos inglesa (1689) cambio del poder político de la monarquía británica al Parlamento inglés (pág. 91)

Enlightenment the Age of Reason; movement that began in Europe in the 1700s as people began examining the natural world, society, and government (p. 95)
Ilustración Era de la Razón; movimiento iniciado en Europa en el siglo XVIII cuando las personas empezaron a examinar la naturaleza, la sociedad y el gobierno (pág. 95)

environment the climate and landscape that surrounds living things (p. 7)
medio ambiente clima y paisaje donde habitan seres vivos (pág. 7)

Era of Good Feelings a period of peace, pride, and progress for the United States from 1815 to 1825 (p. 302)
Era de los Buenos Sentimientos período de paz, orgullo y progreso en Estados Unidos de 1815 a 1825 (pág. 302)

Erie Canal the canal that runs from Albany to Buffalo, New York; completed in 1825 (p. 309)
canal de Erie canal que va de Albany a Buffalo, Nueva York; completado en 1825 (pág. 309)

executive branch the division of the federal government that includes the president and the administrative departments; enforces the nation's laws (pp. 167, 185)
poder ejecutivo división del gobierno federal que incluye al presidente y a los departamentos administrativos; hace cumplir las leyes de la nación (pág. 167, 185)

executive orders nonlegislative directives issued by the U.S. president in certain circumstances; executive orders have the force of congressional law (p. 192)
órdenes ejecutivas órdenes no legislativas dictadas por el presidente de Estados Unidos en circunstancias específicas; tienen la misma validez que las leyes del Congreso (pág. 192)

Exodusters African Americans who settled western lands in the late 1800s (p. 379)
Exodusters afroamericanos que se establecieron en el Oeste a fi nales del siglo XIX (pág. 379)

F

factor a crop broker who managed the trade between southern planters and their customers (p. 457)
agente agrícola persona que administraba el comercio entre las plantaciones del Sur y sus clients (pág. 457)
fascismo sistema político en el que se considera que el estado o gobierno es más importante que las personas (pág. 830)

federal system a system that divided powers between the states and the federal government (p. 188)
sistema federal sistema en el que se distribuye el poder entre los estados y el gobierno federal (pág. 188)

federalism U.S. system of government in which power is distributed between a central government and individual states (pp. 168, 185)
federalismo sistema de gobierno de Estados Unidos en el que el poder se divide entre una autoridad central y estados individuales (pág. 168, 185)

Federalist Papers a series of essays that defended and explained the Constitution and tried to reassure Americans that the states would not be overpowered by the proposed national government (pp. 171, 186)
Federalist Papers serie de ensayos que defendían y explicaban la Constitución para convencer a los estadounidenses de que el gobierno nacional propuesto no tendría más poder que los estados (pág. 171, 186)

Federalist Party a political party created in the 1790s and influenced by Alexander Hamilton that wanted to strengthen the federal government and promote industry and trade (p. 263)
Partido Federalista partido político creado en la década de 1790 e influenciado por las ideas de Alexander Hamilton para fortalecer al gobierno federal y fomentar la industria y el comercio (pág. 263)

Federalists people who supported ratification of the Constitution (pp. 170, 185)
federalistas personas que apoyaban la ratificación de la Constitución (pág. 170, 185)

Fifteenth Amendment (1870) a constitutional amendment that gave African American men the right to vote (p. 626)
Decimoquinta Enmienda (1870) enmienda constitucional que daba a los hombres afroamericanos el derecho al voto (pág. 626)

54th Massachusetts Infantry African American Civil War regiment that captured Fort Wagner in South Carolina (p. 593)
54to Batallón de Infantería de Massachusetts regimiento afroamericano de la Guerra Civil que tomó el fuerte Wagner en Carolina del Sur (pág. 593)

First Battle of Bull Run (1861) the first major battle of the Civil War, resulting in a Confederate victory; showed that the Civil War would not be won easily (p. 578)
primera batalla de Bull Run (1861) primera batalla importante de la Guerra Civil, en la cual ganó el ejército confederado; demostró que la guerra no se ganaría fácilmente (pág. 578)

First Continental Congress (1774) a meeting of colonial delegates in Philadelphia to decide how to respond to the closing of Boston Harbor, increased taxes, and abuses of authority by the British government; delegates petitioned King George III, listing the freedoms they believed colonists should enjoy (p. 113)

Primer Congreso Continental (1774) reunión de delegados de las colonias en Filadelfi a para decidir cómo responder al cierre del puerto de Boston, al alza de impuestos y a los abusos de la autoridad por parte del gobierno británico; los delegados hicieron peticiones al rey Jorge III, enumerando los derechos que consideraban justos para los colonos (pág. 113)

folktale a story that often provides a moral lesson (pp. 466, 485)
cuento folclórico narración que con frecuencia ofrece una moraleja (pág. 466, 485)

Fort Sumter a federal outpost in Charleston, South Carolina, that was attacked by the Confederates in April 1861, sparking the Civil War (p. 570)
fuerte Sumter puesto de avanzada federal en Charleston, Carolina del Sur, cuyo ataque por parte de los confederados en abril de 1861 dio origen a la Guerra Civil (pág. 570)

forty-niner a gold-seeker who moved to California during the gold rush (p. 409)
del cuarenta y nueve buscador de oro que se mudó a California durante la fiebre del oro (pág. 409)

Fourteenth Amendment (1866) a constitutional amendment giving full rights of citizenship to all people born or naturalized in the United States, except for American Indians (p. 622)
Decimocuarta Enmienda (1866) enmienda constitucional que otorgaba derechos totales de ciudadanía a todas las personas nacidas en Estados Unidos o naturalizadas estadounidenses, con excepción de los indígenas americanos (pág. 622)

Freedmen's Bureau an agency established by Congress in 1865 to help poor people throughout the South (p. 617)
Oficina de los Libertos ofi cina creada por el Congreso en 1865 para ayudar a los pobres del Sur del país (pág. 617)

Freeport Doctrine (1858) a statement made by Stephen Douglas during the Lincoln-Douglas debates that pointed out how people could use popular sovereignty to determine if their state or territory should permit slavery (p. 557)

Doctrina de Freeport (1858) declaración hecha por Stephen Douglas durante los debates Lincoln-Douglas que señalaba que el pueblo podía usar la soberanía popular para decidir si su estado o territorio debía permitir la esclavitud (pág. 557)

Free-Soil Party a political party formed in 1848 by antislavery northerners who left the Whig and Democratic parties because neither addressed the slavery issue (pp. 497, 593)

Partido Tierra Libre partido político formado en 1848 por abolicionistas de los estados del Norte que habían abandonado el Partido Whig y el Partido Demócrata porque ninguno de los dos partidos tenía una postura sobre la esclavitud (pág. 497, 593)

French Revolution French rebellion that began in 1789 in which the French people overthrew the monarchy and made their country a republic (p. 255)

Revolución Francesa rebelión francesa iniciada en 1789 en la que la población francesa derrocó a la monarquía y convirtió el país en una república (pág. 255)

frontier an undeveloped area (p. 364)

frontera área que no está siendo utilizada por el ser humano (pág. 364)

Fugitive Slave Act (1850) a law that made it a crime to help runaway slaves; allowed for the arrest of escaped slaves in areas where slavery was illegal, and required their return to slaveholders (pp. 498, 545)

Ley de Esclavos Fugitivos (1850) ley que hacía que ayudar a un esclavo a escapar de su amo fuera un delito; permitía la captura de esclavos fugitivos en zonas donde la esclavitud era ilegal para devolverlos a sus dueños (pág. 498, 545)

G

Gadsden Purchase (1853) U.S. purchase of land from Mexico that included the southern parts of present-day Arizona and New Mexico (p. 405)

Compra de Gadsden (1853) compra por parte del gobierno de Estados Unidos de territorio mexicano que incluía la región ocupada actualmente por el sur de Arizona y Nuevo México (pág. 405)

Gettysburg Address (1863) a speech given by Abraham Lincoln in which he praised the bravery of Union soldiers and renewed his commitment to winning the Civil War (p. 602)

Discurso de Gettysburg (1863) discurso de Abraham Lincoln en el que alababa la valentía de las tropas de la Unión y renovaba su compromiso de triunfar en la Guerra Civil (pág. 602)

Ghost Dance a religious movement among Native Americans that spread across the Plains in the 1880s (p. 376)

Danza de los Espíritus movimiento religioso de los indígenas norteamericanos que se extendió por la región de las Planicies en la década de 1880 (pág. 376)

Gibbons* v. *Ogden (1824) a Supreme Court ruling that reinforced the federal government's authority over the states (p. 437)

Gibbons contra *Ogden* (1824) decisión de la Corte Suprema que reforzó la autoridad del gobierno federal sobre los estados (pág. 437)

Great Awakening a religious movement that became widespread in the American colonies in the 1730s and 1740s (p. 94)

Gran Despertar movimiento religioso que tuvo gran popularidad en las colonias norteamericanas en las décadas de 1730 y 1740 (pág. 94)

Great Compromise (1787) an agreement worked out at the Constitutional Convention establishing that a state's population would determine representation in the lower house of the legislature, while each state would have equal representation in the upper house of the legislature (pp. 166, 183)

Gran Compromiso (1787) acuerdo redactado durante la Convención Constitucional en el que se establece que la población de un estado debe determinar su representación en la cámara baja de la asamblea legislativa y que cada estado debe tener igual representación en la cámara alta de la asamblea (pág. 166, 183)

H

habeas corpus the constitutional protection against unlawful imprisonment (p. 595)

hábeas corpus protección constitucional contra el encarcelamiento ilegal (pág. 595)

hajj a pilgrimage to Mecca made by devout Muslims (p. 21)

hajj peregrinación a La Meca realizada por los musulmanes devotos (pág. 21)

Hartford Convention (1815) a meeting of Federalists at Hartford, Connecticut, to protest the War of 1812 (p. 291)

Convención de Hartford (1815) reunión de federalistas en Hartford, Connecticut, para protestar por la Guerra de 1812 (pág. 291)

Homestead Act (1862) a law passed by Congress to encourage settlement in the West by giving government-owned land to small farmers (p. 378)

Ley de Heredad (1862) ley aprobada por el Congreso para fomentar la colonización del Oeste mediante la cesión de tierras del gobierno a pequeños agricultores (pág. 378)

Hudson River school a group of American artists in the mid-1800s whose paintings focused on the American landscape (p. 315)

Escuela del Río Hudson grupo de artistas estadounidenses de mediados del siglo XIX que pintaban diversos paisajes del territorio estadounidense (pág. 315)

hunter-gatherer a person who hunts animals and gathers wild plants to provide for his or her needs (p. 7)

cazador y recolector persona que caza animals y recolecta plantas para satisfacer sus necesidades (pág. 7)

I

immigrant a person who moves to another country after leaving his or her homeland (p. 75)

inmigrante persona que abandona su país para establecerse en un país diferente (pág. 75)

immune having a natural resistance to disease (p. 476)

inmune la condición de tener resistencia natural contra la enfermedad (pág. 476)

impeach to bring charges against a public official (p. 191)

someter a juicio político presentar cargos en contra de un funcionario público (pág. 191)

impeachment the process used by a legislative body to bring charges of wrongdoing against a public official (p. 624)

juicio político proceso por el cual un cuerpo legislativo presenta cargos en contra de un funcionario público (pág. 624)

impressment the practice of forcing people to serve in the army or navy; led to increased tensions between Great Britain and the United States in the early 1800s (p. 282)

leva práctica que obligaba a las personas a servir en el ejército o la marina; aumentó las fricciones entre Gran Bretaña y Estados Unidos a principios del siglo XIX (pág. 282)

indentured servant a colonist who received free passage to North America in exchange for working without pay for a certain number of years (p. 70)

sirviente por contrato colono que recibía un pasaje gratuito a América del Norte a cambio de trabajar sin salario por varios años (pág. 70)

Indian Removal Act (1830) a congressional act that authorized the removal of Native Americans who lived east of the Mississippi River (p. 340)

Ley de Expulsión de Indígenas (1830) ley del Congreso que autorizaba la expulsión de los indígenas norteamericanos que vivían al este del río Mississippi (pág. 340)

English and Spanish Glossary

Indian Territory an area covering most of present-day Oklahoma to which most Native Americans in the Southeast were forced to move in the 1830s (p. 340)
Territorio Indígena área que abarcaba la mayor parte del actual estado de Oklahoma a la que la mayoría de las tribus indígenas del sureste fueron obligadas a trasladarse durante la década de 1830 (pág. 340)

indict to formally accuse (p. 226)
acusar presentar cargos formales en contra de alguien (pág. 226)

Industrial Revolution a period of rapid growth in the use of machines in manufacturing and production that began in the mid-1700s (p. 424)
Revolución Industrial período de rápido desarrollo debido al uso de maquinaria en la fabricación y producción; comenzó a mediados del siglo XVIII (pág. 424)

inflation increased prices for goods and services combined with the reduced value of money (p. 161)
inflación subida en los precios de los bienes al mismo tiempo que se reduce al valor del dinero (pág. 161)

interchangeable parts a process developed by Eli Whitney in the 1790s that called for making each part of a machine exactly the same (p. 426)
piezas intercambiables proceso desarrollado por Eli Whitney en la década de 1790 para que todas las piezas de una máquina fueran exactamente iguales (pág. 426)

interest group a group of people who share common interests for political action (p. 237)
grupo de interés grupo de personas que comparten intereses comunes en iniciativas políticas (pág. 237)

interstate commerce trade between two or more states (p. 160)
comercio interestatal intercambio comercial entre dos o más estados (pág. 160)

Intolerable Acts (1774) laws passed by Parliament to punish the colonists for the Boston Tea Party and to tighten government control of the colonies (p. 112)
Leyes Intolerables (1774) serie de leyes aprobadas por el Parlamento para castigar a los colonos que participaron en el Motín del Té de Boston y para aumentar su control sobre las colonias (pág. 112)

ironclad a warship that is heavily armored with iron (p. 582)
acorazado buque de guerra fuertemente protegido con hierro (pág. 582)

Iroquois League a political confederation of five northeastern Native American nations of the Seneca, Oneida, Mohawk, Cayuga, and Onondaga that made decisions concerning war and peace (p. 15)
Liga de Iroqueses confederación política formada por cinco naciones indígenas del noreste de Estados Unidos (los senecas, los oneidas, los mohawks, los cayugas y los onondagas) para tomar decisions relacionadas con asuntos de guerra y paz (pág. 15)

J

Jacksonian Democracy an expansion of voting rights during the popular Andrew Jackson administration (p. 330)
democracia jacksoniana ampliación del derecho al voto durante el popular gobierno del president Andrew Jackson (pág. 330)

Jamestown the first colony in the U.S.; set up in 1607 along the James River in Virginia (p. 68)
Jamestown primera colonia en territorio estadounidense; fundada en 1607 a orillas del río James en Virginia (pág. 68)

Jay's Treaty (1794) an agreement negotiated by John Jay to work out problems between Britain and the United States over northwestern lands, British seizure of U.S. ships, and U.S. debts owed to the British (p. 257)
Tratado de Jay (1794) acuerdo negociado por John Jay para resolver los problemas entre Gran Bretaña y Estados Unidos por los territorios del noroeste, la confiscación británica de barcos estadounidenses, y las deudas que los estadounidenses les debían a los británicos (pág. 257)

Jim Crow law a law that enforced segregation in the southern states (p. 631)
ley de Jim Crow ley que imponía la segregación en los estados del Sur (pág. 631)

John Brown's raid (1859) an incident in which abolitionist John Brown and 21 other men captured a federal arsenal in Harpers Ferry, Virginia, in hope of starting a slave rebellion (p. 558)
ataque de John Brown (1859) incidente en el que el abolicionista John Brown y otros 21 hombres capturaron un arsenal federal en Harpers Ferry, Virginia, con la esperanza de iniciar una rebelión de esclavos (pág. 558)

joint-stock company a business formed by a group of people who jointly make an investment and share in the profits and losses (p. 28)
sociedad por acciones negocio formado por un grupo de personas que hacen una inversión juntos y comparten las ganancias y las pérdidas (pág. 28)

judicial branch the division of the federal government that is made up of the national courts; interprets laws, punishes criminals, and settles disputes between states (pp. 167, 185)
poder judicial división del gobierno federal formada por las cortes nacionales; interpreta las leyes, castiga a los delincuentes y resuelve las disputas entre estados (pág. 167, 185)

judicial review the Supreme Court's power to declare acts of Congress unconstitutional (p. 274)
recurso de inconstitucionalidad (revision judicial) poder de la Corte Suprema para declarar inconstitucionales las leyes del Congreso (pág. 274)

Judiciary Act of 1789 legislation passed by Congress that created the federal court system (p. 248)
Ley de Judicatura de 1789 ley aprobada por el Congreso para crear el sistema federal de cortes (pág. 248)

K

Kansas-Nebraska Act (1854) a law that allowed voters in Kansas and Nebraska to choose whether to allow slavery (p. 549)

Ley de Kansas y Nebraska (1854) ley que permitía a los votantes de Kansas y Nebraska decidir si permitían la esclavitud (pág. 549)

Kentucky and Virginia Resolutions (1798–1799) Republican documents that argued that the Alien and Sedition Acts were unconstitutional (p. 267)
Resoluciones de Kentucky y Virginia (1798–1799) documentos republicanos que argumentaban que las Leyes de No Intervención Extranjera y Sedición eran inconstitucionales (pág. 267)

Kitchen Cabinet Pres. Andrew Jackson's group of informal advisers; so called because they often met in the White House kitchen (p. 332)
gabinete de la cocina grupo informal de consejeros del presidente Andrew Jackson; llamado así porque solían reunirse en la cocina de la Casa Blanca (pág. 332)

kivas underground ceremonial chambers at the center of Anasazi communities (p. 12)
kivas cámaras ceremoniales subterráneas en el centro de las comunidades anasazi (pág. 12)

knights warriors who fought on horseback in return for land from nobles (p. 25)
caballeros guerreros que luchaban a caballo a cambio de tierras de los nobles (pág. 25)

Know-Nothing Party a political organization founded in 1849 by nativists who supported measures making it difficult for foreigners to become citizens and to hold office (p. 510)
Partido de los Ignorantes organización política fundada en 1849 por un grupo de nativistas; apoyaba medidas que dificultaban que los extranjeros obtuvieran la ciudadanía y que tuvieran cargos públicos (pág. 510)

Ku Klux Klan a secret society created by white southerners in 1866 that used terror and violence to keep African Americans from obtaining their civil rights (p. 629)
Ku Klux Klan sociedad secreta creada en 1866 por blancos del Sur que usaba el terror y la violencia para impedir que los afroamericanos obtuvieran derechos civiles (pág. 629)

English and Spanish Glossary

L

Land Ordinance of 1785 legislation passed by Congress authorizing surveys and the division of public lands in the western region of the country (p. 155)
Ordenanza de Territorios de 1785 legislación aprobada por el Congreso en la que se autorizaban las mediciones de terreno y la división de territories públicos en el oeste del país (pág. 155)

legislative branch the division of the government that proposes bills and passes them into laws (pp. 167, 185)
poder legislativo división del gobierno que propone proyectos de ley y los aprueba para convertirlos en leyes (pág. 167, 185)

Lewis and Clark expedition an expedition led by Meriwether Lewis and William Clark that began in 1804 to explore the Louisiana Purchase (p. 356)
expedición de Lewis y Clark expedición encabezada por Meriwether Lewis y William Clark que empezó en 1804 para explorar la Compra de Luisiana (pág. 356)

Lincoln-Douglas debates a series of debates between Republican Abraham Lincoln and Democrat Stephen Douglas during the 1858 U.S. Senate campaign in Illinois (p. 555)
debates Lincoln-Douglas serie de debates entre el republicano Abraham Lincoln y el demócrata Stephen Douglas durante la campaña de 1858 para el Senado estadounidense en Illinois (pág. 555)

Line of Demarcation boundary between Spanish and Portuguese territories in the New World (p. 43)
Línea de Demarcación límite entre los territorios españoles y portugueses en el Nuevo Mundo (pág. 43)

Long Walk (1864) a 300-mile march made by Navajo captives to a reservation in Bosque Redondo, New Mexico, that led to the deaths of hundreds of Navajo (p. 375)
Larga Marcha (1864) caminata de 300 millas que hizo un grupo de prisioneros navajos hasta una reserva indígena en Bosque Redondo, Nuevo México, en la que murieron cientos de ellos (pág. 375)

loose construction a way of interpreting the Constitution that allows the federal government to take actions that the Constitution does not specifically forbid it from taking (p. 254)
interpretación flexible interpretación de la Constitución que permite al gobierno federal tomar acciones que la Constitución no prohíbe de manera específica (pág. 254)

Louisiana Purchase (1803) the purchase of French land between the Mississippi River and the Rocky Mountains that doubled the size of the United States (pp. 271, 356)
Compra de Luisiana (1803) adquisición del territorio francés localizado entre el río Mississippi y las montañas Rocallosas que duplicó el tamaño de Estados Unidos (pág. 271, 356)

Lowell system the use of waterpowered textile mills that employed young, unmarried women in the 1800s (p. 431)
sistema de Lowell uso de molinos de agua en la industria textil, dando empleo a muchas mujeres jóvenes solteras en el siglo XIX (pág. 431)

Loyalists colonists who sided with Britain in the American Revolution (p. 120)
leales colonos que apoyaron la causa británica durante la Guerra de Independencia estadounidense (pág. 120)

M

Magna Carta (1215) a charter of liberties agreed to by King John of England, it made the king obey the same laws as citizens (p. 152)
Carta Magna (1215) carta de libertades firmada por el rey Juan de Inglaterra que decía que el rey debía obedecer las mismas leyes que los ciudadanos (pág. 152)

majority rule the idea that policies are decided by the greatest number of people (p. 223)
gobierno de la mayoría idea de que las políticas se adoptan según lo que decida el mayor número de personas (pág. 223)

manifest destiny a belief shared by many Americans in the mid-1800s that the United States should expand across the continent to the Pacific Ocean (p. 397)
destino manifiesto creencia de muchos ciudadanos estadounidenses a mediados del siglo XIX de que Estados Unidos debía expandirse por todo el continente hasta el océano Pacífico (pág. 397)

Marbury v. *Madison* (1803) U.S. Supreme Court case that established the principle of judicial review (p. 273)
Marbury contra *Madison* (1803) caso de la Corte Suprema de Estados Unidos que estableció recurso de inconstitucionalidad (pág. 273)

Massacre at Wounded Knee (1890) the U.S. Army's killing of approximately 150 Sioux at Wounded Knee Creek in South Dakota; ended U.S-Indian wars on the Plains (p. 375)
masacre de Wounded Knee (1890) matanza de aproximadamente 150 indios siux en Wounded Knee Creek, Dakota del Sur; dio por terminadas las guerras entre estadounidenses e indígenas en las Planicies (pág. 375)

mass production the efficient production of large numbers of identical goods (p. 427)
producción en masa producción eficiente de grandes cantidades de productos idénticos (pág. 427)

matrilineal related to ancestry traced through the maternal, or mother's, line (p. 15)
materno basado en linaje seguido por línea materna, o de la madre (pág. 15)

Mayflower Compact (1620) a document written by the Pilgrims establishing themselves as a political society and setting guidelines for self-government (p. 76)
Pacto del Mayflower (1620) documento redactado por los peregrinos en el que se establecían como sociedad política y establecían principios para gobernarse a sí mismos (pág. 76)

McCulloch v. *Maryland* (1819) U.S. Supreme Court case that declared the Second Bank of the United States was constitutional and that Maryland could not interfere with it (p. 337)
McCulloch contra *Maryland* (1819) caso de la Corte Suprema de Estados Unidos que declaraba que el Segundo Banco de la Nación era constitucional y que Maryland no podía intervenir en sus operaciones (pág. 337)

mercenaries hired foreign soldiers (p. 131)
mercenarios soldados extranjeros a sueldo (pág. 131)

middle class the social and economic level between the wealthy and the poor (p. 511)
clase media nivel social y económico ubicado entre la clase rica y la clase pobre (pág. 511)

Middle Passage a voyage that brought enslaved Africans across the Atlantic Ocean to North America and the West Indies (p. 477)
Viaje Intermedio viaje a través del océano Atlántico para transportar esclavos africanos a América del Norte y a las Antillas (pág. 477)

migration the movement of people from one region to another (p. 7)
migración movimiento de personas de una región a otra (pág. 7)

minutemen American colonial militia members ready to fight at a minute's notice (p. 115)
minutemen milicanos norteamericanos en la época colonial que estaban preparados para combater en cualquier momento si la situación lo requería (pág. 115)

Missouri Compromise (1820) an agreement proposed by Henry Clay that allowed Missouri to enter the Union as a slave state and Maine to enter as a free state and outlawed slavery in any territories or states north of 36°30′ latitude (p. 310)
Compromiso de Missouri (1820) acuerdo propuesto por Henry Clay en el que se aceptaba a Missouri en la Unión como estado esclavista y a Maine como estado libre, además de prohibir la esclavitud en los territorios o estados al norte del paralelo 36°30′ (pág. 310)

English and Spanish Glossary

Monroe Doctrine (1823) President James Monroe's statement forbidding further colonization in the Americas and declaring that any attempt by a foreign country to colonize would be considered an act of hostility (p. 304)
Doctrina Monroe (1823) declaración hecha por el presidente James Monroe en la que se prohibía la colonización adicional de las Américas y se declaraba que cualquier intento de colonización por parte de otro país se consideraría un acto hostil (pág. 304)

Mormon a member of the Church of Jesus Christ of Latter-day Saints (p. 360)
mormón miembro de la Iglesia de Jesucristo de los Santos de los Últimos Días (pág. 360)

Morrill Act (1862) a federal law passed by Congress that gave land to western states to encourage them to build colleges (p. 378)
Ley de Morrill (1862) ley federal aprobada por el Congreso que otorgaba tierras a los estados del Oeste para fomentar la construcción de universidades (pág. 378)

Morse code a system developed by Alfred Lewis Vail for the telegraph that used a certain combination of dots and dashes to represent each letter of the alphabet (p. 441)
clave Morse sistema desarrollado por Alfred Lewis Vail para el telégrafo en el que una combinación de puntos y rayas representa cada letra del alfabeto (pág. 441)

mosques buildings used for Muslim prayer (p. 21)
mezquitas casas de oración musulmanas (pág. 21)

mountain men men hired by eastern companies to trap animals for fur in the Rocky Mountains and other western regions of the United States (p. 358)
montañeses hombres contratados por compañías del este para atrapar animales y obtener sus pieles en las montañas Rocallosas y en otras regiones del oeste de Estados Unidos (pág. 358)

N

national debt the total amount of money owed by a country to its lenders (p. 250)
deuda nacional cantidad total de dinero que un país debe a quienes se lo prestaron (pág. 250)

National Grange a social and educational organization for farmers (p. 382)
National Grange organización social y educativa para los agricultores (pág. 382)

nationalism a sense of pride and devotion to a nation (p. 302)
nacionalismo sentimiento de orgullo y lealtad a una nación (pág. 302)

nativists U.S. citizens who opposed immigration because they were suspicious of immigrants and feared losing jobs to them (p. 510)
nativistas ciudadanos estadounidenses que se oponían a la inmigración porque sospechaban de los inmigrantes y temían que se apropiaran de sus empleos (pág. 510)

Nat Turner's Rebellion (1831) a rebellion in which Nat Turner led a group of slaves in Virginia in an unsuccessful attempt to overthrow and kill planter families (p. 487)
Rebelión de Nat Turner (1831) rebelión de un grupo de esclavos encabezados por Nat Turner en Virginia en un intento frustrado de derrocar y asesinar familias que eran dueñas de plantaciones (pág. 487)

naturalized citizen a person born in another country who has been granted citizenship in the United States (p. 234)
ciudadano naturalizado persona nacida en otro país que ha obtenido la ciudadanía estadounidense (pág. 234)

Neutrality Proclamation (1793) a statement made by President George Washington that the United States would not side with any of the nations at war in Europe following the French Revolution (p. 256)
Proclamación de Neutralidad (1793) declaración en la que el presidente George Washington anunció que Estados Unidos no sería aliado de ninguna de las naciones europeas en guerra después de la Revolución Francesa (pág. 256)

New Jersey Plan a proposal to create a unicameral legislature with equal representation of states rather than representation by population; rejected at the Constitutional Convention (pp. 166, 183)
Plan de Nueva Jersey propuesta para la creación de un gobierno de una cámara con la misma representación para cada estado sin importer el tamaño de su población; fue rechazada en la Convención Constitucional (pág. 166, 183)

nominating conventions a meeting at which a political party selects its presidential and vice presidential candidate; first held in the 1820s (p. 330)
convenciones de nominación reunión en la que un partido político elige a sus candidatos a la presidencia y la vicepresidencia; se realizaron por primera vez en la década de 1820 (pág. 330)

Non-Intercourse Act (1809) a law that replaced the Embargo Act and restored trade with all nations except Britain, France, and their colonies (p. 284)
Ley de No Interacción (1809) ley que reemplazaba a la Ley de Embargo, restableciendo el comercio con todas las naciones, excepto Gran Bretaña, Francia y sus colonias (pág. 284)

Northwest Ordinance of 1787 legislation passed by Congress to establish a political structure for the Northwest Territory and create a system for the admission of new states (p. 155)
Ordenanza del Noroeste de 1787 legislación aprobada por el Congreso para establecer una estructura política en el Territorio del Noroeste y crear un proceso de admisión de nuevos estados (pág. 155)

Northwest Passage a nonexistent path through North America that early explorers searched for that would allow ships to sail from the Atlantic to the Pacific Ocean (p. 55)
Paso del Noroeste ruta inexistente buscada po muchos exploradores a lo largo de América del Norte para cruzar en barco del océano Atlántico al océano Pacífico (pág. 55)

Northwest Territory lands including present-day Illinois, Indiana, Michigan, Ohio, and Wisconsin; organized by the Northwest Ordinance of 1787 (p. 155)
Territorio del Noroeste región que incluía los actuals estados de Illinois, Indiana, Michigan, Ohio y Wisconsin; creado por la Ordenanza del Noroeste de 1787 (pág. 155)

nullification crisis a dispute led by John C. Calhoun that said that states could ignore federal laws if they believed those laws violated the Constitution (p. 335)
crisis de anulación controversia iniciada por John C. Calhoun que decía que los estados no tenían que hacer caso a las leyes federales si consideraban que desobedecían la Constitución (pág. 335)

O

oral tradition passing down stories, poems, and songs by word of mouth (p. 466)
tradición oral transmitir verbalmente relatos, poemas y canciones de generación en generación (pág. 466)

Oregon Trail a 2,000-mile trail stretching through the Great Plains from western Missouri to the Oregon Territory (p. 359)
Camino de Oregón ruta de 2,000 millas que cruzaba las Grandes Planicies desde el oeste de Missouri hasta el Territorio de Oregón (pág. 359)

overseer men hired by farmers and planters to oversee and direct the work of slaves on plantations (p. 464)
capataz hombres contratados por los agricultores y plantadores de supervisar y dirigir el trabajo de los esclavos en las plantaciones (pág. 464)

P

Paleo-Indians the first Americans who crossed from Asia into North America sometime between 38,000 and 10,000 BC (p. 7)
paleoindígenas primeros habitantes de América que cruzaron de Asia a América del Norte entre 38,000 y 10,000 a. C. (pág. 7)

English and Spanish Glossary

Panic of 1837 a financial crisis in the United States that led to an economic depression (p. 339)

Pánico de 1837 crisis financiera en Estados Unidos que provocó una depresión económica (pág. 339)

Patriots American colonists who fought for independence from Great Britain during the Revolutionary War (p. 114)

patriotas colonos que lucharon para independizarse de Gran Bretaña durante la Guerra de Independencia estadounidense (pág. 114)

petition to make a formal request of the government (p. 225)

peticionar hacer una solicitud formal al gobierno (pág. 225)

Pickett's Charge (1863) a failed Confederate attack during the Civil War led by General George Pickett at the Battle of Gettysburg (p. 601)

ataque de Pickett (1863) ataque fallido del ejército confederado, al mando del general George Pickett, en la batalla de Gettysburg durante la Guerra Civil (pág. 601)

Pilgrim a member of a Puritan Separatist sect that left England in the early 1600s to settle in the Americas (p. 75)

peregrino miembro de una secta separatista puritan que se fue de Inglaterra a principios del siglo XVII para establecerse en América (pág. 75)

Pinckney's Treaty (1795) an agreement between the United States and Spain that changed Florida's border and made it easier for American ships to use the port of New Orleans (p. 257)

Tratado de Pinckney (1795) acuerdo entre Estados Unidos y España que modifi có los límites de Florida y facilitó a los barcos estadounidenses el uso del Puerto de Nueva Orleáns (pág. 257)

placer miner a person who mines for gold by using pans or other devices to wash gold nuggets out of loose rock and gravel (p. 410)

buscador de oro con batea persona que busca oro con bateas u otros aparatos similares para lavar las pepitas de oro y separarlas de las piedras y la gravilla (pág. 410)

plantation a large farm that usually specialized in growing one kind of crop for profit (p. 52)

plantación gran fi nca que por lo general se especializaba en un cultivo específico para obtener ganancias (pág. 52)

planter a large-scale farmer who held more than 20 slaves (p. 454)

hacendado agricultor a gran escala que tenía más de 20 esclavos (pág. 454)

Plessy v. Ferguson (1896) U.S. Supreme Court case that established the "separate-but-equal" doctrine for public facilities (p. 631)

Plessy contra Ferguson (1896) caso en el que la Corte Suprema de Estados Unidos estableció la doctrina de "separados pero iguales" en los lugares públicos (pág. 631)

political action committee (PAC) an organization that collects money to distribute to candidates who support the same issues as the contributors (p. 237)

comité de acción política (PAC, por sus siglas en inglés) organización que recolecta dinero para distribuirlo a los candidatos que apoyen los mismos asuntos que los contribuyentes (pág. 237)

political party a group of people who organize to help elect government officials and influence government policies (p. 263)

partido político grupo de personas que se organiza para facilitar la elección de los funcionarios del gobierno e influye en las políticas del gobierno (pág. 263)

poll tax a special tax that a person had to pay in order to vote (p. 631)

impuesto electoral impuesto especial que tenía que pagar una persona para poder votar (pág. 631)

Pony Express a system of messengers that carried mail between relay stations on a route 2,000 miles long in 1860 and 1861 (p. 367)

Pony Express sistema de mensajeros que llevaban el correo entre estaciones de relevo a lo largo de una ruta de 2,000 millas en 1860 y 1861 (pág. 367)

popular sovereignty the idea that political authority belongs to the people (pp. 185, 542)

soberanía popular idea de que la autoridad política pertenece al pueblo (pág. 185, 542)

Populist Party a political party formed in 1892 that supported free coinage of silver, work reforms, immigration restrictions, and government ownership of railroads and telegraph and telephone systems (p. 383)
Partido Populista partido político formado en 1892 que apoyaba la libre producción de monedas de plata, reformas laborales y restricciones de la inmigración, además de asignar al gobierno la propiedad de los sistemas ferroviario, telegráfico y telefónico (pág. 383)

Pottawatomie Massacre (1856) an incident in which abolitionist John Brown and seven other men murdered pro-slavery Kansans (p. 551)
masacre de Pottawatomie (1856) incidente en el que el abolicionista John Brown y siete hombres más asesinaron a habitantes esclavistas de Kansas (pág. 551)

precedent an action or decision that later serves as an example (p. 247)
precedente acción o decisión que más tarde sirve de ejemplo (pág. 247)

privateer a private ship authorized by a nation to attack its enemies (p. 256)
corsario barco privado autorizado por una nación para atacar a sus enemigos (pág. 256)

prospect to search for gold (p. 410)
prospectar buscar oro (pág. 410)

Protestant Reformation a religious movement begun by Martin Luther and others in 1517 to reform the Catholic Church (p. 53)
Reforma Protestante movimiento religioso iniciado por Martín Lutero y otros en 1517 para reformar la Iglesia católica (pág. 53)

Protestants reformers who protested certain practices of the Catholic Church (p. 54)
protestantes reformistas que protestaban por ciertas prácticas de la Iglesia católica (pág. 54)

pueblos above-ground houses made of heavy clay called adobe that were built by Native Americans of the southwestern United States (p. 11)
pueblos casas de arcilla gruesa, llamada adobe, construidas más arriba de la superficie por indígenas del suroeste de Estados Unidos (pág. 11)

Puritans Protestants who wanted to reform the Church of England (p. 75)
puritanos protestantes que querían reformar la Iglesia anglicana (pág. 75)

Q

Quakers Society of Friends; Protestant sect begun in 1640s in England whose members believed that salvation was available to all people (p. 85)
cuáqueros Sociedad de Amigos; secta protestante fundada en la década de 1640 en Inglaterra cuyos miembros creían que la salvación estaba al alcance de todos (pág. 85)

Quartering Act (1774) One of the Coercive or Intolerable Acts that helped fan the falames of revolution in the English colonies. It required each colonist to provide a place in their home, or quarter, for British soldiers. (p. 112)
Ley de Acuartelamiento (1774) Uno de los actos coersitivos o intolerables que ayudó a inspirar la revolución en las colonias inglesas. Requería que cada colono proveyera alojamiento en su casa para los soldados británicos. (pág. 112)

R

Radical Republicans members of Congress who felt that southern states needed to make great social changes before they could be readmitted to the Union (p. 622)
republicanos radicales miembros del Congreso convencidos de que los estados del Sur necesitaban hacer grandes cambios sociales antes de volver a ser admitidos en la Unión (pág. 622)

ratification an official approval (p. 154)
ratificación aprobación formal (pág. 154)

reason clear and ordered thinking; Greek philosopher Aristotle believed it was the basis of a good life (p. 23)
razón ideas claras y ordenadas; el fi lósofo griego Aristóteles pensaba que la razón era la base de una vida buena (pág. 23)

Reconstruction (1865–1877) the period following the Civil War during which the U.S. government worked to reunite the nation and to rebuild the southern states (p. 614)
Reconstrucción (1865–1877) período posterior a la Guerra Civil en el que el gobierno de Estados Unidos trabajó por reunifi car de la nación y reconstruir los estados del Sur (pág. 614)

English and Spanish Glossary

Reconstruction Acts (1867–1868) the laws that put the southern states under U.S. military control and required them to draft new constitutions upholding the Fourteenth Amendment (p. 623)
Leyes de Reconstrucción (1867–1868) leyes que declaraban a los estados del Sur territorio sujeto al control militar estadounidense y los obligaban a reformar sus constituciones de manera que defendieran la Decimocuarta Enmienda (pág. 623)

Redcoats British soldiers who fought against the colonists in the American Revolution; so called because of their bright red uniforms (p. 115)
casacas rojas soldados británicos que lucharon contra los colonos en la Guerra de Independencia estadounidense, llamados así por el color rojo fuerte de sus uniformes (pág. 115)

Republican Party a political party formed in the 1850s to stop the spread of slavery in the West (p. 553)
Partido Republicano partido político formado en la década de 1850 para detener la expansión de la esclavitud en el Oeste (pág. 553)

reservations federal lands set aside for American Indians (p. 372)
reservas territorios federales reservados para los indígenas norteamericanos (pág. 372)

Rhode Island system a system developed by Samuel Slater in the mid-1800s in which whole families were hired as textile workers and factory work was divided into simple tasks (p. 431)
sistema de Rhode Island sistema desarrollado por Samuel Slater a mediados del siglo XIX mediante el cual se contrataba a familias completas para trabajar en la industria textil y en el que el trabajo de las fábricas estaba dividido en tareas sencillas (pág. 431)

Rush-Bagot Agreement (1817) an agreement that limited naval power on the Great Lakes for both the United States and British Canada (p. 292)
Acuerdo de Rush-Bagot (1817) acuerdo que limitaba el poder naval de Estados Unidos y la Canadá británica en los Grandes Lagos (pág. 292)

S

salutary neglect an English policy of relaxing the enforcement of regulations in its colonies in return for the colonies' continued economic loyalty (p. 98)
negligencia saludable una política inglesa de regulaciones menos estrictas en sus colonias a cambio de la lealtad continua económica de las colonias (pág. 98)

Santa Fe Trail an important trade trail west from Independence, Missouri, to Santa Fe, New Mexico (p. 360)
Camino de Santa Fe importante ruta comercial que va desde Independence, Missouri, hasta Santa Fe, Nuevo México (pág. 360)

search warrant a judge's order authorizing the search of a person's home or property to look for evidence of a crime (p. 225)
orden de registro orden de un juez que permite registrar el hogar y las pertenencias de una persona en busca de pruebas de un delito (pág. 225)

secede to formally withdraw from the Union (pp. 497, 543)
separarse salirse formalmente de la Unión (pág. 497, 543)

Second Battle of Bull Run (1862) a Civil War battle in which the Confederate army forced most of the Union army out of Virginia (p. 579)
segunda batalla de Bull Run (1862) batalla de la Guerra Civil en la que el ejército confederado obligó a gran parte del ejército de la Unión a abandoner Virginia (pág. 579)

Second Continental Congress (1775) a meeting of colonial delegates in Philadelphia to decide how to react to fighting at Lexington and Concord (p. 116)
Segundo Congreso Continental (1775) reunión de delegados coloniales en Filadelfi a para decidir cómo reaccionar ante la lucha en Lexington y Concord (pág. 116)

Second Great Awakening a period of religious evangelism that began in the 1790s and became widespread in the U.S. by the 1830s (p. 518)

Segundo Gran Despertar período de evangelización religiosa iniciado en la década de 1790 que se extendió por Estados Unidos para la década de 1830 (pág. 518)

sectionalism a devotion to the interests of one geographic region over the interests of the country as a whole (pp. 310, 497, 543)

regionalismo lealtad a los intereses de una region geográfica más que a los del país entero (pág. 310, 497, 543)

segregation the forced separation of people of different races in public places (p. 631)

segregación separación obligada de personas de diferentes razas en lugares públicos (pág. 631)

Seneca Falls Convention (1848) the first national women's rights convention at which the Declaration of Sentiments was written (p. 532)

Convención de Seneca Falls (1848) primera convención nacional a favor de los derechos de la mujer, en la cual se redactó la Declaración de Sentimientos (pág. 532)

Seven Days' Battles (1862) a series of Civil War battles in which Confederate army successes forced the Union army to retreat from Richmond, Virginia, the Confederate capital (p. 579)

batallas de los Siete Días (1862) serie de batallas de la Guerra Civil en las que las victorias del ejército confederado obligaron a las tropas de la Unión a retirarse de Richmond, Virginia, la capital confederada (pág. 579)

sharecropping a system used on southern farms after the Civil War in which farmers worked land owned by someone else in return for a small portion of the crops (p. 632)

cultivo de aparceros sistema usado en las granjas sureñas después de la Guerra Civil en el que los agricultores trabajaban las tierras de otra persona a cambio de una pequeña porción de la cosecha (pág. 632)

Shays's Rebellion (1786–87) an uprising of Massachusetts's farmers, led by Daniel Shays, to protest high taxes, heavy debt, and farm foreclosures (p. 161)

Rebelión de Shays (1786–87) rebelión de agricultores de Massachusetts, encabezados por Daniel Shays, para protestar por los altos impuestos, las grandes deudas y el embargo de las granjas (pág. 161)

Siege of Vicksburg (1863) the Union army's six-week blockade of Vicksburg that led the city to surrender during the Civil War (p. 585)

Sitio de Vicksburg (1863) bloqueo de seis semanas realizado por el ejército de la Unión en Vicksburg para forzar la rendición de esa ciudad durante la Guerra Civil (pág. 585)

slave codes laws passed in the colonies to control slaves (p. 74)

códigos de esclavos leyes aprobadas por las colonias para controlar a los esclavos (pág. 74)

sodbusters the name given to Plains farmers who worked hard to break up the region's tough sod (p. 380)

sodbusters nombre dado a los agricultores de las Planicies que se esforzaron mucho para trabajar el duro terreno de la región (pág. 380)

Spanish Armada a large Spanish fleet defeated by England in 1588 (p. 54)

Armada española gran flota española derrotada por las tropas de Inglaterra en 1588 (pág. 54)

speculator an investor who buys items at low prices in hope that their values will rise (p. 250)

especulador inversionista que compra artículos a precios bajos con la esperanza de que su valor aumente (pág. 250)

spirituals emotional Christian songs sung by enslaved people in the South that mixed African and European elements and usually expressed slaves' religious beliefs (p. 466, 585)

espirituales canciones religiosas emotivas cantadas por los esclavos del Sur que combinaban elementos de origen africano y europeo y solían expresar sus creencias religiosas (pág. 466, 585)

spoils system a politician's practice of giving government jobs to his or her supporters (p. 332)

tráfico de influencias práctica de los políticos de ofrecer empleos a las personas que los apoyan (pág. 332)

English and Spanish Glossary

Stamp Act of 1765 a law passed by Parliament that raised tax money by requiring colonists to pay for an official stamp whenever they bought paper items such as newspapers, licenses, and legal documents (p. 107)

Ley del Sello de 1765 ley aprobada por el Parlamento para recaudar impuestos en la que se obligaba a los colonos a pagar un sello oficial cada vez que compraran artículos de papel, como periódicos, licencias y documentos legales (pág. 107)

standard time the system set up by the railroad companies that divided the country into four time zones (p. 370)

hora estándar el sistema establecido por las compañías de ferrocarriles que dividieron al país en cuatro zonas de tiempo (pág. 370)

staple crop a crop that is continuously in demand (p. 86)

cultivo básico cultivo de demanda constante (pág. 86)

states' rights doctrine the belief that the power of the states should be greater than the power of the federal government (p. 335)

doctrina de los derechos estatales creencia de que el poder de los estados debe ser mayor que el del gobierno federal (pág. 335)

strict construction a way of interpreting the Constitution that allows the federal government to take only those actions the Constitution specifically says it can take (p. 254)

interpretación estricta interpretación de la Constitución que sólo permite al gobierno federal hacer las acciones mencionadas específicamente en ella (pág. 254)

strike the refusal of workers to perform their jobs until employers meet their demands (p. 433)

huelga negativa de los empleados a trabajar hasta que sus empleadores satisfagan sus demandas (pág. 433)

suffrage voting rights (p. 153)

sufragio derecho al voto (pág. 153)

T

tariff a tax on imports or exports (p. 159)

arancel impuesto pagado por las importaciones o exportaciones (pág. 159)

Tariff of Abominations (1828) the nickname given to a tariff by southerners who opposed it (p. 334)

Arancel de Abominaciones (1828) sobrenombre dado a un arancel por los habitantes del Sur que se oponían a éste (pág. 334)

Tea Act (1773) a law passed by Parliament allowing the British East India Company to sell its low-cost tea directly to the colonies, undermining colonial tea merchants; led to the Boston Tea Party (p. 110)

Ley del Té (1773) ley aprobada por el Parlamento británico que le permitía a la British East India Company vender té a bajo costo a las colonias directamente, afectando a los comerciantes de té coloniales; dio origen al Motín del Té de Boston (pág. 110)

technology the tools used to produce goods or to do work (p. 426)

tecnología herramientas utilizadas para producer bienes o realizar un trabajo (pág. 426)

teepees cone-shaped shelters made of buffalo skins used by Native Americans in the Plains region (p. 14)

tipis viviendas en forma de cono hechas de piel de búfalo que usaban los indígenas norteamericanos en la región de las Planicies (pág. 14)

telegraph a machine perfected by Samuel F. B. Morse in 1832 that uses pulses of electric current to send messages across long distances through wires (p. 441)

telégrafo máquina perfeccionada por Samuel F. B. Morse en 1832 que emplea impulsos eléctricos transmitidos por cables para enviar mensajes a grandes distancias (pág. 441)

temperance movement a social reform effort begun in the mid-1800s to encourage people to drink less alcohol (p. 520)

movimiento de abstinencia movimiento de reforma social iniciado a mediados del siglo XIX para promover el que las personas bebieran menos alcohol (pág. 520)

Ten Percent Plan President Abraham Lincoln's plan for Reconstruction; once 10 percent of voters in a former Confederate state took a U.S. loyalty oath, they could form a new state government and be readmitted to the Union (p. 615)
Plan del Diez por Ciento plan de Reconstrucción del presidente Abraham Lincoln; si el 10 por ciento de los votantes de un estado que había sido confederado juraba lealtad a la nación, podían formar un Nuevo gobierno y ser readmitidos en la Unión (pág. 615)

textile cloth (p. 425)
textil tela (pág. 425)

Thirteenth Amendment (1865) a constitutional amendment that outlawed slavery (p. 615)
Decimotercera Enmienda (1865) enmienda constitucional que prohibió la esclavitud (pág. 615)

Three-Fifths Compromise (1787) an agreement worked out at the Constitutional Convention stating that only three-fifths of the slaves in a state would count when determining a state's population for representation in the lower house of Congress (pp. 167, 184)
Compromiso de las Tres Quintas Partes (1787) acuerdo negociado durante la Convención Constitucional en el que se estableció que solamente tres quintas de los esclavos en un estado contarían para al determiner la representación de ese estado en la cámara baja del Congreso (pág. 167, 184)

Toleration Act of 1649 a Maryland law that made restricting the religious rights of Christians a crime; the first law guaranteeing religious freedom to be passed in America (p. 72)
Ley de Tolerancia de 1649 ley de Maryland que calificaba como delito la restricción de los derechos religiosos de los cristianos; fue la primera ley que garantizó la libertad religiosa en América (pág. 72)

total war a type of war in which an army destroys its opponent's ability to fight by targeting civilian and economic as well as military resources (p. 604)
guerra total tipo de guerra en la que un ejército destruye la capacidad de lucha de su oponente mediante ataques a la población civil y a la economía así como a los recursos militares (pág. 604)

totems images of ancestors or animal spirits; carved onto tall, wooden poles by Native American peoples of the Pacific Northwest (p. 13)
tótems imágenes de antepasados o espíritus de animales; a menudo talladas en altos troncos de madera por los indígenas americanos de la costa noroeste del Pacífico (pág. 13)

town meeting a political meeting at which people make decisions on local issues; used primarily in New England (p. 91)
reunión del pueblo reunión política en la que las personas toman decisiones sobre temas locales; se usan principalmente en Nueva Inglaterra (pág. 91)

trade unions workers' organizations that try to improve working conditions (p. 433)
sindicatos organizaciones de trabajadores que intentan mejorar sus condiciones laborales (pág. 433)

Trail of Tears (1838–39) an 800-mile forced march made by the Cherokee from their homeland in Georgia to Indian Territory; resulted in the deaths of almost one-fourth of the Cherokee people (p. 343)
Ruta de las Lágrimas (1838–39) marcha forzada de 800 millas que hicieron los cheroquíes desde su territorio natal en Georgia hasta el Territorio Indígena, y en la que perdió la vida casi una cuarta parte del pueblo cheroquí (pág. 343)

transcendentalism the idea that people could rise above the material things in life; a popular movement among New England writers and thinkers in the mid-1800s (p. 513)
trascendentalismo creencia de que las personas podían prescindir de los objetos materiales en la vida; movimiento popular entre los escritores y pensadores de Nueva Inglaterra a mediados del siglo XIX (pág. 513)

transcontinental railroad a railroad system that crossed the continental United States; construction began in 1863 (p. 368)
tren transcontinental línea que cruzaba Estados Unidos de un extremo a otro; su construcción se inició en 1863 (pág. 368)

English and Spanish Glossary

Transportation Revolution the rapid growth in the speed and convenience of transportation (p. 435)

Revolución del Transporte rápido desarrollo de la velocidad y comodidad de los medios de transporte (pág. 435)

Treaty of Fort Jackson (1814) a treaty signed after the U.S. victory at the Battle of Horseshoe Bend; the Creek were forced to give up 23 million acres of their land (p. 290)

Tratado del Fuerte Jackson (1814) tratado que se firmó tras la victoria de Estados Unidos en la batalla de Horseshoe Bend; los indígenas creek se vieron obligados a ceder 23 millones de acres de su territorio (pág. 290)

Treaty of Fort Laramie (1851) a treaty signed in Wyoming by the United States and northern Plains nations (p. 372)

Tratado del Fuerte Laramie (1851) tratado firmado en Wyoming por Estados Unidos y las naciones indígenas de las Planicies del norte (pág. 372)

Treaty of Ghent (1814) a treaty signed by the United States and Britain ending the War of 1812 (p. 291)

Tratado de Gante (1814) tratado firmado por Estados Unidos y Gran Bretaña para dar fi n a la Guerra de 1812 (pág. 291)

Treaty of Greenville (1795) an agreement between Native American confederation leaders and the U.S. government that gave the United States Indian lands in the Northwest Territory and guaranteed that U.S. citizens could safely travel through the region (p. 259)

Tratado de Greenville (1795) acuerdo entre los líderes de la confederación de indígenas norteamericanos y el gobierno estadounidense que otorgó a Estados Unidos tierras indígenas en el Territorio del Noroeste y garantizó la seguridad a los ciudadanos estadounidenses que viajaran por la región (pág. 259)

Treaty of Guadalupe Hidalgo (1848) a treaty that ended the Mexican-American War and gave the United States much of Mexico's northern territory (p. 405)

Tratado de Guadalupe Hidalgo (1848) tratado que daba por terminada la Guerra contra México y daba a Estados Unidos gran parte del norte del territorio mexicano (pág. 405)

Treaty of Medicine Lodge (1867) an agreement between the U.S. government and southern Plains Indians in which the Indians agreed to move onto reservations (p. 373)

Tratado de Medicine Lodge (1867) acuerdo entre el gobierno de Estados Unidos y los indígenas de las Planicies del sur en el que los indígenas aceptaron irse a las reservas (pág. 373)

Treaty of Paris of 1783 a peace agreement that officially ended the Revolutionary War and established British recognition of the independence of the United States (p. 144)

Tratado de París de 1783 acuerdo de paz que oficialmente dio por terminada la Guerra de Independencia estadounidense y en el que Gran Bretaña reconocía la independencia de Estados Unidos (pág. 144)

Treaty of Tordesillas (1494) a treaty between Spain and Portugal that moved the Line of Demarcation (p. 43)

Tratado de Tordesillas (1494) tratado entre España y Portugal que modifi có la Línea de Demarcación (pág. 43)

Tredegar Iron Works a large iron factory that operated in Richmond, Virginia, in the early to mid-1800s (p. 458)

Tredegar Iron Works gran fábrica de acero que operaba a mediados del siglo XIX en Richmond, Virginia (pág. 458)

triangular trade trading networks in which goods and slaves moved among England, the American colonies, and Africa (p. 93)

comercio triangular redes comerciales en las que los bienes y los esclavos se intercambiaban entre Inglaterra, las colonias americanas y África (pág. 93)

U

Uncle Tom's Cabin (1852) an antislavery novel written by Harriet Beecher Stowe that showed northerners the violent reality of slavery and drew many people to the abolitionists' cause (pp. 499, 546)
La cabaña del tío Tom (1852) novela abolicionista escrita por Harriet Beecher Stowe que mostró a los habitantes del norte del país la violenta realidad de la esclavitud e hizo que muchos se unieran a la causa abolicionista (pág. 499, 546)

Underground Railroad a network of people who helped thousands of enslaved people escape to the North by providing transportation and hiding places (p. 492, 526)
Tren Clandestino red de personas que ayudó a miles de esclavos a escapar al Norte ofreciéndoles transporte y lugares para esconderse (pág. 492, 526)

USS *Constitution* a large warship (p. 282)
USS *Constitution* gran buque de guerra (pág. 282)

utopian communities places where people worked to establish a perfect society; such communities were popular in the United States during the late 1700s and early to mid-1800s (p. 514)
comunidades utópicas lugares en los que un grupo de personas trabajaba para establecer una sociedad perfecta; se popularizaron en Estados Unidos a finales del siglo XVIII y principios y mediados del XIX (pág. 514)

V

vaqueros Mexican cowboys in the West who tended cattle and horses (p. 399)
vaqueros arrieros mexicanos que vivían en el Oeste y se ganaban la vida ocupándose del ganado y los caballos (pág. 399)

veto to cancel a law (p. 192)
vetar cancelar una ley (pág. 192)

Virginia Plan (1787) the plan for government proposed at the Constitutional Convention in which the national government would have supreme power and a legislative branch would have two houses with representation determined by state population (pp. 165, 183)

Plan de Virginia (1787) plan de gobierno propuesto en la Convención Constitucional por el que el gobierno nacional tendría poder supremo y habría un poder legislativo con dos cámaras en las que la representación de cada estado sería determinada por su población (pág. 165, 183)

Virginia Statute for Religious Freedom (1786) a document that gave people in Virginia freedom of worship and prohibited tax money from being used to fund churches (p. 153)
Estatuto de Virginia para la Libertad Religiosa (1786) documento que reconocía a los habitantes de Virginia la libertad de culto y prohibía utilizar los impuestos para financiar iglesias (pág. 153)

W

War Hawks members of Congress who wanted to declare war against Britain after the Battle of Tippecanoe (p. 286)
halcones de guerra miembros del Congreso que querían declarar la guerra a Gran Bretaña tras la batalla de Tippecanoe (pág. 286)
Ley de Poderes de Guerra (1973) ley que
Whig Party a political party formed in 1834 by opponents of Andrew Jackson and who supported a strong legislature (p. 339)
Partido Whig partido político formado en 1834 por oponentes de Andrew Jackson que apoyaba una asamblea legislativa con mucha autoridad (pág. 339)

Whiskey Rebellion (1794) a protest of small farmers in Pennsylvania against new taxes on whiskey (p. 260)
Rebelión del Whisky (1794) protesta de pequeños agricultores de Pensilvania contra los nuevos impuestos sobre el whisky (pág. 260)

Wilderness Campaign (1864) a series of battles between Union and Confederate forces in northern and central Virginia that delayed the Union capture of Richmond (p. 603)
Campaña de Wilderness (1864) serie de batallas entre la Unión y los confederados en el norte y el centro de Virginia que retrasaron la captura de Richmond por parte de la Unión (pág. 603)

English and Spanish Glossary

Wilmot Proviso (1846) a proposal to outlaw slavery in the territory added to the United States by the Mexican Cession; passed in the House of Representatives but was defeated in the Senate (pp. 496, 542)

Condición de Wilmot (1846) propuesta de prohibir la esclavitud en el territorio anexado a Estados Unidos por la Cesión Mexicana; aprobada por la Cámara de Representantes, pero rechazada por el Senado (pág. 496, 542)

Worcester v. Georgia (1832) the Supreme Court ruling that stated that the Cherokee nation was a distinct territory over which only the federal government had authority; ignored by both President Andrew Jackson and the state of Georgia (p. 342)

Worcester contra Georgia (1832) decisión de la Corte Suprema que establecía que la nación cheroquí era un territorio distinto sobre el que sólo el gobierno federal tenía autoridad; fue ignorada por el presidente Andrew Jackson y por el estado de Georgia (pág. 342)

X

XYZ affair (1797) an incident in which French agents attempted to get a bribe and loans from U.S. diplomats in exchange for an agreement that French privateers would no longer attack American ships; it led to an undeclared naval war between the two countries (p. 265)

asunto XYZ (1797) incidente en el que funcionarios franceses intentaron obtener sobornos y préstamos de diplomáticos estadounidenses a cambio de un acuerdo por el cual sus corsarios no atacarían más a los barcos estadounidenses; provocó una guerra no declarada entre las fuerzas navales de ambas naciones (pág. 265)

Y

yeomen owners of small farms (p. 461)

pequeños terratenientes dueños de granjas pequeñas (pág. 461)

Index

Index

Index

Index

Index

Art and Photography Credits

 Video reference screens © 2010 A&E Television Networks, LLC. All rights reserved.

Cover: *Cannon* Malcolm MacGregor/Getty Images; *paper texture* Tolga Tezcan/Getty Images

Front Matter: *Signing the Declaration of Independence* ©Bettmann/Corbis; *Independence Hall* ©Dennis Degnan/Corbis; *Migrant Mother* Library of Congress Prints and Photographs Division, Washington, D.C. [LC-DIG-fsa-8b29516]; *Dust Bowl* NOAA George E. Marsh Album; *people with flags* ©Moodboard/Superstock.

Module 1: *Buffalo* ©Annie Griffiths/Corbis; *mammoth skeleton* ©Richard Cummins/Corbis; *Egyptian pyramids* ©Jupiterimages; *Olmec head* ©Yoshio Tomii/SuperStock; *Michelangelo David* ©Rabatti-Dominigie/AKG Images; *Roman columns* ©Christopher Groenhout/Lonely Planet Images; *maize* Picture Research Consultants, Inc.; *Tikal* ©Getty Images; *Mesa Verde Cliff Palace* ©Photodisc/Getty Images; *bird shaped pipe* akg-images/Werner Forman; *sewing awl* ©Werner Forman/AKG Images; *painted effigy jar* Courtesy National Museum of the American Indian, Smithsonian Institution. 3/9547; 115 (t) *Iroquois longhouse* ©Marilyn Angel Wynn/Getty Images; *Iroquois longhouse illustration* The Granger Collection, NYC; *Mali salt market* ©John Elk III; *Ashante gold jewelry* ©Robert Estall photo agency/Alamy; *Roman Senate* ©PRISMA/Ancient Art & Architecture Collection Ltd; *Charlemagne* ©INTERFOTO/Alamy; *Crusades painting* Iberfoto/Photoaisa; *rat* ©GK Hart/Vikki Hart/Photodisc/Getty Images; *Johann Gutenberg* The Granger Collection, NYC; *signing Magna Carta* ©Bettmann/Corbis.

Module 2: *Ships* © Rebecca Marvil/Index Stock Imagery/photolibrary.com; *Christopher Columbus* ©SuperStock, Inc./SuperStock; *Henry Hudson* © Tate Gallery, London/Art Resource, NY; *1570 compass* National Maritime Museum, Greenwich, London; *Galileo telescope* ©G. Tortoli/Ancient Art and Architecture Collection; *Francisco Pizarro* ©Time Life Pictures/Getty Images; *Christopher Columbus* ©SuperStock, Inc./SuperStock; *Estevanico* The Granger Collection, NYC; *de Las Casas* PRC Picture Research Consultants, Inc.; *Martin Luther* ©AKG Images; *printing press* Saint Bride Printing Library; *Spanish Armada* ©Mary Evans Picture Library; *Spanish coin* Bridgeman Art Library.

Module 3: *Plymouth Colony garden* ©Superstock; *Taj Mahal* ©David Ball/Corbis; *Peter the Great* ©Superstock; *Chief Pontiac* The Granger Collection, NYC; *Sandwich Islander* ©Culver Pictures, Inc.; *Virginia landscape* Colonial Williamsburg Foundation; *Fall of New Amsterdam* ©Superstock; *Appalachian Mountains* ©Superstock; *Boston satellite photo* NASA; *Port of Marseille* ©Superstock; *slave ship* Bridgeman Art Library.

Module 4: *War re-enactment* © James Lemass/Index Stock Imagery/photolibrary.com; *tax stamp act 1765* ©Everett Collection Inc./Superstock; *Declaration of Independence* The Granger Collection, NYC; *ships in battle* Falmouth Art Gallery, Cornwall, UK/The Bridgeman Art Library; *Simon Bolivar* ©North Wind Picture Archives/Alamy; *Patrick Henry* Virginia Historical Society; *tax stamp act 1765* ©Everett Collection Inc./Superstock; *Boston Massacre engraving* Peter Newark's American Pictures; *Boston Massacre* ©Bettmann/Corbis; *Boston Tea Party* American Antiquarian Society; *Battle of Lexington* The Granger Collection, NYC; *William Franklin* The Granger Collection, New York; *Benjamin Franklin* ©clipart.com; *Signing the Declaration of Independence* ©Bettmann/Corbis; *American flag (detail)* ©Getty Images/PhotoDisc; *Mum Bett* The Granger Collection, NYC; *British Soldier* ©Collection of The New-York Historical Society, neg. 31665; *Colonial Soldier* #1921.101, ©Collection of The New-York Historical; *Crossing the Delaware* ©SuperStock; *Marquis de Lafayette* Chateau de Versailles, France/Giraudon/Bridgeman; *Bernardo de Galvez* ©Hotel Galvez; *Battle of Saratoga pistol* Saratoga National Historic Park; *Valley Forge* ©SuperStock/SuperStock; *Francis Marion ship* The Granger Collection, NYC.

Module 5: *Nancy Pelosi swears in Congress* ©2009 Jay Mallin; *James Madison miniature* Library of Congress Prints & Photographs Division, Washington, D.C. [LC-USZC4-4097]; *Continental bills* ©North Wind Picture Archives/Alamy; *Castillo de San Marcos* ©Nik Wheeler/Corbis; *Kremlin* ©Andrea Jemolo/Corbis; *women voting* The Granger Collection, NYC; *Mayflower reconstruction* ©Bettmann/Corbis; *Thomas Jefferson* ©Bettmann/Corbis; *signing Magna Carta* ©Bettmann/Corbis; *King William & Queen Mary* ©Michael Nicholson/Corbis; *John Locke* AISA/World Illustrated/Photoshot; *U.S. Constitution* National Archives (London); *Shays's Rebellion* The Granger Collection, NYC; *James Madison* ©Stock Montage/Getty Images; *Signing the Constitution* ©Hall of Representatives, Washington, DC/Bridgeman Art Library; *cl) Roger Sherman* ©Independence National Historical Park; *James Wilson* ©North Wind Picture Archives/Alamy.

Module 6: *Students* ©Sam Dudgeon/Houghton Mifflin Harcourt; *Woman Suffrage poster* Picture Research Consultants, Inc.; *teen voting* ©Tony Freeman/PhotoEdit, Inc.; *Brown v. Board of Education* ©Bettmann/Corbis; *Independence Hall* ©Dennis Degnan/Corbis; *John Rutledge* ©North Wind Picture Archives/Alamy; *Gouverneur Morris* ©Bridgeman Images; *photo of U.S. Constitution* ©Houghton Mifflin Harcourt; *Supreme Court* ©Jurgen Vogt/The Image Bank/Getty Images; *Sonia Sotomayor* AP Photo/Collection of the Supreme Court of the United States, Steve Petteway; *American flag (detail)* ©Getty Images/PhotoDisc; *John Thune* ©Michael Reynolds/epa/Corbis; *Congress* ©Mark Wilson/Getty Images; *signing document* ©Brooks Kraft/Corbis; *US Capitol building* ©Barry Howe/Corbis; *woman's hands* © Yang Liu/CORBIS; *smiling girl* ©Norm Detlaff/AP Images; *suffragette with banner* ©Bettmann/Corbis; *reading Nixon headline* ©Bettmann/CORBIS; *woman with megaphone* David Young-Wolff/PhotoEdit, Inc.; *African American voting* Library of Congress Prints and Photographs Division, Washington, D.C. [LC-USZ62-100971]; *suffragettes petition* Library of Congress Prints and Photographs Division, Washington, D.C. [LC-USZ62-78691]; *FDR portrait* © Oscar White/CORBIS; *FDR button* ©Bettmann/Corbis; *African American woman voting* ©1978 Matt Herron/TakeStock; *NYC union* ©New York Daily News Archive/Getty Images; *man addressing jury* ©Moodboard/Alamy; *female student raising hand* ©Ariel Skelley/Corbis; *Declaration of Independence photo* ©Houghton Mifflin Harcourt; *Constitution* National Archives (London); *swearing in US citizen* ©David Butow/Corbis; *U.S. Marine* ©Brownie Harris/Corbis; *election day* ©kleo67/Alamy; *teen volunteers* ©Ariel Skelley/Corbis.

Module 7: *Washington, D.C., at night* ©Miles Ertman/Masterfile; *George Washington* ©Museum of the City of New York/Corbis; *John Adams* ©RMN-Grand Palais/Art Resource, NY; *Thomas Jefferson* Independence National Historical Park Collection; *Storming the Bastille* © RMN-Grand Palais / Art Resource, NY; *guillotine* ©Bridgeman-Giraudon/Art Resource, NY; *Rosetta Stone* Art Resource, NY; *Toussaint L'Ouverture* The Granger Collection, NYC; *first cabinet* The Granger Collection, NYC; *New York City* ©Francis Guy/Corbis; *Benjamin Banneker* ©North Wind Picture Archives/Alamy; *Alexander Hamilton* © Stock Montage/Getty Images; *Thomas Jefferson* ©Stock Montage/Getty Images; *Chief Little Turtle* ©North Wind Picture Archives/Alamy; *burning Jay in effigy* The Granger Collection, NYC; *riverboat* ©Houghton Mifflin Harcourt; *George Washington* ©Museum of the City of New York/Corbis; *Alexander Hamilton* Stock Montage/Getty Images; *John Adams* The Art Archive/Chateau de Blernacourt/Dagli Orti; *John Jay* The Bridgeman Art Library; *Thomas Jefferson* Independence National Historical Park Collection; *James Madison* ©Superstock; *Albert Gallatin portrait* National Portrait Gallery, Smithsonian Institution; *1798 political cartoon* Library of Congress Prints and Photographs Division, Washington, D.C. [LC-USZC4-2711]; *John Adams* ©RMN-Grand Palais/Art Resource, NY; *Thomas Jefferson* ©Bettmann/CORBIS; *Supreme Court* ©Jurgen Vogt/The Image Bank/Getty Images.

Module 8: *Battle of New Orleans* Library of Congress Prints & Photographs Division, Washington, D.C. [LC-DIG-pga-01838]; *1807 Embargo Act* © North Wind/North Wind Picture Archives—All rights reserved; *Amistad Slave Mutiny* ©New Haven Colony Historical Society; *Andrew Jackson* Library of Congress Prints and Photographs Division, Washington, D.C. [LC-USZC4-6466]; *James Monroe* ©National Portrait Gallery, Smithsonian Institution, Washington, DC/Art Resource, NY; *1807 Embargo Act* © North Wind/North Wind Picture Archives—All rights reserved; *Henry Clay* The Granger Collection, NYC; *Tecumseh* The Granger Collection, NYC; *Henry Harrison* National Portrait Gallery, Smithsonian Institution; *Dolley Madison* ©New-York Historical Society/Bridgeman Art Library; *burning of Washington, D.C.* ©Bettmann/CORBIS; *Andrew Jackson* White House Collection, copyright White House Historical Association.

Module 9: *Erie Canal re-enactment* ©Lee Snider/Corbis; *James Monroe* ©National Portrait Gallery, Smithsonian Institution, Washington, DC/Art Resource, NY; *seal of Liberia* PRC Picture Research Consultants; *John Quincy Adams* Library of Congress Prints and Photographs Division, Washington, D.C. [LC-USZC4-5801]; *Allegiance To No Crown* National Portrait Gallery, Smithsonian Institution / Art Resource, NY; *James Monroe* ©National Portrait Gallery, Smithsonian Institution, Washington, DC/Art Resource, NY; *pioneers flatboat* ©Bettmann/Corbis; *Fairview Inn painting* Maryland Historical Society, Baltimore, Maryland; *The Oxbow* ©Francis G. Mayer/Corbis; *Audubon heron* PRC Picture Research Consultants; *George Catlin Little Wolf* ©Art Resource, NY; *UVA Rotunda* ©Andre Jenny/Alamy; *American Spelling Book* American Antiquarian Society.

Module 10: *Jackson statue* Library of Congress Prints and Photographs Division, Washington, D.C. [LC-DIG-ppmsca-18037]; *Jackson ticket poster* ©David J. Frent; *Sequoya* The Granger Collection, NYC; *Martin Van Buren* ©National Portrait Gallery, Smithsonian Institution/Art Resource, NY; *Zulu conflict* The Bridgeman Art Library; *Arguing the Point* R.W. Norton Art Gallery, Shreveport, LA. Used by permission; *parade* ©David Young-Wolff/PhotoEdit; *woolen mills* American Museum of Textile History; *cotton picking* ©Bridgeman Images; *Mission San Carlos* Gift of Mrs. Eleanor Martin. Fine Arts Museum of San Francisco; *Jackson political cartoon* The Granger Collection, NYC; *Trail of Tears* ©Superstock; *Cherokee* ©Art Resource, NY; *Creek* ©Art Resource, NY; *Seminole* ©Art Resource, NY; *Choctaw* Smithsonian American Art Museum, Washington, D.C.

Module 11: *Covered wagons* ©James L. Amos/Corbis; *sunrise over mountain* ©Alan Majchrowicz/Getty Images; *railroad track marker* Southern Pacific Lines/Courtesy of Picture Research Consultants, Inc.; *Sitting Bull* ©Corbis; *Commodore Perry* Library of Congress Prints and Photographs Division, Washington, D.C. [LC-USZC4-1307]; *Louis Pasteur* The Art Archive / Musée d'Orsay Paris / Dagli Orti; *Orient Express poster* The Granger Collection, New York; *sunrise over mountain* ©Alan Majchrowicz/Getty Images; *Jim Beckworth* ©Bettmann/Corbis; *Mormon trek* Used by permission, Utah State Historical Society; *Pacific Ocean sea stacks* ©Joseph Sohm-Visions of America/Corbis; *Mississippi River* ©Ron Chapple Stock/Alamy Images; *California cornucopia* ©Collection of the New-York Historical Society, USA/The Bridgeman Art Library; *Nat Love* Library of Congress Prints and Photographs Division, Washington, D.C., [LC-USZ62-46841]; *Wyatt Earp* ©Bettmann/Corbis; *Pony Express stamp* Courtesy Wells Fargo Bank; *Transcontinental Railroad* © Bettmann/CORBIS; *Buffalo Hunt* ©Superstock; *Reno's retreat* ©The Stapleton Collection/Corbis; *Custer's Last Stand* ©Bettmann/Corbis; *Sarah Winnemucca* The Granger Collection, NYC; *sod house family* Western History Collections, University of Oklahoma; *African American family* The Granger Collection, NYC; *Guthrie Oklahoma* ©Corbis.

Module 12: *Alamo* ©Jack Lewis/Texas Department of Transportation (TxDOT); *Commodore Perry* Library of Congress Prints and Photographs Division, Washington, D.C. [LC-USZC4-1307]; *miner wooden rocker* ©The Oakland Museum, The City of Oakland; *Texas settlers* ©Bettmann/Corbis; *Texas state flag* ©Stockbyte/Getty Images; *American Progress* Library of Congress Prints and Photographs Division, Washington, D.C. [LC-USZC4-668]; *vaqueros* ©INTERFOTO/Alamy; *California Bear flag* Society of California Pioneers; *miner* Collection of Matthew Isenburg; *Anglo and Chinese miners* Courtesy of the California History Room, California; *woman with three miners* ©Art Resource, NY; *San Francisco harbor* Library of Congress Prints and Photographs Division, Washington, D.C. [LC-USZC4-7421]; *hands nuggets* © George F. Mobley/National Geographic/Getty Images; *panning for gold* ©Bettmann/Corbis; *The Way of the Empire* ©Superstock; *Grand Tetons Snake River* ©Lester Lefkowitz/CORBIS.

Module 13: *Textile mill* © Marilyn Root/Index Stock Imagery/photolibrary.com; *Robert Fulton* Fenimore Art Museum, Cooperstown, New York/ Photo by Richard Walker; *steam engine* Picture Research Consultants, Inc.; *Neptune* NASA; *Borden's milk* ©Southeast Museum; *Crystal Palace* © CORBIS; *Eli Whitney* Samuel Finley Breese Morse, Eli Whitney (1765–1825), Yale University Art Gallery. Gift of George Hoadley, B.A. 1801/Art Resource, NY; *block making machine* Library of Congress Prints and Photographs Division, Washington, D.C. [LC-USZ62-110389]; *transformer manufacture* Library of Congress Prints and Photographs Division, Washington, D.C. [LC-USE6-D-002859]; *guns galore* ©Hulton Archive/Getty Images; *car assembly line* ©Bob Krist/Corbis; *mill girl* Jack Naylor Collection; *steamboats at dock* Library of Congress Prints and Photographs Division, Washington, D.C. [LC-D401-19395]; *John Deere plow* Courtesy John Deere & Company Archives; *telegraph key* © A. Dagli Orti/ De Agostini Picture Library/Getty Images; *sewing machine* ©Science and Society/ SuperStock.

Module 14: *Slave plantation* ©L.J. Schira/Hulton Archive/Getty Images; *Eli Whitney cotton gin* ©Bettmann/Corbis; *Tredegar Iron Works* Library of Congress Prints and Photographs Division, Washington, D.C. [LC-B817-7542]; *Queen Victoria* ©Hulton-Deutsch Collection/ CORBIS; *freed slave badge* Collection of the American Numismatic Society, New; *1861 barber shop* Courtesy of the Valentine Richmond History Center; *Slave Cabins* Library of Congress Prints and Photographs Division, Washington, D.C. [LC-USZ62-16178]; *slave auction* Library of Congress Prints and Photographs Division, Washington, D.C. [LC-USZ62-76081]; *Nat Turner Rebellion* The Granger Collection, New York.

Module 15: *Ride for Liberty* The Granger Collection, New York; *lower deck slave ship* ©Bettmann/Corbis; Uncle Tom's Cabin Picture Research Consultants, Inc.; *King Afonso* ©The New York Public Library/Schomburg Center for Research in Black Culture/Manuscripts, Archives and Rare Books Division; *crusher squeezes juice* British Library, London, UK/The Bridgeman Art Library; *lower deck slave ship* ©Bettmann/Corbis; *Elmina Castle* ©Michael Dwyer/Alamy; *slaves picking cotton* ©North Wind Picture Archives/ Alamy; *slave with owner's child* The Granger Collection, New York; *African American church* South Carolina Historical Society; *William Lloyd Garrison* Trustees of the Boston Public Library; *Sojourner Truth* Courtesy of the Massachusetts Historical Society; *"Outrage," February 2, 1837 Handbill* Rare Book and Special Collections Division, Library of Congress, Washington, D.C. (41); *Henry Clay* National Portrait Gallery, Smithsonian Institution / Art Resource, NY; Uncle Tom's Cabin Picture Research Consultants, Inc.

Module 16: *Busy Port* ©Superstock; *proclaim liberty banner* Courtesy of the Massachusetts Historical Society; *Women Rights report* Picture Research Consultants, Inc.; *Braille typewriter* Photo © David Modica, courtesy American Printing House for the Blind Museum; *immigrants at Battery* Peter Newark's American Pictures; *"Outrage," February 2, 1837 Handbill* Rare Book and Special Collections Division, Library of Congress, Washington, D.C. (41); *Irish immigrant family* Wm. B. Becker Collection/American Museum of Photography; *Walden Pond* ©Corbis; *The First Harvest in the Wilderness*, 1855 (oil on canvas), Durand, Asher Brown (1796–1886) / Brooklyn Museum of Art, New York, USA / Gift of the Brooklyn Institute of Arts and Sciences / The Bridgeman Art Library; *Revival camp* The Granger Collection, New

York; *temperance pledge* ©Getty Images; *Oberlin College students* Courtesy of Oberlin Archives; *Am I Not a Woman* The Granger Collection, New York; *Harriet Tubman* Library of Congress Prints and Photographs Division, Washington, D.C. [LC-USZ62-7816]; *North Star*, June 2, 1848. Edited by Frederick Douglass and Martin Delany. Newspaper. Library of Congress, Serial and Government Publications Division, Washington, D.C. (2-10); *Angelina Grimke* The Granger Collection, New York; *Sarah Grimke* The Granger Collection, New York; *National Anti-Suffrage Headquarters* ©Stock Montage, Inc.; *Declaration of Sentiments from Report of the Woman's Rights Convention, Held at Seneca Falls, New York July 19 and 20, 1848. Rochester: North Star Office, 1848.* Elizabeth Cady Stanton Papers, Library of Congress, Manuscript Division, Washington, D.C. (111.01.01) [Digital ID# us0111_01a]; *Lucy Stone* ©Bettmann/Corbis; *Susan B. Anthony* ©Bettmann/Corbis; *Abigail Adams* Courtesy of the Massachusetts Historical Society; *Suffrage car* Library of Congress Prints and Photographs Division, Washington, D.C. [LC-DIG-ggbain-12924].

Module 17: *Women in museum* © Dave G. Houser; Uncle Tom's Cabin Picture Research Consultants, Inc.; *Napoleon III* The Art Archive/Private Collection/Dagli Orti; *Sepoy Mutiny* India Office Library & Records, The British Library; *Charleston Mercury* Library of Congress, Rare Book and Special Collections Division, Alfred Whital Stern Collection of Lincolniana [Digital ID# lprbscsm scsm0241]; *Henry Clay addressing Senate* Picture Research Consultants, Inc.; *Fugitive Slave Law convention* The Granger Collection, New York; *John Doy abolitionists* Kansas State Historical Society, Topeka, Kansas; *Brooks attacking Sumner* The Granger Collection, New York; *Abraham Lincoln* Library of Congress Prints and Photographs Division, Washington, D.C. [LC-DIG-ppmsca-19204]; *Stephen A. Douglas* Library of Congress Prints and Photographs Division, Washington, D.C. [LC-DIG-cwpbh-00882]; *John Brown* Fotosearch/Getty Images.

Module 18: *Union drummer boys* Library of Congress Prints and Photographs Division, Washington, D.C. [LC-B8171-7514]; *Emancipation poster* ©Superstock; *Kaiser Maximillian* ©Hulton-Deutsch Collection/Corbis; *Surrender at Appomattox* ©Superstock; *Scott's Great Snake* Library of Congress Geography and Map Division, Washington, D.C. [Digital ID # g3701 scw0011000]; *Union gunboats* ©North Wind Picture Archives/Alamy; *ironclad* Naval Historical Center; *4th U.S. Colored Infantry* Library of Congress, Prints and Photographs Division, Washington, D.C. [LC-DIG-cwpb-04294]; *recruitment poster (inset)* Courtesy of the Massachusetts Historical Society; *infantry family* ©Bettmann/Corbis; *Clara Barton* American Antiquarian Society; *Lincoln giving speech* Library of Congress Prints

and Photographs Division, Washington, D.C. [LC-DIG-ppmsca-19926]; *Surrender at Appomattox* ©Superstock; *copperheads cartoon* The Granger Collection, New York; *Lincoln cartoon* ©Hulton Archive/Getty Images; *copperheads cartoon* The Granger Collection, New York.

Module 19: *Charleston Ruins* Still Picture Records Section, Special Media Archives Services Division (NWCS-S), National Archives [111-B-744]; *Lincoln assassination* © Kean Collection/Getty Images; *Johnson impeachment* The Granger Collection, New York; *Hiram Revels* Herbert F. Johnson Museum of Art, Cornell University; *Suez Canal* ©Michael Maslan Historic Photographs/CORBIS; *barge leaving Richmond* Library of Congress Prints and Photographs Division, Washington, D.C. [LC-DIG-cwpb-04079]; *African American couple* University of Texas at El Paso Library, Special Collections; *Freedmen's Bureau school* ©Corbis; *Andrew Johnson* Library of Congress Prints and Photographs Division, Washington, D.C. [LC-BH83-171]; *Thaddeus Stevens* ©Corbis; *first vote* © North Wind/North Wind Picture Archives—All rights reserved; *Ku Klux Klan* ©Bettmann/Corbis; *visit from Ku Klux Klan* The Granger Collection, New York; *Henry Grady* ©Bettmann/Corbis; *Atlanta Georgia 1887* Courtesy of the Charleston Renaissance Gallery, Robert M. Hicklin Jr., Inc., Charleston, South Carolina.

Epilogue: *U.S. troops in France* © Bettmann/Corbis; *March on Washington* © Robert W. Kelley/Time Life Pictures/Getty Images; *The Final Frost Barrier* The Granger Collection, New York; *Vietnamese parade* © Paula Bronstein/Getty Images; *World Trade Center rubble* © Reuters/Corbis.

Reference: *Lincoln Memorial at night* ©John Aikins/Corbis Sept. 11, 2001 ©Reuters/Corbis.

Multimedia Connections: Video reference screens © 2010 A&E Television Networks, LLC. All rights reserved.

Tikal Mayan pyramid ©Imagebroker/Alamy; *Ponce de Leon in Florida* ©Cummer Museum of Art & Gardens/Superstock; *American Revolution* ©Ted Spiegel/Corbis; *Lewis Clark re-enactment* ©Charles Rex Arbogast/AP Images; *old paper with creases* ©Corbis; *gold miners* The Granger Collection, New York

Symbols of the United States: *American flag* ©Photodisc/Getty Images; *Star Spangled Banner* The Granger Collection, New York; *Uncle Sam recruitment poster* Library of Congress Prints and Photographs Division, Washington, D.C. [LC-USZC4-3859]; *Mt. Rushmore* ©reb/Fotolia; *The Third-Term Panic (political cartoon)* Library of Congress Prints and Photographs Division, Washington, D.C. [LC-DIG-ppmsca-15785].